THE ELUSIVE EDEN

THE ELUSIVE EDEN

A New History of California

THIRD EDITION

Richard B. Rice
California State University, Hayward

William A. Bullough
California State University, Hayward

Richard J. Orsi
California State University, Hayward

Boston   Burr Ridge, IL   Dubuque, IA   Madison, WI   New York
San Francisco   St. Louis   Bangkok   Bogotá   Caracas   Kuala Lumpur
Lisbon   London   Madrid   Mexico City   Milan   Montreal   New Delhi
Santiago   Seoul   Singapore   Sydney   Taipei   Toronto

McGraw-Hill Higher Education 🞰
*A Division of The **McGraw-Hill** Companies*

THE ELUSIVE EDEN: A NEW HISTORY OF CALIFORNIA
Published by McGraw-Hill, an imprint of The McGraw-Hill Companies, Inc. 1221 Avenue of the Americas, New York, NY, 10020. Copyright © 2002, 1996, 1988 by The McGraw-Hill Companies, Inc. All rights reserved. No part of this publication may be reproduced or distributed in any form or by any means, or stored in a database or retrieval system, without the prior written consent of The McGraw-Hill Companies, Inc., including, but not limited to, in any network or other electronic storage or transmission, or broadcast for distance learning.

This book is printed on acid-free paper.

5 6 7 8 9 0 QWF/QWF 0 9 8 7 6 5 4

ISBN   0-07-241810-9

Executive editor: *Lyn Uhl*
Developmental editor: *Kristen Mellitt*
Marketing manager: *Janise Fry*
Project manager: *Jean R. Starr*
Production supervisor: *Susanne Riedell*
Photo research coordinator: *Jeremy Cheshareck*
Cover design: *Mary E. Kazak*
Cover image: *Steve Turner Gallery, Beverly Hills*
Typeface: *10.5/12 New Baskerville*
Printer: *Quebecor World Fairfield Inc.*
Compositor: *Electronic Publishing Services, Inc., NY*

Library of Congress Cataloging-in-Publication Data

Rice, Richard B.
    The elusive eden : a new history of California / Richard B. Rice, William A. Bullough, Richard J. Orsi.—3rd ed.
        p. cm.
    Includes bibliographical references and index.
    ISBN 0–07–241810–9
    1. California—History. I. Bullough, William A., 1933– II. Orsi, Richard J. III. Title.

F861 .R49   2002
979.4—dc21

                                                2001044905

We dedicate this book to our families, who shared the burden:

Eve, Lindy, Katie, and John
Pat and Greg
Dolores, Peter, Jared, Becky, Renata, Raymonde, and John

CONTENTS

PART VI

CALIFORNIA AND THE NATION, 1880–1920

MAPS

FEATURE ESSAYS

PREFACE

Many of the changes in this edition of *The Elusive Eden* result from comments and suggestions by students and colleagues; the same principles, however, have guided our thinking about each version. Convictions resulting from our collective seventy-plus years of teaching the state's history—that Californians, natives and newcomers alike, study their state's past out of genuine (sometimes avid) interest and that they like a good story—persisted unabated. Consequently, the book's original organizational format remains, with only a few changes. After an introductory prologue of three chapters (Part I), the book is arranged in a series of generally chronological parts, each consisting of three chapters and dealing with a recognized era. The first chapter in each set is a detailed narrative about a specific person or event directly related to the history of the period under study. The two subsequent chapters are traditional, chronologically based accounts of the broader history of the period. For this edition the last chapter has been completely rewritten to reflect recent scholarship and to bring the history up to date.

The narrative chapters are designed to give the reader a feel for the "texture" of history by suggesting how individuals and groups grappled with and shaped historical change. In some cases these chapters include passages from primary sources to provide a distinct flavor of the time. We hope that each will capture the interest of readers, provoke thought and debate, and encourage them to seek further information about the topics introduced. The narrative chapters also illuminate the drama and excitement of history, investigate subjects of current interest, and strive to elaborate the cultural diversity of California. They focus on all sections of the state: north and south, central valleys and coast, urban and rural settings. Two deal with women (Chapters 10 and 19), one with Indians (Chapter 4), one with the Mexican heritage (Chapter 7), two with the ethnic minority experience (Chapters 22 and 25), and one with recent environmental controversy (Chapter 28). An introductory paragraph to provide context and elaborate purpose precedes each narrative chapter.

Because of the organizational framework the authors have chosen, the narrative chapters also do not appear in strict chronological order. They may highlight events occurring in the beginning, middle, or even the end of the period of history in the unit. The authors believe, however, that they provide a commentary on the main themes of the chronological chapters that follow and that the advantages to be gained in reader interest and opportunity for discussion outweigh the disadvantages of historical discontinuity.

In our approach to issues such as ethnic minorities and gender, we have adhered to the conviction that respect for these topics and for history itself mandates that they be woven into the historical fabric rather than treated in a patchwork of detached chapters, as if they were somehow isolated from the warp and woof of human affairs. Accordingly, accounts of the changing status of women and the struggle of ethnic minorities to survive and progress in frequently hostile social environments—as well as the contributions of both to California history—are, with a few exceptions, integral parts of chapters, and therefore not highly visible in the table of contents. Cultural development is treated with a specific section at the end of each part, beginning with Part II, and in Feature Essays distributed throughout the book.

Dealing with the vast scope, incredible diversity, and fascinating nuances of California history continues to confront us with painful decisions in this edition. Finding space to deal with additional ethnic and gender issues and recent developments make judgments about abbreviating or deleting treatments of events or personalities more difficult than ever. With those who find their favorite episodes in the story of the state neglected, we can only empathize; some of our own individually cherished episodes fell victim to our collective editorial axe. We have expanded lists of suggested reading at the end of each part to compensate for the loss and to include important recent scholarship. Interested readers will find general bibliographies of the state's history listed in the suggested readings following the Prologue.

In this version of the book, like the first two, each of us undertook principal responsibility for specific chapters: Professor Rice for Chapters 7–9, 19–24, and 30; Professor Bullough for Chapters 10–12, 16–18, and 25–27; Professor Orsi for Chapters 1–6, 13–15, and 28 and 29. Initials of specific authors appear at the end of each Feature Essay. Although collaboration continued to inform our collective effort, each of us assumes responsibility solely for the content of his parts of the book.

ACKNOWLEDGMENTS

So many people helped us to complete this book that it is impossible to mention every one of them. We extend our heartfelt gratitude to all, particularly colleagues in the Department of History and the Library of California State University, Hayward. We are also indebted to the staffs at the Huntington Library; the Bancroft Library; the Newberry Library; the California State Library; Stanford University Library; the California Historical Society; the California State Railroad Museum; the Tulare County Library; the Kings County Library; Trinity County Historical Society; the California Department of Water Resources; the California Department of Transportation; the California Air Pollution Control Board; the United States Geological Survey; the San Francisco Bay National Wildlife Refuge; and Save San Francisco Bay Association.

Some individuals deserve special mention. Lowell John Bean, Professor Emeritus of Anthropology at California State University, Hayward, graciously read drafts of several chapters dealing with Native Americans and offered insights and suggestions that greatly improved the finished product. We also thank these reviewers for their comments: Francisco E. Balderrama, California State University—Los Angeles, Kate Briegel, California State University—Long Beach, Mary Ann Irwin, Diablo Valley College, Ann De Jesús Riley, Hartnell College, Mark Stemen, California State University—Chico, Nancy J. Taniguchi, California State University—Stanislaus, Richard S. Unruh, Fresno Pacific University, and George L. Vásquez, San José State University. Kristen Mellitt, McGraw-Hill's Developmental Editor for History, has patiently managed the publication of this edition. Special thanks go to Patricia Bullough for her contribution to the essay on John Steinbeck and to Pauline Thompson for her essay on Anna Morrison Reed. Finally, we wish to acknowledge the very special contributions of the late Eve Rice to the book: her essay on Eric Hoffer, her suggestion of the title *The Elusive Eden,* and her constant and unstinting support.

Richard B. Rice
William A. Bullough
Richard J. Orsi

ABOUT THE AUTHORS

RICHARD B. RICE received the B.A., M.A., and Ph.D. in history from the University of California, Berkeley. He was a staff assistant to the president and assistant to the vice president of the University of California before going to California State University, Hayward, where he also served as a department chairman, division head, and dean. He taught United States and California history at Hayward from 1960 to 1995, part of that time as an Emeritus Professor on a faculty early retirement program.

WILLIAM A. BULLOUGH is Professor Emeritus of History at California State University, Hayward. In 1970, he received his Ph.D. degree from the University of California, Santa Barbara, after teaching in the state's public schools for ten years. He is the author of *Cities and Schools in the Gilded Age: The Evolution of an Urban Institution* (1974), *The Blind Boss and His City: Christopher Augustine Buckley and Nineteenth-Century San Francisco* (1979), and articles in *The San Francisco Irish, 1850–1976,* (James P. Walsh, ed., 1978), *The Historian, Pacific Historical Review,* and *California History.* Professor Bullough is an accomplished photographer who has published and exhibited his prints and written articles for *Darkroom Photography.* He is currently engaged in an investigation of the work of several nineteenth-century photographers of California for use as historical documents and assembling a selection of his own images for publication as a photo essay tentatively titled *Pastime.*

RICHARD J. ORSI is Professor Emeritus of History at California State University, Hayward. A graduate of Occidental College in Los Angeles, he received his doctorate from the University of Wisconsin, Madison. He has published articles and book reviews in *California History, Pacific Historian, Agricultural History,* and *The Journal of American History.* He is the author of *A List of References for the History of Agriculture in California* (1974) and is nearing completion of another book, "A Railroad and the Development of the American West: The Southern Pacific Company, 1860–1930." He has received fellowships from the Woodrow Wilson Foundation, the Huntington Library, and the Newberry Library. He is the former editor of *California History,* the quarterly of the California Historical Society. He also edited (with Alfred A. Runte and Marlene Smith-Baranzini) *Yosemite and Sequoia: A Century of California National Parks* (1993), along with several other anthologies of essays interpreting Califronia's history.

PART ONE

PROLOGUE

California, The Land of Promise
California's promotional literature has long portrayed
the state as an Eden. This booster pamphlet was published by the California State Board of Trade in 1897.
Courtesy of the Huntington Library.

CHAPTER ONE

CALIFORNIANS AND THEIR HISTORY: MYTHS AND REALITIES

CALIFORNIA'S LOVE AFFAIR WITH HISTORY

Californians have long identified with their state's past. As early as the 1870s, historians started producing local and state histories, and in the 1890s efforts began to restore the old Spanish missions and other crumbling historic structures. In recent years, however, a veritable mania for history has seized the state. Authors have turned out increasing numbers of books. New local and state historical journals have been founded, and old ones have modernized formats and increased circulation. Bookshelves groan under a new burden of Californiana, and specialized libraries, bookstores, and museums have sprouted to gather, preserve, and propagate historical knowledge. Students in high schools, colleges, and extended education programs flock to courses in state and local history. Local historical societies have proliferated, as have attempts to preserve sites, buildings, and artifacts. To the delight of residents and visitors alike, entire neighborhoods of historic buildings have been res-

cued from wreckers and restored. San Francisco, Sacramento, Alameda, San José, Eureka, Ferndale, San Diego, Pasadena, and Los Angeles, along with dozens of gold-rush towns, now sport colorful Mexican-era adobe "old towns" or streets of pioneer cottages or graceful Victorian homes.

By 1982, according to the California Heritage Task Force, the state led the nation in "heritage resources"—officially designated historic sites and historically oriented organizations. California boasted 1,170 buildings and sites listed in the National Register of Historic Places, 72 national historic landmarks, 959 California historic landmarks, 36 state historic parks, 878 important Native American archeological sites, 362 museums, 256 historical societies, more than 60 local governments with heritage preservation boards, and at least 35,000 historically or architecturally significant buildings. California also led the nation in annual income from tourism ($27 billion, nearly twice the value of the state's farm produce), a large part of which derived from visits to historic sites. The past, the Task Force concluded, is an important economic resource that should be systematically conserved and marketed. In California, history has become big business.

THE NEW EDEN

Ironically, for all their fixation on history, for all their vivid images of certain historic persons and events, Californians' understanding of their state's past is distorted by legend and myth. Most Californians see the state's history as a romantic, anecdotal story featuring famous people and heroic events: Cabrillo's voyage of discovery in 1542, the Serra-Portolá expedition in 1769, the Bear Flag Revolt of 1846, the gold rush of 1849, the completion of the transcontinental railway in 1869, the "boom of the '80s," the Progressive triumph over big business in 1910, and so on. These events, not the complicated social processes associated with them, are seen as making history. Californians, for example, know much about Junípero Serra and his heroic efforts to found the first Spanish missions at San Diego and Monterey in 1769 and 1770, but little about the function of the missions in the long-term relationship between Hispanic colonists and Indians, perhaps the major historical dynamic prior to the 1840s. They have read how the Central Pacific Railroad conquered the invincible Sierra Nevada and seen illustrations of Leland Stanford driving the last golden spike, but understand little about the role of railroads in social, economic, cultural, and political change.

In the popular tradition, history is also composed of the exploits of the famous and powerful, heroes and villains alike: Father Serra, Jedediah Smith, John C. Frémont, David Broderick, Stanford and the other members of the "Big Four," Denis Kearney, Hiram Johnson, Sunny Jim Rolph, Upton Sinclair, Earl Warren, Richard Nixon, Ronald Reagan, Jerry Brown, Howard Jarvis, and

others. In the popular history, California was built by great individuals, who were usually politicians and old-line Americans—and invariably white and male. Playing less publicized or important roles were the masses of poor people, women, and ethnic minorities (Indians, European and Asian immigrants, Hispanics, and blacks). These people are barely visible in the typical publication, museum, or historical park.

Popular history also emphasizes the theme of California's uniqueness. The state appears as a land apart from the rest of the world. A distinctive population, settlement history, and particularly climate and geography have combined to create a singular civilization in California. The region is variously described as "the great exception," "an experimental society," and "the cutting edge of American civilization," an ultimate frontier where new values, behaviors, and institutions have been pioneered.

The California of popular history is, finally, a "Garden of Eden," a unique, benevolent land where innovative and enterprising people have fulfilled individual and national aspirations. A relentless current of untarnished success runs through popular California history on many levels, especially economic progress. Society in frontier California is commonly portrayed as democratic and classless. Accessible and abundant resources, coupled with the egalitarian instincts of the people, shattered the rigid class structures of older societies. People succeeded through diligence and intelligence, not inherited wealth or influence, and failed because of their own weakness. Starting out equally, most thrived, and California quickly emerged as a homogeneous, middle-class society.

To the extent that ethnic minorities appear in this popular history, California also epitomizes the great American "melting pot." In the tolerant atmosphere of a new

Casa del Oro and Carson Mansion
Modern restorations throughout California convey a romanticized impression of the state's past. Casa del Oro in Monterey *(left)* was a simple store in the 1840s; along with other buildings from the Hispanic eras, it has been upgraded, sterilized, and surrounded with lavish landscaping and courtyards, creating an illusion of a vanished aristocratic community. In Eureka, the Carson Mansion *(right)* suggests an affluence that did not generally characterize the early years of the American period. *Photographs by William A. Bullough.*

frontier, where there was enough land and opportunity to go around, virtually everyone was welcomed, and different ethnic groups related to one another harmoniously.

In the popular mind, California is in virtually every way the ultimate achievement of the American dream and one of the greatest success stories in human history. "California history," concluded a recent pamphlet by the State Department of Parks, "is a romantic tale of a land blessed by nature and inhab-

ited by men of greatness." That single, brief, unabashedly chauvinistic statement captures the essence of popular mythology about the state.

THE TRADITIONAL VIEW OF CALIFORNIA HISTORY

Californians' capacity to romanticize their history typifies the normal tendency of each generation to glorify the past, to remember only what it feels comfortable remembering. But it also reflects the fact that, until recently, history has been written by and for affluent white men and, predictably, dwelt on the achievements of that group while overlooking the experiences and contributions of others. In addition, during the last century, California history has often been linked to boosterism. Many early state historians, such as John H. Hittell, were boosters, and their writings were, at least in part, promotional tracts for local resources and culture. The boosters' inevitable emphasis on such traditional and safe themes as growth, progress, success, social equality, and exciting romance on the frontier has permeated popular culture and some scholarly historical thought as well. In a region where most residents are newcomers or the children of newcomers, personal and family memories about the past are sufficiently short to make many people susceptible to the boosters' claims.

Californians are also unknowing victims of their own successful preservation efforts. Libraries, museums, state parks, and restorations concern themselves primarily with the documents, buildings, and artifacts of the wealthy, powerful, and famous individuals, who constituted a small minority of all past generations. By contrast, the shanties, factories, tools, and clothing of the poor and most of the middle class—by far the majority of the people—were common, unadorned, and cheaply constructed. Readily dismantled and burned or discarded in trash heaps, they rarely survive into the present.

Restorers then clean, paint, and rebuild the structures and artifacts of the elite and surround them with gardens, fountains, and courtyards. Usually, objects are restored to a higher level of elegance than they ever had originally. The results are vivid, colorful images with a dramatic impact on visitors. But they suggest a sanitized past of affluence, sta-

bility, and democracy—in other words, a false history, one without failure, poverty, inequality, racism, disease, or conflict. California restorers have thus erected Spanish missions containing little evidence that their major inhabitants were ill-treated and rebellious Indians. Restorers have also recreated mines without miners, lung disease, or strikes; farms without stooped crop pickers; lovely Victorian neighborhoods with no adjacent slums; and entire worlds with few or no women.

California's professional historians also bear part of the blame for the state's skewed history. Often sharing the boosters' patriotic vision of their home state, they have sometimes perpetuated old stereotypes and myths. Some state historians who have advanced beyond boosterism have been limited by parochialism; working in state and local history, a notoriously traditional field to begin with, they have until recently been remote from major centers of scholarship. As a result, some California historians have been slow to adopt the current interests, theories, and research methods of modern national historians. Many of their works uncritically celebrate California's historical successes, treat the state in a vacuum without comparing it with the outside world, or persist in using older interpretive ideas that scholars elsewhere have discredited.

For seventy years, for example, most California historians have continued to see the complex period of economic and social change between the 1860s and 1920 within the traditional "Populist-Progressive" framework. The unifying theme of that period, they maintain, was the struggle between common people and rising corporate monopolies—the Southern Pacific Railroad, in California's case. In standard California histories, democratic reformers and corporate bosses still stalk each other doggedly across those decades. Most national historians within the last thirty years, however, have abandoned that view as simplistic and have proposed alternative unifying themes such as industrialization, modernization, ethnocultural conflict, and the organizational revolution, few of which California historians have explored. Instead, through their textbooks, reference works, and more specialized and popular writings, they have laid the factual and interpretive foundation for historical restorations, influenced the traditional teaching of state history in colleges and public schools, and helped to reinforce popular misconceptions of California history.

RECONSIDERING CALIFORNIA HISTORY

Over the last few decades, modern scholarship has increasingly questioned popular myths of California history. In part, changes within the historical profession itself have contributed to the reevaluation of the state's past. Influenced by other social sciences, such as anthropology, sociology, economics, and political science, historians have adopted more sophisticated theories of interpreting social change and new methods of measuring it. They have framed questions more carefully, gathered and evaluated evidence more systematically, and broadened their perspective by comparing California to other western states and even to other countries. In order to recapture the history of ordinary people, who left few official records, some historians have turned more to nonwritten evidence. Social structure, economics, and culture have replaced politics as the principal focus of research. At the same time, new manuscripts, documents, census records, and nonverbal sources such as photographs, artifacts, and archeological evidence have released a flood of additional data. Armed with fresh materials, professional interests, and tools of analysis, state historians have begun to test old assumptions about California's past and, increasingly, to find them inaccurate, simplistic, or limiting.

Also, ideas about race, ethnicity, gender roles, and other questions have changed dramatically since the 1950s, requiring a reevaluation of such important topics as the Spanish missions; Asian, Hispanic, and European immigration; and the experience of black people and women. New ethnic and feminist organizations have demanded that historical stereotypes be corrected, insisted that more attention be paid to their group's participation in the state's development, and sponsored exhibits, publications, archival collections, and public school programs. Although some efforts have degenerated into their own brand of group boosterism, the upsurge of ethnic and women's studies has enlivened and strengthened historical thinking, both popular and scholarly. New specialized histories of these groups have appeared, records have been unearthed, old museums have been improved and entirely new ones have been founded, and public school and college textbooks have been expanded and rewritten. Historians have begun to recover the long-ignored story of the people who at all times have constituted the majority of Californians.

Similarly, contemporary conflicts over water, energy, and wilderness have sparked a new environmental history, and debates over agricultural policy have bred studies of land, labor, irrigation, mechanization, and the crucial role of government in economic development. Much rethinking remains, and will always remain, to be done. Nevertheless, the recent generation has produced a new history that, although not as simply understood as the boosters', is more subtle, complex, and realistic, and is better able to embrace the rich diversity of California's past and present.

This volume attempts to reexamine California history in light of recent scholarship at the state and national levels. While the traditional political subject matter will be covered, we have chosen to emphasize social, economic, and cultural history. We will also focus not on the few rich and famous people, but rather on the masses of ordinary Californians, their labors, recreations, families, failures, and achievements.

Bringing the common people to the fore—reading "history from the bottom up"—exposes California as something other than the model frontier democracy of popular myth. California has never been a harmonious, homogeneous, middle-class society. The major hallmark of the state has been its diversity, rooted in its contrasting natural environments and the varied backgrounds and experiences of its settlers. Some succeeded economically, some failed. Some acquired power, others did not. Some were oppressors, some were oppressed, some were both, and many were neither. Society in California has been as hierarchical, and the chasm between the poor and the rich as great, as in any American region.

Since the first human settlement there, ethnic and cultural diversity particularly has characterized the region. But California has never been the classic "melting pot." Usually, groups in power insisted that minorities relinquish their cultures, adopt those of the dominant groups, and accept social, economic, and political inferiority. The minorities rarely gave in without a struggle. Interaction, assimilation, and conflict among ethnic and cultural groups have always shaped California history.

Persistent inequality, attempts by groups to subordinate others, and intergroup tension, then, have been major themes of California history. Usually, however, conflict has not been a simple matter of rich versus poor, workers versus employers, reformers versus conservatives, whites versus ethnics, or north versus south. Instead, conflict among and within groups has been bewilderingly complex and ever changing. In California, democracy was the child not of homogeneity and agreement, but of diversity and competition among groups.

Success or failure in California was a function not only of personal, but also of group, effort. Instead of celebrating the achievements of frontier rugged individualism, this volume will emphasize the important role of human interaction and organization. To the settlers of recent centuries, California was often no paradise on earth, but rather a rugged, harsh land that yielded its treasures reluctantly. California developed into an enormously successful civilization not only because it had great heroes ("men of greatness"), but because countless ordinary residents banded together into ingenious and flexible organizations to overcome monumental barriers to development. California history records the works of farm organizations, labor unions, business associations, professional groups, political parties, community organizations, water agencies, churches, schools, universities, and a succession of other voluntary and official agencies. The great difficulties of settlement in California made the building of diverse, flexible, and strong governments particularly essential to foster and regulate economic growth, modify natural conditions, and mediate among contending factions. Groups who could organize effectively often succeeded; those who could not often failed. California today stands as a testament to the power of cooperation and collective action.

All human societies have interacted with

nature in distinctive ways that have influenced regional history. This volume will explore this relationship as one of the central themes of the California experience. Nature endowed California with singular location, topography, climate, and resources. Indians, Hispanic colonists, American pioneers, and modern residents all developed their own approaches to the natural environment, approaches that both reflected and shaped their cultures. Gradually, the people acquired greater power to manipulate their environment—particularly water—in order to extract resources, build more complex economies, and support ever larger populations. Along with that power came, over the last century, a growing awareness of nature's sensitivity and unpredictability and of the human capacity for dangerous, perhaps catastrophic, error. To the rest of the world, California has contributed models both of ruthless environmental destruction and of conservation and preservation.

For all of California's distinctiveness, however, nature's sway over history and the region's uniqueness and inventiveness have too often been exaggerated. Following the lead of the great frontier historian Frederick Jackson Turner, many observers have assumed that pioneers, in confronting raw nature in the wilderness, shed previous ways as impractical and invented new cultures attuned to their natural conditions. Since California was the ultimate frontier, with the most singular of environments, it followed logically that it must also be the most experimental of American regions.

But comparisons of California with other frontiers and settled areas show that continuity, not deviation, of cultures marked the western experience. Settlers did not discard their ancestral cultures, but clung to them even more fiercely as a defense against the disorganizing wilderness. Culture proved resilient to environmental pressures, and Californians imposed their cultures on nature, at least eventually. The region's civilization thus came to resemble the outside world of which it was a part. No one force, not even nature, determined California history. The people found the land and made of it what they willed.

CHAPTER TWO

THE NATURAL SETTING

CALIFORNIA, AN ISLAND WORLD

At first, Europeans conceived of California as an island. Even before the region was discovered, the name appeared in a popular mythic romance, *Las Sergas de Esplandián*, written in the early sixteenth century by the Spanish author Garcí Ordoñez de Montalvo. "Know ye," wrote Montalvo, "that at the right hand of the Indies there is an island named California, very close to that part of the Terrestrial Paradise. . . . The island itself is one of the wildest in the world on account of the bold and craggy rocks. . . . The island everywhere abounds with gold and precious stones, and upon it no other metal was found." A few decades later, perhaps in jest, Spaniards gave the name "California" to the area north and west of Mexico, which they at first reached only by ship and thought to be a bleak island. Eventually, explorers established that California was part of the North American mainland. In this case, however, the Europeans' naive early impressions, though geographically false, turned out to be ecologically true.

Although physically attached to North America, California is still most accurately thought of as an ecological "island." Its geological history is distinct from that of the rest of the continent. Winds, currents, mountains, and deserts isolate the region biologically just as effectively as if it were girthed by an ocean moat. Its unique climates and landscapes create a potential for diverse and distinctive life forms unmatched elsewhere on the continent. As many have observed, California is the place of the extreme, the unusual, and the spectacular. It is "the land of contrast," "a land apart," a veritable "island upon the land." Throughout its human occupation, California's exceptional landscapes, climates, and life forms have bred distinctive economies and cultures. Only against such a powerful and dynamic natural setting can we understand the drama of human history in this singular region.

THE DYNAMIC LANDSCAPE

Nature is often incorrectly assumed to be static and eternal, a stable benchmark

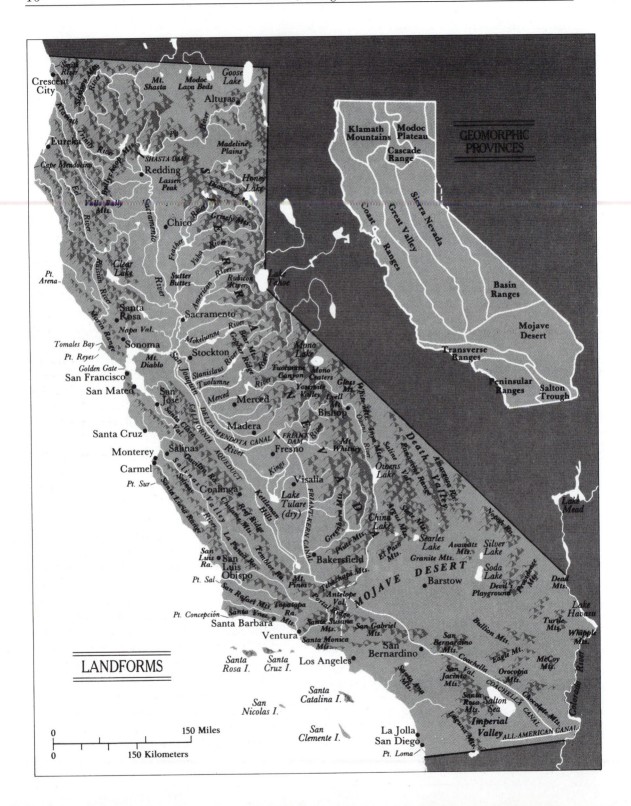

LANDFORMS

GEOMORPHIC PROVINCES

Klamath Mountains
Modoc Plateau
Cascade Range
Coast Ranges
Great Valley
Sierra Nevada
Basin Ranges
Mojave Desert
Transverse Ranges
Peninsular Ranges
Salton Trough

Crescent City
Smith River
Siskiyou Mts.
Mt. Shasta
Modoc Lava Beds
Goose Lake
Alturas
Madeline Plains
Eureka
Klamath River
Trinity River
Cape Mendocino
SHASTA DAM
Redding
Lassen Peak
Honey Lake
Eel River
Yolla Bolly Mts.
Chico
Grizzly Mts.
Feather River
Yuba River
Pt. Arena
Clear Lake
Russian River
Sutter Buttes
American River
Rubicon River
Lake Tahoe
Santa Rosa
Napa Val.
Sacramento
Bear Mts.
Gopher Ridge
Mono Lake
Tomales Bay
Sonoma
Mokelumne River
Pt. Reyes
Mt. Diablo
Stockton
Stanislaus River
Tuolumne
Tuolumne Canyon
Mono Craters
Golden Gate
Glass Mt.
San Francisco
San Mateo
San José
Merced
Madera
Yosemite Valley
Mt. Lyell
Bishop
White Mts.
Santa Cruz
FRIANT DAM
Fresno
Mt. Whitney
Monterey
Salinas
Carmel
Coalinga
Kings
Visalia
Owens Lake
Pt. Sur
Lake Tulare (dry)
China Lake
Death Valley
Kettleman Hills
Reef Ridge
Searles Lake
Avawatz Mts.
Silver Lake
San Luis Ra.
San Luis Obispo
Bakersfield
El Paso Mts.
Granite Mts.
Soda Lake
Pt. Sal
Mt. Pinos
Tehachapi Mts.
MOJAVE DESERT
Barstow
Devil's Playground
Dead Mts.
Pt. Concepción
Topatopa Ra.
Antelope Val.
Lake Havasu
Santa Barbara
Santa Ynez
Santa Susana Mts.
Santa Monica Mts.
San Gabriel Mts.
San Bernardino Mts.
Bullion Mts.
Turtle Mts.
Whipple Mts.
Ventura
San Bernardino
Coachella Val.
Eagle Mt.
McCoy Mts.
Los Angeles
San Jacinto Mts.
Orocopia Mts.
Santa Rosa I.
Santa Cruz I.
Santa Ana Mts.
Santa Rosa Mts.
Salton Sea
Chocolate Mts.
Colorado River
San Nicolas I.
Santa Catalina I.
Imperial Valley
San Clemente I.
La Jolla
San Diego
Pt. Loma
COACHELLA CANAL
ALL-AMERICAN CANAL
Laguna Mts.

0   150 Miles

0   150 Kilometers

against which to measure the ups and downs of human affairs. Actually, nature is dynamic. Oceans rise and fall on the land. Whole continents meander around the globe. Mountain chains burst from the earth, then sink down again. Plants and animals evolve, some going on to become new species and some dying out altogether. Climates change from frigid to torrid, from humid to arid. Radically different ecological communities succeed one another on the same landscape. So it has been for billions of years. Although the change has usually been slower than the creeping of a glacier, it has been no less revolutionary.

No place illustrates nature's dynamism better than California. For hundreds of millions of years, the region's landscape has been evolving. The present coast generally coincides with the border between the North American and Pacific plates of the earth's crust. These plates continually interact, grinding together, pushing apart, or slipping sideways against each other. The gnashing of plates has made the Pacific Coast, unlike most of North America, a particularly active geological region, with abundant earthquakes, volcanic action, and elevation and subsidence of land. Over the last one hundred million years, mountains have risen, pushed upward by subterranean pressure or formed by lava from volcanic eruptions, only to be whittled down by water and wind erosion and then reborn elsewhere. As the earth heaved and sank, the sea roamed back and forth across the landscape. At times, nearly all of California was under water; at others, the coastline was many miles west of its present location. Marshes and forests flourished in turn, and then were buried under hundreds of feet of sediment.

Then, about thirty million years ago, the present landscape began to emerge. The western, or Pacific, plate began to drift northward along the San Andreas Fault, its border with the North American Plate. Over millions of years, it carried part of the Baja California Peninsula north to form the present coast from San Francisco Bay south to the Imperial Valley. Between ten and twenty million years ago, the Sierra Nevada mountain range loomed up and tilted to the west. It is still rising. The younger Coast Range took shape, and the great Central Valley, then a vast inland arm of the sea, was gradually sealed off and filled with eroding sediment from surrounding mountains. About two million years ago, the world's climate turned cold, inaugurating a series of ice ages. Although great glaciers moved southward from the polar region over much of North America, they missed California. Smaller glaciers, however, did grind down the slopes of the High Sierra, sculpting out valleys such as Yosemite.

When the ice finally began to melt, only about twenty thousand years ago, the coastline was twenty miles west of its current location. Herds of mammoths shared the cool, moist country with giant ground sloths, camels, and saber-toothed cats. Marshes and redwood forests covered the land. As the receding glaciers melted, oceans rose and salt water again flooded the land. The climate grew hotter and drier, and the southern deserts began to develop. Many animals and plants became extinct or, like the redwoods, retreated to tiny ranges. About ten thousand years ago, the sea reached the present shore, penetrated the Golden Gate, and started flooding a north–south valley in the Coast Range. San Francisco Bay was not formed for another several thousand years. When Indians first settled that area, the bay did not

California Topography
Adapted from David Hornbeck, *California Patterns: A Geographical and Historical Atlas* (Mountain View, Calif.: Mayfield Publishing Co., 1983).

exist; their ancient villages are now buried under its waters. California as we know it, with its sea cliffs, harbors, forests, grasslands, and deserts, is comparatively young—only a few thousand years old—and still forming. It is a fragile, and by no means immutable, land.

A MOSAIC OF CLIMATES

As California's landscape emerged a few thousand years ago, so did its modern climate. The state's climate results from the interaction of ocean currents and temperatures, air-pressure systems, wind and storm patterns, and the location of major mountains and valleys. Most of the densely populated, low-lying areas along the coast and in interior valleys have a Mediterranean climate—a moderate, subtropical climate with rainy winters and dry summers. Although this climate type is rare, a few other regions have similar climates, including the Mediterranean region, North Africa, the Near East, and parts of Chile, Australia, and South Africa.

Geographical position and landscape cause California's climate to differ greatly from those of neighboring regions, the cool Pacific Northwest rain forest and the arid Southwest and Great Basin. A dominant marine influence moderates California's climate. The wide California Current carries a stream of relatively cool water (warm in winter) from the northwestern Pacific Ocean southeastward along the coast. Prevailing westerly winds sweep air masses from the ocean, whose temperature is relatively stable, across the region, cooling it in summer and warming it in winter.

A large high air-pressure zone called the Pacific High usually hovers about one thousand miles west of the coast. It intensifies the moderating ocean winds and regulates the flow of weather systems, and hence of pre-

cipitation. In the late spring and early summer, as air and water temperatures increase, the Pacific High moves northward, forcing storms originating in the Gulf of Alaska to track across the Pacific Northwest and into the northern Great Plains. Most of the state is therefore practically free of rainfall from April through September. In autumn, though, the Pacific High drifts southward, opening the door to a succession of winter storms that deliver most of California's precipitation. Mountain chains, particularly the northwestern Siskiyou, the Coast Range, and the Sierra Nevada, slow down the storms and extract their moisture before they move eastward. As a result, California is well watered in comparison to arid inland states. Almost all precipitation falls in the winter, however, and it runs off quickly or is stored in forest watersheds, underground basins, and deep mountain snows.

Actually, because of its immense size and diverse topography, California encompasses a mosaic of climates that duplicate the weather of most areas of the world, including temperate rain forest in the northwestern part of the state, arctic and alpine climates on the tops of the highest mountains, and arid steppe and desert climates to the south and southeast. Even the Mediterranean climate zones are heterogeneous. Local climates vary according to three criteria: distance southward from the northern border; distance eastward from the coast; and elevation. Generally, it is cooler in summer and wetter in winter in the north than in the south, along the coast than inland, and at higher than at lower elevations. Moreover, low-elevation gaps in the Coast Range allow more ocean air and marine influence to reach the interior at some points, such as opposite the Golden Gate and Carquinez Strait. Elsewhere, high coastal peaks inhibit the flow of marine air and cast rain shadows that reduce land to the east to searing deserts, as in the southern San Joaquin Valley and the Mojave and Colorado deserts east of the San Gabriel and San Bernardino mountains.

Climatic contrasts can be enormous. The northwest coast has one of the coolest average summer high temperatures (rarely more than 70 degrees F) and one of the highest average annual rainfalls (more than one hundred inches) in the contiguous United States. Yet the Imperial Valley in the southeast is one of the hottest and driest places in the Western Hemisphere, with summer temperatures in excess of 120 degrees and an annual rainfall of less than three inches. Some of the coldest temperatures ever recorded in the United States were taken near Donner Pass in the High Sierra (less than −60 degrees), while the highest (more than 130 degrees) has been recorded at Death Valley, two hundred fifty miles to the southeast. Local variations can be nearly as great. Average annual rainfall at San José, for example, is about thirteen inches; twenty miles west and across the Santa Cruz Mountains—at Boulder Creek, in the redwood forest—it is sixty inches. On a hot summer day in the city of Los Angeles, it is not unusual for the temperature to be 75 degrees at the beaches, 85 degrees in Westwood, 95 degrees downtown, and 105 degrees in the San Fernando Valley. California's local climates—and hence its resources, plant and animal communities, and human settlement patterns—vary more than in any other land of similar size in the world.

DISTINCTIVE PLANT LIFE

Because of its singular geographical location, heterogeneous landscape, and disparate climates, California's resources are unique and diverse. Microenvironments of distinct location, elevation, soil, and climate nurture a more varied wildlife than anywhere in North America. California alone, for example, has three times as many native plant species as the entire northeastern United States.

As befits an "island upon the land," many plants are endemic, or found only in this state. Such plants are particularly common along the central coast, from the northern San Francisco Bay region south to Point Conception; in this zone, unique in North America, cool, moist northwestern and hot, dry southwestern climates overlap. Mountains in the north and east of the state, and deserts in the southeast, keep endemic plants from spreading and insulate them from invasion by outsiders. Indicative of California's tendency toward diverse, specialized environments and species are the state's coniferous trees. Of the seventy-three varieties of conifers in the American West, fifty-four are native to California, including about one-quarter of all the species of pines in the world. Of the state's conifers, twenty-one are endemic, including the coast redwood (*Sequoia sempervirens*), giant sequoia (*Sequoiadendron giganteum*), Monterey pine, digger pine, and many species of cypress.

Some endemic species are ancient ones that were common as long ago as the dinosaur era, but survive now only in small, specialized environments. The graceful coast redwood, though hardy within its range, can exist naturally only in the cool, moist, foggy low-lying belt along the coast from Big Sur to the Oregon border. The gnarled bristlecone pine survives only above ten thousand feet of elevation in the eastern White Mountains. Some individual trees have lived for more than six thousand years, ranking them among the world's oldest living organisms. California has also given birth to the world's tallest species (coast redwood) and the bulkiest (giant sequoia).

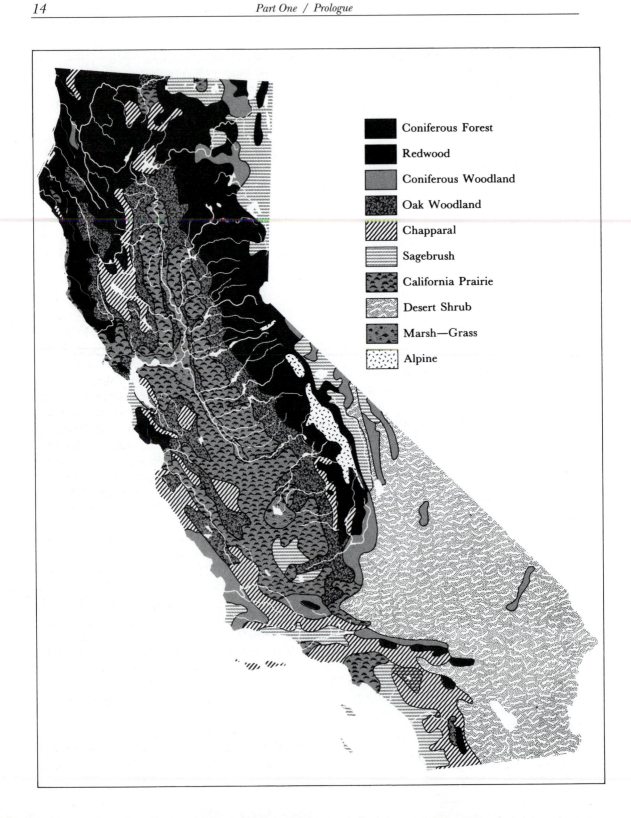

Coniferous Forest

Redwood

Coniferous Woodland

Oak Woodland

Chapparal

Sagebrush

California Prairie

Desert Shrub

Marsh—Grass

Alpine

A LAND OF MANY WORLDS

California is an assemblage of small worlds, each one unique, with a combined capacity for production and self-sufficiency greater than that of most nations. The subregions offer a mix of resources and economic potentials unrivaled by any other state.

The state has twelve hundred miles of beautiful seacoast—gentle and warm with wide beaches in the south, rugged, cold, and windswept in the north. Abundant fisheries lie just off the coast in the nutrient-rich waters of the California Current, in rocky tidepools, and in shoreline bays and salt marshes. Before Europeans arrived, the fisheries supported immense populations of birds, sea mammals, and native peoples. In the last century, harvesting of salmon, cod, halibut, tuna, crab, and shellfish, and, until recently, the whale, developed into one of the nation's largest fishing industries.

Inland from the shore is a coastal plain composed of the valleys of rivers that flow into the Pacific. The coastal plain has fertile soil, moderate temperatures, and generally higher rainfall than the interior. Wide and warm in the south, the plain becomes increasingly narrow, intermittent, and forbidding until it peters out in precipitous cliffs and fog banks north of Morro Bay. At several points, natural harbors break up the plain. Two bays, San Francisco and San Diego, are among the largest and most sheltered in the world. Since the early days of European exploration, they have made California a focal point of Pacific maritime commerce.

Several coastal points have ready access to the interior, especially the path through San Francisco Bay, the Carquinez Strait, and the Sacramento–San Joaquin river system, the only navigable sea-level route through the Coast Range into the interior between Mexico and the Columbia River. To the east of Los Angeles, a gentle, low-lying, one-thousand-mile pathway stretches across southern Arizona, New Mexico, and Texas to the Mississippi Valley; this made Los Angeles the major southwestern terminus for the American railroad system. For thousands of years, the coastal valleys have supported large human populations. They have great potential for urbanization, particularly at San Francisco, San Diego, and Los Angeles, as well as for intensive agriculture.

California's mountains also constitute an important resource. Varying from low hills to medium peaks, the Coast Range flanks the entire coast. In the north, the Siskiyous, Klamaths, and the southern extension of the Cascade volcanic range through Mount Shasta and Lassen Peak separate the state from Oregon. California's most monumental chain, the Sierra Nevada, stretches southward from the Cascades in a belt forty to eighty miles wide and four hundred miles long on the state's eastern border. With many peaks over ten thousand feet high, it insulates the state from the Great Basin. The Tehachapis, San Gabriels, and San Bernardinos—rare east-west mountains collectively called the Transverse Ranges—slice through the state about one hundred fifty miles north of the Mexican border, dividing southern and northern California into distinct geological, biological, climatic, and cultural regions. As noted earlier, all of these mountain chains isolate California from the rest of North America and inhibit the migration of plants and animals to, from, and within the state. Until the recent development of the railroad, automobile, and airplane, they also deterred the flow of overland immigrants and commerce.

California's mountains also house mineral treasures. More than one hundred million

California Vegetation Zones
Adapted from *Historical Atlas of California,* by Warren A. Beck and Ynez D. Haase. Copyright © 1974 by the University of Oklahoma Press.

Sierra Snowpack
Melting Sierra snows feed the Yuba River, near Cisco Grove. Like many Sierra streams, the Yuba's water eventually descends through reservoirs and the Sacramento River to the Delta and San Francisco Bay, slaking the thirst of farms, cities, and industries along the way. *Courtesy of the California Department of Water Resources.*

years ago, while subterranean rocks were heating and cooling, molten gold collected in faults and fractures. After the Sierra Nevada had been raised up, yellow metal from the lodes eroded and was deposited as placer gold at lower elevations along the beds of ancient and modern rivers in the western foothills of the Sierra. In the 1840s and 1850s, the gold was discovered with

great fanfare. Mining developed into the state's first great industry, triggering the first of many population booms.

Also serving as watersheds, the mountains collect precipitation from winter Pacific storms, store it in rocks, soils, and snows as deep as fifty or seventy-five feet and then, in spring and summer, dispense it gradually into rivers that deliver water and fertile silt to the lowland valleys. Steep mountain slopes also create much potential for hydroelectric power generation.

In mountain coolness and moisture large forests thrive—redwood along the northern coast, oak on the central and southern coast and Sierra foothills, and pine and fir elsewhere. The trees shelter rodents, birds, grazers, and predators, and they play an important part in maintaining the mountain watershed. Their roots solidify soils, slow runoff, reduce erosion, and increase the water-storage capacity. Interspersed with rugged peaks, glacial valleys and waterfalls, and sparkling alpine lakes, the state's mountain forests have attracted artists, sightseers, campers, and defenders of wilderness. Forests blanketed more than half the state until heavy logging began in the mid-nineteenth century. Lumbering, however, has since become a major industry in northern and Sierra counties, and forests are being stripped from the land faster than nature can regenerate them. Because the needs of lumbering, mining, irrigation, hydroelectric generation, tourism, and wilderness preservation often conflict, California's mountains and forests have been the focus of bitter political, economic, and ideological struggles.

Dramatic though the mountains are, the great Central Valley is in many ways California's most remarkable geographical feature. Composed of the drainage basins of the Sacramento and San Joaquin rivers, the north–south valley between the Coast Range and the Sierra is a flat territory, nearly at sea level, five hundred miles long and thirty to seventy miles wide. It is filled with fertile alluvial soils—hundreds of feet deep in some places—washed from the surrounding mountainsides. The largest expanse of flat land west of the Rocky Mountains, the Central Valley is about the size of the states of Vermont, New Hampshire, Massachusetts,

Sierra Nevada Forest, Yosemite National Park
Photograph by William A. Bullough.

Connecticut, and Rhode Island combined. Annual rainfall in the valley varies enormously, from more than thirty inches at Redding in the north to less than seven inches at Bakersfield in the south. The valley's west side, in the rain shadow of the Coast Range, is also far more arid than its east side.

All of the valley lies near abundant water resources, however. Large, perennial rivers originate in the Sierra to the east, snake slowly back and forth across the gentle country, and keep underground water basins overflowing to ground levels. Before the dams and flood-control and drainage projects of the last century, marshes covered much riverside land. In especially rainy years, the valley was transformed into a series of lakes. With immense agricultural potential in its soils, flat terrain, water, and hot climate, the valley, in the twentieth century, developed into the world's largest irrigated area and the nation's most productive farm region.

Another key topographical region of the state is the Sacramento–San Joaquin Delta, formed by the confluence of the two major river systems before they enter San Francisco Bay. The Delta has been central to California's development, serving as a natural reservoir, collecting, filtering, and dispersing about one-half of the state's water. Since it is at or below sea level, it is also the point at which salt water surging eastward from the bay mixes with fresh water flowing westward from the interior. The cleansing action of its marshes and sloughs maintains the purity of San Francisco Bay. In the last century, growing demands have been placed on the Delta to furnish navigable waterways, sewer drainage, and reclaimed farmland—as well as water for local agriculture, industry, and cities, and, increasingly, for export to the south. The Delta and the contradictory pressures exerted on its resources are a microcosm of twentieth-century California water management, with its potential for stimulating economic growth, aggravating environmental problems, and provoking conflicts among rival interests.

In stark contrast to the well-watered Delta are the fierce deserts east of the Sierra Nevada and in the southeastern corner of the state. The deserts are generally composed of flat terrain, broken occasionally by alkali sinks, seasonally dry rivers and creeks, and ranges of rocky hills and mountains.

Though the deserts support only limited natural plant and animal life, at or beneath the surface were valuable deposits of gold, silver, copper, borax, lime, salt, and other minerals that, before being depleted, supported valuable mining industries. In a few areas, fertile soil has been deposited by modern streams (the Mojave and Colorado valleys) or ancient rivers (the Salton Sink, or Imperial Valley). Where outside water can be acquired, the desert's hot climate is ideal for growing rare crops, such as dates, melons, strawberries, and winter fruits and vegetables. After it received irrigation water in the early twentieth century, the dunes and alkali plains of the Imperial Valley developed into one of California's most productive croplands. The Imperial Valley, and the Coachella Valley just to the north, became the only below-sea-level agricultural areas in North America.

WATER

In terms of its influence on human settlement, the uneven distribution of water is the most significant pattern in California's natural environment. Because of California's location, climate, and topography, water is relatively abundant by western standards. From Indian days to the present, a generous water supply has attracted much larger human populations to California than to other western areas. Yet California is still an arid region. It receives less than half the average annual rainfall of the South Atlantic and Gulf Coast states, and its mean water runoff per acre is a small fraction of that in states east of the Mississippi.

Complex drought patterns have always shaped California's human history. First of all, there is a seasonal water imbalance. Almost eighty percent of the state's rain falls between November and March. The period from May through September, the normal agricultural growing season, is virtually rainless. Agriculture and urbanization are difficult or impossible in most parts of the state without large-scale man-made water developments.

There are also extreme regional variations in rainfall and access to water. Northern and southern California are fundamentally dissimilar water regions. In the north, the climate is more humid, the storms more frequent and moisture-laden, and the mountains higher and more advantageously positioned to capture and store water. Nearly ninety percent of moisture falls and is available north of an east–west line just south of Monterey—roughly the northern half of the state. Climatically much more a part of the arid Southwest, the southern counties are by nature largely desert. Northwesterly storms often expend their fury and their moisture before they ever reach the southern districts. Yet, because of other resources—primarily petroleum and natural gas, fertile soil, a gentler winter climate, and proximity to strategic pathways into the interior—the coastal strip from Santa Barbara through Los Angeles to San Diego began to be densely populated in the 1880s. Today it houses more than half the state's population, with a seemingly insatiable thirst for more water than is available locally.

Further complicating California's water situation are prolonged, cyclical water shortages, one- to ten-year periods when the Pacific High stays in northern latitudes and insufficient winter rain falls over part or all of the state. Acute, long-term drought has recurred every decade or two for at least the last two centuries that records have been kept, with sometimes catastrophic loss of property, livestock, and human life. Severe drought has intensified squabbles over water and heightened pressures to construct facilities large enough to store more than a one-year supply.

Ironically, water is sometimes too abundant. During particularly fierce winter storms and, occasionally, entire years of abnormally high precipitation, far more rain falls than can be absorbed, evaporated, or evacuated in natural drainage systems. California is flood-prone, particularly the low-lying areas along northwestern coast rivers and in the Central Valley. Great floods have annihilated towns, farms, mines, irrigation works, transportation lines, and human lives. The flood of early 1862 turned the Central Valley into a giant lake, destroyed about half of the property value in the state, and touched off lethal epidemics. A 1938 flood in the Los Angeles area inundated 300,000 acres, destroyed $78 million in property, and killed 87 people. Heavy rains in 1982, 1983, 1986, and 1995 unleashed huge earthslides, isolated towns, wiped out entire neighborhoods, and killed scores of people.

Agricultural, industrial, and urban development in California since the 1880s has thus necessitated the most elaborate facilities for water impoundment, storage, control, and interregional transfer in human history. Indeed, water redistribution has become the central problem of the state's modern period. In the early twentieth century, burgeoning San Francisco and Oakland grasped the watersheds of the central Sierra Nevada one hundred miles away, dammed its rivers, and sucked in mountain water by canal and conduit to make urban development on San Francisco Bay possible. Simultaneously, booming Los Angeles looked two hundred miles northward to the Owens River east of the Sierra, acquired water rights in the district, and imported virtually its entire water supply by aqueduct, much to the consternation of Owens Valley farmers and townspeople. When drought struck in the 1920s, southern cities again looked outward and tapped the mighty Colorado River across the state. After the 1940s, when development in postwar southern California consumed even these supplies, the region, with the assistance of federal and state agencies, increasingly imported water from northern watersheds through the Delta and southern San Joaquin Valley and over the Tehachapis. During the last one hundred years, the state's farmers, who consume nearly ninety percent of the managed supplies of water, also sank wells, built dams and canals, and transferred water—sometimes over hundreds of miles—to irrigate crops.

By the 1980s, the California water-distribution system had evolved into a maze of dams, canals, reservoirs, pipelines, pumping plants, underground storage basins, and flood-control projects. Except for a few wild north-coast rivers, virtually every major stream from Mexico to the Oregon border has been reduced to an artificial, human-managed waterway, broken by reservoirs, pumping stations, and hydroelectric generation facilities and leveed or channelized with rock and concrete. In some cases, the flow of rivers has been reversed to move water in directions nature never intended. The California water system ranks among the greatest accomplishments of human intelligence, organization, and technology.

Complex water development has shaped California history in countless ways. In addition to encouraging economic and population growth, large-scale water transfers have made economic development expensive, limited the future growth of areas giving up water, caused severe environmental problems in the regions of origin and of delivery, and greatly aggravated interregional conflict. They have affected even the institutional structure: building and managing such massive systems has given birth to a labyrinth of water agencies and greatly augmented the power of the state and federal governments to regulate local interests. The great expense of irrigation and land reclamation has tended to favor large as opposed

to small farms, wealthy as opposed to poorer growers, and commercial and specialized as opposed to general and subsistence production. In the last century, water has become California's major political, economic, and ideological battleground. The historian Donald Worster has described California as a classic "hydraulic" civilization, like ancient Mesopotamia and Egypt—centralized and hierarchical, dependent on its water facilities, and vulnerable to severe disorder should they collapse.

ENVIRONMENT AND HISTORY

California's natural environment so dramatically differs from that of the rest of North America that observers often rely on it to explain the state's distinctive history. Several widely shared fallacies about the interaction of environment and history, however, have clouded even the understanding of some scholars. Popular and professional writers commonly celebrate the legacy of California's environment as if it were uniformly positive. Like Garcí Ordoñez de Montalvo, most have seen California as "very close to . . . the Terrestrial Paradise," or as stated more recently in a historical summary by the State Department of Parks, a "land blessed by nature." Furthermore, topography, climate, and location have been frequently viewed as the most powerful, and perhaps all-powerful, forces shaping the state's development, responsible for everything from moral values and religious beliefs to institutions, land-tenure patterns, agricultural structures, politics, literature, architecture, and clothing styles.

Largely as a result of the molding influence of a distinctive natural environment on pliable human cultures, many have maintained, California developed a society as unique as its plant forms. "The regional consciousness of California," wrote geographer

James Parsons four decades ago, "has had its origins in the common problems and interests imposed by geography." Remoteness from the rest of the world and a singular climate, particularly its gentleness and its water patterns, he asserted, "strongly influenced the settlement history of the state and the character of its economy and culture." Geography, Parsons concluded, "has had obvious and far-reaching importance for agriculture, industry, and the entire mode of life within the state . . . [and] helps account for whatever quality of regional identity, of uniqueness, that here exists."

These theories contain kernels of truth. Certainly, environment has influenced the state's history. Nature served as a general framework, creating potentials and setting directions for human activities. Because the area's resources are abundant and diverse, California has nurtured populous, complex, and successful civilizations for thousands of years. Without modifying their environment to any extreme degree, the local Indians hunted and gathered natural products and lived more affluently than did most other native peoples. In the past two hundred years, a succession of immigrants created technologies and organizations to harvest California's resources—land, grass, fur-bearing animals, gold, forests, water, climates, scenery, hydroelectric potential, petroleum and natural gas, and transportation sites— even more efficiently and profitably. Each resource in turn gave birth to thriving industries and settlements. On the basis of a prolific and distinctive natural endowment, by the 1990s Californians were able to build their state into the most populous, diverse, productive, and wealthy region in the Amer-

Principal Earthquake Faults
Adapted from Robert Durrenberger, *California: Patterns on the Land* (Mountain View, Calif.: Mayfield Publishing Company, 1976), p. 11.

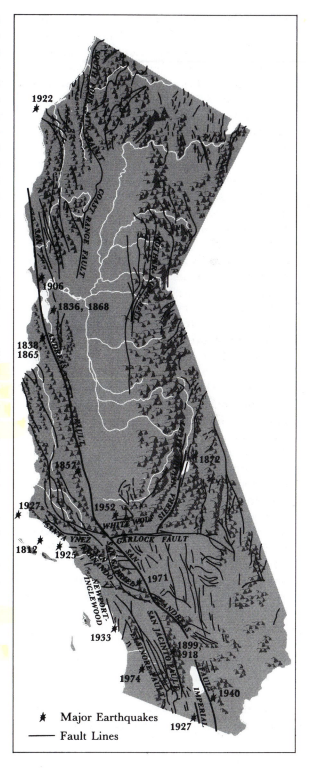

icas. Thus far, most would agree, California's history is largely a success story, a testimonial to the capacity of human intelligence to exploit nature's benevolence.

Nevertheless, the geographical-determinist interpretation of California's past and present, however tempting, is complacent, simplistic, and ahistorical. It also encourages people to believe that social and economic conditions in California are basically "natural" and therefore inevitable, blinds them to the existence of serious problems, and paralyzes attempts to develop realistic public policies.

Although its resources are remarkable, California is not a paradise on earth. Nature placed severe limits on the aspirations of Californians, generated many of their thorniest problems, and undid much of their handiwork. Nature furnished bountiful foods for Indians who were willing to remain separated from the outside world, to spread their populations thin, to adapt to conditions as they found them, and to be content with a subsistence economy. The land raised obstacles to more modern peoples, however. Geographical isolation imposed by mountains, deserts, and the direction of winds and ocean currents complicated exploration, delayed settlement and development of resources, undermined administration, and retarded the establishment of outside markets for the region's products. Diverse climates and resources, in tandem with internal natural barriers, bred incompatible local economies and cultures, interrupted communication, and wracked the state with interregional conflicts. Internal secessionist movements, for example, have plagued California more than any other state.

Although usually present in sufficient quantity, resources have also proven difficult to exploit because they are isolated or poorly distributed. This is especially true of water.

The San Andreas Fault at the Edge of the Carrizo Plain
In this view looking south along the San Andreas Fault in the Carrizo Plain area, between Bakersfield and San Luis Obispo, offset streambeds illustrate the northward drift of the western (Pacific) plate. At this point along California's major fault line, single earthquakes have been known to cause the ground to leap as much as 30 feet laterally in only a few seconds, sending out destructive shock waves for hundreds of miles. *Photograph by Robert Wallace. Courtesy of the United States Geological Survey, Menlo Park.*

Invariably, modern people have wanted to live and work in places where water is in short supply. Imbalances between water supply and human demand have retarded the growth of agriculture and cities and made economic development costly and risky. Like the state's minerals, forests, and soils, water could be used only with technologies that inflicted great environmental damage. Massive relocation of water has destroyed some thriving natural communities, polluted others, overwhelmed drainage systems, poisoned soils, and caused land to subside. These and many other problems created by environmental manipulation are complex and difficult to resolve. They threaten the state's present and future prosperity.

California's environmental balances are not only fragile and easily upset, but the landscape is new and still forming and its natural forces are potent and unpredictable. The region is more prone than others to natural calamity—earthquakes, droughts, floods, volcanic eruptions, forest fires, and tidal waves. If Californians have been blessed by nature, they have also been cursed.

Nature alone, moreover, cannot sufficiently explain California's human history. Lines of cultural development have not been predetermined by natural conditions. Nature offered many alternatives. In all periods, there was wide latitude for the people to shape their own history through individual and social choices growing out of their values, institutions, technologies, and social and economic preferences. In fact, successive groups of Californians used culture to modify the environment to suit their needs, a phenomenon that has grown apace with advancing technology, energy, and organization. If there were to be a single interpretation of the state's long and contradictory history, it would not be the power of nature to mold a distinctive, indigenous culture, but rather the expanding ability of humans, for good or ill, to impose their cultures on the landscape and to recast nature in their own image.

By overplaying the supremacy of nature and underplaying the resilience of culture, geographical determinism consistently exaggerates California's separateness. Often asserted, but rarely proved, "uniqueness" has become an assumed California attribute, a cliché of popular speech and writing. However much the region may be legitimately considered "a land apart," California's peoples at most times and in most important ways resembled, more than they diverged from, the larger cultures to which they belonged. Native Americans, whose societies evolved here for thousands of years and who came closest to being dominated by nature, resembled other hunter-gatherer peoples in general and surrounding western tribes in particular. And even the Indians had a measure of control over their environment and partially freed themselves from its confines. After 1769, Hispanic California was but one segment of a long colonial frontier stretching across northern Mexico, sharing in broader colonial goals, culture, economy, institutions, and Indian policies. Similarly, in the period of United States domination since the 1840s, California can be most completely understood as a region firmly rooted in a rapidly modernizing American culture, not as a radical departure from it.

THE WORLD BEFORE EUROPEANS CAME

The California of today little resembles the pre-European natural world. For more than two centuries, waves of immigrants wielding a growing power over their environment substituted man-made for natural landscapes in most settled, low-lying areas. In both the speed and the extent of environmental change, California has exceeded the rest of the world. The plants, the animals, the people, and even the shape of the land have been radically transformed. California today is the farm, the strip mine, the reservoir, the suburb, the factory, the business park, the freeway, the parking lot.

However, before Spaniards began colonization in 1769, a scant three or four human lifetimes ago, rivers ran freely to the ocean. Valleys and hills were studded with oak groves and carpeted with chest-high bunch grasses that, for the most part, no longer survive. Millions of acres of fresh- and salt-water marshes bordered rivers and bays, particularly in the Delta. Large bodies of water, such as Tulare Lake, then second in size only to Lake Tahoe, dotted the San Joaquin and other valleys. Now, their bottoms largely dried by water diversion and pumping, they are used to raise grain and cotton. Redwood forests covered the western slopes of the Coast Range north of Big Sur, including many of the hills ringing San Francisco Bay. More than ninety percent of the virgin groves have since been cut down. Whales, seals, and otter shared the sites of present-day seaports with hundreds of millions of gulls, egrets, herons, pelicans, and migratory waterfowl. Thousands of condors and eagles ruled the sky.

Grizzlies, not humans, sat at the top of the food chain. Ten thousand of the aggressive, powerful bears roamed California in packs, fearing no other beings. They ate meat from beached whales, salmon from the rivers, and acorns from the oak trees, and they intimidated mountain lions and humans into abandoning their kills. Although webs of grizzly trails crisscrossed the state, intersecting human thoroughfares, the people avoided them. Bears and Indians competed for the same foods and habitats, but man usually deferred to beast. The world was different then, as was the people's place in it.

THE DAMNDEST FINEST RUINS

Californians blissfully ignore a basic fact about their "Eden": unimaginable fury created much of the scenic grandeur that provides their pleasure and the abundant resources that sustain their prosperity. Nature, however, periodically compels them to recognize that they live in earthquake country, and after each reminder they launch earnest preparations for the inevitable "Big One." But by the time memory fades, dust settles, and rubble disappears, they resume the bravado-bordering-on-bombast that characterizes Lawrence W. Harris' "The Damndest Finest Ruins," published in the San Francisco *Examiner* shortly after the 1906 quake.

> Put me somewhere west of East Street where there's nothin' left but dust,
> Where the lads are all a'bustlin' and where everything's gone bust,
> Where the buildings that are standin' sort of blink and blindly stare
> At the damndest finest ruins ever gazed on anywhere.
>
> Bully Ruins—bricks and wall—through the night I've heard you call
> Sort of sorry for each other 'cause you had to burn and fall,
> From the ferries to Van Ness you're a Godforsaken mess,
> But the damndest finest ruins—nothin' more or nothin' less.

THE DAMNDEST FINEST RUINS (continued)

The strangers who come rubberin' and a'huntin' souvenirs,
The fools, they try to tell us it will take a million years
Before we can get started, so why don't we come to live
And build our homes and factories upon land they've got to give.

"Got to give!" Why on my soul, I would rather bore a hole
And live right in the ashes than evermore to Oakland's mole,
If they'd all give me my pick of their buildin's proud an slick
In the damndest finest ruins still I'd rather be a brick.

In 1935, Charles F. Richter of Cal Tech introduced the standard of earthquake measurement that bears his name, a logarithmic scale on which each whole number magnitude (energy released at epicenter) is 31.5 times greater than its predecessor, from 1.0 (six ounces of dynamite) to 9.0 (200,000,000 *tons*). The incredible Magnitude 8.3 force that created the "damndest finest ruins" burst from beneath the Pacific off Humboldt Bay early on April 18, sped south along the San Andreas Fault at two miles a *second*, demolished coastal towns, sank at least one steamer, and hammered ashore at Point Arena. The shock raced across the Golden Gate and smashed into San Francisco, continued down the peninsula to wreck Stanford University and Agnews State Insane Asylum, sprinted through the Salinas Valley and Coastal Ranges, flattened Hollister and other towns, and rattled through the Tehachapis into southern California. Within minutes, many hundreds (some say thousands) in San Francisco were dead, debris clogged streets, water and gas pipes burst, and chimneys toppled. Fires merged into an inferno that consumed working-class Tar Flat and elite Nob Hill without distinction; when the flames died, more than 200,000 were homeless and signs warned of hazards:

SEWERS BLOCKED
Don't Use Toilets
Epidemics Threatened
OBEY ORDERS OR GET SHOT

Although Californians and their historians call the episode the "San Francisco" earthquake, it was neither a local incident nor the first or last of its kind. Indians' oral tradition includes tales of shaking earth, but Spaniards provided the first written accounts. Near the Santa Ana River in 1769, shocks staggered Gaspar de Portolá's band as it headed north from San Diego in search of Monterey Bay. Padre Juan Crespí recorded the incident and named the stream *el río del dulcilismo nombre de Jesús de los temblores* (River

THE DAMNDEST FINEST RUINS (continued)

of the Sweetest Name of Jesus of the Earthquakes). Another quake in 1812 destroyed Spanish missions at Santa Ynez and Santa Barbara. Episodes appear on the record in all parts of the state from then until early 1994 when the Magnitude 6.7 Northridge Quake devastated parts of the San Fernando Valley.

To remind succeeding generations of the 1906 disaster, photographers left numerous images, some of them made with great effort. Chicagoan George R. Lawrence, who raised his panoramic camera 2,000 feet above the Bay with seventeen kites, tripped his shutter from the ground, but Clara Smith of Marysville herself rode a helium balloon to make her panorama. Most, however, remained earth-bound to produce photographs, stereo cards, and lantern slides like those that follow for sale to the curious; in the process, they added an important adjunct to the historical record.

A   B

Presidio commander Gen. Frederick Funston temporarily usurped civil authority and ordered his troops to blast lines to contain the flames. Their inexperience with explosives spread fires, and by the second day most of the center city *(A)* was engulfed. The towering Call Building would soon be gutted, as would the Byzantine-spired Temple Emanu-El also seen in Eadweard Muybridge's 1878 photo panorama. Neither earthquake nor fire distinguished among classes. A gutted mansion *(B)* stands on Nob Hill, where only the home of silver-baron James Flood survived to become the Pacific Union Club in 1911. A middle-class home on Steiner Street

C

D

E

F

(C) escaped the flames, but probably not the wrecker's ball. At Howard and 18th Streets, the columns of a working-class apartment house *(D)* prepare to collapse. On Geary Street, a Japanese woman *(E)* prepares an outdoor meal. People of all races and classes enacted similar scenes throughout the city; if fire and earthquake did not destroy their homes, damage and escaping gas made them unsafe to enter. Churches were no longer sanctuaries of safety or refuge: St. Dominic's Catholic Church *(F)*, a ruined synagogue

G   H

I   J

(G), and Stanford University's Chapel *(H).* To aid the homeless, the city mustered its meager resources to establish refugee camps like one in Golden Gate Park *(I),* where the army provided organization, tents, food, blankets, and emergency medical care. Crisis usually elicited the best among San Franciscans, but not always. Looters descended on places like a Market Street jewelry store *(J),* and untrained patrolmen often executed Mayor Eugene Schmitz's "shoot-on-sight" order with excessive zeal and tragic errors. Earthquake and fire destroyed familiar institutions and landmarks like the newly completed City Hall *(K)* and the popular

K

L

M

Tivoli Opera House *(L)* and the notorious Poodle Dog French Restaurant *(M)*, which faced each other across the intersection of Mason and Eddy streets. Nevertheless, clearing and rebuilding began almost immediately, and the city celebrated its rise from the ashes by hosting the Panama-Pacific Exposition in 1915. *(WAB)*

PHOTO CREDIT: Photographs Courtesy Special Collections, California State University Library, Hayward.

CHAPTER THREE

THE NATIVE PEOPLES

THE "DIGGER" STEREOTYPE

Most modern Californians know little of the original residents of their state. What information they do possess is often tainted by misunderstanding and racial bias. When white Americans first encountered Great Basin and California natives in the mid-nineteenth century, they derisively called these foraging peoples "Digger Indians," a name suggesting extreme racial and cultural inferiority. Reflecting the animosity Americans felt toward all natives, the name "Digger" and the stereotypes associated with it became deeply ingrained in pioneer culture. One nineteenth-century historian spoke for an entire age when he condemned the California Indian as "one of the most degraded of God's creatures."

He was without knowledge, religion or morals, even in their most elementary forms. He lived without labor, and enjoyed all the ease and pleasure he could. Physically, he was not prepossessing, although having considerable endurance and strength. His skin was nearly as dark as that of the negro, and his hair as coarse as that of a horse, while his features were repulsive.

To gratify his appetite and satiate his lust were his only ambition. He was too cowardly to be warlike, and did not possess that spirit of independence which is commonly supposed to be the principal attribute of his race. In so genial a climate as ours, nature easily provided for all his wants. The best part of his time was spent in dancing and sleeping. (William Halley, *Centennial Yearbook of Alameda County,* 1878)

Such negative stereotypes salved the consciences of white nineteenth-century Californians as they murdered Indians, stole their land, destroyed their cultures, enslaved their children, and confined the survivors on barren reservations.

Unfortunately, the pioneers' perception of Indians continues to influence popular attitudes. Many people persist in seeing California's original peoples as the most primitive of North American Indians, without a significant culture, and certainly no match for the better-known agricultural groups of the Southwest or the noble buffalo hunters of the Great Plains. Partly for this reason, during the last one and one-half centuries, native cemeteries have been desecrated and converted into parking lots, ancient village shell mounds have been excavated and used to pave streets, priceless archaeological sites have been deliberately plundered and vandalized, and unique rock carvings and paintings have been defaced with graffiti. Until recently, most historical restorations and published popular works, including public school textbooks, ignored, ridiculed, or trivialized the California Indians. Even some professional historians, neglecting Indian sources and anthropological writings, have perpetuated old stereotypes, describing natives with such loaded adjectives as "prehistoric," "primitive," "savage," and "Stone Age." Perhaps more important, they dismiss Indians as quaint oddities, irrelevant to the flow of California history.

In recent decades, however, anthropologists have developed more sophisticated theories and methods for understanding native peoples, amassed new archeological evidence, analyzed oral traditions among surviving individuals, and read historical documents more objectively. California's Indians have become some of the most studied and written-about native peoples in the world. Leading scholars such as Alfred L. Kroeber, Sherburne F. Cook, Robert F. Heizer, and Lowell John Bean have demonstrated that native cultures were complex and dynamic. Well after the successive invasions of Spaniards, Mexicans, and Anglo-Americans, Indian peoples actively continued to shape California's land and history.

NATIVE ORIGINS, LANGUAGES, AND POPULATIONS

California's Indians are popularly viewed as static remnants of ancient Stone-Age peoples. Nothing could be farther from the truth. Before and after the advent of whites in their lands, native cultures constantly changed and adapted to shifting social and ecological conditions. The pace of change

Tattooed Yuki Indian
The first systematic attempt to gather information about the California Indians was made by Stephen Powers in *Tribes of California* (1877). This is one of the volume's many vivid illustrations of native life at a time when it was rapidly disappearing. *Courtesy of the Bancroft Library.*

was usually much slower than in more modern civilizations, however.

Sometime between 50,000 and 15,000 B.C. the ancestors of the Native Americans migrated eastward across ice or land bridges that then spanned the Bering Strait between Asia and North America. Migrating quickly southward in pursuit of large, now-extinct game animals such as the bison, mammoth, and giant sloth, the new peoples had penetrated most of North and South America by 12,000 B.C. By 10,000 or 9000 B.C., offshoots of many Indian peoples had found their way into isolated California. Small and nomadic, the earliest groups subsisted primarily by hunting large game with spears; they developed little material culture or distinctiveness from each other.

Between 6000 and 3000 B.C., the Ice Age

ended, temperatures rose, rainfall decreased, lush vegetation receded, and huge
game animals died out. Indians adapted successfully to the changing environment, and
over the centuries they gradually came to
survive by fishing, hunting smaller animals,
and harvesting wild plants. With more diverse and stable food supplies, the Indians'
population grew. The natives settled in villages, adapted to their varying ecosystems,
and developed more elaborate social systems, religions, and arts. By 1000 B.C., complex, specialized cultures, similar to those
that European explorers encountered after
1542, were firmly established. Over thousands of years, California natives had transformed themselves from nomadic hunters
into one of the most complex hunter-gatherer civilizations in human history.

Diverse patterns of interaction between
population and resources distinguished California Indians from other North American
natives. California was originally settled by
fragments of many cultural groups. After arriving, they adjusted to sharply different climates and resources and developed distinctive local and regional cultures. Natural
barriers, the difficulties of travel within the
region, and limited contact with outside cultures reinforced local differences. By the
onset of European colonization, California
Indians had divided and subdivided into
many small, independent groups. There
were more than one hundred different
tribes, each with a unique economy, technology, arts, religion, and social organization.
California natives spoke between sixty-four
and eighty different languages belonging to
five of the major North American language
families. Most language stocks spoken on the

California Indian Tribal Boundaries
Tribes of California drawn by A.L. Kroeber.
Reprinted in Robert F. Heizer and Albert B. Elsasser,
The Natural World of the California Indians (Berkeley:
University of California Press, 1980), p. 5.

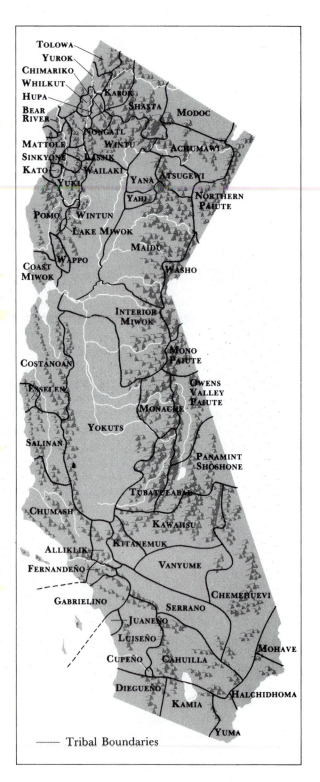

—— Tribal Boundaries

Indians Hunting Near San Francisco Bay
Visiting artist Louis Choris depicted hunters belonging to San Francisco Bay or San Joaquin Valley tribes in 1816. Strong and flexible, Indian bows were constructed especially for hunting small game at short or medium distances. The men were crack shots. *Courtesy of the Huntington Library.*

continent were used here. In practice, the Indians spoke hundreds of local dialects that were unintelligible to speakers of the same basic language. In its diversity of cultures, California was unmatched in all of North America.

Also unmatched was the population. Demographers estimate that between three hundred thousand and one million Indians inhabited the region on the eve of colonization in the eighteenth century. Although populations in desert or mountain environ-ments were sparse and scattered over vast territories, some valley or coastal tribes, such as the Yokuts of the San Joaquin Valley and the Chumash of the Santa Barbara Channel, were large and thickly settled, with densities of ten to twenty persons per square mile and communities in excess of one thousand individuals. With an overall density of one-half person per square mile, California was one of the most intensively populated regions north of Mexico. Then, as it does today, California housed roughly one-tenth of the inhabitants of that part of North America on only one-twentieth of the land area.

California's large native population undermines the traditional view that European colonization of the New World consisted of the occupation of a mostly vacant, unused wilderness. Like much of North and South America, California was hardly a wilderness. Its Indian groups were large and thriving, and very little of the land was unharvested. European colonization of California was most fundamentally a conquest, not of land, but of peoples.

ECONOMY: FOODS

Flourishing populations and cultures were made possible by a productive and reliable economy. The great majority of California groups practiced a subsistence economy based on the hunting and gathering of naturally occurring foods and materials. Blinded by cultural bias, early Europeans saw the absence of agriculture and higher industry among the hunter-gatherers as a sign of racial inferiority. These people, the outsiders assumed, were so primitive and unintelligent that they could not follow the examples of the Pueblo groups to the east and grow their own food. Instead, Europeans charged, the lazy and simple Californians wandered about, mindlessly picking foods that nature happened to provide.

Actually, because rain rarely fell during the growing season, agriculture would have been difficult for most California Indians, while naturally occurring foods were bountiful for those who knew how to exploit them. The hunting-and-gathering economy was systematic, rational, and based on immense environmental knowledge. For many groups, it yielded a higher and more dependable standard of living than could have been achieved through farming.

Carefully spreading their populations evenly so as not to tax natural resources, the Indians harvested hundreds of varieties of plants, animals, and minerals for food and building materials. More than elsewhere in North America, staple foods varied from group to group according to their environments. Among most coastal, valley, and foothill tribes, acorns from ten species of oaks provided an abundant and nutritious staple, one distinctive to California. Concentrated geographically and seasonally and requiring no cultivation, acorns could be harvested more efficiently than farm crops. With their meat encased in hard shells, they were also relatively nonperishable and could be stored without further processing. By using the labor of all its able-bodied members during a few weeks in autumn, a family could harvest enough acorns for a basic food supply of two years, protecting it from possible shortages.

High in tannic acid, acorns are inedible in their natural state, however. To exploit them as food, Indians learned something of their chemistry and developed techniques for removing the poisonous acid. When the acorns were ready for use, women husked and ground them into flour with mortars. They then washed the flour in finely sewn baskets or earth pits to leach out the tannin. The meal was eaten as mush, baked into cakes, or added to other foods. Probably invented by Indian women several thousand years earlier, acorn-processing technology had spread to most California tribes by 1000 B.C. The increased food supply resulting from acorn processing probably caused the elaboration of cultures that began about that time. Indians also adapted the method to other naturally poisonous plants, such as the buckeye. The example of acorn processing demonstrates that human ingenuity and cultural change and diffusion, in addition to the bountiful natural environment, were responsible for the blossoming of California Indian life.

In zones lacking oak trees or replete with

Women Processing Acorns in the Sacramento Valley, ca. 1840
Acorn processing was a constant task for tribeswomen with oak groves in their territories. Along with other strenuous female responsibilities, this practice led early American observers to jump to the false conclusion that Indian women were oppressed by their men. "On the women, all the drudgery seems to be thrown," observed Charles Wilkes, the American military officer in charge of the expedition that produced this illustration. Actually, all tribal members worked hard for the welfare of the group, and responsibility for acorn processing and plant gathering, vital to tribal survival, earned women respect and status within Indian communities. Illustration from Charles Wilkes, *Narrative of the United States Exploring Expedition during the Years 1838, 1839, 1840, 1841, and 1842* (1845). *Courtesy of the California State Library.*

other foods, the people developed other staples. Some tribes organized their lives around fisheries. Locating their villages along the rivers of the well-watered northern coast, the Yurok and Karok preyed on the salmon swimming to and from upstream spawning grounds. The Chumash invented long oceangoing plank canoes to harvest fish, seals, sea otter, and beached whales from the coast, offshore islands, and kelp beds of the rich Santa Barbara Channel. Combining fishing with acorn gathering, the affluent Chumash built large, well-ordered towns and made highly refined baskets, jewelry, stone sculptures, and pictographs. The Chumash carried civilization to its highest level in pre-European California.

Other cultures arose from still different resource bases. With buoyant tule canoes, the Costanoan (or Ohlone) groups in tidelands along Monterey and San Francisco bays gathered shellfish and other salt-marsh foods. In the Sierra Nevada, the Miwok relied on pine nuts; in southern deserts, the Cahuilla harvested the mesquite and screw bean. Groups in especially harsh environments, such as the Yuma and Mohave of the Colorado River, the Cahuilla of the Palm Springs area, and the Paiute of the Owens Valley, developed agriculture. Like the Chu-

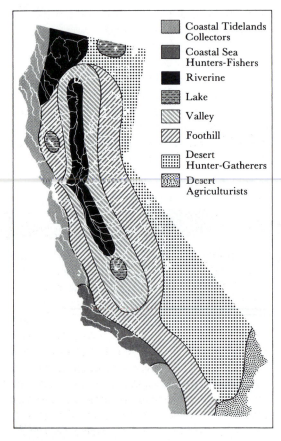

Coastal Tidelands
Collectors

Coastal Sea
Hunters-Fishers

Riverine

Lake

Valley

Foothill

Desert
Hunter-Gatherers

Desert
Agriculturists

Indian Ecological Zones
From Robert F. Heizer and Albert B. Elsasser, *The
Natural World of the California Indians* (Berkeley: University of California Press, 1980), p. 60.

mash, many tribes were fortunate enough to harvest more than one staple. The Yokuts had access to both fine oak groves and river salmon. On elevated riverbanks in the northern San Joaquin Valley, they established large villages and an organized way of life that approached the prosperity of the Chumash. Most groups located villages and adjusted boundaries so that they had access to water, fuel, and several different ecosystems for maximum variety and abundance.

Even the staples, however, were not relied on to the extent that Great Plains cultures needed buffalo and the Pueblo depended on maize. Californians consumed seeds, nuts, roots, stems, and leaves from a multitude of grasses, shrubs, and trees. These products often required special processing. Using ingenious snares, weapons, decoys, and trickery, natives also hunted rodents, reptiles, birds, insects, and larger grazers such as deer, elk, and bighorn sheep. Only the powerful grizzly, the Indians' major foraging competitor, and some sacred animals such as the coyote and other predators, failed to make their way into native cooking baskets.

As could be expected, varying resources gave birth to different cultures. There were numerous "ecological types" of California Indian cultures, classified according to the distinctive ways in which local societies exploited diverse climates, topographies, and flora and fauna: coastal tideland collectors; sea hunters and fishers; riverine fishers; lakeshore fishers, hunters, and gatherers; valley and plains gatherers; foothill hunters and gatherers; desert hunters and collectors; and desert agriculturists. Some language groups included several ecological types.

ECONOMY: INDUSTRY AND TRADE

Many California regions contained surpluses of foods and raw materials, and some Indians became particularly skilled at extracting and manufacturing. Industry and commerce thus emerged thousands of years ago and became more extensive with passing centuries. Groups in unique geological areas mined and quarried for rare minerals such as volcanic black obsidian, which was preferred for arrow and spear points, cutting edges, and scraping tools. Other groups quarried granite for grinding mortars, steatite for carving into bowls and sculpted figures, salt for seasoning and preserving, tar for caulking and gluing, and shells for money or jewelry. One of the largest mining operations was the Costanoan cinnabar mine near present-day New Almaden, from which natives extracted a brilliant red pigment prized across western North America. Other artisans, and sometimes entire tribes, specialized in manufacturing redwood dugout canoes, arrows, tools, shell money, and other valuable products.

Surplus food, manufactured items, and hunting and gathering rights were exchanged within and among groups. Elaborate trade systems developed, complete with fairs, treaties, merchants, marketing centers, commercial organizations, and fixed-value currencies. Trade linked tribes of various environments, languages, and cultures in networks that stretched inland from the coast, sometimes hundreds of miles, far beyond California's current borders. Expanding industry and commerce broadened the tribes' resource base, ensured a higher and more secure standard of living, and encouraged more complex cultures. By providing alternative ways of acquiring necessities, trade also reduced intertribal conflict, thus helping to make California Indians generally peaceable peoples.

Plentiful and varied foods, a genial climate, and the opportunity to trade made the Californians prosperous by the standards of hunter-gatherer peoples. Contrary to perceptions of white pioneers who did not understand the native economy, Indians had a well-developed work ethic. While labor was rarely grueling, it was constant and carefully planned. Drudgery was lightened because Indians often worked in groups, with plenty of lively music and gossip. The native diet was balanced, dependable, and high in protein and vitamins; it was nutritionally superior to that of average Europeans at the time of colonization, and certainly to that of Indians in the Spanish missions of the eighteenth and nineteenth centuries. Men and women were active, healthy, and physically robust, with greater strength and endurance than the more sedentary Europeans.

The first Californians avoided the famines and forced migrations that periodically dislocated other pre-Columbian peoples, although lean drought years did occasionally force them to shift to less desirable foods. They led relatively stable, predictable lives, in settled villages within carefully prescribed homelands.

SCIENCE, ECOLOGY, AND AGRICULTURE

The hunter-gatherer cultures that Europeans first encountered in the sixteenth century flourished only because of the resourcefulness and accumulated knowledge of the native peoples. Over many centuries, Indians patiently observed and experimented with animals, plants, and minerals and developed tools to use them efficiently. Lacking written languages and books, the natives assimilated the ancestral knowledge of their families and tribes, built on it, and transmitted it to succeeding generations through their oral tradition. Eventually, Indians evolved an understanding of their immediate natural world that was more sophisticated than that of all but the most learned of Europeans of the colonization era or even of present-day Americans.

Indians precisely and scientifically classified plants and animals into categories similar to those of modern botany and zoology. They learned the habits of creatures, discovered the food chains and other relationships among living beings, and perceived the environmental factors that made organisms thrive or decline. As part of their religious rites and to keep track of the seasons, Indians methodically followed the celestial movements of the sun, moon, planets, and stars. Some tribes, such as the Chumash, built observatories to mark and predict solstices. It was on such a practical, yet scientific, foundation that Indians developed efficient systems to gather natural foods and construction materials.

Also through experimentation, Indians detected and exploited the chemical properties of plants. Like other North American groups, native Californians extracted medicines from seeds, roots, bark, and leaves to relieve pain, combat infection, and promote healing. Although not all of their medicines have been shown to be effective, Indians did discover many chemically sound agents that became the basis for modern medicines. California natives also set bones, practiced surgery, and understood some basic principles of dream analysis and psychotherapy. Found universally in native California, shamans were religious specialists who also healed through the use of medicines and magic to eject evil spirits from the body. Overall, in light of the superstition, brutality, and quackery then dominating European medicine, California Indians could cure most illnesses at least as effectively as their conquerors. Later Spanish and Mexican settlers commonly consulted Indian healers, particularly for the treatment of serious infections.

The Indians did not simply react passively to what they found in California. They used their knowledge to reshape nature and increase its harvests. For easier access to plants that were valued for food, rituals, healing, or basket materials, they sowed wild seeds and transplanted wild plants closer to villages. To increase the productivity of oak, mesquite, and other trees and shrubs, they pruned away dead and nonbearing branches and thinned the plants for optimum use of water, sunlight, and nutrients.

The natives' major manipulation of nature was fire burning. After observing that natural fires controlled underbrush, made seed grasses lusher the next year, and at-tracted game, Indians began to burn valleys, foothills, and mountain meadows systematically each autumn or spring. Over centuries, Indian burning dramatically influenced the flora and fauna in heavily settled regions, maximizing grasslands and large trees, driving back chaparral, increasing the population of grazers, encouraging the growth of groves of acorn-bearing oaks, and giving the landscape a tended, parklike quality that amazed early explorers. The original Californians were skilled resource managers who consciously influenced the distribution of species and increased the land's capacity to support life. Modern experts have only recently rediscovered the Indian use of controlled burns to maintain forests and grasslands.

Where naturally occurring foods were deficient, some desert tribes devised forms of agriculture suited to their particular environments. The Yuma, Mohave, and Halchidhoma practiced floodplain farming, which they adapted from the irrigation methods of the agricultural Indians to the east. In the fertile mud left behind after the annual spring flooding of the Colorado River, they planted traditional Native American crops of maize, beans, pumpkins, and calabashes, along with a few European imports such as watermelon, oats, and wheat, whose seeds they began to receive in trade from Mexican Indians in about 1700. The Cahuilla of the Salton Sink cultivated soils with high moisture along streams, in marshy areas around natural oases, and in places where the underground water table rose close to the surface. Where necessary, they dug wells and carried water to irrigate their crops. Preserved by drying in the desiccating desert heat, farm produce furnished about half of the food of these tribes.

The Owens Valley Paiute built the largest true irrigation works in the region. Using communal labor, they dammed the streams flowing down the steep east face of the Sierra

Nevada, dug grids of large canals, and irrigated wild grasses and tubers in fields that often ran to several square miles each. A few other southern tribes, such as the Tipai and Ipai east of San Diego, probably farmed as well. Actually, most tribes were aware of agriculture through observation, trade for cultivated products, or communication with outsiders, but rejected it on ecological or cultural grounds. Groups with richer environments considered hunting and gathering more productive and reliable.

RELIGION

Religion combined with economic necessity to reinforce ecological values. To native Californians, the close interaction of humanity and environment was a constant reality and the central theme of their culture. Appreciating their dependence on their surroundings, Indians saw themselves not as above nature, but as an integral part of it. Respect for nature permeated their life, philosophy, and religion.

Like practically everything else, beliefs and rites differed greatly from group to group. Some tribes were monotheistic and believed in a single great deity presiding over all creation. Most, however, believed in many equal gods—or, more appropriately, spirits—who were embodied in animals, places, and natural processes and who controlled the resources on which human society depended. To survive in such an animistic universe, people had to keep on the good side of the spirits, who could be particularly angered by waste of plants, animals, and other materials. Carefully observed rituals to conciliate these spirits accompanied all important occasions—birth, puberty, marriage, sex, childbearing, hunting, gathering, sickness, and death. Specific observances varied from the unadorned individual and family rituals of the seminomadic Great

Basin tribes to the complex ceremonies of the more affluent groups, which might attract thousands of people. Common features among California religions were offerings by priests, shamans, cult leaders, and individual Indians to assure the spirits' continued benevolence.

Thus rituals, and even entire religious complexes, were basically ecological. Yurok and Karok rites, for example, discouraged overfishing of the salmon and contamination of the rivers on which the tribes depended. The World Renewal ceremony of the northwestern salmon-fishing groups, the major annual religious gathering of riverside villages, redistributed resources to poorer tribal members and appeased supernatural forces in order to avert floods, earthquakes, and failure of the salmon run. Similar in intent was the elaborate yearly dance of the Kuksu Cult among the Pomo, Patwin, and Maidu. By countless simpler tribal and personal rituals, natives across California expressed kinship with plants and animals, thanked spirits for past favors, and prepared themselves for respectful and orderly behavior toward nature during hunting, fishing, and gathering.

By careful gathering practices and social organization, reinforced by rituals, the Indians avoided straining their resources. They harvested plants and animals selectively to leave enough for each species to reproduce. To keep their own numbers in balance with resources, Indians practiced strict population control through marriage customs, sexual taboos, continence, abortion, and chemical contraceptives derived from plants. Before the Europeans arrived, California Indians had already established the values and practices of environmental management. As a result, dense populations of Indians had inhabited the region for millennia without noticeably polluting the soil and water, reducing their capacity to sustain life, or destroying other species. When invaders con-

Indian Village Scenes
Differences in local climate and building materials contributed to variations in Indian architecture: *(upper left)* tule-thatch Yokuts houses protected from the hot San Joaquin Valley sun by a shade; *(upper right)* earth-covered Maidu lodges in the equally hot Sacramento Valley; *(lower left)* Miwok bark-slab lodge, Yosemite Valley; *(lower right)* Sierra Nevada bark-slab community house. From Stephen Powers, *Tribes of California* (1877). *Courtesy of the Bancroft Library.*

quered them, native groups relinquished a land that was still unspoiled.

POLITICS AND SOCIETY

California Indians generally organized themselves into small political units. The reasons were historical and ecological. Originally, many small offshoots of distinct groups settled the region and further specialized their cultures while adapting to local ecosystems.

Geographical barriers isolated tribelets, and local food resources were usually insufficient to sustain large population concentrations. Oceans, mountains, and deserts insulated the Californians from outside invaders who might have forced them to unite in their own defense.

Over much of the region, the word "tribe" itself must be applied with caution. In California, "tribes" were large groups of people with a related language and culture and who occupied a general area, but who had little organization or consciousness of a common identity. Among almost all these broader cultural bodies, land ownership, sovereignty, and cohesive action resided in small, independent groups that have come to be called "tribelets." Tribelets contained from about a hundred to several thousand related persons, inhabiting anywhere from several to a dozen villages. Their territories ranged from fifty square miles in rich environments to as much as six thousand square miles in barren ones. The Yokuts, for example, numbered at least 25,000 persons and occupied 22,000 square miles of the San Joaquin Valley, but they were divided into more than 60 autonomous tribelets. Tribelets developed local economies, dialects, and religious practices that were variants of their larger tribal cultures.

A formal authority structure bound the people of a tribelet together. Usually inheriting their position within elite families, chiefs presided—assisted by family and ritual leaders—over the harvesting, storage, and exchange of resources. Their considerable power derived from their wealth, prestige, and ability to persuade, as well as from a tradition of community consensus. Second in power to chiefs, shamans served as the principal religious figures, performed medical and psychiatric functions, and advised chiefs and other headmen.

Most groups were relatively affluent and peaceful and preferred to avoid violent conflict through trade, intermarriage, and mediation. Nevertheless, all tribes maintained military organization to defend against encroachment, and armed conflict did sometimes erupt when outsiders stole property, attacked villages and travelers, murdered or practiced witchcraft against family members, or trespassed on prized hunting and gathering grounds. If peaceful resolution of grievances failed, warfare was the only means of compensation or revenge. Actual fighting, while sometimes vicious, was usually sponta-

neous and small in scale. In the absence of much larger-scale military cooperation, the conflict rarely spread beyond a few villages. Occasionally, one group conquered another or subjected it to imperial tribute. The Mohave and the Yuma of the Colorado River, large and highly organized tribes, had the strongest tradition of militarism. These groups supported a class of professional warriors, reared boys from an early age in the values and skills of combat, and waged war frequently to acquire and defend rich agricultural land, or simply for pleasure and glory. Influenced by the Colorado cultures, the Ipai and Tipai of the San Diego area were also particularly aggressive in protecting their borders against intruders, as early Spanish explorers and missionaries would discover.

However much all Indians might have appeared alike to some pioneer Europeans and Americans, California native societies were complex and highly differentiated. The basic unit of southern and south central tribes, and that which delimited personal behavior and located the individual in the larger society, was the *lineage,* a large extended family of persons related to one another, usually through the male line. Several related lineages constituted a *clan.* Clans and lineages were highly structured and exerted much authority over their members. In most of northern and central California, by contrast, membership in the community derived from simple residence, not family descent.

Families differed sharply from one another in status and wealth, and individuals' places in the tribelet were usually marked from birth by their family. Generally, California families were divided into four classes: elites, commoners, vagabonds, and slaves. A small minority of elite, or aristocratic, families controlled most ritual, property, trade, and means of production, such as the best oak groves, fishing spots, and in the case of the Chumash, the oceangoing boats essential to the marine economy. They also furnished most of the important specialists to the tribe: chiefs, diplomats, shamans, merchants, and highly skilled craftsmen. Far less well off, the majority of commoners traveled less, spent most of their time in subsistence activities, and supported their betters with labor, taxes, fees, and gifts. In some areas, a small number of vagabonds lived on the fringes of legitimate society, although they were sometimes absorbed into tribes and started low-status families. A few tribes kept slaves, usually female war captives who were held for ransom or eventually assimilated into the victorious tribe.

California Indian societies were not democratic or egalitarian by modern standards. Individuals inherited unequal status, duties, and privileges from their ancestors, with only slight opportunity for upward mobility through working hard or acquiring shaman or craft skills. Nevertheless, since everyone sanctioned the class system, and since most tribes alleviated poverty by redistributing resources, there appears to have been little internal dissent. Force was not usually needed to maintain social order.

Sex roles were similarly structured. The burden of labor was distributed fairly evenly between men and women. However, demarcations in male and female functions, behaviors, privileges, dress, and even manners of speech were rigid. The woman's world was local and limited primarily to gathering and processing plant materials, preparing food, maintaining the household, making clothing, rearing children, and nursing and midwifery. More flexible and encompassing, the male sphere extended to politics, religion, and harvesting and processing of animal, rock, and wood products, as well as dealing with outside groups in trade, diplomacy, and warfare.

Some sharing of labor and mixing of gender roles did occur. During intensive work periods, such as acorn-gathering season, men performed what would normally have been women's work. When salmon ran the rivers and rabbits were being driven by large village groups, women helped to fish and hunt. Occasionally, women served as shamans, especially among the northwest and north-central tribes, and, more rarely—as among the Pomo, Chumash, and Miwok—as property owners and co-chiefs. Nevertheless, tradition confined women more firmly and allowed more role-crossing by men than by women. With clearly lower status in families and tribelets, women were usually expected to move to the village of their husbands upon marriage and to defer to fathers, husbands, and male family and tribelet leaders in general.

Male supremacy was not absolute, however. The work of women was central in an economy based largely on plant gathering, and women were accorded great respect and, within their sphere, independence and autonomy. Moreover, the contributions of women were central to the progress of native civilization. Primarily responsible as they were for harvesting and processing plants, it is likely that it was Indian women who experimented with and discovered new methods of exploiting and manipulating nature, such as in acorn processing, agriculture, fire burning, and the development of new uses for plants in medicine, the arts, and basket-making.

Sex roles were strongly sanctioned by the Indian religions and were taught to children at an early age. Although Indian sex roles in some ways resembled those of their European counterparts, there were also striking differences. Later, at the Spanish missions, deeply ingrained sex roles complicated the assimilation of natives. Particularly, the Europeans insisted that men perform farm tasks—planting, tending, and harvesting of plants. This required the men to do what many of them considered to be women's work. Such cultural differences encouraged

"A Sweat and a Cold Plunge"
Male sweathouses were common among many California native groups. In these large buildings, sometimes called "temescals," the adult men slept, socialized, and performed male rituals. For example, purification rites were performed before hunts to appease the animal spirits and to remove bodily scents that might alert game to the men's presence. After sweating before fires in the sealed buildings, the men plunged into cool water. The ritual was repeated until both body and soul were cleansed. From Stephen Powers, *Tribes of California* (1877). *Courtesy of the Bancroft Library.*

Indians to resist assimilation and bred conflict between colonizers and natives.

THE ARTS

Because they were extensions of Indian economic and religious life, the arts were also segregated according to gender. Men dominated wood, bone, and stone carving and painting, music, and oral literature, all of which were closely associated with religion. While the fashioning of bone and stone effigies was nearly universal in California, rock carvings (petroglyphs) and rock paintings (pictographs) reached their highest development among southern tribes, particularly the Chumash. In order to honor the gods, bring success in hunting, and establish boundaries, Indian artists engraved and pecked designs, often with recognizable animal and geometrical shapes, into the sides of boulders and the walls of caves. During the centuries just before the Europeans arrived, Chumash and southern Yokuts artists started painting abstract pictographs—brilliant multicolored arrangements of human, animal, celestial, and symbolic shapes—usually in remote caves. Pictographs evolved from the introduction of new religious cults, as well

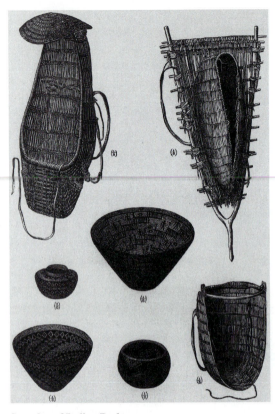

Sampler of Indian Baskets
The two baskets at the top of the illustration were used by women to carry infants. The others served diverse purposes. Although native Californians preferred baskets because they were portable and of greater use in a mobile, gathering way of life, some southern California tribes also made and used pottery or, like the Chumash, carved steatite bowls. From Stephen Powers, *Tribes of California* (1877). *Courtesy of the Bancroft Library.*

as rituals that included the use of hallucinogenic drugs.

Often recounted by elders in the male sweathouses, the oral literature of California Indians was rich in symbolism, imagery, and poetic expression. Learned by rote and passed from generation to generation, the literature included myths, stories, prayers, songs, and epic poems incorporating the accumulated philosophy, ethics, mores, history, science, and folk traditions of the people.

Common themes were the unity of the natural and the supernatural realms, the power of animal spirits, and the interdependence of human beings and nature.

Women dominated a highly creative form of California art—basketry. Woven from dozens of materials of various textures and colors, the light, portable baskets served essential purposes in a gathering economy. Women produced baskets in many shapes and sizes for all manner of uses in gathering, processing, storage, and cooking. Baskets were also used in rituals, as hats, and as valuable trade items. Over thousands of years, tribes developed distinctive methods of construction and decorative styles, which the most skilled women further refined. The best baskets were gracefully proportioned, beautifully decorated with woven geometrical, animal, and symbolic designs, and so finely stitched that they could hold water. Some ceremonial baskets, such as those of the Pomo, were inlaid with feathers and mother-of-pearl. California Indian women developed the art of basketry to an extraordinarily high level.

ON THE EVE OF EUROPEAN COLONIZATION

The thousand or so years before Europeans invaded California was an especially dynamic time for the native peoples. Their economic productivity increased dramatically through their mastery of the environment, more efficient hunting and gathering, increased agriculture, and trade. Cultures became more elaborate and societies more organized. Some tribes migrated to new territories and ejected or absorbed earlier occupants. The cultures that the Europeans found took shape.

Although the autonomous tribelet remained the primary unit of organization in most areas, broadening relationships knit the small groups together in ever more intricate patterns. Alliances transcending the tribelets developed, often linking groups of different languages and cultures. Increasing commerce gave rise to formalized inter-tribelet trade relationships and business institutions. At the same time, new prophets began to preach new forms of religion. Using expanded intertribal contacts fostered by commerce, these more emotional religions spread from group to group. Eventually, people from many tribelets shared allegiance to cults and began gathering for ceremonies at regional religious centers. Because prohibitions against marriage with close family members forced people to seek partners outside of their lineage and tribelet, family alliances also evolved beyond the borders of tribelets. By the time the Europeans appeared, lineages and clans in some regions had expanded to encompass numerous tribelets and even entire cultures. More people traveled, resided in more than one locale in the course of their lives, and became multilingual and multicultural. California Indians were less insular and more aware of the broader world around them, including that outside of California proper.

The native Californians also became more affluent in the centuries before white contact. As they became more organized, Indians harvested, processed, and distributed resources more efficiently. Their standard of living rose, and populations and settlement densities increased, particularly in the most favored environments. Urbanization occurred, as smaller villages waned in significance and people clustered around the most important ceremonial and trade centers. Greater productivity and population concentration encouraged job specialization. More individuals focused their energies on tasks they could perform most efficiently and received the necessities of life through purchase or barter.

Prosperity did not breed equality, however. Property-owning and merchant classes expanded, increased in power, and removed themselves further from commoners. Cemeteries used in the last centuries before the European invasion testify to an increase in the wealth of some families, but also to growing segregation between the rich and the poor. Indian societies were becoming more hierarchical and interdependent in the centuries before the European invasion. Although change had been slow, the natives did have a tradition of adaptation that gave them alternatives for adjusting to the European presence.

California Indian civilization was thriving, but fragile. The people were productive, healthy, humane, and peaceful, and they had achieved a remarkable harmony with nature, exploiting and manipulating resources without threatening individual species or general environmental balances. Yet their technology and organization were simple in comparison with those of the Europeans. They had not developed written languages, had not domesticated work animals, had not learned to use metals, and had not invented the wheel and other simple machines. Their wood, sinew, and stone weapons were no match for European steel and firearms. Most important, like Native Americans throughout the Western Hemisphere, the Californians lacked immunities to the virulent Old World diseases brought by early explorers and settlers. Although larger organizations were emerging, Indian societies remained locally autonomous, for the most part. Their lives were easily disrupted, and they lacked mechanisms for broader cooperation in government and warfare. The natives were vulnerable to a concerted challenge from aggressive, more technologically and militarily sophisticated outsiders. Moreover, the Indian way of life rested precariously on a delicate balance with natural resources. Spaniards and other invaders not only assaulted the natives physically; they upset their equilibrium with nature and threw whole cultures into disarray.

SUGGESTIONS FOR FURTHER READING

California History, General

Hubert Howe Bancroft, *History of California* (7 vols., 1884–1890); Theodore H. Hittell, *History of California* (4 vols., 1885–1897); Robert Glass Cleland and Glenn S. Dumke, *From Wilderness to Empire: A History of California* (1962); Andrew F. Rolle, *California: A History* (1987); John W. Caughey and Norris Hundley, Jr., *California: History of a Remarkable State* (1982); James J. Rawls and Walton Bean, *California: An Interpretive History* (1998); James D. Hart, *A Companion to California* (1987); Earl Pomeroy, *The Pacific Slope* (1968).

Bibliographies, General

Doyce B. Nunis, Jr., and Gloria Ricci Lothrop, *A Guide to the History of California* (1989); Robert E. Cowan and Robert G. Cowan, *A Bibliography of the History of California, 1510–1930* (4 vols., 1933–1964); Margaret M. Rocq, *California Local History: A Bibliography and Union List of Library Holdings* (2 vols., 1970, 1976); Francis J. Weber, "A Bibliography of California Bibliographies," *Southern California Quarterly* (1968); Rodman W. Paul and Richard W. Etulain, *The Frontier and the American West* (1977); Oscar O. Winther and Richard A. Van Orman, *The Trans-Mississippi West: A Guide to Its Periodical Literature, 1811–1967* (1972).

Bibliographies, Specific

James Abajian, *Blacks and Their Contributions to the American West* (1974); Newton D. Baird and Robert Greenwood, *An Annotated Bibliography of California Fiction, 1664–1970* (1971); Lowell John Bean and Sylvia Brakke Vane, *California Indians: Primary Resources* (1977); Pamela Bleich, "A Study of Graduate Research in California History in California Colleges and Universities," *California Historical Society Quarterly* (various issues, 1964–1966); Lynn Donovan, "California Historical Society Collections on the History of Women in California," *California Historical Quarterly* (1973); Clifford Drury, *California Imprints, 1846–1876, Pertaining to Social, Educational, and Religious Subjects* (1970); Francis Farquhar, *Yo-semite, the Big Trees, and the High Sierra: A Selective Bibliography* (1948); Gladys Hansen, *The Chinese in California: A Brief Bibliographic History* (1970); Adelaide R. Haase,

Index to the Economic Material in the Documents of the States of the United States: California, 1849– 1904 (1908); Robert F. Heizer, *The Indians of California: A Critical Bibliography* (1976); Lawrence B. Lee, *Reclaiming the American West: An Historiography and Guide* (1979); David A. Leuthold, *California Politics and Problems, 1900–63: A Selective Bibliography* (1965); Doyce B. Nunis, Jr., *Los Angeles and Its Environs in the Twentieth Century: A Bibliography of a Metropolis* (1973); Richard J. Orsi, *A List of References for the History of Agriculture in California* (1974); J. Carlyle Parker, *An Index to the Biographies in Nineteenth Century California County Histories* (1980); Mitchell Slobo-dek, *A Selected Bibliography of California Labor History* (1964); Norton B. Stern, *California Jewish History: A Descriptive Bibliography* (1967); Francis J. Weber, *A Select Bibliography: The California Missions, 1765–1972* (1972), and *A Select Bibliography of California Catholic Literature, 1856–1974* (1974); Rich-ard Yates and Mary Marshall, *The Lower Colorado: A Bibliography* (1974).

Interpreting California History

Carey McWilliams, *California: The Great Exception* (1949); Kevin Starr, *Americans and the California Dream, 1850–1915* (1973), *Inventing the Dream: California through the Progressive Era* (1985), and *Material Dreams: Southern California through the 1920s* (1990); Lawrence Clark Powell, *California Classics: The Creative Literature of the Golden State* (1971); George H. Knoles, ed., *Essays and Assays: California History Reconsidered* (1973); Dennis Hale and Jonathan Eisen, *The California Dream* (1968); James D. Houston, *Californians: Searching for the Golden State* (1985); Gerald D. Nash, "California and Its Historians: An Appraisal of the Histories of the State," *Pacific Historical Review* (1981); California Heritage Task Force, *California's Historical and Cultural Resources* (1984); Joel Kotkin and Paul Grabowicz, *California, Inc.* (1982); Robert V. Hine, *California Utopianism: Contemplations of Eden* (1981); Peter W. Williams, "Reflections in/on/of a Golden State," *American Quarterly* (1976); James J. Rawls, "The Rise and Fall of the California Dream," *California Historical Courier* (1979); William Everson, *Archetype West: The Pacific Coast as a Literary Region* (1976); Doyce B. Nunis, Jr., "California, Why We Come; Myth or Reality," *California Historical Society Quarterly* (1965); James J. Parsons, "The Uniqueness of California," *American Quarterly* (1955); Dan Walters, *The New California: Facing the 21st Century* (1986); "Envisioning California," special issue of *California History* (Winter 1989–90); David Wyatt, *The Fall into Eden: Landscape and Imagination in California* (1986); Mike Davis, *City of Quartz: Excavating the Future of Los Angeles* (1990); Claire Perry, *Pacific Arcadia: Images of California, 1600–1915* (1999); and the four-volume "California History Sesquicentennial Series," series editor Richard J. Orsi, published simultaneously as special expanded issues of *California History* and as separate volumes by the University of California Press: Ramon A. Gutierrez and Richard J. Orsi, eds., *Contested Eden: California Before the Gold Rush* (1997–98), James J. Rawls and Richard J. Orsi, eds., *A Golden State: Mining and Economic Development in Gold Rush California* (1999), Kevin Starr and Richard J. Orsi, eds., *Rooted in Barbarous Soil: People, Culture, and Community in Gold Rush California* (2000), and John F. Burns and Richard J. Orsi, eds., *Taming the Elephant: Politics, Government, and Law in Pioneer California* (2002).

Atlases and Maps

Michael W. Donley, et al., *Atlas of California* (1979); Robert W. Durrenberger and Robert B. Johnson, *California: Patterns on the Land* (1976); David Hornbeck and David L. Fuller, *California Patterns: A Geographical and Historical Atlas* (1983); Warren A. Beck and Ynez D. Haase, *Historical Atlas of California* (1974).

Geographies

David W. Lantis, et al., *California: Land of Contrast* (1977); David Hartman, *California and Man* (1968); Crane Miller and Richard Hyslop, *California: The Geography of Diversity* (1983).

Environment and Ecology

Alan A. Schoenherr, *A Natural History of California* (1992); Elna Bakker, *An Island Called California: An Ecological Introduction to Its Natural Communities* (1982); John W. Caughey, "The Californian and His Environment," *California Historical Quarterly* (1972); Raymond F. Dasmann, *California's Changing Environment* (1981); Mary Austin, *Land of Little Rain* (1903); Edmund C. Jaeger, *The California Desert* (1965);

Monterey Bay Aquarium, *A Natural History of the Monterey Bay National Marine Sanctuary* (1999); John Muir, *The Mountains of California* (1894).

Flora and Fauna

John Williams and Howard C. Monroe, *Natural History of Northern California* (1976); Edmund C. Jaeger and Arthur C. Smith, *Introduction to the Natural History of Southern California* (1966); Tracy I. Storer and Lloyd P. Tevis, Jr., *California Grizzly* (1955); Arthur C. Smith, *Introduction to the Natural History of the San Francisco Bay Region* (1959); Joel W. Hedgepeth, *Introduction to the Seashore Life of the San Francisco Bay Region* (1962).

Geological History

N. E. A. Hinds, *Evolution of the California Landscape* (1952); Arthur D. Howard, *Evolution of the Landscape of the San Francisco Bay Region* (1962), and *Geologic History of Middle California* (1979); Mary Hill, *Geology of the Sierra Nevada* (1975) and *California Landscape: Origin and Evolution* (1984); Robert Iacopi, *Earthquake Country* (1964); John McPhee, *Assembling California* (1993); Michael Collier, *A Land in Motion: California's San Andreas Fault* (1999); Bill Guyton, *Glaciers of California* (1998).

Climate

Ernest L. Felton, *California's Many Climates* (1965); Harold Gilliam, *The Weather of the San Francisco Bay Region* (1966); Harry P. Bailey, *The Climate of Southern California* (1966).

Water

Norris Hundley, Jr., *The Great Thirst: Californians and Water, 1770s to 1990s* (2001); William Kahrl, *The California Water Atlas* (1979); Donald J. Pisani, *From Family Farm to Agribusiness: The Irrigation Crusade in California, 1850–1931* (1984); Merrill R. Goodall, et al., *California Water: A New Political Economy* (1978); Joe S. Bain, et al., *Northern Califor-nia's Water Industry* (1967); Erwin Cooper, *Aqueduct Empire: A Guide to Water in California* (1968); David Seckler, *California Water: A Study in Resource Management* (1971); "Water in California," a special issue of *The Pacific Historian*

(1983); Donald Worster, "Hydraulic Society in California: An Ecological Interpretation," *Agricultural History* (1982), and *Rivers of Empire: Water, Aridity, and the Growth of the American West* (1985).

Regional Divisiveness

Michael DiLeo and Eleanor Smith, *Two Californias: The Truth About the Split-State Movement* (1983); Rockwell D. Hunt, "History of the California State Division Controversy," Historical Society of Southern California, *Annual Publications* (1924); Roberta McDow, "To Divide or Not to Divide," *Pacific Historian* (1966), and "State Separation Schemes, 1907–1921," *California Historical Society Quarterly* (1970); Bruce Robeck, "Urban-Rural and Regional Voting Patterns in California Before and After Reapportionment," *Western Political Quarterly* (1970); Michael P. Rogin and John L. Shover, *Political Change in California: Critical Elections and Social Movements, 1890–1966* (1970).

Geography and Agricultural History

Lawrence J. Jelinek, *Harvest Empire: A History of California Agriculture* (1982); Ellen Liebman, *California Farmland: A History of Large Agricultural Landholdings* (1983); Howard F. Gregor, "The Industrial Farm as a Western Institution," *Journal of the West* (1970), and "The Large Industrialized American Crop Farm," *The Geographical Review* (1970); Paul S. Taylor, "The Foundations of California Rural Society," *California Historical Society Quarterly* (1945); Varden Fuller, "The Supply of Agricultural Labor as a Factor in the Evolution of Farm Organization in California" (Ph.D. dissertation, University of California, Berkeley, 1939); Paul W. Gates, "Corporate Farming in California," in Ray Allen Billington, ed., *People of the Plains and Mountains: Essays in the History of the West Dedicated to Everett Dick* (1973).

Indians, General

Joseph L. Chartkoff and Kerry Kona Chartkoff, *The Archaeology of California* (1984); Michael Moratto, *California Archaeology* (1984); Lowell J. Bean, "California Indians: Diverse and Complex Peoples," *California History* (Fall 1992); Alfred L. Kroeber, *Handbook of the Indians of California* (1925); Robert Heizer

and Mary Ann Whipple, *The California Indians: A Source Book (1971);* Robert Heizer, *Handbook of North American Indians,* Volume 8: *California* (1978); Jack D. Forbes, *Native Americans of California and Nevada* (1969); Sherburne F. Cook, *The Population of the California Indians, 1769–1970* (1976); George H. Phillips, *The Enduring Struggle: Indians in California History* (1981); James J. Rawls, *Indians of California: The Changing Image* (1984); Theodora Kroeber, et al., *Drawn from Life: California Indians in Pen and Brush* (1977); Lowell J. Bean and Thomas C. Blackburn, *Native Californians: A Theoretical Retrospective* (1976); Thomas C. Blackburn and Travis Hudson, *Time's Flotsam: Overseas Collections of California Indian Material Culture* (1990); Sylvia Brakke Vane and Lowell John Bean, *California Indians: Primary Resources, A Guide to Manuscripts, Artifacts, Documents, Serials, Music, and Illustrations* (1990); "Indians of California," special issue of *California History* (Fall 1992); M. Kat Anderson, Michael G. Barbour, and Valerie Whitwourth, "A World of Balance and Plenty: Land, Plants, Animals, and Humans in a Pre-European California," William S. Simmons, "Indian Peoples of California," and William Preston, "Serpent in the Garden: Environmental Change in Colonial California," all chapters in *Contested Eden: California Before the Gold Rush,* Ramon A. Gutierrez and Richard J. Orsi, eds. (1997–98).

Tribes, Specific

Lowell John Bean, *Mukat's People: The Cahuilla Indians of Southern California* (1972); James F. Downs, *The Two Worlds of the Washo: An Indian Tribe of California and Nevada* (1966); Bernice Eastman Johnston, *California's Gabrielino Indians* (1962); William McCawley, *The First Angelinos: The Gabrielino Indians of Los Angeles* (1996); Leif C. W. Landberg, *The Chumash Indians of Southern California* (1965); Frank Forest Latta, *Handbook of Yokuts Indians* (1949); Malcolm Margolin, *The Ohlone Way: Indian Life in the San Francisco-Monterey Bay Area* (1978).

Economy

Chester King, "Chumash Inter-Village Economic Exchange," *The Indian Historian* (1971); William Wallace, "Indian Use of California's Rocks and Minerals," *Journal of the West* (1971); James T. Davis, "Trade Routes and Economic Exchange Among the Indians of California," in Robert F. Heizer, ed., *Aboriginal California: Three Studies in Cultural History* (1963).

Science, Ecology, and Agriculture

Thomas C. Blackburn and Kat Anderson, eds., *Before the Wilderness: Environmental Management by Native Californians* (1993); Robert F. Heizer and Albert B. Elsasser, *The Natural World of the California Indians* (1980); Malcolm Margolin, ed., "California Indians and the Environment," special issue of *News from Native California* (Spring 1992); David Rich Lewis, *Neither Wolf Nor Dog: American Indians, Environment, and Agrarian Change* (1994); Travis Hudson and Ernest Underhay, *Crystals in the Sky: An Intellectual Odyssey Involving the Chumash Astronomy, Cosmology, and Rock Art* (1978); E. F. Castetter, et al., *Yuman Indian Agriculture* (1951); Jack D. Forbes, "Indian Horticulture West and Northwest of the Colorado River," *Journal of the West* (1963); Harry Lawton, et al., "Agriculture Among the Paiute of Owens Valley," *Journal of California Anthropology* (1976); Henry T. Lewis, ed., *Patterns of Indian Burning in California* (1973); E. K. Balls, *Early Uses of California Plants* (1975); Lowell John Bean and Harry W. Lawton, "Some Explanations for the Rise of Cultural Complexity in Native California with Comments on Proto-Agriculture and Agriculture," in Henry T. Lewis, ed., *Patterns of Indian Burning in California* (1973); Lowell John Bean and Katherine S. Saubel, *Temalpakh: Cahuilla Indian Knowledge and Usage of Plants* (1972).

Culture, Religion, and Arts

Cambell Grant, *The Rock Paintings of the Chumash: A Study of California Indian Culture* (1965); James R. Moriarty, "A Reconstruction of the Development of Primitive Religion in California," *Southern California Quarterly* (1970); Theodora Kroeber, *The Inland Whale: Nine Stories Retold from California Indian Legends* (1959); Thomas C. Blackburn, *December's Child: A Book of Chumash Oral Narratives* (1975); Malcolm Margolin, ed., *The Way We Lived: California Indian Stories, Songs, and Reminiscences* (1993); Lowell John Bean, ed., *California Indian Shamanism* (1992).

Social and Political Structure

Lowell John Bean and Thomas F. King, *Antap: California Indian Political and Economic Organization* (1974); Tom King, "New Views of California Indian Societies," *The Indian Historian* (1972); Edith Wallace, "Sexual Status and Role Differences," in Robert Heizer, *Handbook of North American Indians*, Volume 8: *California* (1978).

Mission Santa Barbara
The restored Mission Santa Barbara recalls Spain's attempt in the eighteenth century to implant European civilization on the Pacific coast. *Photograph by Richard Orsl.*

PART TWO

EUROPEANS AND INDIANS: THE CALIFORNIA EXPERIENCE

Few eras of American history have been as romanticized as the period of Spanish and Mexican rule in California. Many popular writers and restored historic sites have testified that life in California from the Serra-Portolá expedition to settle the province in 1769 until the outbreak of war between Mexico and the United States in 1846 was peaceful, harmonious, and perhaps even rudely aristocratic. In the time-honored popular legend, the dominant plot in California, as elsewhere in the New World, was the progressive European conquest and colonization of the wilderness. The central characters were the heroic explorers, soldiers, missionaries, and ranchers, who with sword, cross, and branding iron transplanted Mediterranean civilization to the American frontier. This drama took place against a gold-lit setting of ornate Spanish missions adorned with tall bell towers, red-tiled roofs, and gracefully arched porticoes, or of expansive feudal ranchos with whitewashed adobe *casas grandes* and colorful gardens bubbling with the music of fountains and the laughter of *señoritas* and *caballeros*. The land was benevolent and productive, the people graceful and honorable. Hispanic California, as popular legend would have it, was a languid Eden of simple ease and pleasure.

The colonial Hispanics are commonly portrayed as treating the Indians humanely and paternalistically. The elaborately restored missions today stand as colorful monuments to Spain's attempt to Christianize and bring the blessings of progress to the "lowly" native Californians. In a famous 1917 essay, the noted historian Herbert E. Bolton captured the prevailing popular sentiment on this subject when he characterized the missions as "a force which made for the preservation of the Indians, as opposed to their destruction, so characteristic of the Anglo-American frontier." "In the English colonies," he concluded, "the only good Indians were dead Indians. In the Spanish colonies it was thought worth while to improve the natives for this life as well as for the next." In the rare instances when the popular tradition focuses any attention on the natives themselves, they are usually depicted as docile children of nature, few in number, backward remnants of the Stone Age noted mostly for their meek acceptance of the superior culture taught to them by the kindly Franciscan missionaries. Unable or unwilling to resist, so this view goes, the Indians thrived under Hispanic paternalism until the more racist Anglo-Americans rudely pushed them from the land after the 1840s.

However, as the following narrative of Estanislao's rebellion suggests, the true story is starkly different, more complicated, and filled with deprivation, confusion, and conflict. The good life was indeed elusive in Hispanic California. The realities of settling a remote, thinly populated, semi-arid region repeatedly undermined the official colonization policies relied on by both Spain and, after independence, Mexico. The goals of the few settlers along the coast were continually frustrated by a multitude of geographic, economic, and administrative problems, both within the colony and outside it. As late as the 1840s, after three-quarters of a century of effort, the region's economy remained colonial, its institutions fragmented, its military power negligible, and its population small and scattered.

Not the least of the hindrances to Spanish and Mexican success in California were the diverse native peoples, who, despite suffering calamities caused by colonization, proved remarkably resistant to efforts to assimilate and control them. Contact with the intruders greatly changed and threatened Indian cultures, but after the first shock of colonization, natives adapted, reorganized, and reasserted their power. Indian resistance soon developed into the major force frustrating Spanish and Mexican colonial ambitions. Far from being bit players, the Indians were lead actors, and the clash between their civilization and that of the invaders was the central dramatic theme of Hispanic California.

CHAPTER FOUR

ESTANISLAO'S REBELLION, 1829

When Spain began to colonize California in 1769, the mission served as the principal instrument of conquest of land and native peoples. Missions were socio-religious settlements in which the Indians were to be gathered, controlled, Christianized, culturally assimilated, and economically exploited. After Mexico gained its independence from Spain in 1821, many groups in the new nation sharply criticized the numerous missions that had been founded all along its northern frontier. Nevertheless, Mexico's financial, military, and governmental instability and disagreements over replacement Indian policies prevented the disestablishment of the missions until the 1830s and 1840s. Although Estanislao's rebellion occurred relatively late in the period of colonization, it illustrates the weaknesses of the Hispanic colony of California, the missions' influence on native cultures, the contradictions and conflicts that undermined the missions, and the important role Indians played in shaping California history.

One day in February 1829, two Indian *vaqueros*, or cowboys, from Mission San José rode their horses eastward from San Francisco Bay over the lonely coastal hills into the valley of the San Joaquin River. Weary of tending the mission's cattle, Macario and Benigno joined two old Indian fishermen at the marshy riverbank and settled down to fish and perhaps to reminisce about old friends and old ways. Thus preoccupied, the loafers failed to notice the stealthy approach of seven riders until it was too late. Quickly surrounded and captured, the *vaqueros* recognized one of the horsemen as the renowned Estanislao, a former neophyte (Indian converted to Christianity) at Mission San José and now the commander of a large renegade band of Christian defectors and gentiles (unconverted Indians) who were defying colonial authority in the interior.

Estanislao had the prisoners stripped of their horses, gear, and clothing. Benigno quickly went over to his captors, but Estanislao freed Macario to warn Father Durán at the mission that the rebels would soon storm the ranchos, towns, and missions. Boasting that he also had firearms, Estanislao taunted the colonists to try to stop him, if they were brave enough. With that, Estanislao's party crossed the river and vanished into the valley wilderness to the east. Shaken and naked, Macario trudged back to the settlements bearing Estanislao's challenge.

Estanislao had been born in about 1800 in the San Joaquin Valley. Before the first Spanish explorers arrived, the valley was a vast, fertile land. Melting snows in the Sierra Nevada to the east fed streams that tumbled onto the flat valley floor, nourishing abundant plant, animal, and human life. With underground waters nearly reaching the surface, the valley was, in the words of Pedro Fages, who first explored it in 1772, "a labyrinth of lagoons and Tulares [marshes]." Along the major rivers stood thick forests of oak, poplar, and willow, interlaced with wild berry and grape vines. Father Narciso Durán, who, as missionary at Mission San José, made numerous trips into the valley in search of converts or runaways, marveled that its landscape was "like a park because of the verdure and luxuriousness of its groves and trees." Salmon and trout freely swam the rivers, waterfowl nested the sloughs, and deer, elk, pronghorn, and grizzly bears roamed the plains and marshes. Indeed, as Fages observed, the San Joaquin Valley teemed with "every kind of animal, terrestrial and aerial."

Fages also found the valley to be thickly settled with people. Occupying most of the valley floor, Yokuts tribelets located their villages on mounds or the highest riverbanks to escape annual flooding. Their salmon-fishing and hunter-gatherer economy, supplemented by trade with other interior and coastal peoples, made the Northern Valley Yokuts—who included Estanislao's people, the Lakisamni—prosperous. Along the major rivers, where most valley people lived, the population density of ten persons per square mile equaled that of any part of California. Not particularly warlike, the Yokuts welcomed Fages when he arrived in 1772. He described them as "good looking, excellently formed, frank and liberal."

For several decades after the Spanish colonists arrived in 1769, the Yokuts remained largely untouched by the European presence. From beachheads at San Diego and Monterey, the Spaniards established a string of forts, towns, missions, and ranches along five hundred miles of coastal valleys. Leading the early colonial thrust were the missions, where the Spaniards hoped to gather the natives, convert them to Spanish culture and religion, and transform them into a working citizenry to develop the colony. To control northern California, the Spaniards founded communities on San Francisco Bay, just over the Coast Range from Yokuts territory: a presidio (fort) at San Francisco in 1776, missions at San Francisco (1776) and Santa Clara (1777), and a pueblo (civilian town) at San José (1777). Mission San José, established in 1797 about fifteen miles northeast of the pueblo, completed the early Bay Area settlements. Although many coastal tribes soon fell into the orbit of the missions and other Spanish settlements, colonial contact with interior groups such as the Yokuts was at first restricted to occasional visits by explorers, missionaries, or outlaws. The Yokuts' world went on much as before.

After 1800, however, the European influence penetrated deeper into California's heart, and revolutionary change swept the Yokuts and other inland groups. Relations between the Yokuts and the Spaniards had begun to deteriorate even before 1800. As early as the 1770s, deserters from the colonial army began attacking villages and assaulting Indian women. The natives retaliated by capturing and executing some of the offenders. Soon, runaway mission neophytes were fleeing into the interior, spreading deadly diseases and grim news of conditions in the missions. By the early 1800s, when the colonials turned to missionizing the interior, the tribes were already wary of the Spaniards. When Father Juan Martín arrived in 1804 to scout for a new mission site, he found that mission runaways roamed throughout the valley on horseback, warning

Mission San José in 1853
The great California photographer Carleton E. Watkins made one of the first photographic images, a daguerreotype, of Mission San José in 1853. By this time, the imposing buildings that had impressed foreign visitors had fallen into disrepair. The large church to the right was demolished in the great 1868 earthquake, one of the state's most violent, along the Hayward Fault. Not until 1985 did a combined church and civic effort succeed in restoring the historic building. *Courtesy of the Bancroft Library.*

gentiles that "the fathers do nothing but kill Indians." European venereal disease was also rampant, and wherever Martín went, the villagers hid their women and refused to allow children to be brought to the missions to be educated.

Mission San José mirrored the contradictory Hispanic Indian policy that reshaped Yokuts' life and led to Estanislao's rebellion. Perched on the shoulder of the coastal hills overlooking southern San Francisco Bay, San José flourished amid sun-drenched valleys, ever-flowing streams, and a large local population of Costanoans. Although founded in 1797, relatively late in the Spanish mission period, by 1820 it grew into one of the most productive of the missions, exceeded in population only by San Luis Rey. Clad in coarse wool shirts, pants, and blankets, its 1,700 neophytes tended grain fields, gardens and orchards, and thousands of sheep, cattle, and horses that ranged in valleys as far away as forty miles inland. The mission compound resembled a medium-size town with flour mill, tannery, soap factory, winery, and weaving, blacksmith, tailor, harness, pottery, and candlemaking shops.

Fathers Narciso Durán and Buenaventura Fortuny, who shared management of the mission after 1806, started an impressive building program that produced shops, warehouses, schoolrooms, guesthouses, several blocks of Indian barracks, and a large church and rectory. The mission's sailboats plied the bay, carrying the community's products to merchant ships anchored off San Francisco, thirty miles to the north. In good years, in addition to meeting its own

Christianity and Spanish culture voluntarily. They had to be brought to the mission and, once baptized, forced to remain there, even after they had demonstrated their conversion. A stern taskmaster, Durán freely disciplined recalcitrant neophytes with shackles, stocks, pillory, and, most often, the lash. Single women and girls over age eleven, especially the many gentile captives, were locked up each night because, in the words of another Franciscan, they were so "obstinate in their evil intercourse." San José's *monjerio,* where the women were imprisoned at night, was one of the mission's most prominent buildings. Its few windows were placed high on twenty-four-foot walls to prevent entry or escape. José María Amador, an overseer under Durán, testified in his memoirs to the mission's climate of compulsion:

> The treatment accorded the Indians was stern. Their shortcomings were pardoned but rarely or through very special consideration. A very minor dereliction was punished with fifteen lashes, a more serious one with twenty-five. A person who was absent from work over two weeks without permission or through laziness or anything else not thoroughly justified suffered fifty lashes. Other serious infractions, such as quarrels at the *rancherias,* fights or the use of arrows brought one hundred lashes and a set of shackles in the guard house for one or two weeks during hours off from work, while at the same time working at a loom, gathering wood or performing other tasks during the daily hours of labor.

Among the California Indians, unaccustomed to corporal punishment, such treatment was likely to breed further resistance, rather than acceptance, of missionization.

Most tragically, the neophytes fell ill and died at staggering rates. The mission's poor nutrition, concentrated population, and casual sanitation compounded the Indians' lack of natural immunities to European diseases. Venereal disease, cholera, dysentery, tuberculosis, influenza, and childhood illnesses, particularly measles, swept away the weakened neophytes. During one of the ferocious epidemics, as many as one-third of the Indians might die, often a dozen or more in a single day. Even in "normal" years, about ten percent of San José Indians, including twenty percent of the children, perished. So often did death visit the mission that Father Durán assigned five boys the full-time task of informing him of impending deaths so that he might comfort families and administer last rites. Despite frequent punishment, the boys could not keep up with the pace of illness, and did not always tell Durán in time. While making an entry in the mission's "Register of Deaths" after such an occurrence, Durán revealed his sadness and disillusionment. "I am weary," he added in the margin, "of so many sick and dying Indians, *who are more fragile than glass.*" A low birth rate, principally because Indian women often deliberately aborted their fetuses, further depleted the mission's population. By the 1820s, the local Costanoans were virtually extinct.

Beneath its prosperous facade, San José was an unstable community with extraordinarily high turnover. Life in the mission was a short-term experience for most neophytes. Although the fathers had baptized almost 5,600 persons in the first thirty years, the population held at only 1,700 in 1826. Nearly 4,000 individuals had entered and vanished from the community, most through death, many through defection. As early as 1806, José Arguëllo, commander of the San Francisco presidio, complained that San José's neophytes had "always given signs of agitation and sedition." By the 1820s, the mission had become a hotbed of fugitivism. In that decade, more than one thousand neophytes, seeking release from the dangers and constraints of mission life, fled to the sanctuary of interior tribes, often in organized escapes. In just two days, May 25 and 26, 1827, four hundred disgruntled neophytes, one-quarter of the residents, deserted into the *tulares* of the San Joaquin Valley.

As with other missions, San José's constantly draining population was maintained by dispatching soldiers to catch the fugitives and by recruiting new converts, whether they were willing or not. After 1810, missionaries from San José and the other nearby missions journeyed among the Yokuts, sometimes converting whole villages and bringing them to live at the mission. Increasingly engaged in battle with interior Indians, colonial armies also returned with gentile captives, many of whom were impressed into the mission community. By these means, some Yokuts, including Estanislao, had been removed to Mission San José by the 1820s. Homesick and unaccustomed to the climate of the coast, valley neophytes defected more readily, and were harder to recapture, than coastal Indians.

Complicating the situation after 1800, the introduction of Spanish horses revolutionized the culture of interior groups such as the Yokuts and made the Indians more mobile and powerful. The mounted tribes took to raiding ranch and mission herds of horses, which, from their point of view, were grazing on former Indian lands and destroying the natives' subsistence base. Quickly becoming widespread, horse raiding threatened the fragile colonial economy. Expeditions from San José to punish horse raiders, capture runaway neophytes, or seek new mission recruits began to embroil the mission in growing strife with the Yokuts in 1805, when Indians attacked a party led by Father Pedro de la Cueva near the Stanislaus River. Indian ambushes and horse raids and retaliatory colonial expeditions followed, including major skirmishes in 1813, 1816, 1819, 1823, and 1826. Estanislao's rebellion thus emerged from a long tradition of conflict between Indians and Hispanic settlers.

Although Estanislao was a major Indian resistance leader, the fragmented records of colonial California disclose surprisingly little personal information about him. He was probably born among the Yokuts about 1800 and brought to the mission with other tribespeople at some later date. Whatever his origins, Estanislao adapted readily to the new culture and demonstrated leadership qualities. By trade a cowboy or mule tamer, he had been chosen for the position of *alcalde*, the highest Indian official in the mission hierarchy, with limited authority over Indian work and life routines. From the time Governor Felipe de Neve instituted the office in the 1770s, against the wishes of Junípero Serra and the other missionaries, Indian *alcaldes* had often used their power to organize resistance movements.

The specific incidents leading to Estanislao's rebellion are uncertain. Because his position required him to dispense punishments and take part in expeditions to catch runaways and chastise interior tribes, Estanislao may have become enraged at the Indians' plight. He probably also learned of neophyte resistance at other missions and of the rumored demise of the mission system. He may have taken an active part in organizing the rebellion from the beginning, or tribespeople may have thrust leadership on him at the last moment. Although Estanislao's specific goals and motives remain obscure, the general circumstances precipitating the rebellion are reasonably clear: widespread Indian dissatisfaction with the mission system, shaky civil and military authority in colonial California, the emerging horse culture and growing power of the interior tribes, and the legacy of conflict between the San Francisco area colonists and the valley Indians.

Just before the rebellion, pressure from

the government to disband, or "secularize," the missions unsettled mission Indian society further. José María Echeandía, a new governor sent from Mexico to initiate secularization, proclaimed in 1826 that married Indian Christians could leave under certain circumstances, thus throwing the missions into turmoil. Rumors of impending freedom spread rapidly among the neophytes, and discipline collapsed. So many of them abandoned the missions without permission that production declined dramatically. The remaining Indians grew insubordinate. Those who had been legally freed congregated in the colonial towns, ranches, and forts, where they were exploited and driven to begging or thievery to support themselves. Many were flogged, jailed, or returned to the missions. Faced with these problems and loud protests from the Franciscans, Echeandía modified his order, but not before the experiment had produced harsher controls on the mission population and increased Indian resentment. At least one soldier who fought against Estanislao, Antonio María Osio, attributed the rebellion to Echeandía's secularization orders.

Discontented and now favored with a courageous leader, San José's Indians were ripe for revolution by 1828. In the fall of that year, when the neophytes were visiting relatives in the valley, several hundred led by Estanislao remained at the villages of the Lakisamni along the Stanislaus River, just east of its junction with the San Joaquin. Indicative of a broad conspiracy, several hundred more runaways from missions Santa Clara, San Juan Bautista, and Santa Cruz, under the command of another *alcalde*, Cipriano of Santa Clara, joined Estanislao's rebels. Through returning neophytes, Estanislao, in typical native fashion, boasted that the rebels did not fear the soldiers because, in Father Durán's words, they "are few in number, are very young, and do not shoot well." In light

of the approaching rainy season, on November 9 Durán wrote to Ygnacio Martinez, commandant of the San Francisco presidio, recommending that he send a small force immediately "to take the two ring-leaders, dead or alive, and to punish with a good cudgeling as many as deserved it."

Sometime in late 1828, Martinez did dispatch an expedition under Sergeant Antonio Soto, a seasoned Indian fighter. Little is known of Soto's campaign except for Osio's recollections in his *Historia de California*, set down fifty years later. According to Osio, Soto set out hastily from San Francisco with fifteen or twenty men and arrived several days later at the Lakisamni villages, about sixty miles east of Mission San José. The party discovered that the Indians had adopted new tactics. To neutralize the colonials' cannon, muskets, and horses, the rebels had moved their village from the open riverbank into a willow thicket, surrounded by marshes and interlaced "by a great quantity of runners and stems of grapevines" that made it impenetrable even to the rays of the sun.

As the colonials approached, the Indians, in the tradition of Yokuts warfare, bombarded them with obscenities and insults calculated to lure them into the thicket. Enraged at being ridiculed as cowardly, Soto and six of his best men dismounted and thrust carelessly into the wood. After allowing the soldiers to move unchecked to the center of the forest, the Indians suddenly attacked. Taking advantage of the dim light, thick underbrush, and their familiarity with the terrain, the invisible warriors avoided the soldiers' tough leather jackets and instead aimed their sure arrows at the intruders' heads. Forced to fight its way desperately out of the thicket, Soto's party lost two soldiers. Seriously wounded, all the survivors—including Soto, who had himself been shot in the eye—fled from the woods with barbed ar-

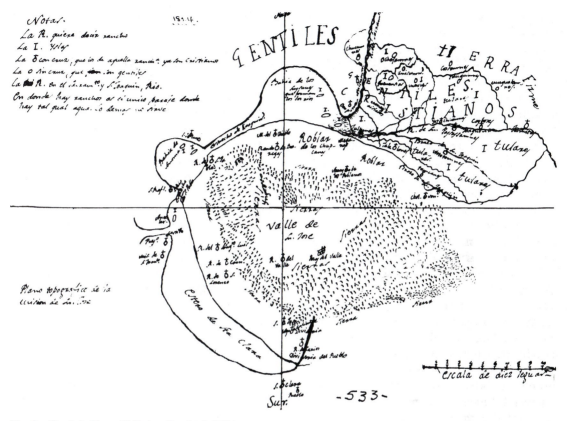

Narciso Durán's Map of Mission San José, 1824
Narciso Durán's topographical map of Mission San José's territory shows San Francisco Bay at the lower left and the complex of rivers in the San Joaquin Valley, beyond the Coast Range, at the upper right. This was the home of the Yokuts. Christianized native villages are marked with a +, gentile villages with a 0. The mission appears along the vertical center line in the lower part of the map. *Courtesy of the Bancroft Library.*

rows still protruding from their faces. Traveling "with much effort because of the great pain which the wounded suffered," the party retreated to San José, where Soto died a few days later. The jubilant Indians, according to Osio, "solemnized" their triumph "with great celebrations and dances, putting on exhibit the corpses of the soldiers who had been killed so that the neighboring tribes, who had been invited, might admire their great valor and bravery."

Although winter rains soon flooded the valley's rivers and marshes, preventing colonial authorities from retaliating immediately, Estanislao lost no time in consolidating his forces. News of his crushing defeat of Soto spread rapidly across the valley, bringing offers of support from aroused Yokuts and perhaps the more distant Miwok of the Sierra foothills. By spring, Estanislao had forged a broad alliance and assembled at his stronghold an army of 500 to 1,000 neophyte and gentile warriors, one of the largest Indian forces ever to fight against whites in California. A dozen tribelets had moved to the stronghold, and more Christian runaways continued to filter in. The rebels had also developed a system for supplying the stronghold with food by runners from outlying villages. Emboldened by success, Estanislao intensified his raids on the livestock of Bay Area missions and ranches. By the time he captured Macario and Benigno in late February 1829, he felt confident enough to issue another challenge to the Mexicans. Macario's story of his encounter with Estanislao prompted Father Durán to write another letter to Martinez on March 1, calling for immediate action against the rebels.

Government officials were in a difficult position. They were fully aware that the rebellion constituted a serious challenge to their authority and, if left unpunished, could lead to broader resistance. Military problems typical in Hispanic California, however, hindered their ability to fight Estanislao. In theory, the colonials possessed a superiority derived from European horses, steel blades, firearms, and cannon. In reality, much of their edge was blunted when the Indians themselves acquired horses. Moreover, the impoverished colony could support but few professional soldiers, several dozen at each presidio and a half-dozen in each mission guard. During larger Indian campaigns, these meager forces had to be augmented by unreliable civilian militiamen and Indian auxiliaries, neophyte and gentile. Rarely paid, the colonial soldiers wore ragged uniforms, were forced to fight with insufficient and dilapidated equipment, and often had to forage for food. Poorly disciplined, the disgruntled troops were prone to mutiny and fights with soldiers from other presidios. F. W. Beechey, a British naval officer who observed an expedition against valley tribes from Mission San José in 1826, dismissed California's military organization as "ludicrous."

Nonetheless, officials moved to crush Es-

tanislao's rebellion when good weather returned. They entrusted the task to Ensign José Antonio Sanchez of the San Francisco presidio, a courageous veteran of more than twenty Indian campaigns. From the beginning, the expedition was ill-fated. Sanchez marched out of San Francisco on May 1, 1829, with only eleven soldiers and one cannon. At Mission San José, some of the guards from missions Santa Clara and Santa Cruz joined him. Commandant Martinez's appeal a week earlier for assistance from the nearby San José pueblo apparently had fallen on deaf ears, for only seven militiamen and five civilians turned out. At that, all civilians and one militiaman returned home because Sanchez lacked horses and harness to mount them. After several days of making cartridges and preparing what equipment he did have, Sanchez set out from Mission San José on May 4 with a less-than-imposing force of twenty-eight soldiers, six militiamen, and seventy Indian auxiliaries. As on other campaigns, the auxiliaries not only proved useful as guides and fighters, but also rounded up and slaughtered cattle for food en route and built tule rafts to ferry the troops across the still-swollen valley rivers.

After slogging through the wet San Joaquin Valley for several days, the colonial army arrived at the Indian stronghold early on May 7. Sanchez found Estanislao's warriors already alerted to his advance and gathered with their horses at a fortress in the middle of a thick forest nearly surrounded by a bend of the Stanislaus River. A canopy of tall oaks shaded a jungle of small trees and bushes overhung with wild vines. The undergrowth thinned to a grassy parkland toward the landward side of the forest, but as it neared the riverbank, it became a dense tangle of shrubbery that was impenetrable to outsiders.

After dismounting and unsuccessfully trying to set fire to the damp brush, Sanchez divided his forces into three squads. One guarded the horses, while another flanked the village by fording the river. Sanchez led the third on an immediate charge into the center of the woods. He advanced without resistance until blocked by the river and three thick log palisades ringing the Indian camp; since routing Soto, Estanislao had apparently fortified his defenses with techniques he had learned from the colonials. Stymied, Sanchez retreated to the edge of the woods, where Indians had already attacked one of his other parties. Sanchez ordered the cannon to be brought up, but at the first shot the wheel broke, and after two more shots, in Sanchez's words, "the piece was useless." The Mexicans continued their fire with carbines. Always keeping under the cover of the brush, the warriors retaliated with a barrage of arrows, along with some gunfire, although Sanchez maintained in his report that the Indians had powder, but no bullets. Finally, after a long battle under a scorching sun, Sanchez, "perceiving that little if any damage was being done to the enemy," withdrew his exhausted men to a camp along the river several thousand yards distant.

At daylight on May 8, Sanchez, leaving half his troops to guard the perimeter of the woods against Indian escape, entered the forest to attack the stockade directly. When he reached the fortifications, Sanchez made a final attempt to avoid bloodshed. Through an interpreter, he warned the runaways to return to their missions or else be killed. According to Sanchez's report, Estanislao answered "that he had to defend himself and he would not hesitate to die in the underbrush." Hoping to divide the Indians, Sanchez offered to allow the gentiles to return to their villages unharmed. Although twelve leaders came forward to confer, Sanchez could not convince them to abandon the renegade neophytes.

Sanchez then ordered an attack. For three hours, the two sides battled fiercely. The Mexican soldiers made little headway against the invisible enemy. They failed to penetrate the stockade, and few Indian casualties could be counted. In contrast, eleven auxiliaries and eight soldiers were wounded, three seriously. Ammunition ran out, and most firearms were broken or lost. "The weapons," Sanchez later reported, "were almost entirely useless." Discipline also collapsed. When he ordered a counterattack to rescue four surrounded soldiers who were fighting for their lives, the troops and auxiliaries refused to budge.

Convinced that his insubordinate army, "fatigued from fighting on foot in the impenetrable brush in the extreme heat," could not mount another charge, Sanchez ordered a retreat to Mission San José. Leaving two dead behind, the soldiers mounted more than twenty wounded on horses and rode off in defeat. In his memoirs, Juan Bojorges, who had fought in the battle, reported that as the soldiers fled the thicket, Estanislao came out behind them, fired one parting gunshot, threw his hat in the air, and shouted insults in Spanish. "When we reached San José on our march to San Francisco," Bojorges recalled, "news of our defeat had already reached there. The bells were tolled and there were many demonstrations of great sorrow."

Sanchez's defeat exposed the colonial government's military weakness and the potential power Indians could achieve by adapting and uniting. The debacle finally convinced the leaders to mobilize all available military resources. Martinez chose Ensign Mariano Guadalupe Vallejo of the Monterey presidio to command the combined forces of the two northern presidios, including Sanchez and his weary San Francisco troops, along with all the mission guards who could be spared. In writing to Vallejo on May 16, Martinez emphasized the crisis facing the colony. Estanislao's renegades, he warned, were "extremely insolent, committing murders and stealing horses, stripping bare the unwary, seducing the other Christians to accompany them in their evil and diabolical schemes, openly insulting our troops and ridiculing them and their weapons." The rebels were exploiting "the manpower of the wild Indians, and the terrain and positions which they are occupying . . . [and] the losses which we have suffered." Martinez ordered Vallejo "to administer a total defeat to the Christian rebels and to the wild Indians who are aiding them, leaving them totally crushed" and to "retaliate in full for all damage inflicted" an open-ended charge that Martinez may later have had cause to regret.

Despite colonial determination, the new expedition assembled at Mission San José under much uncertainty. Although he would later become a power in California, the twenty-one-year-old Vallejo had been on only two Indian campaigns and had just been made an officer. The Monterey soldiers, who had not been fully paid and rationed in nearly two years and who had mutinied six months earlier, were rumored to be on the verge of another rebellion. (They did revolt later in 1829.) Moreover, there was talk of rivalry between Vallejo and Sanchez, who understandably rankled at his defeat and replacement by the young stripling from Monterey. Just returned from a successful campaign against tribes farther south in the San Joaquin Valley, the Monterey troops undoubtedly taunted Sanchez's men, and fights between the two garrisons later marred the expedition. Moreover, the recent Indian campaigns had strained the supply of firearms, powder, and bullets, and just as the army was about to depart, Vallejo discovered that a cannon needed to breach the rebel stockade had a rotten bed and two broken wheels. Although he delayed departure to repair the cannon, it still broke down repeatedly during the coming campaign.

Finally, on May 26, Vallejo rode out with 107 soldiers and 50 auxiliaries, armed with the cannon, its ammunition, and 3,500 musket cartridges—one of the largest Hispanic armies to march against the California Indians. When he arrived at Estanislao's stronghold on May 29, Vallejo discovered that the natives had improved their fortifications with interconnected trenches covering much of the thicket floor. Other new conditions, however, favored the colonials. More regular soldiers were in the field with increased firepower, including a cannon that worked at least some of the time. Also, summer heat had dried the ground, allowing the invading forces more mobility, particularly for their artillery, and making it possible to burn the Indians' cover. Nevertheless, the Mexicans hardly overwhelmed Estanislao's people.

On arriving in the valley, Vallejo sent his troops to surround the stronghold, set fire to the woods, and ordered an assault on foot against the fort from several directions. Meanwhile, the cannon bombarded the stockade from the opposite riverbank. Cannonballs weakened the log walls and unleashed showers of jagged splinters that wounded many Indians. After several hours of exchanging musket balls for arrows at close quarters, the Mexicans had fought their way to the first wall, where the attacks stalled. Their own brush fire burning rapidly down on them and an Indian counterattack in the rear that threatened to capture their horses and supplies forced them to retreat from the forest.

Vallejo again invaded the thicket the next morning, but the Indians, apparently no longer confident in their fortifications, had escaped overnight by swimming the river. Although the Mexicans discovered only a few corpses, bloodstains in the trenches indicated that there had been many Indian casualties. Joaquin Piña, a cannoneer from Monterey, recorded in his diary that the artillery and musket balls had shattered the stockade.

Vallejo picked up the trail of the fleeing natives and caught them the next morning ten miles south along the Tuolumne River at another fortress that had been fortified with a log stockade and, in Vallejo's words, "a system of pits and trenches constructed even better than the first." Still more gentile allies had now joined Estanislao.

After surrounding and setting fire to the woods, Vallejo attacked with the bulk of his forces into the forest. Under heavy fire from the rebels and penetrating the underbrush "with much labor," twenty-five neophyte auxiliaries with axes hacked out a wide trail so that the cannon and infantry could approach the stockade. When the gun was positioned ten yards from the wall, Vallejo, through an interpreter and a gentile food runner who had been captured the day before, again appealed to Estanislao's warriors to give up. Only one Indian defected to the Mexican side, a neophyte named Matias, who begged for mercy and warned the soldiers that their gentile captive was secretly making signs encouraging the rebels to continue fighting. According to Piña, "the prisoner was consequently immediately shot."

Then began the major battle of Estanislao's rebellion. Vallejo's troops advanced from several directions toward the trenches at the center of the forest. The fighting became ferocious. In Piña's words, "the enemy were established in a position very advantageous for impeding our advance." For four hours, with only brief respites, the battle raged. Although the Mexicans, apparently out of cannonballs, blasted the stockade with grapeshot and musket fire, the Indians held their position.

At that point, the colonial assault stalled. Their ammunition for cannon and muskets exhausted, some soldiers jumped into the trenches and fought hand-to-hand with their daggers. The Indian auxiliaries, according to Piña, "became frightened both because of the fury of the attack by arrows . . . and because of the thunder of the cannon," and "as a result, we could not make them move any further." By that time, the fire Vallejo had set earlier raged completely around them. To save his army, Vallejo ordered his troops to retreat quickly through the fire, which was accomplished "in good order," according to Piña, "in spite of emerging nearly roasted in the tremendous blaze of the underbrush." When they reached open country, the soldiers heard a yell from the burning forest and fired one last shot in return. Complete silence followed. "One would not have believed," marveled Piña, "so many Indians could still be inside the woods."

Vallejo immediately had the forest surrounded to prevent the Indians from escaping. That night the soldiers killed a few Indians who were trying to swim out along the river. Early the next morning, the Mexicans captured three women, including a runaway neophyte named Agustina, who testified that many Indians had died in the battle. With Matias and Agustina as guides, Vallejo's men reconnoitered the trenches and fort, but found only a few survivors or bodies. Evidently, most natives, including Estanislao, had escaped into the valley or the mountains to the east under cover of water and darkness, taking their horses and most of their dead with them.

Although Vallejo and his defenders later denied it, the soldiers committed atrocities that day as they prepared to return home. One chronicler of the campaign, Antonio María Osio, emphasized that the most guilty were the auxiliaries, "ancient enemies of Estanislao's villages," who "burst out like starving hounds and instantly began an atrocious massacre." Other, fuller accounts, though, show that all parties participated, including auxiliaries, soldiers, civilians, and Vallejo himself. Piña's diary is probably the most reliable, because he wrote it just after the event and because he reported the atrocities in detail, despite his clear loyalty to Vallejo, his commander. Vallejo either abetted the cruelty or lost control of his army.

A number of surviving Indians, mostly women or aged and infirm men, were tortured and killed. As the soldiers swept through the forest, according to Piña, "three old women" found hiding in some grapevines "were immediately pulled out of the bushes and shot on the spot." Auxiliaries captured a Santa Clara neophyte whom they accused of having tortured two of Sanchez's soldiers a month earlier. With Vallejo's permission, the auxiliaries formed a circle around the captive and fired seventy-three arrows into him. When the rebel still refused to die, a soldier mercifully shot him in the head with a carbine. The Indians hanged the body in the top of a tree. Auxiliaries and soldiers also killed and hanged Matias, to whom Vallejo had promised safety, and four other men and women. Although the vengeful soldiers also clamored for the lives of Agustina and her two female companions, Vallejo refused and placed them under guard for return to the missions.

Its food and ammunition depleted, the army departed for Mission San José that afternoon. The soldiers drove before them several female Indian captives and a herd of eighteen recaptured horses—rather small booty for such an ambitious undertaking. Miraculously, no Mexican soldiers perished in the fighting; only thirteen, including two auxiliaries, were wounded. Several of these may have died later from their wounds, however. Indian losses, although unknown, must have been great. Dozens, perhaps hundreds, of Indians fell in the three days of fighting. As Vallejo's party rode away from Estanislao's wrecked fortress, a half-dozen bodies swung from the tops of valley oak trees, grim warnings to other would-be Indian rebels.

By any standard, the Mexican defeat of Estanislao was an inglorious victory. Suffering slight losses of their own, the colonial armies, though embarrassed, did finally succeed in demolishing two Indian fortress-towns, dissipating a large resistance force, and driving a formidable Indian leader into submission. But if colonial authorities thought that by quelling this rebellion they had taught the interior tribes a lesson and thereby quenched the flame of resistance, they were sadly mistaken. Most of the rebels had escaped, after all, and even the colonials realized that their victory had been less than total. Responding to Vallejo's report, which was much more favorable than the facts warranted, Commandant Martinez rejoiced "exceedingly that this scum has been chastised," but regretted "that due to lack of munitions and supplies you did not inflict a complete rout upon those rebellious and insolent Christians."

Persistent reports of atrocities also embarrassed the government. Father Durán and other leaders demanded that Governor Echeandía punish Vallejo and his cohorts for unnecessary cruelty and violation of laws governing the treatment of Indian prisoners. Although an investigating officer concluded that "those in the party hanged and killed two old, defenseless Indian men and three women" and shot another captive, he recommended only a mild chastisement for one low-ranking Monterey soldier. To this day the affair remains a stain on the record of Vallejo, one of California's most revered heroes.

The broader problem of Indian resistance remained unresolved. The economic, political, and cultural forces that precipitated the rebellion persisted. Neophytes continued to

Estanislao as a Great Plains Warrior
This plaque, at Caswell Memorial State Park along the Stanislaus River, depicts Estanislao as a Great Plains warrior, complete with eagle feathers, pigtails, and choke collar. The drama of the Plains Indian wars of the late nineteenth century made a great impression on the American popular mind, and all natives began to be seen in terms of Plains Indian imagery. Reflecting common ignorance about the state's original inhabitants, some early California local histories described Indians as roaming the landscape on horses, hunting the buffalo, and living in tepees. *Photograph by Richard J. Orsi.*

flee the missions, new powerful Indian leaders emerged, and horse stealing increased. In the 1830s and 1840s, resistance disrupted colonial authority even further. In 1832, Father Durán complained from San José that the colonials "were almost on foot because of the incessant horse thefts committed by apostate Christian Indians in league with the pagans. . . . Their insolence causes some to prophesy that in a very few years we shall find ourselves in a sad necessity of abandoning our outposts and uniting at one point for our common defense." By fomenting disor-

der and delaying exploration and settlement of the interior, resurgent Indian power shaped the subsequent history of California.

When his rebellion collapsed, Estanislao nearly vanished from the pages of written history. Shortly after Vallejo's return to the settlements, Estanislao and some followers reappeared at Mission San José seeking mercy and protection. Father Durán helped secure them pardons from Governor Echeandía. Remarkably, Estanislao returned to the *tulares* a year later, this time with Durán's permission. That the authorities punished

no repentant neophytes, not even their notorious leader, may seem incredible, given
the seriousness of the uprising and the
depth of colonial emotions about it. Common throughout the mission period, such le-
nience represented a less harsh, more pater-
nalistic, but no less real, dimension of
mission life.

Estanislao lived in obscurity at Mission
San José until he died in the late 1830s during one of the epidemics that were decimating the Yokuts. Although a river and a
county (Stanislaus) were named after him,
generations of Californians remained ignorant of his exploits. In the 1950s, when the
state created a new recreation area, Caswell
Memorial Park, near the site of the Indian
stronghold along the Stanislaus River, it finally erected a small monument commemorating the heroism of Estanislao and his people. A sad testament to the persistent
misunderstanding of the original Californians, the plaque pictures Estanislao in the
dress of a Great Plains warrior.

CHAPTER FIVE

EXPLORERS AND INDIANS

THE MEETING OF INDIANS AND EUROPEANS

In describing California exploration between 1542 and 1603, historians stress the exploits of the daring European mariners who battled the elements to discover and chart this remote coast. A neglected, concurrent theme was the interaction between these early explorers and the native Californians. The Europeans were confronting strange peoples as well as strange lands, and investigating the inhabitants of new territories was a major goal of exploration. Thus the pioneer expeditions left valuable records of native cultures and initial Indian-white relations.

In addition to ending California's geographical isolation, the first European ships shattered the predictable world of the natives. The sudden, unexpected arrival of beings so strange and unaccounted for in the Indians' universe was a cataclysmic event that modern people, accustomed to change, have difficulty comprehending. According to historical myth, the naive and peaceful California Indians, overwhelmed at meeting the powerful Europeans, became meek and fearful. In this legend, the natives, immobilized by culture shock and unable to compete with the stronger weapons and organization of the outsiders, lethargically accepted conquest.

Expedition accounts, however, show that the Indians were not uniformly terrified and passive when they first encountered Europeans. As could be expected from such diverse peoples, they responded differently according to their particular culture, prior information about the newcomers, and the behavior of the explorers. Also, despite trying circumstances, the natives met the intruders actively and assertively. Early contacts between the two peoples foreshadowed the complexity of later Indian-white relations—a complexity that was evident centuries later in Estanislao's rebellion.

DISCOVERY AND NAMING

Remote and self-contained, California's peoples had remained sheltered from the major currents of history for thousands of years. This isolation ended in the mid-sixteenth century, however, and the region began to

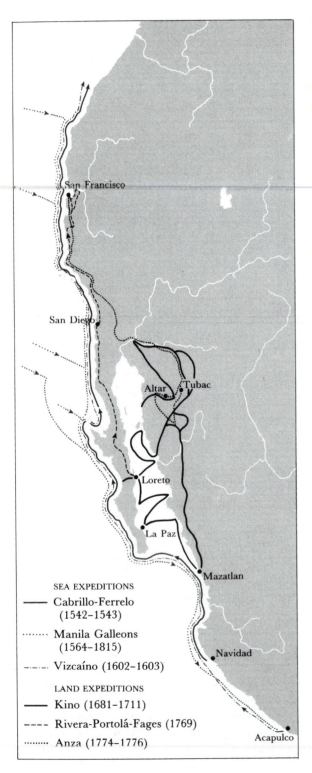

SEA EXPEDITIONS

—— Cabrillo-Ferrelo
(1542–1543)

········ Manila Galleons
(1564–1815)

–·—·– Vizcaíno (1602–1603)

LAND EXPEDITIONS

—— Kino (1681–1711)

–––– Rivera-Portolá-Fages (1769)

········ Anza (1774–1776)

be influenced dramatically by events in the outside world, often thousands of miles distant. This was an age of imperialism, when European nations competed with one another to subjugate the lands and peoples of Africa, Asia, and North and South America. On the strength of Christopher Columbus's pioneering voyages in the 1490s, Spain established an early hegemony in the New World, particularly in and along the Caribbean Sea. By 1515, Spain had set up a colonial system on the islands of Hispaniola and Cuba based on the military conquest, religious conversion, cultural assimilation, and economic exploitation of natives.

In 1519, an expedition under the ambitious adventurer Hernan Cortés landed on the east coast of Mexico, bent on conquering the Aztecs, a wealthy Indian civilization in the interior. With only a small force, Cortés marched inland, shrewdly forging alliances along the way with Indian groups opposed to the powerful Aztecs. Relying on his native allies, Cortés captured the Aztec capital, Tenochtitlán (present-day Mexico City) in 1521. Populous, rich in resources, and boasting highly developed agriculture and mining, the former Aztec empire immediately became the center of Spanish expansionism. In the 1520s, the Spanish government established the viceroyalty of New Spain to govern its North American possessions from a capital at Mexico City. For the next three centuries, Spanish viceroys administered a gigantic territory stretching from Central America and the West Indies northwestward and including Florida and much of the present-day southwestern United States.

California was discovered as a result of Spain's consolidation of its Mexican empire.

Explorers of California

Adapted from *Historical Atlas of California*, by Warren A. Beck and Ynez D. Haase. Copyright © 1974 by the University of Oklahoma Press.

From the 1520s to the 1540s, the Spaniards, exploiting dissension among the natives, subdued one group after another and relentlessly pushed their frontier northward from Mexico City. They were lured on by rumors of other wealthy Indian tribes ripe for plunder and by the dream of finding the Strait of Anián, the legendary deep-water passage through the North American continent to the riches of the Far East that inspired explorers in that era. From Acapulco and other Pacific ports, sea expeditions explored Mexico's northwest coast in the late 1520s and early 1530s. Plagued by mutiny, hostile Indians, and the great hardships of sailing uncharted seas, these early expeditions accomplished little. In 1533, one group of mutineers did cross the Gulf of California and reach Bahía de la Paz, near the tip of the Baja Peninsula. When the rebels tried to land, however, Indians killed all but two of them. Somehow sailing the ship back to Mexico, the survivors spread tales of an island surrounded by pearl beds. Finally, in 1535, Cortés himself led a fleet of three ships to take formal possession of Baja and its inhabitants.

Believing the discovery to be an island, early explorers announced that they had found "California," the rugged, pearl-rich island home of Calafia, a mythical Amazon queen in *Las Sergas de Esplandián*, a popular Spanish romance by Garcí Ordoñez de Montalvo. During subsequent voyages under Ulloa in 1539 and Alarcon in 1540, explorers circumnavigated the Gulf of California, discovered the mouth of the Colorado River, and determined that the land was a peninsula. The name stuck, however, and "California" eventually came to mean all the territory from the tip of Baja northward to the still undiscovered Strait of Anián.

CABRILLO'S VOYAGE

Encouraged by the discoveries, colonial authorities determined to explore Mexico's northwest coast further, particularly in hopes of claiming the elusive strait. To this end, Viceroy Antonio de Mendoza dispatched an expedition of three ships—the *San Salvador*, the *Victoria*, and a vessel of unknown name—under the command of Juan Rodríguez Cabrillo. Contrary to a well-established legend that he was Portuguese, Cabrillo had been born in Spain. An able navigator and shipbuilder, he was a veteran of the conquest of Mexico.

Cabrillo's fleet sailed from Navidad on June 27, 1542, rounded the tip of Baja California, and cruised northward along the peninsula. At first, summertime seas and winds made navigating easy, and Cabrillo leisurely charted islands and bays, landing occasionally to take possession. Along what Cabrillo observed was a "bare and arid" coast, the expedition encountered only a few Indian fishermen, some of whom fled at the

Juan Rodríguez Cabrillo
Courtesy of the California State Library.

sight of the strangers. Some, however, came on board to trade and communicate in signs. News of the Spanish presence had already reached even these isolated tribes. The Indians told Cabrillo that other white men had landed to the east, probably a reference to Ulloa's expedition three years earlier. The explorers heard similar stories all along the California coast.

On September 28, Cabrillo's small craft anchored in "a very good closed port" that Cabrillo christened San Miguel (later renamed San Diego by Vizcaíno). That day, the Spaniards went ashore for the first time on the coast of present-day California. Their first encounter with upper California natives heralded trouble for the future. When the explorers approached some Indians, all but three ran away. Even the remaining natives "displayed much fear" and had to be won over with gifts. But that night, when a ship's party landed to fish, Indians attacked with bows and arrows, wounding three men. A few days later, friendlier Indians told the Spaniards that the hostile natives had been alarmed because white men, dressed and armed like Cabrillo's, were wreaking havoc to the east. The chronicler of the expedition recorded that the Indians "showed by signs that these carried crossbows and swords; they made gestures with the right arm as if using lances, and went running about as if they were going on horseback, and further showed that these were killing many of the native Indians, and for this reason they were afraid." On October 3, their stores somewhat replenished, the explorers departed from San Diego and resumed their voyage northward.

Cabrillo encountered many natives on the coast and offshore islands between San Diego and Point Conception. The Spaniards were particularly captivated by the Santa Barbara Channel, which the expedition's chronicler described as rich with marine life, "very

beautiful and well-populated valleys," and "fine plains and many trees and savannas." Cabrillo's men marveled at the Chumash, especially because of their nautical skill, well-constructed canoes, and advanced Indian culture. Although aware of the plundering by the *conquistadores* in the interior, the Chumash appeared confident in the power of their numbers and unafraid of the newcomers. As the explorers traversed the coast, jubilant tribesmen in canoes rowed out from the shore, some accompanying the Spaniards for long distances. Many natives came aboard to trade or confer. One delegation of chiefs reveled with the Europeans, "danced to the sound of a tambourine and a Castillian bagpipe," and slept on board overnight. Chumash affluence also impressed the explorers. The chronicler related that the spacious plazas of their large towns were surrounded by "round houses, well covered down to the ground. They wear skins of many different animals, eat acorns and a white seed the size of maize, which is used to make tamales. They live well." The friendliness and sophistication of the Chumash, however, did not stop the Spaniards from kidnapping a half-dozen native children on their return trip to be taken back to New Spain and trained as interpreters for future voyages.

As autumn approached, Cabrillo's expedition ran into problems typical of early navigators along the California coast. Having left Mexico too late in the year for such an ambitious voyage, the ships were battered, separated, and delayed by continuous fall and winter storms. "Contrary winds" out of the northwest, threatening to drive them aground, repeatedly forced them far out to sea and made it difficult to chart the coast accurately or to take on water and supplies. Confined by the weather to their tiny, poorly provisioned hulls, the crews were racked by hunger, dissension, and illness, particularly scurvy. In the face of such adversity, it is remarkable that Cabrillo and the other explorers accomplished what they did.

On October 18, after rounding Point Conception and leaving the shelter of the channel, Cabrillo's ships were immediately blasted by "a great storm." Driven out to sea, the Spaniards took refuge for a week at a small harbor on the lee side of San Miguel Island. Here, Cabrillo broke his arm while trying to rescue some of his men who had been attacked by Indians. Departing San Miguel despite Cabrillo's injury, the Spaniards began a long ordeal of deprivation and suffering. Making scant headway against constant storms and prevented from landing by gales and rough seas, the ships fought their way northward for nearly a month until they reached a point somewhere between Monterey Bay and the present-day Oregon-California border. Ill, exhausted, out of supplies, and discouraged at not having found the Strait of Anián, the Spaniards turned around. Within a few days, strong winds had blown them back to San Miguel Island. Here, on January 3, 1543, Juan Rodríguez Cabrillo died from an infection in his broken arm.

Perilously low on supplies after two months on San Miguel, the expedition left the island on January 19 under the command of Bartolomé Ferrer (or Ferrelo), the first mate. Desperately seeking provisions in order to head northward again, the Spaniards were buffeted from one hazardous anchorage to another throughout February and early March. Although they did regain the northern California coast, they could not land; weather and hunger once again repelled them. With their ships repeatedly scattered by fierce storms and their stores whittled down to "some damaged biscuit," the seamen finally abandoned the cause and allowed the winds to beat them southward. On April 14, 1543, Cabrillo's surviving crew

staggered into Navidad, convinced that only divine intervention had rescued them from certain doom.

Cabrillo's voyage undoubtedly disappointed officials in New Spain. The costly expedition had unearthed no precious metals, discovered no Strait of Anián, encountered no opulent Indian civilization. Cabrillo had been able to make only fragmentary charts of the coastline; these were especially sketchy north of Point Conception. Furthermore, the California pictured in the explorers' accounts was remote and inaccessible, with a rugged coast guarded by treacherous winds and currents. Named for a fabled paradise, California had turned out to be nothing but a desolate wilderness.

Cabrillo, however, did establish Spain's claim to the western coast of North America as far north as Oregon. His preliminary examination of the Baja and the southern California shorelines also provided at least a crude guide for later mariners. Cabrillo's reports, moreover, meticulously described Indian food, dress, architecture, technology, and reactions to the Europeans. These documents vividly portray Indian life at the moment Europeans arrived. For more than a generation, however, Spanish interest in California waned. Instead, colonial leaders concentrated on putting down native resistance and developing the resources in Mexico and the other, more profitable regions of New Spain, and did little to explore the northern coast.

FRANCIS DRAKE IN CALIFORNIA

The second reported European landing in upper California was accomplished not by Spaniards, but by Englishmen. By the 1570s, English privateers, with the encouragement of their government, were preying on Spanish shipping in the Americas. In 1579, the most famous of the "sea dogs," Francis

Francis Drake Being Welcomed by the California Indians
This fanciful view from a later English illustration depicts an actual ceremony of welcome and crowning described in the narratives of Drake's voyage. The architecture of Indian buildings shown here is totally unlike the domed tule dwellings of the Coast Miwok. *Courtesy of the Bancroft Library.*

Drake, sailed the *Golden Hind* through the Straits of Magellan and took to raiding Spanish treasure ships and pillaging seaports up the western coast of South and Central America. His leaky ship bulging with booty, Drake escaped north into the Pacific, intent on finding the Northwest Passage (Strait of Anián) and returning to England. According to contemporary published accounts of the voyage, Drake reached the coast somewhere in Oregon and drifted back southward, look-

ing for a place to prepare the *Golden Hind* for the long voyage home. On June 17, 1579, at around thirty-eight degrees north latitude, in the vicinity of San Francisco Bay, Drake cast anchor in "a convenient and fit harbor," which he named Nova Albion (New England) because its "white bancks and cliffes, which lie toward the sea" reminded him of home.

Having clashed with Latin American Indians, Drake built a fort on the beach protected by piles of stones. Drake's crew remained encamped there for more than a month while they careened, repaired, and provisioned the *Golden Hind.* Like other early explorers of the California shoreline, Drake's men detested its harsh climate and rugged landscape. Although it was summer, the shivering Englishmen, by now accustomed to tropical weather, grumbled constantly because of the "nipping colds" and "those thicke mists and most stinking fogges." The "insufferable sharpeness" of the wind, thought Francis Fletcher, a chronicler of the voyage, was the cause of "the generall squalidnesse and barrenesse of the countrie."

The Englishmen took more kindly to the Coast Miwok Indians, however. Unlike the Spaniards, Drake's men were uninterested in settling permanently or subjugating Indians, and they approached the natives in a relaxed manner. Drake's visit was the most intense contact between Europeans and native Californians in the exploration period. Chroniclers described the culture shock experienced by both groups, as well as the considerable potential for positive interaction. Soon after the sailors' arrival, word spread among local villages, and throngs of armed warriors fell on the English encampment, ready to make "war in defense of their countrie." When the English made signs of friendship, the natives dropped their weapons and stood awestruck, as Fletcher observed, "as men ravished in their minds, with the sight of things they had never seene or heard of before that time."

The English also were deeply moved and puzzled by meeting the strange people. After ritual exchanges of gifts, the Indian women, in an apparent mourning ceremony, began "crying and shrieking piteously, tearing their flesh with their nailes from their cheekes in a monstrous manner, the blood streaming

downe along their brests, . . . [and] with furie cast themselves upon the ground . . . on hard stones, nobby hillocks, stocks of wood, and pricking bushes." The English were more unnerved by the frenzy of the Indian women than they had been by the belligerence of the warriors. Fearing that Satan was present, Drake and his crew immediately fell to their knees and commenced praying and singing psalms, "lifting up our eyes and hands to heaven . . . beseeching God, if it were his good pleasure, to open by some means their blinded eyes." The fascinated natives, quickly calmed, sat down, and watched attentively. At prayers' end, they applauded with enthusiasm and pleasure. Whenever Indians came, thereafter, they asked the English to sing.

After the initial shock of meeting, the peoples adjusted to one another remarkably well. Within a few days, hundreds of Indians from a wide territory had converged on Drake's camp in columns, singing, dancing, and bringing gifts. Throughout Drake's sojourn, many Indians remained at the camp, working, trading, eating, and worshiping with the Englishmen. Clearly impressed with the wondrous "magic" of the Europeans, natives with sores presented themselves to be healed.

Drake's crewmen also soon discarded their fears, opened up the fortress, and allowed the natives to socialize freely. After completing their repairs, the Englishmen toured inland villages to learn more about their inhabitants. Although the English never lost their contempt for "heathen" customs, particularly the self-torture of the women, which recurred often during their stay, they soon grew to like, if not admire, their friendly hosts. The English marveled at the Indians' skill with bow and arrow, their uncanny fishing ability, and the ease and freedom of their demeanor. Native strength and endurance particularly impressed the English. The men, wrote Fletcher, are "commonly so strong, that that which 2 or 3 of our men could hardly beare, one of them would take upon his back, and without grudging carrie it easily away up hill and downe hill an English mile. . . . They are also exceedingly swift in running, and of long continuance." The English "took pitty" on the afflicted Indians who begged for cures and used what lotions they had to ease their pain, "beseeching God, if it made for his glory, to give cure to their diseases by these means." Drake's men probably also had sexual relations with native women. Overall, Fletcher concluded, the Indians "are a people of a tractable, free and loving nature, without guile or treachery."

On July 23, 1579, his ship and crew refreshed, Drake sailed away in the *Golden Hind*, leaving behind a brass plate, nailed to a post, recording his visit and laying claim to Nova Albion in the name of Queen Elizabeth of England and her successors. The disappointed Indians wept "bitter teares," climbed to the highest hills, and lit beacon fires to their departing friends. After a brief stop at the Farallon Islands to take on a store of seals and sea birds, Drake, discouraged by fierce northerly winds from further seeking the Northwest Passage, resumed his voyage westward across the Pacific. More than a year later, the *Golden Hind* returned home with its treasure to a jubilant queen and nation, the second vessel to sail around the world.

Drake's placid visit to California left a legacy of historical controversy. Long sought by historians, a crudely fashioned brass plate bearing Drake's inscription finally surfaced in Marin County in 1937. Put on display at the University of California's Bancroft Library, the plate quickly became one of California's most celebrated historical artifacts. Because of its peculiar phrasing and letter-

ing, though, skeptics questioned the plate's authenticity from the beginning. In the 1970s, to resolve decades of debate, the library subjected the plate to analysis by independent laboratories. On the basis of its chemical composition, along with the methods evidently used to flatten and cut the brass, the tests showed that "Drake's Plate" was almost certainly a modern forgery.

A somewhat more substantial controversy surrounding Drake is the recurrent debate over the precise location of Nova Albion: San Francisco Bay or the more commonly accepted Drake's Bay in western Marin County. Although most evidence, particularly the presence of white cliffs and blustery climate vividly described in the narratives, seems to favor the latter site, the accounts of the voyage are vague enough to have encouraged seemingly endless quibbling among local boosters, popular writers, and historians and anthropologists. Over the years, the number of ships under Drake's command, the possibility that he left some of his party behind in California, and other minor issues have also been debated. Historian Harry Kelsey, writing in the *Western Historical Quarterly* in 1990, has even demonstrated that there is room for doubt that Drake ever made it to California at all and that the entire story may have been a fabrication. Barring the dramatic discovery of lost manuscripts or archaeological evidence, the many controversies spawned by Drake's visit may never be settled.

For all the scholars' sound and fury, Francis Drake's sojourn in California actually signified little. Drake's around-the-world voyage was indeed one of the grand events of European exploration. It also served as one of the foundations of Great Britain's claim to the Oregon Country two centuries later. The voyage's narratives, moreover, are one of the best sources of information on the dynamics of Indian-white contact. Nevertheless, Drake's

"Drake's Plate"

The inscription on "Drake's Plate" at the Bancroft Library in Berkeley reads: "BEE IT KNOWNE VNTO ALL MEN BY THESE PRESENTS, IVNE.17.1579. BY THE GRACE OF GOD AND IN THE NAME OF HERR MAIESTY QVEEN ELIZABETH OF ENGLAND AND HER SVCCESSORS FOREVER. I TAKE POSSESSION OF THIS KINGDOME WHOSE KING AND PEOPLE FREELY RESIGNE THEIR RIGHT AND TITLE IN THE WHOLE LAND VNTO HERR MAIESTIES KEEPEING. NOW NAMED BY ME AN TO BEE KNOWNE V(N)TO ALL MEN AS NOVA ALBION. G. FRANCIS DRAKE." Ironically, after the library announced that the plate is probably a hoax, the number of sightseers coming to view it increased. *Courtesy of the Bancroft Library.*

influence on the course of California history was negligible; the sea dog came and went, leaving little in his wake except antiquarian controversy. The first published account of the landing, Richard Hakluyt's *Principall Navigations* (1589), did possibly help to rekindle Spanish interest in the region in the 1590s. A new movement to explore and settle California was already under way by 1589, however, and there is no direct evidence that Drake's claim of possession influ-

enced Spanish policy substantially. Ultimately, Spain cast its authority over California just as it would have done had Drake never landed at Nova Albion.

THE MANILA GALLEON AND REVIVED EXPLORATION

In the late sixteenth century, Spain once again looked toward California, but for new reasons and from another direction. Fernando Magellan's voyage in 1521 had established Spain's claim to the Philippines. By mid-century, Spaniards had colonized those islands and developed a lucrative trade in bullion and rare Asian products between Mexico and the new territory. To shield valuable cargoes from English and Dutch pirates, Spain eventually concentrated this trade in one ship that sailed annually between Acapulco and Manila. Seeking advantageous winds and currents, the famed "Manila galleons" eventually charted a new return route, heading north from the Philippines, east across the northern Pacific to a point somewhere off the upper coast of California, and then rapidly southward to Acapulco. Despite its navigational superiority, this route proved long and extremely hazardous for people and cargo. After sailing for half a year or more over open seas without touching land, the galleons reached California waters in bad repair and out of supplies, with crew and passengers dying or ill and too weak to go ashore. Limping down the coast to Mexico, the ships were easy pickings for pirates lurking off the Baja Peninsula. The loss of several treasure-laden galleons revived Spanish interest in California as a possible supply station for the Mexico-bound ships.

After some abortive attempts, the search for a harbor in California began in earnest in the 1580s. At first, Manila galleons themselves conducted explorations on their return voyage. Authorities in the Philippines directed Pedro de Unamuno, commander of the 1587 galleon, to examine California thoroughly. Arriving off central California in early October 1587, Unamuno found a safe anchorage, probably in Morro Bay. On sighting evidence of numerous Indians, Unamuno led a party of twelve heavily armed soldiers and a priest ashore to make contact with the inhabitants. The skittish natives, however, fled their villages and evaded the

strangers. During several days of hide-and-seek, the landing party traveled many miles inland and inspected abandoned villages of large dugout houses. As the Spaniards returned to the ship, a large force of warriors ambushed them. Pelted by arrows and javelins, five of the explorers, including one Filipino native, were wounded, two of them mortally. When Spanish harquebus fire failed to cow the tenacious Indians, the explorers retreated to the beach. Under cover of darkness, they finally escaped to their ship on a makeshift raft.

This skirmish frightened the Spaniards. Citing his depleted powder supply, the suffering of the wounded, and the overwhelming number of warlike Indians, Unamuno ordered the ship to sneak out of the harbor before dawn. Beset by fogs and heavy seas, which made exploring the coast treacherous, Unamuno abandoned the mission a week later and made haste for Acapulco. Concerned about the Indians' aggressiveness, officials in Mexico specifically ordered later explorers not to leave the protection of their ships and venture inland, thereby exposing their entire expeditions and their precious cargoes to attack.

Despite the disappointing results of Unamuno's voyage to California, the continued loss of Manila galleons kept alive Spanish interest in a relief colony there. Still lacking accurate charts and information about California's resources and inhabitants, the Spanish government decided in 1594 to resume exploration of the remote and troublesome province. In 1595, Sebastián Rodríguez Cermeño, a Portuguese-born navigator, sailed from the Philippines in charge of the heavily loaded galleon *San Agustín*, under orders to search the California shoreline for a suitable haven. Reaching the coast north of present-day Eureka, the *San Agustín* sailed southward, hugging the land. In an incident unfortunately typical of early explorations, a storm threatened to wreck the ship on the rocks and forced Cermeño to anchor in a harbor on November 6. The harbor, which he christened the Port of San Francisco, is the present-day Drake's Bay, where the famous sea dog had probably landed fifteen years earlier.

Boatloads of Indians soon surrounded the *San Agustín.* After receiving gifts of cloth, the natives welcomed the strangers ashore. Landing with twenty-two men armed with harquebuses, swords, and shields, Cermeño performed the customary ceremonies of possession and, with Unamuno's experience in mind, built a fortress on the beach. Cermeño's party remained here for a month, assembling the small sailing launch *San Buenaventura,* which had been brought along for shoreline exploration, touring the interior (in violation of his instructions), and conferring and trading with many Coast Miwok villages. During one of the longest encounters between California natives and Spanish explorers, Cermeño's scribe, Pedro de Lugo, compiled extensive and detailed reports of Indian dress, foods, and reaction to Europeans. In keeping with Drake's experience, most local groups were friendly. Some, however, were initially defiant until convinced of the visitors' peaceful intentions. Typically, Spanish presents and trade worked miracles, transforming bands of bristling warriors into gracious hosts. Lugo observed that, though the Indians went about "naked without covering and with their private parts exposed," they were "a well-made people, robust and more corpulent than the Spaniards in general."

On November 30, 1595, disaster struck. A fierce storm demolished the *San Agustín,* sinking all the galleon's cargo and provisions and killing about a dozen people. Completely out of food, Cermeño ordered a sweep through the countryside to gather acorns, wild nuts, and salvage from the ship-

wreck. Most Indians relinquished these goods peacefully, but when the Spaniards attempted to retrieve ship planks from one village, the enraged natives attacked, wounding one man. Driving the natives off with harquebus volleys, the Spaniards stripped the village of the wood, as well as its store of food. On December 8, eighty survivors, along with their meager supplies, crammed into the launch and set sail for Mexico.

The return voyage of the *San Buenaventura* was one of the most heroic exploits of New World exploration. Now at their peak during the winter storm season, gales thrashed the tiny vessel continually, while fogs obscured the rugged shore. Although they passed just a few miles away, Cermeño's party, as did all the early explorers, failed to see the mist-enshrouded Golden Gate, and the vast, sheltered San Francisco Bay remained undiscovered. Huddled in the tiny, open boat, the survivors suffered grievously from thirst, hunger, and exposure to the elements. The party survived by catching fish, gathering plants on offshore islands, and trading for food with Indians. Bitter acorns and roots made some Spaniards violently ill. Deaf to the pleas of his crew, Cermeño doggedly stopped whenever the weather cleared to take soundings and make observations and charts. Only after struggling as far south as Baja California, which had been fairly well charted, did Cermeño finally capitulate and order a speedy passage to Acapulco. Nearly naked and gaunt from starvation, the men of the *San Buenaventura* arrived in Mexico at the end of January 1596. As far as is known, all survived the ordeal.

Despite his remarkable achievement, Cermeño received an icy welcome. Angered by the loss of a cargo worth one million pesos, Mexican officials charged that he had wandered too far from the ship, had exposed his expedition to unnecessary danger, and had failed to examine California carefully enough to discover a sheltered port. An investigation cleared Cermeño of personal blame but pronounced the expedition a failure. As a result, Cermeño's charts, for which he and his crew had paid dearly, were suppressed, although they were the most accurate to date for some stretches of the coast. Authorities also abandoned further attempts to explore California from the Philippines in the valuable and ponderous merchant ships, with exhausted crews and supplies. Subsequent Manila galleons were ordered to avoid the treacherous coast. Future expeditions to California were to venture northward from Mexico in light, maneuverable, specially equipped ships, burdened only with supplies and trade goods for Indians.

VIZCAÍNO'S EXPEDITION

The viceroy of New Spain at the time of Cermeño's voyage, Gaspar de Zúñiga y Acevedo, Conde de Monterrey, enthusiastically promoted the exploration of California. On orders from the Spanish government, Zúñiga organized a special expedition to chart the California coast accurately and to locate a sheltered port for future settlement. He placed Sebastián Vizcaíno, a veteran explorer and developer of pearl fisheries on the Baja Peninsula, in charge of this venture. To avoid the problem that had thwarted earlier efforts, Zúñiga and Vizcaíno devoted more than a year to planning the expedition, outfitting the vessels, and assembling the most expert cartographers and officers, along with seasoned soldiers and sailors who "knew how to handle arms well." In his detailed instructions, Zúñiga particularly cautioned Vizcaíno against going inland and arousing the natives. Determined to leave early enough in the year to reach California

before stormy weather began, Vizcaíno loaded his force of more than 130 men aboard three small ships, the *San Diego*, the *Santo Tomás*, and the *Tres Reyes*, and sailed from Acapulco on May 5, 1602.

Despite the painstaking preparations, Vizcaíno's voyage proved just as difficult as those of his predecessors. Unseasonably strong northwest winds continually forced the ships to tack back and forth, "an insufferable labor," according to Father Antonio de la Ascensión, one of the expedition's chaplains. Vizcaíno's careful coastal survey, along with frequent stops to replenish the large crew's supplies, also impeded progress. The expedition failed to turn the southern tip of Baja until July 5 and did not reach San Diego until November 10, more than six months after departure. The season was already too late to challenge California's tempestuous waters. Logging a tortured course up the coast into the teeth of gales and storms, Vizcaíno, true to his instructions, charted bays, islands, and landmarks from San Diego northward. The names he gave them, from saints' days on the Catholic liturgical calendar, have lasted to the present day.

Vizcaíno's relations with southern California Indians resembled those of Cabrillo sixty years earlier. He found the coast and offshore islands densely populated from San Diego to Point Conception. As in Baja, some groups offered resistance. After Vizcaíno's men had come ashore at San Diego, throngs of enraged Indians brandishing bows and arrows charged them along the beach. The natives calmed down when Father Ascensión advanced alone to embrace and regale them with gifts of bead necklaces. During the Spaniards' ten-day sojourn, Ascensión recalled, the "contented and happy" Indians came often to trade animal skins for European goods. The natives learned some Spanish words and, like the Baja Indians, reported news of white men in the interior, which Vizcaíno recognized as accounts of Juan de Oñate's reconquest of New Mexico a few years earlier.

The people of the Santa Barbara Channel particularly impressed Vizcaíno's party. At Santa Catalina Island, the explorers stayed a week among the Gabrielino, who, according to Ascensión, received them with such familiarity that it appeared "they had seen Spaniards before." (Cabrillo had stopped there for a few hours in 1542.) Vizcaíno erected a tent and altar, and the chaplains preached and said mass before "a great number of young Indians," who seemed curious about the strangers' religion. Ascensión admired the islanders' swift plank canoes, "pleasing and easy" methods for stalking and harpooning large fish and seals, and system of trade and communication with the mainland and other islands. The Indians also stole skillfully from the Spaniards. Ascensión complained that they were "very light-fingered and clever" and "beat the gypsies in cunning and dexterity." While scouring the island, soldiers triggered one serious incident when they desecrated a shrine by casually shooting two sacred crows guarding it, causing the Indians "to weep and show great emotion."

News of the Spanish presence preceded them to the Chumash. As they had done for Cabrillo, native boatmen met the ships whenever they neared land. The Chumash insisted that the Spaniards accept their hospitality on shore. One especially outgoing Indian leader came aboard and, seeing no females on the ships, offered the strangers ten women apiece if they would visit the villages. Father Ascensión reported that, when "all of us laughed very much," the chief, thinking that they doubted his sincerity, offered to remain on board as a hostage if the Spaniards would go ashore. Although he presented the Indian with gifts and sent him home to pre-

pare for the visit, Vizcaíno seized the advantage of a rare southeast wind that had just come up, and on December 3 the explorers sailed off to the north, intending to take up the chief's offer on the return voyage. Within a day, however, the wind had reversed, and the Spaniards once again were combating the elements. Adverse weather prevented them from contacting many Indians north of Point Conception.

On December 16, the explorers rounded a rocky promontory flanked by pine forests (Point Piños) and struggled into a tiny, northward-facing inlet. The expedition was in crisis. Scurvy ravished the ships. Almost all the men suffered to some degree from severe body pains, swollen gums, and loose teeth. Most, including officers and priests, were too weak to rise from their beds, and, according to Father Ascensión, "no one was found who could even manage the sails of the ships." So far, sixteen had perished, "while others were dying each day without any remedy." Ignorant of the true cause of the disease—insufficient fresh fruit and vegetables in the crewmen's diet—Ascensión blamed California's sharp, northwesterly winds for inflicting a pestilence.

Stalled by weather and illness, the expedition had not found a site for a port. Fearing that this failure jeopardized his chances for royal pensions and positions, Vizcaíno transformed his present rocky, windswept anchorage into the long-sought California harbor. Shrewdly naming it Monterey Bay in honor of the viceroy, the explorer penned glowing descriptions of his "discovery" into his reports and a letter to the king. Monterey, he boasted, was a large, protected harbor, "the best port that could be desired, for besides being sheltered from all the winds, it has many pines for masts and yards, and live oaks and white oaks, and water in great quantity, all near the shore." According to Vizcaíno, the region also teemed with gentle natives eager to subject themselves to the gospel and Spanish authority, and the climate was so benevolent and the soil so fertile that "any seed sown there will give fruit." Actually, the local Costanoan population was sparse and the climate foggy and windy. Indeed, Vizcaíno's reports and charts so exaggerated the bay's virtues that, a century and a half later, Portolá's expedition failed to recognize the place.

Vizcaíno spent several weeks at Monterey trying to regroup. After an emergency council, he sent the *Santo Tomás*, with the disabled seamen aboard, back to Mexico on December 29 to request relief supplies and crew. Five days later, the remaining vessels departed in an attempt to push as far as Cape Mendocino that winter.

Another fierce storm struck the *San Diego* and the *Tres Reyes* on January 5 and continued for more than two weeks. Unusual southerly winds blew them quickly and nearly uncontrollably northward and separated them. The *San Diego*, commanded by Vizcaíno, was beaten about by swiftly reversing winds, with sails furled, unable to turn back or take shelter. By this time, everyone aboard suffered grievously from scurvy and exposure. Only six men could rise from their beds; only two could climb the mast. During a particularly violent blast, a loose crate broke Vizcaíno's ribs. The explorers entered Drake's Bay, the scene of Cermeño's shipwreck, but could not land to salvage the *San Agustín*'s cargo. When the weather finally moderated, Vizcaíno found himself off an uncharted white promontory, which he named Cape San Sebastián (in what is now southern Oregon).

On January 19, to save themselves from destruction, the entire crew, including the sick, joined in a supreme effort, lifted the sails, and set off for New Spain. On March 21, 1603, the *San Diego* struggled into port at

Acapulco. The *Santo Tomás* and *Tres Reyes* had already returned. Altogether, more than forty mariners, or about one-third of the expedition, had perished.

CALIFORNIA FORSAKEN

Vizcaíno's voyage was the crowning achievement of early Spanish exploration of California. The most accurate survey north of the Baja Peninsula, Vizcaíno's detailed charts and logs influenced serious mapmaking for nearly two centuries. In the 1760s, they guided the Serra-Portolá expedition to settle California. Vizcaíno also located a potential port, Monterey, which became the focus of later colonizing efforts. Vizcaíno's embellishment of Monterey's attributes, however, along with his failure to discover San Francisco Bay, would greatly complicate the difficult task of settlement.

Although Vizcaíno, Ascensión, and Zúñiga sang Monterey's praises, immediate colonization of the region did not result. Never more than lukewarm, official Spanish interest in California evaporated after Vizcaíno's return. Zúñiga soon departed his post, and the new viceroy scoffed at his predecessor's colonial ambitions. By that time, most authorities had concluded that California was too close to Mexico to be of much assistance to the Manila galleons, and hence not worth the effort to explore and settle it. Moreover, sixty years of exploration had produced negative impressions of California. Although accounts sometimes did acclaim the area's beauty, the ripeness of the natives for Christianity, or the Strait of Anián, which was still believed to beckon just beyond the horizon, their most vivid images were of the biting wind, the land's unforgiving ruggedness, and the mariners' toil and suffering.

In 1606, a royal order prohibited further exploration of California, and for more than 150 years, no known ships visited the remote coast. Once again, popular maps began to imagine California as an island. The fact that it was part of the mainland had to be rediscovered in 1702 during a land expedition to the Colorado River area by Eusebio Kino, the great Jesuit missionary-explorer of Sonora and Arizona.

EXPLORERS AND INDIANS: AN ASSESSMENT

Since all exploration records come from the Europeans, it is impossible to know exactly how California Indians perceived the strangers and what goals they pursued in their relations with them. Some observations are possible, however, on the basis of the explorers' description of Indian actions, the nature of native cultures, and the patterns of Indian-white encounters elsewhere in the New World. In general, the stereotypes that have limited thinking about Indians clearly do not fit the realities of first contact.

Indian response to the Europeans was not uniform or predictable. Some natives evidently behaved in keeping with stereotypes. Astounded by events for which they were totally unprepared, they fled at the Europeans' arrival or quavered in fear before them. Bewildered by the origin and meaning of the strange intruders and their deadly weapons, these natives could account for them only by fitting them into their own mythology as powerful gods or ghosts of departed ancestors, beings to be feared and avoided.

Others, however, perhaps the majority, seemed uncowed. Although alarmed, Indians did not necessarily see the newcomers as an insurmountable threat. In theory, firearms, steel blades, and other European weapons were a powerful advantage. In reality, the simple arms of the day were unreliable, particularly because of a scarcity of ammunition and gunsmiths on remote frontiers. The population of coastal tribes such as the Chu-

mash was large in comparison to the exploring parties. Arriving weak and hungry from an arduous voyage, the Europeans, moreover, appeared inept in an environment that yielded abundant resources to the Indians. Against a handful of such woeful opponents, natives could, if they chose, muster scores of vigorous, skilled bowmen accustomed to fighting on home ground. Unsurprisingly, the European invasion did not immobilize the Indians.

Initially, most Indians greeted the intruders with suspicion, if not outright hostility; most tribes already knew of the Spanish assault on inland natives and were accustomed to defending their territories aggressively. Thus California Indians usually perceived the Europeans as dangerous interlopers to be resisted and driven away. At European landings all along the coast, including Baja California, San Diego, Morro Bay, and Drake's Bay, tribes prepared for war and attacked immediately, with no apparent provocation other than violation of their boundaries. Sometimes, Indians prevented landings. At Morro Bay, for instance, aroused natives repelled Unamuno's party and thwarted an entire expedition. Indicatively, in this battle Spanish gunfire did not scatter the warriors but served only to enrage them further. Only after becoming convinced that the strangers intended no harm did most native groups lay aside their arms and initiate peaceful relations.

Indian defiance hindered exploration. In fact, it had become so widespread by the 1590s that explorers were instructed to be prepared for violence anywhere. The constant threat of Indian resistance put the Europeans on the defensive from the start, confined them to a narrow coastal strip, forced them to expend scarce time and energy fortifying beach camps, and generally made the ordeal of exploration even more complicated. The possibility of armed conflict was also one reason why officials prohibited visits by Manila galleons after Cermeño's ill-fated voyage of 1595. Additional landings might have improved knowledge about California, perhaps even led to the discovery of San Francisco Bay and to earlier colonization.

Not all natives resisted the Europeans, however. From the beginning, some saw the strangers as objects of wonder, or perhaps of pity, but not as serious threats. The powerful Chumash, and other tribes that came to trust the explorers, approached them fearlessly, as equals, eager to learn about European tools, ornaments, language, and religion. Like Indians throughout the New World, the California natives also perceived in the Europeans an opportunity for profit. They traded foodstuffs, baskets, and other goods for fascinating and valuable European items that were sure to bring status and wealth. Indians also labored for the Europeans in return for trade goods. When Cabrillo's expedition, in dire need of supplies, landed in the Santa Barbara Channel in 1542, Chumash villagers worked for three days carrying wood, food, and water to the ships. Indeed, Cabrillo, Drake, Cermeño, and other explorers would have had difficulty surviving had they not obtained supplies and services from the natives.

For their own part, the explorers also failed to act according to stereotype. Despite frequent battles, the explorers were more favorably inclined toward the California Indians than later officials and missionaries would be. Typical of Europeans encountering other civilizations, the explorers condemned native nudity, "heathenism," and thievery. But the explorers usually were as curious about the Indians as the natives were about them, and those who remained among the Indians found much to admire. The chroniclers of the Cabrillo, Drake, Cermeño, and Vizcaíno expeditions commonly praised the natives' complex culture, trade systems, well-ordered villages, artfully constructed boats and tools, and ingenious methods of hunting and fishing. The visitors also marveled at the natives' strength, agility, and robust health, as well as their honesty, generosity, friendliness, fearlessness, and quickness to learn European ways—hardly the attributes of passive, cowering people. In general, while the explorers certainly regarded the Indians as primitive inferiors, they nevertheless portrayed them as a skilled, vigorous, and likable, though often defiant, people.

During these brief visits, the explorers do not appear to have greatly changed native cultures. Through trade and shipwreck, European products entered into Indian material culture. Some natives acquired beads, cloth, glassware and pottery, tools, coins, and other metal objects. These products, however, were relatively few in number and kind, and the Indians lacked the skills, raw materials, and technology to reproduce them. These goods thus did not revolutionize Indian life. Similarly, European explorers did not alter Indian language, religion, or other aspects of culture.

Some biological interchange between explorers and Indians also was likely. Sexual relations between the natives and the visitors probably occurred during the long stays of Drake and Cermeño, and perhaps those of Cabrillo and Vizcaíno, and some children of mixed blood may have been born after the ships had sailed away. Also, given what happened elsewhere in the New World, Indians may have contracted deadly European diseases from the explorers, who were often sick when they arrived. Soon after the outsiders had come and gone, natives may have sickened or died from mysterious afflictions against which their medicine was powerless. Such fleeting encounters, however, seem to have unleashed no great epidemics; by the time Spaniards returned to colonize a century and a half later, Indian populations were thriving.

All in all, then, the first contacts between Europeans and Indians exposed a wide range of possible relations—violence, friendship, economic exchange, and cultural and biological interaction. Later, in the longer and more intense period of colonization, Indian-white relations would be similarly complex and contradictory.

Although the explorers' visits made little difference in the culture and everyday life of most natives, the advent of what they perceived of as odd beings from parts unknown, in large birds flying swiftly over the water, must have shattered the psychological and cultural certainties of the Indians. The first coming of the whites made a profound impression on the coastal peoples who witnessed it. They passed news of the event to other groups, and it was remembered in tribal lore for centuries. In this sense, the soldiers and missionaries who came to settle in 1769 did not arrive as total strangers.

CHAPTER SIX

SPANISH CALIFORNIA

IMPERIAL PROBLEMS AND THE FOUNDING OF SPANISH CALIFORNIA

After a century and a half of neglect, European imperial rivalries rekindled Spanish interest in Alta (upper) California. In 1763, as a result of the Seven Years' War, Great Britain seized Florida from Spain, as well as Canada and the eastern Mississippi Valley from France, Spain's ally. Although France compensated Spain with New Orleans and the Louisiana country, which sprawled northwestward to the Rocky Mountains, Spain now had to worry about the unsettling presence of the powerful, unfriendly, and Protestant British on its northern frontier. In addition, word spread through Europe that the Russians planned to expand their fur-trading business in Alaska southward along the Pacific Coast toward northern Mexico. By this time, Indians on the southern Great Plains had acquired European horses, and their resurgent power threatened struggling frontier outposts in Texas, New Mexico, Sonora, and Arizona. With Spanish sovereignty on the defensive throughout North America, in 1765 the Spanish government dispatched Visitor-General José de Gálvez to reform the corrupt bureaucracy of New Spain, shore up the territory's northern frontier defenses, and establish a colony in Alta California to forestall the Russian advance.

Through more than two centuries of experience in the New World, Spain had developed a strategy for seizing territory from hostile Indians. Lacking sufficient volunteer settlers to occupy such vast, remote regions, Spain resorted to a government-coordinated military, civilian, and religious conquest of the frontier. Soldiers led the assault, governed the settlements, and built fortified outposts (presidios) to put down the expected Indian resistance. Civilians established agricultural towns (pueblos) and livestock grazing enterprises (ranchos) to sustain the colony and cultivate products for export. Though few in number, soldiers, town dwellers, and ranchers constituted the local ruling class. Central to Spain's plan were the missions, religio-economic institutions operated by orders of Spanish priests to pacify Indians, convert them to Catholicism, teach them European skills and culture, and transform them into a laboring population. By the mid-eighteenth century, strings of presidios, pueblos, ranchos, and missions had established a fragile hold on Florida, Texas, New Mexico, Sonora, Arizona, and the Baja California Peninsula.

In 1768 and 1769, Gálvez prepared his expedition for the arduous passage to Alta California. To lead and serve as governor of the new colony, he chose Spanish-born Captain Gaspar de Portolá, the experienced and loyal governor of Baja California. Gálvez entrusted the new missions to a group of Franciscan priests from the Baja missions, under the direction of Father Junípero Serra. Gálvez chose wisely; the mettle of Portolá and Serra would be indispensable during the coming ordeal.

Gálvez's plan relied on the reports of the early explorers, especially Vizcaíno. The expedition was to found presidios and missions both at San Diego and at Monterey, 400 miles farther north. From these widely separated beachheads, five additional missions and at least one more presidio were to be established among the dense coastal Indian populations. To avoid the difficulties encountered by the early explorers, Gálvez organized a four-pronged sea and land expedition from the Baja Peninsula to converge on the well-charted bay of San Diego. In January and February 1769, the ships *San Antonio* and *San Carlos*—carrying supplies and 100 seasoned sailors to put down the resistance expected from the San Diego Indians—sailed separately from La Paz. In March, the first land expedition of leather-armored troops departed under the able command of Captain Fernando Rivera, driving cattle and horses. In May, Portolá and Serra led a final contingent of soldiers and Baja mission Indians out across the rugged, arid wastes toward San Diego.

The trials of the first colonists foreshadowed a troubled future for Alta California.

Despite the Spaniards' precautions, the country proved no more receptive than it had to earlier voyagers. Enduring delay, hardships, and Indian resistance, the four parts of the expedition straggled into San Diego in disarray from March through June. More than half of the three hundred colonists died, particularly on board ship, where scurvy and dysentery took a heavy toll. Many, especially among the mission Indians, deserted the floundering expedition and returned to Mexico. The weakened survivors spent weeks erecting fortifications at San Diego, burying the dead, and trying in vain to heal the sick. Far behind schedule, the expedition ran low on supplies. Soldiers, sailors, craftsmen, and clerics lacked the skills to forage in a wilderness, even one as bountiful as California. When an additional provision ship sent from Baja perished at sea, starvation loomed. Desperately, Portolá ordered the *San Antonio* back to Mexico for reinforcements and supplies.

Leaving Serra behind to care for the sick and construct the mission, Portolá rode out of camp on July 14, 1769, with an emaciated troop of sixty leather-jacketed soldiers to find Monterey. Suffering from exposure, hunger, and illness, Portolá's party beat a tortured path northward through the uncharted country, hugging the coast wherever possible. Like earlier explorers, Portolá was harassed by some Indians and aided by others. Keeping themselves alive by trading for food from friendly natives, occasionally shooting animals, and ultimately slaughtering their own mules, the Spaniards took months to reach the latitude of the "port" of Monterey. Although they scoured the rugged, cold, and windy coastline, they could not recognize the place from Vizcaíno's overblown description.

Puzzled, Portolá pressed northward along the coast. On November 2, he found the way blocked by a giant "arm of the sea or estu-

JUNÍPERO SERRA
Apostle of California

Junípero Serra and the California Indians
Serra, as portrayed in a nineteenth-century illustration. *Courtesy of the Huntington Library.*

Miguel José Serra, who would become the "Apostle of California," was born to a humble farm family on the Spanish Mediterranean island of Majorca on November 24, 1713. A bright child, he attended Franciscan schools. After graduate studies in philosophy and theology, Serra was ordained a Franciscan priest, taking the name Junípero after the brother of St. Francis, founder of the order. Serra's fame as a compelling preacher and learned professor of philosophy spread quickly, and he seemed destined for a distinguished ecclesiastical career in Spain. But Junípero also embodied Franciscan virtues of personal humility, asceticism, fierce religious devotion, and militant activism in the cause of the faith. He passionately longed to spread the gospel among the unconverted and one day to die a martyr's death. Forsaking his comfortable seminary, Serra embarked in 1749 for New Spain and the rigors of a missionary life among the Indians.

For the next twenty years, Serra served in various Franciscan missions in eastern and northern Mexico. There he learned the religious and economic techniques that Spanish missionaries had developed to minister to New World Indians, and he became known as an able administrator and champion of native welfare. In 1767, he was appointed to take charge of the fifteen Baja California missions that the Spanish government had just stripped from the Jesuits.

Serra had been on the peninsula only a few months when José de Gálvez arrived to plan the occupation of Alta California. Seized by a vision of new vineyards of souls to

JUNÍPERO SERRA
Apostle of California (continued)

harvest, Serra volunteered for the expedition. Impressed with Serra's enthusiasm, Gálvez chose the friar to lead the Franciscans who were to found the new missions. On the journey north with Portolá in early 1769, Serra suffered grievously from ulcerated legs and feet, an ailment that plagued him for the rest of his life. Despite excruciating pain, Serra refused to be sent back. For much of the journey he could not walk or take the saddle unaided, and Serra's neophyte companions had to lift him on and off his mule or carry him on a stretcher. Such was the dedication of the "Apostle of California" to spread the faith among the Indians.

Father-President Serra took up residence at Mission San Carlos near Monterey, but, though his legs troubled him constantly, he spent most of the next fifteen years traveling along the coastal frontier, baptizing Indians, founding missions, and helping the new communities survive the difficult early years. Unlike some missionaries, Serra, in the spirit of St. Francis, loved and admired the Indians. He described them as having "fine stature, deportment, conversation, and gaiety" and rejoiced that they were "so amenable and so well fitted . . . to receive the Holy Gospel." Although already infirm by the time he reached Alta California, Serra struggled to master the many, complex Indian languages so that he could better understand the natives. He sweated with the Indians in mission shops and fields, shared food, tears, and laughter in their homes, and soon counted natives among his closest friends. Stubborn and aggressive when it came to the welfare of his Indians or missions, the otherwise meek Franciscan worked tirelessly to provide food and shelter for the neophytes. He berated churchmen and government officials alike for their neglect of the missions, and repeatedly defended the natives against assault and exploitation by soldiers and civilians. On the other hand, like most of his contemporaries, Serra saw the Indians as being, at best, innocent children, and like all good fathers of that era, he believed that his brood needed strict discipline, occasionally with the lash, laid on as gently as possible.

Junípero Serra died at San Carlos on August 28, 1784, leaving behind a firmly established mission system of nine communities and 5,000 Christian Indian residents. Nearly to his dying day, he ignored his failing health and limped miles to baptize or administer last rites to isolated natives. Later generations of all faiths hailed him as the founding hero of modern California, and his statue represents the state in the Rotunda of the Capitol in Washington, D.C.

Serra's biographer Maynard Geiger has captured the complexities of this remarkable man: "By some Serra was considered too aggressive, zealous, and demanding. . . . Though he fought for the Indians, he believed in and practiced corporal punishment when their misdeeds called for it. He had the qualities of a fine administrator. The mystic and the man of affairs were harmoniously blended in him." A Franciscan contemporary perhaps put it better when he wrote of Serra that "notwithstanding his many and laborious years, he has the quality of a lion which succumbs only to fever." (RJO) ary" (San Francisco Bay). Mistaking this harbor for Drake's Bay, Portolá realized he had passed Monterey and started to retrace his steps southward. Again failing to find Vizcaíno's "port," the Spaniards retreated to San Diego, where they arrived in late January 1770, disheartened, exhausted, and nearly starved.

Conditions were no better at the new settlement. A log stockade had been built, along with some stick-and-mud mission buildings. But help had not arrived from Mexico. The garrison was nearly out of food, and men continued to die. Not content with taking supplies, Indians had attacked a number of times, on one occasion killing a Baja Indian boy and wounding several other colonists. The Spaniards were reduced to exchanging their clothes for food from the few natives who would deal with them. The venture was saved when the *San Antonio* finally sailed in on March 19, one day before the expedition was to return to Mexico.

Refreshed by food and rest, the Spaniards improved their buildings and planted crops. Leaving behind a contingent to occupy San Diego, Portolá and Serra headed north with a land and sea force, which finally identified the port of Monterey. True to his orders, Portolá founded a presidio and the Mission San Carlos Borromeo there. He proclaimed Monterey the capital of Alta California, and San Carlos its mother mission and headquarters for Father-President Serra. His task completed, Portolá turned over command to Lieutenant Pedro Fages and, presumably with a prayer of thanksgiving, set sail for Mexico on July 9, 1770.

THE FOUNDING OF SAN FRANCISCO

Over the next five decades, the colony progressed slowly. By 1772, Serra had established three more missions, equally spaced between San Diego and San Carlos: San Gabriel, San Luis Obispo, and San Antonio.

Spanish Missions, Presidios, and Pueblos to 1824
Adapted from Historical Atlas of California, *by Warren A. Beck and Ynez D. Haase. Copyright © 1974 by the University of Oklahoma Press.*

He left each in the care of a small detachment of Franciscans, soldiers, and converted Indians from other missions. Because many died or deserted and some of the original soldiers and sailors were ordered back to

Mexico, the settlers of California as late as 1773 numbered fewer than one hundred non-Indians, or *gente de razón* ("civilized people"). There were no non-Indian women or children. Although it did not suffer the starvation conditions of 1769 and 1770, the California colony in the 1770s remained weak, scattered, and dependent on supplies from Mexico.

In the early 1770s, ships and overland parties from Monterey discovered the Golden Gate and Carquinez Strait, charted the large bay that had stymied Portolá, and determined that it was not Drake's Bay after all, but a hitherto unknown harbor of immense importance. The Spaniards named it San Francisco Bay and immediately drafted plans to occupy the region. In the winter of 1775–1776, Captain Juan Bautista de Anza led 240 San Francisco-bound colonists, including the first women and children, along a trail he had blazed two years earlier from Tubac in southern Arizona along the Gila River, across the Colorado River, and over the desert to San Gabriel. Although hot, dry, and more than five hundred miles long, this new path was safer and easier than the sea or land routes from Baja. The several caravans that traversed the route were largely responsible for the modest increase in the population of nonnative residents in Alta California during the second half of the 1770s.

After resting at San Gabriel, the San Francisco colonists traveled to Monterey. Although feeding and outfitting the expedition strained the food stores of the fledgling Mission San Carlos, preparations for the settlement went forward. In late June 1776, soldiers and settler families left Monterey for San Francisco. Serra sent along fathers Francisco Palóu and Pedro Cambón and three Indian neophytes to start a mission. The party arrived at the tip of the San Francisco Peninsula on June 27. Although a supply ship was blown out to sea and arrived a month late, the settlers laid out a plaza on a windswept bluff overlooking the mouth of the bay and started building the fortress, church, houses, warehouses, and jails of the San Francisco presidio. Work also began on the Mission San Francisco de Asís at a sunnier and better-watered site several miles to the southeast. During the hectic early weeks, friendly Costanoan Indians cut and hauled wood and helped in the construction. Rudimentary pole and mud structures were completed by mid-September.

On October 9, 1776, settlers and Indians gathered for a joyous ceremony to formalize the founding of Mission San Francisco. Father Palóu recalled that High Mass was followed by "repeated salvos of muskets, rifles, and swivel-guns that were brought from the bark for this purpose, and also with rockets." Apparently stunned by the fierce explosions, all the Indians in the vicinity of the mission immediately disappeared. They returned several days later, packed up their belongings, and vanished down the peninsula. Mission San Francisco did not record its first Indian baptism for nearly a year, and according to Palóu, "the rest of the heathen came no more."

THE MISSIONS

The missions became the largest and most productive Spanish communities in Alta California. Between 1769 and his death in 1784, the tireless Father Serra established the first nine missions, located every fifty to seventy-five miles between San Diego and San Francisco. A far cry from their twentieth-century restorations, the early missions were tiny, tenuous settlements, marked by stick, mud, and thatch buildings, marginal agriculture, and small neophyte populations. Flood, disease, water shortage, and Indian resistance often forced missionaries to move the compounds several times before they settled at permanent sites.

Serra's successor as father-president, the

Mission San Carlos, 1794
One of the oldest drawings of a California mission, this sketch was made by artist J. Sykes, who accompanied Captain George Vancouver's British naval expedition to the Pacific. This and other views illustrate the rudeness and disorder in the difficult early years of a mission's existence. At first, buildings were simple stick-and-thatch structures, and, as was the case at San Carlos, the neophytes continued to wear native garb and live in native dwellings for some time. When Vancouver visited, San Carlos was becoming a more mature settlement. The present stone chapel was under construction at the left of the drawing. It was completed in 1797, nearly thirty years after the mission's founding. *Courtesy of the California State Library.*

tactful and capable Fermín de Lasuén, founded nine additional missions during his tenure between 1785 and 1803 to reduce the distance between missions and thereby strengthen the colony. More important, Lasuén fostered irrigation, agricultural expansion, and industrial diversification needed to make the missions more productive and self-sufficient. Under his administration, the neophyte population reached about 20,000 by the turn of the nineteenth century. Reflecting the missions' greater maturity, wealth, and labor forces, more elaborate stone, abode, and tile-roofed chapels and outbuildings replaced the shabby pioneer structures after 1790. Ultimately, by the early 1820s twenty-one missions spanned the five hundred miles between San Diego and San Francisco Solano (Sonoma).

In keeping with the close relationship be-

tween church and state in Spain and its empire, the missionaries played diverse and sometimes contradictory roles in the colonization of California. Most of the 142 Franciscans who served before the 1840s were deeply religious, idealistic, and devoted to saving Indian souls. Yet most insisted that native converts also adopt the rest of European culture. When Indians resisted acculturation, the missionaries often despaired of conversion as well. Typical of European and colonial thinking of the time, the missionaries' attitudes toward Indians varied from kindly paternalism at best to aggressive racism at worst. As a result, missionaries attempted to regulate the lives of converted Indians down to minute details of waking, sleeping, eating, working, worship, amusement, family, and sex, provoking much neophyte resistance. Converted neophytes were thus ill-equipped to live independently in the colonial society.

Spanish law vested the missionaries with official positions as teachers of Indians and custodians of their persons, labor, and properties until they were ready for life in the secular settlements. These responsibilities undermined religious goals and embroiled the missionaries in conflicts with those whose interest in Indians was more selfish. Both Serra and Lasuén, like Narciso Durán after them, battled continually with civilians and military leaders over control of Indian workers, the degree of military protection for the missions, governmental requisitioning of supplies and money from the missions, and the time to free the neophytes. On the one hand, the Franciscans sometimes successfully defended their charges from exploitation beyond mission boundaries. On the other, they also fought against and delayed the integration of the mission Indians into the secular settlements. Conflict between the Franciscans and other leaders over Indian policy reduced the coordination and effectiveness of California communities.

THE PRESIDIOS AND PUEBLOS

To control Indians and discourage its imperial rivals, Spain tried to establish a strong military presence in California. Fortified with stockades, firearms, and artillery, presidios watched over local districts and guarded the strategic approaches to California at San Diego, Monterey, San Francisco, and ultimately Santa Barbara. Five or ten heavily armed soldiers were assigned to each mission to discipline neophytes, catch runaways, and put down resistance from gentiles. Like their counterparts on the Anglo-American frontier, California soldiers also performed nonmilitary services. They surveyed land, carried mail, worked as craftsmen, and designed and erected public works

such as buildings, roads, and bridges. Marketplaces and government centers, presidios developed into California's early small villages. Scattered around the stockades were farms, barracks, warehouses, stores, houses, a church, and saloons and other places of soldierly amusement.

Spaniards deemed more specialized agricultural towns necessary to support the presidios and missions, to establish local government, and to reduce the cost and uncertainty of supplying the colony from Mexico. Governor Felipe de Neve founded the first two *pueblos de gente razón* ("towns for civilized people"). In 1777, some of the immigrants from Anza's expedition, joined by others from San Francisco and Monterey, sixty-eight persons in all, established the pueblo of San José near the foot of San Francisco Bay, just east of the new Mission Santa Clara. Intended to serve the northern presidios and missions, San José became the first chartered civil community in California. Four years later, on the banks of the Río de Porciúncula, ten miles west of San Gabriel, Neve settled eleven families recruited from northern Mexico and taken over Anza's trail. Initially called Nuestra Señora la Reina de los Angeles de la Porciúncula (soon shortened to Los Angeles), the southern pueblo benefited from fertile soil and plentiful water and soon developed into the largest secular settlement in Spanish California. A third pueblo, Villa de Branciforte, was established in 1797 near Mission Santa Cruz by soldiers, artisans, and derelicts banished from Mexico. Its population was ill-suited for farming, and the community all but vanished after two decades.

As on most isolated frontiers, Spanish settlers congregated together for safety and more efficient production, and the pueblos were central to the secular life of the colony. From 1769 to the end of Spanish rule, almost all *gente de razón* inhabited the three pueblos or the less organized presidio communities. According to the Laws of the Indies, Spain's general colonial regulations, the pueblos were to be carefully ordered. Authorities provided each pueblo with a formal charter granting its lands and establishing its government. To encourage migration and development, the government supplied residents with food, clothing, tools, and livestock, along with house lots, strips of farming and grazing land, and several years' salary while harvests were insufficient. In return, settlers had to agree to serve in the militia, improve their lands, work on public projects and communal lands, and turn over their crops to the government.

Rudimentary urban planning based on the Laws of the Indies was instituted. Rectangular plazas served as the focal point for entertainments, religious festivals, and military parades. The church, government buildings, and residences of prominent citizens fronted the plazas. Although grids of streets were planned to emanate from the plazas, the thoroughfares that actually developed were usually meandering lanes, haphazardly lined with tiny adobe, tar-and-stick-roofed houses. Small strip farms ringed the village outskirts. Beyond were open ranges for cattle, horses, sheep, and goats. Public lands interspersed throughout provided room for future expansion and for raising crops and herds for town revenue. Knitting the settlement together were open, publicly maintained ditches (*zanjas*) that carried water for irrigation, drainage, and consumption by people and livestock. Though they remained poor and disorganized and rarely developed according to plan, California's communities testified to the introduction of European concepts of order.

Drawn from the diverse population of Mexico, residents of the settlements were of varied racial origin. Only a few—particularly colonial governors, high-ranking military officers, and Franciscan missionaries—were Spanish-born. Some others were of Spanish

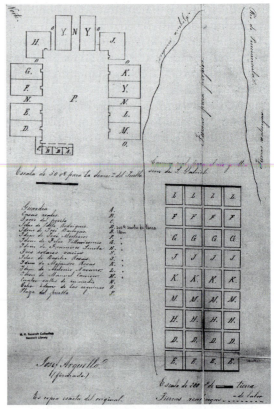

José Argüello's Plan of the Los Angeles Pueblo, 1786
This early plan of Los Angeles demonstrates the inception of urban planning in California. At the upper left is the plaza, surrounded by the pueblo's major buildings. The main irrigation ditch leaves the river at the top and threads down through the middle of the town, past the town's farm plots. *Courtesy of the Bancroft Library.*

blood, but born in Mexico. Most early Californians were of mixed Spanish, Mexican Indian, and African ancestry. Although town records differentiated between people of light and dark skin, most settlers were poor, and there appears to have been little prejudice and discrimination among those classified as *gente de razón*.

Between the *gente de razón* and California Indians, however, there were sharp distinctions and strained relationships. In the pueb-

attitudes
pueblo

los, most citizens lived intermixed in simple dwellings, but at least one run-down district housed low-caste residents, usually Indian gentiles, unconverted and thus unmissionized. Their native villages uprooted, they were conscripted or came voluntarily to work in the towns as domestic servants and farm laborers.

Los Angeles, for example, within a few years of its founding in 1781, was dependent on poorly paid gentile laborers, who were cheated, flogged, jailed without cause, and required to toil against their will. Having brought few women from Mexico, townsmen also forced Indian women and girls into becoming their servants and concubines. In order to preserve and discipline its labor force, Los Angeles, by the end of the 1780s, had adopted complicated and often-ignored regulations to govern working conditions and Indian-white relationships. The town banned extreme cruelty toward Indians, prohibited sex between Indians and *gente de razón*, required Indians to live in specific neighborhoods, forbade them from working or sleeping in settlers' houses or congregating in large groups, and banished Indian amusements from the town. Missionaries and Los Angeles leaders complained that the cheap labor system made the *gente de razón* idle, encouraged natives to remain out of the missions and retain heathen practices, and spread the colonists' vices and venereal diseases to the Indians. The advantages of exploited native labor were too strong, however, and the authority of the missionaries too weak. The system continued, with abuses unabated, and by 1803 Los Angeles had a population of 359 *gente de razón* and 200 Indian gentiles.

ECONOMIC DEVELOPMENT, LABOR, AND SOCIETY

Born in deprivation, Alta California struggled for decades to sustain itself. Virtually cut off from the outside world and hampered by lack of rainfall, capital, labor, supplies, machinery, transportation, markets, and business institutions, Spanish Californians devoted their energy to subsistence, rather than commerce. Raising products for food and simple processing was their principal endeavor. Fortunately, the colonists could draw on a heritage of Mediterranean and Mexican Indian irrigated agriculture. At the pueblos—and, to a lesser extent, at the presidios and ranchos—settlers dug ditches to divert water from streams onto their fields. They practiced a blend of European and American Indian farming techniques that had evolved in colonial Mexico. Relying on Indian laborers, the settlers cultivated small plots of corn, wheat, barley, beans, squash, melons, and a few other vegetables and fruits. Poultry roamed freely through the communities. Later, in more substantial towns such as Los Angeles, improved irrigation allowed the planting of larger orchards and gardens. Pueblo agriculture grew slowly, however. Because town populations were small, many citizens idle, and the water supplies erratic, pueblos were fortunate to be able to feed themselves, much less produce a surplus.

The most successful agriculture emerged at the missions. Trained in farming under semiarid conditions, the Franciscans adapted European and Mexican Indian methods to California. The missionaries also benefited from a larger labor supply and more disciplined organization than existed in the pueblos. Although first conversions were slow in coming, the missionaries, reinforced by military authorities, soon gathered large flocks of neophytes. By 1784, the nine existing missions, with a combined number of *gente de razón* of no more than one hundred, had enrolled 5,800 Indians; by the early nineteenth century, the twenty missions had an Indian population of about 20,000.

Missions functioned as industrial schools, not only converting Indians to Catholicism, but also teaching them European handicrafts and agricultural skills to make the community self-sufficient. Accustomed to highly refined skills in their own cultures, Indians quickly learned to plow, plant, harvest, tend livestock, and construct implements from stone, wood, leather, and what little iron could be obtained from the outside. The priests disciplined the neophytes, introduced specialization of tasks, designated the most skilled Indians as work leaders, and instituted European group labor practices. In the missions, as in the other settlements, it was Indian labor that sustained the struggling colony.

Neophyte labor enabled the missions to cultivate more land, to construct larger and more reliable irrigation systems, and to attain higher efficiency than the other Spanish settlements. Starting with simple diversion ditches, missions eventually developed elaborate waterworks with storage reservoirs, masonry aqueducts, and miles of ditches. The masonry dam in the mountains behind Mission Santa Barbara, for example, was one hundred feet long, seventeen feet thick, and seventeen feet high. Its main stone canals, each three miles long, piped water down to buildings, shops, work yards, washing basins, and, of course, the fields. The greater storage capacities of mission irrigation systems allowed larger, more diverse, and more dependable farms. Missionaries sowed European crops, such as wheat, barley, oats, citrus and deciduous fruits and nuts, grapes, hemp, and flax, as well as American Indian crops, such as corn, beans, squash, melons, cotton, and tobacco. At their peak in the early 1820s, the missions collectively cultivated between 5,000 and 10,000 acres and annually produced more than 100,000 bushels of crops, mostly wheat and corn. Particularly successful in horticulture was Mis-

sion San Gabriel, which cultivated nearly two hundred acres of fruit trees.

It is easy to exaggerate the sophistication and productivity of mission farms. Even at its zenith, mission agriculture languished because of limited markets and cash to buy necessary imported items, interruptions of supplies from Spain during the Mexican Revolution, and high rates of death and fugitivism among neophyte laborers. Inefficient cultivation, soil depletion, and lack of fertilization (livestock were allowed to roam wild) also caused crop yields to decline. Moreover, mission gardens had to sustain a large Indian population (21,000 in 1820) in addition to filling requisitions of supplies for presidios and pueblos, whose support from the Spanish government also declined. Particularly during droughts, both mission Indians and *gente de razón* went hungry. Even in times of comparative plenty, the neophytes suffered from a lean and unbalanced diet. The padres reluctantly released Indians periodically to collect wild foods. Such forays undoubtedly weakened mission discipline and encouraged contact between neophytes and gentiles. Nevertheless, despite these problems, the missions introduced crops and techniques of modern Euro-Indian farming that served later generations as models of the miracles that water development could perform in California's rich environment.

As at the pueblos and ranchos, the missions' major industry was raising livestock, particularly cattle. Coastal valleys and hills furnished good conditions for open-range grazing: plentiful and nutritious grasses, acorns, and shrubbery; ponds and perennially flowing streams to water stock; and a gentle climate that reduced the necessity to control and shelter animals. Moreover, livestock compensated somewhat for the region's marketing problems. Livestock reproduced in the wild, maintained themselves inexpensively (in effect, they were stored live on the hoof), and were then rounded up and butchered as needed. The cattle yielded not only meat—which was consumed fresh or was dried and salted for future use—but also horns, hides, and tallow for soap, oils, candles, and lubricants. The missions also raised sheep for mutton and wool, hogs for lard, and horses, mules, and oxen for transportation and farm work. Breeding stock brought between 1769 and 1781 had propagated into two million head of cattle, sheep, goats, horses, and mules by 1830. Although a few private ranchos developed before 1821, most livestock roamed the large mission ranges, tended by Indian vaqueros.

Although officials encouraged manufacturing to make the colony self-supporting, only the missions succeeded in diversifying their economies to any extent. Indian workers at mature missions such as San José processed raw materials and farm produce into cloth, blankets, rope, pottery, bricks, tiles, leather goods, candles, soap, furniture, and iron hardware. All missions had grain and saw mills, driven by water, animal, or human power. Some missions specialized—such as San Gabriel in making wine, and San Juan Capistrano in smelting and casting iron—and traded with other missions and secular communities. The missions' crude industrial products, however essential to life on an isolated frontier, had scant outside markets, though.

Outside the missions, the underdeveloped economy and sparse population inhibited job specialization and industry. A few soldiers and townspeople worked as carpenters, masons, blacksmiths, musicians, or merchants, but adversity forced most people, including artisans, into subsistence tasks. There were virtually no doctors, lawyers, teachers, or other trained professionals, other than the few priests and high-ranking military officers.

During Spanish rule in California, from 1769 to 1821, the economy advanced little. The expansion of farming, livestock ranching, and simple industry barely compensated for the increase in numbers of *gente de razón*, mission neophytes, and partially assimilated gentiles, or for the decline in subsidies from the Spanish government. The standard of living for ordinary people rose little. Although it usually produced sufficient food except during extreme drought periods, California exported little until after 1800. This commerce was limited to some surplus grain sold to the Russian colony at Fort Ross in bountiful years and a modest and illegal, but growing, hide-and-tallow trade with British and American merchant ships. California also lacked organized transportation. Without industry and a reliable revenue, the colony remained dependent on outside manufactures and financial support from the Spanish government, which after 1800 could not furnish it. Economic adversity discouraged immigration, sapped the settlers' initiative, reduced government revenues, undermined the effectiveness of presidios, pueblos, and missions, and soured relations among governors, soldiers, missionaries, and Indians.

Spanish California was a far cry from the pastoral land celebrated in romantic legend. The province was a crude frontier, with virtually no contact with the outside world. Poverty and thin population weakened its institutions and diluted its culture. Since virtually no schools existed outside the missions, most *gente de razón*, even high-ranking persons, were illiterate. Nor did folk art flourish beyond the limited music, architecture, and decorative arts of the missions. Settlers were further hindered by a weak authority structure. Limited by insufficient money, officers, soldiers, arms, courts, and administrators, the colonial government enforced laws and policies haphazardly. Colonial politics degenerated into factionalism among the missionaries, governors, military commanders, and rival cliques of *gente de razón*. Partly as a result, vice and violence abounded, particularly in the towns. Californians also died at high rates from epidemics, poor diet, water pollution, and unscientific medicine. Earthquakes collapsed buildings, floods washed away settlements, droughts seared crops, and plagues of insects and rodents were a constant annoyance.

Unsurprisingly, the rest of the Spanish empire disparaged California, and immigrants rarely sought its shores voluntarily. The number of *gente de razón* reached 500 by 1779 but grew only to 1,800 in 1800 and 3,300 in 1821, largely because of natural increase. New Mexico's population, by comparison, was ten times larger. Californians also scattered themselves among three dozen struggling settlements along a 500-mile frontier. In 1821, a mere vestige of European civilization was clinging to a fragile hold on the coast.

THE EUROPEAN CONQUEST OF NATURE

The Indians' impact on land, water, plants, and animals, while significant, had been gentle and evolutionary. Like most Europeans and American colonists, however, the Spaniards arrived in California with a more powerful technology and economy and little ecological sensitivity. By stressing that God had devised nature for humankind's sole benefit, the Judeo-Christian religious tradition appeared to sanction extreme environmental exploitation. Over the centuries, Europeans had denuded much of their own continent of forests, reduced fertile valleys and hillsides to wastelands, and eradicated many species of plants and animals. By the eighteenth century, they were fast on their way to destroying large stretches of the New World as well. In California, the Spaniards

both intentionally and unintentionally introduced physical, economic, and biological changes that triggered an environmental revolution after 1769.

Spanish colonization had astounding ecological effects. Within a short time, settlers cut down local forests for fuel and building materials, causing wood shortages and flooding. In their irrigation systems, Spaniards also introduced large-scale water impoundment and transfer. Along with destructive plowing and soil management practices, European monoculture (the raising of a single crop) eroded topsoils, exhausted nutrients, and drove out more diverse native species. After a few years, much mission and pueblo land had to be abandoned, to be reclaimed usually by foreign weeds rather than native grasses and trees.

Seeds from new crops such as oats, along with useless weeds brought in baggage and grain sacks from Mexico, spread wildly beyond cultivated fields. Birds, livestock, and wind bore them miles inland in a single season. Perennial native grasses and plants could not compete with hardier invading annuals—particularly on land disturbed by cultivation or livestock grazing—and rapidly receded from settled areas. The Spaniards compounded their grassland problems when, to halt the destruction of dry range for livestock, they used arms and treaties to force Indians to cease their traditional autumn fireburning. Quickly, the unproductive chaparral encroached on grasslands, requiring the colonists to begin clearing brush laboriously.

Livestock ranching, the most destructive new Spanish practice, wreaked environmental havoc far out of proportion to the small number of colonists. Dense herds of horses and aggressive longhorn cattle devoured vegetation, eroded hillsides, collapsed the protective banks of streams, drove back native deer and elk, and paved the way for mission/native relations

other invading species. By competing for grass seeds and acorns, the cattle also threatened Indian hunting and gathering and forced the natives from the land. The Spaniards themselves soon realized the dangers of their livestock industry. As early as the 1780s, authorities began ordering mass slaughters of surplus cattle that were devastating some ranges.

In the more densely colonized coastal areas of southern California and the Monterey and San Francisco bay regions, grasses were depleted, lands were eroded, and many native species were vanishing by the early nineteenth century. By the 1820s, new ecological patterns were advancing inland ahead of settlement, spread by herds of cattle and horses that had run wild from the coastal communities. Trailing along, European weeds and grains had largely replaced native bunch grasses in parts of the interior by the 1840s. Simultaneously, other foreigners were assaulting fur-bearing animals. During the two decades after 1820, American and British mountain men trapped the mink, otter, and beaver to near extinction in the central valleys, while Russian and American fur companies slaughtered the seals and sea otter along much of the coast. Although Hispanic settlers were relatively few and their technology and markets limited, they drastically altered California's fragile natural landscapes and wildlife, particularly along the coast.

MISSIONS AND THE ACCULTURATION OF INDIANS

Indian-Hispanic interaction greatly influenced colonial policy in California. As the colony's founders had intended, the missions became the major focus for Indian-Hispanic relationships. Though much written about, the California missions remain an enigma. A strong popular tradition, but-

tressed by the romantic mission restorations, persists in historian Herbert Bolton's belief that the missions were benevolent institutions that transmitted Christianity and European culture and shielded California's weak natives from abuse by soldiers and civilians. However, Indians, most anthropologists, and a growing number of historians view the missions as examples of European brutality toward less-developed peoples. The missions, they charge, were based on the ethnocentric assumption that Indians were inferior; using compulsion to concentrate, exploit, and whip native groups into docile submission, the missionaries shattered Indian culture without leaving anything in its place. As a result, critics conclude, missions destroyed, more than they protected, Indians. Because they rely on limited evidence and oversimplify complex events, both arguments are unsatisfactory. The missions were paradoxical communities, and the behavior of both colonists and Indians was varied and often contradictory.

As suggested by the experience of Estanislao's people at Mission San José, there was a wide range of Indian-colonial relationships, some of which were positive. Indians responded differently to colonization according to their culture and the history of their relations with Europeans and other tribes. Initially, some natives were attracted by the magical new culture, the valuable trade items it offered, and the opportunity to exploit the foreigners as allies against enemies. These groups freely interacted with the newcomers, often providing food, labor, protection, and assistance as guides. In 1774, for example, the Yuma rescued Anza's first trailblazing expedition, which was lost and near annihilation in the desert. The natives helped the Spaniards ford the Gila and Colorado rivers, directed them to trails and water holes, and guarded their equipment and livestock while Anza forged ahead to the coast with a smaller party. Indians also aided new Spanish missions and other settlements during their early ordeals.

Similarly, most Indian neophytes entered the missions willingly, at least during the founding years. Although Indians resisted giving up native ways and few converted at first, the Franciscans eventually wooed them with colorful liturgy, music, gifts or trade, food supplies, and the promise of shelter from enemies. Moreover, to many natives faced with declining supplies of acorns, grass seeds, and wild game because of spreading domestic livestock herds, association with missions was a useful response to the deterioration of their resource base caused by the arrival of the Spaniards. The missionaries focused on converting village and family heads who would bring along others. Once converted, the Indians were considered lifelong Christians and could not legally leave the mission. Only rarely did all local Indians evacuate to the missions, however. Some continued to live in a native fashion, usually falling eventual victims to disease or escaping into the interior when colonials destroyed their food supply. Other gentiles gravitated to presidios, pueblos, and ranchos, where they were usually relegated to low-caste, servile positions.

Through contact with the missions, converted and unconverted Indians learned Spanish, the fundamentals of Catholicism, and agricultural and industrial skills. They also acquired metal knives, saws, arrowheads, fishhooks, plows, and kettles, along with other items that modified their economies and cultures. Nonmission Indians obtained Spanish products and economic techniques through trade, association with civilians and soldiers, and interaction with neophytes. Spanish culture thus dispersed inland beyond the missions' orbit, especially among southern California's semiagricultural Indians, who were particularly receptive. By the

1830s, the Cahuilla, Cupeño, Ipai, and Tipai herded sheep, cattle, horses, and poultry; raised wheat and other foreign crops using Spanish methods of irrigation; and had, in general, become more agricultural.

Few Indians were completely Hispanicized, however. Even highly assimilated mission natives took what was valuable or necessary from the new culture, while adhering to much of their own. To the disgust of the missionaries, many neophytes superficially converted and participated in the economic regimen at the missions while still following family and tribal traditions, sometimes secretly. They often lived in tule houses and dressed in indigenous costume, continued hunting and gathering, spoke old dialects, used native tools and crafts, remained loyal to traditional leaders, celebrated native rites, and consulted shamans in time of illness. Some neophytes also refused to accept common European practices, such as work schedules and rigid sexual and family codes. What resulted in the missions was not a totally assimilated Indian laboring class, as colonial leaders had expected, but rather an amalgam of old and new cultures.

Nevertheless, missions permanently altered the culture of neophytes and gentiles. For some, the destruction of the old natural environment prevented reversion to traditional ways. Even after they were free to go, Hispanicized neophytes huddled around the crumbling old missions and pueblos, sometimes for generations, practicing a form of Catholicism blended with aboriginal rites, laboring for farmers and townspeople, and hunting and gathering whenever possible. When he visited the ruins of Mission San Carlos in the 1870s, forty years after its secularization, Scottish author Robert Louis Stevenson found a community of neophyte musicians still intact, performing and passing on the music introduced by the Franciscans.

EARLY INDIAN RESISTANCE: THE SAN DIEGO AND COLORADO RIVER REBELLIONS

As Estanislao's rebellion suggests, not all Indians accepted missionization. The advent of explorers and the founding of missions in their territory provoked some tribes to immediate resistance. The presence of colonists, particularly their relocation of some natives to a mission, violated tribal territories, disrupted family and community life, challenged the authority of Indian leaders, upset the balance of power among tribelets, and caused immediate, observable declines in natural resources. The arrival of foreigners also coincided with outbreaks of strange diseases that the Indians soon attributed to the newcomers. Colonials, especially soldiers who lacked the missionaries' zeal for saving souls, destroyed wild foods, drove away game, assaulted native men and conscripted their labor, raped women, and kidnapped women and children into concubinage and servitude. Although missionaries complained bitterly and some military commanders attempted to end these practices, the abuse of natives remained a problem. Unsurprisingly, many Indians not only rejected missionization, but moved their villages beyond the Spanish frontier and shunned all contact with the foreigners.

Other natives retaliated whenever an opportunity arose. As they had done to Cabrillo and Vizcaíno, San Diego Indians attacked the Portolá-Serra party several times in 1769 and 1770. By force of arms, the Spaniards imposed an uneasy peace, but conversions were few and natives seethed at Spanish abuses. Finally, in November 1775, escaped neophytes and gentiles of the Ipai and Tipai, led by the neophyte Francisco, forged an alliance of perhaps as many as forty villages to eject the foreigners and reestablish the old way of life. About eight hundred warriors stormed the presidio, burned the mission, and killed three colonials, including Father Luis Jayme. Only later in 1776, when soldiers converged on San Diego from throughout the colony, did the Spaniards regain control over the region. Other minor revolts, conspiracies, and attacks on travelers and priests by neophytes and local gentiles occurred prior to the early nineteenth century at missions San Gabriel, La Purísima, San Luis Obispo, Santa Clara, San Francisco, San Miguel, and San Antonio. All attempts failed to put up more than sporadic resistance, however, not simply because of Spanish firepower, but because feuding local tribelets were rarely able to ally themselves.

The most important early Indian insurrection occurred on the Colorado River. In 1780, to pacify Yuman groups and guard the crossing of the Colorado on Anza's trail, Spaniards established soldiers and settlers at two missions, Purísima Concepción and San Pedro, near present-day Yuma. Directing these missions was Father Francisco Garcés, famed Franciscan explorer-priest who had accompanied Anza and was liked by local Indians. Although they initially welcomed the missionaries, the Yuma divided into pro- and anti-Hispanic factions when Spanish soldiers abused them and stole prize farmland. The last straw fell in the summer of 1781, when settlers whom Lieutenant Governor Fernando Rivera was bringing from Mexico to found Los Angeles wantonly trampled Indian crops. On July 17 and 18, evidently after careful planning, the Yuma assaulted both missions, killing Rivera, Garcés, three other Franciscans, and more than thirty soldiers and settlers who had stayed behind when the expedition had continued on to San Gabriel. Military campaigns by Spain and later Mexico failed utterly to defeat the Yuma, who remained the undisputed lords of the Colorado River for the next seventy years. One of the most far-reaching events in early Cali-

San Francisco's Presidio, 1816

This published version of Louis Choris's 1816 drawing of the San Francisco Presidio, perched above the Golden Gate, reflected a then-common view among enlightened Europeans that, in Spanish California, Indians lived in a climate of force and fear. Here, mounted soldiers watch over and drive Indians as they would beasts of burden. The fort's farm fields are at lower left. Although the treatment of Indians was often harsh at the presidios, this particular image illustrates the dangers inherent in reading historical documents superficially. Choris's original drawing, made in California, depicted no menacing soldiers. They were inserted in the drawing later by printers in Europe to conform with their expectations of how missions were supposed to look. *Courtesy of the Huntington Library.*

fornia history, the "Yuma Massacre" closed Anza's trail, virtually ending immigration, stifling population growth, and forcing New Spain to supply the province by the expensive and unreliable sea route. No single defeat weakened the colony more.

DISEASE, FUGITIVES, AND HORSES

By the early nineteenth century, contact with the new colonial society, particularly its diseases, missions, and horses, had altered native life and intensified Indian defiance, further weakening the colony. When neophytes refused to renounce their traditions, missionaries meted out harsh punishments. For even minor breaches of work, sexual, or religious rules, missionaries and native overseers lashed, shackled, pilloried, and jailed neophytes, or assigned them extra labor and short rations. Chronic runaways were chained to logs or boulders, which they had to drag about to do their work. Although these practices were commonplace in eighteenth-century Europe and colonial America, California Indians considered such cruel forms of corporal punishment to be suitable only for enemies. Natives also chafed at overcrowding and food shortages. The conflict between cultures was great, and the missionaries' insistence on speedy, total assimilation at the threat of compulsion provoked resistance as well as compliance.

European diseases swept away Indians throughout the New World, including California. Concentrated in unsanitary mission compounds and weakened by poor diets, neophytes were no match for contagious

Old World diseases for which they lacked immunity. Epidemics of smallpox, dysentery, malaria, influenza, venereal disease, and childhood illnesses began immediately with the building of the first missions and reached a peak between 1800 and 1820. The 1806 measles epidemic at San Francisco-area missions, for example, wiped out more than one-third of the neophytes, including practically all children under ten years of age. Disease was virulent even in nonepidemic years, and by 1815 the indigenous Indian population of the Bay region was virtually extinct. Sherburne F. Cook, a leading authority on Indian demography, has estimated that few children born in the California missions before 1820 lived to adulthood. Mission diseases also spread quickly to local gentiles and, through them and neophyte runaways, into the interior.

Between 1769 and 1846, the population of California Indians declined from more than 300,000 to about 100,000, primarily because of disease. Large coastal and Central Valley tribes were nearly annihilated. Disease eradicated entire tribelets, disorganized families, demoralized survivors, decimated leadership groups, touched off power struggles among successors, and weakened native allegiance to traditional religions, which appeared to have lost their protective powers. As elsewhere on the New World frontier, it was the ravage of disease, more than superior European technology, that allowed the outnumbered and weaker invaders to overwhelm the California natives.

Women bore the brunt of violence, disease, and colonial missionization policies, posing an ominous threat to demographic survival of indigenous peoples and cultures. Within and outside of the missions, it was Indian women who suffered most from disease, dying younger and in higher numbers than men. Those who survived were often weakened or rendered infertile by venereal disease, especially syphilis, which quickly became virulent after Spanish occupation of California. The babies born to infected mothers were often born dead, disabled, or themselves infected with venereal disease. Women were also removed from native communities when Hispanic men, who lacked mates in their own settlements, kidnapped Indians into forced concubinage or prostitution, relocated women to the missions in larger numbers than men, and, in a few cases, intermarried with native females. In some instances, colonial armies killed or dispersed nearly all men in a village community, while forcing surviving women and children into missions.

In combination with the traditionally low native birthrate and large numbers of Indian deaths in battle, sharp reductions in the female population shattered family structures and caused catastrophic declines in reproduction. Thus, many local Indian societies and cultures were doomed to demographic extinction, whether or not they were missionized. If anything, these patterns decimating native societies accelerated after the American conquest of California in the late 1840s. Indeed by the 1850s, many tribes suffered from severely unbalanced gender ratios; in the state overall, only one-third of Indians were female.

Dangerous conditions in the missions, along with resistance to acculturation, caused discontent among many neophytes. They refused to speak Spanish, went on hunger strikes, stole livestock and other property, and occasionally assaulted mission officials. Abortion and infanticide, important signs of protest against assimilation, were leading causes of death in the missions. Fugitivism particularly disrupted the mission community. Neophytes fled by the thousands to the sanctuary of the interior tribes to return to traditional ways or escape punishment, hunger, and disease. Although officials sent expeditions to retrieve runaways and punished culprits severely, they could not stem the tide of defection. There were too many Indians and too few soldiers, and the interior was too rugged. Sherburne Cook found that the missions lost about ten percent of their population to fugitivism each year, with higher proportions in some years. In 1817, for which good records exist, nearly 2,500 mission Indians became fugitives, many permanently. By 1827, when the American fur trapper Jedediah Smith visited the San Joaquin Valley, he encountered Spanish-speaking Indians, presumably escaped neophytes, everywhere. After 1800, the influx of embittered, partially assimilated runaways like Estanislao's followers was embroiling the Yokuts and other interior groups in colonial conflicts and speeding up the process of cultural change.

Fugitivism and the dramatic decline of coastal gentile populations drove authorities to adopt new methods of maintaining the mission population, including converting interior Indians and bringing them to the missions. Although forcing Indians to convert to Christianity violated church and civil law, means of "impressment" were sometimes used. These appeared superficially voluntary to satisfy legal technicalities, but in reality they involved varying degrees of compulsion. After 1800, colonial expeditions into the interior became brutal campaigns to recapture runaway neophytes and punish the tribes that sheltered them. The soldiers frequently returned with gentile prisoners, particularly women and children. Many captives were driven to the missions, where they were detained until they agreed to convert. In one typical example in 1805, a punitive expedition against a village near the Stanislaus River, perhaps among Estanislao's people, killed ten Indians and seized twenty-seven

gentiles, including twenty-five women and girls. While the men were imprisoned at hard labor in the San Francisco presidio, the females were held at Mission San José. After the natives had served their sentence, *all* "chose" to be converted and remain at the mission. Given the antipathy of Indians toward missions, it is hardly believable that such conversions were truly voluntary.

Closely linked to the influx of mission defectors was the arrival of horses in the interior. Alerted by previous experience to the revolutionary impact of horses on natives, the Spaniards initially prohibited Indians in California from possessing, or even riding, horses. Nevertheless, Indian labor was so essential to the livestock industry that the law proved unenforceable, and neophytes quickly became skilled horsemen. Mission Indians rode horses while visiting the interior; neophyte horse thieves pilfered stock and traded it to gentile tribes; and runaways frequently took along stolen herds to ingratiate themselves with gentile protectors. "Today they come," one missionary complained about the neophytes in 1818, "and tomorrow they leave, not on foot but on horseback, so that, with such guests, there is not a safe horse in the whole valley of the north." Within a short time, inland gentiles acquired horses and the skills to ride and herd them.

As on earlier Spanish colonial frontiers, the horse, once introduced, wrought a cultural transformation. Horse meat became a new staple for the Yokuts and other interior groups. With a more flexible economy, the mounted tribes became more mobile, powerful, and militaristic, better equipped to resist colonial patrols and strike back fiercely in guerrilla attacks. The horse and the increasing need to defend against foreigners forced inland groups like the Yokuts, Cahuilla, and Cupeño to become more centralized and assertive. In some cases, tribes decimated by disease or warfare joined into new social units. Leaders with broader support—many of them former neophytes like Estanislao—emerged to unite the tribelets and direct their new activities. The horse encouraged broad cultural change. By the 1820s, visitors to the interior found not only stolen horses but also saddles, bridles, firearms, cattle, and other European products. Some tribes were observed hunting wild game on horseback in the manner of the Great Plains Indians.

Once set into motion, cultural change moved with astonishing speed. Whereas there were only a few horses in the interior at the turn of the nineteenth century, two decades later most San Joaquin Valley and southern desert tribes were mounted. When the supply of illicit trade horses proved insufficient, inland tribes raided coastal missions and ranchos, striking quickly, stealing small herds, and vanishing. Indian villages cooperated to mount larger-scale attacks, to slaughter the horses and distribute the horse meat, and to hold horse-trading fairs. By the 1820s, growing Indian resistance and horse raiding were depleting mission and ranch herds, threatening life on the more remote ranchos, discouraging settlement of new territory, and fomenting dissension among the colonists. Located near passes in the Coast Range, the Monterey and San Francisco regions, particularly Mission San José, bore the brunt of these assaults, but Indians attacked all settlements southward to San Diego. Officials feared the colony was seriously threatened. As early as 1819, Father Durán warned from Mission San José that unless the powerful San Joaquin Valley tribes were quickly stripped of their horses, "California might in time become the theater of a second band of Apaches."

The colony struggled in vain to squelch the horse revolution. At first, officials planned to build missions in the interior to pacify the tribes, but expense, remoteness, and native resistance doomed this project. Instead, colonials resorted to punitive expeditions from the presidios. Between the early 1800s and the 1840s, dozens of campaigns by soldiers, aided by neophytes, civilian militiamen, and gentile auxiliaries, assaulted and burned offending villages to punish horse eaters, retrieve stolen horses, and capture mission runaways. If the actual thieves could not be found, colonists sometimes vented their fear and hatred against any available group of natives. When the Indians resisted, violent skirmishes ensued. Greatly outnumbering the colonials, native warriors sometimes won, but since they possessed few firearms, many Indians lost their lives. Soldiers typically took captives back for confinement at the missions and presidios.

Brutality abounded on both sides. Indians frequently tortured prisoners or mutilated the bodies of dead Hispanic soldiers, while colonials commonly acquired battle trophies by cutting off heads, ears, or genitalia from fallen warriors, some of whom were still alive. As happened after Vallejo's 1829 campaign against Estanislao, not all of the soldiers' prisoners made it back to the settlements; some were tortured or murdered. Legendary Hispanic benevolence toward Indians was not a deep-seated social practice, but a shallow official rhetoric that quickly evaporated in the fierce heat of cultural conflict and violence on the frontier.

For all their brutality, by the 1820s punitive expeditions had accomplished little except to inflame Indian-Hispanic relations further. Few neophytes or horses were recaptured. Unchastised gentiles redoubled their raids. The horse culture spread to new groups. Resistance and fugitivism at the missions increased. Emboldened, mission Indians in that decade mounted two of their largest insurrections—one among the Chumash in Santa Barbara-area missions in 1824, and Estanislao's rebellion in 1829. In both instances, the rebels attempted, in the latter case successfully, to ally themselves with San Joaquin Valley tribes. By the time of Estanislao's rebellion, warfare had erupted all along the frontier, and foreigners ventured into the interior only with a heavy guard.

What might have happened had Indian resurgence continued to gain momentum can never be known; in the 1830s, some of the fiercest epidemics ever to strike the natives swept the interior, destroying entire tribelets and greatly weakening survivors. The Yokuts, a key group in the emerging new culture, were hard hit. One catastrophic epidemic in the summer of 1833—probably malaria introduced by British trappers from the Pacific Northwest—killed about 20,000 Indians, perhaps seventy-five percent of the population of the San Joaquin Valley. One of the trappers, J. J. Warner, reported that on his way south in 1832, "the banks of the Sacramento and San Joaquin, and numerous tributaries of these rivers, were studded with Indian villages from one to twelve hundred inhabitants each." But by 1833, when he returned north, "death had obtained a victory. The first struck down were buried. But the increasing dead gave not time to the living to dispose of their departed fellows. The decaying bodies compelled us nightly to pitch our tents in the open prairie." Except for scattered remnants, Yokuts culture was shattered forever. Other California Indians fought on into the 1870s, however, attacking settlements, stealing livestock, and frustrating the ambitions of later pioneers.

SPANISH CALIFORNIA ON THE EVE OF MEXICAN INDEPENDENCE

By 1820, although half a century had passed since the arrival of Serra and Portolá, Spain's weak California colony was still struggling. It had a subsistence economy; its tiny non-Indian population was expanding only slowly; its society was loosely organized. Disease and native resistance crippled its major institution, the mission. Colonials had disrupted coastal Indian societies but, despite disease and native population decline, failed to dominate interior groups. The consequences for Hispanic civilization in California were enormous. Indian resistance, within and outside of the missions, disorganized the economy, eroded the colony's authority structure, and delayed exploration and settlement of the interior.

After 1810, while revolution raged in Mexico, Spain ignored California, its most remote province. Vital supplies and military reinforcements ceased arriving; buildings, equipment, and firearms deteriorated to the point of uselessness. If anything, Spanish control over California was more tenuous in 1820 than it had been ten years earlier.

SUGGESTIONS FOR FURTHER READING

Estanislao's Rebellion

José María Amador, "Memorias sobre la Historia de California," and Joaquin Piña, "Diario de la expedición al valle de San José," June 13, 1829 (Bancroft Library, University of California, Berkeley); Sherburne F. Cook, "Colonial Expeditions to the Interior of California: Central Valley, 1820–1840," *University of California Anthropological Records* (1962);

Jack Holterman, "The Revolt of Estanislao," *The Indian Historian* (1970); Francis F. McCarthy, *The History of Mission San Jose, California, 1797–1835* (1958); Wallace Smith, *Garden of the Sun* (1939); George Tays, "Mariano Guadalupe Vallejo and Sonoma—A Biography and a History," *California Historical Society Quarterly* (1937–1938); Alan Rosenus, *General M.G. Vallejo and the Advent of the Americans: A Biography* (1995).

Background, Discovery, and Naming

Robert Ryal Miller, *Mexico: A History* (1985), and "Cortés and the First Attempt to Colonize California," *California Historical Quarterly* (1974); Donald C. Cutter, "Sources of the Name 'California,'" *Arizona and the West* (1961).

Spanish Colonization, General

David J. Weber, *The Spanish Frontier in North America* (1992); John A. Schutz, *Spain's Colonial Outpost* (1985); David J. Weber, ed., *New Spain's Far Northern Frontier: Essays on Spain in the American West* (1979); Charles E. Chapman, *A History of California: The Spanish Period* (1925); Hubert H. Bancroft, *California Pastoral, 1769–1848* (1888); Ramon A. Gutierrez and Richard J. Orsi, eds., *Contested Eden: California before the Gold Rush* (1997–98).

Spanish Exploration

Maurice G. Holmes, *From New Spain by Sea to the Californias, 1519–1668* (1963); Herbert E. Bolton, ed., *Spanish Exploration in the Southwest, 1542–1706* (1959); Henry R. Wagner, *Spanish Voyages to the Northwest Coast of America in the Sixteenth Century* (1929), and *Juan Rodríguez Cabrillo: Discoverer of the Coast of California* (1941); Harry Kelsey, "The California Armada of Juan Rodríguez Cabrillo," *Southern California Quarterly* (1979), and *Juan Rodríguez Cabrillo* (1986); Donald C. Cutter, *The California Coast: A Bilingual Edition of Documents from the Sutro Collection* (1969); W. Michael Mathes, *Vizcaíno and Spanish Exploration in the Pacific Ocean, 1580–1630* (1968); Harlan Hague, "'Here Is the Road': The Indian as Guide," *The Californians* (1985).

Drake in California

Warren L. Hanna, *Lost Harbor: The Controversy over Drake's California Anchorage* (1979); Henry R. Wagner, *Drake on the Pacific Coast* (1970); Robert F. Heizer, *Francis Drake and the California Indians, 1579* (1974), and *Elizabethan California* (1974); Francis Fletcher, *The World Encompassed* (1628); James D. Hart, *The Plate of Brass Reexamined* (1977); Harry Kelsey, "Did Francis Drake Really Visit California?" *Western Historical Quarterly* (1990); John Sugden, *Sir Francis Drake* (1991).

Founding the California Colony

Herbert I. Priestly, *José de Gálvez, Visitador-General of New Spain* (1916); Charles E. Chapman, *The Founding of Spanish California: The Northwestward Expansion of New Spain* (1916); Theodore E. Treutlein, "The Portolá Expedition of 1769–1770," *California Historical Society Quarterly* (1968), and *San Francisco Bay: Discovery and Colonization* (1968).

Junípero Serra

Maynard J. Geiger, *The Life and Times of Fray Junípero Serra* (1959), and "Fray Junípero Serra: Organizer and Administrator of the Upper California Missions, 1769–1784," *California Historical Society Quarterly* (1963); *The Writings of Junípero Serra* (4 vols., 1955); "Serra and His California," *The Californians* (1984).

Missions

Herbert E. Bolton, "The Mission as a Frontier Institution in the Spanish American Colonies," *American Historical Review* (1917); John Francis Bannon, "The Mission as a Frontier Institution: Sixty Years of Interest and Research," *Western Historical Quarterly* (1979); James J. Rawls, "The California Mission as Symbol and Myth," *California History* (Fall 1992); Maynard Geiger, *Franciscan Missionaries in Hispanic California, 1769–1848: A Biographical Dictionary* (1969), and *Mission Santa Barbara, 1782–1965* (1965); Zephyrin Engelhardt, *The Missions and Missionaries of California* (4 vols., 1908–1915); Francis F. Guest, *Fermín Francisco de Lasuén: A Biography* (1973); Robert Archibald, "Indian Labor at the California Missions: Slavery or Salvation," *Journal of San Diego History* (1978), "The Economy of the Alta California Mission, 1803–1821," *Southern California Quarterly* (1976), and *Economic Aspects of the California Missions* (1978); Richard Steven Street, "First Farmworkers, First *Braceros*: Baja California Field Hands and the Origins of Farm Labor Importation in California Agriculture, 1769–1790." *California History* (Winter 1996–97).

Presidios and Pueblos

Leon G. Campbell, "The Spanish Presidio in Alta California During the Mission Period, 1769–1784," *Journal of the West* (1977); Diane Spencer-Hancock and William E. Pritchard, "El Castillo de Monterey, Frontline of Defense," *California History* (1984);

Richard S. Whitehead, "Alta California's Four Fortres-ses," *Southern California Quarterly* (1983); Joseph P. Sánchez, *Spanish Bluecoats: The Catalonian Volunteers in Northwestern New Spain, 1767–1810* (1990); Francis F. Guest, "Municipal Institutions in Spanish California, 1769–1821" (Ph.D. dissertation, University of Southern California, 1961), and "Municipal Government in Spanish California," *California Historical Society Quarterly* (1967); John W. Reps, "Expansion of the Spanish Borderlands: Urban Settlement of Arizona and California in the Hispanic Era," in his *Cities of the American West* (1979); Gilbert R. Cruz, *Let There Be Towns: Spanish Municipal Origins in the American Southwest, 1610–1810* (1988); Oscar O. Winther, "The Story of San José, 1777–1868: California's First Pueblo," *California Historical Society Quarterly* (1934); Andrew F. Rolle, *Los Angeles: From Pueblo to City of the Future* (1981).

Politics and Government

Edwin A. Beilharz, *Felipe de Neve, First Governor of California* (1972); Donald A. Nuttall, "The Gobernantes of Spanish Upper Cali-fornia," *California Historical Society Quar-terly* (1972); Daniel S. Garr, "Power and Priorities: Church-State Boundary Disputes in Span-ish California," *California History* (1978); Theodore Grivas, "Alcalde Rule: The Nature of Local Government in Spanish and Mexican California," *California Historical Society Quarterly* (1961).

Social, Economic, and Cultural Development

Douglas Monroy, *Thrown Among Strangers: The Making of Mexican Culture in Frontier California* (1990); Robert R. Alvarez, Jr., *Familia: Migration and Adaptation in Baja and Alta California, 1800–1975* (1987); Manuel P. Servín, "California's Hispanic Heritage: A View of the Spanish Myth," *San Diego History* (1973); Oakah L. Jones, *Los Paisanos: Spanish Settlers on the Northern Frontier of New Spain* (1978); Leon G. Campbell, "The First Californios: Presidial Society in Spanish California," *Journal of the West* (1972); David Hornbeck, "Land Tenure and Rancho Expansion in Alta California," *Journal of Historical Geography* (1978); Marie E. Northrup, *Spanish-Mexican Families of Early California, 1769–1850* (1976).

European Conquest of Nature

Alfred W. Crosby, Jr., *The Columbian Exchange: Biolog-ical and Cultural Consequences of 1492* (1972), and *Ecological Imperialism: The Biological Expansion of Eu-rope, 900–1900* (1986); Burton L. Gordon, *Monterey Bay Area: Natural History and Cultural Imprints* (1977); Michael Barbour and Valerie Whitworth, "California's Grassroots: Native or European?" *Pacific Discovery* (Winter 1992).

Native Acculturation and Indian-Colonial Conflict

Albert L. Hurtado, *Indian Survival on the California Frontier* (1988), "Sexuality in California's Franciscan Missions: Cultural Perceptions and Sad Realities," *California History* (Fall 1992), and *Intimate Frontiers: Sex, Gender, and Culture in Old California* (1999); Edward H. Spicer, *Cycles of Conquest: The Impact of Spain, Mexico, and the United States on the Indians of the South-west, 1533–1960* (1962); Sherburne F. Cook, *The Conflict Between the California Indian and White Civi-lization* (1976); Francis F. Guest, "An Examination of the Thesis of S. F. Cook on the Forced Conversion of Indians in the California Missions," *Southern Cali-fornia Quarterly* (1979), and "Cultural Perspectives of Cali-fornia Mission Life," *Southern California Quar-terly* (1983); Wilbur R. Jacobs, "Sher-burne Friend Cook: Rebel-Revisionist (1896– 1974)," *Pacific Histor-ical Review* (1985); C. Alan Hutchinson, "The Mexi-can Government and the Mission Indians of Upper California, 1821–1835," *The Americas* (1965); George H. Phillips, "Indians and the Breakdown of the Spanish Mission System in California," *Ethnohistory* (1974), *Chiefs and Challengers: Indian Resistance and Cooperation in Southern California* (1975), "Indians in Los Angeles, 1781–1875: Economic Integration, So-cial Disintegration," *Pacific Historical Review* (1980), and *Indians and Intruders in Central California, 1769–1849* (1993); Thomas Blackburn, "The Chu-mash Revolt of 1824: A Native Account," *The Journal of California Anthropology* (1975); Sylvia M. Broad-bent, "Conflict at Monterey: Indian Horse Raiding, 1820–1850," *Journal of California Anthropology* (1974); Jack D. Forbes, *Warriors of the Colorado* (1965); Robert F. Heizer, "The Impact of Colonization on the Native California Societies," *Journal of San Diego*

History (1978); Martha Voght, "Shamans and Padres: The Religion of Southern California Mission Indians," *Pacific Historical Review* (1967); *The Autobiography of Delfina Cuero, A Diegueño* (1970); Robert H. Jackson, "Patterns of Demographic Change in the Alta California Missions: The Case of Santa Ines," *California History* (Fall 1992), "Patterns of Demographic Change in the Missions of Central Alta California," *Journal of California and Great Basin Anthropology* (1987); David H. Thomas, ed., *Columbian Consequences: Archaeological and Historical Perspectives on the Spanish Borderlands West* (1989); Daniel Reff, *Disease, Depopulation, and Culture Change in Northwestern New Spain, 1518–1764* (1991); Robert H. Jackson, *Indian Population Decline: The Missions of Northwestern New Spain, 1687–1840* (1994); Robert H. Jackson and Edward Castillo, *Indians, Franciscans, and Spanish Colonization: The Impact of the Mission System on California Indians* (1995); Randall Milliken, *A Time of Little Choice: The Disintegration of Tribal Culture in the San Francisco Bay Area, 1769–1810* (1995); Lisbeth Haas, *Conquests and Historical Indentities in California, 1769–1936* (1995).

PART THREE

THE PASTORAL ERA

In 1821, after more than ten years of revolutionary turmoil, Mexico won its independence from Spain, thus gaining sovereignty over California. But Mexican control of the province was relatively short-lived and in many respects seemed a mere continuation of the Spanish experience, prompting historian Charles Chapman to assert that "strictly speaking, there was no Mexican period of California history." This, however, is a simplification that ignores the fundamental economic and social changes occurring in the period. Development of the hide-and-tallow trade after 1822 materially altered the province's economy. Secularization of the missions in the mid–1830s dramatically changed not only the Indian's place in society but also the whole social structure. The rancho society that arose in conjunction with both these events had important economic consequences as well. Finally, the American frontier movement reached the province in 1841, the beginning of the end of Mexican rule.

Many aspects of rancho life in the Mexican era have led writers to romanticize it. After all, the great rancheros really did live in spacious homes with many Indian servants; they dressed in fine clothes and celebrated any significant occasion with feasting and dancing. Accordingly, the tendency has been to describe the Californians of this era, as Carey McWilliams put it, as "one big, happy, guitar-twanging family," dancing the fandango and living

"Rodeo Riders"
Since California cattle ran wild over thousands of acres of range land, the rodeo, an annual roundup, was necessary for sorting out ownership and branding. It became a festive occasion in Mexican California. *Courtesy of the Bancroft Library.*

out their days basking in the sun. Mexican California, however, produced a much more complex society than legend suggests.

While inheriting Spain's culture and institutions, the new nation also inherited its problems in administering California. Isolation, poverty, lax authority, military weakness, and conflict with Indians characterized Mexican rule and ultimately contributed to its overthrow. Impoverished and torn by factionalism, the Mexican government failed to establish its authority in the province or to prevent the intrusion, in the 1840s, of Americans who played an important role in the loss of California to the United States. While early British and American settlers became naturalized Mexican citizens and made important contributions to the life of the province, these later American arrivals did not. By 1846, they constituted a growing unassimilated population, restless and unhappy with Mexican policy. Many of them became participants in the Bear Flag Revolt and the subsequent American conquest that ended the Mexican period in 1846.

Even though the Bear Flag Revolt took place at the end of the Mexican period, it vividly illustrates the problems Mexico faced from the very beginning in administering the isolated province. In constant financial trouble, the Mexican government rarely sent funds to pay for the government or defense of California. By the mid-1830s most soldiers in the California presidios had not been paid for ten, even fifteen, years, and civil and military officials were reduced to squabbling over the revenues produced by the hide and tallow trade that developed after 1822. The competition for control of these trade duties contributed to a growing rivalry between northern and southern *californios*—a conflict characterized by bombastic verbal threats and, for the most part, bloodless military action. The conflict in 1846 between José Castro, California's military *comandante*, based in Monterey, and Governor Pío Pico, based in Los Angeles, was simply an extension of experience going back to the 1820s.

The participation of Americans in the "revolutions" by which the *californios* settled their grievances against the Mexican government and with each other was an ominous sign. Throughout the period Mexico and the Californians feared the growing presence of American mountain men, settlers such as William B. Ide, and the ubiquitous John C. Frémont, but seemed powerless to deal with the growth of an American frontier population in California. The Bear Flag Revolt, therefore, contains many of the elements of the Mexican experience in California. A curious episode that has been both lampooned and romanticized in popular histories, it served as the first step in the separation of California from Mexico by the United States.

CHAPTER SEVEN

THE BEAR FLAG REVOLT

The decade from 1836 to 1846 saw increasing tension between Mexico and the United States. Immigrants from the United States led the 1836 revolt that carved the Lone Star Republic out of Mexico's borderlands, and the prospect of American annexation of Texas embittered relations with Mexico for years. Meanwhile, the arrival of the American frontier movement in California, beginning in 1841, spread the fear among Mexican authorities that this isolated, weakly defended province, too, might go the way of Texas. In 1845, the United States finally annexed Texas and President James K. Polk sent troops into the borderlands in dispute between Texas and Mexico; they clashed with Mexican soldiers and war began. But, before news of the war reached California, events there took the province along the road of "another Texas." Thus, the Bear Flag revolt not only revealed Mexico's problems in administering California, but it was also the prelude to the war with Mexico in California.

The spring of 1846 in California seemed like so many that had gone before—warm days, cool nights, and a sense of peace and contentment in the air. The simple frontier province, an appendage of the Federal Republic of Mexico since 1821, was dominated by the *californios* with their great ranchos, huge herds of cattle, and easygoing way of life. Hospitable and proud, they enjoyed their colorful rodeos and fandangos and, like many colonial peoples, profited from the trade of hides and tallow from their cattle for finished goods from Europe and the United States. But Don José Castro, *comandante general* of the Department of California, had more important matters on his mind than rodeos and fandangos, for beneath the seemingly serene surface of life in the province major forces were on a collision course. Since January, in fact, events had been unfolding that were soon to throw California into turmoil. Born into a modest family and raised near Monterey, José Castro had been a youthful protégé of Pablo Vicente de Solá, the last Spanish governor of California. Politically active from an early age, Castro served briefly as interim governor in the mid-1830s. Now, at age thirty-six, he was California's *comandante general*, the chief military official of this isolated Mexican province, with headquarters in Monterey. While he was not a large landholder,

José Castro
A lieutenant colonel in the Mexican army, Castro was addressed as "General" by virtue of his position as *comandante general* of California. *Courtesy of the Bancroft Library.*

Castro was a man of influence and considerable power, especially among the lower classes, and some people expected him to displace the present governor of California, Pío Pico. Clever and ambitious, José Castro took his responsibility for the security of the province seriously.

That security, however, now seemed threatened by an American military expedition moving boldly along the foothills of the great Central Valley. John C. Frémont of the U.S. Corps of Topographical Engineers was leading his second expedition to California. At thirty-three, Frémont was already a

well-known figure whose reports of his western explorations had excited the nation. Courageous, witty, and magnetic, yet often arrogant, he elicited a fierce loyalty from his followers. Now accompanied by sixty armed, rough-looking ex-mountain men, his presence worried many Californians, particularly General Castro.

Two years earlier, Frémont had led a "scientific" expedition over the Sierra Nevada to California. Why was he back now? Castro wondered. Mindful of the strained relations between Mexico and the United States following the latter's annexation of Texas in 1845 and the speculation that war was imminent, Castro kept a wary eye on the expedition moving through the interior.

In January, Frémont and a handful of his men, in the company of Thomas O. Larkin, the American consul in Monterey, appeared in Monterey seeking supplies from the *comandante*. While marked by the cordial hospitality characteristic of the *californios*, the meeting with Castro led to a misunderstanding. Frémont assumed he had been given approval to move freely about the province, while Castro believed that Frémont had assured him his expedition would not approach the coastal settlements before continuing north to Oregon. It was a misunderstanding that had unfortunate consequences.

On leaving Monterey that January, Frémont gathered his men near San José and camped a few miles south, at the vacant Rancho Laguna Seca. Here, his cordial relations with the Californians began to deteriorate. Soon after his arrival at Laguna Seca, Sebastián Peralta, a local ranchero and *mayordomo* at Mission Santa Clara, appeared, claiming that some of the horses Frémont's men had acquired in the interior had previously been stolen from him. Frémont refused to consider their return and rudely ordered Peralta away. The latter took his complaint to

John C. Frémont
Few persons have provoked more controversy among historians than John C. Frémont. Self-serving and opportunistic, he also played an important role in the conquest of California in 1846–1847 and was easily elected one of the first United States senators from the state. *Courtesy of the California State Library.*

the *alcalde* of San José, who wrote Frémont on February 20, asking him to explain the matter in person. Frémont wrote back indignantly, accusing Don Sebastián of attempting to "obtain animals under false pretenses." Peralta, he said, "should have been well satisfied to escape without a severe horse-whipping." As for his coming to San José, Frémont added, "my duties will not permit me to appear before the magistrates of your towns on the complaint of every straggling vagabond who may chance to visit my camp."

On February 22, the Frémont expedition

got under way again, but, to the dismay of the Californians, it did not head in the direction of Oregon. Leaving his camp near San José, Frémont moved south over the Santa Cruz Mountains and a few days later rode along the shore of Monterey Bay. As it neared Monterey, the expedition turned south along the Salinas River and encamped at William P. Hartnell's Rancho Alisal, only twenty-five miles from Monterey.

General Castro reacted quickly to this penetration of armed Americans into the immediate vicinity of northern California's most important settlement. He saw it as an ominous move at such a time of tension and a violation of his understanding that Frémont's men would remain in the Central Valley. He dispatched a sharp note notifying Frémont that his presence there was prohibited by law and that he must "retire beyond the limits of the department."

Frémont replied promptly and curtly that he would not obey an order he regarded as insulting to himself and the government of the United States. The next day, he moved into the Gavilan Mountains between the Salinas and San Joaquin valleys and occupied a formidable position (near the present-day Frémont Peak) overlooking San Juan Bautista and the main road to Monterey. Here Frémont constructed a crude log fortification and brashly hoisted the American flag while the people of Monterey eagerly awaited Castro's reaction.

Incensed, Castro sent a small military force to keep an eye on Frémont and issued a call to the local citizenry to join him in "repelling the invasion." He was not eager to attack Frémont's nearly impregnable position, manned by sixty sharp-shooting frontiersmen (especially when only a handful of citizens answered his call to action). So Castro's troops marched back and forth on the plain below Frémont's hilltop, collected some cannon, and from time to time galloped a short way up the road toward the peak, while Frémont readied an ambush should they come nearer. For three days the tense confrontation created great excitement in the area.

One of those most distressed by the affair was Thomas O. Larkin, the American consul. Larkin had been in California since 1832. Unlike most foreigners who had come in the early days of the hide-and-tallow trade, Larkin had retained his American citizenship and married an American woman whom he had met on the ship that carried them to California. He proved to be a shrewd businessman and became one of the most influential residents of Monterey. Recognition of his success came with his appointment as United States consul in 1843 and as President Polk's secret agent in 1845. Thereafter, he reported at great length on the disorder and uncertainty of government in California and the strained relations between California and Mexico. Worried that the British might at any time "pluck the ripe pear," Larkin, in his reports, dwelt on the infirmity of Mexico's hold on the province.

With considerable skill, Larkin had worked to neutralize British influence and to promote closer American relations with California. By 1846 he was convinced that many prominent Californians were willing to consider the creation of an independent California that might eventually seek the protection of the United States. Small wonder that, as Frémont lay behind his barricade in the Gavilan Mountains, Larkin worked feverishly to keep the peace. On March 6 he sent a note to Castro counseling caution and trying to explain Frémont's action as a possible misunderstanding. On March 8 he wrote to Frémont urging him to move farther away immediately or, through a "proper representation to the general and prefecto," obtain permission to stay. Prudently, he also wrote the American naval commander off the coast of Mexico suggesting that a ship be sent north. A month later the U.S.S. *Portsmouth* was in Monterey, and it moved to San Francisco in June.

Larkin's note to Frémont may have had some effect, along with Frémont's recognition that hostile action against the Mexican government in California would set off a serious international incident. On March 10, Frémont left his fortress and moved slowly east into the San Joaquin Valley. By March 21 he was camped on the American River near Sutter's Fort; three days later he headed up the Sacramento Valley toward Oregon, leaving behind a greatly relieved General Castro.

Frémont's departure, however, did not end Castro's troubles. There remained the most serious problem of all—the appearance of the vanguard of the American frontier movement in California. Ever since Jedediah Smith penetrated the eastern frontier in 1826, American beaver trappers had entered California over the Sierra or through the deserts of the Southwest. Rough, fiercely independent individuals, most came for a season and left with their packs of beaver skins. A few had remained over the years, many of them unassimilated "floaters," roaming in and out of the California settlements. Their growing numbers were a source of concern to Californians—especially when they joined in the petty political wars so characteristic of Mexican California.

But in 1841 a far more menacing movement of Americans began when the first frontier settlers, drawn by glowing reports of earlier visitors and the conscious enticement of others, made their tortuous way over the Sierra. Thirty-four arrived in 1841, another thirty-eight in 1843, and fifty-three more in 1844. Then in 1845 the number jumped to an alarming 260. One group, led by a former Massachusetts school teacher, William B. Ide, numbered more than 100. These were

land-hungry farm folk who had ignored no-
tices published by the Mexican government
in midwestern newspapers that they could
not remain in California without passports
and Mexican approval. Once in California,
they bought or rented land and kept to
themselves in the interior valleys north of
San Francisco and Sacramento, posing a
growing threat to Mexican control of the region.

José Castro watched the arrival of the
American settlers with apprehension, conscious that these were the kind of migrants
who had poured into Texas in the 1830s and
led the revolt that tore the territory from
Mexico. In 1845, he had received orders
from Mexico to stop the entry of Americans
into California from Oregon and the east.
But, lacking funds and soldiers, Castro could
do no more that autumn than summon
newly arrived residents to meetings at localities from Sonoma to Sacramento where he
wrung from them promises to obey the laws
and apply for proper permission to remain.
Now, with the coming of spring, there was
talk that thousands of Americans would be
heading to California by May.

The *comandante's* desire to protect California against foreign intruders, however, was
plagued by internal conflict, especially by a
festering struggle for power with his former
ally, Don Pío Pico. Together, in 1844, Castro
and Pico had led the revolt that forced out
the last Mexican governor of California. In
the aftermath, Pico had assumed the title of
governor while Castro became *comandante*,
thus dividing the civil and military powers
between them, an arrangement eventually
endorsed by the Mexican government.

This arrangement had pleased neither
man. Pico moved the capital from Monterey
to Los Angeles where he controlled the government through the southern-dominated
provincial assembly. Castro remained in

Monterey where he controlled the customs
house and thus the funds of the territory.
Sharp conflict arose over Castro's allocation
of these funds, which favored the military,
and each leader began to defend his own interests and complain to Mexico City about
the other.

With all these problems in mind—his rivalry with Pico, the Frémont expedition, and
the American overland movement—Castro
summoned a military *junta* in Monterey at
the end of March 1846. The *junta* recommended that the general prepare to defend
California by fortifying the northern towns,
that he invite Governor Pico north to participate in the effort, and that he establish military headquarters at Santa Clara. Castro
agreed, but when he began to carry out
these recommendations, his actions were
seen in a considerably different light by his
various antagonists. Pío Pico became convinced that Castro was amassing troops to
march south to overthrow him as governor;
refusing to come north he began to assemble his own military force. In the north the
rumor spread that Castro was preparing to
throw the Americans out of California by
force, and anxious settlers began to consider
active resistance. When word reached them
that Frémont had returned to the valley, they
looked to him for guidance.

Frémont had left the Gavilan Mountains
in a surly mood. Although incensed by the
tone of General Castro's order to leave California, he had no real choice in the matter.
Certainly the orders for his expedition did
not include starting a war with Mexico. Moving east and north at a leisurely pace, Frémont entered the Sacramento Valley and, a
few weeks later, reached the 22,000-acre Rancho Bosqueto of Peter Lassen, between present-day Chico and Red Bluff. He spent the
first three weeks of April 1846 at Lassen's
ranch, having sent men off to the San

Joaquin Valley for fresh horses. During this time Frémont made a number of sorties to explore the valley and the rugged Coast Range. His men, meanwhile, spent their time getting to know the settlers along the river by joining them in raids on Indian villages and in all-night fandangos. Finally, on April 24, Frémont headed for Oregon, marching east of Mount Shasta through the Pit River and Tule Lake region.

By early May, Frémont was at Klamath Lake where, on the night of May 8, he received news that an American officer, Lieutenant Archibald Gillespie, was trying to overtake him with an important message from Washington. Taking a handful of men, Frémont rode back into Gillespie's camp the next night.

Just what Gillespie told Frémont that night has long remained a mystery, since he had memorized the contents of the papers he carried from Washington and destroyed them when he entered Mexican territory. Moreover, Frémont's many versions of the meeting were contradictory. It seems clear, however, that Gillespie was convinced—by what he had seen and heard in Mexico and by his contact with American naval officers in the Pacific—that war was imminent. The two young men talked long into the night about the possibility of war and what course of action they should follow. As a consequence, Frémont, who perhaps also wanted to settle accounts with Castro, decided to lead his expedition back into California. The next day, accompanied by Gillespie, he began to cautiously retrace his route to Lassen's ranch, where he arrived on May 24. Five days later he was encamped at a secure point on the southeastern slopes of the Sutter, or Marysville, Buttes, just north of Sutter's Fort.

Frémont's reappearance marked the beginning of the end of Mexican California.

The camp at the buttes immediately became the rallying point of worried settlers, most of them Americans who had entered California illegally and had not become Mexican citizens. Singly and in small groups, often led by the lanky, weathered ex-mountain man Ezekiel Merritt, Frémont's "field lieutenant" among the immigrants, they converged on Frémont to voice their concerns. It was rumored, they said, that Castro had issued a proclamation threatening to drive all unnaturalized foreign settlers out of California and was gathering a military force at Santa Clara to do so. They also claimed that Castro was urging the Indians to burn the settlers' wheat fields and steal their animals. Many of them feared they would have to fight for their property or flee. More and more of the "floaters" like Merritt began to hang around Frémont's camp.

Reacting first to the rumored Indian attacks, Frémont decided to "anticipate the Indians and strike them a blow which would make them recognize that Castro was far and I was near." Frémont's force swept down from the buttes, crossed the Sacramento River, and rode south, raiding the string of Maidu villages along the river. Years later, Frémont noted in his *Memoirs* that "several Indians were killed in the dispersion," and expressed satisfaction that his action had been beneficial. Confident that he had eliminated a real threat to the settlers by his surprise attack on the Maidu, and still smarting from his earlier encounter with the *comandante*, Frémont turned his attention to General José Castro.

With military preparations made all the more urgent by Frémont's return to the Central Valley, Castro visited Colonel Mariano Vallejo, commander of the northern military district, at Sonoma in early June to arrange for the transfer of a large herd of horses to his headquarters at Santa Clara. Soon news arrived at Frémont's camp that Castro's men were driving some 170 horses around the bay, stopping at Sutter's Fort on the way. Reasoning that if those horses could be prevented from reaching Santa Clara Castro would have trouble carrying out any threats against the northern settlers, "Zeke" Merritt and ten others rode out from the buttes in pursuit. Meanwhile, a call went out to the settlers to meet at Frémont's camp. Thus began, on the spur of the moment, a series of events that culminated in what became known as the Bear Flag Revolt.

Merritt's men included Robert Semple, a dentist and printer whose height (6 feet, 8 inches) excited comment wherever he went; Granville Swift, noted as a crack shot and the fastest reloader on the coast; and other expe-

Route of the Bear Flag Party
The Bear Flag party captured Castro's horses, then took Sonoma, where the Republic of California was established. Mariano G. Vallejo, his brother, and his brother-in-law were sent to Sutter's Fort as prisoners.

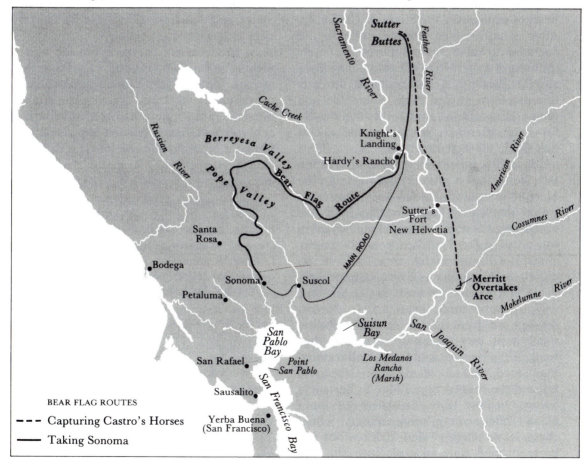

The Bear Flag
The Bear Flag was raised at Sonoma by William B. Ide's men as the flag of the California Republic. Some accounts state that a green turf was painted under the bear, as in the present state flag of California. *Courtesy of the Bancroft Library.*

proclamation promised security of life and property to all who would not take up arms against them. In all this, Ide took care to keep the revolt unrelated to the government of the United States. Still, he thought it was a good idea to keep the commander of the American warship at San Francisco, the *Portsmouth*, informed and sent him a letter for this purpose on June 15. The next day an officer from the *Portsmouth* visited the garrison and assured the "Bears" of American neutrality in the matter.

The political necessities taken care of, the men, now calling themselves *osos* (bears) looked to their defenses. Expecting General Castro to move quickly to retake Sonoma, they readied the little fortress in preparation. The men were divided into an artillery company (of ten men) and a rifle company (also ten men), and supplies were requisitioned from the local citizenry. To alleviate a shortage of gunpowder, George Fowler and Thomas Cowie rode off to the rancho of Henry D. Fitch on the Russian River for a keg of powder. William Todd and another Bear rode west to carry the message of the revolt to other settlers. Meanwhile, Ide's "proclamation" drew new recruits daily to Sonoma. Within a week, the Sonoma garrison numbered more than ninety men and was still growing, as the Bears waited nervously for Castro's expected attack.

At Santa Clara, Castro was stunned to hear of the capture of Sonoma and on June 17 issued two proclamations of his own that rivaled Ide's in wordiness and bombast. Exhorting Californians to "arise in mass," he called on them to rally to his banner and to help put down the rebellion. A second proclamation assured foreign residents of their security provided they remained peaceable, and warned of dire consequences for those who did not. Organizing the men who answered his call to arms into three small companies, he sent one led by Joaquin de la Torre across the bay from San Pablo to San Rafael to quash the Sonoma insurgents.

At Sonoma, when Fowler and Cowie failed to return from their mission to obtain powder, Ide's lieutenant, Henry L. Ford, sent more men to Fitch's rancho. On their return they reported that Fowler and Cowie had been captured and brutally murdered by a force of Californians under Juan Padilla. Concerned now for the safety of Todd and his companion, Ford sent a message to "Zeke" Merritt at Sacramento to bring more men to Sonoma and set out with a rescue party of some eighteen men. Near the present-day town of Novato, Ford's party followed Padilla's trail to a small rancho where a few men could be seen outside an adobe house. Charging the house, Ford's force was surprised as men came "pouring out of the house" and more appeared from the nearby woods. Padilla had been joined by Torre's detachment. Ford's men took cover in the woods and soon drove Torre's troops off toward San Rafael and rescued Todd, who had been captured and held prisoner in the house. One of Torre's men had been killed and several wounded, and the Bear Flag Revolt was beginning to take on substantial proportions.

On June 20, Captain Frémont was camped on the American River near Sutter's Fort, waiting anxiously for news of the Sonoma attack and of the activities of General Castro. What he heard that day propelled him into action, and into the Bear Flag Revolt. Two of the settlers returned from the south bay area to report that Castro had sent forces to attack north of the bay. Then Merritt received Ford's call for help. Frémont quickly gathered thirty settlers, in addition to his company of sixty, and headed for Sonoma. On June 25, this "army" of mountain men, drifters, farmers, and Frémont's Delaware Indian bodyguard rode into the plaza of Commander Ide's capital. Dressed in buckskin, the famous Hawken long rifles across their saddles, and pistols and skinning knives at their waists, they were a formidable sight.

Frémont's intervention in the Bear Flag Revolt required some delicacy. As an American army officer, his participation in any conflict with the Californians could well cost him his appointment. Moreover, Ide clearly sensed that Frémont was a threat to his position as commander. Relations between the two cooled rapidly when Frémont disagreed with Ide's plans to extend the rebellion around the San Francisco bay area.

However, the paramount issue of the moment was the disposition of Castro's forces under Torre. With more than 200 men now at Sonoma, the Bears had emerged as a potent military force, strong enough to go in pursuit of Torre. Claiming "that he had come down, *not to take part in the matter*, only to see the sport, and *explore* about the Bay," Frémont disguised his appearance and rode south toward San Rafael with Lieutenant Ford and 125 men.

Upon reaching the mission at San Rafael the Bears were disappointed to find Torre gone, and for the next two days, scouts tried to locate the Californians. One such party under Frémont's chief scout, Kit Carson, cold-bloodedly shot José de los Reyes Berreyesa, father of Sonoma's *alcalde*, and his twin nephews, Ramón and Francisco de Haro. A message from Castro to Torre was found on one of the victims, but there was much controversy in later years over what Carson and others called retaliation for the murder of Fowler and Cowie. On the same day, another scouting party captured an Indian with a message from Torre to Castro stating that the former planned to attack Sonoma on June 29. Ford and Frémont hurried back to Sonoma to protect the Bear Flag capital, only to find they were victims of a ruse. With Frémont and Ford riding hard to Sonoma, Torre commandeered a launch at Sausalito and escaped with his soldiers back across the bay to join Castro's forces at San Pablo. Thus, by diverting Frémont from the main scene of action, Torre had averted a possible disaster for the *comandante*.

At Sonoma, Ide's forces had also heard the rumor of an impending attack and were waiting, cannons and rifles ready, when Frémont's men rode into the hamlet near dawn. Fortunately, the defenders recognized their friends' voices and held their fire. Chagrined by Torre's ruse, Frémont then led another expedition to Sausalito and, with the aid of an American trader, crossed the Golden Gate to the old ungarrisoned Castillo de San Joaquin overlooking the shores of the bay, where he spiked its ancient guns. The next day, July 2, the officials at Yerba Buena were taken prisoner, one of the captors reporting that "the Captain of the Port, couldn't go, because he had died the day before." Even so, his replacement put up a struggle because "he had a game of billiards to finish."

Frémont's "nonparticipation" in the Bear Flag Revolt came to an end when he returned to Sonoma. Ide's companions had loaded a launch with a cannon and a hundred muskets from the Sonoma arsenal, hoping to arm settlers on the eastern side of San Francisco Bay whom, they had heard, wished to join the revolt. Frémont opposed the idea and forced postponement until after July 4. A disappointed Ide noted:

> Two hundred and seventy-two men had signed our roll. We were in quiet, and for the time, in undisturbed possession of all California north and east of the San Joaquin River. We had taken possession of Yerba Buena and spiked the cannon there. All that was necessary was to have pursued our victory, to have made it complete.

For the moment, though, all joined in a celebration of the independence of the United States and the birth of the California Republic.

On July 5, Frémont moved to assume the dominant role in the revolt. He called a meeting that was attended by his original company, the Bear Flag men, and even a handful of navy officers from the *Portsmouth*, whose captain had been keeping a close eye on all that was going on at Sonoma. Frémont told the men of the serious military situation confronting them and offered his experienced leadership. In short order, the men at Sonoma enrolled in what was now called the California Battalion, and under Frémont's direction it was organized into four companies. In the process of reorganization, William B. Ide was demoted to the position of private in one of the companies, his dream of glory rapidly evaporating. With almost 350 men, Frémont now had control of a major army by California standards. Leaving one company of fifty men at Sonoma, Frémont headed for Sacramento on the first leg of a wide movement aimed at flanking General Castro's Santa Clara headquarters.

Frémont was now in charge, but em-

Two Mountain Men
Not all mountain men wore fringed deerskin clothing, but when they rode into Sonoma, and later into Monterey, with Frémont they were an awesome sight. Mountain men and "floaters" like Ezekiel Merritt made up a large portion of the California Battalion in 1846–1847. *Courtesy of the Bancroft Library.*

barked on a risky course. If the United States were at war with Mexico, as most people expected would soon be the case, his actions were commendable. But there was no evidence available to him that war had broken out, and in the absence of war, Frémont was certainly risking dishonor and court-martial. He was in luck, however, because the United States had in fact been at war with Mexico since May 13, 1846. News of the early battles of the war became known in May and June at Mazatlan on the Pacific coast. On June 8 the American naval commander there, Commodore John D. Sloat, set sail for Monterey in accordance with his long-standing instructions that, in the event of war, he was to seize California before any other power could do so. On July 2, Sloat sailed into Monterey, but without evidence of a clear declaration of war he hesitated to act. When he learned of the Bear Flag Revolt and Frémont's association with it, Sloat raised the American flag on July 7 and sent orders to commander John B. Montgomery on the *Portsmouth* to take Yerba Buena and San Francisco Bay. Frémont's men and the Bear Flaggers, the California Battalion, were soon fighting under the American flag. The Bear Flag Revolt was over, and the short-lived California Republic came to an end.

The end was also near for Mexican California and José Castro's career as *comandante general*. Despite his popularity among his own people and despite his urgent proclamations, Castro failed to collect more than 160 men at Santa Clara and was no match for the American forces now converging on him from Monterey and the north. Nor was there comfort in the knowledge that Governor Pico's armed forces in the south had been collected not to help him but to attack him. He could only retreat, importuning Pico to come to his aid, while his armed force melted away as he moved south. In mid-July Castro and Pico met near San Luis Obispo and were reconciled, Pico having learned of the Bear Flag action and the American occupation. Together they retreated south to the Los Angeles region, but the continuing sectional, as well as personal, rivalry weakened their resistance to the Americans who landed at San Diego and San Pedro in August. As the invaders approached Los Angeles, a dejected Castro occupied a mesa south of town with barely a hundred discontented men, and he and Pico both prepared to flee to Mexico. The night of August 9, having disbanded his forces, José Castro slipped away to the northern Mexico province of Sonora, where he spent the next year petitioning the beleaguered Mexican government for assistance that never came. California was firmly in American hands.

The conquest over, William B. Ide returned to his cabin on the Sacramento River that November, eventually to become the owner of the Rancho La Barranca Colorado. His desire for prestige and influence was finally satisfied when Colusi County was formed in 1850 (including the present counties of Colusa, Tehema, and Glenn). In a brief but satisfying two years before his death from smallpox in 1852, Ide held, at various times, the following county positions: associate justice and member of the Court of Sessions, county judge, deputy county clerk, county treasurer, county clerk, clerk of the Ninth District Court, clerk of the County Court and of the Court of Sessions, clerk of the Probate Court, county recorder, and county auditor.

Castro's departure from Los Angeles coincided with the arrival of John C. Frémont's conquering California Battalion. Frémont was eventually named military governor of California, only to act so impetuously that he was court-martialed. Nevertheless, his

unique personality and opportunism enabled him not only to survive conviction but
also to move forward to important political
success as one of California's first U.S. senators and later as the Republican party's first
candidate for president.

As the Mexican War drew to a close in
1848, the military governor of California,
Colonel Richard B. Mason, made a conciliatory gesture to José Castro, inviting him to
come back to his home. Castro accepted the
offer and returned to Monterey. Homecoming did not bring happiness, however, for he
was often seen sitting in local restaurants, a
proud and bitter figure, muttering darkly
about "the reconquest of the region." Only
on moving to Baja California in the 1850s
did he regain his former status, serving as
governor and military *comandante* until his
death in 1860.

CHAPTER EIGHT

MEXICAN CALIFORNIA, 1821–1848

The Bear Flag Revolt set in motion a process that ended the twenty-five-year rule of Mexico in California. From the very beginning, Mexico, absorbed by internal difficulties, had failed to establish a firm hold on its northern province. Mexican independence was declared on September 28, 1821, by a revolutionary junta presided over by ex-royalist Agustín Iturbide, who quickly proclaimed himself emperor of Mexico and just as quickly fell from power the next year. In 1824 a new constitution established the Federal Republic of Mexico, a form of government inaugurated in the United States just thirty-five years earlier and a dramatic change from the autocratic Spanish colonial system. However, few Mexicans had experience with representative government. Armed conflict was frequent, political instability became the rule, the formation of effective policy became almost impossible, and the Mexican government was in constant financial need. Under the Constitution of 1824, California, like Mexico's other frontier provinces of Texas and New Mexico, became a territory theoretically governed directly by the Mexican Congress. But the Congress failed to establish any clear policies for administration and financial support of the territories, which remained in a state of confusion and destitution. The new political order in Mexico also seemed to promise Californians access to political offices previously denied them, producing strong personal and sectional rivalries and a growing desire for home rule. California under Mexico thus remained a neglected and isolated province where the descendants of soldiers and early *pobladores* (settlers) struggled to build a new society of their own.

ESTABLISHMENT OF MEXICAN GOVERNMENT IN CALIFORNIA

Isolated as they were, Californians had little to do with Mexico's long (1810–1821) war for independence. When they learned that the Mexican revolution had succeeded, they pledged allegiance to the new government and awaited its actions. In 1822 Iturbide's government established a new structure of local government with the selection of a new governor and the election of a *diputación*, or provincial assembly, to advise the governor;

an *ayuntamiento,* or town council, for each of the two pueblos, San José and Los Angeles; and a provincial representative to the new Mexican Congress.

The new governor, Luis Antonio Argüello, was the first *hijo del país,* or native son, appointed to the position and he enjoyed wide popular support. Argüello's chief concern as governor was revival of the economy. The revolution had all but eliminated coastal shipping between California and Mexico, causing the last Spanish governor, Pablo Vicente de Solá, to relax many of the traditional restrictions on trading with foreigners. In 1822, just before leaving office, Solá allowed William E. P. Hartnell and Hugh McCullough, who represented the British firm of John Begg & Co., to sign three-year contracts with almost all the missions for their production of hides and tallow. Argüello granted similar privileges to William Gale, who was acting on behalf of the Boston firm of Bryant & Sturgis, which eventually dominated the trade. The prospect of increased revenue from trade in hides and tallow may also have encouraged Argüello to issue several large land grants between 1823 and 1824 in the hope of increasing production.

Argüello's appointment ended in 1825, when the first governor appointed under the Republic arrived at San Diego. José María Echeandía, a gaunt, hypochondriacal lieutenant colonel in the Army Corps of Engineers, had hoped to be appointed director of engineers in Mexico and no doubt reluctantly left his wife and four daughters in Mexico City when he departed for the "frontier." He has probably been underestimated as governor, partly because he immediately contributed to the developing rivalry between north and south. Announcing that the foggy climate of the capital, Monterey, was bad for his health, he made San Diego his chief place of residence and the unofficial capital, a move that pleased southerners and

offended northerners. But Echeandía deserves credit for dealing, as best he could under difficult circumstances, with several major problems: rebellious soldiers and Indians, the ominous appearance of American fur trappers from the east, and the Mexican government's desire to end the mission system by secularization.

Echeandía inherited a demoralized military establishment. Many of the soldiers sent to California were undisciplined ex-convicts, misfits, and vagabonds, the source of constant conflict with missionaries and townspeople who labeled them *cholos* (scoundrels). The government was far in arrears in their pay, and Echeandía lacked the funds necessary to correct this condition. Consequently, a serious mutiny erupted at Monterey in 1829, led by a former soldier-convict, Joaquín Solís. Solís and a force of unpaid soldiers marched south against the governor, only to flee back to Monterey when Echeandía appeared on the battlefield near Santa Barbara with his own troops. The problem of the soldiers' pay remained unsolved, however.

A related problem was the Mexican policy of sentencing convicts to a life in California as punishment for their crimes. A substantial population of disreputable persons therefore roamed the province, foraging, stealing, fighting, and provoking consternation and resentment among the townspeople, whose protests, relayed by Echeandía, finally convinced the government to end the practice of dumping convicts in California. Echeandía, meanwhile, absorbed much of the blame for the trouble these criminals caused.

Within a year of his arrival, Echeandía was also confronted with the breakdown of the province's security on its eastern border. In 1826 Jedediah Smith led a party of American fur trappers from the Rocky Mountains across the Mojave Desert to Mission San

Gabriel, the first Americans to enter California from the east. Appalled by the precedent, Echeandía refused Smith permission to hunt beaver in the province and, after weeks of indecision, ordered him to return to the United States. But, with good reason, he worried that Smith would be followed by others.

However, Echeandía devoted most of his attention to Indian affairs. He arrived in San Diego shortly after a serious Indian revolt in the southern missions and only with difficulty persuaded the frightened padres to continue to clothe and feed the families of his soldiers. He also made a modest attempt to begin secularizing the missions, to the Franciscans' great dismay. Echeandía sympathized with the democratic principles of the revolution and the government's determination to integrate the Indians into Mexican society. Influenced by a report by the government's Commission for the Development of the Californias, he announced a plan in 1826 whereby certain Indian families might leave a few specified missions. As the mission fathers predicted, few left and Echeandía was further discouraged by accounts that those who did were incapable of an independent existence.

The fact that it took four more years for Echeandía to develop another plan for secularization reflected not only the failure of his first attempt but also his realization that the economic well-being of Californians depended on the production of hides, tallow, and foodstuffs at the missions. The missions supported two-thirds of the Mexican population of California, and the Franciscans insisted that disruption of the system would be disastrous. It was a real dilemma: secularization of the missions seemed necessary not only in order to integrate the Indians into Mexican society, but also to promote California's economic development, in particular

immigration and private ranching on former mission lands; yet secularization could ruin the existing supply system. California could not grow if the mission system remained intact but seemingly could not survive without it. Echeandía issued a new proposal in January 1831, but before it could be implemented a new government came to power in Mexico and Echeandía was replaced.

The new governor, Colonel Manuel Victoria, contrasted sharply with his predecessor. Reactionary, militaristic, and ruthless, he had little faith in republicanism and little respect for the *californios*. Reflecting the conservative, proclerical new regime in Mexico, he halted plans for secularization, refused to call the territorial *diputación* into session, and ruled in a dictatorial fashion, all of which offended the emerging local elite.

Victoria's harsh regime came to an end with the first of many "revolutions" of the period. On November 29, 1831, several prominent southern Californians issued a *pronunciamiento* against Victoria, demanding that he be expelled and replaced by ex-Governor Echeandía. Victoria gathered a small band of soldiers and marched south to meet the rebels in combat. At Cahuenga Pass, just north of Los Angeles, the opposing forces met and exchanged harmless volleys until one of the rebels, José María Avila, dashed forth, wounded Victoria with his lance, and killed the governor's aide before he himself was killed. Victoria made his way to the nearest mission, San Gabriel, where, on December 9, he arranged to turn his authority back to Echeandía. On January 17, 1832, after less than a year in office, he sailed for Mexico.

Having deposed Victoria, the Californians quarreled among themselves. Southern Californians, particularly Juan Bandini, Pío Pico, and José Carrillo, who had led the revolt against Victoria, were unhappy with Echeandía's assumption of both military and civil authority. The territorial *diputación,* meeting in Los Angeles, elected Pío Pico as governor, but Echeandía managed to overturn the appointment. Meanwhile, northern Californians led by Captain Agustín Zamorano (Victoria's former secretary, better known for bringing the first printing press to California) disputed Echeandía's return to power, and opposing "armies" were again in the field. Bloodshed was averted with a truce whereby Zamorano retained military command north of San Fernando while Echeandía commanded the area to the south.

The events in California convinced Mexican officials that experience was a highly desirable quality for their next appointee, and they found it in forty-year-old General José Figueroa, who was named governor on May 9, 1832. Figueroa had been *comandante general* of Sonora and Sinaloa and a judge in the Supreme Tribunal of War and Marine. He was proud of his Indian blood and sympathized with the liberal aims of the Mexican revolution. He was, without doubt, the most capable Mexican governor of California. Despite some shortcomings (he is said to have abandoned a wife and two children and been a compulsive gambler), his engaging personality and political abilities soon endeared him to prominent Californians, particularly in the north, where he assumed office in January 1833. He also won the support of southern Californians by issuing a proclamation of amnesty for all participants in the revolt against Victoria.

Figueroa's instructions emphasized promoting colonization, especially in the areas threatened by Russian or American activity. Accordingly, one of his first acts was to send Ensign Mariano Guadalupe Vallejo north to reconnoiter the Russian base at Fort Ross and to select a site for a presidio north of San Francisco. Vallejo, who then commanded the San Francisco presidio, was also authorized

Mariano Guadalupe Vallejo
Haughty and reserved, but honest and loyal, General Mariano Guadalupe Vallejo controlled vast landholdings and the military compound at Sonoma. In Thomas O. Larkin's view he was "the most independent man in California." While Vallejo was not politically inclined, his support was critical to the ambitions of Juan B. Alvarado and José Castro. *Courtesy of the California State Library.*

to grant land to qualified settlers who would move into the northern frontier. Within the next few years, Vallejo established the towns of Petaluma and Santa Rosa and directed the development of a substantial rancho economy in this area, effectively cutting the Russians off from expanding inland—a major factor in their decision to abandon Fort Ross at the end of the 1830s. In the process, Vallejo became one of the largest landowners in northern California.

SECULARIZATION OF THE MISSIONS

The most pressing problem for Figueroa remained Indian policy and the future of the missions. As early as 1813 the Spanish government had ordered secularization of all missions that had been in existence for ten years, but the Mexican revolution had prevented enforcement of the decree. Almost immediately after independence, contradictory pressures built up in Mexico over ending the mission system. Idealistic followers of democratic revolutionary principles saw the missions as lingering vestiges of Spanish colonialism and worked to make Indians throughout Mexico free citizens. Others, in league with Californians, hoped to take advantage of the dissatisfaction with the mission system to appropriate the missions' lands, herds, and wealth for themselves. Charges that the missions failed to assimilate the Indians, but treated them cruelly, deluged Mexico City.

Although the mission system had many flaws, much of the criticism was sheer hypocrisy, coming as it did from California soldiers, civil officials, and a growing class of rancheros, who themselves exploited and abused Indians and were seeking even freer access to mission lands and neophyte labor. Nevertheless, because of confusion and conflict over their status and future, the missions were disintegrating by the time of Figueroa's appointment, their neophytes were in flight or defiance, and their production declining.

THE GÓMEZ FARÍAS PLAN

José Figueroa's arrival in Monterey coincided with another political change in Mexico. New elections in 1833 brought to power an unlikely coalition of military figures led by the unprincipled General Antonio López de Santa Anna and liberal democrats led by Valentín Gómez Farías. Although elected president, Santa Anna decided to spend a few months resting at his estate near Jalapa, leaving Vice President Gómez Farías as acting chief executive—the first civilian to govern Mexico since independence. For many years, especially since his service on the Commission for the Development of the Californias, Gómez Farías had favored integration of the Indians into Mexican society through secularization of the missions. He also shared the anxiety of many Mexicans about Russian encroachment on the weak California settlements. Seizing the opportunity afforded by Santa Anna's absence, he advanced a plan to combine secularization of the California missions with a colonization scheme to strengthen the settlements between San Francisco and Fort Ross.

The first step in this plan was a law, introduced in Congress in April and signed by Gómez Farías in August 1833, ordering the complete dismemberment, or secularization, of the Baja and Alta California missions. The clergy's temporal authority over the Indians was to be removed, the missions converted into ordinary churches, and the missionaries replaced by parish priests. A second bill, also introduced by the Gómez Farías government in April, provided a detailed plan for distribution of the vast properties of the missions, not only to the neophytes but also to a number of other groups, including soldiers, colonists, naturalized foreigners, and convicts. Significantly, those who already held land in the region were not included. The bill also dealt with the formation of town governments, establishment and staffing of schools, and administration of the land and property distribution. Unfortunately, the proposed property-distribution bill was never adopted and the opportunity for an orderly secularization process coordinated with colonization was lost.

Gómez Farías not only saw colonization as an important adjunct to secularization, he also regarded it as an effective means of defense. Accordingly, he planned and organized a major expedition under the leadership of José María Híjar aimed at occupying mission lands on the northern frontier between San Francisco Bay and Fort Ross. The importance attached to this project is indicated by the fact that Híjar, a friend of Gómez Farías from Guadalajara, was appointed director of colonization *and* governor of California, to replace Figueroa on arrival in California. José María Padrés, also a friend of Gómez Farías and a familiar figure in California, was named second in command of the colony and appointed military *comandante* of California. The Híjar-Padrés expedition, consisting of some 250 people, left Mexico City in April 1834. Since the law outlining land and property distribution of secularized missions had not been adopted, Gómez Farías gave Híjar a hastily drawn, but similar, set of instructions for implementing the secularization act of August 1833.

SECULARIZATION UNDER FIGUEROA

Meanwhile, Governor Figueroa, while anxious to carry out the intent of his own instructions for secularizing the missions, had doubts about the wisdom of wholesale emancipation of the Indians. Experience under Echeandía had been that the neophytes, when freed from the missions, soon lost their property and gravitated toward a degraded status as servants of local *gente de razón*. Father Narciso Durán, the leading Franciscan in California, persistently pointed this out to Figueroa in a campaign to prevent or delay secularization. Moreover, Figueroa, painfully aware that for twenty years the military and civil personnel and their families in California had survived only with the help of the missions, was reluctant to move precipitously. Nevertheless, under great pressure from Californians, who cov-

eted mission lands, he referred the question to the territorial *diputación*, which with Figueroa's assistance drew up a plan that the governor issued on August 9, 1834.

This plan of secularization provided that ten missions would be converted to towns, and the padres replaced by parish priests at once; six of the remaining eleven were to be secularized in 1835, and five in 1836. The plan also provided for distribution of land and property and for administration of the process. Unlike Gómez Farías's plan, Figueroa's called for distribution of mission lands and property only to neophytes in grants to each family of thirty-three acres of cultivable land, whether irrigated or not, along with grants "in common" of "enough land to pasture their stock," an amount that the administration could increase or decrease. Also, it called for dividing one-half of the mission herds of livestock proportionately among the Indian families, with all surplus livestock and property remaining in the care of an appointee of the governor. Finally, it provided that the "emancipated" Indians, at the discretion of the governor, could be forced to work on the mission's undistributed lands. Thus the way was opened for the *californios* to acquire mission lands while still partially retaining the mission supply system.

Figueroa's plan had hardly gone into effect when the governor received word that Híjar and half the members of his colony had landed at San Diego, while Padrés and the rest of the colonists were expected in Monterey momentarily. At the same time an overland courier from Mexico City brought instructions from President Santa Anna, who had now taken over the government from Gómez Farías, canceling Híjar's appointment as governor and Padrés's appointment as military *comandante*. Bitterly disappointed, Híjar and Padrés finally agreed to settle the colony in the Sonoma area, north of San Francisco. Although the colony was criticized for including too many people not suited for agriculture, California desperately needed the skilled craftsmen and schoolteachers who made up the majority of the colonists. In any event, the settlement in Sonoma went badly, and rumors abounded that a revolution was brewing.

Figueroa was not one to ignore such rumors, and his relations with Híjar and Padrés worsened with reports that they were plotting against his administration. Finally, in the spring of 1835, he ordered that all colonists be free to settle wherever they might wish, in effect dispersing the colony, and instructed Vallejo to arrest Híjar and Padrés and ship them back to Mexico. By May 1835, this had been done, and Figueroa was at work on a manifesto designed to explain his actions for posterity. Unfortunately neither Híjar nor Padrés produced an account of the matter, and as a consequence historians have generally accepted Figueroa's criticism of the colony and its leaders. Probably the most knowledgeable student of the subject, C. Alan Hutchinson, maintains, however, that Figueroa's document was badly biased and unworthy of such an otherwise capable public servant. Figueroa eventually resigned in poor health and turned his office over to the young José Castro. The ex-governor died in September 1835, shortly after completing his manifesto.

Despite the trouble over the Híjar-Padrés colony, secularization proceeded quickly, but it ran afoul of the overwhelming unwillingness of the Californians to cease exploiting natives, and of the inability of the weak central government to alter local conditions. Though Figueroa personally sought to protect Indian rights, he lacked funds and soldiers to enforce secularization on his own. Instead, he was forced to appoint leading *gente de razón* such as Pío Pico and Mariano Vallejo to oversee the distribution of mission assets. After Figueroa's death, his successors ignored the intentions behind secularization.

Predictably, local administrators and their supporters made off in most cases with the bulk of the missions' cattle, horses, equipment, and cash—in some instances even taking altar pieces and bells. Neophytes received allotments of land and livestock that were too small to support them. Encroaching *gente de razón* quickly forced neophytes to sell out, while local officials made little attempt to protect them. Even the respected William Hartnell, appointed *visitador de misiones* in 1839 to investigate complaints about secularization, could not halt the abuses and resigned bitterly after two years as the most fertile mission lands fell into the hands of local rancheros. The Indians themselves participated in the destruction of the missions, having no love for a system that had kept them forcibly institutionalized. Many abandoned their lands and refused to work on the "surplus" mission lands. Although a few neophytes remained in the mission Indian pueblos, most soon drifted away. Some congregated around towns and ranchos, where they were exploited as before. Others fled to the interior, resumed the native life, and gave new impetus to the cultural revolution of gentile tribes. From the 1830s to the 1850s, many returned to the coast time and again, now heading Indian cavalry attacks on the settlements and their herds.

The decline of the missions continued until the end of the Mexican period, and the failure of secularization to improve Indian-white relations stands as a stark illustration of the general failure of Hispanic Indian policy in California. Like Spain, Mexico had continued the disruption of coastal Indian societies but, despite the population decline caused by the ravages of European diseases, had failed to dominate interior groups. Thus Indian resistance and aggression effectively inhibited settlement of the interior, a critical factor in the success of the American frontier movement into California after 1840.

POLITICAL TURMOIL

Figueroa's departure plunged the province into political turmoil once again. José Castro and Nicolas Gutiérrez each served a short term as acting governor until Mexico sent Colonel Mariano Chico to take the office in 1836. Chico was so impolitic—attempting to pass off his mistress as his "niece," for example—that he lasted only three months; another "revolution" sent him back to Mexico. His rejection also signified California's discontent with the new centrist government, which had suddenly discarded the liberal constitution of 1824. Gutiérrez followed Chico and was similarly ousted after a disagreement with Juan Bautista Alvarado, the dashing twenty-seven-year-old president of the *diputación*. Alvarado and José Castro collected a small "army" of seventy-five men, recruited Isaac Graham, an American ex-trapper running a distillery in the Pájaro Valley, and about fifty of his cohorts, and marched on Monterey. One cannon shot induced Gutiérrez to leave, whereupon the *diputación* elected Alvarado governor and Mariano Vallejo comandante general.

Upon assuming the governorship, Alvarado was soon involved in another conflict between forces from the north, led by José Castro, and the south, led by Alvarado's uncle, Carlos Carrillo. After one man had inadvertently been killed, Castro persuaded the southerners to accept a compromise, awarding them, in effect, a subgovernor (an arrangement authorized by Mexico's establishment of the *prefectura*, creating such an office). By 1838 the Mexican government had formally appointed Alvarado as governor and Vallejo as *comandante general*, and California enjoyed relative political peace for the next four years. Under Alvarado, secularization was essentially completed, development of the rancho economy accelerated, and the hide-and-tallow trade continued to dominate the economy.

THE HIDE AND TALLOW TRADE

The demise of the missions fundamentally changed California's economic development. By the time of secularization, the missions had established a flourishing cattle economy, controlling 10 million acres of land and counting in their herds some 400,000 head of cattle,

Hide and Tallow Trade Ports of Call

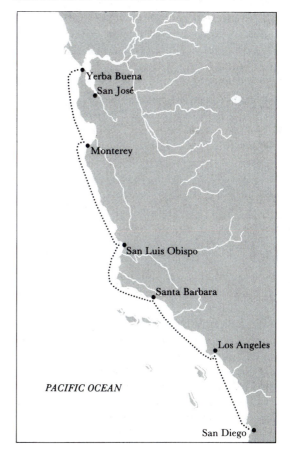

nearly the same number of sheep, and tens of thousands of horses. Also, over the years the Franciscans had developed a modest trade with other parts of the Spanish empire in cowhides and the tallow rendered from animal carcasses. At the same time, a limited, clandestine trade with foreign fur traders and whalers had acquainted the outside world with the province's developing cattle economy. When the Mexican revolution disrupted California's communication with the rest of New Spain, this illicit trade increased. By the time of Mexican independence, the foundation had been laid for what became the key to the economic survival of Mexican California—the production of hides and tallow for export.

The decision of the new Mexican government to open California to trade with foreigners was crucial for the development of the hide-and-tallow trade. Mexico opened the ports of Monterey and San Diego to foreign ships, levying substantial duties on the goods they carried. Local officials soon relaxed these regulations in the interest of promoting increased revenues through increased trade. Thus Governor Argüello permitted company representatives to build storehouses on shore and carry on trade at many other points along the coast.

Resident foreign company representatives such as Hartnell, Gale, and many others played an essential role in the growth of the hide-and-tallow trade by linking California with British and American companies, particularly the growing leather-goods industry in and around Boston. Moreover, lacking the necessary training, Californians left commercial activities to the foreigners, who soon controlled most of the business aspects of the trade. By the mid-1830s, British and American trading ships were a permanent part of the California scene, and the region's economic ties to New England were especially strong.

The classic contemporary description of the California hide-and-tallow trade is Richard Henry Dana's *Two Years Before the Mast*, published in 1840. Dana was a nineteen-year-old Harvard student when he signed onto the ship *Pilgrim*, which was bound for California, where he spent sixteen months in the hide-and-tallow trade. *Two Years Before the Mast* grew out of this experience (and led, incidentally, to some important legal reforms concerning the treatment of sailors in the merchant marine).

Dana described in vivid detail the process whereby ships put in at Monterey, paid duties on their cargo, and then plied the coast as "floating department stores." Often they were supplied with additional goods from Hawaii, where several American firms maintained large stocks of merchandise. Small schooners made frequent runs between Hawaii and California, resupplying the trading ships and bringing native Hawaiians (Kanakas) to work as sailors and "hide droghers."

Ships such as the *Pilgrim* carried a vast array of goods. Gold thread, holy pictures, musical instruments, bells, and other items useful for religious services were brought to the mission fathers. For the *californios*, Dana reported, the cargo consisted of "everything under the sun":

We had spirits of all kinds (sold by the case), teas, coffee, sugars, spices, molasses, hardware, crockery, tin-ware, cutlery, clothing of all kinds, boots and shoes from Lynn, calicoes, and cotton from Lowell, crapes, silks; also shawls, scarfs, necklaces, jewelry, and combs for women; furniture; and, in fact, everything that can be imagined, from Chinese fireworks to English cart-wheels. . . .

The arrival of a company ship produced great excitement as local residents flocked to choose from its cargo and days of buying, selling, and entertainment followed. Eventually, foreign merchants such as Abel Stearns and Thomas Larkin established retail businesses that provided these goods year-round, but shipboard sales remained a fixture of the trade throughout the Mexican period. Most transactions were on credit, there being little currency available in California, and purchases were paid for in hides—"California bank-notes," usually worth a dollar or two apiece—while resident company representatives, or "supercargoes," assembled hides and tallow at collection points along the coast.

Bringing the hides and tallow on board ship was a particularly difficult task, since San Francisco, San Diego, and Monterey were the only convenient harbors. Everywhere else, ships had to anchor three to four miles offshore while goods were ferried to and from the beach in small boats. Dana drew a memorable picture of hides piled on the beach and hide droghers carrying them, balanced on their heads, through the surf to the boats. The leather bags of tallow, called *botas*, were then loaded into the small boats and rowed out to the ship, exceedingly hazardous work in heavy seas.

Once collected along the coast, hides had to be cured. Accordingly, the trading companies maintained large warehouses at the safe harbor of San Diego, where the curing process began. San Diego was considered the best place on the coast for this work because southern California had the biggest missions and ranchos, and because cured hides could be loaded without getting them wet in the surf; once cured, hides would spoil if they became wet. Each raw hide was soaked in the ocean to soften it, then pickled in a vat of brine, cleaned of fat and other residue, spread in the sun, scraped free of grease, and dried. Dana reported that each man in his crew cured 25 hides a day and noted their long faces when they were informed that the company's storehouse held 40,000 hides.

The hide-and-tallow trade was of vital importance to California. It became almost the sole source of revenue for the government, a fact that accounts for the persistent efforts of southerners to get the capital and customs house moved to Los Angeles or San Diego. Unfortunately, it has been estimated that one-fourth to one-third of legitimate duties were evaded by smuggling. Nevertheless, the hide-and-tallow trade permitted the development of the rancho society that is so closely identified with the Mexican period. It provided almost all the manufactured items obtained by Californians, who had little incentive to develop domestic industry to replace mission industries, and enabled them to make raising cattle their sole means of support. With secularization of the missions, the ranchos produced most of the available goods and services, and the great rancheros became more firmly established as a landed elite.

RANCHO AND PUEBLO SOCIETY

The popular conception of life in Mexican California has probably been unduly influenced by descriptions of the almost feudal estates of the ranchero class. Contemporary accounts, biographies, memoirs, popular histories, and modern-day films and pageants have all romanticized the "pastoral era" and engendered a stereotype built on the best features of life on the ranchos. This glowing picture has some basis in fact. These proud upper-class *californios* created what historian Douglas Monroy has called a "seigneurial" culture in which "a pattern of submission, hi-

RICHARD HENRY DANA, JR.
Success and Disappointment

Richard Henry Dana, Jr.
Courtesy of the Huntington Library.

Richard Henry Dana's *Two Years Before the Mast* is considered California's first great literary classic and offers an example of the writer who, in one great flash of genius, produces a monumental work that he never again equals. Barely into his twenties when he wrote the book, Dana's inspiration or compulsion to write must have been great. His first draft of the manuscript was lost on the Boston dock when he returned from California in 1836, yet he managed over the next three years to rewrite the whole book at night,

erarchy, and obligation" governed relations between the rancheros and their women, children, and Indian laborers. They controlled huge tracts of land with thousands of head of cattle, horses, and sheep; their adobe homes were often very large and well furnished; they were attended by great numbers of Indian servants and *vaqueros;* they dressed splendidly and were lavish in their hospitality with much music, singing, and dancing. Weddings and fiestas were regarded as opportunities to display an open-handed generosity that symbolized their social status. For them, perhaps, it *was* an idyllic time.

But until secularization and development of the rancho economy the great ranchos were few and far between. Society was dominated by a small elite consisting of the mission fathers, civil and military officials, and

RICHARD HENRY DANA, JR.
Success and Disappointment (continued)

from skimpy notes, after a full day's study as a law student. He produced what Lawrence Clark Powell has called "a prose of utmost precision, clarity, and beauty, prose that is in perfect register, so that there is no blur between it and the life it describes, prose of such transparency that we can look through it to life itself."

Dana's glowing descriptions of the *Pilgrim*'s first California landfall, of the coastal towns, and of the climate attracted widespread attention, especially among his fellow New Englanders, many of whom ultimately made the trek west. He disparaged the Californians as unable to produce anything for themselves, as dependent on Indian servants and labor, and as foolishly improvident, thus fostering attitudes that many of his readers carried west when they migrated.

Dana himself returned to California in 1859 on the first leg of a round-the-world trip that he described in his three-volume *Journal,* his only other published work. Although he visited the Mariposa mines of John C. Frémont, Yosemite Valley, his old southern California haunts, and the San Francisco Bay region where he had friends, and survived a fire at sea that destroyed the ship on which he had embarked for Hawaii, Dana's *Journal* revealed little of the inspiration of *Two Years Before the Mast.* The trip did serve to rekindle his love of the sea, however, and he wrote his wife that he was "made for the sea" and that his "life on shore is a mistake." He wished, he said, that they could have "had no profession and no home, and roamed over the world together, like two civilized and refined gypsies."

Years later Richard Henry Dana, Jr., a highly respected and successful lawyer, still looked back over the years with a sense of regret, writing "My life has been a failure compared to what I might and ought to have done. My great success—my book—was a boy's work, done before I came to the bar." Could he have but looked a hundred years and more into the future to see the enduring popularity of his "boy's work," his gratification might well have overcome his disappointment. (RBR)

only a handful of large landowners, most claiming direct Spanish descent. Wealth, family influence, land, and ethnicity all served to distinguish them from the vast majority of the non-Indian population—the mestizo *pobladores* (settlers), who were soldiers, ex-soldiers, colonists, and their families. Most of these settlers lived in the pueblos and presidio towns, where they owned lots on which they built small adobe homes and farmed adjacent public land. Others lived on small grants of land, where they carried on subsistence farming. Women had much of the responsibility for the farming and livestock operations of this family-based economy, and often worked as seamstresses and cooks as well. Some women also worked at the missions, supervising kitchens and manufacturing of clothing or teaching neophytes domestic tasks. The men often worked as

Andrés Pico
Pío Pico's brother, Andrés, dressed in the finery of the great ranchero. In the 1850s Andrés Pico served in the state legislature and authored the resolution, adopted in 1859, dividing the state at the Tehachapi Mountains. The U.S. Congress, immersed in the slavery controversy, did not act on the proposal. *Courtesy of the Western History Collection, Los Angeles County Museum of Natural History.*

vaqueros, saddlemakers, blacksmiths, and at other skilled pastoral trades. Families were small, with an average of three or four children, and all were expected to contribute to the needs of the family. With the exception of domestic chores, there was no division of labor on the basis of gender. For most Californians, it was a typically hard frontier life.

Secularization of the missions in the 1830s produced a significant change in this social structure, expanding the large landholding class, greatly weakening the church, and essentially stripping the missionaries of their influence. Indeed, by 1845 there were only six Catholic priests in Alta California. Thus, by the 1840s the ruling elite consisted of civil and military officials; an expanded class of great rancheros, some owning 200,000 acres of land or more; and a few leading merchants and other assimilated foreigners. Far below them in power and influence there also devoloped a significant class of mestizo rancheros—ex-soldiers, colonists, and others—who had received smaller grants of land for past services and who engaged in cattle ranching and subsistence farming on a significant but lesser scale. In the pueblos and presidio towns the *pobladores* still constituted sixty to eighty percent of the non-Indian population and an important source of seasonal labor. At all times the Indian was at the bottom of the social scale, performing almost all the manual labor on the ranchos and in the pueblos and acting as servants to the *gente de razón.*

The large ranchos were a natural outgrowth of the secularization of the missions and the government's desire to promote the hide-and-tallow trade. A few private land grants had been made in the Spanish period, some carved from mission lands for soldiers who married mission Indians. Most were sizable—such as the Rancho Simi, a tract of more than 100,000 acres granted to an uncle of Pío Pico, and the Rancho San Pedro, a 75,000-acre area granted to Juan José Domínguez. Still, by 1820 only twenty such grants had been made, and there were probably no more than fifty by 1830. But between 1834, when secularization began, and 1846, more than 700 private land grants were made covering more than 8 million acres of land—in itself a measure of the fundamental economic and social change connected with secularization. Under Mexican law, individual grants were limited in size to 11 square leagues, or nearly 50,000 acres, but since some rancheros owned more than one grant, there were some very large holdings.

The well-favored found it easy to obtain land. The applicant presented a petition to the governor, including a *diseño*, or map, of the desired land, then set about marking the boundaries of the grant, a decidedly casual process. Riders, each trailing a lasso of a certain length, rode quickly from one identifiable object to another making rough approximations of the distance between them. Key points might be a creek bed, large tree, skull, or large rock, any of which might disappear or change position with time. Some grants were "floating grants," a specific number of leagues that the grantee might locate anywhere within a large, vaguely defined area. Most rancheros were equally casual about complying with other grant requirements, such as occupying the lands, making improvements, and properly recording the grant, resulting in tragic loss for many of them when called on to prove title to their holdings after the gold rush.

A significant number of these ranchos were owned and operated by women. Some sixty grants, over 335,000 acres, were made to women, including the 4,449-acre Rancho Rodeo de las Aguas, of which María Rita Valdez de Villa was a joint grantee, and the 4,439-acre Rancho Purísima Concepción near San José, granted to Juana Briones de Miranda. Moreover, under Mexican law, married women retained ownership of any separate property possessed prior to marriage and were granted community property rights. Consequently, there were also large landholdings owned and operated by widows of California rancheros. Doña Vicente Sepúlveda, for example, managed Rancho Los Palos Verdes for thirty years after the death of her husband, while in Contra Costa María Manuela Valencia de Briones managed the Rancho Boca de la Cañada del Pinole, both over 13,000-acre ranchos.

Many rancheros moved onto their land and built large adobe homes, architectural forerunners of the California ranch-style house. One-story, tile-roofed structures, with long covered porches and often an inner courtyard, they were usually built on a hill with plenty of open space around as a precaution against raids by Indians from the Central Valley. Some were unusually large. The *casa* of Don Bernardo Yorba near Los Angeles, for example, reportedly consisted of thirty rooms plus another twenty-one for servants' quarters and workrooms. Well-to-do rancheros imported furniture and other fine articles from New England, while even the lesser rancheros managed to have such luxuries as embroidered bedspreads and pillowcases. Many of the larger landholders lived in town while their more isolated ranchos were operated by relatives or mestizo *mayordomos*. These rancheros constituted from ten to twenty percent of the non-Indian pueblo population and were frequently the chief local civil and military figures, as well as the social leaders of the province.

The ranchero was the unquestioned master of his estate. Fathers locked up unmarried daughters, arranged marriages, and often controlled the lives of children after marriage. Yet there was a reciprocal obligation to treat women and children with respect and consideration, and women were provided legal protections against abusive husbands. Children were instructed in religious values and proper conduct from an early age. Disobedience and disrespect for one's elders was regarded as a "grave offense." There was little formal education for young Californians, and most were illiterate or, at best, semiliterate; the sons of the rancheros, however, might be sent abroad

RANCHO SAN PEDRO
A CLASSIC SPANISH LAND GRANT

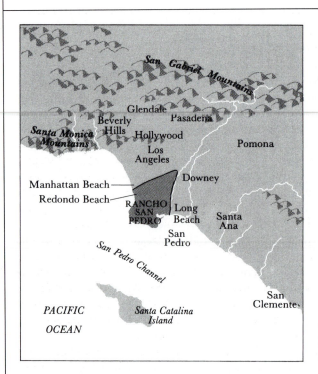

The original extent of the Rancho San Pedro, outlined on a current map of the Los Angeles region.

For many modern Californians, their state's Spanish-Mexican heritage evokes images of great land grants that became the ranchos of the pastoral era; and although the vast majority of such grants were made under Mexican rule, they are still thought of as "Spanish land grants" in the popular mind. Rancho San Pedro was one of the few genuinely Spanish land grants, the first in Alta California, and its history is closely integrated with the history of the Los Angeles region.

Juan José Domínguez, a foot soldier with Portolá's 1769 expedition who retired in 1782, was the original grantee of Rancho San Pedro. In 1784 Governor Pedro Fages, his former commander, approved Domínguez's petition for permission to use the grant for raising cattle. As was customary, the permission included no specific title to the land, and no survey or map of the grant was recorded. Domínguez and two friends, however, had marked out the tract, which roughly included the area bounded on the west and

RANCHO SAN PEDRO
A CLASSIC SPANISH LAND GRANT (continued)

south by the ocean, on the east by the Los Angeles River, and on the north by a line running from the present-day city of Compton to a point midway between Hermosa Beach and Redondo Beach. The line was described generally as "commencing at a large sycamore tree [on the] road leading from San Pedro to Los Angeles . . . thence running [westerly] to a stone placed near the high road," and so on, with the typical *un poco más o menos* (a little more or less) added to cover discrepancies in estimates of the amount of land involved—in this case, more than 75,000 acres.

As Domínguez grew older, he left the management of his grant to others, which led to the kinds of disputes common among all California rancheros. For example, Domínguez and an old friend, Manuel Nieto, who had obtained a neighboring grant, were constantly arguing over lands along their common boundary, the Los Angeles River, because it would change course as much as half a mile during winter flooding. Another conflict involved the Sepúlveda family, who—by virtue of permission granted them by Domínguez's executor to pasture cattle in the western portion of Rancho San Pedro—eventually carved more than 30,000 acres out of the Domínguez ranch to create Rancho Los Palos Verdes for themselves. Juan José's heirs, nephew Cristóbal and grand-nephew Manuel, spent years petitioning for regranting of the rancho and for confirmation of their title from the Mexican government. As with most large land grants, there were family squabbles over shares in the rancho and a long struggle for confirmation of title from the United States Land Commission after the Mexican War.

Meanwhile, during the Mexican War, the Battle of Domínguez Ranch, sometimes called the "Battle of the Old Woman's Gun," took place on the rancho in 1846, when the Californians, using a small cannon they had hidden in an old woman's yard, beat back an American force advancing on Los Angeles. In the 1850s part of the rancho was sold to Phineas Banning and some associates who began the development of San Pedro harbor. The first railroad in the area was built through Rancho San Pedro, and in the 1920s the Domínguez Hills oil field, one of the richest in California, was discovered on the rancho.

Surprisingly, the Domínguez family has held on to much of the rancho. When Manuel, who had been mayor of Los Angeles and a member of the 1849 constitutional convention, died in 1882, he left his wife and daughters more than 24,000 acres of the rancho still intact. Through judicious development the family has retained control of a substantial portion until modern times, a rare circumstance that makes Rancho San Pedro not only the oldest but one of the few grants to remain in one family's possession for such a long period of time. (RBR)

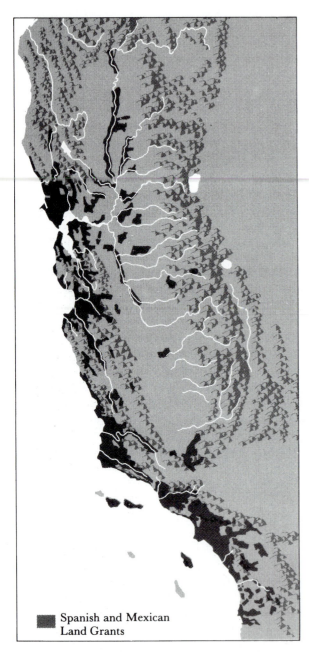

Spanish and Mexican
Land Grants

Spanish and Mexican Land Grants

for schooling. Girls of all classes were seldom provided such opportunities.

The work of the rancho focused on producing hides and tallow for export and food for its own personnel. During the annual rodeo, neighboring families rounded up cattle from the open range for identification and branding. The Californians, both men and women, were widely regarded as the best riders in the world. The rodeo, a major social event, was often accompanied by a gala celebration, with days of feasting, singing, and dancing. The men of the rancho usually conducted the great *matanzas*, or slaughters. Cattle were driven to areas convenient for the transport of hides and tallow to the trading ships along the coast. There they were slaughtered and skinned, and their hides stretched out to dry. Meat was dried, and tallow melted and placed in skin bags. The remaining carcasses were left for wild animals. Guadelupe Vallejo, in reminiscing about his days at Mission San José, noted that many a serenade was broken up by grizzly bears wandering through the streets on their way to and from the mission's *calavera*, or slaughter corral.

While cattle were the main product of the ranchos, sheep and horses were abundant; sheep provided wool for cloth and blankets. In addition, a few hogs were raised, mainly for lard, since both Californians and Indians regarded pork with disfavor. The missions and pueblos—and to a lesser extent, the ranchos—also produced substantial quantities of wheat, using primitive methods. Iron-tipped wooden plows broke the soil, which was sometimes smoothed out with tree branches prior to planting. The wheat was harvested by hand and often threshed by dumping the cut wheat into a hard-packed corral and running horses around and around over it. The wheat was then winnowed by tossing it in the wind until the chaff blew away. This process could take many weeks.

Ranch women shared the burden of administering a sometimes extensive organization, managed a large corps of household workers, and participated in cattle drives and rodeos. Their daughters usually married in their teens and spent much of their young lives bearing children, many of whom died within six months. Still, among the ranchero class, large families were not uncommon. Maria Teresa de la Guerra, daughter of José de la Guerra y Noriega, married William E. P. Hartnell and presented him with eighteen children. Don José himself was survived by more than a hundred descendants. Preparing food was also a major responsibility, and while all celebrations were accompanied by great feasts, Californians, as one writer noted, ate well at all times:

> A family breakfast would include eggs or *frijoles* (beans) . . . coffee with rich cream, or chocolate, or tea, honey and *tortillas*. Dinner came at noon and was a solid meal of beefsteak and boiled beef, stewed chickens or hash made of *carne seca* (dried beef) mixed with scrambled eggs, onions, tomatoes well seasoned and sprinkled with red chili pepper, beans prepared with plenty of gravy, *tortillas*, and *vino del país*. . . . Supper was slightly less solid . . . consisting of soup, roast duck perhaps, or *guisado de carne* richly flavored, sweet potatoes, *frijoles*, and lettuce salad.

Male or female, young or old, the rancheros loved entertainment. Weddings, baptisms, feast days, rodeos, and visitors provided occasions for celebrations that sometimes lasted for days. Dancing, a special enjoyment, included the lively *jaramba* and the sedate *contradanza*. The more formal affairs on the ranchos were called *bailles*, while the less formal events were known as *fandangos*.

This elaborate way of life depended on an abundant supply of cheap Indian labor; large numbers of ex-neophytes performed most household duties. Mariano Vallejo's wife, Benicia, described her household staff as follows:

> Each of my children, boy or girl, has a servant who has no other duty but to care for him or her. I have two servants for myself. Four or five grind the corn for the tortillas, for here we entertain so many guests that three grinders are not enough. Six or seven serve in the kitchen. Five or six are constantly busy washing the clothes of the children and servants, and nearly a dozen are required to attend to the sewing and spinning.

Ex-neophytes and gentile Indians performed the ranch work, while competent ex-neophytes sometimes acted as *mayordomos*, supervising the work of the Indian labor force. Only a few were paid even a subsistence wage, while most worked simply for food and shelter. Nevertheless, their importance cannot be ignored. Almost all foreign observers were quick to note the dependence of the rancho economy and way of life on the Indians. The seeming indolence of the Californians, and their avoidance of all manual labor, merely reflected that dependence. On the other hand many Indians, their culture and economy destroyed by European contact, were dependent on the ranchos for food and shelter. This mutual dependence was fundamental to the rancho economy and social system.

The expansion of trade after 1822 contributed to the growth of towns where hides and tallow were exchanged. Los Angeles and Monterey, surrounded by the most productive ranchos, became the respective centers of influence in the south and north, while San José developed as a prosperous pueblo in the San Francisco Bay region. (Yerba Buena, forerunner of the city of San Fran-

Doña Marcelina's Grapevine
This Edward Vischer drawing shows rancho life near Santa Barbara, with guitar players, strolling señoritas, and Indian servants—a way of life that lasted well into the 1870s. Ironically, southern California boosters chopped down this grapevine and sent the pieces east to advertise California's fertile soil. *Courtesy of the Huntington Library, San Marino, California.*

cisco, was not founded until 1835.) Santa Barbara, while relatively isolated, exported many hides.

The constitution of 1824 accorded each town, or pueblo, a representative *ayuntamiento*, or council, but the key figure remained the *alcalde*, who was not only the chief executive officer but also the chief judicial figure for the community. Most disputes were settled by the *alcalde* through a conciliatory process, although he referred more serious matters to the governor. The lack of a court system proved difficult for Americans to adjust to, but the *alcalde* was a respected figure and regarded as a true city father.

Town life, particularly in Los Angeles and Monterey, was rather more complicated than life on the remote ranchos. Here military and civil officials, and a growing population of merchants and prominent foreigners, shared power and status with those rancheros who maintained town houses. They dressed more fashionably and their social activities were more elaborate, although they displayed the same generosity and hospitality that characterized the country people.

In the pueblos and mission towns the non-Indian population lived in small adobe buildings that usually had thatched roofs and earth floors, and, in many respects, they tried to emulate the life of the upper classes, although family size was generally smaller, averaging three to four children per family. They ate simple but plentiful food and enjoyed feasting, singing, and dancing. Bull and grizzly-bear fights, cockfighting, and horse racing were common entertainments in the pueblos. With secularization, substantial numbers of Indians took up residence in squalid quarters, and pueblo life changed markedly. At one time, conditions in the Indian section of Los Angeles became so bad that the townspeople forced its removal across the river.

In spite of the stratified social structure of Mexican California there is a certain element of truth in the depiction of the *gente de razón*, the small non-Indian population, as "one big happy guitar-twanging family." Religious ties, especially godparent relationships between members of different classes, a common culture, common social activities, and the nature of rancho life, all made for personal loyalties binding groups together. In this sense, California society attained a remarkable cohesion that transcended class status in many ways.

Mexican California thus remained, as in the Spanish period, much like an overseas colonial possession—isolated and neglected. Left to their own resources and absorbing much of the revolutionary ideology of the day, Californians made drastic changes in their own religious and economic institutions, producing the great rancho society and cattle economy with all its romantic elements. Still, it remained very much a frontier society, and one that was soon to be challenged.

CHAPTER NINE

FOREIGN PENETRATION OF CALIFORNIA

No feature of the Mexican period in California had more far-reaching consequences than foreign penetration of the province. Prior to Mexican independence, Spain's colonial policies kept California essentially closed to foreign settlement, although contact with British, American, and Russian fur traders and whalers heightened interest in the area and, after 1810, encouraged a clandestine trade during the war for Mexican independence. A good deal was learned about California during these years, especially that it was an attractive land—and almost defenseless. Foreign observers were quick to see that Spain, and later Mexico, did not have a firm hold on the province. With independence, the bar to immigration was withdrawn and hide-and-tallow traders, especially Britishers and Americans, made their way to California. These early immigrants were welcomed, became assimilated, and made important contributions to the region's economic development. But the nature of foreign immigration changed when the American frontier movement reached California in 1841. Mexican authorities regarded these pioneer settlers as a threat, but were never strong enough to stop their migration.

THE RUSSIANS IN CALIFORNIA

The establishment of the Russian colony at Fort Ross, not far from San Francisco, in 1812 was an early sign of Spain's weakness. In 1806 Count Nikolai Rezanov visited San Francisco seeking supplies for the starving and scurvy-ridden outpost of the Russian-American Fur Company at Sitka, Alaska. Trade with foreigners was illegal, but his betrothal to Concepción Argüello, the daughter of San Francisco's *comandante,* helped him to secure the provisions he sought. Unhappily, Rezanov died on the return trip to Russia and the young Concepción faithfully waited years for his return before learning of his death, their love affair providing raw material for romantic California literature. Rezanov's visit, however, did lead to the establishment of a Russian settlement north of San Francisco as a base for shipping food to the Alaskan fur-trading posts and for hunting sea otter and seals along the California coast. In 1810 Ivan Kuskov scouted the Bodega Bay area and returned two years later to establish Fort Ross, a picturesque wooden structure on a bluff near the sea. Using Bodega Bay as their port, the Russians ultimately extended their influence several miles inland and employed several hundred Aleut hunters along the coast and in San Francisco Bay and more than 200 Indian farm workers. Ignoring Spanish orders to leave, Kuskov established trade with the Californians, supplying them with manufactured implements, utensils, furniture, and boats in return for foodstuffs.

But several factors prevented the Russian foothold in California from prospering. The climate of Fort Ross was unsuited to raising wheat and the colony could never meet the needs of the Alaskan trading posts. In addition, any attempt to expand inland was blocked by Mexican development of the region east of Fort Ross, and decline of the sea otter population made the fur trade unprofitable. Finally, Mexico's opening of California to foreign trade reduced the need for the establishment. Consequently, Fort Ross was definitely a losing proposition by 1839. When the Russian-American Fur Company made an agreement with the Hudson's Bay Company to provision the Alaskan posts

from Oregon, the way became cleared to get rid of Fort Ross. Also, by then the Russians believed that California would ultimately be absorbed by the United States. In 1841, they sold out to John A. Sutter.

A few other foreigners made their way to California before 1820, but their arrival was usually more accidental than not. In 1814, for example, John Gilroy, a Scottish sailor on an English ship, was left in Monterey because of illness. Later baptized and naturalized, he married a daughter of Ignacio Ortega and became a ranchero; the present-day town of Gilroy bears his name. In all, probably no more than twenty foreigners took up permanent residence in California in the Spanish period, and they were soon absorbed by the local population.

THE HIDE-AND-TALLOW TRADERS

Mexico's opening of the ports of San Diego and Monterey to trade also opened the door to substantial additional foreign settlement. Beginning with Hartnell and Gale in 1822, the hide-and-tallow trade brought fifteen to twenty new foreign settlers each year. Some, like Gilroy, became residents by force of circumstance, leaving no memorable record, but many others were essential to the suc-

Fort Ross, circa 1830
Cut off from expansion inland by Mexican development of the Sonoma region, the Russians sold the fort to John Sutter in 1841. *Courtesy of the California State Library.*

cessful development of California's commerce, especially since Californians lacked both the experience and the inclination to manage commercial affairs. With few exceptions, hide-and-tallow traders were assimilated into the local elite. They became Catholics and naturalized citizens, arranged marriages with ranchero families that gave them access to land, Hispanicized their names, and adopted California ways and dress.

William E. P. Hartnell was typical of the resident business agent. He came to California after two years with John Begg & Co. in Peru, converted to Catholicism, married Maria Teresa de la Guerra, and acquired Rancho Patrocinio del Alisal, twenty miles inland from Monterey. Naturalized in 1830, he held numerous civil posts. His most important assignment, as *visitador de misiones* of the secularized missions, proved to be a hopeless effort to stem the tide of plunder following secularization. A cultivated man who spoke French, German, and Spanish fluently, Hartnell became one of the most respected foreign residents of Mexican California. Many others followed Hartnell's example—among them William G. Dana, Henry Delano Fitch, and John R. Cooper (all Yankee sea captains of the trade), Alfred Robinson, and William Heath Davis, Jr., all of whom contributed to stronger economic ties with the United States.

Abel Stearns, another New Englander turned Californian, was naturalized in Mexico, entered California in 1829, and went into business selling hides and spirits in Los Angeles. Not a handsome man, he was known as *Cara de Caballo*, or "Horseface," but this did not prevent him from winning the hand of a southern California beauty, Doña Arcadia Bandini. Stearns's business flourished, he acquired huge landholdings, and he became the wealthiest man in southern California, also holding a number of important local offices. He was almost unique in being childless.

Like Stearns, Hugo Reid, a Scotsman, came to California in the early 1830s from Mexico and became prominent in southern California affairs. Reid wed an Indian neophyte, Victoria, who received a sizable land grant from Mission San Gabriel upon her marriage, and Reid obtained Rancho Santa Anita for himself. He devoted his attention to Indian customs and wrote some of the earliest criticism of the mission system, based largely on Doña Victoria's recollections of her childhood at the mission.

Thomas Oliver Larkin was a singular exception to the pattern of assimilation of the hide-and-tallow trade immigrants in that he did not become naturalized. He came to California in 1832 and in the following year married Rachel Hobson Holmes, whom he had met on board ship. (She thus became the first American woman to reside in California.) Settling in Monterey, Larkin opened a store and proceeded to make himself perhaps the most successful merchant in the province. A canny businessman, he established close relations with Mexican officials, frequently lending money to the hard-pressed government. Yet he did not particularly sympathize with Mexican rule and in later years worked for American acquisition of California. Larkin did not become a ranchero, although he dealt in real estate, but he built a fine house in Monterey, pioneering the "Monterey" style of architecture. So successful were his dealings in merchandise, lumber, and real estate that his sight drafts on funds he had on deposit in the United States circulated like bank notes in currency-starved California. Although remaining an American citizen, Larkin became a respected and influential figure in California affairs. In 1843 President James K. Polk appointed him U.S. consul in Monterey, and later confidential agent. Larkin's lengthy dispatches and observations are an important resource for the history of the period.

Like Hartnell, Stearns, and Larkin, most foreigners connected with the hide-and-tallow trade performed a valuable function in the cattle economy. They were, in fact, encouraged to become permanent residents through such devices as the Mexican colonization laws of 1824 and 1828, which made naturalized citizens eligible for land grants. Welcome additions to the ranks of the *californios*, many occupied prestigious positions in the province.

THE MOUNTAIN MEN

The arrival of the mountain men was viewed in a decidedly different light. Seemingly safe from American expansionism behind the wall of the Sierra Nevada and the deserts of the Southwest, Californians were justifiably alarmed when Jedediah Smith broke through these barriers and appeared with a large group of men at Mission San Gabriel in 1826. Smith's feat was the direct result of the development by William H. Ashley, one of the great fur-industry entrepreneurs, of the rendezvous, whereby beaver trappers exchanged pelts for merchandise at an annual meeting in the Rocky Mountains. This extended their range some 1,500 miles and brought Smith to California.

Jedediah Smith was a literate, observant young man, in addition to possessing the heroic qualities so often associated with his kind. His own story of his 1826 expedition lay forgotten in the attic of descendants of General Ashley until its discovery in 1967. It was published in 1977 as *The Southwest Expedition of Jedediah S. Smith: His Personal Account of the Journey to California, 1826–1827*, and it is a fascinating story of the opening of California to the American frontier movement. In partnership with William L. Sublette and

David E. Jackson, Smith took over Ashley's Rocky Mountain Fur Company in 1826 and decided to lead an expedition through the Great Basin (probably the least-known part of North America at the time) to the Southwest to open new beaver country. Leaving the rendezvous, Smith and seventeen men traveled south to the Great Salt Lake and then southwest to the Colorado River. At the Mojave villages, near the present-day town of Needles, Smith decided to push west into California, making his way through the Mojave Desert to an outlying rancho of Mission San Gabriel in November 1826, guided by two neophytes who had fled from the mission. He announced his arrival in a note to Father José Bernardo Sanchez requesting his permission to replenish his supplies. Smith received a reply in Latin, prompting him to observe that "as I could not read his Latin nor he my english [sic] it seemed we were not likely to become general correspondents."

Nevertheless, the amiable Father Sanchez welcomed Smith's party, providing them with comfortable quarters and good food while Smith traveled to San Diego, seeking permission to trade and hunt beaver. Aware that Smith's presence was a dangerous sign, Governor Echeandía received him with great suspicion and detained him for six weeks. Eventually, the governor released him, with instructions to leave California the way he had come. Smith departed from San Gabriel in January 1827, retracing his path until he passed through the San Gabriel Mountains at Cajon Pass. There he asserted that he had fulfilled the governor's instructions and turned north, crossing the Tehachapi Mountains through the old Tejon Pass, picking up runaway mission Indians as guides. After trapping in the San Joaquin Valley until April, Smith left his party on the Stanislaus River and, taking two men, crossed the Sierra Nevada mountains at what is now

Ebbets Pass. They were the first white men to make the passage. After a harrowing trek across the parched Great Basin, Smith reached the 1827 rendezvous at Bear Lake, in northern Utah.

Mindful of the men he had left at the Stanislaus River, Smith was off again within ten days. Following his route of the previous year, Smith, with eighteen men and two Indian women, traveled uneventfully until he reached the Mojave villages. There, the Mojave, peaceful the year before, attacked as Smith's company crossed the river, killing the women and ten men and wounding several others. The survivors limped into San Gabriel, where Smith obtained horses and supplies and hurried north to join the company he had left at the Stanislaus River the year before. In need of supplies, Smith rode into Mission San José for assistance, but Father Durán seized him and packed him off to Governor Echeandía, then on one of his infrequent visits to Monterey. Echeandía clapped him in jail, but soon released him on the condition that Smith and his trappers leave California. After making the first recorded journey by land up the coast of California into Oregon, Smith reached the Umpqua River in mid-July, when Indians killed all but Smith and two other members of the party. The three survivors fled to the Hudson's Bay Company post at Fort Vancouver. Reequipped, Smith returned to the Rockies. Three years later, in May 1831, he was killed by Comanche on the Santa Fe Trail.

Jedediah Smith was in California for only two brief periods, yet he had a major impact on the state's history. It was he who first opened California to the east, bringing it within reach of the American frontier movement. He was the first to cross the Sierra Nevada and to travel between the Sierra and Great Salt Lake, and he opened a trail between California and Oregon that was soon improved and traveled by Hudson's Bay

Company trappers. A pious, thoughtful young man, his descriptions of the terrain he covered and the people he saw are a unique contribution to the history of western America.

Other mountain men soon followed Smith into California. In 1827, James Ohio Pattie and his father, Sylvester, joined a party heading down the Gila River to the Colorado. Here, the Yuma Indians ran off their horses and, after an unsuccessful attempt to float down the river to the Gulf of California, the expedition forged west across the desert somewhat south of the trail blazed by Anza fifty years before. Emerging in Baja California, south of San Diego, they were turned over to Governor Echeandía by missionaries. The governor's worst fears, raised by the appearance of Jedediah Smith, were now being realized, and he had the Patties imprisoned. The *calabozo* (jail) was too much for Sylvester Pattie, who sickened and died. James Ohio Pattie later claimed that his own release was due to the fact that he had brought with him a supply of smallpox vaccine; when an epidemic thought to be smallpox broke out, he was freed on the condition that he vaccinate Californians. Pattie wrote of his experiences in a book, *The Personal Narratives of James Ohio Pattie*, published in 1831, in which fact and fiction became a bit confused. It was an important work, however, in publicizing California among its American readers.

A less colorful, but nevertheless important, figure in the list of mountain men who broke down California's isolation from the east was Ewing Young. Like the Patties, Young worked out of Santa Fe and helped develop the overland trail to California called the Old Spanish Trail. In the 1830s he brought large trapping parties into California, ranging all the way north to Oregon and the Klamath Lake region. Several of the men in Young's expeditions elected to stay in California under the liberalized Mexican colonization laws of 1828, which encouraged for-

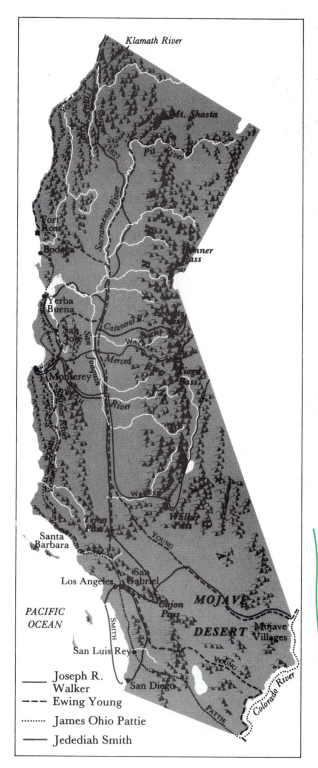

Joseph R. Walker
Ewing Young
James Ohio Pattie
Jedediah Smith

eign settlement. Among them was Isaac Williams, whose Rancho Santa Ana del Chino gave him, by the end of the Mexican period, an income of $30,000 per year. Jonathan Trumbull Warner and William Wolfskill also became prominent figures, while others took up occupations in the pueblos. A few became part of an unassimilated and unpredictable floating population of foreigners who were contemptuous of Mexican authority and often appeared in the ranks of opposing forces in the frequent political turnovers. In 1840 Governor Alvarado sent Isaac Graham, a notorious member of this group, and several dozen of his cohorts to Mexico in chains, an indication of the seriousness of the problem they presented.

The opening of the central route over the Sierra was pioneered by Joseph Reddeford Walker in 1833. Leading a large force of trappers, he crossed the Great Basin to the Humboldt River, proceeded across the desert, and came to the lake and river east of the Sierra that now bear his name. Following the river, his group made the first east-to-west crossing of the Sierra and were probably the first whites to see the grandeur of Yosemite Valley and the region's giant sequoias. Walker left the West having led the first organized party along what would become a main route to California for thousands of migrants.

The importance of the mountain men to California history can scarcely be exaggerated. They blazed the trails that opened the region to the east, they publicized it on the American frontier, and they led the first pioneer settlers over the Sierra passes and the Old Spanish Trail. More than any others they brought the American frontier movement, with all its potential for disruption of the romantic rancho era, to the "land of promise" in the Far West.

Routes of the Mountain Men

MAVERICKS

Two nonconformists who came to California in the 1830s, "Dr." John Marsh and John A. Sutter, made important contributions to the penetration of the province by the American frontier movement. Marsh came from Santa Fe in 1836, escaping an unhappy life and, some say, the law. A graduate of Harvard University, he convinced local residents that his bachelor of arts degree was a certificate to practice medicine, and began a career as a doctor in Los Angeles, accepting hides in payment of his fees. In 1837 he purchased a large rancho on the eastern slope of Mount Diablo, across the bay from San Francisco, where he lived a reclusive life. His importance, however, was as a publicist. Convinced that California could be another Texas, the articulate Marsh wrote dozens of letters extolling its virtues to acquaintances in the East. Widely published in the Midwest, his letters stimulated a significant movement of frontier settlers to California.

John Sutter, originally Johann Augustus Sutter, was a Swiss emigré who, in 1834, left bad debts, an unhappy wife, and several children behind to seek his fortune in America. After spending some time in the fur trade in the Rocky Mountains and St. Louis, he came to California by way of Hawaii, Alaska, and eventually Oregon. Upon arrival he wangled a huge grant of land in the unoccupied Sacramento Valley, as well as extensive civil authority from Governor Alvarado, who appointed him local military commander and judge "to represent . . . all the laws of the country in the area." Selecting a site at the junction of the Sacramento and American rivers, Sutter in time developed a little barony that he called New Helvetia. In 1841 he bought out the Russians at Fort Ross for a trifling down payment and a large promise to pay. With the cannon from Fort Ross, Sutter erected his own fort, which not only was a major defensive bulwark against Indian raids, but also made him largely independent of Mexican control. He established a

Sutter's Fort
Sutter's fort dominated the interior of northern California in the 1840s. Sutter encouraged and protected American frontier settler migration from 1841 to 1846. Ironically, when John C. Frémont placed one of his men in charge of the fort at the time of the Bear Flag Revolt, Sutter became a virtual prisoner in his own house. *Courtesy of the Bancroft Library.*

large cattle and sheep business, planted a sizable wheat crop, built a grist mill and a distillery, and employed large numbers of Hawaiians, Indians, and Californians. Indeed, one of his clerks noted that Sutter seemed to feel obligated to give employment to anyone who sought it.

Sutter's importance to the development of California, however, is not merely the result of his colorful character and his independent feudal domain. New Helvetia lay at the terminus of the main westward trails. Sutter encouraged American migration along these trails and frequently sent supplies east over the Sierra to emigrant parties in trouble, receiving them with warm hospitality when they arrived. He gave them work, sold them land, leased them Indian laborers, gave them passports, and otherwise promoted the advance of the American frontier.

FRONTIER SETTLERS

By 1840 California had a permanent foreign resident population of perhaps 380, almost all of them men who came with the hide-and-tallow trade or in search of beaver. For the most part, they had been accepted and assimilated by the local society, but the growing number of former mountain men such as Isaac Graham and his friends created some anxiety among officials. Then, in 1841, a portentous change occurred as the first elements of the American frontier movement began to make their way over the Sierra.

The appearance of land-hungry American farm families stemmed from the activities of the mountain men, the repeated and glowing reports of California's attractions, the pressures of the depression years of the 1830s, and British-American rivalry in the Northwest. The United States' claim to Oregon in particular attracted the attention of frontier settlers, and in the 1840s migration along the Oregon Trail increased rapidly. Until 1849 the number of pioneers moving

to Oregon was eight to ten times the number coming to California, but the movement along the Oregon Trail stimulated interest in California as well.

The first organized company of frontier settlers to leave Missouri for California was the Bidwell-Bartleson party of 1841. In 1840, letters from John Marsh and speeches by trapper Antoine Robidoux excited enough interest to lead to the formation of the Western Emigration Society, in which some 500 people pledged to assemble the next spring at Sapling Grove, on the Missouri River, and go to California. Over the winter, however, reports that Isaac Graham and his cronies had been rounded up and sent to prison in Mexico dampened this enthusiasm. In the spring of 1841, only one of the original members of the society, former teacher John Bidwell, appeared at the designated meeting place. Sixty-eight new members eventually joined him and then elected John Bartleson as captain of the company. It was a poor choice since Bartleson was unqualified and even abandoned the party temporarily at one point; when he returned, he found that Bidwell had assumed effective leadership.

Despite warnings against overland travel to California that Mexican authorities published in midwestern newspapers, Bidwell's pioneers left Sapling Grove on May 19, 1841, in company with some Oregon-bound settlers and missionaries, under the guidance of Thomas "Broken Hand" Fitzpatrick, one of the best mountain men. The journey along the Platte River, through South Pass and on to Bear Valley and Soda Springs in northern Utah, was untroubled. At Soda Springs, the turning point for California, half of Bidwell's group decided to go on to Oregon, and some others turned back to Missouri. The remaining thirty-two headed for California—including Nancy Kelsey and her infant daughter, Rebecca, the first white women to travel west to California by wagon. Inexperienced and ignorant of what lay before them, they managed to make their way to the Humboldt River, having abandoned their wagons and heavy possessions along the way. From the Humboldt Sink they struggled across the Nevada desert, eventually reaching the Walker River, and made the difficult passage across the Sierra at Sonora Pass in late October, fortunate that the snows were late that year. Upon reaching the San Joaquin Valley, the party made its way to Marsh's rancho at the base of Mount Diablo, their food supplies exhausted. Marsh sold them meat and flour at what they considered exorbitant prices and, also for a stiff fee, obtained passports for them from reluctant Mexican authorities. When the party subsequently dispersed, several went to work for Sutter, whose generous treatment of them contrasted sharply with Marsh's. Bidwell later acquired the Rancho Chico north of Sacramento and eventually became one of the state's most prominent men.

Not long after the Bidwell party arrived, another group arrived from Santa Fe under the leadership of William Workman and John Rowland. Some twenty-five Americans, in company with New Mexican traders, followed the Old Spanish Trail to southern California, where they had little difficulty in obtaining permission to settle. Workman and Rowland, along with another member of the group, Benjamin D. Wilson, became prominent rancheros in the Los Angeles area. Wilson, known as Don Benito, married Ramona Yorba (whose father owned the Rancho Santa Ana) founded the town of Alhambra, and was the second mayor of the city of Los Angeles. The nearby Mount Wilson is named for him. That same year the first small group of what became a substantial movement of pioneers from Oregon made their way down from the north. The ease with which the migrants of 1841 obtained permission to settle illustrates the breakdown of Mexican authority in the province. After the Texas revolution of 1836, Mexico looked with disfavor on American migration to its territories, yet the ability and willingness of local officials to grant passports (often for profit) undermined government policy.

No organized groups of migrants arrived in 1842, but the movement resumed in 1843, when Lansford W. Hastings arrived with part of a group of settlers he had taken to Oregon the year before. In the same year, Joseph B. Chiles, who had come with Bidwell and returned east in 1842, recruited a party of about fifty that he took along the Oregon Trail to Fort Hall. From there, Chiles and some ten men proceeded to California via the Pit River, while the remaining settlers, led by the veteran Joseph Reddeford Walker, came south by way of the Owens Valley and Walker Pass. The year 1844 saw the first wagons roll across the Sierra and what was to be the main route to California open when the Stevens-Murphy party crossed the mountains over what is now called Donner Pass.

To this point the migration, while unwelcome, had remained small. In 1845, however, its nature changed as more than 250 Americans poured over the Sierra. Among them were half a dozen large groups such as the Grigsby-Ide party of 50 men and their families. Moreover, they brought with them reports that thousands more planned to make the trek the next year, and, in fact, some 1,500 did.

The pioneers of 1846 arrived to find California in American hands. The most famous overland group, the Donner party, was one of these. A large company of some eighty-seven men, women, and children, the Donner party suffered from inexperience, lack of leadership, dissension, and delay. Their first mistake was attempting the so-called Hastings Cut-Off, leaving the Oregon Trail to travel south of the Great Salt Lake, which proved to be a difficult and time-consuming journey. With delays occasioned by disagreements and dawdling, the party arrived too late in the year at the Truckee River, nearly 6,000 feet high in the Sierras. There they were trapped by heavy snowfall. Demoralized, short of supplies, and without effective leadership, they failed to make the crossing and remained snowbound on Alder Creek and Donner Lake, where thirty-nine died and some of the starving members were reduced to cannibalism. Relief parties organized at San Francisco and Sutter's Fort finally managed to bring forty-eight survivors over the mountains; their story became a source of morbid fascination for future generations.

Mexican authorities were alarmed by the sudden increase in American immigrants in 1845. Propagandists such as Marsh and Lansford Hastings, who published his fanciful *Emigrant's Guide* in 1844, were boldly promoting settlement in California, and the new immigrants were not so easily absorbed into California society as earlier ones. The farm families who settled in the interior were reluctant to become Mexican citizens or Catholics. Yet they bought or rented land, received questionable grants of land, or simply squatted on it, constituting a growing threat to Mexican control of the interior. Essentially, they were beginning to do what Spain and Mexico had never been able to do—colonize California effectively—and local authorities seemed unable to stop them.

THE BREAKDOWN OF MEXICAN GOVERNMENT

Increasing evidence of Mexico's inability to control affairs in California foreshadowed the end of the Mexican period. Governor Alvarado's administration had been characterized by rapid development of the rancho economy and the hide-and-tallow trade as the mission system was dismantled, and by relative political stability. Sectional rivalry over the location of the capital and customs house continued, but for the most part Alvarado successfully avoided conflict over these issues. He did, however, fall into disagreement with General Vallejo, his uncle (though only two years his senior), over the military capabilities of the government. Vallejo, who as military *comandante* despaired of disciplining "an army of unpaid relatives and friends," bombarded Mexico City with reports urging the strengthening of defenses and calling for a reunited political and military authority, a plan that Alvarado opposed.

Late in 1842 Mexico responded to Vallejo's entreaties by appointing General Manuel Micheltorena as governor and *comandante general*, replacing Alvarado and Vallejo. An attractive and gracious man, Micheltorena arrived with a force of 300 men to bolster the defenses of the province. Unfortunately, this army consisted mostly of ex-convicts and, as usual, the governor could not pay them. Consequently, they took to foraging, which outraged the local population. Although Micheltorena attempted with some success to administer California, he could never overcome the rampages of his convict army or the fact that he was an outsider. In November 1844, another "revolution" broke out, engineered as in 1836 by Alvarado and José Castro with support from southern Californians led by Pío Pico. Both sides had foreign contingents in their forces. Micheltorena was supported by Sutter and a motley group under Isaac Graham, who still smarted from his treatment by Alvarado in 1840. Castro, Pico, and Alvarado were joined by foreigners in the south, including Stearns, Workman, and Rowland. The armies confronted each other at Cahuenga Pass in February 1845 in an artillery duel that killed a horse and wounded a mule. When the foreigners on both sides held a meeting and agreed to refrain from combat, Micheltorena's support vanished, and he agreed to leave California with his soldiers. He was replaced by another regime that returned to the principle of separation of civil and military authority. Pío Pico, as senior member of the *diputación*, became interim governor, while José Castro assumed the position of *comandante general*, an arrangement that, as the Bear Flag Revolt revealed, merely heightened sectional rivalry and weakened authority.

Probably no issue was more important, or better demonstrated the weakness of government in California, than the Indian problem. All through the Mexican period, the Indians of the interior, who had developed a taste for horse meat, periodically drove off large numbers of horses from the mission and rancho herds, as well as cattle that they slaughtered for hides. In the south they were also frequently in league with unscrupulous horse traders from New Mexico. During the 1830s the Indian raids were so serious in the San Diego district that most of the ranchos there were abandoned at one time or another, and the population of the area declined by almost 50 percent. Efforts to control the Indians were never really successful. In the north, Vallejo spent years chasing Indians as far as the Tuolumne and Stanislaus rivers after raids on local missions and ranchos, and Sutter's records recount many punitive expeditions after Indians had stolen horses and burned his fields.

The political turmoil and military weakness did not go unnoticed by foreigners. In April 1846, Thomas Larkin wrote his unofficial vice-consul in San Francisco, William Leidesdorff, that "the pear is near ripe for the falling." Not many expected it to fall into any but American hands.

AMERICAN INTEREST

Since the 1820s the United States had looked westward with an acquisitive eye and acted to protect its western territorial interests. The Monroe Doctrine of 1823 was in part an effort to maintain these interests against Russian encroachment, and led in 1824 to an agreement in which Russia relinquished its claims south of 54° 40' north latitude, while the United States abandoned its claims north of that line. At the same time, American fur companies such as those of William Ashley and Jedediah Smith competed with the British Hudson's Bay Company for furs and national hegemony in the Pacific Northwest. In the process they opened the Northwest, particularly Oregon, to the American frontier movement.

In the 1830s a number of developments sharpened American interest in California. Texas, for one, was very much on the minds of Americans and Mexicans. After the revolution of 1836, Texas remained independent for almost ten years, but annexation by the United States was continually under consideration. The issue muddied political waters in Mexico and the United States for many years and fueled the American expansionist impulse.

In the 1830s the American government began to focus its attention more directly on California. In 1835 Andrew Jackson offered Mexico half a million dollars for San Francisco Bay and the territory north of it without success. He also tried to use Texas's revolt against Mexico as an opportunity to negotiate for the area from San Francisco north, but again failed. Interest in the region remained high, however, and the United States began to send military exploration parties to wander, sometimes uninvited, in and out of Mexican territory, specifically California. A naval expedition led by Lieutenant Charles Wilkes spent the years 1838 to 1842 on the West Coast, charting the waters and observing conditions there. While ostensibly devoted to surveys in the interest of the whaling industry, Wilkes's expedition included a

The Pueblo of Monterey, 1842
This lithograph portrays California's capital, Monterey, at the time of the arrival of the U.S. Squadron of the Pacific under Commodore Thomas ap Catesby Jones. Decades after its founding, Monterey, now under Mexican authority, still bore the marks of the rude frontier life in Hispanic California. The harbor lacks wharf facilities, and the pueblo's houses are scattered and virtually devoid of ornamental greenery. Walls confine household livestock—and guard against the ever-present danger of Indian attack. *Courtesy of the Bancroft Library.*

sizable party that went overland from Oregon to San Francisco through the Sacramento Valley. At the same time, a great deal of concern was expressed over the Isaac Graham affair, and American naval forces in the area were strengthened.

A good deal of this activity was a reaction to the interest of other countries in the "ripening pear" on the Pacific. In 1839, Alexander Forbes, British vice-consul in Tepic, Mexico, published his *History of California*, the first English-language book on the territory, in which he proposed that Mexico's British creditors cancel Mexican bonds and take over California in return. Sir George Simpson of the Hudson's Bay Company seemed to endorse this plan when he visited San Francisco in 1841. Many other such plans were voiced freely by British representatives in the West—to the consternation of Americans such as Larkin who worked to

prevent such schemes, whether British, French, or Russian. Actually, the British government never took the suggestions of its western agents seriously, and British policy did not include any suggestion of seeking control of California aggressively. Still, Anglo-American rivalry in Oregon and the Americans' traditional Anglophobia contributed to the persistent belief that the British were maneuvering to do so.

Interest continued, therefore, in negotiating with Mexico for the cession of California, or part of it, to the United States. In fact, Daniel Webster, secretary of state under President John Tyler, worked out a complicated deal in 1842 by which the United States would pay Mexican debts to British and American creditors in return for Texas and part of California and Oregon as far north as the Columbia River. This tripartite arrangement was opposed by American expansionists who objected to giving up the territory north of the Columbia. When Commodore Thomas ap Catesby Jones seized the port of Monterey in October 1842, in the mistaken belief that war had broken out, the plan collapsed. Jones learned he was in error within hours and retired with apologies, but his action was a clear signal of American intentions.

The election of James K. Polk as president in 1844 made it even more obvious that the spirit of Manifest Destiny was reaching a climax in the United States. Polk, a protégé of Andrew Jackson, shared his predecessor's distrust of British intentions and had campaigned for the presidency on a platform of aggressive expansionism and resistance to British imperialism in America. This meant primarily the annexation of Texas and occupation of the disputed Oregon territory, but Polk, supported by a growing clamor in the American press, made it clear that he also intended to acquire California. Like presidents before him, Polk attempted to acquire the region by purchase, sending John Slidell to Mexico with an offer of up to $40 million for Upper California and New Mexico. At the same time he took another tack, probably well aware that Slidell's mission had no real chance of success. In 1845 he appointed Consul Larkin a "confidential agent" with instructions to try to persuade Californians to declare their independence from Mexico and seek the protection of the United States.

Larkin was not unsuccessful in his assignment. He enlisted the aid of important foreign residents, including General Vallejo's brother-in-law Jacob Leese in Sonoma, Abel Stearns in Los Angeles, and J. J. Warner in San Diego. Since the Californians had always resented Mexican interference in their affairs, many, including even General Vallejo, were also receptive to Larkin's proposals. However, John Charles Frémont's arrival on

the scene was the first of a series of events that made Larkin's plan superfluous.

JOHN C. FRÉMONT

Few Americans captured the imagination of their time as did John C. Frémont. Although of illegitimate birth, he obtained a commission in the Army Corps of Topographical Engineers and won the hand of the beautiful Jessie, daughter of Thomas Hart Benton, the powerful expansionist U.S. senator from Missouri. After leading five major expeditions into the American West, Frémont wrote and published reports, with the aid of his talented and ambitious wife, that profoundly affected Americans. Containing masterful descriptions of the flora, fauna, and geology of the regions he traversed, and carefully mapped routes for future migrants, Frémont's reports particularly appealed to a generation of Americans moved by the spirit of Manifest Destiny. These accounts also made Frémont a romantic hero, and he and his wife achieved a popularity enjoyed by no other couple of the age.

For two decades Frémont—a natural showman, an adventurer, and an opportunist whose ambition and ego were almost boundless—was a prominent national figure. He was one of the first two U.S. senators from California, the Republican party's first candidate for president, and, as a Civil War general, one of the first to attempt to free southern slaves. He was criticized as merely a follower of the trails that others blazed, court-martialed for his refusal to obey army orders, and forced by Lincoln to curtail his efforts to emancipate slaves in his Missouri command. He also resigned his commission before the Civil War was over and engaged in political maneuvers that almost cost Lincoln his reelection. Historians have tended to view him as either a hero or a scoundrel, but, in either case, his significance to the American westward movement is undeniable.

Frémont's second and third expeditions were probably the most important, his first, in 1842, having been no more than a reconnaissance of the Oregon Trail as far as South Pass. On the second, in 1843 and 1844, he traveled west to the Columbia River, turned south, and crossed the Sierra by way of Carson Pass in the middle of winter. After resting at Sutter's Fort, Frémont's company traveled the length of the San Joaquin Valley, crossed Tehachapi Pass to the Mojave Desert, followed the Old Spanish Trail into southern Utah, and then struck out for St. Louis by way of the Sevier River and Bent's Fort on the Arkansas River. From November 1843 to July 1844, no word was heard in the East from Frémont, and anxiety for the "lost expedition" mounted. When he emerged from the wilderness and published his report of the journey, it became an immediate popular success and the chief source of information for would-be migrants.

In 1845, Frémont set off on another expedition to map the trail west through the Rocky Mountains. It was not in his instructions to enter California, but he did; one section of his company crossed the Sierra at Walker Pass in the south, while Frémont led another group up the Truckee River and over Donner Pass, arriving at Sutter's Fort in early December. His arrival sparked the chain of events that culminated in the Bear Flag Revolt, which itself can be considered the beginning of the Mexican War in California. When Frémont assumed command of the Bear Flag party, he positioned himself to play an important role in that war.

THE PRIZE OF WAR

In March 1845, Congress finally adopted a joint resolution to annex Texas. Along with

Texas, the United States also acquired its new territory's disputes with Mexico, particularly one involving its western border. Texans had themselves been expansionists, some envisioning a Texas that encompassed all of the Southwest and California. In any event, by 1845, Texans claimed a western border at the Rio Grande del Norte, from its mouth to its source. Mexico asserted that the border was on the traditional line, the Nueces River, and prepared to occupy the ground between the two rivers. Congress's resolution of annexation was silent on the matter. James K. Polk's election to the presidency in 1844 brought an unabashed expansionist to power in the United States. Polk supported the Rio Grande line and sent General Zachary Taylor to the region with instructions to regard a Mexican crossing of the Rio Grande as an act of war. When Polk signed the resolution admitting Texas to the Union as the twenty-eighth state in December 1845, both sides prepared for war.

In the spring of 1846, as José Castro and John C. Frémont moved toward their own fateful confrontations, Mexican and American soldiers jockeyed along the disputed Texas border. Finally, in May, American forces under Taylor entered the no-man's-land between the Nueces and Rio Grande rivers and came under Mexican fire. The expected war had begun.

There were two distinct phases to the war in California. The first consisted of the almost uncontested seizure of the province by American forces. Reports of Taylor's activities in Texas reached Commodore John D. Sloat, who commanded the Pacific squadron at Mazatlán, in June 1846. Since Sloat's instructions were to occupy California upon a declaration of war between the United States and Mexico and he was fearful of British designs, he rushed north to Monterey Bay. But Sloat did not occupy the town, since he lacked evidence of an actual declaration of war. His hand was forced, however, when he learned of the successes of the Bear Flaggers and of Frémont's having joined them. On July 7, 1846, he raised the American flag at Monterey and issued a proclamation stating that "henceforth California will be a portion of the United States." It was a conciliatory document, promising Californians U.S. citizenship, religious freedom, and freer trade. Two days later, the American flag was raised at Sonoma, Sutter's Fort, and San Francisco.

On July 15 the aged and ill Sloat turned over his command to Commodore Robert F. Stockton, a much more aggressive commander. A prominent easterner, Stockton was flamboyant, adventurous, and ambitious. On questionable authority, he promoted Frémont to the rank of major, and later to lieutenant colonel. Stockton also enlisted the California Battalion as horse marines and sailed off with them for Los Angeles—to the discomfort of most of Frémont's hardy but seasick mountain men. On July 28 Frémont and his men landed at San Diego, while Stockton landed at San Pedro with a force of marines and sailors. Marching north, Frémont joined Stockton and on August 13 they occupied Los Angeles, as Pío Pico and José Castro fled to Mexico. In Los Angeles, Stockton issued offensive statements against California authorities and unnecessarily imposed martial law and a strict curfew. Leaving Captain Archibald Gillespie and but fifty men as a garrison, Stockton and Frémont returned north.

Where courteous and diplomatic actions might have been called for, Gillespie chose to enforce Stockton's martial law and curfew harshly and rigorously. Led by José María Flores, the Angelenos rebelled, attacked Gillespie, and, after a short siege, forced his surrender on September 29. Meanwhile, warned of Gillespie's plight, Stockton re-

cruited a force to sail to San Diego, while Frémont marched south with the 300-man California Battalion. At the same time, General Stephen W. Kearny was approaching from the east.

General Kearny had been sent to the southwest to obtain control of lands that President Polk hoped to acquire from Mexico. He took possession of New Mexico at Santa Fe without encountering any opposition and proceeded west to California with some 300 men. When he met Kit Carson returning east with the report that California had been occupied without resistance, Kearny sent most of his force back to Santa Fe and persuaded Carson to guide his remaining troops to the West Coast. In early December, Kearny reached San Pascual, an Indian village east of San Diego, his men and animals showing the effects of the long 2,000-mile march. Confronted by a large force of Californians under Andrés Pico (Pío Pico's brother), Kearny sent his exhausted men on a charge that strung the company out widely. The Californians, riding superior horses and armed with long lances, struck the disunited Americans. Sixteen or eighteen Americans were killed, and an equal number, including Kearny, were wounded seriously. Pico's men came away virtually unscathed and proceeded to pin Kearny down in a desert siege. At this point, Carson and Lieutenant Edward F. Beale slipped through the lines to San Diego, where Stockton organized a relief force. With this aid, Kearny finally reached San Diego on December 12.

The second phase of the war in California, the reconquest of the south, followed. It took Kearny and Stockton another month to march north to Los Angeles, which was recaptured on January 10, 1847. Flores, leaving Andrés Pico in command of the Californians, fled to Sonora. Reluctant to surrender to the harsh Stockton, Pico rode north to capitulate to Frémont at San Fernando. Learning that Frémont had already pardoned a relative, Jesús Pico, for violating his parole in the rebellion, Andrés correctly gambled on similar treatment. On January 13 the two men agreed to the Cahuenga Capitulation, ending the revolt without rancor.

With California at last securely in the hands of the United States, Commodore Stockton, again on questionable authority, appointed Frémont governor and sailed off for Mexican waters. In spite of the presence of Kearny, a brigadier general who had been sent west with specific orders to organize a government in the conquered province, Frémont issued orders establishing his government in Los Angeles. When Kearny attempted to exert his authority, Frémont, a mere lieutenant in the army a few months previously, infuriated him by arrogantly refusing to comply, asserting that his orders from Stockton came from a superior command. After dispatches from Washington confirmed Kearny's position, Frémont was forced to return to the East with Kearny, was placed under arrest, and court-martialed. Though defended by his powerful father-in-law, Senator Benton, Frémont was convicted of mutiny, disobedience, and conduct to the prejudice of good order and military discipline, but he was recommended for clemency. President Polk confirmed his guilt on only the second two counts, granted clemency, and ordered him back to duty. Frémont, however, resigned his commission rather than admit the justice of the decision; the court-martial, oddly enough, only enhanced his attractiveness as a political figure. Meanwhile, Kearny had left the able Colonel Richard B. Mason behind as military governor.

The war with Mexico left little other imprint on California and finally ended when the Treaty of Guadalupe Hidalgo was signed on February 2, 1848, and ratified by the U.S. Senate on March 11. By its terms, as had been expected, California was ceded to the United States. The "ripe pear" had been picked.

CULTURE IN SPANISH AND MEXICAN CALIFORNIA

California's isolation and its relatively primitive existence made it a cultural desert. Indeed, officials appointed to serve in California found it difficult to persuade their womenfolk to follow them into what was perceived as a social wasteland. The difficulty of life in provincial California is reflected in the exceedingly limited and short-lived attempts at education and in the near absence of arts and letters, although the more affluent rancheros imported some fine furniture and a few *objets d'art*. Perhaps the most significant cultural contribution of the period was the development of the architecture of the missions, ranchos, and Monterey-style homes.

Education was badly neglected, both inside and outside the missions. Mission schooling was limited to musical training and development of industrial arts. As many as fifty elementary schools existed at various times outside the missions, but none lasted any reasonable length of time. Some Spanish governors, notably Diego de Borica and Pablo Vicente de Solá, set up schools in old granaries or barracks, with retired soldiers who could read and write and do simple arithmetic serving as teachers. Using disciplinary methods such as a small cat-o'-nine-tails, they often stifled student interest as effectively as they imparted learning, as Mariano G. Vallejo vividly recalled. As late as 1845, scarcely one hundred native Californians were able to read and write.

A lucky few young Californians were given

Petaluma Adobe
The double veranda of the restored main building at Mariano Vallejo's Petaluma Rancho (circa 1840)—the largest non-ecclesiastical adobe building in Hispanic California—attests to the influence of the new Monterey style. *Photograph by Richard J. Orsi.*

personal instruction by priests, military officers, and foreigners. As youths, Juan B. Alvarado, José Castro, and Mariano G. Vallejo were taken under the wing of Governor Solá, who taught them from his personal library, and, of course, his protégés became important figures in Mexican California. Near Monterey, William P. Hartnell, with the financial assistance of Governor Figueroa, conducted classes for his own and neighbor children, but his Colegio de San José closed soon after Figueroa's death. The most favored were those boys whose families could afford to send them to Hawaii, Chile, or even Europe for their education. Girls were much less likely to receive any formal schooling other than training in cooking, sewing, and household management.

Given the scarcity of literate persons in California, it is not surprising that it produced little in the way of an indigenous literature. However, the writings of Francisco Palóu—including *Noticias de la Nueva California*, which was the first book written in California, and *Vida de Junípero Serra*—are basic works on the early history of Spanish California. Mexican California, which did not have a printing press until the 1830s, is distinguished more by the descriptive writings of foreign residents and visitors than by any native work. The most famous, of course, is Richard Henry Dana's *Two Years Before the Mast* (see page 138), but many argue that Alfred Robinson's *Life in California* offers superior descriptions of the era. The mountain men also contributed to this literature, notably James Ohio Pattie's *Personal Narrative*, while John C. Frémont's reports on his expeditions were widely read. Although written in the 1820s, Jedediah Smith's account of his pioneering 1826 expedition to California was not published until 1977.

The most pervasive cultural influence of Spanish and Mexican California has been its architecture. The "Mission" style, which was popularly revived at the turn of this century, evolved in the Spanish period, especially after 1790. The early missions were essentially mud huts with thatched roofs, but as the Indian neophytes acquired construction skills, mission fathers replaced the early structures with the now-familiar adobe and stone buildings. Reflecting Roman-Moorish influences, the California mission became characterized by thick walls and tile roofs (as a result of experience with earthquakes and fire), long colonnades, and archways. Like other southwestern missions, they lacked ar-chitectural adornments, lending a simple, clean line to the style, which remains popular in modern California.

The Spanish and Mexican periods also saw the evolution of the early ancestors of today's ubiquitous California ranch-style house. Square or oblong, made mostly of thick adobe walls, with spacious rooms and long covered porches, rancho houses proved to be comfortably cool in summer heat but warm in the winter. A fusion of the California rancho house with New England architecture has become known as the "Monterey" style, attributed to Thomas O. Larkin, who developed the style in designs for his own home, the customs house, and other buildings in the old capital. The wide upper-story balcony, adobe construction, and white woodwork typical of this style can be seen in the restored buildings of modern Monterey.

SUGGESTIONS FOR FURTHER READING

José Castro and the Bear Flag Revolt

H. H. Bancroft, *History of California*, vol. 5 (1886); John A. Hussey, "Bear Flag Revolt," *American Heritage* (1950); Neal Harlow, *California Conquered* (1982); Simeon Ide, *A Biographical Sketch of the Life of William B. Ide* (1880, 1967); Fred B. Rogers, *William B. Ide: Bear Flagger* (1962), and *Bear Flag Lieutenant: The Life Story of Henry L. Ford* (1951); Harlan Hague and David J. Langum, *Thomas O. Larkin: A Life of Patriotism and Profit in Old California* (1990); John A. Hawgood, *First and Last Consul: Thomas Oliver Larkin and the Americanization of California* (1962), and "John C. Frémont and the Bear Flag Revolution: A Reappraisal," *Southern California Quarterly* (1962); John C. Frémont, *Memoirs of My Life* (1887); Ferol Egan, *Frémont, Explorer for a Restless Nation* (1977); Andrew Rolle, *John Charles Frémont: Character As Destiny* (1991); George P. Hammond, *The Larkin Papers* (10 vols., 1951–1966).

Politics and Secularization

George Tays, "Revolutionary California: The Political History of California During the Mexican Period, 1822–1846" (Ph.D. dissertation, University of California, Berkeley, 1932); Woodrow James Hansen, *The Search for Authority in California* (1960); C. Alan Hutchinson, *Frontier Settlement in Mexican California: The Híjar-Padrés Colony and Its Origins, 1769–1835* (1965), and "The Mexican Government and the California Indians," *The Americas* (1965); David J. Langum, *Law and Community on the Mexican California Frontier* (1987);

Manuel P. Servín, "The Secularization of the California Missions: A Reappraisal," *Southern California Quarterly* (1952); Gerald J. Geary, *The Secularization of the California Missions, 1810–1846* (1934); David J. Weber, *The Mexican Frontier, 1821–1846: The American Southwest Under Mexico* (1982); Robert Ryal Miller, *Juan Alvarado, Governor of California, 1836–1842* (1998).

The Rancho Society

Robert G. Cleland, *The Cattle on a Thousand Hills* (1951); W. W. Robinson, *Land in California* (1948), and *Ranchos Become Cities* (1939); Robert Cameron Gillingham, *The Rancho San Pedro* (1961); Doyce B. Nunis, Jr. ed., *The California Diary of Faxon Dean Atherton* (1964); Alfred Robinson, *Life in California* (1846, 1970); Richard Henry Dana, *Two Years Before the Mast* (1840); Douglas Monroy, *Thrown Among Strangers: The Making of Mexican Culture in Frontier California* (1990); Robert A. Alvarez, *Familia: Migration and Adaptation in Baja and Alta California, 1800–1975* (1987); Antonia Castañeda, "Gender, Race, and Culture: Spanish-Mexican Women in the Historiography of Frontier California," *Frontiers*, XI (1990); Gloria A. Miranda, "Racial and Cultural Dimensions of Gente de Razón Status in Spanish and Mexican California," *Southern California Quarterly* LXX (1988) and "Hispano-Mexican Childrearing Practices in Pre-American Santa Barbara," *Southern California Quarterly*, LXV (Winter, 1983); Albert Camarillo, *Chicanos in a Changing Society: From Mexican Pueblos to American Barrios* (1979); Madie Brown Emparan, *The Vallejos of California* (1968); George Tays, "Mariano Guadalupe Vallejo and Sonoma—A Biography and a History," *California Historical Society Quarterly* (1937– 1938); Federico A. Sanchez, "Rancho Life in Alta California," *Masterkey*, 60, nos. 2–3 (1986); Albert L. Hurtado, "California In-dians and the Workaday West: Labor, Assimilation, and Survival," *California History* (Spring, 1990).

Foreigners in California

James R. Gibson, *Imperial Russia in Frontier America* (1976); John A. Hawgood, "The Pattern of Yankee Infiltration in Mexican Alta California, 1821–1846," *Pacific Historical Review* (1958); Irving Stone, *Men to Match My Mountains: The Opening of the Far West, 1840- 1900* (1956); Robert G. Cleland, *This Reckless Breed of Men: The Trappers and Fur Traders of the Southwest* (1950); John D. Unruh, Jr., *The Plains Across: The Overland Emigrants and the Trans-Mississippi West, 1848–1860* (1979); Harrison C. Dale, *The Ashley-Smith Explorations and the Discovery of a Central Route to the Pacific* (1918, 1941); Andrew Rolle, "Jedediah Strong Smith: New Documentation," *Mississippi Valley Historical Review* (1953); George R. Brooks, ed., *The Southwest Expedition of Jedediah Smith: His Personal Account of the Journey to California, 1826–27* (1977 and 1989); Dale L. Morgan, *Jedediah Smith and the Opening of the West* (1953); David J. Weber, "Mexico and the Mountain Men," *Journal of the West* (1969); Adele Ogden, "Hide and Tallow: McCullough, Hartnell and Company, 1822–1828," *California Historical Society Quarterly* (1927), "Boston Hide Droughers Along the California Shores," *California Historical Society Quarterly* (1929), and "Alfred Robinson, New England Merchant in Mexican California," *California Historical Society Quarterly* (1944); Andrew F. Rolle, *An American in California: The Biography of William Heath Davis* (1956); Susanna Bryant Dakin, *The Lives of William Hartnell* (1949); George R. Stewart, *Ordeal by Hunger: The Story of the Donner Party* (1960); Thomas Frederick Howard, *Sierra Crossing: First Roads to California* (1998); Erwin G. Gudde, *Sutter's Own Story* (1936); Richard Dillon, *Fool's Gold: The Decline and Fall of Captain John Sutter of California* (1967); Kenneth N. Owen, ed., *John Sutter and a Wider West* (1994); Robert Ryal Miller, *Captain Richardson: Mariner, Ranchero, and Founder of San Francisco* (1995); George Harwood Phillips, *Indians and Intruders in Central California, 1769–1849* (1993); and *Indians and Indian Agents: The Origins of the Reservation System in California, 1849–1852* (1997).

American Takeover

Charles G. Sellers, *James K. Polk, Continentalist* (1966); Norman A. Graebner, *Empire on the Pacific*

(1955); Ernest A. Wiltsee, "The British Vice-Consul in California and the Events of 1846," *California Historical Society Quarterly* (1931); Reuben Underhill, *From Cowhides to Golden Fleece* (1939); Werner H. Marti, *Messenger of Destiny: The California Adventures, 1846–1847, of Archibald H. Gillespie* (1960); Russell M. Posner, "A British Consular Agent in California: The Reports of James A. Forbes, 1843–1846," *Southern California Quarterly* (1971); Dwight L. Clarke, *Stephen Watts Kearny, Soldier of the West* (1961); Ramon Guttiérez and Richard J. Orsi (eds.), *Contested Eden: California Before the Gold Rush* (1998). See also suggested readings for "José Castro and the Bear Flag Revolt."

Hydraulic Gold Mining

While Alfred A. Hart was documenting the construction of the Central Pacific Railway during the 1860s, he also recorded hydraulic gold miners at work. Twenty years later, their activities would precipitate the "debris wars" between the miners and valley farmers. Even when Hart made the photograph, however, environmental damage from hydraulic mining was evident. *Courtesy Henry E. Huntington Library.*

PART FOUR

GOLD AND THE AMERICANIZATION OF CALIFORNIA

Assessments of the California gold rush often treat it as little more than the colorful "Days of '49," a brief and exciting interlude in a thoroughly romantic narrative. It was that, but it was much more. Indeed, for John W. Caughey, acknowledged dean of California historians, gold was the "cornerstone" of much of the state's late-nineteenth-century history. Events that began at Sutter's Mill on the American River had momentous consequences for the state, for the nation, and even for the world.

The rush for gold accelerated California's development and compressed its history. In an historical instant, hundreds of thousands of argonauts provided the region with a new population composed principally of Americans impelled equally by a quest for wealth and a sense of their Manifest Destiny. In just over a year, they bypassed the traditional territorial period and made California the thirty-first state. Mining stimulated explosive economic growth: manufacturing to provide tools and other essentials, financial institutions to manage anticipated wealth, commercial and transportation facilities to distribute money and goods, and agriculture to feed a hungry populace. Just as quickly, familiar social and cultural institutions appeared, a process epitomized by the "instant city," San Francisco.

The lure of the mines also created a unique and diverse population that quickly made natives of the region—Indians and *californios*—minorities in their own homeland and exposed less admirable elements in Americans' notion of their Manifest Destiny. Among them was a sense of superiority that was too often translated into unrestrained expressions of prejudice and bigotry. The velocity of events placed a heavy burden on traditions and on institutions of law and justice, frequently with violent results. Energetic and ambitious gold-seekers ruthlessly exploited the land and its resources, inflicting great ecological damage with little concern for consequences. In addition, they introduced squabbles over land and water rights, reckless speculation in urban and rural real estate, and a host of other problems that would plague the state for generations.

Thus, within the span of a very few years, the gold rush transformed what had been for a century the Hispanic frontier province called Alta California into a thoroughly American state of the Union, embodying both the positive and negative attributes of the nation. Indeed, the rapid Americanization of California, although it is mundane by comparison, at least matches and probably surpasses the discovery of gold in both immediate and long-term historial importance.

CHAPTER TEN

DAME SHIRLEY: A YANKEE LADY IN THE CALIFORNIA MINES

Men dominated the non-Indian population of gold rush California (more than ninety percent in 1852), and the male-female ratio began to approach parity only during the late 1860s. Impressions introduced by fiction such as Bret Harte's "Outcasts of Poker Flat" and "The Luck of Roaring Camp" and perpetuated by entertainment media stereotype a substantial proportion of the female ten percent, often as prostitutes. In reality, women of all sorts traveled to California, even aboard the first steamship from Panama in 1849. Although few in number, they were important social, cultural, and economic influences. Indeed, one of them penned perhaps the most perceptive existing account of early gold rush life and society. "Dame Shirley," for whom life in the mines was principally an adventure, did not typify female gold rush Californians, but her letters provide not only information about the lives of women in the mines and the composition of mining camp populations, but also details about the miners' work and play, attempts to civilize their environment, personal characteristics, prejudices, and much more.

Late in the summer of 1851, a Yankee lady arrived at Rich Bar on the East Branch of the North Fork of the Feather River, "at almost the highest point, . . . where gold has been discovered, and indeed, within fifty miles of the summit of the Sierra Nevada itself." In the first of twenty-three letters to her sister Molly at home in "the States," she anticipated inevitable questions:

> How did such a shivering, frail, homeloving little thistle ever float safely to that far away spot, and take root so kindly . . . in that barbarous soil? . . . And for pity's sake, how does the poor little fool expect to amuse herself there?

During the following year, she provided answers by "taking pains to describe things exactly as I see them, hoping thus you will obtain an idea of life in the mines *as it is*." She succeeded—probably far better than she expected.*

Best known by her childhood sobriquet and pen name, "Dame Shirley," Louisa Amelia Knapp Smith Clapp assumed that

---

* The "Shirley Letters" first appeared in print in the short-lived San Francisco magazine, *The Pioneer*, in 1854 and 1855.

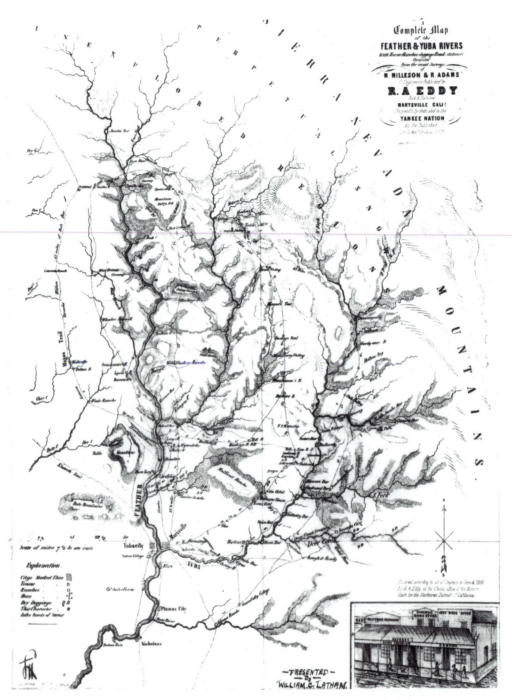

A Complete Map of the Feather and Yuba Rivers . . .
Produced in 1851, the map shows both Dame Shirley's route and her destination. She and her husband departed from relatively civilized Marysville on a two-week journey over barely marked trails. After traveling for 100 miles, they reached Rich Bar, on the very edge of California's "Unexplored Regions" and not far from an area identified only as "Perpetual Snow." *Courtesy California State Library.*

she would be the "only petticoated astonishment" in the mines; she was not, but she was a remarkable person indeed. Born in 1819 in Elizabeth, New Jersey, she was descended from prominent New England families. When her father died in 1832 and his wife followed him to the grave in 1837, they left seven orphans. Despite the loss of their parents, the children were well provided for, loved, and educated. Louisa, who became the ward of a prominent attorney, attended the Female Seminary in Charlestown and Amherst Academy, where she received a contemporary young woman's standard training in writing, literature, languages, and music. Subsequently, she taught school and began a lifelong friendship-by-correspondence with career diplomat Alexander Hill Everett. Although he was twenty years older than Louisa, Everett's interest in her was more than fatherly. She did not return his affection, but she did respond to his encouragement of her literary pursuits and began to publish her work. Later in the 1840s, Louisa Smith met Fayette Clapp, five years her junior but, like her, a descendant of respected New Englanders. Although Clapp began his higher education in theology, when he received his degree from Brown University in 1848, his interest had shifted to medicine. For about a year, he studied with a cousin, Dr. Sylvanus Clapp, and attended classes at Castleton Medical College in Vermont. In 1849, he contracted gold fever, married Louisa, and sailed for California with his bride.

Little is known about the couple's voyage around the Horn or their stay in San Francisco, but they soon left the foggy city for the more wholesome climate and greater opportunity of the region around Marysville. Then, in June 1851, Dr. Clapp (who had somehow obtained his medical credentials from Castleton while living in California) departed for Rich Bar on the Feather River,

hoping to establish a practice, recover his health, and perhaps strike it rich. Late in the year, he felt confident enough to return for his wife, who had spent the summer on a ranch in the vicinity of Marysville. The prospect of a winter in the mountains "perfectly enchanted" her, to the dismay of her local acquaintances:

> Some said that I ought to be put in a strait jacket. . . . Some said that I should never get there alive, and if I *did,* would not stay a month; others simply observed . . . that even if the Indians *did not* kill me, I should expire of *ennui* or the cold before spring. One lady declared in a burst of outraged modesty, that it was absolutely indelicate, to think of living in such a large population of men; where at most there were two or three women.

Louisa decided to go, but soon after the couple began the trek to Rich Bar in September 1851, her enchantment diminished and her friends' warnings began to seem prophetic.

The 100-mile expedition over barely marked trails commenced on muleback. On the first stage of the journey, a defective saddle dumped Louisa in the dust, "which filled eyes, nose, ears, and hair," and the couple did not even reach Marysville until after midnight. A few days later, the doctor and the animals set out for Bidwell's Bar, a "rag city" thirty miles upriver, and his wife followed by stagecoach. Fleas and other pests so infested Bidwell's accommodations that the Clapps decided to press on to Berry Creek House, another ten miles distant. They missed the trail, became hopelessly lost, and spent the night under the stars. When they did arrive at the way station, after a thirty-mile detour:

> Every one that we met [there], congratulated us upon not having encountered any Indians; for the paths which we followed were Indian trails, and it is said, that they would have killed us for our mules and our

clothes. A few weeks ago, a Frenchman and his wife were murdered. . . . They generally take women captive, however, and who knows how narrowly I escaped becoming an Indian chieftainess, and feeding for the rest of my life upon roasted grasshoppers and flower seeds?

The night's hazards neither extinguished Louisa's enthusiasm and sense of humor nor increased her husband's caution or skills as a pathfinder. When the trek resumed, the doctor's errors resulted in another night in the open, this time in Indian *and* grizzly country. But after two weeks on the trail and more near disasters, the couple arrived safely at Rich Bar.

The journey to the diggings added several new elements to Louisa's experience, including her first encounter with "live" Indians. From the stagecoach window on the way to Bidwell's Bar, she observed Indian women collecting flower seeds to flavor their acorn bread. The sight produced an ambivalent reaction:

> Each one carried two brown baskets, . . . woven with a neatness which is absolutely marvellous [sic], when one considers that they are the handiwork of such degraded wretches. . . . It is evident by the grace with which they handle them, that they are exceedingly light.

The gleaners, with "their regular motion . . . dark shining skin, beautiful limbs, and lithe forms, . . . [were] by no means the least picturesque features of the landscape."

Later, at Wild Yankee's Ranch, "a *herd* of Indians . . . crowded into the room to stare at us." One, she observed, presented a remarkable contrast to the "general hideousness" of the others:

> A girl of sixteen, perhaps; with those large magnificently lustrous eyes, . . . shyly glided, like a dark, beautiful spirit into the corner of the room. A fringe of silken jet swept heavily upward from her dusky cheek, [and from it] the richest color came and went like flashes of lightning. Her flexible lips curved slightly away from her teeth like strips of cocoa-nut meat, with a mocking grace infinitely bewitching. She wore a cotton chemise, disgustingly dirty, I must confess, girt about her slender waist with a crimson handkerchief; while over her night black hair, . . . was a purple scarf of knotted silk.

Shirley was "perfectly enraptured with this wild-wood Cleopatra," but later in her letter she expressed attitudes characteristic of even the most sympathetic white nineteenth-century Americans:

> I always *did* "take" to Indians; though it must be said that those who bear that name here, have little resemblance to the glorious forest heroes that live in the Leather Stocking Tales [of James Fenimore Cooper]; and in spite of my desire to find in them something poetical and interesting, a stern regard for truth compels me to acknowledge, that the dusky beauty above described, is the only moderately *pretty* squaw that I have ever seen.

Dame Shirley arrived at Rich Bar a year after the first gold discovery there, when few of the original 500 miners remained in the camp. Reluctant to risk the hazards of winter or having squandered their accumulated gold on gambling, most had drifted away in pursuit of other *bonanzas* (rich strikes), real or rumored. In the summer of 1851, about 200 men lived there in rude log cabins, tents made of calico, *ramadas* constructed of brush, and a variety of even less permanent shelters. A fortunate few resided in one of the community's more substantial lodgings. The Clapps, for example, enjoyed the comforts of the Empire Hotel, "the only two-story building in town." About the Empire Dame Shirley wrote:

> you will find two or three glass windows, an unknown luxury in all other dwellings. It is built of planks of the roughest possible de-

scription; the roof, of course, is covered with canvas, which also forms the entire front. . . . You first enter a large apartment, level with the street, part of which is fitted up as a bar-room, with that eternal crimson calico, which flushes the whole social life of the "golden State," with its everlasting red. . . . A table covered with a green cloth—upon which lies a pack of monte cards, a backgammon board, and a sickening pile of "yellow-kivered" literature—with several uncomfortable looking benches, complete the furniture of this most important portion of such a place as "The Empire."

The remainder of the room was a store where clothing, tools, and groceries were stocked, "cheek by jowl . . . in hopeless confusion."

Four steps led up to the hotel's parlor, with its selection of well-worn furniture and a "quite decent looking-glass," and four more rose to the upper floor and four tiny bedrooms. The Empire was crude, with "floors so very uneven, that you were always ascending a hill or descending a valley" and interior walls consisting mainly of canvas. Shirley called it "just a piece of carpentering as a child two years old, gifted with the strength of a man, would produce." Nevertheless, this "impertinent apology for a house" cost its builders $8,000, since every item in it had to be freighted from Marysville at a rate of 40 cents a pound. Originally, the hotel was built as a brothel, but it failed, which Dame Shirley attributed to "the everlasting honor of the *miners*." By the time the Clapps arrived, it was owned and operated by Curtis A. Bancroft, a brother of future California historian Hubert Howe Bancroft, and his wife.

Dame Shirley was surprised to learn that she was not the only female inhabitant of the camp. Four others lived at Rich Bar, but the Yankee lady was not at first particularly impressed by them. Mrs. Bancroft was "a gentle

and amiable looking woman, about twenty-five years of age," but, Dame Shirley continued:

> I will give you a key to her character which will exhibit it better than weeks of description. She took a nursing babe of eight months old, from her bosom, and left it with two other children—almost infants—to cross the plains [with her husband] in search of gold.

At the Empire, Shirley found the woman calmly cooking dinner for the hotel's half-dozen guests, while her youngest child, just two weeks old and born in the mines, "lay kicking furiously in his champagne basket cradle."

A second Rich Bar woman was Mary Stanfield, the "Indiana Girl," who assisted her father, the proprietor of the Indiana Hotel. During the previous winter, she had packed a fifty-pound sack of flour through five feet of snow over the mountain to the mining camp. According to Dame Shirley, she was a:

> gigantic piece of humanity [who] wears the thickest kind of miners' boots, and has the dainty habit of wiping her dishes upon her apron. . . . The far-off roll of her mighty voice, booming through two closed doors and a long entry, added greatly to my severe attack of nervous headache.

One of Dame Shirley's few regrets was that the Indiana Girl left the settlement before the two met in person.

Dame Shirley did meet the other two Rich Bar women. One was the diminutive "Mrs. R---" who tended bar and otherwise assisted at the "Miners' Home," which her husband owned and where miners congregated to eat and drink. The place was:

> a canvas house, containing a suite of three "apartments" . . . which, considering that they are all on the ground floor, are kept surprisingly neat. There is a bar-room, blushing all over with red calico, a dining

room, kitchen and a small bed-closet. The little sixty-eight pounder woman is queen of the establishment.

Tiny "Mrs. R---" was also a favorite of the miners, one of whom explained to the Clapps that she "earnt her *old man* . . . nine hundred dollars in nine weeks, clear of all expenses, by [taking in] washing! Such women ain't common; if they were, a man might marry and make money by the operation." The man's chauvinism annoyed Dame Shirley, but she had to concede that she had "known of sacrifices, requiring, it would seem, superhuman efforts, made by women in this country, who at home were nurtured in the extreme of elegance and delicacy."

The fourth Rich Bar woman was Nancy Ann Bailey, the young wife of a miner and the mother of two children; she died of peritonitis shortly after the Clapps' arrival, and Shirley described her funeral, which began at the Baileys' cabin:

> On a board, supported by two butter-tubs, was extended the body of the dead woman, covered with a sheet; by its side stood the coffin of unstained pine, lined with white cambric.
>
> The bereaved husband held in his arms a sickly babe ten months old, which was moaning piteously at its mother. The other child, a handsome, bold-looking little girl six years of age, was running gaily around the room, perfectly unconscious of her great bereavement. . . .
>
> About twenty men, with the three women of the place, had assembled at the funeral. An *extempore* prayer was made, filled with all the peculiarities usual to that style of petition. Ah! how different from the soothing verses of the glorious burial service of the church.
>
> As the procession started for the hill-side grave-yard—a dark cloth, borrowed from a neighboring monte table, was flung over the coffin. Do not think that I mention any of these circumstances in a spirit of mockery; far from it. Every observance, . . . that

was *procurable,* surrounded this funeral. All the gold on Rich Bar could do no more; should I die tomorrow, I should be marshaled to my mountain grave beneath the same monte-table cover pall, which surrounded the coffin of poor Mrs. B.

A sobering experience for Dame Shirley, the funeral improved her attitude toward her female companions. In an early letter, she commented sarcastically, "Splendid materials for social parties this winter, are they not?" But later observations reflect a different opinion, even admiration.

In the fall of 1851, the Clapps moved to Indian Bar, a mile or so downstream, where rumors of a rich strike produced a bustling new community. The bar was littered with miners' dwellings like those at Rich Bar, and there was a hotel, the Humbolt ("without the *d*," Dame Shirley noted, although she insisted on restoring it in her letters). At Indian Bar, she had her own log cabin, which she described to her sister:

> The room into which you have just entered is about twenty feet square. It is lined over the top with white cotton cloth, the breadths of which have been sewed together only in spots, stretch gracefully apart in many places, giving one a bird's-eye view of the shingles above. The sides are hung with a gaudy chintz, . . . a perfect marvel of calico printing. . . .
>
> The fireplace is built of stones and mud, the chimney finished off with alternate layers of rough sticks and this same rude mortar; contrary to the usual custom, it is built inside, . . . and you can imagine the queer appearance of this unfinished pile of stone, mud and sticks. The mantelpiece . . . is formed of a beam of wood, covered with strips of tin procured from cans, upon which still remain in black hieroglyphics, the names [of their former contents]. . . . Two smooth stones—how delightfully primitive—do duty as fire-dogs. I suppose that it would be no more than civil to call a hole two feet square in one side of the room, a

window, although it is as yet guiltless of glass. . . . I must mention that the floor is so uneven that no article of furniture gifted with four legs pretends to stand on but three at once, so that the chairs, tables, etc., remind you constantly of a dog with a sore foot.

Comments on improvised furniture and candlesticks, Dr. Clapp's pipes and tobaccos on the mantel, and the couple's meager library arranged on a candle-box bookshelf completed the guided tour.

Dame Shirley's home was elegant by mining camp standards, but it was not the most luxurious in the district. Honors for that—and for sheer ingenuity—belonged to five miners who apparently spent as much energy on creature comforts as they did on prospecting. Their cabin boasted an efficient fireplace for heat and cooking and windows made by mortaring empty jars into the walls. From mounds of discarded materials that cluttered the camp, they devised an array of functional candlesticks and lanterns and built bunks and other furniture. A visit inspired Shirley to comment, "Really, everybody ought to go to the mines, just to see how little it takes to make people comfortable in the world."

Miners' cabins could be innovative and even homey; but gold, not comfort, was the principal concern at Rich Bar, and finding it was an arduous, hazardous, frequently disappointing pursuit. Dame Shirley tried panning just once and wrote, "I wet my feet, tore my dress, spoilt a pair of new gloves, nearly froze my fingers, got an awful headache, and lost a valuable breastpin, in this my labor of love." Her efforts were rewarded with $3.25 worth of gold dust, which miners assessed as a fine prospect for one panfull. But Dame Shirley was not impressed; she sent her treasure to her sister with a terse comment: "I am sorry I ever learned the trade."

For Shirley, searching for gold was a lark; for miners it was backbreaking toil. By the 1850s, the gold pan and its successor, the rocker or cradle, were no longer the principal tools of extraction. As early as the Clapps' arrival on the Feather River in 1851, the individual prospector and the rudimentary methods of 1848 and 1849 were on their way to extinction:

Here in the mountains, the labor of excavation is extremely difficult, on account of the immense rocks which form a large portion of the soil. Of course, no man can "work" a "claim" alone. For that reason, . . . they congregate in companies of four or six, generally designating themselves by the name of the place from whence the majority have emigrated. . . . In many places, the surface soil, or in mining phrase, the "top-dirt," "pays" when worked in a "Long Tom." This machine, . . . is a trough, generally about twenty feet in length, and eight inches in depth, formed of wood, with the exception of six feet at one end, called the "riddle," . . . which is made of sheet iron, perforated with large holes about the size of a large marble. Underneath this cullender-like portion of the "long tom," is placed another trough, about ten feet long, the sides six inches perhaps in height, [with slats across its bottom], called the "rifflebox." . . . [Several] spadesmen throw in large quantities of the precious dirt, which is washed down to the "riddle" by a stream of water leading into the "long-tom" through gutters or "sluices." When the soil reaches the "riddle," it is kept constantly in motion by the man with the hoe. Of course, by this means, all the dirt and gold escapes through the perforations into the "riffle-box" below, one compartment of which is placed just beyond the "riddle." Most of the dirt washes over the sides of the "riffle-box," but the gold being so astonishingly heavy remains safely at the bottom of it [behind the slats].

Because much "top dirt" in California mining districts had already been thoroughly prospected, more complex methods became necessary:

Miners at Work
Dame Shirley's descriptions, as well as daguerreotypes from the early years of the gold rush, document rapid changes in mining methods. At first, a few basic tools and hard work sufficed *(top left)*. By 1850 and 1851, elaborate flumes *(top right)* and water wheels to drive machinery *(bottom left)* were essentials. The physical labor required of miners, however, rarely diminished *(bottom right)*. *Courtesy of the Bancroft Library.*

Many of the miners decline washing the "top dirt" at all, but try to reach as quickly as possible the "bed-rock," where are found the richest deposits of gold. The river is supposed to have formerly flowed over the "bed-rock," in the largest "crevices" of which, it left, . . . the largest portions of the so eagerly sought for ore. . . .

When a company wishes to reach the bed-rock as quickly as possible, they "sink a shaft," . . . until they "strike" it. Then they commence "drifting coyote holes" . . . in search of "crevices," which, . . . often pay immensely. These "coyote holes" often extend hundreds of feet into the side of a hill. . . . [The miners] generally proceed, until the air is so impure as to extinguish [their] lights.

At that point, they began again, after scraping tunnel walls with knives, searching for a crevice possibly overlooked.

Such burrows could fill with water from underground springs, making them unworkable, causing them to cave in, and even drowning the miners. But water was also essential to placer mining, and it was transported over great distances to "dry diggings" by difficult and ingenious methods:

> In most cases, it is brought from ravines in the mountains. A company, . . . has dug a ditch about a foot in width and depth, and more than three miles in length, which is fed in this way. . . . When it reaches the top of the hill [at Rich Bar], the sparkling thing is divided into five or six branches, each one of which supplies [several] "long-toms." . . . This "race" . . . has already cost the company more than five thousand dollars.

To recover part of their investment, builders often formed ditch companies that sold water to other miners.

On some occasions, miners attempted to get at bed-rock by constructing a "flume, an immense trough, which takes up a portion of the river, and, with the aid of a dam, compels it to run in another channel, leaving the vacated bed of the stream for mining purposes. . . . Sometimes these fluming companies are eminently successful; at others, [they] are a dead failure." Unfortunately, failure was more frequent than success.

Most of the miners whom the Clapps encountered remained eager participants in "Nature's great lottery scheme," despite the ever-lengthening odds against them:

> They are always looking for "big strikes." If a "claim" is paying them a steady income, by which . . . they could lay up more in a month than they could accumulate in a

year at home, still, they are dissatisfied, and, in most cases, will wander off in search of better "diggings." There are hundreds now pursuing this foolish course, who, if they had stopped where they first "camped," would now have been rich men. Sometimes a company of these wanderers will find itself upon a bar, where a few pieces of precious metal lie scattered upon the surface of the ground; of course, they immediately "prospect" it, which is accomplished by "panning out" a few basinsful of the soil. If it "pays," they "claim" the spot, and build their shanties; the news spreads that wonderful "diggings" have been discovered at such and such a place. . . .

Hordes of enthusiastic gold-seekers inevitably followed the news; just as certainly, so did gamblers, "those worse than fiends, rush vulture-like upon the scene." The more industrious miners worked their claims for adequate rewards, but too many, in their quest for immediate riches, either lost their earnings in games of faro or monte or hurried off in quest of even richer strikes.

But all was not drudgery in the diggings. At Indian Bar, Paganini Ned, the mulatto cook at the hotel, was equally skilled in culinary arts and violin. The meal that he prepared to welcome Dame Shirley to Indian Bar—complete with oyster soup, dessert, claret, and champagne—she called an accomplishment "the memory of which the world will not willingly let die." And she was just as impressed by Ned's musical talents when he and another man treated her to an impromptu serenade.

Isolation from creature comforts and diversions not only made most miners appreciate talents like Ned's but also forced them to organize for sociability, as well as for the task of extracting gold. In mining camps, an unwritten law, almost universally obeyed, forbade working claims on Sundays. On their day of rest, miners occupied themselves with such chores as washing and mending clothes and repairing shelters, tools, and equipment. They also told stories, played cards, gossiped, and hunted and fished, not only to while away time but also to vary monotonous diets. Some even captured wild animals to raise as pets.

Among residents of the mining camps, exceptional acts of kindness and solicitude often occurred. When Nancy Ann Bailey died, her husband's comrades attended the funeral, consoled the man, and helped with the care of his children. Similarly, when an accident mangled the leg of a young miner, his friends acted as nurses both before and after Dr. Clapp amputated the limb. During winter months, when supplies were scarce, miners frequently shared what they had while awaiting the first pack trains of spring.

During the same months, they were hardest pressed for amusement. Observing holidays, including those of the many foreigners in the mines, furnished diversion. Dame Shirley was amazed at the variety among the residents of Rich Bar:

> You will hear on the same day the lofty melody of the Spanish language, the piquant polish of the French, . . . the silver, changing clearness of the Italian, the harsh gargle of the German, the hissing precision of the English, the liquid sweetness of the Kanaka, and the sleep-inspiring languor of the East Indian.

But her own countrymen's attitude toward foreigners and their languages perplexed her. Most of them believed that when they had "learned *sabe, vamos,* . . . *poco tiempo, si,* and *bueno,* . . . they had the whole of the glorious Castillian at their tongue's end." Others simply assumed that "by splitting the tympanum of an unhappy foreigner, in screaming forth their sentences in good, solid English," they could be understood by anyone. Yankees also joined exuberantly in foreigners' festivities. When a company of Chileans celebrated the anniversary of their country's independence, for example, Dame Shirley observed that:

> It was impossible to tell which nation was the most gloriously drunk; but I *will* say, even at the risk of being thought partial to my own beloved countrymen; "that though the Chilenos reeled with better grace, the Americans did it more *naturally!*"

Traditional American holidays, including the Fourth of July, provided welcome departures from routine in the mines. In 1852, Independence Day festivities at Rich Bar drew residents of camps from up and down the river. When the day's proceedings began at the Empire, politicians introduced one another and a speaker imported for the occasion "pronounced beautifully a very splendid Oration." At the dinner later, "the toasts were quite spicy and original." By nightfall, two "new ladies from the hill" appeared, "so lately arrived from the States, with everything fresh and new, they quite extinguished poor Mrs. B. and myself, trying our best to look fashionable in our antique mode of four years ago." One of the newcomers favored celebrants with "three or four beautiful songs," and substantial quantities of "the spirit" disappeared. Still, "everything passed off quite respectably at Rich Bar . . . [despite] a small fight in the bar-room . . . during which much speech and some blood were spouted."

Dame Shirley also described a rather less civilized Christmas and New Year's celebration that followed months of confinement, cold, and boredom:

> The Saturnalia commenced on Christmas evening at the Humboldt, which on the very day, had passed into the hands of new proprietors. The most gorgeous preparations were made for celebrating the *two* events. The bar was re-trimmed with red calico, the bowling alley had a new lining of

the coarsest and whitest cotton cloth, and the broken lamp shades were replaced by whole ones. All day long, patient mules could be seen descending the hill, bending beneath casks of brandy and baskets of champagne, and, for the first time in the history of that celebrated building, the floor . . . *was washed,* at a lavish expenditure of some fifty pails of water, the using up of one entire broom, and the melting away of sundry bars of the best yellow soap.

Throughout the day, troops of miners— "an army of India-rubber coats (the rain was falling in riversful)"—descended on Indian Bar, and at night the celebration began:

> At nine o'clock in the evening, they had an oyster and champagne supper in the Humboldt, which was very gay. . . . I believe that the company danced all night; at any rate, they were dancing when I went to sleep, and they were dancing when I woke the next morning. The revel was kept up in this mad way for three days, growing wilder every hour. On the fourth day, they got past dancing, and, lying in drunken heaps about the bar-room, commenced a most unearthly howling. . . . Many were too far gone to imitate anything but their own animalized selves. . . . Some of these bacchanals were among the most respectable and respected men upon the river . . . [who] had never been seen intoxicated before.
>
> Toward the latter part of the week, people were compelled to be a little more quiet from sheer exhaustion; but on New Years' day, . . . at Rich Bar, the excitement broke out again, if possible, worse than ever.

Dame Shirley forgave the excesses, writing to Molly that "the miners as a class, possess many truly admirable characteristics."

No regular authority existed in remote mining districts, even after California's admission to the Union in 1850. The situation forced their residents to attend to legal and political affairs, especially those pertaining to mining activities:

> As there are no state laws upon the subject, each mining community is permitted to make its own. Here, they have decided that no man may "claim" an area of more than forty feet square. This he "stakes off" and puts a notice upon it, to the effect that he "holds" it for mining purposes. If he does not choose to "work it" immediately, he is obliged to renew the notice every ten days; for without this precaution, any other person has the right to "jump it," that is, to take it from him. There are many ways of evading the above law . . . [such as hiring someone else to work a claim]. After all, the "holding of claims" by proxy is considered rather as carrying out the spirit of the law, than as an evasion of it. But there are many ways of *really* outwitting the rule, . . . which give rise to innumerable arbitrations, and nearly every Sunday there is a "miners' meeting" connected with this subject.

Some camps relied on general meetings to settle disputes; others elected claims officers or committees to maintain registers and resolve conflicts. Frequently, too, miners' meetings assumed authority for other matters of law, and on occasion state or county governments sent officials to the mining camps, with varied results.

On the Feather River, a man called the Squire (perhaps Thomas D. Bonner, who recorded the memoirs of black pathfinder James P. Beckwourth) was appointed justice of the peace. Dame Shirley doubted his ability to uphold the law in the camps, and his first "opportunity to exercise (or rather to *try* to do so) his judicial power upon a criminal case" confirmed her opinion. After a Swede called Little John squandered unexplained money on gambling and was arrested for theft, the Squire attempted to conduct the subsequent trial:

> When the . . . mighty people had assembled at the Empire, they commenced proceedings by voting in a president and jury of

their own; though they kindly consented . . . that the "Squire" might *play at judge,* by sitting at the side of *their* elected magistrate! This honor, the "Squire" seemed to take as a sort of salvo to his wounded dignity, and with unprecedented meekness accepted it.

At the trial, Little John maintained that the sudden wealth that was evidence against him was a gift from his father. Nevertheless, despite a vigorous defense by an appointed counsel and the Squire's opinion of innocence:

the jury brought in a verdict of guilty, and condemned [Little John] to receive thirty-nine lashes at nine o'clock the following morning, and to leave the river, never to return to it, within twenty-four hours; a "claim" of which he owned a part, [was] to be made over to Mr. [Bancroft], to indemnify him for his loss.

More serious episodes, however, received almost no response from miners' tribunals. When, during "a drunken frolic," one man stabbed another with "not the slightest provocation," a puzzled Dame Shirley wrote that "The people have not taken the slightest notice of this affair, although for some days the life of the wounded man was despaired of." As public disorders increased in frequency and changed in character during the spring and summer of 1852, her letters hinted at the nature of the transformation; like her compatriots, she began to refer to all miners of Hispanic origins as "Spaniards"— when fewer than 300 individuals from Spain were in California.

During April 1852, the miners' meeting at Rich Bar made the point more emphatically when it passed laws "to the effect that no foreigner shall work the mines." Immediate results were migration of most Spanish-speaking miners to Indian Bar, an increase in the number of establishments catering to them there, and a vigorous complaint from Shirley: "On Sundays, the swearing, drink-ing, gambling, and fighting which are carried on in some of these houses, are truly horrible." Clearly, too, earlier camaraderie among miners was evaporating. When an American stabbed a "Spaniard" because the latter requested payment of a debt, Shirley protested that "Nothing was done, and very little was said about this atrocious affair." But there was more to come.

Following the July 4 celebration, several "of the *elite* of Rich Bar, drunk with whisky and patriotism," attacked and injured several "Spaniards." For this incident, Dame Shirley concluded, "Sir Barley Corn was to blame, for many of the ringleaders are fine young men, who, when sober, are . . . friendly to the Spaniards." But she also sensed a "gradually increasing state of bad feeling exhibited by our countrymen . . . toward foreigners." She feared that the episode was not the last of its kind, despite efforts by "the more intelligent foreigners, as well as the judicious Americans."

Numerous "drunken fights . . . with the usual amount of broken heads, collar bones, stabs, etc." punctuated July 1852, when almost every Sunday was "enlivened by some such merry event." In one incident, a "Spaniard" stabbed an Irishman in a dispute over a Mexican woman. The Irishman (a naturalized U.S. citizen) died, his attacker escaped, rumors of conspiracies spread, and conflict seemed imminent. The "Spaniards thought the Americans had risen against them; and our countrymen fancied the same of foreigners." When armed Americans and foreigners converged on Indian Bar, Shirley and the other women in the camp retreated to the hill to observe. Two miners—an Englishman who survived and a "Spaniard" who died—were wounded when a rifle discharged accidentally; the "frightful accident recalled the people to their senses, and they began to act a little less like madmen, than they had previously done."

Events of the "fatal Sabbath," as residents

began to call it, had important results. Perhaps in imitation of San Francisco, Indian Bar organized a Vigilance Committee. In its first official act, the committee sent a posse after "Spaniards" suspected of instigating the previous Sunday's disturbance and tried "a *Mejicana,* who had been foremost in the fray. . . . She was sentenced to leave the Bar by day-light." The vigilantes next "tried five or six Spaniards who were proven to have been ringleaders in the Sabbath-day riot. Two of them were sentenced to be whipped, the remainder to leave the Bar that evening; the property of all to be confiscated to the use of the wounded persons. Oh Mary! imagine my anguish when I heard the first blow fall upon those wretched men." Punishment could have been worse, however; most in the community clamored for a hanging.

The committee's work continued during July with the conviction of a black cook (not Paganini Ned) for murder. Sentenced to hang, he cut his throat in a suicide attempt while in custody. Then:

> Their majesties the mob, with that beautiful consistency which usually distinguishes those august individuals, insisted upon shooting [the prisoner].

As the committee deteriorated, Dame Shirley wrote, "The state of society has never been so bad as since the appointment of [the vigilantes]." She believed that committee leaders also led a group of rowdies called the "Moguls," who:

> parade the streets all night, howling, shouting, breaking into houses, taking wearied miners out of their beds and throwing them into the river, and in short, "murdering sleep," in a most remorseless manner.

Fall did not increase public peace, but during late September and early October the Clapps escaped from the disorders when they journeyed to the American Valley near present Quincy. The doctor was a delegate to

a nominating convention being held there, and Shirley decided to accompany him. She said little about the convention, except that "Horse-racing, and gambling, in all their detestable varieties" seemed to characterize frontier politics. But she was moved by the sight of pioneer women who were widowed on the trail and arrived in California "looking as haggard as so many Endorean witches; burnt to the color of a hazel-nut, with their hair cut short, and its gloss entirely destroyed by the alkali, whole plains of which they are compelled to cross on the way." Dame Shirley was delighted to end her "dreadful pleasure tour of the American Valley" and return to her cabin.

It was a disappointing homecoming. Indian Bar had changed during her absence. Signs of the impending harsh winter were visible everywhere, and new mining operations undertaken to salvage the community's faltering economy were a disaster:

> To our unbounded surprise, we found . . . that nearly all the fluming companies had failed—contrary to every expectation, on [their] arriving at bed-rock no gold made its appearance.
>
> Of course the whole world (*our* world) was, to use a phrase much in vogue here, "dead broke." The shop-keepers, restaurants, and gambling-houses . . . had trusted the miners to the degree that they themselves were in the same moneyless condition.

In fact, "nearly every person on the river received the same stepmother's treatment from Dame Nature, in this her mountain workshop." The miners dispersed almost as quickly as they had gathered: "It is said, that there are not twenty men remaining on Indian Bar, although two months ago, you could count them up in the hundreds." Those who stayed "amused themselves by prosecuting one another right and left," keeping the Squire's court busy for the first time.

Since the Clapps had no reason to remain at Indian Bar, they planned to leave in late November. Despite the hardships of her year on the Feather River, however, Dame Shirley regretted the decision. To her sister, she lamented that she had never learned to sketch from nature. Nevertheless, her letters sparkled with vivid descriptions of the spectacle surrounding her and revealed her love for the mountains, even in bitter winter when:

> the Storm King . . . stole silently down, and garlanded us in a wreath of shining snowflakes, and lo! the next morning you would have thought that some great white bird had shed its glittering feathers all over rock, tree, hill and bar.

And while waiting to leave the mountains, she penned her farewell:

> My heart is heavy at the thought of departing forever from this place. I *like* this wild and barbarous life; I leave it with regret. The solemn fir trees, "whose slender tops *are* close against the sky" here, the watching hills, and the calmly beautiful river, seem to gaze sorrowfully at me, as I stand in the moon-lighted midnight, to bid them farewell. . . . Yes, Molly, smile if you will at my folly; but I go from the mountains with a deep heart sorrow. I took kindly to this existence, which to you seems so sordid and mean. Here, at least, I have been contented.

She probably never again experienced quite such contentment. After the Clapps returned to San Francisco in November 1852, the doctor left. He sailed to Hawaii, returned to New England in 1854, and then drifted to Illinois and finally to Missouri. Dame Shirley remained in California and divorced her husband *in absentia* in 1857; he remarried and served as a Union Army surgeon during the Civil War. As Louisa Clapp (sometimes Clappe), she made numerous friends in San Francisco and taught in local public schools until 1878, when failing health forced her return to the East to live with family and friends. She died in 1906, leaving in her letters an incomparable legacy: the opportunity for later generations to share with gold rush Californians the experience that they called "seeing the elephant."

CHAPTER ELEVEN

THE NEW *EL DORADO*

On May 12, 1848, Sam Brannan waved a quinine bottle filled with glittering dust at San Franciscans, shouted his fabulous news, and perhaps calculated its impact on his own fortunes. "Gold!" he cried, "Gold, gold from the American River!" Reaction was immediate. Within days, half of San Francisco's population had departed. Within weeks, settlements from Sonoma to San Diego became virtual ghost towns. And within months, reports of the discovery crossed oceans and continents to lure adventurers from all points of the globe to the new *El Dorado*.

THE GREAT DISCOVERY

The sequence of events that set the world in motion began almost by chance. John Sutter decided to build a sawmill in partnership with an employee, James Wilson Marshall, in 1847. Born in New Jersey in 1810, Marshall learned his father's skills as a carpenter and wheelwright, drifted into the Ohio Valley during the 1830s, and joined a wagon train to Oregon in 1844. He later wandered south to California where he worked for Sutter, joined the Bear Flag Revolt, and soldiered in the Califor-

nia Battalion. Shortly after the Cahuenga Capitulation, he returned to Sutter's employ.

Marshall somehow convinced Sutter that partnership in a sawmill would be profitable and set out to locate a suitable site. He found what he needed on the South Fork of the American River, thirty miles from New Helvetia near a Maidu village called Cullumah (Coloma), and building began. A crew composed of village Indians and Mormon veterans of the Mexican War began construction, and the mill neared completion in late 1847. To accelerate the process, Marshall directed the river's flow through the millrace each night, allowing erosion to deepen the channel and carry away the debris of the previous day's labor. On January 24, 1848, during his regular morning inspection, he made the discovery that changed the course of history. Marshall spotted a gleam in the bottom of the ditch, scooped up a handful of gravel, examined it, and concluded that he had found gold. Crude tests—comparing flakes with a five-dollar gold piece and pounding a nugget on an anvil—convinced him, and he took samples of his find to Sutter. More tests persuaded

John Sutter and James Marshall
Sutter *(left)* and Marshall *(right)* were, quite unexpectedly, among the losers in "Nature's great lottery scheme."
Courtesy of the Bancroft Library.

the partners that they had indeed found gold, and they decided that secrecy was the only sensible policy. Somewhat surprisingly, their orders to remain silent were generally obeyed. Workers at the mill, for the moment at least, remained at their tasks and reasonably silent, prospecting individually on their own time.

Most Californians who heard of the strike doubted its significance, but a few capitalized on advance knowledge to reap handsome rewards. Sutter and Marshall, however, were not among them; both ultimately joined the ranks of gold rush casualties. When Sutter died in a Philadelphia hotel room in 1880, he was alone and destitute; squatters and speculators had stripped him

of his estates and California had terminated his $250 monthly pension. Marshall remained at Coloma and died nearby in 1885, a drunkard with $218 to his name; he had spent most of his life trying to collect private debts, to secure confirmation of his land claims, and to convince the state and the nation that he deserved some sort of compensation. To add to the irony, Sam Brannan, the man who announced *la bonanza* (rich vein or fair weather) to the world fared no better.

SOURCES OF *LA BONANZA*

The lure of gold that brought fortunes to some and ruin to others was certainly nothing new in human history. The metal's

SAM BRANNAN: FORTY-EIGHTER

Sam Brannan *Courtesy of the Bancroft Library.*

Although he was not yet thirty when he arrived in California, Sam Brannan was an Elder of the Mormon Church, chosen in 1846 to lead East Coast Saints "out of Babylon." He chartered the ancient *Brooklyn* and loaded her with supplies (including his printing press) and 200 Mormons bound for California. Upon their arrival, the flock set about its mission: preparation for the coming of the Nauvoo Saints, who were already on the overland trail from Illinois. But Brigham Young, who assumed church leadership after the murder of Joseph Smith, chose the Valley of the Great Salt Lake, not California, to be the Mormons' new Zion.

Conflict with Young over that decision and other matters eventually led to Brannan's excommunication, but personal ambition competed with religious zeal from the time of his arrival on the West Coast. Publication of the *California Star*, speculation in Yerba Buena (San Francisco) real estate, and other ventures made him rich, and he built the finest house in the village using tithes and labor commandeered from the Brethren. Few *Brooklyn* comrades, however, attended the galas held there; nor did Brannan share his affluence with the church.

Late in 1847, he embarked on a new venture: a general store at Sutter's Fort, where

SAM BRANNAN: FORTY-EIGHTER (continued)

workers began to pay for purchases with gold. The elder went to Coloma to investigate, confirmed the source of his customers' wealth, and began to stockpile goods in his warehouse. In May 1848 he returned to San Francisco to break the news, and as prospectors spread throughout the Sierra, Brannan & Co. followed them. Profits from sales (the Sutter's Fort store grossed up to $5,000 a *day*) went into new stores, land speculation, and investments in railroads, shipping, and waterfront development. Brannan also involved himself in local politics and in the Vigilance Committees of 1851 and 1856.

Success and fame brought the final conflict with Brigham Young. When the Leader heard of Brannan's wealth, he sent emissaries to collect $40,000 of "the Lord's money." But the San Francisco elder had an ultimatum of his own: the money in return for a receipt "signed by the Lord." This finished Brannan as a Mormon, but as California's first millionaire he used his resources to promote the state as well as to increase his wealth. He helped to organize the Society of California Pioneers and endowed fire companies, drill teams, and other civic and social associations. He founded a bank and a mint and financed a mail service, and in 1861 he bought an immense tract of Napa Valley land where he built his estate, Calistoga.

During the 1860s, however, Brannan began to suffer reverses. A dandy and a social lion, he also made enemies, including a squatter whose bullet left him partially paralyzed. Speculation in Hawaiian land and Nevada silver and plans to finance a revolution in Mexico depleted his assets. Finally his wife, who preferred cultured Europe to raw California, sued for divorce and was granted half of his fortune in cash.

The settlement brought poverty and the pain of paralysis and arthritis led to alcohol, which alienated friends. Still, Brannan remained ambitious. During the 1870s, he promoted settlement on Sonora land granted in recognition of his services to Mexico. Later, he sold real estate near San Diego and, in the garb of a *campesino* (peasant), raised figs at Escondido. All of the ventures failed, and Sam Brannan finished his days supported by brother Odd Fellows lodge members and relatives. When he died in 1889, only his landlady, Magdalena Moreno, was present to ease his passing. (WAB)

beauty, malleability, and scarcity have historically inspired quests both real and imaginary, for motives both economic and emotional. Yet in at least one sense the rush to California was unique. Most of the ore was placer gold—transported, deposited, and eventually extracted by the action of water— and located in areas of dense Indian habitation. Generations of native Californians could not have missed its glitter as they crossed streams or followed trails where rivers once ran, but unlike their Central and South American counterparts, they considered gold of little use. Thus the wealth of the Sierra waited thousands of years to be "discovered" by people sufficiently "civilized" to appreciate it.

Incredible natural forces formed California's mountains during the Mesozoic Era (200 to 70 million years ago), and distributed and deposited their gold. Over millennia, upheavals fragmented ore-bearing rock

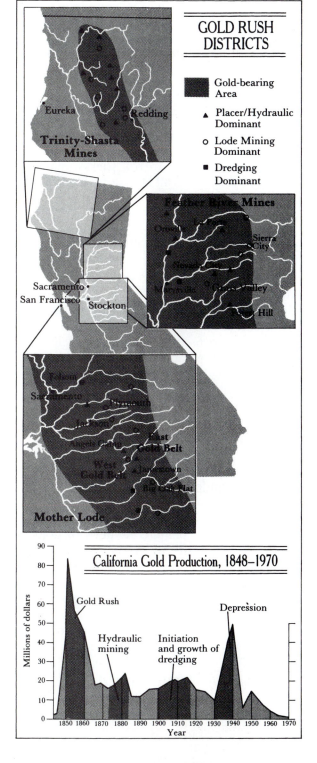

Gold Regions of California

and erosion scattered it. Rivers carried it in their currents and dropped it in holes in their beds or pockets along their banks. During the Tertiary Period of the Cenozoic Era (70 to 3 million years ago), streams altered courses and left deposits buried under layers of rock and gravel or exposed as cliffs. The process created the fabled Mother Lode, a band more than 100 miles long and up to 20 miles wide along the Sierra's western slope, and similar deposits in the Feather-Yuba River and Trinity-Shasta-Siskyou regions of California. Nature also trapped gold in the bowels of the earth, where magma cooled in fissures. Throughout the gold rush decades, miners scoured the Sierra for such veins, believing them to be origins of placer gold and richer even than the Mother Lode itself.

Potential *bonanzas* provided a main ingredient in the mythology of gold stretching from Jason's quest for the Golden Fleece to the search for *El Dorado* ("the golden one") to Garcí Ordoñez de Montalvo's tales of Calafia's island. They also inspired the legend of Cíbola and speculation by California explorers and visitors from Sebastián Vizcaíno to Richard Henry Dana. But until 1841 there was no tangible basis for such myths in California. Then Francisco López found a pocket in San Feliciano Canyon (now Placerita Canyon) north of Mission San Fernando. The discovery generated some enthusiasm among Mexican officials, a modest influx of miners from Mexico, and the first twenty ounces of California gold sent to the U.S. Mint. But well before the Treaty of Guadalupe Hidalgo was signed, the *placero* was exhausted.

THE GOLD RUSH OF 1848

Skepticism resulting from the San Feliciano episode may explain the restraint of the gold rush of early 1848, even though some news did leak out. Sutter's emissary, sent to Monterey to register his American River claim, crowed about the discovery to men he met along the way. Children of the cook at the sawmill chattered about it to a teamster delivering supplies. Workers at Sutter's Mill began to pay for purchases at Brannan's nearby store in nuggets and dust. Indeed, Sutter himself could not resist gossiping to friends such as John Bidwell and Mariano Vallejo. Not even samples, however, convinced most Californians. Nor were news-hungry journalists impressed; the first report appeared as a kind of postscript on the last page of the *Californian* of March 15. Subsequently, editor Edward C. Kemble included accounts of events at Coloma in the *California Star*, the province's only other newspaper. He compared the new strike to the San Feliciano episode, and in April he traveled to Sutter's Mill to investigate for himself. Back in San Francisco, he wrote enthusiastically about the beauty of the region but said little about the mines.

Still, some did take the strike seriously. A mill worker, for example, found a rich deposit and conveyed his success to friends from Mormon Battalion days. They visited Coloma and returned home to find their own *bonanza* near Mariposa. As weather improved in the spring, others appeared to investigate. John Bidwell arrived from his ranch near Chico, noted geological similarities between the American River terrain and his own region, and went home to open the Feather River diggings. Pierson B. Reading visited the mill, made observations similiar to Bidwell's, returned north, and began successful prospecting near Shasta and on the Trinity River. At about the same time, Charles M. Weber of Stockton put Indians to work taking gold from the Stanislaus and Mokelumne Rivers.

Although Marshall's workers remained at their tasks long enough to complete the mill, they too contracted gold fever. In March, their exodus began, marking the beginning of the end for Sutter's fortunes. By early April, a skeleton crew remaining at the sawmill had little timber to cut; most of Sutter's logging crews had gone prospecting. Work at New Helvetia ground to a halt as workers abandoned flour mill and tannery projects and left thousands of hides and bushels of grain to rot. Clerks, teamsters, and carpenters all abandoned Sutter's high wages in favor of the seduction of gold.

This handful of local miners and a few more from southern California monopolized the gold fields from January until May, when Brannan's announcement ended the interlude. The effect in San Francisco was electric, despite Edward Kemble's pronouncement that the episode was "a sham, got up to guzzle the gullible." With little thought for preparations or provisions, residents departed in droves. Some set sail aboard anything that would float; others struck out overland on horses or mules, trailed by scores more on foot. By mid-June, only 200 souls—a fourth of the population—remained in town, as real estate brokers, physicians, merchants, and lawyers boarded doors and windows and followed clients to the mines. Sailors deserted ships, often led by their officers, and soldiers from local garrisons were close behind. As news of gold rippled through the province in May and June, residents of other towns repeated the San Francisco exodus. Like a magnet, news from the mill on the American attracted the populace of the province: *californios, gringos,* and a few Indians. It seemed, the editor of the *Californian* wrote, that "the whole country from San Francisco to Los Angeles, and from the seashore to the base of the Sierra Nevada responds to the sordid cry of . . . **GOLD!**"

SPREADING THE NEWS

Californians could not monopolize the *bonanza* for long, however. Traders carried the news to Hawaii, to the Pacific Northwest, to Mexico, and to the Pacific coast of South America. By the end of 1848, confirmation of the discovery reached China, the east coast of the United States, and Europe.

The gold rush of 1848 increased California's non-Indian population to about 20,000; Hawaiians and Hispanic Americans accounted for most of the growth. Migration from "the States" was not dramatic until early 1849, despite reports that found their way east of the Mississippi. Thomas O. Larkin sent the *Californian's* announcement to the State Department, but apparently no one read it. The New York *Herald* printed a letter from California that predicted a "Peruvian harvest" of gold. In mid-September, the New Orleans *Picayune* published an interview with Lieutenant Edward F. Beale, on his way to Washington with confirmation of the discovery. During subsequent months, eastern newspapers printed stories from California, often grossly exaggerated, and samples of dust appeared. Nevertheless, Americans remained skeptical until their president verified the strike.

On December 7, 1848, Lieutenant Lucien Loeser arrived in Washington with a dispatch from military governor Richard B. Mason and 230 ounces of gold. Loeser's route was circuitous, and by the time he arrived, President James Knox Polk already had a copy of Mason's report, confirming the presence of gold—perhaps enough to finance the Mexican War "a hundred times over." Polk appended the document to his annual message to Congress, and when Loeser's sample arrived, he had it tested and placed on display in the War Office.

Response was instantaneous. Horace Greeley's description of the "California frenzy" appeared in the New York *Tribune* on January 30, 1849:

> A resident of New York coming back after a three month's absence, without having heard of California fever, would be almost doubtful of the identity of the place. He would find it impossible to account for the remarkable activity in certain branches of trade which are not usually subject to sudden change. He would wonder at the word "California," seen everywhere in glaring letters, and at the columns of vessels advertised in the papers as about to set sail for San Francisco. And finally, he would be puzzled at seeing a new class of men in the streets, in a peculiar costume—broad felt hats of reddish brown hue, loose rough coats reaching to the knee, and high boots. . . . Even those who have watched the gradual progress of the excitement are astonished at its extent and intensity. The ordinary course of business seems for the time to be changed. The bakers of sea-bread keep their ovens hot day and night, . . . without supplying the demand; the provision stores of all kinds are besieged by crowds of purchasers; manufacturers of India rubber goods, gutta percha, oil cloth, etc. have very large demands to supply; the makers of rifles, pistols and bowie knives can scarcely furnish as many of the articles as called for; and even the vendors of nostrums share a part in this windfall of business. . . . In fact, goods of every description sell just at present, and articles which have long been unsalable are packed up and sent away. Boxes, barrels and bales crowd the sidewalks, and hundreds of drays convey to the wharves the freight now being stored away in seventy vessels [bound] for the Gold Regions.

Greeley did not exaggerate, and before mid-year similar accounts appeared in journals from Hamburg to Hong Kong. As a result, by the end of 1849, California's non-Indian population had leapt to nearly 100,000.

When the state conducted its own census in 1852, the count exceeded 200,000.

BY SEA TO CALIFORNIA

Residents of East Coast states felt the bite of the gold bug first, and most of them chose to journey to California by sea. Departure points were close at hand, ships were available in most ports, the northeastern maritime tradition remained strong, and routes were already well known.

For many argonauts, the route across the Isthmus of Panama seemed most promising. Shorter and theoretically faster and safer than the five-month, 17,000-mile Cape Horn passage, it was open in all seasons. It was reasonably familiar, and in 1847 Congress had subsidized the United States Mail and the Pacific Mail companies, which were to begin steamship service between the two coasts of the nation in 1849. Hopes for a safe, swift journey by ship to the isthmus, across to the Pacific, and then by sea to San Francisco seldom materialized, however. Steamships could accommodate only a few of those eager for passage, so ancient sailing vessels, often grossly overloaded, were pressed into service. Since tickets covered only the ocean legs of the trip, travelers negotiated with Panama natives for transportation forty miles up the Chágres River and twenty more miles overland to the Pacific—only to encounter new problems. The first Pacific Mail steamer, the *California*, did not arrive until mid-January, when more than 700 ticketholders vied for its 250 berths. All sorts of vessels dumped as many as 1,000 passengers daily on the Atlantic side of the isthmus, but far fewer were available on the Pacific side. Consequently, by the end of February several thousand argonauts waited in Panama to complete the journey to the gold fields. Delays could deplete both resources and health, but conditions improved in 1850 when steamship lines coordinated services

and again in 1855 when a transisthmian railway was completed. From then until completion of the railroad across the continent in 1869, the Panama passage remained the favored route between California and "the States" for those who could afford it.

A greater volume of sea-borne traffic to California arrived by way of the long and hazardous Cape Horn route around the tip of South America. About half of those who rounded "Cape Stiff" formed joint stock companies, some of them well capitalized and outfitted. Members of the Northwestern Mining & Trading Company of Boston, for instance, refitted an old ship, turned her into a "floating drygoods emporium," and sailed replete with uniforms, a cook, and a brass band. The company hoped to sell the ship and cargo to finance the voyage, but too many others had similar plans. When the San Francisco waterfront became a graveyard for derelict ships and a dump for surplus merchandise, most companies disbanded to search for gold as individuals or with a few companions.

The voyage around the Horn did little to prepare argonauts for mining. Even seaworthy ships manned by competent crews (and they were few) took fearful beatings from the elements, and so did their passengers. Seasickness, spoiled food and stagnant water, boredom, and confinement in close quarters added to the misery. Months of inactivity and poor diet inevitably took a toll when the hard labor of mining began. But the Cape Horn passage had at least one positive result: to pass the time, travelers kept journals that made the migration one of the best documented in history.

CROSSING THE PLAINS

For those who crossed the Plains, journeys began in spring, when grasses provided food for animals and warmer weather melted some of the snow barriers in the mountains.

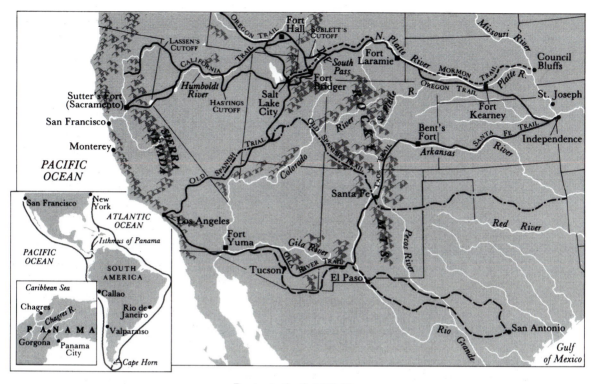

Routes to the Gold Fields

Knowledge of the Donner tragedy inspired caution in most, but a few parties tempted the elements by leaving too early or late or by traveling on their own, often with disastrous results. After the trek from Council Bluffs in 1849, for example, the Royce family rested at Salt Lake City, instead of joining an organized party with a guide. The decision put them far behind schedule, and following hand-written directions for crossing the Humboldt Sink cost them more time and severely fatigued their oxen. Even though Sarah Royce walked and carried her child to conserve their animals' energy, the family had to abandon its wagon and finish their journey on foot. They were among the last to cross the Sierra in the bitter winter of 1849, and only the timely arrival of a rescue party prevented another tragedy. A similar error was more costly to Roys Oatman and his family in 1851. After they left their train and set out alone on the Gila Trail, Apaches killed most of them and took a daughter, Olive, into captivity for five years.

Fortunately, most of those who crossed the Plains in 1849 and the early 1850s, when the California Trail was but a line on a map, traveled in companies. During March and April, they transported wagons and supplies to departure points such as Independence, Missouri, where they bought animals and additional provisions. The wisest among them hired experienced guides, and when all was ready the trains departed, many wagons abreast. For, as a member of one of the first companies to head west observed,

> Our daily task will be to get past those in advance of us, and to so travel that no trains will overtake us. In this way only can we hope to maintain our animals. The locusts of Egypt could scarcely be a greater scourge

than these great caravans, as grass and whatever else is green vanish completely before them.

Very soon kegs of nails, anvils, iron stoves, and other heavy cargo—jettisoned to lighten loads—littered the Plains.

The greatest menace to early argonauts was not Indians, as many had anticipated. That would come, but early gold-seekers were their own worst enemies. Some brought cholera up the Mississippi River from New Orleans, and it took a terrible toll. Burials occurred almost daily. So did accidental wounds from guns or axes, fractures caused by animals or wagon wheels, and injuries sustained while hauling wagons up and down mountains and across rivers. Equally dangerous, perhaps, were temptations to rely on useless guidebooks published in 1849 and 1850 or to leave established routes for unproven "cut-offs" to California.

Despite the hazards, between 25,000 and 30,000 crossed the Plains in 1849, pausing to rest at trading posts and among the Mormons at Salt Lake City. In the gold fields, they joined another 40,000 who arrived by one of the sea routes and a few thousand more who followed land routes across Mexico and the Southwest. During the 1850s, more than 200,000 arrived by overland routes, but not all remained; indeed, records of the U.S. Customs House at San Francisco indicate annual departures as high as seventy percent of arrivals.

San Francisco Maritime Arrivals and Departures

	Arrivals	Departures
1850	36,000	26,000
1852	64,000	23,000
1855	31,700	23,000
1858	40,700	28,000
1860	30,800	14,500

Although similar data do not exist for overland routes, estimates suggest that between 500 and 1,200 traversed the Plains eastward during each year of the 1850s.

Of those who remained, nearly one-fourth were foreign-born; they came from points in the United States and from around the globe to contribute to the Babel that Dame Shirley described. Despite vast differences, however, they had some things in common, whether they were from New England or Canton. They were young (less than thirty years old, on average) and male (more than ninety percent); in gold rush California "a gray beard *was* almost as rare as a petticoat." The argonauts also were typically enthusiastic and optimistic. Stephen J. Field, for example, would ultimately be a member of the first California legislature, write the state's first civil and criminal codes, serve as chief justice of the state supreme court, and be appointed to the U.S. Supreme Court in 1863. But when he arrived in San Francisco in 1849, he was just another exuberant adventurer:

> There was something exhilarating and exciting in the atmosphere which made everyone cheerful and buoyant. . . . Everyone in greeting me said, "It's a glorious country," or "Isn't it a glorious country?" . . . or something to that effect. In every case the word "glorious" was sure to come out. . . . I had not been out many hours before I caught the infection, and though I had but a single dollar in my pocket and no business whatever and did not know where I should get my next meal, I found myself saying to everybody I met, "It's a glorious country."

Glorious or not, many argonauts—perhaps most of them—regarded California as less than a fit place for permanent residence. Instead, it was a final frontier to be exploited and divested of its treasure before returning home.

SEARCHING FOR *LA BONANZA*

In addition to being predominantly young, enthusiastic, and male, early argonauts shared another attribute. Since the cost of transportation and equipment was substantial—$750 to $1,000 in an era when "a dollar could do wondrous things"—a winnowing process occurred. Few of the first gold seekers belonged to the laboring classes; most were professionals, semiprofessionals, skilled craftsmen, and small merchants. Ultimately, their talents became assets to life and society in California, but at mining—in many cases at physical labor itself—they began as rank amateurs. Buying patented manuals or gold-finding devices increased disadvantages, since few of the authors or inventors had ever seen a mine.

For most Forty-Niners and those who followed them during the 1850s, searching for gold meant learning an unfamiliar skill by trial, error, and imitation. Fortunately, many of the techniques eventually used were outlined in translations of Georgius Agricola's sixteenth-century treatise, *De Re Metallica*, and the Sierra strike attracted potential teachers as well as novices: Sonorans from Mexico, southerners from earlier strikes in the Carolinas and Georgia, coal and iron miners from both Pennsylvania and Britain, lead miners from the Midwest, and experienced Europeans.

Equally fortunate were early conditions; amateurism at first mattered little. Abundant surface deposits of placer gold were easily mined with rudimentary tools and little skill. Spoons, knives, shovels, and even cooking utensils sufficed to scoop pay dirt from river banks and beds. Readily mastered washing techniques separated gold from sand and gravel without complex equipment. Mexicans and southerners introduced panning to wash small amounts of pay dirt, flush away sediment, and leave only the heavier gold

behind. Mexicans used a wooden *batea* with sloped sides, southerners a metal pan designed for the purpose. As washing greater quantities of dirt became necessary, Georgians and Carolinians introduced another device—the "rocker" or "cradle." Simple enough to be constructed on the spot, the cradle was a variation on panning, but its operation required a team of at least three miners: one to shovel dirt into a hopper, one to pour in water, and one to "rock the cradle." The process carried away debris and left gold particles behind cleats or "riffles" that were inspected and cleaned periodically. Crude as it was, cradling permitted groups of miners to wash more dirt than they could by panning individually.

Mining conditions changed rapidly, however. By 1852, surface deposits were discovered, claimed, and depleted by the 100,000 miners swarming the hills; then it became necessary to process tons of dirt to recover ounces of gold. Ore-bearing gravels were sought deeper in the earth, and the "long toms" and other devices that Dame Shirley described became essential. No longer could an individual or a few partners work a claim. More and more frequently, miners organized companies to supply the labor and attract the capital needed to construct flumes, dams, and sluices and to dig ditches to transport water from distant sources. Companies also tunneled into hillsides to reach gold-bearing tertiary gravels. But the work was expensive, up to $20 a foot. If pay dirt was found, hauling it out of tunnels for crushing and washing also required costly equipment. All too often, months or years of effort and investment brought disappointment, disaster, or both.

› MECHANIZED MINING

In 1852, while working a low-yield Nevada County claim, Anthony Chabot devised a more efficient means for moving large quantities of earth to uncover gold deposits. He attached a hose to his flume and used water pressure to erode topsoil. A year later, Edward E. Matteson refined the method by attaching a nozzle to the hose; hydraulic mining—California's principal contribution to mining technology—was born.

The technique was an immense success as early as 1854 when the Sacramento *Weekly Union* described "a claim on Iowa Hill [that] had been worked . . . by the application of hydraulic power until it was *one hundred and twenty feet from the top of the hill to the bed rock of the claim.*"

> With a perpendicular column of water 120 feet high, in a strong hose, . . . ten men who own the claim are enabled to run off hundreds of tons of dirt daily. So great is the force employed, that two men with the pipes, by directing streams of water against the base of a high bank, will cause immense slides of earth, which often bring with them large trees and heavy boulders. To carry off these immense masses of dirt, they have constructed two sluices. . . . After these immense masses of earth are undermined and brought down by the streams forced from the pipes, those same streams are turned upon the tons of fallen earth, and it melts away before them, and is carried away through the sluices with almost as much rapidity as if it were a bank of snow. No such labor-saving power has ever been introduced to assist the miner in his operations.

Decades later, valley farmers would launch attacks on hydraulic miners, whose debris choked irrigation streams and flooded towns, and still later, environmentalists would condemn their devastation of the landscape. But at the time Californians accepted the damage as the inevitable price of progress.

Another form of placer mining, dredging, caused equally severe environmental damage, but it became important only after an 1884 court decision restricted hydraulic mining. Dredging had been tried in 1850, when a group of New England capitalists converted a river steamer to work the Yuba River near Marysville. The efforts failed, but the Risdon Iron Works of San Francisco later developed a bucket dredge, based on a New Zealand design and first put into operation near Oroville in 1898. From then until the 1940s, the process remained an important mining method in California, and it was profitable even if each cubic yard of earth yielded less than a half-ounce of gold. Eventually these clattering monsters—often several stories high—worked around the clock to gouge tons of rock and gravel from river beds, process it to wash gold free, and dump the piles of tailings that remain visible alongside rivers from the Smith and Trinity in the north to the Stanislaus and San Joaquin in the south.

Least significant in early California was tunnel mining, also called quartz, hard-rock, or lode mining. Most early efforts to burrow into underground deposits of placer gold were bankrupt by the mid-1850s; lack of both capital and experience destroyed them. Argonauts learned from Cornishmen and others to sink reasonably safe shafts and to ventilate them at great depths, and Mexican miners introduced the *arrastra* to crush ore brought to the surface; through a circular rock-lined trough, an animal dragged stones around a central pivot to grind gold-bearing quartz. Chileans made the device somewhat more efficient by substituting an axle and stone wheel for the cumbersome grinders. Experienced Hispanics also taught neophytes to use mercury or quicksilver to extract gold from pulverized rock.

Tool-making and foundry operations such as the Risdon, Union, and Vulcan works in San Francisco soon refined crude implements. They produced improved equipment

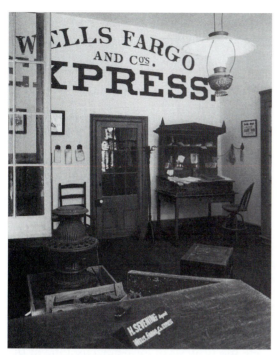

Wells Fargo & Company Express Office, Columbia
Beginning in 1852, Wells Fargo & Company offices such as this one in Columbia provided residents of remote mining communities with banking, transportation, and mail services to keep them in touch with the outside world. *Photograph by William A. Bullough.*

for drilling and tunneling, rail cart and elevator systems to transport ore to the surface, pumps to reduce flood hazards, the California stamp mill to smash rock more efficiently, and steam engines to power them all. Mining entrepreneurs such as Alvinza Hayward in Amador County and his counterparts in Trinity and Nevada Counties used such locally developed advances in mining technology with substantial success during the 1860s and 1870s. In the process, they helped to sustain the state's gold production after the initial boom years. The new equipment and techniques became even more significant, however, when they were applied in the Comstock silver mines in Nevada during

the 1860s and as they gave impetus to California manufacturing.

LIFE IN THE MINES

Shortly after completing a voyage around Cape Horn in December 1849, Dr. J. D. B. Stillman described conditions surrounding the Sacramento hospital that he established with two partners:

> The people at home can have no conception of the amount of suffering in the vicinity. Hundreds are encamped in tents, throughout the rains and storms, scantily supplied with food and covering. Men are driven from the mines for want of food, and are begging for employment. Yesterday there were twenty-five deaths. The sickness does not arise from the severity of the climate but largely from overwork, scanty and bad food, disappointment and homesickness.

Clearly life in the mines could be devastating, both physically and emotionally. But Stillman's presence illuminates another aspect of gold rush history: civilization arrived with the first argonauts, and the doctor and his hospital are but one example. Gold seekers dispersed rapidly from the American River region northward to the Feather River and Trinity-Shasta-Siskyou diggings and southward to the Amador and Mariposa districts, bearing elements of societies they had left behind.

Little can be added to Dame Shirley's eloquent descriptions of life in mining camps, except to emphasize the reluctance of most of their residents to revert to primitivism. To be sure, some tolerated bedrolls, brush huts, and crude nourishment. Others, however, built sturdy cabins and furniture to make life more comfortable. Drinking, gambling, and carousing often characterized miners' diversions. But a book was as prized as a deck of cards; the arrival of a live performer, physician, or clergyman was cause for jubilation. Photographers (who often doubled as barbers or dentists) found eager clients for their tintypes, daguerreotypes, and other services. And a "petticoated astonishment" brought out the best more often than the worst in the miners. Mining camps were more than bastions of unfettered male hedonism; they kept miners in touch with the societies they had left and brought not only saloons, brothels, and gambling dens but also schools, churches, newspapers, and similar institutions to the frontier.

The settlements also introduced rudimentary political structures to the wilderness. California's vast mining regions were quite literally lawless; therefore, committees elected in each camp or district devised rules for mining operations. They specified methods for making and maintaining claims, recorded titles and transfers, and settled ownership disputes. Often, a rough logic prevailed. Where gold deposits were rich, claims might be limited to a ten-foot square. In another region, a miner stood at the center of his prospective "dig" and heaved his pick at the points of the compass to establish his corners. Local conditions dictated expedients, but principles originated by local committees were sound enough to be incorporated into the state's mining code, its land ownership laws, and its water policies.

Other aspects of mining-camp law proved far less worthy of emulation, however. Initially, little serious crime required attention. When it occurred, miners' tribunals—often supervised by a locally elected justice of the peace or *alcalde*—convened to deal with theft, claim jumping, and the like. Since there were no jails, punishments were immediate: fines, banishment, or flogging. The influx of a varied, highly competitive population altered the situation. Newcomers

included fugitives memorialized in the contemporary ballad:

> What was your name in the States?
> Was it Thompson or Johnson or Bates?
> Did you murder your wife and flee for your life?
> O, what was your name in the States?

Early miners rarely asked such questions of their comrades. But as crime and competition for gold increased, so too did suspicion and demands for swift justice.

Unfortunately, popular tribunals all too easily degenerated into lawless mobs. The first recorded incident occurred in January 1849 at Dry Diggings (subsequently Hangtown and now Placerville). Five miners who spoke only French and Spanish were caught stealing, tried, and flogged. Two of them (some accounts say three) were accused of a previous theft and murder and lynched, despite the protests of local citizens. One of the most infamous episodes involved a Mexican woman, Juanita, at Downieville. During a boisterous July 4 celebration in 1851, a drunken miner entered her cabin and she stabbed him. A mob tried her and, because she would not recant her action, sentenced her to die. A physician certified that she was pregnant, and Stephen J. Field condemned the action as a travesty of justice, but to no avail. Juanita was hanged from the Yuba River bridge.

Historian Hubert Howe Bancroft exaggerated when he described the trees of mining districts as "tasseled with the carcasses of the wicked." Nevertheless, incidents were sufficiently numerous to cast a dark shadow over the early history of the state. Through the first half of the 1850s, mob justice occurred frequently, not only in the mines but also in San Francisco, Los Angeles, and other towns. Some of those punished were criminals, but others were targets of local political animosities, moral prejudices, economic frustration, or nativist and racist sentiments.

BONANZA TO BORRASCA

During the first half of the gold rush decade, mining changed significantly from an individual pursuit of instant wealth to an organized corporate enterprise that required specialized skills and equipment and substantial capital. The transformation had a major impact on the development of California society, especially on the expectations of the thousands of argonauts who crossed the isthmus, rounded the Horn, or traversed the Plains in search of fortune. For many of them, the anticipated *bonanza* soon became *una borrasca* (a storm or tempest). The value of gold extracted by various means during the first dozen years of the California gold rush was spectacular indeed.

1848	$245,000	1854	$69,433,931
1849	10,151,360	1855	55,485,395
1850	41,273,106	1856	57,509,411
1851	75,938,232	1857	43,628,172
1852	81,294,700	1858	46,591,140
1853	67,613,487	1859	45,846,599

Totals must be multiplied at least tenfold to place them in the context of present dollar values. They must also be assessed in terms of the worth of gold in the nineteenth century, $16 an ounce, and the number of miners at work: 5,000 in 1848; 40,000 in 1849; 50,000 in 1850; 100,000 in 1852. Between 1852 and 1860, the number remained fairly stable.

Gold production tended to decrease as the number of miners increased, and that had important implications. Initially, the quest for gold was fairly democratic. Deposits encompassed some 35,000 square miles, room for a multitude of prospectors. In addition, the treasure was located in the public domain, apparently there for the finding and taking. Under the circumstances, few willingly submitted to legal, political, or economic authority or accepted work for wages. During the halcyon years of 1848 to 1850, when each miner searched for the "big strike," a daily wage was defined as the value a person extracted from the ground. As the volume of gold diminished and miners more frequently worked for others, however, the term acquired a more conventional meaning and rewards diminished significantly.

Average Daily Wage for White Miners

1848	$20	1852	$6
1849	16	1853–55	5
1850	10	1856–60	3
1851	8		

Chinese, Indians, and other nonwhite miners received considerably less. For individuals arriving in California expecting to make their fortunes, disappointment at declining potential was severe.

Through the 1850s, Californians' compensation compared favorably with the average daily wage in "the States," $1.00 to $1.25 for a skilled eastern miner, but living costs in California were far higher. More important, declining wage levels and the fact that after 1855 most miners were employees, not independent prospectors, suggest that the average argonaut did not find the anticipated *bonanza*. Rare enough even in 1848 and 1849, big strikes became rarer still in later years. Once placer deposits were depleted, mining became an increasingly complex and corporate enterprise. Individual prospectors virtually disappeared, replaced by wage earners working for entrepreneurs who organized labor forces, supplied essential machinery, and furnished the capital often obtainable only at exorbitant interest rates. The situation was not what most participants in "nature's great lottery scheme" anticipated, and many of them vented their frustration on native *californios* and Indians.

CALIFORNIOS IN THE MINES

More effectively than war with Mexico, waves of argonauts flooding the region accomplished the American conquest of California. Two-thirds were Yankees who carried with them their customs, attitudes, and prejudices—including the nativism that prevailed in "the States" at mid-nineteenth century. Eventually, many in California— especially the Chinese—became targets for American biases. But the first to suffer from imported bigotry were natives of the region, *californios* and Indians, who were reduced to minority status in their own homeland. For the Spanish-speaking, loss of lands would later complete what Leonard Pitt called "the decline of the *californios.*" But even before the Mexican War of 1846, an influx of Yankees prompted Doña Angustias de la Guerra Ord to observe, "Now, . . . it rains on the sheepfold."

Californios in the mines did not experience the buffets of the impending tempest immediately. During the rush of 1848, about 1,300 of them were successful participants. Members of the Coronel, Sepúlveda, and Carrillo families in Los Angeles, for example, organized a party that headed for the Stanislaus River. They mined on their own, traded trinkets for nuggets with some Indians, and hired others to work for them. Antonio Coronel accumulated forty-five ounces of gold in just one day, and an associate found a 12-ounce nugget. Another *compadre* gathered a "towelful of nuggets" in a few hours; then he sold his claim to another who extracted fifty-two pounds of gold in a week. A third owner of the site also became rich.

When the mining season of 1848 ended, successful *californios* returned to their homes

to enjoy their wealth and lay plans for 1849. By then, however, conditions were less congenial. During Coronel's return journey, a belligerent ex-Bear Flagger attacked and severely injured one of his companions. In the diggings, the party encountered Yankee hostility and open threats to all "foreigners." They also witnessed California's first lynching, the flogging and execution of a Frenchman and a Chilean at Hangtown. Even when Coronel's group retreated to more isolated regions, they were informed that the gold belonged exclusively to Yankees. Confronted by overwhelming numbers, obvious hostility, and a real potential for violence, *californios* made the only logical decision; they left the mines.

Coronel later recorded his reaction: "For me, mining is finished." He probably spoke for most of his compatriots, who were rare in the mines after 1849. Occasionally a *patrón* led a party into the southern districts, only to be intimidated by surly *gringos* who resented Hispanics and their competition. Hispanics remained in all mining regions, but most were neither California-born nor independent prospectors. Instead, they were Mexicans and South Americans employed by American companies. A few were also merchants, *arrieros* whose mules carried supplies into remote camps, or cooks in the diggings.

After 1848, Yankees assumed proprietary rights and asserted their sense of ethnic and moral superiority. They argued that the Treaty of Guadalupe Hidalgo made California a "white man's country," conveniently ignoring treaty provisions that protected the rights of provincial residents and offered them citizenship. Like Dame Shirley, Yankees also lumped all Hispanics together as simply "Spaniards," although only 470 individuals from Spain lived in California as late as 1860. As competition and antagonism increased, "Spaniards"—including *californios*— became "Sonorians," "greasers," "*cholos,*" or worse and were associated with gambling, prostitution, and other allegedly "Latin" vices.

Initial efforts to control the Hispanic presence were spontaneous and informal: threats, mob action, claim jumping, and occasional beatings. Quickly, however, local miners' committees gave prejudice a semblance of legality by enacting laws excluding "noncitizens" from many districts. Formal or informal, nativist attitudes could be vindictive and vicious. Miners' tribunals consistently punished aliens more severely than others, often specifying flogging or mutilation. "Their majesties the mob" also took justice into their own hands, as in events at Hangtown in 1849, the lynching of Juanita at Downieville in 1851, the Rich Bar incidents recorded by Dame Shirley, and many more. Nor did anti-Hispanic sentiments abate with admission to the Union and enactment of the Foreign Miners' Tax Law in 1850.

THE FOREIGN MINERS' TAX LAW OF 1850

When the first state legislature convened, Yankee miners appealed for a law to institutionalize their prejudices. Their principal advocate was Senator Thomas Jefferson Green of Sacramento, a Texan who attempted to introduce slavery into the Yuba River mines and whose hatred for Mexicans was notorious. The law that Green drafted and lawmakers approved in 1850 theoretically imposed a twenty dollar monthly fee on *all* noncitizen miners. Support for the measure was not universal, but California's need for revenue convinced most of the legislators to vote for it.

Because the tax was too high for most to pay and selectively enforced, it generated little revenue. Rarely were miners of European origins even asked to pay, but one serious incident did occur when agents in Sonora attempted to collect the tax. Frenchmen and Germans allied themselves with 4,000 unarmed Mexicans to protest the tax, and in the "French Revolution" that followed, dissidents encountered hundreds of armed Americans assembled to support the district tax collector. One Mexican was stabbed in the episode, and the Europeans who instigated the protest were arrested, fined five dollars each, and released. Mexicans, however, were ordered to pay the tax in full. For most of them, the point was made; they packed their belongings and departed.

In one sense, the tax law worked; it drove most Hispanics from the mines. Otherwise it was a failure. It produced neither the anticipated $2.4 million in revenue nor a docile, cheap labor force. Nor did it eliminate only "undesirables," much to the distress of local merchants and corporate mine owners. Tradesmen and would-be employers cited the Treaty of Guadalupe Hidalgo, the U.S. Constitution, and traditional American ideals in appeals to the governor, the legislature, and the state supreme court to repeal or modify the law. Late in 1850, the governor responded by reducing the monthly fee, and early in 1851 agitation by citizens of Sonora, Stockton, and other towns forced the law's repeal. That action, however, did not lure Hispanics back to the mines or halt the "decline of the *californios.*"

"DIGGERS" IN THE MINES

The gold rush experience of California Indians paralleled that of the *californios*, with more devastating results. Argonauts stereotyped them as "diggers," assuming that theirs was a primitive culture based on gathering roots and trapping rodents for sustenance, but James J. Rawls has demonstrated that the term could have a different application. Indeed, Richard B. Mason's report to President Polk estimated that half of the 5,000 gold diggers during the summer of 1848 were Indians. Most worked for wages for individuals such as Marshall, Sutter, or *californios*. Antonio María Suñol, for instance, took twenty from his Bay Area rancho to prospect the American River, and the Coronel-Sepúlveda-Carrillo party included them as well. But pre-1846 non-Hispanic settlers employed the greatest number. Charles M. Weber, who arrived in 1841 and established a rancho near Stockton, had nearly 1,000 Indians working for him along Weber Creek near Placerville, and his Yokuts miners made the first major strike in the Calaveras-Stanislaus region. John M. Murphy married the daughter of a Miwok chief and employed 600 Indians on the North Fork of the Stanislaus, while John Bidwell worked the Feather River with Indians from his Rancho Chico, and emigrant Pierson B. Reading employed others to prospect along Clear Creek in Shasta County and on the Trinity River. Sutter himself often acted as a labor contractor to provide Indian workers.

Not all Indians mined for whites, however. At first amused by effort wasted in search of something neither edible nor wearable, they soon learned that white men prized gold and that it could be traded. Coronel recorded a typical exchange in 1848. Several Miwoks entered his camp, each carrying a bag of dust and obviously interested in trading:

> One . . . took [a saddle blanket] and pointed to the sack filled with gold; he pointed out a certain spot as the amount he was offering. . . . There was then in the area no way to replace the blanket so I refused the offer. . . . He increased it . . . , lowering the place where he pressed the sack with his thumb; I refused again. He increased again and then one of my servants asked me why I did not give it to him—[saying] that he would make some saddle blankets of grass.

The *californio* received seven ounces of gold ($112) for a blanket that cost two *pesetas* (less than 50 cents) when new. Other trades were even more outrageous, including glass beads ounce-for-ounce for gold, and established trading posts made fleecing Indians systematic and endemic. Proprietors set "Indian" prices—often double those charged to whites—and kept lead weights—"digger ounces"—to weigh their dust. They rationalized their policies on grounds that, as one trader put it, "no Christian man is bound to give full value to those infernal redskins; . . . they got no religion, and tharfore no conscience, so I deals with them accordin'."

SOLVING THE "INDIAN PROBLEM"

Journals written in 1848 refer frequently not only to native Californians but also to Walla Walla, Chinooks, and an occasional Delaware in the mines. By late 1849, however, few are mentioned; by the 1850s, almost none. During the early gold rush, *californios* and others familiar with local Indians prevailed in the diggings, but the experiences of later arrivals involved violent encounters or sensationalized tales of savagery and slaughter. Among the first to appear were Oregonians, fresh from the Whitman massacre at Walla Walla in 1847 and subsequent Cayuse wars. Those incidents and clashes on the trail to California conditioned their attitudes; when they encountered Indians working productive mines, they were outraged. In March 1849, Oregon miners attacked a Maidu village on the American River; Indians retaliated by killing five Oregonians. The dead men's compatriots assembled in force, pillaged another village, slaughtered many inhabitants, and took a score prisoner. That the captives belonged to the tribe that killed the five Oregonians is unlikely; nevertheless, seven of them were marched to Coloma and summarily executed. When James Marshall and others protested, their lives also were threatened.

Indian-fighting subsequently degenerated into scalping, beheading, and other forms of mutilation and sadism, to the disgust of Californians like the one who asked, "What courage is displayed by such warfare as this, what honor is to be gained in it, and why have so many of your Oregon men shot down scores of Indians like wolves?" But "Oregon men" were not the only ones involved; gold-seekers from all over "the States" brought their hostilities and prejudices with them. Some antagonisms resulted from stereotypes in the minds of individuals who, like Dame Shirley, had never before seen a "real" Indian, and imagination could produce fantasies of incredible proportions. In 1850, for example, Governor Peter Burnett reported to the president that 100,000 armed braves were awaiting a signal to wage a war of extermination against whites—when the entire Indian population of the new state barely equaled that number.

Private forces conducted sporadic forays against Indians, until militia forces funded by state and national governments added a semblance of legitimacy to the campaign. About 15,000 Indians were killed by the 1860s; many more died of disease and starvation. Some of those involved in the warfare claimed that they opposed Indian peonage, a labor system equated with racial slavery. Many resented Indian competition with white labor for the state's gold or acted on the assumption that "the only good Indian is a dead Indian." And a vicious few simply enjoyed the killing. Historian Hubert Howe Bancroft justly called the episode "one of the last human hunts of civilization, and the basest and most brutal of them all."

In 1850, to solve the "Indian problem," state legislators enacted laws—similar to the "black codes" adopted in the post-Civil War South—providing that Indians judged to be vagrants could be indentured to private individuals as laborers. Governors Peter Burnett and John McDougal advocated extermination, while others leaned toward the somewhat more humane policy of removal. Federal officials, however, considered annihilation repugnant and removal impractical and sanctioned an alternate approach. In 1850 Congress appointed three commissioners to implement a segregation program. The trio negotiated agreements with a score of tribes that accepted relocation in areas remote from white settlement, but the solution was untenable. Californians protested that the 12,000 square miles allocated to Indians constituted one-eighth of the state's area, and in 1852 the U.S. Senate rejected all of the treaties. A year later, Congress approved a measure proposed by Edward F. Beale, U.S. Indian Superintendent for California, to establish several reservations of up to 30,000 acres each. Only Fort Tejón in the southern San Joaquin Valley and Tehachapi Mountains attracted many Indians or functioned well even temporarily, and by the early 1860s political manipulation and the incompetence of Beale's successors reduced California reservations to near ruin. Fort Tejón itself was abandoned in 1868.

Some California Indians resisted removal, as in the Modoc War of 1872–1873. In northeastern California, fifty poorly armed warriors, led by Chief Kientepoos (Captain Jack) and accompanied by women and children, fortified themselves in lava beds and held off 400 U.S. Army regulars. After months of fighting that cost the lives of seventy-five Americans and five Indian warriors (and scores of Indian women and children) and a half-million dollars, the Modocs were defeated and Captain Jack was executed. Other tribes, like the Mill Creeks during the 1850s and 1860s, attacked whites who raided villages, raped women, stole children, and in-

A Fight with the Indians
An engraving from a Sacramento newspaper depicts a Trinity County incident in which residents reportedly avenged the murder of a local butcher by slaughtering more than a hundred local Indians. It also illustrates the attitudes of most settlers in California during the gold rush era. *From the collection of Peter E. Palmquist.*

vaded territories. But most —like the Yahi described in Theodora Kroeber's *Ishi* and the Yosemite who, during the retaliatory "Mariposa Wars" of the 1850s, followed Chief Tenaya into the Sierra wilderness and ultimately joined Mono Lake Paiutes—retreated before the inevitable. Against devastating numbers and debilitating disease, however, neither resistance nor retreat was effective; by 1870, only 30,000 Indians survived anywhere in California.

Whether directly attacked or not, Indians could not endure the cultural conflict ushered in by the gold rush. Miners—and later loggers and farmers—rendered streams and forests of their habitat virtually useless to them. In contrast to earlier Spaniards and Mexicans, new settlers penetrated into areas that were isolated native habitats, even in remote portions of the state. With evident satis-

faction, an editor of the *Humboldt Times* in 1857 observed,

> Seven years ago, [this region] . . . was innocent of any knowledge of the Anglo-Saxon race. The Indian roamed over its wilds . . . until the bold and enterprising hand of the white man came. Now the scene is changed. . . . Another cycle of seven years and the last vestiges of the race will be well nigh obliterated, . . . crushed out like other imbecilities, under the iron heel of progress and the steady and resistless march of civilization, and places [the Indians] once occupied will resound with the busy hum of industrious whites, and the loom, the plough, and the anvil will supersede the Indian arrow and hunting knife.

During the 1850s and 1860s, most white Californians undoubtedly shared the writer's sentiment.

CHAPTER TWELVE

THE THIRTY-FIRST STATE

Carey McWilliams reinforced John W. Caughey's observation that gold was the cornerstone of California's nineteenth-century experience when he described a "gold-energy equation" that telescoped history and gave events unprecedented velocity. Developments that took decades elsewhere occurred in years; those that required centuries took decades. Only months after the first Forty-Niners arrived, a convention at Monterey drafted a state constitution and applied for admission to the Union. San Francisco emerged as an "instant city" with a cosmopolitan population, mature social and economic institutions, nascent manufacturing establishments, and a developing cultural life. Just as quickly, California entered the mainstream of national affairs and became embroiled in the slavery issue, the rising tide of nativism, and changes in American political and economic life. Rapid progress brought conflict and turbulence.

THE MILITARY INTERREGNUM

From the Cahuenga Capitulation in January 1847 until late 1849, political authority in California struck a precarious balance between American military government and institutions retained from the Mexican era, a hybrid arrangement that satisfied no one. A series of military governors administered the province as a whole, none for very long. Five served during the first ten months of occupation: Commodores John D. Sloat and Robert F. Stockton, General Stephen W. Kearny, and Colonels John C. Frémont and Richard B. Mason. General Persifor F. Smith replaced Mason in February 1849, followed by General Bennett Riley in April. In 1848 Mason issued his *Laws for the Better Government of California* in an attempt to reduce confusion, but inconsistency, not the absence of laws, inhibited effective administration.

Local government adhered to Mexican forms, in keeping with the Treaty of Guadalupe Hidalgo. An *alcalde*, whose office combined executive, legislative, and judicial authority, governed each settlement. Most *alcaldes* were *californios*, but not all. U.S. Navy Lieutenant Washington Bartlett was the first American *alcalde* in Yerba Buena (San Francisco) and John W. Geary was the last. In

Monterey, Walter Colton was appointed in 1846, and in Marysville, Stephen J. Field was elected in 1849. Appointed *ayuntamientos* or town councils advised the *alcaldes*.

Military government and remnants of the Mexican system contradicted Americans' political traditions, and inaction in Washington magnified their discontent. Late in 1846, when it was apparent that Mexican lands in the West would fall under U.S. jurisdiction, Pennsylvania Congressman David Wilmot introduced his proposal to exclude slavery from new territories in advance of acquisition, embroiling Congress in controversy. Northern representatives supported the principles of Wilmot's Proviso, Southerners demanded an extension of the Missouri Compromise line, and nativists opposed annexing "foreigners": Hispanics and Indians. None would compromise, and California's status in the Union drifted without definition, even after the war ended.

THE CONSTITUTION OF 1849

Thousands of Americans swarming into California became impatient with chaotic political arrangements, and in February 1849, San Franciscans defied the military governor and replaced the local *alcalde* and *ayuntamiento* with a traditional town government. During succeeding months, Americans at San José, Monterey, and Sacramento expressed discontent with both local arrangements and congressional delays by demanding immediate action. To forestall popular agitation, military governor Bennett Riley exceeded his authority in June 1849 and—probably with support from President Zachary Taylor—ordered election of delegates to a constitutional convention to meet in Monterey in September.

None of the forty-eight constitution makers who assembled were miners; only twelve—including William Gwin of San Fran-

cisco, with three months in the province, and Captain Henry W. Halleck, the military representative—arrived in California after 1847. Eight delegates were *californios*, among them Pablo de la Guerra, José Carrillo, and Mariano Vallejo. The majority were pre-Mexican War settlers in California—men such as Thomas O. Larkin, Esteban Foster, Abel Stearns, and convention president Robert B. Semple. Most were young; three-fourths were under forty, average age was thirty-six, and nine were under thirty. But more than half had prior political experience, in either California or "the States."

Several potentially divisive issues might have disrupted or even dissolved the convention. One was the choice between state or territorial status, but that question was resolved—with tacit approval from Washington—in favor of statehood. The volatile issue of slavery provided surprisingly few problems; even delegates of Southern origin joined in unanimous opposition to the institution. Their action reflected neither abolitionist sentiments nor sympathy for black equality, however; instead, racism and hostility toward competitive slave labor motivated their votes. Indeed, when a former Kentuckian proposed the exclusion of free blacks from the state, the convention balked mainly because the measure would violate the U.S. Constitution and delay admission to the Union.

The most serious controversy at the convention—and the one that nearly ended it—involved boundaries. Some delegates ardently advocated a state bordered by the Rocky Mountains, while a more judicious faction argued for the Sierra and compromisers proposed several intermediate lines. Heated debates focused on related issues: governing nearly a quarter of the nation's area, potential intrusion of slavery, inclusion of the Mormon state of Deseret (present-day Utah), responsibility for Indian affairs, and the safety of settlers in the vast region. Disputes might have ended the convention, but the logic of the small-state faction prevailed. Delegates adopted the state's present boundaries: 42° north latitude eastward to 120° west longitude, then southward to 39° north latitude in the center of Lake Tahoe; from there, southeasterly to intersect with the Colorado River at 35° north latitude, and along the center of the river to Mexico.

Expediency guided the convention's action on the issues of statehood, slavery, and boundaries. It also prompted one of the unique features of California's first constitution: the Monterey Convention retained elements of Mexican law that protected the property rights of married women. Delegates may have responded to the nation's first feminist conference held at Seneca Falls in New York in 1848, but more probably they were trying to make the state attractive to women such as Luzena Stanley Wilson and Julia Shannon. With her husband, Wilson operated hotels in Sacramento, but when they moved to Nevada City she struck out on her own, "borrowed" lumber, and built a table and kitchen. She later reported that:

> When my husband came back [that] night, . . . he found twenty miners eating at my table. Each man as he rose put a dollar in my hand and said I might count on him as a permanent customer. . . . I shortly thereafter took my husband into partnership.

Shannon, California's first known female photographer, advertised in San Francisco between 1850 and 1852: daguerreotypes "taken by a real live lady" ("Give her a call, gents") and services as a midwife (with references from several local physicians). She apparently did well; according to the *Alta California*, she lost two buildings valued at $7,000 in a fire that destroyed the city in May 1851.

Whatever motivated constitution writers, their action was a radical one at mid-nine-teenth century. Nearly as radical were provisions reflecting Jacksonian preferences for the individual over the corporate entrepreneur, prohibiting the use of paper money, imposing stringent regulations on corporate organization, especially banks, and restricting the issue of securities.

The remainder of the Constitution of 1849 was conventional. It banned dueling and mandated the legislature to create a public school system, to establish a university, and to secure federal land-grant aid for educational purposes. For the most part, the delegates followed existing models. From the U.S. Constitution, they took the principles of separation of powers, a bicameral legislature, and checks and balances. They also borrowed freely from other state constitutions: Iowa's because it was the most recently admitted western state and New York's because it was most recently revised. The result was an organic law that dealt with principles of government and wisely left enacting laws to legislative action.

Before the convention adjourned, it raised two issues that had important long-range implications. Underrepresented southern Californians (only eleven delegates) protested revenue policies that placed burdens almost exclusively on real property (such as grazing lands) and exempted personal property (such as mining profits). Their position later proved to be astute, but they were outvoted in 1849. And when the convention adopted a Great Seal for the state, Mariano Vallejo recalled *californios'* humiliation by Bear Flaggers in 1846 and objected to including a grizzly in the design, unless a *vaquero* held the beast on a *reata*. He was overruled in a decision that reflected the widening gulf between newly arrived Yankees and long-time Hispanic residents of California and involved an irony that Vallejo might have appreciated: Californians gave the grizzly prominence on both their seal

The Great Seal of the State of California
Despite Mariano Vallejo's objections, the grizzly remained on the Great Seal, but the *vaquero* and *reata* did not. The Roman goddess of wisdom, invention, and the arts, Minerva, surveys the scene, and over all is the state's motto: "Eureka," or "I have found it!"

and their flag, and then proceeded to exterminate the noble beast.

STATEHOOD

The Monterey Convention completed its task in just six weeks, prompting some criticism for unseemly haste, expediency, and self-interest. Nevertheless, Californians approved the constitution in November 1849 by a vote of 12,064 to 811. Voters also made Peter H. Burnett the state's first governor and John McDougal lieutenant governor and chose members of a legislature and a representative to Congress. For the next eleven months, however, Congress approved neither the Monterey Constitution nor California's petition for statehood, and uncertainty hampered the government that met in San José in December 1849. The state had no authority from Washington, it could not send representatives to Congress, and its

very existence was of dubious legality. Nevertheless—perhaps to demonstrate faith in inevitable recognition—legislators began immediately to conduct state business by electing two U. S. Senators: John C. Frémont and William M. Gwin.

Unlike delegates to the Monterey Convention, most members of the first legislature lacked previous political experience. Some were principally concerned with their own interests or with timely response to Senator Thomas Jefferson Green's frequent calls for adjournment to his nearby saloon. The habit inspired a nickname, "The Legislature of a Thousand Drinks," and perhaps influenced inaction on an important early order of business: designating a state capital. Neglect resulted in a bidding war among rival towns and kept state government on the move until 1854, when Sacramento became the permanent capital. In the interim, the capital shifted six times among San José, Vallejo, Benicia, and Sacramento.

On the other hand, the first government included many competent and serious individuals. Among them was Assemblyman Stephen J. Field who drafted the state's first civil and criminal codes, using those of his native New York as models. Legislators also formulated policies for establishing local governments and law enforcement agencies, creating new counties, and collecting revenue to support the government. Although these were important accomplishments, California's attention remained focused on Washington, for without approval from Congress, decisions made at San José meant nothing.

In the nation's capital, partisan controversy, efforts to preserve a balance of power in Congress, and especially the slavery issue delayed action on California's petition. Finally, a proposal supported by leading Whigs and Democrats granted something to everyone and at last broke the impasse. Known as

Statehood Celebration
On October 29, 1850, San Franciscans celebrated California's admission as the thirty-first state. *Courtesy of the Bancroft Library.*

the Compromise of 1850, this Omnibus Bill admitted California to the Union as a free state, defined the Utah and New Mexico territories and allowed them to decide the slavery question locally when they were organized as states, abolished the slave trade (but not slavery) in the District of Columbia, and enacted a more stringent federal fugitive slave code. The bill became law on September 9, 1850; when the news reached Californians a month later, they responded with parades, illuminations, and jubilant celebrations throughout the new state.

EARLY POLITICAL RUMBLES: BRODERICK AND GWIN

During the 1850s, California's political affairs were influenced less by changing administrations, conflicting ideologies, party realignments, or national issues than by two individuals: David C. Broderick and William M. Gwin. The pair had several things in common. Both were Democrats who arrived in California in 1849, ambitious men who cov-

eted a seat in the U.S. Senate, and experienced politicians able to establish solid personal support. But there the similarities ended.

Born in Washington, D.C., Broderick was the son of Irish immigrants. As a youth in New York City, he received no formal education but a thorough schooling in rough-and-tumble city politics. Blunt, affable, and occasionally unscrupulous, he was a saloon keeper, hack driver, and unsuccessful congressional candidate before moving west. In San Francisco, he renewed acquaintances with former New Yorkers, became involved in Democratic politics, built a machine centered on local volunteer fire companies, and increased his personal wealth by speculation in waterfront lots and a private mint. His opposition to slavery and Jacksonian principles gave him local appeal, especially among wage earners, and as a member of the first state senate, Broderick used patronage to control the San Francisco party and muster statewide support among Northern "Tammany" Democrats.

David Broderick and William Gwin
The rivalry between Democrats David Broderick *(left)* and William Gwin *(right)* dominated the early political life of the new state and added to its turbulence. *Courtesy of the Bancroft Library.*

Fifteen years older than Broderick, Gwin left successful political careers in his native Tennessee and in Mississippi when he emigrated. Trained in law and medicine, he was a Jacksonian Democrat who adhered still to Jeffersonian agrarian principles. His polished manner, origins, and connections made him the natural leader of the Southern "Chivalry" Democrats who settled in California, as did his position on slavery. Gwin supported the institution's exclusion from California, but he consistently rejected federal authority to regulate it. He also became an effective U.S. Senator. None of the transcontinental railway bills that he sponsored became law, but other efforts on the state's behalf—Mare Island Navy Yard near Vallejo and a branch mint in San Francisco—were successful. Gwin's status in the national Democratic party also gave him influence over the distribution of federal patronage in California.

The political milieu in which Broderick and Gwin operated was peculiar indeed. Neither Whigs nor newly organized Republicans influenced California affairs significantly. The antiforeign and anti-Catholic American or "Know-Nothing" party (called *los ignorantes* by *californios*) held power briefly after 1855, but only because of Democratic factionalism. On the surface, local divisions resembled those in the national party, but discord among California Democrats involved mainly state issues and Broderick's ambition.

By 1855, Broderick felt sufficiently secure as leader of the "Tammany" faction to challenge Gwin for his place in the U.S. Senate, but a badly divided legislature chose neither of the rivals—nor anyone else. Instead, it left only John B. Weller, elected to replace Frémont in 1852, to uphold state interests for the next two years. Broderick's premature bid and the Democrats' disunity also allowed Know-Nothings to elect J. Neely Johnson governor and David S. Terry chief justice of the state supreme court in 1855. During national elections a year later, the Republican party compounded the state's political confusion by running John C. Frémont for president. The "Pathfinder" had alienated Californians by inattention to his senatorial duties and by selling his Mariposa estate to corporate mining interests. As a result, he ran far behind Democratic and Know-Nothing candidates in the state. Despite the defeat, the Republican party—organized locally by Leland Stanford, Mark Hopkins, Charles Crocker, and Collis P. Huntington—soon became an important force in state politics.

But in 1857 the major local issue remained the senatorial question. Broderick used his influence in the legislature and carefully distributed favors to secure a full term in the U.S. Senate. Gwin filled the vacant seat for the remaining four years of its term, after promising that he would recommend no federal patronage appointments. Nevertheless, President James Buchanan filled federal positions in California only with "Chivalry" Democrats, and an outraged Broderick openly denounced both his rival and the president. His actions angered his supporters and set in motion events that brought him to an unexpected end.

In the state campaign of 1859, "Chivalry" Democrats swamped disorganized "Tammany" forces. During the contest, former Broderick ally Chief Justice David S. Terry aligned with Gwin in his quest to retain his office. Already enraged by other defections, Broderick denounced the jurist, both viciously and in public. Terry reacted by resigning his office and challenging Broderick to a duel. When the two met in San Mateo County on September 13, 1859, Broderick fired first. His shot went wild, but Terry aimed carefully, mortally wounded his antagonist, and ended one turbulent phase in California's political history. Three decades later, Terry himself met a similarly violent fate.

BUILDING AN AMERICAN STATE

Fortunately, the Broderick-Gwin feud did not absorb all of Californians' political energies during the 1850s. They also attended to the business of establishing state institutions, including schools. The legislature provided for a future state university, mandated the use of property taxes for local school districts, and devised a system to apportion state funds among them. During the 1850s and 1860s, the government's contribution to public education rarely amounted to more than "a pittance almost beneath contempt," but the early legislatures did lay the foundation for future development and expansion.

Failure to support education resulted partially from a constant and serious lack of revenues, and early solutions to the tax problem predicted persistent sectional conflict and even precipitated a separatist movement in 1859. The protests of southern Californians at the Monterey Convention seemed prophetic when an 1851 law exempted mining claims from all property taxes. This was blatantly unfair; in 1852, 6,000 residents of six "cow-counties" in the south paid $42,000 in taxes—twice as much as 120,000 residents of twelve northern mining counties. Californians from south of the Tehachapis complained that they contributed more but received less than their northern counterparts, and it was the taxation issue—not a covert plot to add a slave state to the Union—that renewed demands to divide California. In 1859 Los Angeles assemblyman Andrés Pico introduced—and voters approved—a plan to form a distinct territory from San Luis Obispo southward, but the proposal died in Washington. Congress was in no mood to nurture even a remote potential for the expansion of slavery.

Early legislatures also devoted time and energy to mining questions. Between 1850 and 1852, they passed, rescinded, and reinstated foreign miners tax laws and enacted tax exemptions beneficial to miners and mining entrepreneurs. But they did not devise a comprehensive state mining code. For the most part, miners working claims in the public domain were content to occupy rather than own land and to rely on local codes to protect their interests. Consequently, codified mining laws seemed unimportant until later in the decade, when corporate enterprise increased the significance of land ownership. But the federal government, not the state, ultimately resolved the issue. Congress passed the Mining Act of 1866 which kept mineral deposits in the public domain open to exploitation, confirmed local codes, upheld titles acquired under them, and provided for current occupants of some lands to acquire future title. Although the act was principally intended to prevent mineral lands from falling into the hands of corporate interests, it also gave sanction and legitimacy to California's local laws.

On other matters, early legislatures acted tardily. Not until 1858, for example, did they create a state agency to oversee the disposition of California's public land; by then,

most of it had been sold to speculators. But some issues received remarkably rapid attention. By the end of 1852 the state had on its books measures to regulate government and law enforcement in cities and counties, and—thanks to Stephen J. Field—codes of civil and criminal law and a judicial system.

VIGILANTE JUSTICE: "THEIR MAJESTIES THE MOB"

Codes of law on statute books did not assure the existence of enforcement agents or courts; consequently, early Californians often resorted to the extralegal justice of vigilance committees. Although lines distinguishing activities of popular tribunals from those of lynch mobs are fine and indistinct, vigilantism in the state has been romanticized, defended as citizens' right to take the law into their own hands, and even produced macabre humor. Bret Harte, for example, wrote of a popular tribunal advised to render a "correct" verdict because the defendant was already hanged. In retrospect, however, vigilante justice involved little that was romantic, commendable, or amusing. Nor can it be reconciled with either Hispanic or Anglo-Saxon legal traditions.

Americans did not introduce popular justice to California; in 1836, a "defense committee for the public safety" in Los Angeles removed a man and woman from custody and shot both for allegedly killing the woman's husband. After 1848, however, incidents became more frequent. Since law enforcement and judicial authorities were rare in mining camps, their residents selected officials to uphold the law and maintain order. But, as Dame Shirley observed, "law" frequently degenerated into lynching and "order" into mob rule.

Nor did popular tribunals operate only in mining camps during the 1850s. In Los Angeles, forty-four murders in just over a year confirmed the town's reputation for violence, and in 1851 officials created a vigilance committee that hanged five alleged murderers, at least one of whom was innocent. Early in 1855, Mayor Esteban Foster halted a mob bent on lynching a prisoner, resigned his office, participated in the hanging, and then accepted immediate re-election. The affair was just one of twenty lynchings in Los Angeles during 1854 and 1855, and as fears of Joaquín Murieta and other *bandidos* increased and companies of "rangers" pursued them, hangings in southern California multiplied to eleven in 1857 and seven in just one month in 1863.

Popular justice in southern California and in the mines often involved hostility toward "foreigners," but that was not the case in San Francisco's first incident. In 1849, merchants hired a private police force to keep order on the waterfront and return deserting seamen to their ships. These "Regulators" degenerated into the "Hounds," a gang allied with "Sydney Ducks" from Australian penal colonies. In July 1849, "Hounds" attacked a favorite target, the Hispanic tent colony near Telegraph Hill. They robbed and beat numerous *chilenos*, killed a woman, and raped her daughter. San Franciscans were outraged, and Sam Brannan organized some 200 citizens into a Law and Order party to round up the culprits, try them, and sentence them to fines, imprisonment, and deportation.

The episode terminated the "Hounds"—but not crime or vigilante justice in the city. In February 1851, a popular tribunal headed by William Tell Coleman tried and convicted two "Ducks" suspected of robbing and beating a merchant. The pair escaped the rope because of a divided jury—a fortunate result since one defendant was mistakenly identified and certainly innocent. Later in the year, crime increased, especially after the city's fifth great fire. Despite officials' warn-

ings that public apathy contributed to lawlessness, most residents blamed the courts, politicians, lawyers, and the "Sydney Ducks." In June, with Brannan and Coleman in the lead, some 500 San Franciscans formed the Vigilance Committee of 1851. Days later, the Committee caught, tried, and hanged its first criminal, a "Duck" who allegedly stole a safe. During the following months, vigilantes tried and executed three more Sydney men, one for murder and the others for lesser crimes. Before disbanding in September, committee members searched homes and businesses without due process, deported or whipped individuals suspected of crimes, and abused citizens who were reluctant to cooperate with them.

THE VIGILANCE COMMITTEE OF 1856

Contemporaries and historians alike defend San Francisco's best-known popular tribunal, the Vigilance Committee of 1856, on the basis of several assumptions. They argue that civic authorities refused to maintain law and order or protect the city from fire and arson and that corrupt courts, police, and lawyers permitted rampant vice, crime, and immorality. They also claim that municipal extravagance imposed unbearable tax burdens on citizens and that an inefficient government subservient to David Broderick was unresponsive to the people. Finally, they argue that the nationwide Panic of 1855 spread economic distress among the populace. Close scrutiny, however, suggests that other considerations were involved.

San Francisco leaders such as Brannan and Coleman precipitated many of the city's problems. They demanded cuts in expenditures for police and firefighters, making adequate protection impossible. Even so, the record shows no crime wave in 1856. "Leading citizens" frequented brothels and gambling dens, or owned and tolerated them for economic reasons, so vice persisted. Early in 1856 the city had adopted a new charter, the Consolidation Act, which modernized municipal government, curbed partisan manipulation, and reduced taxes below the norm for other American cities. Broderick, the alleged corrupt influence, supported the reform, but by 1856 his power was in decline, the worst effects of the Panic of 1855 had passed, and the economy showed signs of recovery. In short, early 1856 was a time of civic and economic growth in San Francisco, and traditional explanations of the year's vigilante episode require reevaluation.

Two homicides were the immediate cause. First, gambler Charles Cora shot U.S. Marshal William Richardson. Cora and his mistress, brothel keeper Arabella Ryan, "insulted" the marshal's wife by sitting near the couple in a theater, and Richardson, furious and quite drunk, confronted the gambler with a pistol on the following evening. Cora drew his own weapon, fired once, and Richardson fell. The subsequent trial resulted in a hung jury and the defendant was returned to jail. He was still there on May 14, when James P. Casey shot James King of William, editor of the *Daily Evening Bulletin.*

King, who added "of William" to his name to distinguish himself from others named James King, lost his fortune in the collapse of Adams & Company's banking operation in 1855. Embittered by the reversal, he turned to journalism and used the *Bulletin's* pages to attack those whom he considered responsible: bankers, lawyers, Democrats, police, gamblers, clergymen, immigrants, rival editors, Quakers, and politicians. In one diatribe, King disclosed that Casey had served a prison term in New York. Casey, in turn, threatened the editor and later shot and severely wounded him. The assault, combined with the failure to convict Cora, produced an immediate reaction. Brannan demanded swift justice, but cooler heads

prevailed. Coleman and other leaders of the 1851 committee proposed a new organization, and before the day of King's shooting ended, the Vigilance Committee of 1856 began enrolling volunteers. On May 18, more than 2,000 armed men marched in formation to remove Casey and Cora from jail. King died two days later, and on May 22, after a trial by a popular tribunal, the pair were hanged before a cheering crowd of San Franciscans.

Some local leaders—the mayor, sheriff, and militia commander William T. Sherman—formed a Law and Order party to oppose the committee, expecting that the executions would end the affair. They were wrong. Vigilantes continued to root out "criminals," with the support of local newspapers. The main exception, the *Herald,* suffered dwindling subscription and advertiser lists and entire issues were burned in the streets. Some clergymen, such as Presbyterian minister William Scott, dared to dissent, but pressure exerted by congregations and committee members stifled most. Early in June, municipal authorities appealed for help to the governor, who called out the militia, but the few troops who reported for duty were poorly equipped. When officials attempted to supply them from the federal arsenal at Benicia, vigilantes intercepted the boat and commandeered the weapons.

Thus, with little effective opposition, the Vigilance Committee controlled the city. By the time leaders decided in August to dissolve the membership (but not the executive committee), two more accused murderers had been hanged, a prisoner had committed suicide, and thirty "undesirables" had been deported. Scores also were intimidated or tried but not punished. Among the latter was Chief Justice Terry, arrested for stabbing a vigilante while defending a witness to the arms shipment theft.

On August 18, 1856, vigilantes marched

Membership Certificate, Vigilance Committee of 1856
On the elaborate and highly symbolic membership certificate of Hiram S. Wheeler, the motto of the Vigilance Committee of 1856 reads FIAT JUSTICIA RUAT COELUM: "Let justice be done though the heavens fall." *Courtesy of the Bancroft Library.*

through the city 6,000 strong and disbanded. Leaders proclaimed their purpose served, but records document no significant decrease in crime or increase in convictions in subsequent years. Vigilante justice, moreover, carried a high price tag. Subversion of basic principles—such as the presumption of innocence and rights to representation, trial by jury, and appeal—did not provide a valid basis for reform. Nor did popular emotionalism of the sort generated by King of William.

In another sense, vigilante leadership may have succeeded only too well. During the next decade, the committee's political successor—the People's Reform party—con-

trolled San Francisco's government. But its economy programs left police and teachers unpaid, schools in disrepair, the waterfront and other public facilities dilapidated, and civic morale at a low ebb.

A COSMOPOLITAN SOCIETY

Vigilantism often involved antiforeign sentiments, and the nativism prevalent in "the States" at mid-nineteenth century periodically infected California. Nevertheless, from 1849 onward, migrants of foreign origins poured in to seek their fortunes. Some were impelled by dislocations in Europe—potato famine in Ireland and political repression on the Continent—but for most the lure of gold was motivation enough. Some arrived directly from their homelands, but most migrated west after residence elsewhere in the United States. They represented nearly every major nation on earth, and very quickly a unique, cosmopolitan society evolved in California. By 1860, indeed, nearly forty percent of the state's residents, even excluding the Chinese, were foreign-born, and more than half had at least one foreign-born parent.

During the 1850s, eighty percent of the foreign-born population came from Mexico, Britain and Ireland, the German states, and France; eastern and southern Europe and the Scandinavian countries contributed most of the remainder. For immigrants of European origin, including members of groups that experienced persecution elsewhere, the new state provided a congenial home. In cities of the eastern United States—Boston, Philadelphia, New York, and others—Irish Catholics encountered nativist hostility, bigotry, and even physical attack because of their religion, numbers, and reputation for violence and political volatility. In California, even though they were occasionally stereotyped as "Micks" or "Paddies," they assimilated with relative ease and made important contributions to economic, social, cultural, and political development. Similarly, the thousands of Jews who were among French and German immigrants to the state had been targets of persecution both in the East and in Europe. They also encountered antisemitism in California, but it was significantly less pervasive or virulent than elsewhere at mid-nineteenth century. Jews settled in San Francisco and throughout the gold regions, maintained their own cultural and religious identity, affiliated with local associations such as the Odd Fellows and Masons, and became respected and valued members of gold rush society. Some, like state supreme court justice Solomon Heydenfeldt, participated in the politics of the state or, like Levi Strauss, advanced its economic development.

ANTI-CHINESE PREJUDICE

Non-Europeans found life in gold rush California considerably less congenial, especially the Chinese, whose presence initiated one of the ugliest, most persistent themes in the state's history. Fewer than 1,000 Chinese lived in the United States in 1850; two years later, a state census counted more than 25,000 in California, about ten percent of the population. By 1860, 35,000 had flocked to the "golden mountain" (*chin shan* in Mandarin or *gum san* in Cantonese). Californians regarded the "sojourners" as slaves or coolies, which was inaccurate. But most were bondsmen and women, indentured to merchants in China or San Francisco for passage across the sea and hoping to work off debts for their "credit tickets," amass a modest fortune, and return to China. Experience rarely matched ambition.

Chinese miners worked and reworked the least productive diggings for meager wages and lived in miserable conditions under sur-

veillance by agents for contract holders. Since agreements required that they pay contractors for their subsistence, debts usually became larger, not smaller, and few managed to pay what they owed or save enough to return home. Chinese miners also became prime targets for the hostility of white miners who denounced similarities between contract labor and racial slavery, gambling and other allegedly Oriental vices, and living conditions in Chinatowns. The real source of antagonism, however, was competition. When the Chinese performed domestic service or other undesirable work, they were tolerated; when they worked long hours for under a dollar a day or vied for diminishing gold resources, attitudes changed.

Hostility became apparent in 1852 when mass protests influenced legislators to repudiate contract labor in California and to revive the Foreign Miners' Tax Law. The new version imposed a $3 (later $4) monthly fee on "aliens ineligible to citizenship"—a concept based on a federal statute limiting naturalization to "free, white people." When the law did not discourage competition, white miners resorted to other measures: beatings, queue-cuttings, Chinatown burnings, and lynchings. The Chinese had few defenses against them, especially after the state supreme court ruled in 1854 that, because they shared prehistoric ancestry, Chinese were Indians and therefore could not testify against whites. In 1855, federal courts struck down a state law imposing a $50 entry fee on "aliens ineligible to citizenship." Nevertheless, the euphemism for Asians remained the rationale for selective law enforcement. Stephen J. Field and others denounced Chinese oppression, but most Californians condoned both official and unofficial harassment. As the Chinese left the mines seeking other employment, wage-earner hostility increased, and the "Celestials"—not capital or employers—provided the "indispensable enemy" that unified organized labor in California and made it a major supporter of the federal Exclusion Act of 1882.

Scholars have examined in great detail the oppression that the Chinese endured in nineteenth-century California, but research has shifted to focus on the Chinese themselves. Historian Sucheng Chan, for instance, has described surprising variety in their experience during gold rush decades. Companies of Chinese miners managed to save sufficient capital to buy claims and equipment costing hundreds of dollars. In places like Marysville and Sacramento, independent merchants, artisans, and cooks catered to the needs of compatriots and white residents, and in the San Joaquin Valley Chinese farmers raised crops to supply mining camps and towns. Thus, despite hatred and discrimination, some sojourners managed to succeed; during the 1870s, however, increased competition, diminished opportunity, and economic depression altered conditions drastically for the worse.

BLACK *CALIFORNIOS*

Anti-Chinese sentiment in gold rush California probably mitigated hostility toward black people, who were relatively few despite their presence since 1781 and the Spanish settlement of Los Angeles. At the end of the Mexican period, identifiable black *californios* numbered only a handful, but the gold rush brought increases: to 2,000 by 1852 and 4,000 by 1860. Most of the earliest arrivals were slaves, transported by Southerners to work the mines. After the constitutional ban on slavery in 1849 and statehood in 1850, however, those who remained were technically free, and they were joined by free black people from northern states during the

1850s. A few, like Dame Shirley's Paganini Ned, found work in the mines, but most settled in towns such as Sacramento, Stockton, San Francisco, and Marysville.

Although the state's constitution prohibited the "peculiar institution," its laws rendered the status of free black residents uncertain. Legislation in 1850 denied their right to vote and give testimony against whites, and a local fugitive-slave law passed in 1852 but lapsed in 1856. Thus, black people in the state were neither slave nor citizen; two court cases, one before and one after the U.S. Supreme Court's famous—or infamous—Dred Scott decision in 1857, illustrate their ambiguous status.

Biddy Mason, a slave from Mississippi, arrived in southern California by way of Utah with her three children, several other slaves, and her master Robert Smith in 1851. In Los Angeles and San Bernardino counties, she met several free black people, including Robert Owens, a local businessman and property owner. When Smith decided to move to Texas in 1855, along with his slaves, Owens and others persuaded local authorities to issue a writ of *habeas corpus* and, accompanied by deputies and his own *vaqueros*, removed Mason, her friend Hannah, and their ten children from Smith's camp to the safety of the county jail. The subsequent trial, in which Mason could testify only through white mediators, mustered substantial popular support, and in January 1856 Judge Benjamin Hayes rejected Smith's claim that Mason and her companions were "employees" willing to go to Texas and ruled that "all of the said persons of color are entitled to their freedom and are free forever." Mason remained in Los Angeles where she supported herself as a popular and proficient midwife, bought property, and died in 1891.

Archey Lee, also from Mississippi, arrived

in Sacramento with his owner in 1857. When the master proposed to return to the South, Lee protested that California's constitution made him free and that he should not be returned to slavery. With assistance from white attorneys and encouragement from the local black community, Lee won a hearing and a victory in 1858. A court ruled that accepting employment in the state made Lee's master a resident subject to local laws; he could not own a slave. When the master appealed, the state supreme court upheld the decision but reached a bizarre conclusion: because the youthful master was inexperienced with California law, the original decision should be set aside and Lee returned to slavery. Ultimately, a federal commissioner reversed the high court's decision on grounds that Lee had broken no state or federal law and should be free. Lee quickly exercised his freedom by departing, along with other black Californians, for the Fraser River mines—and more predictable legal climate—in British Columbia.

Although the Mason and Lee cases affirmed the state's ban on slavery, laws still denied black people the rights to vote and to testify in court. During the 1850s, activists organized three statewide Colored Conventions to petition the legislature for change, especially for the suffrage. But lawmakers ridiculed and rejected their appeals, and only in 1863 was the state forced to rescind its restrictions. In the interim, black Californians relied on their own resources. Since state law excluded their children from public schools, black communities in San Francisco, Stockton, Sacramento, and other towns established their own. Churches became social and political as well as religious centers for their communities and raised funds to support legal actions, the convention movement, and even charities for Indians. Philip Alexander Bell's *Pacific Appeal* appeared in 1862, and businesses and

benevolent associations provided a modicum of stability and identity for the state's small black population. Nevertheless, struggles for acceptance persisted. During the later 1860s, Mary Ellen ("Mammy") Pleasant, whose San Francisco business interests had accumulated substantial wealth, had to resort to the courts to establish her right to ride on the city's streetcars, and not until the 1890s did the state admit black children to its high schools.

CALIFORNIOS AND THE LAND-GRANT QUESTION

When California became a state, about 14 million of its acres were included in more than 800 land grants, ranging in size from one square league (4,426 acres) to eleven square leagues. Often inaccurately called "Spanish," the grants were mainly Mexican and protected by the Treaty of Guadalupe Hidalgo.

In Mexican California, large holdings made sense. A small population occupied the province, and vast tracts were vital to cattle grazing. Abundant land also resulted in casual boundaries that lacked the precision of surveyors' metes and bounds and relied on natural features, crude maps called *diseños* (designs), and descriptions that often included the phrase *poco más o menos* (a little more or less). Mexican law stipulated residence and improvement to validate titles, but a home and a few outbuildings sufficed on cattle-raising haciendas. Americans, in contrast, were accustomed to traditional quarter-section (160-acre) public grants, intensively farmed, with fences marking boundaries and improvements clearly visible. Therefore, they frequently squatted on apparently vacant land, and conflict with grantees inevitably resulted.

Inconsistent official opinions compounded discord caused by conflicting Hispanic and Anglo-Saxon land laws and traditions. Captain Henry W. Halleck's 1849 investigation concluded that most Mexican titles were legally flawed and many were outright frauds, but a year later, William Carey Jones examined the matter for the Secretary of the Interior and determined that most grants were legal under Mexican or American law. Jones's wife was John C. Frémont's sister-in-law, and the contested claims included the "Pathfinder's" Mariposa Estate, which may have influenced his decision. Whatever motivated officials, conflicting conclusions increased controversy.

Congress attempted to resolve the problem with the Land Act of 1851. The law created a three-member commission to review titles, required claimants to present their cases within two years, and allowed appeals to the courts by both claimants and the government. During commission meetings held in San Francisco between 1852 and 1856 (one session met in Los Angeles), problems for the 813 claimants were substantial. Titles were considered invalid until otherwise proven, trips to San Francisco were hardships for most, few spoke English, and documents were missing from family and local Mexican archives. Even so, the commission confirmed 512 titles. Holders of 132 denied claims appealed to the courts, more than 100 successfully. Government attorneys appealed more than 400 cases but won only five.

Commission and court decisions could be capricious, however. The Serrano family lost its rancho near San Diego because it presented a temporary permit to establish the origins of its grant; without the document, title would have been confirmed on the basis of longevity of occupancy since 1819. In contrast, Frémont's title to the Mariposa Estate was upheld, even though original grantee Juan B. Alvarado failed to comply with Mexican law requiring occupancy; he had never seen the place. Frauds were also approved. José Limantour's claim to four square leagues that included most of San Francisco was confirmed in 1853, forcing property owners to purchase quitclaim deeds from him. Two years later, Limantour's documents proved to be forgeries, and he departed for Mexico, considerably richer. Even petitioners with confirmed grants faced as many as six hearings before receiving patented titles, and the process could require two decades or more; litigation time averaged fifteen years. In the interim, rancheros watched estates dwindle as squatters invaded and as land was sold to pay attorneys' fees, taxes, and other debts.

The process accelerated the "decline of the *californios*," but they were not the only losers. Prolonged uncertainty deterred settlers from purchasing property for homes or farms and precluded operation of the Preemption Act of 1841, the Homestead Act of 1862, and similar policies. Few would risk buying or improving land without assurance of valid titles. Finally, by the time cases were adjudicated, much of the property was in the hands of speculators, setting the stage for the state's emphasis on agribusiness rather than traditional family farming.

PIONEER AGRICULTURE

Despite land title problems, some agricultural development began during the 1850s, stimulated by the demands of an exploding population. At first, imports from Oregon, Hawaii, and Latin America satisfied needs, but persistent shortages and inflated prices combined with the potential of rich soil and good climate to encourage change. Many of the experienced farmers among the argonauts took a brief fling at mining and then turned to more familiar and hopefully profitable pursuits.

Cattle raising felt the impact of the gold

rush first, as prices soared toward $500 a head. By the mid-1850s, more than three million animals grazed on the "thousand hills" of southern California and the ranges of the San Joaquin Valley, but the golden era ended abruptly. Demand diminished as mines played out and immigration slowed, overgrazing depleted natural grasslands, and many ranchers refused to modernize their methods. Finally, a disastrous flood in the winter of 1861–1862, followed by even more devastating droughts lasting through 1864, eliminated the remnant of the industry that had seemed so promising.

During the same years, however, farmers began to diversify local agriculture. Because of the time and expense involved in shipping produce, even to local markets, they selected growing areas proximate to population and mining centers. They also chose higher rainfall locales or those with artesian wells or flowing streams to provide water. As a result, most early agricultural development clustered in the northern and central regions, especially adjacent to San Francisco Bay and in fertile valley districts such as those near Visalia. By dry farming or planting in the autumn to capitalize on winter rains, pioneer farmers grew standard frontier crops: wheat, barley, oats, and other small grains. Until the 1870s, however, they produced only modest harvests to be milled and sold locally. Traditional methods also permitted cultivation of small-scale vegetable plots and fruit orchards and raising limited quantities of poultry and dairy cattle, but little more. In southern California, renovated Mexican-era irrigation systems or new ones built by Mormons at San Bernardino and German immigrants at Anaheim allowed only limited agricultural development during the 1850s and 1860s.

California conditions that confounded growers of many crops, however, were ideal for wine and brandy production, which had

several more advantages. Argonauts' legendary thirst provided a market, grapes needed minimal irrigation, processing required no complex equipment, and products could be transported without fear of spoilage. Cuttings from mission vineyards provided the original basis for expanding ordinary wine production in areas near missions San Gabriel and San Fernando during the early 1850s. By the 1860s, the industry spread to San Francisco Bay area counties, where conditions were ideal. Individuals such as Agoston Haraszthy—the Hungarian-born father of California viticulture who introduced European grape varieties to the state—made raising grapes for wine-making California's leading fruit industry by 1870. Quality remained inconsistent, but quantity was substantial: two million gallons of wine annually from 40,000 acres of vineyards.

By 1870, 25,000 farms valued at $141 million operated in the state, and reports of twenty-two pound onions, two-hundred pound squash, and two-foot long radishes suggested enormous potential. Nevertheless, agricultural progress during the 1850s and 1860s was erratic. Neither production nor profits approximated expectations, and most farmers shunned experimentation. Disputed titles to Mexican grants inhibited improvement, and labor and capital remained both scarce and expensive. Hostile interests—miners and cattlemen—influenced policies that deterred farmers: apportionment that left agriculture underrepresented, heavy taxes on improved farm land, fence laws that placed burdens for compliance on farmers, and inconsistent water laws that discouraged irrigation. Furthermore, the state remained *terra incognita* to farmers from other regions, and no agency existed to supply information about such matters as climate, rainfall, or effective irrigation practices. Finally, markets offered little incentive; the small, dispersed local population grew slowly after the early

1850s, and the state was too remote from potential alternate customers. Indeed, when the transcontinental rails met in 1869, California had a single potentially profitable agricultural export: its wine.

LAND SPECULATION ON THE URBAN FRONTIER

Speculation in urban real estate is frequently regarded as a recent California phenomenon, but it began even before American possession was confirmed. In 1846, Thomas O. Larkin and Robert Semple bought a plot on the Carquinez Strait from Mariano Vallejo, surveyed a townsite, and called the place Francisca. They advertised its fog-free deepwater port and direct access to the interior in Semple's Yerba Buena *Californian* and began to sell lots. In January 1847, Yerba Buena speculators such as Sam Brannan convinced the local government to change the town's name to San Francisco and to hire surveyor Jasper O'Farrell to lay out a city plan. Contemptuous of would-be competitors, Semple gave away his San Francisco property —worth half a million dollars two years later—and changed his town's name to Benicia.

San Francisco became "the City" in early California, but not without encountering rivals. Directly across the bay, another appeared almost immediately. In 1849, Horace Carpentier arrived aboard the steamship *Panama.* A year later, the young lawyer and two partners squatted on Vicente Peralta's land and somehow convinced the *don* to grant them a lease. Within weeks, they hired a surveyor to plot a town, filed a claim under the Preemption Act of 1841, and began selling lots. Carpentier then appealed to his friend David Broderick, who persuaded the state legislature to incorporate the city of Oakland in 1852. Next, the three partners set up a town government, elected them-

selves to office, and granted Carpentier the town's entire waterfront and rights to collect use fees for thirty-seven years.

Other prospective town-sites—some ambitious to displace San Francisco—appeared around the bay and in southern California during the 1850s. Speculators also were active in the interior, among them Stephen J. Field. Shortly after he arrived in 1849, he journeyed to the junction of the Yuba and Feather rivers where he found real estate promotion in full swing. He was impressed:

> It was a beautiful spot, covered with oaks, and it reminded me of the parks of England. I saw at once that the place, from its position at the head of practical navigation [to the gold regions], was destined to become an important depot for the neighboring mines and that its beauty and salubrity made it a pleasant place for residence.

Field's assets totaled $20, but he subscribed for sixty-five parcels of land at $250 each, precipitating a rumor that "a great capitalist had arrived to invest in lots in this rising town." Because he was an attorney, Field was asked to draw up deeds of sale and record them. He was also elected *alcalde* and justice of the peace, and he participated in naming the town Marysville for the only American woman around. Profits from such ventures could be spectacular, as Field recorded: "At one time I had $14,000 in gold dust in my safe." But so could losses: "I [later] lost all that I made more quickly than I had acquired it and found myself also in debt."

Places such as Marysville, Downieville, Sacramento City, and other towns founded on speculation played an important role in the history of the state, as did settlements that originated as mining camps. In 1850, for example, John Weaver and two companions built cabins near a creek in remote Trinity County, and hundreds of miners congregated to make Weaverville a typically rowdy mining camp. Quickly, however, merchants,

TOM MAGUIRE
Frontier Impresario

Tall, handsome Thomas Maguire undoubtedly cut a dashing figure when he arrived in California in 1849, but he was an unlikely candidate to become a major contributor to the culture of gold rush society. Already in his forties, he was older than most of his fellow argonauts. He was barely educated, and in New York City he had been a hack driver, a saloon keeper, and—even with support from his friend David Broderick—an unsuccessful candidate for political office.

In San Francisco, however, Maguire's career took quite a different turn. During his first years in the city, he operated a series of Jenny Lind Theaters on Portsmouth Square. Fires consumed the first two shortly after they opened, and in 1853 the city bought the third, last, and most elegant for a permanent city hall. Maguire then purchased San Francisco Hall at the corner of Washington and Montgomery streets, and in 1856 he refurbished and reopened the place as Maguire's New Opera House, with the Diana Gam-

Tom Maguire
Courtesy of the Bancroft Library.

TOM MAGUIRE (continued)
Frontier Impresario

bling Hall adjacent and The Snug Saloon in the basement. From then until he returned to the East thirty years later, Tom Maguire was recognized as one of California's preeminent impresarios. By the end of the 1850s, indeed, he owned or operated most theaters in the state, not only in cities such as San Francisco and Sacramento but also in mining communities throughout the Sierra.

Despite the limits of Maguire's formal education, he had a keen eye for talent and a rare gift for promotion. He used both skills to bring an impressive array of nationally and internationally known performers to California audiences. Among those who responded to his inducements were Christy's Minstrels, the Booth family, Lola Montez, Lotta Crabtree, the Bianchi Italian Opera Company, and Adah Isaacs Menken. Productions included vaudeville and burlesque, musicales and recitals, drama ranging from low comedy to Shakespearean tragedy, lecturers including Mark Twain and Artemus Ward, and classical music and grand opera performed by touring American and European troupes. The variety was as impressive as the quality.

The impresario's fortunes began to fade somewhat during the 1870s, due largely to increasing competition and the shift of the center of the city's activity away from the locale of the Opera House; both trends were epitomized by the opening of William Ralston's California Theater on Bush Street in 1869. Two years later, the Opera House was razed to make way for a new thoroughfare—Montgomery Avenue (now Columbus Avenue)—facilitating travel to North Beach. From the beginning of the gold rush, however, Maguire and others like him provided entertainment alternatives to saloons, brothels, and gambling dens to appreciative California audiences. (WAB)

---

artisans, brewers, professionals, clergymen, and other permanent settlers arrived, some with their families. In 1857, the editor of the *Trinity Journal* was able to boast, with evident pride:

> It is pleasant to note the change in the state of society in this place which a few years have effected. Formerly every other house was a gambling saloon, or something equally as bad. Fatal quarrels were of daily and nightly occurrence; drunken men paraded in the streets; blasphemy was heard on every side, and law and order were things heard of but never seen. Now gambling is abolished; a very drunk person is a curiosity; deadly assaults are of rare occurrence. Ladies now promenade our streets and the air resounds with the innocent prattle of little children.

Residents of Weaverville had created in the wilderness a microcosm of urban American society complete with churches, schools, a water system, a fire company, two hospitals, brick business buildings, and a basic town plan. Ethnic associations included the Sons of Hibernia, the German Citizens Society, a Jewish *minyan,* and two Chinese *tongs.* A brass band performed at public and private functions, and a *Turnverein* (gymnastics club) kept its members fit. The Cosmopolitan Art Association, Odd Fellows and Masonic lodges, and active partisan associations contributed to cultural, social, and political life, while two newspapers kept residents in touch with local, state, and national affairs.

CULTURAL AMERICANIZATION

The transformation of California culture from Hispanic to American emanated from San Francisco, the "instant city." A crude village fronting a mud flat in 1848, it astounded a visitor in 1856:

> That a city of the respectability of San Francisco could be raised in the short space of five or six years, appears incredible. Possessing the appearance of an old city of a century, . . . it conveys to the mind the idea of being within a day's journey of the Emporium of the nation.

The vista was no accident; promoters defied politics, logic, and geography to create it. Early in 1847, they surveyed a town site and began selling lots, even under water. When argonauts arrived in 1849, derelict ships moored on the shoreline provided shelter, warehouses, offices, hotels, and even a jail. As vessels sank or burned, debris covered them to provide more land for sale, but such expedience soon gave way to permanence.

Speculators pushed wharves hundreds of yards into the bay, and during the 1860s the city defeated the "Bulkhead Bill" scheme to make the public waterfront a private monopoly. Wells Fargo's and Adams & Company's express and banking operations and the Merchant's Exchange established headquarters in the Montgomery Block, an office building completed in 1853, and made the city the nexus of state economic activity. Three years later, the Consolidation Act stabilized city government, provided a police force, and reorganized volunteer fire compa-

PACIFIC BREWERY.

Junction Oregon and Main Streets, WEAVERVILLE.

F. WALTER & CO.

THE UNDERSIGNED AR. MANUFACTUR-ing, and have always for sale, a superior quality of **LAGER BEER,** which they will deliver, in large and small quantities, in any part of the county, and to FAMILIES when required. Their Brewery is supplied with pure, cool

Spring Water,

and a cellar of ice *temperature,* which enables them to manufacture and preserve the liquid in great purity, and always fit for immediate use.

F. WALTER & CO.

Weaver, June 1, 1858.   20tf.

Pacific Brewery Advertisement
Frederick Walter, a German immigrant, established the Pacific Brewery in Weaverville in 1852. He and entrepreneurs like him brought more than creature comforts to remote mining districts. They also supplied economic, political, and social leadership, as well as the latest marketing methods, to gold rush California. Walter's advertisment appeared regularly in the weekly *Trinity Journal;* both the newspaper and the brewery building still exist. *From the collection of William A. Bullough.*

San Francisco, the "Instant City," in 1852
Courtesy of the Bancroft Library.

ever, were not the city's only contributions to Americanization. In 1848, Timothy Dwight Hunt took leave of his Presbyterian congregation in Hawaii—"for three months with the privilege of continued absence, . . . as Providence should dictate"—to become chaplain to San Franciscans of all Protestant denominations. Five years later, the city boasted thirty houses of worship, including

New England in California
Departing members of the Boston & California Joint Stock Mining and Trading Co. received a repeated admonition: "Take your Bibles in one hand and your good New England civilization in the other" into the wilderness. Many remembered the advice and established a tradition that persisted through the nineteenth century. In 1895, for example, Congregationalists in Lewiston, Trinity County, built their New England-style church overlooking a cemetery dating from the 1850s. *Photograph by William A. Bullough.*

nies to protect citizens and property. Streets that were "impassable, not even jackassable" received attention, and elite neighborhoods on Rincon Hill and at South Park emerged by the mid-1850s. The Parker House and El Dorado hotels, restaurants like the Poulet d'Or (later the "Poodle Dog"), and theaters presenting renowned performers adorned the urban landscape. By 1860, San Francisco's population of 57,000 ranked it fifteenth among American cities and first among those west of the Mississippi River.

Physical and economic development, how-

six Roman Catholic churches and two syna-
gogues. The American Catholic Church created the Archdiocese of San Francisco with
Bishop Joseph S. Alemany in charge, and in
1860, Thomas Starr King arrived in San Francisco to assume the pastorship of the local
Unitarian congregation and became one of
the city's most popular preachers. During
the Civil War years, Starr King's eloquent
speeches secured Californians' support for
the U.S Sanitary Commission and helped to
cement their loyalty to the Union. Equally
eloquent descriptions of California's flora
and fauna placed him among America's foremost naturalists by the time of his death of
diphtheria in 1864 at age forty.

American journalism and literature, too,
arrived by way of San Francisco. Two weekly
newspapers, Sam Brannan's *California Star*
and Robert Semple's *Californian,* merged in
1849 to become the *Daily Alta California.* Literary journals also appeared: *The Golden Era*
in 1852 with 2,200 subscribers in the city and
1,100 more in mining towns; *Hutching's Illustrated California Magazine* in 1856; the *Californian* in 1864; and *Overland Monthly* in
1868. Both newspapers and journals brought
the work of Bret Harte, Ina Coolbrith,
Joaquin Miller, Mark Twain, and others to
eager local readers. And in 1854, John Rollin
Ridge established a national reputation and
created a historical myth with *The Life and
Adventures of Joaquin Murieta.*

But San Francisco did not monopolize
the process of cultural Americanization;
throughout the mining districts, towns followed Weaverville's course, and familiar institutions, including their common schools,
linked residents with the nation. Although
early legislatures sanctioned public education, in 1854 Superintendent of Public Instruction Andrew Jackson Moulder complained that only 4,000 students attended
any state-supported school, and education
remained principally a local function. A
dozen years later, his successor John Swett—
a New Englander called the "Horace Mann
of the Pacific"—influenced passage of a
comprehensive "Act to Provide a System of
Common Schools in California." In the interim, responsibility fell to private groups—
including black churches—and communities
such as North San Juan, where a handful of
residents in 1857 contributed $2,000 to build
a schoolhouse and employ a teacher.

Thus, by the end of the gold rush era, the
thirty-first state, its people, and its institutions were thoroughly Americanized, bound
to the Union during the crisis of the Civil
War and prepared to capitalize on the Comstock silver strike in Nevada and the arrival of
the transcontinental railway in 1869.

SUGGESTIONS FOR FURTHER READING

Dame Shirley and Gold Rush Women

Richard E. Oglesby (intro.), *The Shirley Letters*
(1970); Carl I. Wheat (ed.), *The Shirley Letters from the
California Mines, 1851–1852* (1965); Rodman W.
Paul, "In Search of 'Dame Shirley,'" *Pacific Historical
Review* (1964); Marlene Smith-Baranzini (ed. and
intro.), *The Shirley Letters from the California Mines,
1851–1852* (1998) and "Out of the Shadows: Louisa
Clappe's Life and Early California Writing," *California History* (1999); Sarah Royce, *A Frontier Lady,*
Ralph H. Gabriel, ed. (1932); J. N. Bowman, "Prominent Women in Provincial California," *Southern Cali-
fornia Historical Society Quarterly* (1957); Luzena S.
Wilson, *Luzena Stanley Wilson, '49er* (1937), Andrew J.
Rotter, "'Matilda, for God's Sake Write': Women
and Families on the Argonaut Mind," *California His-*

torical Quarterly (1979); Robert L. Griswold, "Apart but Not Adrift: Wives, Divorce, and Independence in California, 1850–1890," *Pacific Historical Review* (1980); Joan Levy, *They Saw the Elephant: Women in the California Gold Rush* (1989); Jessie Benton Frémont, *A Year of American Travel* (1878); Joan M. Jensen and Gloria Ricci Lothrop, *California Women: A History* (1987).

Miners and Mining

John Walton Caughey, *The California Gold Rush* (1948); Rodman W. Paul, *California Gold* (1947), *Mining Frontiers of the Far West, 1848–1880* (1963), and *The California Gold Discovery* (1966); John W. Caughey (ed.), *Rushing for Gold* (1949), and *The California Gold Rush* (1975); Valeska Bari (ed.), *The Course of Empire: First Hand Accounts of California in the Days of the Gold Rush of '49* (1931); James S. Holliday, *The World Rushed In: The California Gold Rush Experience* (1981); Ralph H. Bieber, "California Gold Mania," *Mississippi Valley Historical Review* (1948); Robert L. Kelley, *Gold vs. Grain* (1959); James E. Davis (ed.), *Dreams to Dust: A Diary of the California Gold Rush, 1849–1850* (1989); Douglas R. Littlefield, "Water Rights during the California Gold Rush: Conflicts over Economic Points of View," *Western Historical Quarterly* (1983); Mary Hill, *Gold: The California Story* (2000); J.S. Holliday and others, "National Gold Rush Symposium," *California History* (1998).

Routes to the Gold Fields

John D. Unruh, *The Plains Across: The Overland Emigrants and the Trans-Mississippi West, 1840–1860* (1979); Oscar Lewis, *Sea Routes to the Gold Fields* (1949); John H. Kemble, *The Panama Route, 1848–1869* (1943); George R. Stewart, *The California Trail* (1962); Ralph P. Bieber, *Southern Trails to California in 1849* (1937); Asa Bement Clark, *Travels in Mexico and California* (1988); Marsha M. Allen, *Traveling West: Nineteenth Century Women on the Overland Routes* (1987).

Politics and Statehood

Theodore Grivas, *Military Governments in California, 1846–1850* (1963); William H. Ellison, *A Self-Governing Dominion: California, 1849–1860* (1950); Cardinal Goodwin, *The Establishment of State Government in California, 1846–1850* (1914); Earl Pomeroy, "California, 1846–1860: Politics in a Representative Frontier State," *California Historical Society Quarterly* (1953); Michael P. Rogin and John L. Shover, *Political Change in California, 1800–1960* (1970); Royce Delmatier and others, *The Rumble of California Politics, 1847–1970* (1970); Spencer C. Olin, Jr., *California Politics, 1846–1920* (1981); Arthur Quinn, *The Rivals: William Gwin, David Broderick, and the Birth of California* (1994); Robert H. Becker, *Diseños of the California Land Grants* (1964) and *Designs on the Land* (1969); Paul W. Gates, "The Adjudication of Spanish-Mexican Land Claims in California," *Huntington Library Quarterly* (1958) and "The California Land Act of 1851," *California Historical Quarterly* (1971); Gordon M. Bakken, *Practicing Law in Frontier California* (1991); Beverly E. Bastian, "'I Heartily Regret That I Ever Touched a Title in California': Henry Wager Halleck, the Californios, and the Clash of Legal Cultures," *California History* (Winter 1993/94); Richard Griswold del Castillo, *The Treaty of Guadalupe Hidalgo: A Legacy of Conflict* (1990); Robert J. Chandler, "The Velvet Glove: The Army during the Secession Crisis in California, 1860–1861," *Journal of the West* (1981).

Race, Nationality, and Ethnic Conflict

Doris M. Wright, "The Making of Cosmopolitan California: An Analysis of Immigration, 1848–1870," *California Historical Society Quarterly* (1940); Bradford F. Luckingham, "Immigrant Life in Emergent San Francisco," *Journal of the West* (1973); Allyn C. Loosely, "Foreign Born Population in California" (M.A. thesis, University of California, Berkeley, 1927); Robert E. Levinson, *Jews in the California Gold Rush* (1978); R.A. Burchell, *The San Francisco Irish, 1848–1880* (1980); Peyton Hurt, "The Rise and Fall of the 'Know-Nothings' in California," *California Historical Society Quarterly* (1930); Gerald Stanley, "Racism and the Early Republican Party: The 1856 Presidential Election in California," *Pacific Historical Review* (1974); Rudolph M. Lapp, *Blacks in Gold Rush California* (1977), "Negro Rights Activities in Gold Rush California," *California Historical Quarterly* (1966), and *Afro-American Californians* (2nd ed.,

1987); Douglas H. Daniels, *Pioneer Urbanites: A Social and Cultural History of Black San Francisco* (1980); James A. Fisher, "The Political Development of the Black Community in California, 1850–1950," *California Historical Quarterly* (1971); Dolores Hayden, "Biddy Mason's Los Angeles, 1856–1891," *California History* (1989); James J. Rawls, "Gold Diggers: Indian Miners in the California Gold Rush," *California Historical Quarterly* (1976); Albert L. Hurtado, *Indian Survival on the California Frontier* (1988); Robert F. Heizer and Theodora Kroeber (eds.), *Ishi, The Last Yahi: A Documentary History* (1979); Leonard Pitt, *The Decline of the Californios* (1966); Albert Camarillo, *Chicanos in California* (1984); Carey McWilliams, *North from Mexico* (1948); D. V. DuFault, "The Chinese in the Mining Camps," *Southern California Quarterly* (1959); Rodman W. Paul, "The Origin of the Chinese Issue in California," *Mississippi Valley Historical Review* (1938); Gunther Barth, *Bitter Strength* (1964); Sucheng Chan, "Chinese Livelihood in Rural California: The Impact of Economic Change, 1860–1880," *Pacific Historical Review* (1984), *This Bittersweet Soil: Chinese in California Agriculture, 1860–1910* (1987), and *Asian Californians* (1990); Lynn M. Hudson, "A New Look, or 'I'm Not Mammy to Everyone in California': Mary Ellen Pleasant, a Black Entrepreneur," *Journal of the West* (1993).

Vigilantes and Vigilantism

Robert W. Blew, "Vigilantism in Los Angeles, 1835–1874," *Southern California Quarterly* (1972); Mary F. Williams, *The History of the San Francisco Vigilance Committee of 1851* (1964); James A. B. Scherer, *"The Lion of the Vigilantes": William T. Coleman and the Life of Old San Francisco* (1939); John W. Caughey, *Their Majesties the Mob* (1960); Robert M. Senkewicz, S. J., *Vigilantes in Gold Rush San Francisco* (1985); Roger Olmsted, "San Francisco and the Vigilante Style," *American West* (1970); Kevin J. Mullin, *Let Justice Be Done: Crime and Politics in Early San Francisco* (1989).

Pioneer Agriculture

Paul W. Gates, *California Ranchos and Farms, 1846–1862* (1947); Gilbert C. Fite, "The Farmers' Frontier in California, 1850–1900," in Fite, ed., *The Farmers' Frontier, 1865–1900* (1966); Paul W. Gates, *California Ranchos and Farms, 1846–1862* (1967), and "Public Land Disposal in California," *Agricultural History* (1975); Rodman W. Paul, "The Beginnings of Agriculture in California: Innovation vs. Continuity," *California Historical Quarterly* (1973); W. W. Robinson, *Land in California* (1948); Ellen Liebman, *California Farmland: A History of Large Agricultural Landholdings* (1983); Vincent P. Carosso, *The California Wine Industry, 1830–1895: A Study of the Formative Years* (1951).

Social and Economic Development

Franklin Walker, *San Francisco's Literary Frontier* (1939); Martin S. Peterson, *Joaquin Miller* (1937); William B. Rice, *The Los Angeles Star, 1851–1864* (1947); Edward C. Kemble, *A History of California Newspapers* (1962); Ella S. Mighels, *The Story of the Files* (1893); Lois F. Rodecape, "Tom Maguire, Napoleon of the Stage," *California Historical Society Quarterly* (1941, 1942); Edmund M. Gagey, *The San Francisco Stage* (1950); Misha Berson, *The San Francisco Stage: From Gold Rush to Golden Spike, 1849–1869* (1989); George Martin, *Verde at the Golden Gate: Opera and San Francisco in the Gold Rush Years* (1993); Nigey Lennon, *Mark Twain in California* (1982); Irving G. Hendrick, *California Education* (1980); Doris Muscatine, *Old San Francisco* (1975); George R. Stewart, *Bret Harte: Argonaut and Exile* (1931); Josephine D. Rhodehamel and Raymund F. Wood, *Ina Coolbrith* (1973); Gunther Barth, *Instant Cities* (1975); Roger W. Lotchin, *San Francisco, 1846–1856: From Hamlet to Modern City* (1974); Bruno Fritzche, "San Francisco, 1846–1848: The Coming of the Land Speculator," *California Historical Quarterly* (1972); Ralph Mann, *After the Gold Rush: Grass Valley and Nevada City* (1982); William A. Bullough, "Entrepreneurs and Urbanism on the California Mining Frontier: Frederick Walter and Weaverville, 1852–1868," *California History* (1991); Eric Niderost, "Pacific Emporium: State versus Local Control of San Francisco Harbor, 1835–1863," (M.A. thesis, California State University, Hayward, 1980); Ira B. Cross, *Financing an Empire: History of Banking in California* (1927); W. Turrentine Jackson, "Wells Fargo

Staging over the Sierra," *California Historical Society Quarterly* (1970); Peter R. Decker, *Fortunes and Failures* (1978); Richard Peterson, "Thomas Starr King in California, 1860–64: Forgotten Naturalist of the Civil War," *California History* (1990); Harlan Hogue and David J. Langum, *Thomas O. Larkin: A Life of Patriotism and Profit in Old California* (1990); Gerald McKevitt, "Hispanic Californians and Catholic Higher Education: The Diary of Jesús María Estudillo, 1857–1864," *California History* (1991); Malcom J. Rohrbough, *Days of Gold: The California Gold Rush and the American Nation* (1997); James F. Varley, *Lola Montez: The California Adventures of Europe's Notorious Courtesan* (1996); Kevin Starr and Richard J. Orsi (eds.), *Rooted in Barbarous Soil: People, Culture and Community in Gold Rush California* (2000); Brian Roberts, *American Alchemy: The California Gold Rush and Middle Class Culture* (2000); James J. Rawls and Richard J. Orsi (eds.), *A Golden State: Mining and Economic Development in California* (1999).

The Bloomer Cut on the Central Pacific Railway Line, West of Auburn, in the 1860s
In late-nineteenth-century California, new railways disrupted society as well as nature. *Courtesy the California State Railway Museum.*

PART FIVE

THE RAILROAD ERA

The railroad was the most significant technology to come of age in the nineteenth century. It brought about new patterns of transportation and communication, which in turn revolutionized economies, institutions, and social behavior. Railroads not only accelerated settlement of the West, but also forged much of what we call "modern" in the American way of life. As much as any region, California experienced these transformations between the 1860s and the early twentieth century.

As is often true of new technologies, however, the railroad's influences in California were complex and contradictory. This was evident at the outset of the railway era. Nineteenth-century Americans usually associated the railroad with individual enrichment and community progress, and Californians had particular reasons for avidly supporting railways. After 1855, the mines petered out, other industries emerged slowly, migration to California slowed to a trickle, and business and employment suffered frequent depressions. Well into the twentieth century, most Californians saw railways as the panacea for the state's problems and clamored for their construction. As one writer put it in 1856, "If we shall live to see the day when the iron horse, with his impetuous speed, shall come from the Atlantic to quench his fiery thirst in the cool waters of the Pacific, then will our fondest visions have been realized and clouds of doubt will no longer obscure the bright future of California."

At least one Californian disagreed. In the 1860s Henry George, who would later become a world-famous social critic, land reformer, and originator of the "single-tax theory," was an itinerant San Francisco-area journalist. In 1868, as the first transcontinental rail line rushed toward completion, he published a dour article in the new *Overland Monthly,* entitled "What the Railroads Will Bring Us." George acknowledged that "the California of the new era will be greater, richer, more powerful than the California of the past," but he also predicted that the railways would aggravate social inequities and make the state more vulnerable to the economic turmoil of the national industrial world. George regretted that "the consequent great increase of business and population will not be a benefit to all of us but only to a portion. As a general rule . . . those who *have*, it will make wealthier; for those who *have not*, it will make it more difficult to get." "The locomotive is a great centralizer," he warned. "It kills little towns and builds up great cities, and in the same way kills little businesses and builds up great ones." George also predicted that the railway would give rise to "large corporations and other special interests," of which California's Central Pacific Railroad, with immense capital, employee force, and political influence, was already a harbinger. "Can we rely," he wondered, "upon sufficient intelligence, independence and virtue among the many to resist the political effects of the concentration of great wealth in the hands of a few?" In light of later events, Henry George's dissenting voice turned out to be prophetic.

For some Californians, the sweet vision of progress that in the 1860s seemed possible through railroad construction soured quickly in the 1870s. Ironically, as happened in the rest of the country, the railway age, a period of great economic development, cultural maturation, and modernization, also brought confusion and conflict to California. Bitter economic and political dissent resulted, with much of citizens' ire being directed toward the Southern Pacific Railroad, the near monopoly formed from the merger of the Central Pacific and most other lines. However, conflict in California was much more complicated than simply opposition by the masses to powerful businesses such as the railroads. Although some groups focused their fight against the power of railroads and other large corporations, other issues associated with the dramatic changes of the period also proved to be battlegrounds: water and agricultural development, urban growth, social inequality, inter-ethnic tension, resource and environmental policies, and sectional and inter-community rivalries. As a result, between the 1860s and the 1880s, California began to reap the profits of the new technological order, while continuing to bear the burdens of the old turbulent mining world.

CHAPTER THIRTEEN

CONFRONTATION AT MUSSEL SLOUGH, 1880

In popular folklore, as in most scholarly histories, the 1870s land war between the railroad and settlers in California's Central Valley was an important event that symbolized the conflict of interest in the late nineteenth century between the masses of ordinary citizens and the era's developing corporations. The Southern Pacific Railroad, part of the near monopoly over transportation assembled by the owners of the Central Pacific, had been provided a land grant by Congress to encourage construction of a southern transcontinental rail line. Some settlers of the Mussel Slough district of the Tulare Basin, contending that the railroad company engaged in fraudulent and corrupt activities, that the grant was illegal, and that the land as a result was vacant, moved onto the land and challenged the railroad's title. The resulting decade-long, land conflict culminated in the famous Mussel Slough incident of May 11, 1880. Relying on local legend and second-hand accounts, historians have generally sided with the settlers. Their contest with the Southern Pacific, scholars have agreed, epitomized the long-term struggle between the public good and the private greed and corruption of big business in the industrial era.

Primary evidence from original letters, railroad records, public documents, and contemporary newspapers illustrates that the actual story is far more complicated than the simplistic morality play of folklore, that guilt and innocence is far more difficult to assess. The drama of Mussel Slough reflects more than a simple struggle between "the people" and "big business." It suggests the sweeping economic, social, and environmental changes of the period, the complex interplay of opportunity and failure, and the bewildering conflicts among many groups that followed in the wake of railroad building in late-nineteenth-century California.

Early on the bright morning of May 11, 1880, U.S. Marshal Alonzo W. Poole and a companion climbed into a buggy and drove out of the town of Hanford. As they made their way north through the unpaved streets of the young village and beyond onto the flat farmland, Poole could not help but notice that it had been a bad spring in the Mussel Slough country. Winter rains had not come. Roadside weeds already shriveled in the dust, irrigation ditches ran dry, and thin clumps of sunburned grain bleached away in the fields. The countryside fairly crackled with impending drought.

Poole detested his mission. After years of struggle with the Southern Pacific Railroad over land titles, the settlers of Mussel Slough had lost their cases in federal court, and Poole was to start dispossessing settlers. His companion, railroad land-grader William H. Clark, knew the country and would identify the disputed tracts. Like many Californians, Poole favored the cause of the settlers, some of whom were his old friends. Setting personal feelings aside, Poole grimly resolved to do his duty.

After bouncing over rutted wagon tracks for two miles, Poole and Clark rendezvoused with Mills Hartt and Walter Crow, two of the many who had purchased land from the railroad and who now expected the marshal to place them finally in possession. Trouble had been rumored for months, and Poole and Clark carried light revolvers. Hartt and Crow, under death threats from the settlers, arrived with pistols, rifles, and shotguns stowed under their wagon seat.

Before the wagons had traveled far toward Crow's tract, news of the marshal's presence sent riders galloping toward the farm from every direction. Along the way, Poole's party met John Storer, who, with Henry Brewer, was occupying Crow's land. Crow repeated his offer to sell the land to Storer and Brewer. They talked calmly, Storer agreed to broach the proposition to Brewer, and the party resumed its drive. Henry Brewer had a valid 80-acre homestead claim with a fence, house, and barn on government land about five miles northwest of Hanford. Adjacent to the south was the disputed plot, a 320-acre unfenced wheat field on railroad grant land, which Brewer and Storer had been claiming and cultivating for several years, but which

Crow had purchased from the railroad in 1878.

At about 10:30 A.M., the marshal's party drove through Brewer's yard and into an open field where the farmer was plowing. They stopped, and Storer rode ahead to confer with Brewer. At that moment, forty or fifty men with rifles on their shoulders rode onto the homestead, bore down on the wagons, and halted about fifty yards away. Agitated, Crow and Hartt reached for their firearms, but the marshal cautioned them not to touch the guns unless they were attacked. The two sides faced each other down across the empty land. A confrontation, brewing for years, had finally arrived. "I think I had better go and meet them," Poole muttered. The marshal jumped down and strode rapidly off toward the riders.

The confrontation between corporation and settlers that reached a climax that 1880 spring morning near Hanford was a true product of the railway age. The Mussel Slough country had dramatically felt the changes, potentials, and conflicts of post–gold rush California. The Tulare Basin, including the Mussel Slough district, was a natural sink in the central San Joaquin Valley. Snow-fed streams, such as the Kings River—a branch of which was named Mussel Slough—meandered westward from the Sierra Nevada and emptied into Tulare Lake. Fertile soils, gentle slopes, and abundant surface and ground water gave the basin unusual agricultural promise. Despite its natural bounty, the Mussel Slough country in the western basin, like most of California, was virtually undeveloped as late as 1870. During the gold rush, the eastern basin, with more rainfall and nearer mining markets, became one of California's first thriving agricultural and cattle-raising areas. Visalia, hub of the region's economy and seat of Tulare County after 1852, quickly grew into the largest valley town south of Stockton. Twenty miles westward, however, the air was dry, the settlers few, and the land sheltered from gold rush frenzy.

Railroad building in the early 1870s touched off changes that culminated in the Mussel Slough incident of 1880. Enticed by a congressional land grant, the Southern Pacific Railroad Company started laying rails south of San José in 1869. Its line was initially planned to run southeastward across the Coast Range, through the Mussel Slough country, down the San Joaquin Valley to southern California, and east across the desert to the Colorado River. Construction halted a few months later at Tres Piños, south of Hollister, where rugged mountains blocked access to the valley. Determined to tap rich lands and traffic, the company's new owners, the famous "Big Four"—Leland Stanford, Collis P. Huntington, Charles Crocker, and Mark Hopkins—decided to extend a branch of their other major railway, the Central Pacific, southward into the valley.

Generally hailed as economic cure-alls, specific railways provoked much conflict, even before they were built. In this case, the Big Four, lacking a federal land grant for their branch line, requested that Visalia and Tulare County provide a cash subsidy and right-of-way through the town, which lay east of the best route down the valley. Although this was a common way to encourage railway construction, the subsidy question produced bitter conflict in the county. Residents of Visalia favored the subsidy to promote the town and their business interests. The most vociferous opponents were stage and wagon companies fearing railroad competition, settlements left off the projected rail line, and cattlemen opposed to the farmers invading their open ranges. From the beginning,

then, Tulare County divided into pro- and anti-railroad factions. Although most local leaders supported the subsidy, in 1870 anti-railroad Governor Henry H. Haight vetoed bills that would have allowed San Joaquin Valley counties to subsidize railroads. The Central Pacific thus bypassed Visalia and most other established communities, and constructed its line along the most direct, inexpensive route through the uninhabited lowlands in the middle of the valley. The railroad decided to build its own market towns to compete with older settlements.

In 1872 crews completed the Central Pacific branch line to Goshen, west of Visalia, where it joined the proposed Southern Pacific route through the Mussel Slough country. To retain their land grant for the rest of the rail line, the Big Four built south of Goshen under the name of the Southern Pacific Railroad Company. To acquire as much land as possible before the completion deadline of 1878 stipulated in its 1866 grant bill, the Southern Pacific Railroad resumed construction on its main line westward from Goshen in 1876 through the Mussel Slough country. The company founded new rail towns at Hanford, Lemoore, and Huron, where in 1877 construction halted near the eastern edge of the mountain barrier. Although an independent railroad linked Visalia to the through line at Goshen in 1874, resentment against the Southern Pacific remained strong among some groups in the valley.

The Mussel Slough country, which lay ten to thirty miles west of Goshen, lacked rail connections in the early 1870s, but the area already quickened to the new transportation system. Since crops could now be hauled by wagon the short distance to Goshen and other rail heads on the Central/Southern Pacific main line, the railroad created markets and encouraged new land uses. Settlers

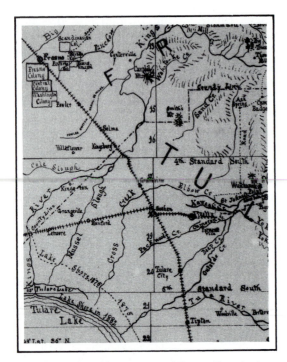

The Mussel Slough of Tulare and Fresno Counties in 1883
This contemporary map illustrates the major features of Mussel Slough geography in the late nineteenth century, as well as the location of the Central/Southern Pacific's main north-south rail line bisecting the valley. Tulare Lake now has nearly vanished, its former bottom drained and covered with large corporate farms. *Courtesy of the California State Library.*

poured into the district, particularly after 1877, when the Mussel Slough district received its own rail line. During the 1870s Tulare County's population increased nearly 150 percent—from 4,500 to 11,300—three times the state's slow rate of growth, with most development coming along Mussel Slough.

Spurred on by new railroad markets, valley settlers revolutionized agriculture and land use. Unoccupied and open grazing lands were quickly subdivided and shifted to hay, grains and, in favored areas where water could be secured, fruit and specialty crops.

Abundant flowing water and gently sloping land simplified irrigation. During the early 1870s, mutual companies of landowners pooled water rights, capital, and labor, and dug canals from the Kings River or Mussel Slough. The ditches supplied water to more than 60,000 acres by 1879, and Mussel Slough had developed into one of California's first intensively cultivated and irrigated small-farm regions. Newly irrigated farms specialized in corn, alfalfa, and, increasingly, vegetables, deciduous fruits, and dairy cattle. Unirrigated farms were limited to less profitable dry-farming of grain, hay, and a few other crops.

Population growth and agricultural change transformed the countryside. In the early 1850s the federal government had surveyed the San Joaquin Valley into a traditional gridiron of "sections" (one square mile, or 640 acres each) and had offered the land for purchase. Indicative of limited land use before railroad building, most public land in the Mussel Slough area remained unsold as late as 1870. As the railroad approached in the early 1870s, however, the vacant land was beset by hundreds of buyers and homesteaders, many of whom were small-scale speculators who held the land in expectation of price increases. Competition for good locations was keen, and furious trading drove prices for unimproved farmland from $1 to $2 per acre in 1870 to $10 to $20 per acre by 1880.

Their scramble for land set many new settlers on a collision course with the Southern Pacific, as well as one another. On the basis of its federal grant, the railroad, although it had yet to complete its line, claimed nearly one-half of the land in the area, the odd-numbered alternate sections located in checkerboard fashion for ten miles on either side of its line east from Goshen to its dead end at Huron. The comparatively new, cumbersome "patenting" procedure for transfer-

A Mussel Slough Farm, 1883
The farm fields, orchards, and house gardens made possible by irrigation and railway development along Mussel Slough are clear in this contemporary woodcut from an early county history. Typical of illustrations in nineteenth-century histories and promotional tracts, a train—a mechanical symbol of economic and cultural progress—chugs in the distance. *Courtesy of the California State Library.*

ring land from the government to the railroad companies broke down completely in the Southern Pacific's case, causing decades of confusion for railroad and settlers alike. The railroad, speculators, local community conflicts, vacillating government officials, and even settlers themselves shared the blame for what happened. Although the 1866 federal land-grant law allowed the railroad to choose its route between San Francisco Bay and the Colorado River, the company's state incorporation charter specified a main line southward along the coast to San Diego. In early 1867 the federal Department of the Interior accepted a map by the Southern Pacific's original owners for a route through the San Joaquin Valley and withdrew from the market vacant public land along the line to await patenting to the railroad. A year later, the department—under pressure from a curious combination of coastal counties intent on securing the rail line and a national ring of speculators led by the notorious California land king William S. Chapman, who hoped to monopolize land along the valley route—suddenly declared the land grant forfeit on the grounds that the new route violated the company's state charter. Protests from valley communities and the Big Four, who had just purchased the Southern Pacific, convinced the department to suspend the order temporarily, however, and the valley land remained reserved for the railroad on official maps at government land offices. In 1870 the railroad and valley people persuaded Congress and the state legislature to confirm the legality of the revised route; and in 1874 the Department of the Interior began issuing the railroad patents for land along the completed segments of track from San José south to Tres Piños and from Goshen south to Bakersfield. For nearly three years in the late 1860s, however, the legal status of the Southern Pacific's grant had been in limbo. Enough uncertainty remained to lead some to take the chance that the railroad's land titles would one day be overturned.

Throughout their conflict with the railroad, Mussel Slough settlers wrapped themselves in the mantle of American yeomanry. Like other God-fearing pioneer farmers, they claimed, they had ventured forth in good faith into the cruel desert wilderness to carve out new homes for their families on what they assumed was public land, open to homesteading. The railroad, they charged, was a corrupt, tyrannical monopoly that was using its illegitimate power to claim their farms and demand ruinous prices.

The Mussel Slough settlers actually included many groups, from honest farmers caught in the web of contradictory land policies to the land sharks haunting all American frontiers. Only a few true homesteaders occupied railroad-reserved lands when the Southern Pacific's grant was reconfirmed in 1870. Mass movement onto the railroad's lands began with John J. Doyle. A typical frontier transient, Doyle had mined, taught school, and farmed in several locations after migrating from Indiana in the mid-1860s. While working a Merced County farm in 1870, he read a prediction in a San Francisco newspaper that the route controversy would one day void the railroad's land grant. Fired with the vision of free land, Doyle sold his farm in 1871 and moved onto reserved railroad land near the hamlet of Grangeville, a few miles north of the proposed rail line through the Mussel Slough country.

A squatter by his own admission, Doyle mounted a challenge to the railroad's title.

Now calling himself a lawyer, he spread word of the company's flawed title throughout the valley. Coinciding with a boom caused by the railroad's building through Goshen to the east, the squatter movement grew quickly. People from hundreds of miles around flocked to cash in on the free land, and by 1875 hundreds of claimants squatted on railroad land in the area. Like many frontier lawyers, Doyle established a land business predicated on overturning railroad titles. He secretly contracted with several hundred neighbors to defeat the railroad's title in exchange for 25 cents per acre in gold.

The lure of fertile lands, free from rent, purchase price, interest, and taxes, produced a speculative mania. Settlers sold farms on government land and moved with their buildings to unoccupied railroad sections; others expanded their legitimate farms to include adjacent railroad lands. By the mid-1870s claims on railroad land changed hands openly at values of up to $500 to $1,000. By 1880 these speculative claims were, in the words of one settler, "the principal stock in trade in the Mussel Slough country."

Because of the frequent exchange of railway land claims, a diverse group finally confronted the Southern Pacific by 1880. A few were bona fide homesteaders whose claims the Department of the Interior had not yet approved. The great majority, though, had established claims since 1871 and were gambling that the company would lose its title. Local land and tax records indicate that some hardly fit the pioneer farmer image. Many did not inhabit their claims, but resided on nearby farms or in the towns. Some had more than one claim to railroad land or possessed additional legal holdings on the even-numbered government sections, occasionally as much as several thousand acres. In fact, many Mussel Slough settlers, particularly the leaders, were primarily land speculators.

Land improvements showed that many claims were speculative. Squatters made only minimal capital investments in their risky enterprises. Some land lay vacant; some was hayed or was used for grazing; and some was plowed and planted in grain fields, mostly by dry-farming methods. Despite settlers' claims that they had invested hundreds of thousands of dollars and years of backbreaking labor in irrigation improvements, most of the water companies were operated by old-timers who rarely took part in squatting ventures, and only some of the odd-numbered railroad sections were being irrigated. Most irrigation facilities were located on secure even-numbered sections, except for minor hand-dug channels that had to be renewed each year. Many squatters sheltered most other improvements, including houses, barns, wells, and fences on the even-numbered sections.

Under Doyle's generalship, the squatters cooperated to attack the railroad's title. They trooped to the federal land office in Visalia to file mass claims under the preemption and homestead laws, charging that the railroad's route and grant were illegal and that the Department of the Interior had reopened the land to settlement in 1868. Although some federal agents sympathized with the squatters, they rejected virtually all the claims on the grounds that the railroad's grant had been confirmed by Congress and was still legally closed to rival entries. When Doyle appealed dozens of cases, the Department of the Interior upheld the decisions of the local office in favor of the railroad. The squatters refiled claims several times under different federal land laws, only to reach the same conclusion. Doyle and other leaders also journeyed to Washington to lobby Congress and to protest against the issuing of

more patents to the railway. Nearly every year after 1874, they unsuccessfully pushed for bills to revoke the Southern Pacific grant or legitimize their claims retroactively.

The settlers later charged that the Southern Pacific had thwarted them with bribery and other illegitimate means. Certainly the railroad possessed financial and political power and was not above using bribery on occasion, but in this case the settlers' major obstacle was their own shaky legal position. Doyle and other inexperienced local attorneys were unfamiliar with the new body of railroad land-grant law that was evolving in the 1870s. Most squatter arguments had already been rendered moot by decisions of Congress, the United States attorney general, the secretary of the interior, or federal courts. If government officials had acceded to the requests of the Mussel Slough settlers, they would have reversed nearly a decade of legal precedent, thereby casting doubt over titles to millions of acres within dozens of railway land grants in nearly all western states. Nevertheless, the undaunted settlers insisted that they were legally and morally correct and that only the corrupt practices of an evil corporation stood between them and their land. Confidently, they sought vindication in an appeal to the federal courts—the Supreme Court, if necessary.

Meanwhile, settlers had to prevent the railroad from selling the land to others. At meetings from February to April 1878, five hundred settlers founded the Settlers' Grand League to resist "the occupation of so-called railroad lands in the Mussel Slough district by the Southern Pacific Railroad Company." Headquartered at Hanford and supported by some local officials, the league functioned in the time-honored tradition of the regulators, claim clubs, and squatters' associations of many American frontiers. It assessed members to finance court appeals, published pamphlets to build public support, and tried to keep local officials from interfering with settlers' use of the lands. The Grand League also used social pressure and boycott to prevent individual members from coming to terms separately with the railroad. The organization assumed the paraphernalia befitting a secret society—secret membership, closed meetings, and costumes of masks, hoods, and long red robes. In its trappings, the league resembled the Ku Klux Klan and other white-supremacy groups then popular in the southern states, from which many Mussel Slough residents had recently migrated. The group's forceful methods provoked dissent and defection and further divided the Mussel Slough settlers.

The settlers threatened violence against the Southern Pacific and its land buyers. League leaders warned the railway that if it tried to sell the land, they would tear up tracks, burn depots, and incinerate the crops and buildings of those who purchased from the company. Land buyers, railway agents, and local residents who criticized the squatters also received anonymous letters ordering them to leave the area. To demonstrate that the threats were not idle, troops of armed and hooded riders roamed the countryside, making nocturnal calls on railroad sympathizers and land buyers. In late 1878, Perry Phillips, who had been feuding with the squatters for years, repeatedly ignored the Grand League's warnings to leave land he had acquired from the railroad. On the night of November 21, one hundred fifty masked and robed riders invaded the land, evicted Phillips's tenant, along with his terrified wife and children, and burned their house and possessions. A few days later, armed men held Phillips and two employees prisoner on another piece of disputed railroad land, while neighbors with fifty-one teams of horses plowed the farm and installed squatter James B. Fretwell in posses-

sion. Although Phillips and the railway protested, local authorities took no action. Denying responsibility, squatters insisted that Phillips's attackers had been "Indians."

In the spring of 1879, when the Southern Pacific continued to sell land and filed trespass complaints against some squatters, the Grand League formalized its armed resistance. At a mass meeting in early March, the league reconfirmed its pledge to resist with force any attempt by the railroad or its buyers to occupy squatters' lands. To enforce its actions, the league organized a cavalry commanded by its president, Thomas Jefferson McQuiddy. Periodically, McQuiddy drilled and paraded the settler militia through the streets of Hanford and other towns.

Widely reported after 1877, the squatters' vigilantism was denounced as illegal and dangerous by many Californians, including some Mussel Slough residents. In the depressed 1870s, however, many blamed the state's ills on the railroad's transportation monopoly, high freight rates, and political influence. Anti-railroad politicians, newspapers, and organizations rallied behind the settlers' cause. The San Francisco *Chronicle*, then the premier anti-Southern Pacific newspaper in the state, reported the anguish of the Mussel Slough settlers in full detail. Abounding in errors and exaggerations and ignoring the chronology of settlement and most of the legal issues, the *Chronicle's* accounts transformed the squatters into innocent homesteaders and land buyers who had been lured onto the land and then deliberately defrauded by an unscrupulous railroad. Fueling the settlers' armed resistance, the *Chronicle* likened them to the colonial patriots at the Boston Tea Party. Unless the Southern Pacific ceased its oppression, the *Chronicle* warned, these farmers would "strike the first blow against land monopoly and corporate greed."

Labor unions and anti-monopoly political

Thomas Jefferson McQuiddy, 1900
A former cavalry officer and secret service agent for the Confederacy, "Major" McQuiddy had come to Mussel Slough by way of Tennessee and Missouri in 1873. He purchased large tracts of even-numbered government sections near Hanford, and like some of his neighbors, moved over to establish claims on odd-numbered railroad sections. An experienced politician and soldier, McQuiddy emerged quickly as a leader in the new community, a natural choice for the Grand League's president and militia commander. *Courtesy of the California State Library.*

which he exhorted the settlers to fight to keep their lands from the Southern Pacific. When Kearney shouted "murder the red-eyed monsters" and promised to lead an army of 40,000 San Francisco workers to defend the settlers from the corporate fiend, the squatters, according to one anti-League settler in the audience, "hurrahed as if they would split their throats." By the end of the 1870s, the Mussel Slough struggle had been engulfed in a rising statewide tide of anti-railroad politics.

Faced with bitter opposition and denounced in many quarters, the railroad was in a quandary. The Southern Pacific defended its land as a legitimate corporate asset, justly earned under congressional law as compensation for the risk and expense of building railroads through uninhabited country. The company's goal, however, was to manage its land grant in a businesslike fashion designed to promote population and community growth, economic development, traffic revenues, and hence corporate profits. As a result, the railway had adopted a conciliatory stance toward settlers from the inception of its land program.

Like other land-grant roads, the Southern Pacific conceived of itself as a land subdivider and distributor, not as a speculator. It applied for land-grant patents as soon as it became eligible by completing a segment of line. Wanting clear land titles, the Southern Pacific avoided selecting tracts already occupied by homesteaders with legitimate rights. The railroad priced its land somewhat below prevailing values on unimproved land and sold it as speedily as possible. To stimulate cultivation, the company favored sales to buyers of small tracts, discouraged speculators from purchasing its lands, charged low prices for good agricultural land (generally $2.50 to $7.00 per acre), and financed a low-interest credit plan. The great majority of

parties also jumped on the settlers' bandwagon. One of these was the Workingmen's Party of California (WPC), a San Francisco-based organization that was building considerable statewide influence with its anti-Chinese and anti-corporate agitation. John Doyle, also an official in the WPC, arranged for the Workingmen to endorse the squatters' cause. In 1879, at the Grand League's invitation, the WPC's fiery leader Denis Kearney delivered passionate orations to crowds at Grangeville, Hanford, and Lemoore in

Southern Pacific Land Agent D. K. Zumwalt
In his popular 1901 novel *The Octopus,* based on the
Mussel Slough land controversy, the great California
writer Frank Norris fashioned one of the most loath-
some characters in American fiction, S. Behrman, the
Southern Pacific Railroad's corrupt land and political
agent for the San Joaquin Valley. Ironically, Behrman's
true-life prototype, D. K. Zumwalt, was a long-time resident and respected leader in Visalia and the valley. On
many occasions, he persuaded Southern Pacific executives to soften policies toward buyers and squatters on
railroad lands. *Courtesy of the California State Library.*

buyers capitalized their land at low initial
sums (about $100 or less for a typical 80- to
160-acre farm) and deferred most of the purchase price until their fields were producing
crops. "We want the country settled because
it does not pay to run Railroads to places
where there are no people," the chief of the
Southern Pacific's Land Department instructed his San Joaquin Valley agent, D. K.
Zumwalt, in 1875. "The company . . . desires
to hold out the strongest inducements to actual settlers to go upon unencumbered land,

to use it and occupy it, and to give such persons who do so, the preference over all others, under all circumstances."

Although the railroad generally enjoyed
cordial relations with homesteaders and buyers on its land, conflicts invariably arose.
Faulty surveys and maps, sloppy administration, or honest errors by settlers, government
land officials, and the railroad resulted in
some overlapping claims. Most conflicts were
resolved amicably, often with the railroad
withdrawing its claim or selling to settlers at
the government price. But some disagreements became tangled and acrimonious,
leaving a residue of bitterness against the
Southern Pacific.

Not all the railroad's contestants were
good-faith homesteaders, however. As typically happened on American frontiers, squatters and resource thieves, many of them
petty speculators, also invaded the railroad's
lands. Though few in comparison to legitimate settlers, these persistent interlopers
used well-known frontier devices to detach
land from the company. They forged claims
and dates of settlement, moved surveyor's
markers, ran their fences onto railroad land,
illegally filed multiple homestead claims on
government and railroad sections under fic-
titious names, and transported cabins from
tract to tract to establish residence in many
places. They also planted crops, grazed livestock, cut down trees, removed gravel and
building stone, and diverted water on railroad land. Railway leaders quickly learned to
distinguish between legitimate and illegitimate settlers. Although the company refrained from pressing its rights against good-
faith settlers, it spared no effort or expense
to defeat the challenges of squatters. Seemingly innocuous cases could establish damaging precedents involving thousands of acres
later.

Torn between a determination to defend
company lands against trespassers and a cor-

porate policy to promote development by accommodating settlers, Southern Pacific leaders dealt indecisively with the Mussel Slough conflict. They were confident that their position on the Mussel Slough lands was ethical and legal according to previous court cases and government decisions. From years of experience, they immediately classified the Mussel Slough settlers as illegitimate squatters. These contestants appeared more dangerous than average, however. Numerous and organized, they successfully mobilized public opinion against the company. Moreover, they attacked not simply the title to small pieces of land, but also the validity of the railway's entire grant of millions of acres. Convinced that important legal issues were at stake, Southern Pacific leaders refused to compromise on the company's land title. "Spare no pains, or any reasonable expense, to win this land for the company," the Land Department instructed its San Joaquin Valley agent.

On the other hand, the Southern Pacific hesitated to oust the squatters. Despite its intransigence on the title issue, the company moved gingerly in dealing with individual claimants to the land. Aware of its opponents' numbers, the wide support they enjoyed, the possibility of political reprisals against the company, and the company's policy of promoting settlement, the railway tried to coax the squatters to acknowledge the company's title and to buy or lease claims legitimately. Essentially, the railroad's solution for its Mussel Slough dilemma was to defend its title tenaciously, while at the same time converting the squatters into customers.

Southern Pacific leaders hoped that the squatters would retain, buy, and work their lands. After receiving patents for Mussel Slough land in late 1877, the company ignored threats and prepared the land for immediate sale. In early 1878, the company sent its experienced land-grader, William H.

Clark, to inspect and price the land according to comparable unimproved land in the vicinity. As was its custom, the railroad's Land Department then reduced Clark's prices by twenty percent. To quell rumors that the company would sell land from under the squatters, Jerome Madden, head of the Land Department in San Francisco, announced that the company would sell no occupied lands without first offering those in possession the option of buying. If occupants decided not to purchase, the company would give them leases to harvest crops and remove improvements. Railway leaders believed that, like most other defeated squatters, the Mussel Slough people would ultimately deal with the railroad.

At the end of April 1878, following usual procedure, Madden sent letters to hundreds of occupants of railroad lands, fixing prices, giving squatters a thirty-day option before their holdings were to be put on public sale, and announcing that they could start purchasing their lands on May 18. Railway leaders anticipated that the prices would provoke resistance. But higher prices than the company normally charged were fair, the railroaders believed, because Mussel Slough land was easily the most valuable land in the entire grant, and it had been the construction of the railroad there that had sparked the local boom.

Madden's letters sent a shock wave through the district. On May 10 the month-old Settlers' Grand League denounced the railroad's prices and warned local residents not to buy the disputed land. Although they continued to hold the railroad's title invalid, the squatters had also argued that, if their challenge were defeated, the railroad could charge only the value of the land as of 1867, when the grant had taken effect, and certainly no more than $2.50 per acre, the official government price for public lands. The settlers contended that their irrigation improvements, not the railroad's construction, had elevated land values. To support their position, the squatters cited recently published Southern Pacific pamphlets that had invited farmers to cultivate the railroad's unpatented lands and, in vague terms, promised such settlers first opportunity to buy, without regard to their improvements, "at various figures from $2.50 upward per acre."

For years after May 1878, settlers and their defenders condemned the Southern Pacific not only for failing to adhere to the $2.50 figure, but also for charging *average* prices per acre of $20 to $50, or even as high as $80. Relying on sources sympathetic toward the settlers, subsequent writers have accepted these figures as accurate. Its alleged charges for Mussel Slough land became prime evidence that the railroad "octopus" was squeezing the very lifeblood from California.

However, Southern Pacific maps, price lists, and sales records for the San Joaquin Valley show that the prices the settlers claimed they were being charged were one-hundred to four-hundred-percent exaggerations of the actual asking prices. Of hundreds of tracts of railroad land in the Mussel Slough district—usually subdivided into 40- to 160-acre lots—almost all were priced between $10 and $20 per acre. Virtually none sold for more than $25, except for a half-dozen tiny suburban plots adjacent to railroad towns.

Squatter leaders knew the true prices. Doyle's farm was priced at $20 per acre, McQuiddy's several claims at $9 to $13.50, and Henry Brewer's, site of the later confrontation between squatters and the railroad, at $19. Though higher than for Southern Pacific lands elsewhere in the valley, the railroad's prices, according to a recent survey of land transactions in the district during the 1860s and 1870s, coincided with those on unimproved lands changing hands on the even-numbered government sections, even among the squatters themselves. As early as 1874, before irrigation improvements were extensive, Henry Brewer, for example, subdivided his legal holding on the public section next to his railroad claim and sold sixty-three acres of it for $15.87 per acre. Throughout the 1870s other squatter leaders routinely bought and sold land on the even-numbered sections for $11 to $25 per acre. Everyone recognized that Mussel Slough land was exceptionally valuable.

Surprised as they were by the squatters' vehemence, Southern Pacific leaders started to sell land. At the same time, they tried to avoid a direct confrontation with squatters. Periodically, Madden sent rounds of letters to occupants renewing the railroad's offer. Although most refused, the company refrained from selling any tracts claimed by squatters to other persons, in the hope that a settlement could be reached. To that end, the railroad in July reduced most prices substantially (ten to twenty-five percent). The company also made purchasing or renting more attractive to buyers who were short of cash by accepting one-fifth crop-share leases, allowing lease payments to be applied toward down payments on later purchases, and permitting buyers to sign contracts before local station agents instead of at the company's Visalia land office. Despite squatter threats, many Mussel Slough settlers took advantage of these concessions, and between May and October 1878, the railroad did a fairly brisk land business.

In the early autumn of 1878, however, Southern Pacific leaders reevaluated their conciliatory position. From their point of view, they had repeatedly compromised and allowed the squatters to use railroad land, in some cases for six or seven years. While much patented railroad land was being kept off the market, Tulare and Fresno counties had recognized the railroad's title and were levying property taxes against the railroad, substantially increasing its overhead. Although it still hesitated to precipitate a confrontation and to provoke public opinion further, the Southern Pacific decided to sell tracts claimed by squatters, but only after the company had received purchase offers and the land agent had given the occupants a final chance to acquire the land.

Although the squatters and many historians charged that the purchasers were outside thugs whom the railroad brought in as dummy buyers, almost all the buyers were local residents. As elsewhere in California, the transition from cattle raising to agriculture was far from orderly, and the district had divided into bitter factions even before the railroad-land issue emerged. Pioneer grazers had occupied available public land and water rights by the late 1860s, prospered modestly, and established themselves as a local elite, bound by business and kinship ties. Then, especially after 1872, when the Southern Pacific arrived at Goshen, farmers began moving in. Some were former Confederates fleeing the post-Civil War chaos in the southern states. By the mid-1870s, newcomers comprised the majority, and the two groups clashed over access to remaining public and railroad lands, the trampling of crops by straying herds, control over local politics, and especially the scarce shares in the irrigation companies, which were controlled by old-timers who had established water rights before 1870. Smoldering feuds erupted into barn and crop burnings, slaughters of livestock, and beatings and shootings. Generally, those willing to buy railroad lands belonged to the somewhat wealthier pioneer faction. Squatters tended to be newcomers. The Mussel Slough land battle thus involved a deep-seated struggle among different kinds of settlers, not just between settlers and the Southern Pacific.

Late in 1878, when recent buyers such as Perry Phillips, Mills Hartt, and Walter Crow tried to cultivate lands claimed by squatters and met with resistance and violence, the Southern Pacific reconsidered its policy further. Squatter rhetoric and vigilantism convinced railway leaders that the settlers intended to use mass violence against the company and its land buyers. Moreover, in November and December 1878, new sales and rentals in the Mussel Slough area declined rapidly, especially after squatters burned Phillips out. By mid-1879, sales had ceased altogether, and revenues were falling elsewhere in the valley. Interviews with prospective buyers convinced Southern Pacific officials that fear of squatter retaliation was to blame. Emissaries from the Grand League were also traveling to other districts to encourage squatters to unite for a common effort.

The deteriorating situation at Mussel Slough was also exposing flaws within the railroad's own structure. The Southern Pacific was not a monolith. Its ownership and control were apportioned equally among the Big Four. Power was further fragmented between two headquarters, in San Francisco and New York. Poor communication, an absence of centralized authority, and internal dissension plagued the company. Although the railway's leaders could agree to defend its land titles, they differed sharply over how to deal with the squatters. Stanford and Huntington, respectively president and vice president of the Central Pacific Railroad, believed that most settlers were innocent dupes of unscrupulous advisers. Sensitive to the political difficulties the controversy was causing, these two men opposed ousting the squatters. Instead, they recommended that the company reduce prices in exchange for the settlers' recognition of the railway's title, even if that meant parting with the land at a loss. On the other hand, Charles Crocker, president of the Southern Pacific Railroad and legally responsible for that railway's land grant, insisted on strict enforcement of both the company's title and its prices, as well as the decisive eviction of all squatters. Divided among themselves and uncertain how to proceed, Southern Pacific leaders moved cautiously, temporizing in the hope that the Mussel Slough people would come to their senses.

With land revenues falling and squatter violence rising in late 1878 and early 1879, Southern Pacific leaders finally began symbolic evictions. Only recourse to court action, they had come to believe, would demonstrate their determination and bring the squatters to a compromise. If nothing else, ejectment suits might discourage squatters in other areas. Company leaders instituted legal proceedings not to dispossess squatters, but to bring them to terms. For this reason, the railway planned to file test cases against only a few leaders and to prosecute the lawsuits slowly, so they could be called off when an agreement was reached.

After informing the squatters that the company intended to sue if they did not buy, lease, or abandon the land, Southern Pacific officials started filing lawsuits in December 1878. The suits caused some squatters to capitulate immediately. By January 1879, dozens were contacting the railway, seeking to buy or rent to avoid being sued, or to have lawsuits dismissed. When these settlers signed contracts, the railway halted legal proceedings and, in the case of impecunious squatters, paid court costs.

As late as April 1879, the Southern Pacific still intended not to prosecute ordinary squatters until cases against the leaders had run their course. That spring, however, squatters organized their militia and stepped up violent threats. An undercover informant alerted the railway in early April that the leaders of the Grand League had persuaded the remaining squatters to sign a secret pact

not to abide by test cases and to resist with force until all claimants were sued and ejected individually. The railway concluded it could delay no longer and began to file lawsuits against masses of squatters. By mid-1880, several hundred cases were before the federal circuit court.

The first court decision, *Southern Pacific Railroad Company* v. *Pierpont Orton*, announced in December 1879, set the pattern for those that followed. In rejecting all the settlers' arguments, Judge Lorenzo Sawyer of the U.S. Circuit Court in San Francisco relied on the 1870 acts of Congress and the state legislature and a long string of federal court precedents involving other western railways. Sawyer ruled that the route change and land grant were legal, that the railroad's filing of its 1867 map had transferred the land titles to the railroad, and that the Interior Department lacked authority to revoke a grant without congressional or judicial direction. Also, the railroad's failure to complete the entire line by the 1878 deadline did not negate the grant along the finished portions. Sawyer held that Orton and others who settled after 1867 were trespassers who had no right to challenge the railroad's title. Ultimately, all the ejectment suits that continued through to a decision favored the Southern Pacific. The court awarded the railway not only eviction orders, but also legal costs and damage judgments. The Mussel Slough squatters had received a stunning blow.

Southern Pacific leaders were confident that their cautious strategy had worked. Many settlers were coming to terms, and more were likely to do so before judgments were entered against them. Altogether, since the spring of 1878 one-half of the 500 to 600 Mussel Slough squatters had resolved their differences with the company. To woo the stragglers, the Southern Pacific in early 1880 liberalized land-sales procedures further and reduced the interest rate on purchases from ten to seven percent. The railway notified squatters that it would withdraw lawsuits if they signed contracts or abandoned claims. To avoid provoking trouble and to allow settlers time to purchase their land or to appeal cases, the company announced it would postpone enforcing the eviction orders and damage judgments until April 1, 1880.

Though shaken, the squatters' alliance did not crumble. A core of about two hundred militant squatters remained inflexible, convinced by the Grand League that Congress or higher federal courts would still vindicate their claims. Doyle caused the state legislature to pass a resolution favoring the squatters and calling on the Congress or the Supreme Court to reverse the *Orton* decision. Meanwhile, leaguers warned that they would resist evictions.

Evidently, however, the legal setback had discouraged many settlers. In February 1880 their leaders quietly approached Crocker with their first serious proposal for a compromise. The settlers wrote they would acknowledge the railroad's title if they could buy at "prices named in your circular inducing settlers to locate upon said lands, viz: from $2.50 to $5 per acre." Although he agreed to meet with the settlers and negotiate prices "upon the basis of the value of the land," Crocker flatly rejected the settlers' reading of the railroad's land pamphlet. What had always been a contest over titles became at a late stage a squabble over prices.

Simultaneously and, it appears, independently, Leland Stanford entered the fray publicly for the first time. Still harboring political ambitions, the former governor offered to confer with the Grand League to see if they could reach "an amicable adjustment of all differences." In Sacramento on March 4, Doyle, McQuiddy, and Stanford reached a preliminary agreement that legal proceedings on both sides would be stayed, that dur-

ing the negotiations the settlers would not raise the question of the railroad's title, and that Stanford would inspect the disputed lands and try to secure reduced prices.

On March 11, 1880, Stanford and an entourage of railway officials arrived in Hanford. With Doyle and other squatter representatives, they spent the day bouncing in wagons over rough roads to view farms and estimate the value of improvements. Before he boarded the return train, Stanford promised that the railroad would regrade the land, and he implied that the price reductions would be substantial. Settler leaders later claimed that the railway magnate had agreed in principle to deduct the cost of the irrigation ditches, reportedly about $400,000, from the value of the land. Spread over 80,000 acres of disputed land, this would have amounted to a reduction of $5 per acre. After Stanford's visit, both sides seemed optimistic about the chances for settlement.

But within a month the mood of compromise soured. This was predictable, given the history of acrimony over Mussel Slough lands. Neither party had retreated greatly. Railwayman and squatter alike underestimated the opponent's commitment to principles, and each assumed it was the other who was giving in. Confident that the lawsuits had forced the settlers to negotiate, the railway concluded it needed to make only modest concessions. For their part, the squatters believed that the railroad was so eager to avoid further agitation that it would give up the land at nominal prices. Indeed, Doyle and other leaders reported to a meeting of the Grand League that they had defeated the railroad on the price issue.

In early April the fragile compromise began to disintegrate. First, Stanford and McQuiddy exchanged letters and telegrams accusing each other of breaking the legal truce. Settlers complained that the railroad's law firm had asked the court for eviction orders against squatters who had not posted bonds for appeals. Stanford countered that the settlers had broken faith first by filing several appeals on grounds that the railroad's title was illegal. On April 21, while charges were still hurtling back and forth, settlers began receiving letters from Jerome Madden reducing prices by $1 to $4 per acre. Madden also informed them that they had ten days to buy or rent at the new prices or, if they had lost lawsuits, to file appeals before the company would take further action. Dismissing these "slight reductions," the settlers' committee warned Stanford that there was "no prospect whatever for a settlement . . . on a basis of less reduction than fifty per cent on your former graded prices." Irked at the settlers' insistence on such a large price cut, Stanford answered bluntly on April 28 that this was the final offer and that the company would start enforcing court orders unless settlers bought lands or appealed cases by May 3. He then whisked off to visit Huntington in New York, en route to an extended vacation in Europe, leaving Crocker to deal with the crisis that was sure to follow.

Why Stanford failed to deliver on his implied promises to the squatters is unclear. From Crocker's later letters to Huntington, however, it appears likely that Stanford made his overtures to the settlers in good faith and that Huntington also still favored further price reductions and compromise. Crocker, however, resenting Stanford's last-minute intervention because it had made the company appear irresolute, refused to go along.

Outrage at the Southern Pacific swept the Mussel Slough country. Even before they received Stanford's final letter, Doyle, McQuiddy, and James Patterson called on the railroad's Hanford land agent with twenty-five armed and masked men and drove him from town. Although a few squatters rushed to sign contracts, Doyle and other leaders

managed to rally the rest for a final legal challenge of the Southern Pacific's title. To carry its appeal to the U.S. Supreme Court, the Grand League decided to hire David S. Terry, the bellicose and controversial former chief justice of the state supreme court. To bolster its unraveling alliance, the league scheduled a mass protest meeting in Hanford for May 11, at which Terry was to deliver a rousing address on the justice of the settlers' cause. As the day approached, tension mounted and emotions became brittle. A developing drought heralded future crop failures and jeopardized the squatters' ability to raise cash to meet the railroad's terms, should that become necessary. Some desperate squatters openly threatened to stop the expected evictions with rifles and shotguns.

In San Francisco, Southern Pacific leaders pondered their next move. Angered by the response to Stanford's offer, they concluded that the squatters had negotiated only to gain time for another title challenge and another year of free crops on the railroad's lands. The ten-day grace period had passed. To the railway, negotiations had failed, and the legal truce was at an end. By then, some railroad land buyers were threatening legal action against the company unless it placed them in possession. Most insistent were Mills Hartt and Walter Crow, members of the pioneer faction who had been at odds with leaguers for years because they and members of their families were willing to buy railroad land. Perhaps using Hartt's belligerent letters as an excuse, Crocker finally asked the circuit court to begin evictions. Madden wrote Hartt on May 8 that a U.S. marshal would arrive in Hanford on the morning of May 11 to place Hartt, Crow, Perry Phillips, and several others in possession.

Still, the Southern Pacific groped for a broader solution. Crocker had ordered only six evictions, all cases in which the railroad had won judgments, the sixty-day appeal period had lapsed, and buyers were demanding possession. Remarkably, given the decade of controversy, the railroad had not determined how to handle the two hundred or so remaining squatters. The company's policy was still to avoid further evictions until conditions forced them. Beyond that, Southern Pacific leaders disagreed. Exasperated with his associates, Crocker wrote to New York on May 7, pleading with Huntington and Stanford to decide on a solution and telegraph him immediately. Although he believed that the company should "assert our rights and maintain them at any hazard or reasonable expense," Crocker promised to abide by their decision. His partners never had a chance to act. Events on May 11 rendered Crocker's letter moot even before they received it.

On the morning of May 11, Marshal Alonzo Poole descended from the buggy and walked across Henry Brewer's wheat field toward the members of the Settlers' Grand League. Poole was immediately engulfed by men on milling horses. He informed them of his mission and tried to read his authorization from the president of the United States. The settlers refused to let him finish, however. Cases were being appealed, they clamored; they would not allow the marshal to enforce the court orders. Poole admitted that the settlers' cause had merits, but he insisted he must do his duty and warned the settlers against interfering with a federal officer. At this, James Patterson, who appeared to be in charge, demanded that the marshal give up his revolver. Poole refused, but indicated he did not intend to use the weapon. Someone shouted, "On peril of your life, surrender your pistol!" When Poole remained steadfast, Patterson allowed the marshal to keep his gun and placed him under armed guard instead.

While Poole and the settlers argued, William Clark, Mills Hartt, and Walter Crow waited nervously in their wagons fifty yards away. Their vision blocked by shuffling horses, they caught only fragments of menacing gestures and unintelligible shouts and curses. In his statement the next day, Clark recalled that all he could see was someone waving a revolver in the air and crying, "God damn you, give up your arms!" At this, Crow reached again for his guns under the wagon seat, but Clark stopped him. "Walter, keep cool," he cautioned. "All depends on keeping cool."

Just then, the settlers' party broke up. Two guarded the marshal. With revolvers leveled, the rest surrounded the wagons. One rider, James Harris, brandished a pistol and demanded that Clark, Hartt, and Crow surrender their weapons. Clark refused, and Crow restrained Hartt from going for his gun. By this time, all the men were tense and confused. A shouting match erupted between several settlers and Crow and Hartt. Dust raised by stomping hooves clouded everyone's vision. In the excitement, a horse carrying one of Poole's guards suddenly lurched and accidentally knocked the marshal sprawling in the dirt.

Thinking the settlers had attacked the marshal, Hartt and Crow instinctively dove for their arms. In an instant, Harris, Hartt, and Crow all fired. Eyewitnesses disagreed over who shot first; Clark and most others said that it had been either Hartt or Crow. Hartt toppled over with a mortal wound; Harris and a settler named Iver Knutson, ironically a friend of Crow, fell dead on the spot. As his team bolted, Crow hit the ground running toward the fallen marshal, reeling off shots from his revolver and shotgun, with settlers in pursuit. Exchanging fire with Poole's guards, he killed both of them. Within a minute, twenty or thirty shots rang out, but Poole, Clark, and most settlers did not fire their weapons.

Shooting ceased abruptly. The field was a chaos of bucking horses, bouncing wagons, and stumbling and panting men. Dust and gunsmoke choked the air. Tragedy had stunned everyone into a horrified quiet. Enemies intermingled and looked after the injured. Hartt and five settlers lay dead or dying; Poole, Clark, and, miraculously, Crow were unhurt. More settlers continued to ride onto Brewer's farm, until soon one hundred men bustled about, demanding to know what had happened. In the confusion, while the dead and wounded were being carried to the shade of an oak tree in Brewer's yard, Poole and Clark warned Crow that the settlers would kill him and told him to flee. Still carrying a shotgun and revolver, Crow slipped away into a stand of wheat and ran toward his father-in-law's house two miles away.

When the smoke had cleared and a measure of order had been restored, Clark and Marshal Poole started driving southeast to safety in Hanford. Within a mile, another troop of settlers, led by Thomas Jefferson McQuiddy, intercepted and surrounded them. Some riders bore rifles on their shoulders in military fashion. McQuiddy handed Poole a paper forbidding the marshal to enforce evictions. "This is a bad business, Major," Clark told the settler leader. "Yes, it's a bad business," McQuiddy returned, "but we are fighting for our homes, and we propose to fight for them."

Nevertheless, McQuiddy warned Poole and Clark that they would never reach Hanford alive. To avoid further trouble, he detailed a guard of four armed men to escort them north to Kingsburg, a town on the main rail line down the valley. As the party was leaving, some riders spotted Crow escaping across the wheat fields. Reaching Kingsburg in the late afternoon, Clark and the marshal first checked into a hotel for the night. A stagecoach driver arriving from the

south warned them that the leaguers were coming after them, and Poole and Clark left on the first northbound train for San Francisco.

That afternoon, a search party found Walter Crow a mile and a half from the scene of the battle. He was lying dead in the muck beside an irrigation ditch, shot in the back with a rifle from close range.

Although only a few dozen persons took part in it, the battle of Mussel Slough was one of the most enduring events in California history. The stunning news pulsed through telegraph wires across the state and nation. Within hours, Huntington and Stanford read about it in New York newspapers. Immediate public reaction was explosive but mixed. Although most Tulare County groups condemned the Southern Pacific, the state's major newspapers, even some that had favored the settlers' cause, branded the squatters as criminals and demanded that they be punished. The San Francisco *Chronicle*, which had encouraged settler vigilantism, now charged that although their cause had been just and the railroad had driven them to extreme acts, the settlers had "by their rash course . . . in opposing armed resistance to the law, placed themselves clearly in the wrong before the tribunal of public opinion and terribly prejudiced their case." Even Ambrose Bierce, a trenchant critic of the Southern Pacific, criticized the squatters in his column in the San Francisco *Post* and chastised their defenders for distorting the legal issues in the case. He accused John Doyle, whom he knew well, of being "the Mephistopheles who for his own aggrandizement has led these settlers into all the trouble in which they find themselves."

Such early critical judgments soon drowned in an outpouring of popular sympathy for the squatters, who were transformed into martyrs in the anti-railroad cru-

"Tragedy Oak"
The dead and wounded Mussel Slough settlers were placed under a sprawling valley oak in Brewer's front yard. The last surviving witness to the battle, the tree was marked with a state historical plaque in 1948. Blighted by pollution and excessive watering from farm irrigation, "Tragedy Oak" may not survive another generation. *Photograph by Richard J. Orsi.*

sade. Businesses in the Mussel Slough area closed their doors in mourning, and several days after the battle, the bodies of settlers killed at Brewer's farm were buried by long processions of weeping mourners. For months after the shooting, farm, labor, and civic groups around the state held mass anti-railroad meetings, many organized by leaders of the Grand League who traveled to other communities to rally public support. Fund drives raised thousands of dollars for the squatters' relief and defense. Tens of thousands of people signed petitions plead-

ing for clemency toward the squatters and a revocation of the Southern Pacific's land grant. Eastern anti-corporate newspapers such as the New York *Sun* hailed the Mussel Slough settlers as an advance guard in the war against monopoly.

Local officials at first refused to arrest those who had resisted Marshal Poole. Despite open rumors regarding the identity of Crow's killer, no one ever was apprehended. In the summer of 1880, after the Southern Pacific had repeatedly pressed the U.S. attorney general to prosecute the case, a federal grand jury in San Francisco indicted eleven settlers, including Doyle, McQuiddy, and Patterson. At the December trial, Doyle, Patterson, and three others were found guilty of obstructing the marshal. During a bizarre eight-month sentence in unlocked cells at the San José jail, the five settlers came and went freely to attend church, lodge meetings, and dinners in their honor. On their return trip home, they were entertained and praised. Neighbors in Hanford gave them a hero's welcome, complete with bands, banners, parades, and anti-railroad orations.

Aided by friends and local officials, Thomas Jefferson McQuiddy evaded capture for years and escaped imprisonment. While he was a fugitive, the major became an underground hero of anti-corporate groups. McQuiddy was nominated for governor in 1882 by both the Anti-Monopoly League and the Greenback Party, but in the election he finished a distant fourth to Democrat George Stoneman. Federal officials delayed prosecuting McQuiddy and finally dismissed charges against him in 1886.

What happened to the masses of squatters? As had been true since the inception of the squatter movement, Mussel Slough residents divided sharply over the next course of action. Though discredited in the eyes of many, the Grand League, still under the sway of Doyle and McQuiddy, struggled into the late 1880s, unsuccessfully trying to keep buyers from dealing with the Southern Pacific and to collect money from claimants to finance more legal challenges. Others, particularly leading businessmen and landowners in the region, despite resentment against the railroad's actions, favored accommodating the company to secure community peace. Some went further. Discontented Mussel Slough people formed an anti-league organization, the Farmers' Club, and condemned the league for having produced only violence, disharmony, and economic stagnation.

Though shocked by the violence, Southern Pacific leaders persisted in their policy of defending the railroad's titles aggressively, while at the same time compromising with individual settlers. The railroad filed more eviction suits, until within a year all the squatters had been sued. The lawsuits and local disenchantment with the league brought claimants to a settlement. In late May 1880 a delegation of community leaders from Hanford and Lemoore negotiated a compromise with Charles Crocker in San Francisco. The railroad president agreed to lower prices by an additional 12.5 percent, retroactively for those who had already purchased.

Although some complained that the price reduction was still too small, after June 1 droves of settlers rushed to take advantage of the railroad's offer, most using Southern Pacific credit plans. When settlers signed contracts, the railroad stopped proceedings against them. In June, in an attempt at further conciliation the company began crediting the amounts squatters paid in court judgments to their purchase and lease accounts. By December 1880 most of the squatters had legalized their claims, and new land sales had revived. By June 1881, except for seventeen small parcels of unoccupied land and a few others still under court judgments, all Southern Pacific land in the Mussel Slough region had been sold or leased. The settlers finally won their long-awaited legal hearing when the U.S. Supreme Court accepted three test cases on appeal. In December 1883, however, the court rejected the settlers' arguments and upheld the lower court's decisions in favor of the Southern Pacific's land titles. John J. Doyle ultimately lost his eviction lawsuit and paid a judgment of $1,214.

"Impending Retribution"
One of the foremost political cartoonists of his era, George Frederick Keller, who drew for San Francisco's satirical magazine *The Wasp,* viewed the growing anti-railroad movement of the early 1880s as "retribution" for the Big Four's oppression of the Mussel Slough settlers. That theme was sounded by cartoons, editorials, and political orations for decades. This cartoon was published on October 7, 1882. *Courtesy of the Bancroft Library.*

A few squatters held out, refusing to bargain with the railroad, obey eviction orders, or pay judgments. Lax local sheriffs and federal marshals delayed serving papers for months, or even years, allowing squatters to use the land in the interim. On some occasions when eviction orders were served, teams of squatters openly followed the officers on their rounds, moving household goods back onto claims and reassembling cabins that the marshal had torn down. Although most remaining squatters vanished or were evicted within a year or two, several were still occupying land in defiance of the court as late as 1887. Some settlers continued to threaten railroad employees and those who cooperated with the company. Although railroad people were never again attacked, sporadic violence persisted for years among settlers competing for railroad land.

The Mussel Slough affair etched in bold relief the struggle between the people and the corporation in late-nineteenth-century America. At Hanford, annual public memorial ceremonies involving settlers and their descendants kept the memory of the battle vivid into the late twentieth century and cemented in local lore a myth of pure pioneers combating the outside monopoly. In California at large, the tragedy strengthened the reputation of the Southern Pacific as an insensitive, if not diabolical, organization. The event became a *cause célèbre* in the rising protest against the railroad's political and economic power.

The battle of Mussel Slough inspired a half-dozen major pieces of fiction and poetry, the most famous of which was Frank Norris's novel *The Octopus,* published in 1901. Naively based on back issues of antirailroad newspapers and pamphlets the settlers had published to defend their actions, the novel reflected the popular legend that had grown up since the 1870s. Norris adopted the settlers' point of view and misrepresented practically every facet of the actual Mussel Slough tragedy. Nevertheless, the popular book intensified public outrage against the Southern Pacific and helped pave the way for the progressives to capture the state government in 1910 and institute stricter controls on corporations. The great progressive president Theodore Roosevelt reportedly told a friend that reading *The Octopus* had convinced him that "conditions were worse in California than elsewhere."

CHAPTER FOURTEEN

THE COMING OF THE RAILROAD

TRANSPORTATION PROBLEMS IN GOLD RUSH CALIFORNIA

In the 1850s and 1860s commerce in California labored under serious geographical burdens. Vast distances separated the state from the outside world, while its large size and rough landscape hindered contact among its own scattered communities. The best means of transportation, those using waterways, were expensive and limited. In the absence of through transportation, goods headed for the interior had to be transferred between riverboats and wagons many times, multiplying costs and delays. Landlocked northern mountains, the southern San Joaquin Valley, and most of the interior of southern California remained isolated and sparsely populated, their resources largely untapped. Importing goods by steamer or clipper ship was particularly expensive, time-consuming, and unreliable. Delays of months in the flow of products and information complicated the state's volatile economy, making supplies and prices unpredictable and businesses more prone to failure than in the rest of the country.

The costs and hazards of ocean and overland travel also discouraged immigration, particularly by women and children. Transportation problems were a major reason why, after the initial gold rush, California's population grew more sluggishly and continued to be more dominated by men than on other frontiers. As mining waned and Californians began exploring new enterprises, they pleaded in newspapers, pamphlets, and public meetings for improved transportation.

EARLY TRANSCONTINENTAL RAILROAD SCHEMES

While California was being settled, steam railroads were revolutionizing trade, industry, agriculture, and urban fortunes in the United States. Even before the Mexican War, prophets of Manifest Destiny envisioned a transcontinental railroad to spread civilization across the forbidding Great Plains, secure American control of the Pacific Coast, and channel the fabled Asian trade through the United States. American acquisition of Texas, Oregon, and California, along with the gold rush, lent urgency to this idea. In the late 1840s and 1850s, conventions in eastern and western cities proposed favorable routes and promoted transcontinental railway bills in Congress. Because laying tracks across two thousand miles of rough wilderness was immediately recognized as beyond the capacity of private business, almost all plans, including legislation proposed in Congress by Senator William Gwin of California in 1853, called for heavy government subsidies.

Little resulted from initial transcontinental railway proposals. Although Americans agreed on building such a line and the need for government subsidy, they clashed over precise routes and conditions of construction. In the East, local rivalries over the route and the sectional struggle between North and South stalled the project. Even Californians, ostensibly the major beneficiaries of the railway, could not agree on its location. San Francisco, Benicia, Vallejo, Sacramento, Stockton, Los Angeles, and San Diego—all claimed to be the logical western terminus and ridiculed the pretensions of competing towns. An 1853 railroad convention in San Francisco, for example, produced little beyond local bickering. When the meeting broke up in disarray, the *Alta California* condemned it as a "miserable abortion." Local and national politics thus doomed early Pacific railway bills, including Gwin's.

PIONEER RAIL LINES

Unable to get the national government to subsidize the Pacific railway, Californians in the 1850s and early 1860s focused on constructing short railways to replace existing stage, wagon, and steamboat lines. Businessmen organized elaborate railroad-building ventures and advertised their towns as the future trade centers of the Pacific Coast. Plagued by delay, incompetent engineering,

corrupt financing, and scarce machinery and labor, most speculative railroads failed to progress from paper and hot air to steel and steam, and were never built. One exception, the Sacramento Valley Railroad, pushed its tracks from the Sacramento steamboat port twenty-three miles northeast up the American River canyon and became the state's first working railroad in 1856. Affording quicker transport to the foothill mines than the wagon roads then in use, the railway was an immediate success, and a new town sprouted at the end of the line.

Other early railways operated in the San Francisco Bay area, the state's wealthiest and most populous region. A railway that had broken ground in 1861 took two years to finish a mile of track between the town of Oakland and its waterfront. In 1864 the San Francisco & San Jose Railroad, also begun in 1861, spanned the fifty miles of bay shore plains and marshes between those communities. A year later, the San Francisco & Alameda Railroad completed a line from Alameda to Hayward, an agricultural settlement fifteen miles to the southeast. Although suffering from poor construction, crushing debts, and opposition from rival communities and transportation companies, early railways sparked agricultural and urban booms and strengthened the bay area's hold on the state's economy.

THEODORE JUDAH, VISIONARY

Above all others, Theodore D. Judah kept alive the hope that railroads would one day bind California and the East. The twenty-eight-year-old Judah had already developed a reputation as an astute builder of eastern canals, bridges, and railroads when the Sacramento Valley Railroad hired him to construct its railway. Judah completed the task in less than two years, a remarkable feat in those days of shaky railway ventures. Typi-

Theodore D. Judah
Courtesy of the California State Railway Museum.

cally, however, the speculative railroad was saddled with debts caused by excessive profits for its organizers and construction company. The bankrupt railroad halted building at Folsom, and Judah left his job as chief engineer in 1856. Although not a skilled businessman, Judah was ambitious and persistent. Intrigued by the idea of a transcontinental railway, he was convinced that a line could be built through the seemingly insurmountable Sierra Nevada, and he scoured the mountains for a route.

Meanwhile, Judah tried to organize a new company to secure the government subsidy vital to his scheme. He authored pamphlets and surveys, addressed public meetings, harried potential investors and political figures in California, and journeyed to Washington to seek aid from the federal government and eastern capitalists. So passionately did the young engineer pursue his vision of a railroad over the central Sierra that scoffers dubbed him "Crazy Judah." Leery investors doubted his business acumen and the feasibility of the Sierra route and branded Judah an impractical pest. Although he did keep the transcontinental railway in the public eye, Judah failed to win government or private funding for his project.

In 1859 Judah and other would-be railway promoters convinced the state legislature to summon another Pacific Railroad Convention to meet in San Francisco. Although local jealousies again prevented agreement on a specific route for the line, the delegates reluctantly passed resolutions favoring a general route from San Francisco Bay eastward through the central Sierra; Judah was appointed to present the plan to Congress. Arriving in Washington in late 1859, Judah struggled during the 1860 session for a bill subsidizing transcontinental railways. Despite his best efforts, the conflict between North and South and the looming presidential election absorbed national energies. Although he believed he had convinced some congressional Republicans to support his plan, southerners opposed such a northerly route, and his bill languished. In the summer of 1860 Judah returned to California. His four frustrating years of promoting wagon-road and railway projects had ended in failure.

THE FOUNDING OF THE CENTRAL PACIFIC RAILROAD

By the time Judah returned from Washington, the lucrative trade between California and the booming Comstock Lode of western Nevada had increased interest in a railroad across the Sierra. A consortium of San Francisco financiers already dominated the Comstock mining trade by controlling steamboats to Sacramento and the ailing Sacramento Valley Railroad, which connected at Folsom to a rugged wagon road through Placerville and over Johnson Pass south of Lake Tahoe to the Comstock Lode towns. The group planned to monopolize the trade by building another rail and wagon route from Folsom through the Sierra north of Lake Tahoe. The railroad rehired Judah to design the new line.

While working for the Sacramento Valley Railroad in 1860, Judah discovered a central Sierra route and secretly mapped out plans to found his own company to tap the Comstock trade and build the western segment of the transcontinental railroad. With the help of a Dutch Flat dentist, Daniel Strong, Judah finally settled on a path that started at Sacramento, rose seventy miles northeastward through 7,000-foot-high Donner Pass, and plunged down the Truckee River canyon to the Nevada border. Although Judah's plan would require the railroad to scale unprecedented grades, combat huge snowfalls, and bore expensive tunnels, the Donner Pass, or Dutch Flat, route was shorter than its rivals and mounted only one summit to cross the Sierra. With a definite route now in hand, Judah, Strong, and a few others formed the Central Pacific Railroad in October 1860. From their own limited resources, however, they could raise only a few thousand of the $115,000 in stock subscriptions legally required to incorporate the company.

Unwisely, Judah openly sought backing in San Francisco. Not only was he rebuffed again, but the Sacramento Valley Railroad got wind of his plan. Outraged that one of its employees had disclosed confidential information and was promoting a rival company, the railroad fired Judah. Its bankers attacked his scheme as poorly planned and impossible to construct, thereby undermining investor confidence in the Central Pacific for years.

At this point, Theodore Judah's railroad resembled most others in California: it existed only on paper and in the mind of its promoter, and was unlikely ever to be built. To salvage his plan, Judah turned to small investors in Sacramento and other towns along the Donner Pass route. In wooing supporters, Judah proposed that the company seek quick profits by monopolizing the Comstock trade by laying tracks to Dutch Flat in the foothills northeast of Sacramento, and simultaneously building a wagon road paralleling the planned rail route from Dutch Flat to Virginia City, Nevada. Such a road would ease rail construction through the remotest stretches of the Sierra and, as the line advanced slowly through the high mountains, offer a continual outlet for the mining trade.

After fruitless public meetings, Judah interested Sacramento hardware merchant Collis P. Huntington in the venture. Huntington brought in his partner Mark Hopkins, along with other Sacramento businessmen, including Charles Crocker and Leland Stanford. The group agreed to buy enough stock to incorporate Judah's company. In April 1861, at a momentous meeting at the Huntington-Hopkins store, the Central Pacific Railroad was reorganized to admit the new investors. Later, a committee composed of Judah and Strong nominated and the board of directors elected Stanford president, Huntington vice president, Hopkins treasurer, and Judah chief engineer. On June 27, 1861, the Central Pacific was legally incorporated, and the struggle began to convert the dream into a reality.

Huntington, Stanford, Crocker, and Hopkins quickly emerged as the most powerful leaders of the new company. The Big Four, as they came to be called, brought much-needed business strength to Judah's struggling venture. Though by no means wealthy, they were respected, successful merchants whose word and credit were as good as gold. Because he knew eastern suppliers and financiers, Huntington was a particularly valuable addition. The Big Four also had important political ties. They had been among the tiny band of militantly anti-slavery men who had founded California's Republican party at Sacramento in 1856. As leaders of the new party, the associates had labored tirelessly in John C. Frémont's losing presidential campaign in 1856, but in November 1860 they had ridden to victory with Abraham Lincoln. With close ties to local and national leaders of the party, newly elected members of Congress, and important officials of Lincoln's incoming administration, the Big Four wielded the political clout that Judah lacked.

THE CIVIL WAR AND THE TRANSCONTINENTAL RAILWAY

Some California settlers hailed from the South, and the racial and sectional issues of the 1850s and 1860s deeply divided the state. When the Civil War finally broke out following the secession of the Confederate states in early 1861, however, vocal Confederate sympathizers were a small minority in California. Although pockets of strong Confederate support existed in southern California and parts of the San Joaquin Valley, more Californians had emigrated from the North than from the South, and the state on the whole remained staunchly loyal to the Union. When secessionist speakers, journalists, politicians, or, occasionally, clergymen became too outspoken, they were silenced by mobs and public opinion or arrested by military authorities. On the tide of pro-Union votes, Republicans, the minority party at the onset of the 1860s, gained sufficient strength to dominate state and local government for most of the decade. By the war's end in 1865, Californians, under the leadership of famed Unionist supporter and Unitarian minister Thomas Starr King, had contributed more than $1 million to the U.S. Sanitary Commission and other Union charities, and volunteers from the state had seen combat with the Second Massachusetts Cavalry and served patrol and garrison duty in the West.

Otherwise, the Civil War's impact on California, though significant, was less direct or immediate. Wartime disruptions forced Californians to rely more on their own resources, accelerating economic development and diversification. New firms manufactured iron, wagons, cigars, sugar, textiles, blasting powder, leather goods, and other products formerly imported. Although the state lost population to the Nevada silver boom during the 1860s, it more than recouped by becoming the financial and commercial center for the Comstock Lode and the entire Pacific Basin.

The Civil War also improved the Central Pacific Railroad's prospects after 1861. Republican leaders in control of Congress and the White House already were committed to federal aid for a transcontinental railway. The war made the project more urgent. Such a railway was vital to the Union effort, its proponents argued. It would assure the allegiance of the frontier and strengthen military control of the Far West. At the same time, the secession of the Confederates from the national government effectively ended southern obstruction of a northern route into California.

THE CENTRAL PACIFIC BESIEGED

Nevertheless, monumental obstacles still blocked the Central Pacific in 1861. Practically every facet of the ambitious project—engineering, building, and financing—lacked precedent. Experts smugly predicted that locomotives would never be able to haul cars over high Sierra grades and that, even if they did, the railroad could not operate profitably through the heavy snows and arctic temperatures of Donner Pass. Furthermore, most construction and operating equipment, including rails, cars, locomotives, and heavy machinery, would have to be shipped expensively around the Horn. Wartime shortages of iron, railroad machinery, and shipping tonnage, along with the federal government's inflationary monetary policies, pushed prices high and caused wasteful delays. Finally, with construction workers scarce in California, the railroad faced great difficulties raising its labor force.

Even using Judah's sanguine estimates, the cost of building the Central Pacific, especially the Sierra segment, would far exceed federal subsidies. The private wealth of the Sacramento businessmen was much too limited, and Judah's group could not expect help from San Francisco financiers either. Already committed to steamship lines or potential rail competitors of the Central Pacific, they were also unlikely to assist ventures to benefit Sacramento, an arch trade rival. Throughout the early 1860s, risky large-scale ventures like the Central Pacific and other would-be transcontinental railroads could raise virtually no cash by selling stocks or bonds on the open market.

Symptomatic of how thin the Central Pacific's resources were, the first stock subscription of 1861 brought in only $10,000 in cash, which the railroad committed to a more detailed survey of the Donner Pass route. The company's funds ran out, however, and Judah had to halt his work prematurely. In the summer of 1861, he returned from the mountains, bearing only the disheartening news that his original survey was seriously flawed. The distance through the Sierra was 140 miles, not 115, and more than three miles of tunnels would have to be bored through some of the hardest granite in

North America. To build the line as far as Nevada would take at least $13 million, or $88,000 per mile, more than fifty percent higher than he had originally estimated and several times the predicted subsidy.

To make matters worse, the Civil War's outbreak and the imminent passage of a Pacific railway subsidy act spawned a host of rival companies to vie for a share in the government's largess. The San Francisco & San Jose Railroad and the Sacramento Valley Railroad, which were both controlled by powerful San Francisco interests and which still boasted the only working tracks in California, were the most formidable competitors. Sacramento's urban rivals—San Francisco, Stockton, Placerville, and Marysville—hitched their fortunes to the Central Pacific's opponents. Encouraged and financed by giants such as the Pacific Mail Steamship, California Steam Navigation, and Wells Fargo companies, who feared losing business and federal mail subsidies, jealous communities and vested interests joined forces to smash Sacramento and its paper railroad.

THE PACIFIC RAILWAY ACT OF 1862

Without much support outside Sacramento, the leaders of the Central Pacific, their private fortunes now committed, turned to securing crucial federal subsidies. To assure that the state would favor their company, the associates ran Stanford for governor on the Republican ticket. In September 1861 he triumphed, bringing with him a group of sympathetic Republican legislators and congressmen. With local matters under a measure of control, Judah, Huntington, other Central Pacific investors, and congressional Republican allies set sail for the East in the fall of 1861. They arrived to find the nation's capital aswarm with railway promoters anxious to cash in on the proposed rail subsidies. However, the Central Pacific's powerful Republican friends, along with several eastern business associates of Huntington's, secured positions on the legislative committees writing the railway bill. They had Judah appointed clerk of both the House and Senate railway committees. Now responsible for administering the committees' business, Judah could guard Central Pacific interests while the transcontinental bill was being shaped.

In the winter and spring of 1862 Judah and Huntington lobbied furiously. To bribe legislators and leaders of other railroads, Judah and Huntington lavishly gave away Central Pacific stock—still worthless, since the company possessed no assets. Central Pacific partisans overcame one major obstacle when they worked out a bargain with the San Francisco & San Jose Railroad. That rival agreed to drop its opposition in exchange for the Central Pacific's promise to assign it the right to build and collect the subsidy for the transcontinental segment between San Francisco and Sacramento.

Judah and Huntington achieved an even more stunning victory in July, when President Lincoln signed the historic Pacific Railway Act. This law empowered the Central Pacific to construct tracks from San Francisco Bay or the navigable waters of the Sacramento River to the eastern boundary of California, and the Union Pacific Railroad to complete the connection from the Missouri River. Both lines were awarded rights-of-way, the right to take timber and stone from the public domain for construction, and grants of ten alternate sections of public land per mile constructed, in a checkerboard pattern within a swath ten miles on each side of the tracks. The act also authorized a loan to the companies of thirty-year government bonds at the rate of $16,000 per mile of track across low-elevation plains at each end of the line, $48,000 per mile in rugged mountains, and $32,000 per mile across the Great Basin. The railroads were to sell the land and bonds to raise capital for construction.

Pathbreaking as it was, the 1862 act by itself probably would never have brought about a transcontinental railway. Not only was the subsidy much lower than the estimated cost of construction, but the law contained serious restrictions. Each company was obligated to complete the entire line by 1876 if the other failed to build its portion, and the U.S. government was to assume the assets of a company that did not meet its responsibilities. To be delivered gradually, after railroads had completed segments of track, the subsidies would not provide capital during the critical early years. Moreover, the government's loan of bonds was secured by a first mortgage against the railroad's property. The company's own bonds were reduced to less valuable second mortgages. Each of these provisions discouraged private investors. As late as 1864 neither the Union nor the Central Pacific company had been able to sell enough of its own securities to complete the mileage needed to qualify for the federal loans.

LOCAL SUBSIDIES AND MOUNTING OPPOSITION TO THE CENTRAL PACIFIC

Determined to amend the act of 1862, Judah and the Big Four sought for the moment to finance construction through local and state subsidies and loans secured by their personal assets. In the nineteenth century, state and local governments commonly subsidized new businesses, particularly transportation ventures. Between 1862 and 1864 Governor

Stanford assured that such support bolstered his own company. He and his allies pushed through many laws favoring the Central Pacific, particularly bills that passed the legislature early in 1863, granting millions of dollars in state bonds and allowing local communities to assist the railroad by subscribing to its stock. After hotly fought elections blemished on both sides by charges of bribery and ballot-box stuffing, the people of San Francisco, Sacramento, Placer, and other counties overwhelmingly approved the purchase of more than $1 million in Central Pacific stock.

The opponents of Sacramento and the Central Pacific redoubled efforts to destroy the infant railroad. In league with railway, steamship, and wagon competitors, communities far from the Donner Pass route tried to get the legislature to revoke Central Pacific subsidies and extend them instead to rivals. They also filed lawsuits challenging the legality of state and local aid, attempted to overturn local subsidy elections, and launched an abusive propaganda war against the Central Pacific. Pamphlets and editorials attacked the Donner Pass route as impractical and condemned the railroad as solely a speculative enterprise that intended to seize subsidies, build the Dutch Flat wagon road, and then go bankrupt. Opponents also claimed that the company's executives had awarded themselves exorbitant construction contracts that would ruin the railroad, and that the company had won its victories only through bribery and corruption. The Central Pacific, its enemies sneered, was the "Great Dutch Flat Swindle."

These accusations were largely self-serving. The Central Pacific was indeed financially weak, and its engineering was untried. Its leaders, particularly Judah and Stanford, were tainted by conflict of interest, and its investors attracted to the enterprise by subsidies. These charges, however, could have

been leveled equally at the critics of the city and the railway, who mostly represented special interests. There is no evidence that the Central Pacific's owners did not intend to build the railway. Popular enthusiasm for railways, not corruption, turned the local subsidy elections, although it appears that Stanford's friends did bribe voters to increase the margin in San Francisco. Conflict of interest, justifiably distasteful to modern sensibilities, was widespread in the nineteenth century, even among otherwise respectable people; once again, most of the Central Pacific's rivals were just as guilty. Likewise, early railroads and other large-scale building projects, including Judah's Sacramento Valley line, commonly employed "dummy" construction companies to overcome insufficiencies of capital and credit.

After 1862 Leland Stanford, as state governor and president of the railroad, led the fight to preserve the Central Pacific's privileged position. The company dispatched organizers to help local supporters get subsidy referendums passed, reached compromises with communities regarding stock purchases, thwarted competing lobbyists in the legislature, and successfully defended almost all of the lawsuits. By 1865 most of the opposition had been subdued, at least for the moment, and the railroad began to receive the much-needed local money.

The anti-Central Pacific campaign of the early 1860s, however, depleted the railroad's funds, delayed subsidies, and probably postponed the railroad's completion. Also, its own tactics, amplified by exaggerations and untruths hurled by partisan opponents, gave the Central Pacific a reputation for corruption and ruthlessness. Many Californians thus were predisposed against the Central Pacific before it had laid even one mile of track. Born in the business and community rivalries inherent in early railway building, these suspicions laid the groundwork for later anti-railroad movements.

BREAKING GROUND

While the battle against its rivals raged, the Central Pacific began construction in late 1862 and early 1863. Although the railroad still could not raise substantial funds, some tangible work, however symbolic, had to be accomplished to shore up public confidence. The railway scraped together capital through new stock subscriptions and levies on its few stockholders, including contributions of $35,000 from each of the Big Four. Work commenced on the Dutch Flat wagon road. In December, Crocker resigned from the board of directors and, in league with other railway investors, founded Charles Crocker & Co., which received the contract to build the first segment of rail line. Finally, on January 8, 1863, ground was broken at the Sacramento riverfront with prayers, speeches, parades, waving American flags, and the music of the Sacramento Brass Band. Governor Stanford ceremoniously turned the first shovelful of dirt to launch the transcontinental railway. After several months, though, work on the roadbed halted about eighteen miles into the empty countryside. Characteristically, grading crews became enmired in the mucky valley earth, and the railroad again ran out of money. No tracks had been laid. In fact, the Central Pacific had no rails, cars, or locomotives—or the cash to buy them.

In March 1863 Collis P. Huntington went east in a desperate attempt to sell $1.5 million in nearly worthless Central Pacific bonds to purchase rolling stock and construction materials. Although the Union Pacific and other eastern builders of the transcontinental railroad had raised virtually no capital in the stringent wartime market, Huntington, relying on old business friends

and the excellent credit of his hardware firm, coaxed financiers into lending him several hundred thousand dollars, secured by some of the bonds and his personal guarantee of repayment. This was the first significant influx of outside funds into the Central Pacific. Using the loan as seed money, Huntington bought rails, locomotives, and other equipment and had it shipped around the Horn, with payment in cash, more discounted bonds, and Huntington's personal promissory notes. The Central Pacific Railroad was finally in business, though heavily in debt.

JUDAH VERSUS THE BIG FOUR

Huntington returned from the East in the summer of 1863 to find the Central Pacific in shambles. Enemies still tied up local subsidies; some stockholders were defaulting on payments due on their subscriptions; and Stanford had lost his party's nomination for a second term as governor. Unless it obtained more capital, and quickly, the company could not finish the fifty miles of track needed by the November 1864 legal deadline. In that case, the railroad would lose the federal subsidy and probably go under, taking with it the personal businesses of its founders. Under mounting pressure, the Central Pacific's leaders fought bitterly over finance, engineering, and control of the railway.

The Big Four, who owned most Central Pacific stock and had already mortgaged their personal assets to begin construction, insisted that delinquent stockholders pay their subscriptions and that all investors be further assessed. Less wealthy minority stockholders, led by Judah, who had received his stock free and had little of his own money in the railroad, were equally determined that the company raise funds by further mortgaging its equipment and uncompleted

THE BIG FOUR
Villains or Heroes?

The Big Four
Leland Stanford (*top left*); Collis P. Huntington (*top right*); Charles Crocker (*bottom left*); and Mark Hopkins (*bottom right*). *Courtesy of the California State Railway Museum.*

THE BIG FOUR (continued)
Villains or Heroes?

The Big Four in many ways typified frontier success. Contrary to the popular "rags-to-riches" myth, nineteenth-century American business and political leaders emerged primarily from northeastern middle- and upper-class families. Leland Stanford (1824–1893), Collis P. Huntington (1821–1900), Charles Crocker (1822–1888), and Mark Hopkins (1813–1878) fit this pattern. All hailed from solid middle-class families with business-ownership backgrounds. All had been born, or had resided, in New York state. As young men, they had followed the lure of gold to California. Each arrived with business and political experience and with capital or goods to invest. Each tried mining "the golden fleece," but soon turned to the more reliable trade of "fleecing" the miners. Weathering flood, fire, depression, and personal adversity, the four established successful supply businesses in Sacramento in the 1850s.

Building the Central and Southern Pacific railroads soon made the associates wealthy and powerful. Their transportation monopoly and aggressive business and political tactics (real and imagined) earned them many enemies after the 1860s. They were widely charged with pocketing excessive profits from public construction subsidies, destroying their competitors unethically, inhibiting California's development by charging shippers "all the market will bear," and corrupting public officials to get their way.

Collis P. Huntington gained particular infamy in 1883, when the chance publication of his private letters to David Colton, a lesser railway official, revealed that the Big Four had indeed bribed congressmen and state politicians. After he ousted the more popular Stanford as president of the Southern Pacific Company in 1890, Huntington came to symbolize the greed and corruption of late-nineteenth-century business. Business rivals and political reformers accused him of every conceivable evil, and journalists and cartoonists made their reputations by pillorying him. Historians have cast Huntington as the state's most despicable villain. One recent writer described him as "the most hated man in California during the final 30 years of the last century."

In the face of harsh public criticism, however, the Big Four saw themselves as honest, loyal California pioneers and took pride in their role in building the state. Their profits, they felt, were just rewards for the great risks they had taken and the opportunities their railroads had generated for increased trade, land values, personal incomes, and community welfare. "I am satisfied with what I have done," Huntington wrote privately near the end of his life. "No man is perfect and the man does not live who can look back and say that he has made no mistakes; but the motives back of my actions have been honest ones and the results have redounded far more to the benefit of California than they have to my own."

The Big Four and their families returned much of their fortunes to the people. Stanford, Huntington, Crocker, and Hopkins often donated land and money for the building of parks, churches, libraries, and other community facilities. In Sacramento, E. B.

THE BIG FOUR (continued)
Villains or Heroes?

Crocker, Charles's brother and an organizer of the Central Pacific, founded the Crocker Art Museum, one of the nation's most renowned small-city museums. A good share of Hopkins's money was given by his heirs to endow the San Francisco Art Institute and the Hopkins Marine Laboratory near Monterey. In one of the most magnificent public bequests in American history, Leland and Jane Stanford donated immense land holdings and practically their entire fortune to create Stanford University, ultimately one of the world's finest institutions, which opened its doors in 1891. In the early twentieth century, Huntington's nephew Henry and widow, Arabella, channeled much of Collis's wealth into the Huntington Library and Art Gallery at San Marino.

Furthermore, while many of his California enemies were also attacking the Chinese and other immigrants, Collis P. Huntington remained a lifelong opponent of racial prejudice. An ardent abolitionist before the Civil War, he later donated hundreds of thousands of dollars to support black churches in California and schools and colleges in the South—most notably Booker T. Washington's Tuskegee Institute in Alabama. Though it was politically unwise, Huntington ordered his companies to give equal employment and pay to black workers, and he publicly opposed exclusion of blacks from public schools and other "Jim Crow" restrictions then being enacted in the South. In newspaper columns and public speeches in the West, Huntington praised the civilization and industriousness of Chinese immigrants. He condemned oppression of the Chinese, American Indians, and, after 1898, Filipino and Japanese immigrants. "If we deny to the individual, no matter what his creed, his color or his nationality, the right to justice which every man possesses," he told a gathering of Southern Pacific leaders in 1900, "there will be no enduring prosperity and [the nation's] decline will surely follow."

Were the Big Four "robber barons" or public benefactors? As with much else about California history, the answer is not simple. (RJO)

---

roadbed. The Huntington faction objected that this would saddle the shaky company with a ruinous debt.

Judah also demanded absolute control over engineering and construction. Fearing that the arrangement drained profits from the Central Pacific into a company in which he held no stock, he blocked the letting of more contracts to Crocker & Co. The Big Four countered that the outside construction firms did shoddy work, charged higher prices, and often defaulted on contracts. Upset at some of the Big Four's questionable methods, Judah was furious when Governor Stanford augmented early construction subsidies by getting the state geologist to declare that the Sierra Nevada began with the first low rises seven miles east of Sacramento, instead of at the steeper grades twenty-seven miles farther east. For their part, the Big Four had long been exasperated by Judah's unrealistic cost estimates, his damaging mistakes in designing roadbed, bridges, and culverts, and his plans to build grandiose stations while the company flirted with bankruptcy. Judah, the associates had concluded, was a careless engineer and an impractical obstructionist who would ruin the railway and their personal fortunes.

In July the Huntington faction won control of the board of directors and demanded that other board members pay their stock assessments or relinquish their seats. When Judah and his supporters refused, the Big Four insisted that Judah buy them out or consent to sell his stock. Eventually, an agreement was reached. Again unable to raise cash, Judah exchanged his stock for $100,000 in Central Pacific bonds and withdrew from the board. He retained his post as chief engineer at a salary of $5,000 per year, as well as an option to buy out the Big Four for $100,000 each. In early October, Judah left by steamer to try to borrow the money from eastern railroad financiers. He contracted yellow fever while in Panama, however, and died in New York City on November 2. The career of one of California's most colorful figures had ended tragically. Even on his deathbed, Theodore Judah believed fervently that he would yet build the first transcontinental railway.

Relying on hindsight and the worshipful memoirs of his wife, Anna, historians have converted Judah into a martyr to the Big Four's greed. Some have speculated that the railroad would have been less corrupt and more public-spirited, and the state better off, if Judah had gained control. Judah's contributions to the Central Pacific were undeniably important. An incurable optimist, he popularized the transcontinental railway, located and defended a feasible route, conceived the original plan for the Central Pacific, and with Huntington lobbied through the Pacific Railway Act of 1862. Judah remains a true hero of California history.

However, in his own era, Judah was only one of many would-be railroad builders. When he left California, the Central Pacific was still a speculative railroad, indistinguishable from many that failed to survive. It owned little equipment and had yet to lay a single rail, haul a passenger or a barrel of flour, or earn one cent of profit. While Judah's engineering talent was adequate for preliminary work, he had made some costly errors and had yet to prove he could solve the unprecedented technical problems looming ahead in the Sierra. Judah had also demonstrated that he shared many of the lax business ethics for which his generation was infamous. However passionate his vision, Judah's business skills and political influence were minimal. The Central Pacific's victories had come primarily in politics, finance, and administration, areas in which the Big Four's contributions were consistently more important than his. If Judah had wrested the Central Pacific away from the Big Four, the railroad would probably have quickly failed. If it had survived, it undoubtedly would have been in the hands of eastern railroad tycoons, such as Jay Gould and Cornelius Vanderbilt, who even more than the Big Four used disreputable methods and disregarded the public welfare.

THE PACIFIC RAILWAY ACT OF 1864

The Central Pacific's 1863 management crisis was the nadir in its history. With the future clouded, the associates resumed work on the roadbed and bridges. The company set October 26 as the date for the laying of the first rails, but it avoided fanfare. "These mountains look too ugly and I see too much work ahead," Huntington complained. At this point, the Big Four were eager for Judah to buy them out.

Even in the gloomy fall of 1863, though, the tide was beginning to turn in favor of the

Central Pacific. Crews were finally driving rails through the streets of Sacramento. On November 9, the first locomotive, *Gov. Stanford*, belched steam and began shuttling supplies, work gangs, and dignitaries back and forth between the river port and the construction front. The railroad's finances also improved dramatically. Starting in September, litigation to block the state and local subsidies began to be resolved in the company's favor. County and municipal subsidy bonds started trickling into the Central Pacific's coffers. State grants soon followed.

With the company's position somewhat bolstered, Huntington again headed east to secure all-important amendments to the Pacific Railway Act. Although the Central Pacific's enemies mounted another campaign to deny aid to the railway, Huntington struck an alliance with the Union Pacific, which was having even greater trouble raising capital and had yet to break ground. Six months of lobbying by Huntington and Thomas Durant of the Union Pacific produced the Pacific Railway Act of 1864, which modified most of the burdensome features of the 1862 law. The new act extended the deadline for completing the first fifty-mile portion to 1865 and doubled the land grant to twenty sections per mile. Most important, the 1864 law reduced the federal subsidy bonds to a second mortgage and allowed the railways to sell their own first-mortgage bonds equal in amount to the government subsidy, thereby doubling the companies' potential construction capital. In 1866, to induce the railroads to build faster, Congress authorized each company to construct as much of the transcontinental line as it could.

The Pacific Railway Act of 1864 was an important turning point for the Central Pacific. Realizing the company's superior position, its rivals either went out of business or reoriented their lines to feed into the Central Pacific. With local and federal subsidies assured, investors grew more confident. For the first time, Huntington could sell the company's securities and government bonds. Investors, however, would purchase the bonds only at heavy discounts. The Central Pacific was lucky to receive one-half the face value of the securities, although it was of course obligated to repay the entire amount, with interest. Laboring under a heavy debt with staggering interest payments, in the next few years the railroad time and again stood days or hours away from financial disaster, especially when the high costs of building over the mountains drained its resources. But Huntington established close ties with American and European investors, and somehow, often by pledging his own or his associates' businesses or by juggling funds in deceptive ways, he always managed to come up with the money to buy supplies and cover interest payments. The Central Pacific's credit remained spotless, and Huntington came to be acknowledged as one of the business geniuses of his era.

COMPLETING THE TRANSCONTINENTAL RAILWAY

Fueled by new capital, construction on the Central Pacific gained momentum after 1863. Locomotives first hauled passengers and freight the eighteen miles between Sacramento and Roseville in April 1864. Although the passenger trains sped along at an astounding twenty-two miles per hour (fifteen miles per hour for freight), traffic was light until June, when the company completed the track to Newcastle and the Dutch Flat Toll Road to the Comstock Lode. The Central Pacific's combined rail and wagon service immediately proved faster and cheaper than what competitors were offering, and most Comstock trade shifted to the new route. Income exceeded operating expenses, making stocks and bonds easier to

Chinese Laborers Filling the Secret Town Trestle
Once they had proven their skills, Chinese immigrants came to comprise a high percentage of the Central Pacific's work force, even after the completion of the first transcontinental line. In the 1870s Collis P. Huntington's friend Carleton E. Watkins, who often worked on assignment for the Big Four, took this famous photograph of Chinese laborers filling in the 1,000-foot-long Secret Town trestle, sixty-two miles east of Sacramento. *Courtesy of the Huntington Library.*

sell. The Central Pacific looked like it might yet turn a profit.

Nevertheless, when the company tried to push its line higher into the Sierra in the winter of 1865, it again bogged down, this time with labor problems. Few men answered the company's call for 5,000 construction workers, and many of those deserted quickly to the Comstock when the railroad had transported them to the mountains, particularly after a taste of working in deep snows at $35 per month. Having employed Chinese construction laborers on the Dutch Flat Road, Charles Crocker, over the objections of some company leaders, or-

dered that Chinese be tried on the heavier Central Pacific work. The experiment was an instant success. Though smaller in stature than Caucasians, the Chinese learned quickly, worked tirelessly, and soon excelled at skilled tasks. Accustomed to a lower standard of living, the Chinese eagerly accepted the work and wages, although they were paid only sixty to ninety percent as much as whites. By May 1865 the Chinese composed two-thirds of the Central Pacific's labor force. For the next four years, the railroad relied on thousands of Chinese in its race to meet the Union Pacific. When its needs exceeded the supply of local immigrants, the

Snowsheds on the Central Pacific
Alfred Hart photographed the Central Pacific's famous snowsheds while they were under construction in the late 1860s. *Courtesy of the Huntington Library.*

railroad arranged with San Francisco labor contractors to bring more from China. So efficient did the Chinese crews become that the company transferred them to its extensions after the transcontinental line was completed. Before long, other western railroads employed Chinese laborers.

Beyond Auburn, Central Pacific crews grappled with some of the most forbidding terrain in the country. The railroad faced a climb of more than 6,000 feet in forty miles over the Sierra crest, culminating in the treacherous cliffs of Donner Pass. Below-zero temperatures and forty-foot snows halted work for weeks at a time. In summertime, the men were harried by insects and swarms

of rattlesnakes whose dens had been disturbed during construction. Illness ravaged the overworked and underpaid workers. Cave-ins and misfired explosions killed and maimed scores of workers. Conditions became so unbearable by the spring of 1867 that even the normally compliant Chinese struck for more pay and shorter working hours. After a week, though, the intransigent Crocker broke the strike by cutting off supplies and starving the Chinese back to work.

Somehow, the Central Pacific inched upward. New railway construction techniques were developed, and the company worked its force of more than 14,000 in round-the-clock shifts. While the Chinese bored away at tunnels a few inches a day from both ends, or chipped out narrow ledges to carry the tracks around precipices, the company took advantage of the Dutch Flat Road to move materials and disassembled rolling stock ahead by wagon—by sled in winter—so that work could proceed on many fronts. To shield its line from the crushing drifts of Donner Pass, the Central Pacific in 1868 began installing miles of long wooden snow-sheds, to this day a distinctive feature of the railway. All of this devoured capital. Many stretches, particularly the tunnels, cost between $150,000 and $1 million per mile, and the company always teetered on the brink of insolvency. Finally, after nearly three years of strenuous mountain construction, trains chugged over the summit in November 1867. In May 1868 they reached Nevada, still only 140 miles from Sacramento.

Once clear of the mountains, the Central Pacific raced across the relatively flat Great Basin to meet the Union Pacific, which was itself stalled in the mountains northeast of the Great Salt Lake. Although plagued by extreme heat and cold and alkali water, Crocker's experienced Chinese and European immigrant crews were honed to a fine working efficiency. During the next year they completed 550 miles.

On May 10, 1869, hundreds of jubilant laborers, executives, dignitaries, and reporters gathered at barren Promontory Point, north of the Great Salt Lake, for a legendary ceremony. After the customary prayers and speeches, Leland Stanford swung his hammer at a golden spike fastening the last rail, and the transcontinental railroad was finally joined. Telegraph wires attached to the spike and hammer announced the grand moment to an eager outside world. Festivities were already in full swing in California. When word arrived at Sacramento, thousands surged through the streets celebrating the city's victory. Their wild cheers quickly drowned in a clangor of church bells, whistles, fire bells, pistol shots, and cannon blasts. To the east, a nation still grieving from years of civil war rejoiced in the country's most heroic building feat and the dawning of a new age of prosperity, westward expansion, and national unity. Prayers and hymns resounded in churches everywhere. A four-mile-long parade danced through the streets of Chicago. In Philadelphia, the Liberty Bell pealed from the tower of Independence Hall.

THE BIG FOUR AND THE EMERGING RAIL SYSTEM

Dramatic though it was, the driving of the golden spike signaled the beginning, not the climax, of California's railway age. Capitalizing on the transcontinental line's potential for stimulating development, promoters organized dozens of railways in the late 1860s and the 1870s. Locomotives soon whistled around the flats of San Francisco Bay and up its rich flanking valleys. Tracks also penetrated the Sacramento Valley north of Marysville and the San Joaquin south of Stockton and entered the distant and lightly populated southern counties. The first operating southern line, the Los Angeles & San Pedro Railroad, connected the old pueblo of Los Angeles to its new harbor at Wilmington in 1869. Within three years, small railroads extended lines into Los Angeles's fertile hinterland. Other railways welded regions together into the first statewide transit system. Of the state's major population centers, only the isolated northwest and central coasts, the Sierra foothills, and the San Diego area lacked direct railroad service by the end of the 1870s. By the early twentieth century, the rail network included these areas.

New railways usually fell quickly into the Big Four's grasp. Often outgrowths of real estate schemes or designed by their promoters for quick speculation rather than long-

Thomas Hill's *The Last Spike*
Commissioned years later by Leland Stanford, Thomas Hill's romantic depiction of the driving of the golden spike at Promontory Point portrays a cross-section of those associated with the building of the transcontinental line: leaders such as Stanford (who stands at center, holding the hammer); Chinese laborers (to Stanford's left); Irish immigrant workers, smoking their characteristic pipes (to the right and below Stanford); Indians (foreground); and a wagon train, the transportation mode being supplanted (background). Also in the painting were persons not present at the spike driving, including Collis P. Huntington, who was in New York at the time. Theodore Judah, dead for nearly six years, is resurrected at the lower right. Scorned by Stanford, the painting now hangs in the California State Railroad Museum at Sacramento. *Courtesy of the California State Railway Museum.*

term efficient operation, the new railways tottered from shoddy construction, light traffic, and ruinous debts, and they could not remain independent. Their builders were all too eager to skim off their profits and unload the shaky companies. The Big Four had reasons of their own for acquiring other lines. The revenues of the Central Pacific were at first disappointing. The Suez Canal, also completed in 1869, siphoned off the Asian trade. Traffic from eastern states in goods, tourists, and immigrants also failed to

match predictions. In the late 1860s and early 1870s the Big Four were deeply in debt and anxious to sell the Central Pacific. Because of the company's troubled finances, its immensity, and the recurrent depressions of the 1870s, the associates could not dispose of the railroad, though they tried repeatedly. The only way to avert disaster, Huntington convinced his partners, was to continue to build new lines, to defeat or absorb potential competitors for California's scant rail traffic, and to make the roads turn a profit. Borrowing heavily and reinvesting profits from constructing the Central Pacific, the associates purchased other transportation companies. The more lines the Big Four acquired, the more deeply involved they became. By the end of the 1870s they had transformed themselves from railroad builders into railroad operators.

Voluntarily or pressured by lowered Central Pacific tariffs they could not afford to match, most California railways came within the control of the Big Four in the 1860s and 1870s. The first to fall was their old nemesis, the Sacramento Valley Railroad, whose owners sold out in 1865. In 1868 the Big Four purchased the railroads around San Francisco Bay, including the San Francisco & San Jose (the only line into San Francisco), the Western Pacific (which was building the final link in the transcontinental railroad, between Sacramento and the bay), and strategic short railways stretching southward from the east bay ports of Alameda and Oakland. Using these lines, Central Pacific trains from the East arrived at the bay a few months after the driving of the golden spike. Sacramento's hard-won fame as the western terminus of the transcontinental proved short-lived. Later in 1869, the Central Pacific moved its terminal to Oakland.

Throughout the 1870s and as late as the early twentieth century, the Big Four and their successors continued to expand their transportation holdings. To reduce water competition, they reached a rate and traffic agreement with the Pacific Mail Steamship Company in 1871. In 1874 they formed their own trans-Pacific firm, the Occidental and Oriental Steamship Company, giving them a large measure of control over San Francisco's oceangoing commerce. The Big Four also absorbed inland riverboat enterprises and San Francisco Bay ferries. Some of the newly acquired routes were integrated as important main lines in the Central Pacific system. Others were reduced to branches or

closed down altogether. While many communities thrived from increased commerce, the hopes of some towns for urban greatness were dashed, and they added their voices to a growing anti-Central Pacific chorus.

The Big Four's prize acquisition was the Southern Pacific Railroad. Because of severe winter weather and high elevations along the Central Pacific–Union Pacific route, a southerly, low-elevation railroad near the Mexican border was likely to carry most cross-country traffic someday. The owners of the San Francisco & San Jose had founded the Southern Pacific in 1865 and secured a federal franchise and land grant to build such a line from San José to the Colorado River. When they purchased the unbuilt Southern Pacific in 1868, the Big Four gained control of the western portion of the southern transcontinental route, thus defeating their most serious competition.

Immediately upon purchasing their new railroad, the Big Four set off to capture the strategic crossing of the Colorado River at Yuma. Between 1869 and 1876, they extended one Southern Pacific line south of San José to Tres Piños and another down the San Joaquin Valley and, in a feat rivaling the crossing of the Sierra, over the rugged Tehachapis into southern California. In exchange for a subsidy from the city, in 1872 the railroad had agreed to build through Los Angeles. With customary fanfare, Los Angeles was connected to the state's northern railway system and the Central Pacific's line to the East on September 5, 1876. Meanwhile, the associates had acquired most other Los Angeles railways, including the line to the harbor, and had already begun building eastward across the cattle ranches of the San Gabriel and San Bernardino valleys and the parched Colorado Desert. The Southern Pacific illegally bridged the Colorado River in 1877, before the federal government had given its approval, and steamed into Yuma.

Southern Pacific Lines
IN
CALIFORNIA AND NEVADA

11-'23   Copyright by Rand McNally & Co Chicago.

In 1879, to the consternation of eastern railroad moguls who coveted the southern transcontinental route for themselves, the Southern Pacific began building across Arizona and New Mexico without a federal subsidy. In 1881, the company's Chinese track-laying crews reached El Paso, Texas, a major rail crossroads. For several years Huntington had been quietly securing control of a string of Texas and Louisiana railroads, and in early 1883 Southern Pacific locomotives entered Houston and New Orleans on these lines, completing the first coast-to-coast railway under one management. Trains between San Francisco and New Orleans, the famed Sunset Route, began operating in February 1883. The acquisition and completion in 1887 of the Oregon & California Railroad between the northern Sacramento Valley and Portland, and the subsequent absorption of other Oregon lines, rounded out the Big Four's unrivaled railroad empire.

THE SOUTHERN PACIFIC COMPANY

By the end of the 1870s the Big Four monopolized California transportation. Capitalized at $225 million, their California railroads in 1877 controlled 2,340 miles of track, including eighty-five percent of the railroad lines in the state and all the important ones in the San Francisco Bay area, Los Angeles, and the Sacramento and San Joaquin valleys. Their successful enterprises had brought the associates great fortunes. From modest beginnings as Sacramento shopkeepers, the Big Four now ranked among America's richest and most powerful business leaders.

Acquiring companies caused acute management problems for the Big Four, however. They generally did not merge new lines, but linked them by complicated lease or stock-ownership arrangements that proved unwieldy, particularly after they had acquired the Texas and Louisiana railroads. To solve these problems and provide a better mechanism for distributing traffic and profits among their far-flung lines, Huntington convinced his partners in 1884 to set up a holding company, the Southern Pacific Company. To broaden its powers and shield it from legal and political attack in the West, the holding company was incorporated in Kentucky. In early 1885 the associates transferred railway stock and leases to the new firm. From headquarters in San Francisco and New York City, the Southern Pacific Company modernized and integrated the Big Four's properties for more efficient and profitable service.

Transportation competition revived somewhat in later years. By constructing some tracks and deftly forcing the Southern Pacific to let it use others, the Santa Fe Railroad entered Los Angeles from the Midwest in the mid-1880s and engaged the Southern Pacific in a rate war that helped to ignite a real estate boom. In the 1890s the Santa Fe bought an independent line up the San Joaquin Valley and built a connection to San Francisco Bay at Richmond. After 1900 both the Union Pacific and a new Western Pacific Railroad completed their own lines to the east. Nevertheless, the Southern Pacific still controlled most important tracks in the major markets and could often convince its rivals to reduce competition. The company influenced California's economic and political life well into the age of automobiles and airplanes.

Southern Pacific Rail Lines in California and Nevada, 1923
In this map of main California and Nevada railroads near their peak of expansion, Southern Pacific Company tracks appear as wide, those of rival companies as narrow, lines. *Courtesy of the California State Library.*

CHAPTER FIFTEEN

CALIFORNIA'S RAILWAY ERA: ECONOMIC DEVELOPMENT AND SOCIAL UNREST

"THE TERRIBLE SEVENTIES"

In 1914 Gertrude Atherton coined the phrase "The Terrible Seventies" to entitle a chapter in her book *California, An Intimate History.* Certainly, the decade after the completion of the transcontinental railway was difficult for some Californians, but not for all. Tens of thousands of farmers, urban laborers, and white-collar workers benefited from the expanded markets, job opportunities, and community life introduced by the railroads. On the other hand, Henry George's gloomy prophecy at the dawn of the railway age came true for many people. Railroads aggravated some old problems and introduced new ones. In general, they most helped those who already had property and influence. They were a boon to industries and communities that were well situated on the new transit system, but undermined those not so fortunately placed. By connecting California more efficiently to the outside world, railways also made the state more vulnerable to nationwide economic dislocations associated with industrializa-

tion. Despite remarkable development after 1869, the next decade was one of the most turbulent in California history. Atherton's phrase, then, is not completely applicable. The 1870s were not as much "terrible" as they were paradoxical.

URBAN GROWTH

Railroads encouraged economic growth in California by reducing transportation costs, making remote lands and resources accessible, widening markets for producers, raising land values, and increasing many people's incomes. One of the first results of the advent of the railroad was phenomenal urbanization. Oakland, a steamboat port that had been settled in the 1850s across the bay from San Francisco, was a prime example.

In 1868, when the ultimate coastal terminus of the transcontinental railway was still in doubt, Horace Carpentier, Oakland's scheming founder and most powerful citizen, assured the city's and his own fortunes by deeding his monopoly of the city's shoreline to the Oakland Waterfront Company, of which he and Leland Stanford were principal owners. In return, the Big Four located the Central Pacific's terminal at Oakland rather than continuing the railroad around the bay to San Francisco. Although the city had to fight a protracted legal battle with the railroad in the 1890s and early 1900s to recapture its waterfront, Oakland's future seemed bright, for the moment at least, and Carpentier was hailed as a local hero.

The Central Pacific trains had immediate and spectacular effects on Oakland. Commuters and travelers jammed downtown shops, hotels, and restaurants. Commerce quickened and land values rose, sparking downtown building booms and new subdivisions filled with ornate Victorian homes. Industries rushed into the city, as firms vied for sites near the rail terminal and proliferating wharves and warehouses. As employment soared, so did population. In 1868 Oakland was a bucolic village of about 2,000 inhabitants, whose streets meandered to avoid the sprawling oak trees after which it had been named. The city's population exploded to 10,500 in 1870, however, and by 1880, with 35,000 residents, it had grown into the second largest city in California and the Far West.

Oakland's rapid modernization after 1869 was typical of rail-era cities. The railroad boom increased the community's size and diversity, expanded its wealth and tax base, and brought new ideas and technologies. Schools, churches, and municipal agencies multiplied, as did social, cultural, and professional organizations. Almost all the oaks were uprooted and the streets straightened and extended. Water, sewer, and gas utilities expanded their service. In 1878, only two years after Alexander Graham Bell had invented it, the telephone arrived in Oakland, easing communication within the city and to

San Francisco. Electricity followed in the early 1880s. Oakland's efficient transit system of horsecar lines, Central Pacific steam commuter trains, and cable cars extended into the countryside, connecting the city to Berkeley to the north and San Leandro and Hayward to the south, and igniting more suburban booms along the way. By the early 1880s Oakland was the hub of a growing east bay metropolitan region, a thriving, attractive, comfortable city, equal or superior in modern facilities to much older eastern centers.

Railroads transformed other towns in similar, though not as spectacular, ways. Already the dominant southern California town, Los Angeles came alive as soon as its citizens voted to subsidize the Southern Pacific Railroad in 1872. Even as the city awaited its outside rail link, trade expanded, downtown buildings rose, outlying property was subdivided for residences, additional farms sprouted in the countryside, and local rail lines gravitated to the future terminus of the southern transcontinental route. By the driving of the last spike on the Southern Pacific's southbound line in September 1876, the city, which had grown little in the 1860s, had tripled its 1870 population of 5,700. Although the boom collapsed in the nationwide depression of the late 1870s, the city could still boast 11,200 residents in 1880, a ninety-five percent increase over ten years earlier. By comparison, rival San Diego, having lost the all-important rail connection, languished with a population of about three thousand for the entire decade. The railroad's arrival began the transformation of Los Angeles from a colonial pueblo into a thoroughly Americanized city, a process to be completed in the 1880s by another railroad-inspired boom.

The laying of tracks through unpopulated lands, such as the central and southern San

Depot at Truckee
On the east slopes of Donner Pass, the High Sierra town of Truckee resembled many communities springing up along rail lines throughout the state. Hitherto a tiny turnpike way station, Truckee became the gateway to California when the Central Pacific located yards and maintenance facilities there in 1868. Within a few years, the town's population had soared, and it had become a major rail operations center as well as one of the leading manufacturers and shippers of ice and lumber in the American West. After the turn of the century, Truckee became California's first winter sports capital and the location for many early outdoor motion pictures. This photograph was taken by Alfred Hart in the late 1860s. *Courtesy of the Huntington Library.*

Joaquin Valley, created opportunities to found new towns. Although outside parties sometimes started settlements adjacent to the lines, the Big Four became the state's major town promoters during the 1870s. Through their construction and real estate development arm, the Contract and Finance Company (after 1879, the Pacific Improvement Company), the associates founded numerous market towns. The railroad laid out the streets in the familiar gridiron pattern and built shops, stations, yards, warehouses, loading docks, stock pens, and housing for its workers. Frequently, the company added a hotel and restaurant to lure travelers and provide a social focus, planted trees to shade

and beautify the new community, and donated lots and cash toward the building of parks, schools, churches, and major businesses. The railroad sometimes installed and operated the first water system, important in attracting people to arid land. It then advertised the townsite and brought in prospective buyers on low-fare excursion trains for festive picnics and lot auctions. With much ballyhoo, instant rail towns materialized within days or weeks of the first sounding of a locomotive's whistle. Although some never progressed beyond way stations, others, such as Modesto, Merced, Fresno, Tulare, Hanford, Niles, and Livermore, developed into prosperous regional trade centers.

SAN FRANCISCO: FROM INSTANT CITY TO PACIFIC METROPOLIS

Before the building of the transcontinental railway, San Francisco was "the City" in California and the Far West. San Francisco's meteoric rise as a gold rush center had resulted primarily from its strategic location on an incomparable deep-water harbor. In the 1860s its residents expected railroads to converge there, and real estate speculators swarmed around the few potential sites for railway operations along the city's southern waterfront. San Francisco's grand ambitions were soon dashed, however. The city lacked sufficient level land for railroad operations and was on the tip of a peninsula, nearly one hundred miles farther from inland mines and farms than its east bay rivals. One of the first California cities blessed with nominal rail service, San Francisco lost the contest for important terminal facilities to competitors with better rail locations—notably Oakland, Sacramento, and Los Angeles. The railroad mania of the 1860s had soured in the great city by the early 1870s. Frustrated San Francisco journalists and business leaders bemoaned the isolation of their city, belittled and tried to undercut urban competitors, and blamed their business woes on the perfidious railroad. For the rest of the nineteenth century, embittered San Franciscans furnished much of the energy behind anti-Southern Pacific politics.

Although disappointed at losing rail preeminence to other cities, San Francisco generally prospered during the railway era. Its head start on rivals was too long, its prestige too great, its facilities too convenient. Major businesses did not desert the city; indeed, they continued to flock there. The Central Pacific itself removed its corporate headquarters from Sacramento to San Francisco in 1873. Despite rail connections to the East, much commerce with the outside world, particularly bulky goods, continued to be shipped by sea. Since Oakland's harbor was still shallow, San Francisco remained the major Pacific Coast port and city; steam ferries shuttled cargo and passengers back and forth between it and Oakland. San Francisco also continued to dominate a diminished, but still significant, coastal trade, as well as riverboat traffic with interior valleys.

San Francisco had become the commercial metropolis of the Pacific Coast by 1880, when the city stood ninth among the nation's cities in manufacturing and population (234,000). Residents came from nearly everywhere on earth; half were foreign-born, and three-fourths had at least one foreign-born parent. San Francisco had developed into one of the nation's most cosmopolitan and ethnically diverse cities.

INDUSTRIALIZATION

In 1860 San Francisco had ranked fifteenth in size among the nation's cities, but only twenty-second in manufacturing and fifty-first in industrial employment because conditions then discouraged heavy industry in the city and state. Coal and iron ore were scarce and expensive. Interest rates as high as fifteen percent a month made investment capital expensive and other speculative ventures—land, transportation, and mining stocks—more appealing. Because of the strong lure of the mines, factory labor remained scarce in San Francisco and other cities. Thus raw materials generally left the state unrefined. Shiploads of logs and raw cattle hides, rather than milled lumber and finished leather goods, departed from California ports.

During the 1860s and early 1870s, changes occurred. Civil War isolation had forced Californians to look to their own resources, but developments within and near the state were more significant. The transformation of western mining into a large-scale industry encouraged economic diversification. Hydraulic and hard-rock mining corporations replaced the prospector-owner placer companies of the early gold rush. Particularly in Nevada's Comstock silver region, shafts and tunnels plunged to unprecedented depths. Mining on such a grand scale required heavy equipment, designed specifically for the Sierra and the Comstock.

San Francisco entrepreneurs responded quickly. The Irish-born Donahue brothers, for example, arrived in 1849 and began turning scrap metal into shovels for miners. Their Union Iron Works thrived, but in 1860 it remained basically a glorified blacksmith shop. The firm shifted to producing mining machines and, a decade later, employed 600 workers to make heavy equipment for mines and other industries. Other factories built cable, pumps, stamp mills, steam engines, and other essentials of the new mining technology, machine tools for manufacturers, and rails, cars, and locomotives for the growing transportation network.

Other economic changes had similar consequences for San Francisco industry. Expanding lumbering required heavy milling equipment and stimulated furniture making and related activities. In the early gold rush, entire buildings had been shipped around the Horn from the East. Thereafter, California's own mills and shops fashioned boards, shingles, posts, windows, grilles, and a phantasmagoria of Victorian gingerbread to adorn the state's growing cities or to ship for export. San Francisco, like Oakland, San José, and other cities, also specialized in processing California's multiplying farm crops. *Bonanza* wheat farms developing in the 1870s needed plows and harvesters designed for unique soil conditions and large-scale operations. Surplus cattle hides inspired a thriving tanning industry, followed by boot-making

and other leather-goods enterprises. The state's growing sheep flocks prompted the 1878 merger of the Pioneer and Mission woolen mills, creating one of the nation's largest producers of high-quality goods. Breweries, wineries, distilleries, grain and cloth mills, and vegetable and fruit canneries sprang up around rail sidings, yards, and waterfronts across the state.

Financing such operations required capital, and that too became available in San Francisco and other cities. Capital accumulated from land and mining-stock speculation and grain production, while the decline of profits from the Comstock Lode forced entrepreneurs into alternative investments. Some, including John W. Mackay—San Francisco's Comstock magnate whose income of $25 a minute made him for a time the wealthiest man in the world—turned to manufacturing. By the time the Bank of California temporarily closed its doors and touched off a panic in 1875, William C. Ralston had invested his own and the bank's funds—not always wisely—in such concerns as lock and clock factories, food and textile plants, and machine-tool shops. Adolph Sutro, Claus Spreckels, James Phelan, and scores of others with more modest fortunes also diversified into manufacturing.

The 1870s also produced the final ingredient essential to industrial development in San Francisco: a labor force. After 1869 many of the Central Pacific's Chinese workers migrated to San Francisco. By 1880 Chinese comprised fifteen percent of the city's total work force of 100,000, and nearly ninety percent in some light industries such as cigar making, textile and clothing manufacture, and shoe production. Other former railroad workers, men idled by depletion of the Comstock and Sierra mines, and additional thousands riding the rails from depressed eastern areas also gravitated toward San Francisco. The growing labor pool helped alter the city's character. No single enterprise dominated, but by 1880 San Francisco had become an industrial city with half its workers employed in manufacturing. Smaller cities experienced similar changes.

RAILROADS AND THE *BONANZA* WHEAT ERA

Although California's climates and soils held rich agricultural potential, progress was uneven during the 1850s and 1860s. While some success was achieved in producing livestock, cereals, vegetables, and fruit, farmers remained troubled by lack of information about growing conditions, vagaries of rainfall, inexperience with arid land agriculture, poor transportation, and, particularly, limited markets. In the nineteenth century, California was hardly an agricultural Eden.

To the surprise of many, the start of transcontinental rail service in 1869 offered little immediate assistance to California's farmers. Shipping time along the Central Pacific route was too long, and extreme winter and summer weather delayed and spoiled cargoes. Freight charges were high—in part because of the Central Pacific monopoly, in part because traffic was low and train operation through rugged territory was expensive. Many California farm products could not hold their own against better and cheaper competitors grown closer to eastern markets. The development of local rail service within the state, however, was a major factor in expanding and modifying agriculture. As illustrated in the Mussel Slough country in the 1870s, the shorter lines unlocked the virgin soils of fertile areas, connected farmers with local market towns and coastal ports, encouraged settlement of new regions, and speeded the development of new crops, machines, and techniques.

A prime example was the transformation of wheat growing in the late 1860s and the 1870s from a decentralized business producing for local consumption into a large-scale, highly structured export industry. Railroad building through the San Francisco Bay region, up the Sacramento Valley, and down the San Joaquin and Salinas valleys triggered a wheat boom in the 1870s. The crop offered an apparently ideal solution to California's agricultural problems. Wheat required little or no irrigation and actually benefited from long dry summers. Its culture was well-known and inexpensive. Although too bulky and low in value to ship east by rail, it was a nonperishable crop that could be transported profitably to distant markets in sailing ships. Growers followed the railroads onto flat valley lands, and wheat acreage soared.

Essential in a poor marketing zone such as California, an elaborate structure emerged overnight to link farmers with consumers around the world. British and American companies bought wheat in California and sold it on exchanges in England and elsewhere. Isaac Friedlander, a German-Jewish immigrant, assembled an international network of banks, warehouses, shipping companies, and grain-sack factories. From San Francisco, Friedlander could forecast wheat output, control finance and supply, and reserve ships to carry the harvest. Although they stabilized the wheat trade, Friedlander and a few others also reaped *bonanza* profits and exercised monopolistic powers that angered growers.

In favored regions, such as Mussel Slough, small farmers raised wheat profitably. But to take advantage of economies of scale, most grain was produced on vast tracts of leased or cheaply purchased land. These ranches employed industrial work forces and huge plows, harvesters, and steam tractors, many developed and manufactured in Stockton and other centers. The largest grower, Hugh J. Glenn, amassed an empire of 66,000 acres in Colusa County, employed nearly 1,000 laborers, invested more than $300,000 in machinery and draft animals, and produced a million bushels of wheat a year by 1880. Growers like Glenn hauled sacks of grain in wagons to railside platforms, where they were snatched up by Southern and Central Pacific wheat specials. These long trains converged on San Francisco Bay and the Carquinez Strait, particularly at Port Costa. Endless strings of boxcars crept across specially built wharves while the wheat was loaded directly into the holds of sailing ships for the voyage to China, Australia, or the British Isles.

During the 1870s and 1880s, California wheat growing developed into the most mechanized and structured form of agriculture in the world, and it became the state's major export industry. Production reached a peak of forty-one million bushels in 1890. During the boom years of the 1870s, the fortunes of Friedlander, Glenn, and other "wheat kings" rivaled those of the Big Four and mining-stock speculators.

The *bonanza* wheat era ended in the 1880s, however. New wheat farms started producing on the Great Plains and in Europe, Asia, and Australia, many using techniques and machines imported from California. Overproduction glutted world markets and sent wheat prices plummeting. At the same time, yield declined sharply on the state's eroded and exhausted soils, and improving irrigation facilities and rail connections to the East encouraged subdivision of wheat lands for more profitable uses. After 1890 wheat became a minor crop in California.

FRUIT AND SPECIALTY-CROP FARMING

Cultivation of specialty crops—such as citrus fruit, deciduous fruit, winter vegetables, melons, rice, and cotton—for which California

would later become famous, emerged slowly after 1870. Although some crops had been grown as early as the mission era, major economic, technological, institutional, and environmental changes were necessary before fruit and specialty-crop agriculture could become a major industry. Fragile, perishable, and unfamiliar to American farmers, the new crops needed specific climates, soils, and handling, which were at first poorly understood. In particular, they required more water than nature provided. Because individual farmers had difficulty solving these complex problems, California agriculture became highly organized in the late nineteenth century.

From the beginning of American settlement, growers formed groups to raise standards, sponsor innovation, combat disease and pests, disseminate information, and, most important, to lobby the government for solutions to farm problems. Farmers first met locally around the state, and in 1854 the California State Agricultural Society was founded to unify their activities. Dominated by the wealthiest and most commercial growers, the society won a modest subsidy from the miner-controlled legislature, managed the state fair and some local expositions, published valuable technical papers, and pressed the state into rewarding crop experimenters with bounties. Specialized organizations arose to meet the needs of growers of livestock, wine grapes, deciduous fruit, oranges, raisins, and nuts.

After the 1880s, when farmers suffered from overproduction, they turned to more powerful marketing cooperatives. The first successful cooperative was the California Fruit Growers' Exchange ("Sunkist"), founded in 1893. The exchange and similar groups for raisers of walnuts, almonds, deciduous fruit, raisins, dairy cattle, poultry, and other products limited production, regulated prices, adopted grading standards, and took charge of packing and marketing in order to eliminate middlemen. Between 1900 and the 1920s, the cooperatives acquired more control of production and convinced the state to erect elaborate governmental machinery to manage supplies, prices, and marketing conditions in the interests of growers. By the early twentieth century, California agriculture was dominated by complex, interlocking organizations that exerted much influence over their members, as well as over public policy.

At the behest of farm pressure groups, all levels of government provided services to modernize agriculture after the 1860s. Federal agencies such as the Army Signal Corps (later the U.S. Weather Bureau) gathered, tabulated, and distributed statistics on climate that enabled farmers to locate fields, choose crops, and design operations more wisely. U.S. Department of Agriculture scientists developed, tested, and introduced revolutionary new crops. Most notable was the Washington navel orange, a superior seedless, winter-ripening fruit that the department imported from Brazil in 1873 to save the struggling Riverside colony. The national and international resources of the department also aided in discovering cures for new crop diseases brought to California as parasites on imported plants and now thriving in the genial climate.

Even more important were state agricultural agencies. The State Board of Agriculture (1863), Board of Viticulture (1880), Horticultural Commission (1883), Board of Silk Culture (1883), Dairy Bureau (1895), and State Veterinarian (1899) were promoted vigorously by farm organizations. Although troubled by poor administration and funding, as well as opposition from rival groups, state agencies sponsored research and published reports, organized conventions of growers, advertised new farm products, and secured tougher regulatory and quarantine legislation. By 1900 the growing state bureaucracies were important forces for agricultural change. In 1919 the legislature consolidated them under the State Department of Agriculture.

Private businesses engaged in agricultural development also encouraged innovation with capital and organization. While they were profiting from land speculation, some developers—such as William S. Chapman, who built up the Fresno area in the 1870s—reorganized land for higher use, promoted compact settlement, financed farm purchases, and encouraged higher-value crops and more efficient farming methods. Before the 1880s private water companies, such as the joint-stock ventures begun by Mussel Slough settlers, built most small irrigation facilities that farmers needed to cultivate the thirsty new crops. Organized colonies—among the most important of which were the Mormons at San Bernardino and the Germans at Anaheim (founded in the 1850s), Riverside, Pasadena, and the Fresno raisin colonies (1870s), and irrigation genius George Chaffey's Ontario and Etiwanda colonies (1880s)—pooled capital, water rights, labor, expertise, and machinery. Cooperatively, they bought and improved land, developed irrigation, introduced new crops, and provided social and cultural amenities to reduce the isolation of the farm frontier.

The major business to promote agriculture was the Southern Pacific. The railroad became convinced by the 1870s that the future of the state, as well as the company, depended on farm progress. The railroad advanced capital to finance many new small farms in emerging regions such as Mussel Slough and encouraged public irrigation and the preservation of forest watersheds. A powerful friend of scientific agriculture, the railroad compiled most climate, crop production, and water statistics used by early experimenters. The company also supported

THE UNIVERSITY OF CALIFORNIA AND
THE BEGINNING OF HIGHER EDUCATION

In an era of rampant self-interest, a few early Californians campaigned for institutions of higher learning. Religious denominations, concerned with educating clergy and lay people to strengthen their new churches, established the first private colleges. The University of the Pacific (Methodist), Santa Clara University (Catholic), and the University of San Francisco (Catholic) originated as sectarian schools in the early 1850s. With sporadic expansion of a public-school system also demanding more teachers, the state established a few normal schools, beginning with one at San Francisco in 1862.

Resistance to financing public schools, particularly colleges, ran high among most transient pioneers, however, and the legislature refused to establish a state university. To overcome this opposition in California and other states, Congress in 1862 passed the Morrill Land-Grant Act, which allocated federal lands to states to establish colleges fostering agricultural, mechanical, and military education. To qualify for the land grants, the legislature in 1868 assumed control of the College of California, a struggling Oakland institution started by Congregationalists and Presbyterians in 1855, and converted it into the state's first public university.

At first, the new university floundered. When its few classes opened at the old Oakland campus in the autumn of 1869, only thirty-eight students showed up, despite the tu-

The University of California, 1874
Carleton E. Watkins photographed the isolated, rural Berkeley campus of the University of California the year after it opened. The mansard roof and dormers of South (*left*) and North (*right*) halls illustrate the influence of the French Second Empire style, a popular Victorian style of the 1870s. *Courtesy of the Bancroft Library.*

THE UNIVERSITY OF CALIFORNIA AND
THE BEGINNING OF HIGHER EDUCATION (continued)

ition of $20 per term. In addition, some mismanagement of the land grant caused delays in realizing the federal subsidy, and the assets of the College of California turned out to be worth less than originally estimated. Responding to continuing public opposition to supporting universities, the legislature also proved stingy. Students faced a bleak social life in the early years as well, particularly after 1873, when the university moved to an isolated rural campus on a Berkeley hillside, where housing and other services were totally lacking. Many commuted miles by slow horsecar from their rooms in Oakland; a few endured a trip of more than two hours by ferry and horsecar from San Francisco.

Nevertheless, the university gradually won increased public approval and financial support and expanded its curriculum. With improved prestige and facilities, it attracted more students, as well as a distinguished faculty to teach them. Over the next few decades, the university added graduate programs, as well as professional schools of medicine (1873), pharmacy (1873), law (1878), dentistry (1881), and veterinary science (1894). By the early twentieth century the University of California had developed into one of the finest public institutions of higher learning in the world, an important cultural center for the state, and a training ground for leaders in the arts, science, business, government, and the professions.

In contrast to many eastern colleges, in 1870 California's new university opened its programs to female students "on equal terms, in all respects, to young men." The university helped make the late nineteenth and early twentieth century a time of great occupational gains for women. Within a few years, its female graduates were embarking on careers as physicians, lawyers, journalists, educators, and engineers.

The University of California also worked to modernize farming. Like other early university programs, the College of Agriculture was at first poorly funded, with few students and a narrow, impractical curriculum. Farmers and laborers initially denounced the college as elitist and agitated to abolish it. Reorganized after 1874 under Dean Eugene W. Hilgard, a German-born soil chemist hired from the University of Mississippi, the College of Agriculture became more scientific. It assembled a faculty of fine teachers and researchers and conducted experiments in soil chemistry, fertilizers, climate, crop testing, irrigation methods, and pest control. Particularly significant were the efforts of Hilgard's staff to develop grape vines resistant to *phylloxera*, a tiny root louse that was destroying the state's vineyards in the 1870s and 1880s. After 1887, the university, in league with the federal government, established a string of experiment stations to adapt crops and techniques to the state's diverse environments and began an ambitious extension service to bring practical information to working farmers. By the turn of the century, the University of California had become a major stimulus to agricultural improvement.

In the wake of the development of railroads and cities, other colleges were founded in California, including major institutions of higher learning such as the University of Southern California (Los Angeles, 1879), Stanford University (Palo Alto, 1891), and Cal-

---

THE UNIVERSITY OF CALIFORNIA AND
THE BEGINNING OF HIGHER EDUCATION (continued)

ifornia Institute of Technology (Pasadena, 1891), as well as distinguished smaller liberal arts colleges such as Loyola University (Los Angeles, 1869), Mills College (Oakland, 1885), Occidental College (Los Angeles, 1887), Pomona College (1887), Whittier College (1901), and Redlands College (1909). By the early twentieth century California possessed a framework of higher education disproportionate to its small population and its isolation from older centers of learning. The state's colleges and universities became important forces for its economic development and growing cultural sophistication. (RJO)

---

the University of California's agricultural programs by lobbying to protect the beleaguered institution's funds and independence and by providing monetary grants and free transportation for university staff and supplies. After 1908, in cooperation with the university, the railroad ran annual instructional trains through rural districts to teach farmers scientific cultivation.

The Southern Pacific's marketing services supplemented those of farm organizations and state agencies. The company's all-weather southern route to the Midwest (completed in 1883), along with the Santa Fe's line to Chicago (1885), linked California farmers to the national market and made possible the expansion of high-value specialty crops. After 1883 the Southern Pacific also instituted faster direct service to the East, ran special fruit trains, and pioneered in the development of ice manufacturing, fruit cooling plants, and refrigerated cars and shipping systems. Because of competition from the Santa Fe, the company reduced its freight rates on a broad range of farm products, though not enough to satisfy many shippers. The Southern Pacific also helped farmers to organize marketing cooperatives and assisted them in mass advertising campaigns to cultivate a taste for oranges, prunes, apricots, and raisins among

reluctant American consumers. Ironically, by the time Frank Norris published his famous novel in 1901, although some conflicts remained over freight rates, California's highly organized growers had become largely reconciled to "the Octopus."

Conversion to modern, higher-profit agriculture was facilitated by innovations in crops and cultivation methods introduced by immigrants with experience in regions with growing conditions similar to California's. As is illustrated by the pioneering role of Hungarian-born Agoston Haraszthy, the production of fine wines was a specialty of immigrants from southern and eastern Europe, including Italians, Frenchmen, and Germans. Similarly, European immigrant orchardists were often the first to introduce fruit culture, as they did in the 1850s and 1860s to convert the Santa Clara Valley into the state's first important fruit district.

The Chinese, who migrated from different types of agricultural regions in the old country, with experience in both arid and semitropical wetlands agricultural environments, played especially valuable roles as farm innovators. Beginning with early mining districts and then spreading throughout the state, it was the Chinese who initiated the truck garden industry, raising vegetables on small rented plots and marketing them directly to towndwellers. Although most of the rural Asians worked as laborers, clearing land and building levees and irrigation works, Caucasian land owners interested in developing their properties commonly contracted with more entrepreneurial Chinese immigrants, who leased land as tenants and independently broke the soil, reclaimed wetlands, and began orchards and vineyards. In this manner, the Chinese were especially important pioneers in the production of strawberries, potatoes, wine grapes, raisins, and deciduous fruit. Although it was in the reclamation and settlement of the Sacramento-San Joaquin Delta that they particularly left their mark, the Chinese served as important farm innovators in the larger Central Valley, the Santa Clara Valley, and other San Francisco districts. Later, after 1890, when they began to come in increasing numbers, Japanese immigrants also served as agricultural innovators in the manner pioneered by the Chinese and Europeans.

Between 1870 and the early 1900s, fruit and specialty-crop agriculture became the state's major industry. Problems were gradually overcome, new crops took root, and some livestock and grain ranches gave way to smaller farms. Orange groves spread through the upland valleys of southern California, lemons along the coast. Viticulture shifted northward to San Francisco Bay valleys, where fine dry-wine grapes flourished, primarily in the vineyards of European immigrants. Deciduous fruit and nut orchards invaded the Bay Area, the Sacramento Valley, and the northern San Joaquin Valley. Millions of raisin-grape vines and acres of drying racks basked in the hot Fresno sun. After 1900, when progress in refrigeration, irrigation, and marketing allowed, lettuce, melons, tomatoes, dates, and other new crops spread along the Salinas River and into the fierce, below-sea-level deserts of the Imperial and Coachella valleys. By 1900 the number of farms had grown to 72,500, collectively valued at $708 million; in 1925, the state's 136,400 farms were worth more than $3 billion. By the early twentieth century, California had become the nation's most diverse agricultural region and its leading producer of wine and table grapes, raisins, winter vegetables, lemons, almonds, walnuts, tomatoes, sugar beets, plums, prunes, apricots, and lesser crops. Bountiful farm harvests sustained urban and industrial growth from 1870 to 1930.

WATER RESOURCES

Mines, farms, cities, and factories could not have expanded had pioneers not reorganized California's natural resources, particularly water. The speculative gold rush mentality prevailed even among later settlers, and most pursued short-term private gain with scant regard for the interests of others, including future generations. This carefree assault on nature had drastic results that are still felt today. To support population and economic growth, California settlers transformed most inhabited low-elevation lands into artificial environments. Rapid development took a high toll in erosion, pollution, resource waste, and declining native species, and the delicate balances of nature, revered by the Indians and modified somewhat by Hispanic settlers, were severely disrupted by the Americans.

In semi-arid California, water manipulation was fundamental. San Francisco, Oakland, Los Angeles, and other boom towns developed hearty thirsts. Water companies satisfied these by drilling wells, tapping local rivers, and building reservoirs to catch the runoff from surrounding highlands. By the 1870s expanding city water systems were dominated by large corporations, such as San Francisco's Spring Valley Water Company, which often intervened in local politics, encroached into the countryside, and aroused the opposition of farmers and small-town dwellers who also needed the water.

Contradictory water laws at first inhibited development of agricultural water. During early statehood, the legislature, in the traditionalism typical of frontier governments, adopted the "riparian" doctrine—an old principle in Anglo-American common law that gave landowners along watercourses the sole right to divert water. Growing from experience in the well-watered East, the riparian doctrine restricted irrigation and discouraged agricultural and urban growth in drier lands such as California. Later in the 1850s the legislature confused the water issue further by also legalizing the Hispanic "prior appropriation" doctrine, which allowed miners and others to preempt water rights on public lands on a first-come, first-served basis and to transport water to areas removed from the water source for "beneficial use." Bitter disputes between riparian and appropriation claimants resulted in endless litigation that was usually, though not always, won by riparians. In 1870 only 60,000 acres, a tiny fraction of the state's cultivated lands, was being irrigated.

During the next twenty years, expanded irrigation fostered modest plantings of fruit and specialty crops. By 1889, one million acres, or twenty-six percent of the state's crop acreage, was being irrigated—most by small private water companies, and the rest by cooperative colonies and individual farm wells. Throughout this time, however, water rights remained uncertain, irrigation projects were delayed, and water deliveries were erratic. Decades of legal confusion finally climaxed in *Lux* v. *Haggin* (1886). In this case, in which two giant land interests fought over control of the flow of the Kern River, the state supreme court determined that the riparian rights of downstream landowners (the Miller-Lux Land and Cattle Company) superseded the appropriation rights of upstream water users (James B. A. Haggin and Lloyd Tevis). Irrigation and agriculture had suffered a serious setback.

Under pressure from agricultural interests, the legislature passed the Wright Irrigation Act in 1887. This path-breaking law authorized the formation of local irrigation districts, bestowed on the districts the power of eminent domain—authority to condemn private water rights and irrigation facilities for public use—and empowered districts to levy taxes and sell bonds to build reservoirs and canals. Although several dozen districts immediately sprouted up, few survived because of poor management and lawsuits by riparian owners and some small farmers who objected to higher land assessments and taxes. Their funds drained by litigation, most districts lapsed without delivering a drop of water. As late as 1910, the nine functioning districts covered only 600,000 acres and had raised only $23 million through bond issues.

Reforms passed in 1911, 1913, and 1917 strengthened the planning and state supervision of the districts and greatly expanded the scope of California irrigation. Between 1909 and 1920, sixty new districts were founded. Irrigated acreage grew from 2.6 million to 4.2 million, and capital invested in irrigation from $19 million to $195 million. Public water accounted for most of the increase. The golden age of California irrigation had dawned. After 1900, acreage, production, and the profitability of fruit and specialty crops increased sharply. Once established by the Wright Act, public management of irrigation water spread to other western states, and ultimately the federal government. The National Reclamation Act, which passed Congress in 1902, inspired the construction of still larger federal irrigation systems in twentieth-century California.

THE ASSAULT ON NATURE AND THE BEGINNING OF ENVIRONMENTAL CONCERN

Environmental alteration after the gold rush was especially rapid because of dramatic population growth, the settlers' intense profit motives, the powerful new industrial organization and technology, widespread water development, and casual public planning and control. With the abandon described by Dame Shirley, miners ripped open hillsides, cut down watershed forests, disrupted streambeds, polluted water supplies, and stripped away topsoils. Much of the Sierra foothills became, in Mark Twain's words, a "torn and guttered and disfigured" region. Meanwhile, farmers, livestock raisers, and market hunters capitalizing on early food shortages preyed ruthlessly on shore birds, waterfowl, eagles, condor, deer, elk, pronghorn, mountain lion, wolf, and other native species, seriously depleting their numbers by the 1870s. By the early 1900s some species, such as the California grizzly, which had awed Indians and Hispanic colonists, had vanished from the state. Many others, including the elk, bighorn, and condor, were driven into tiny, remote enclaves.

Overpopulated herds of cattle, sheep, and horses reduced large stretches of fragile grasslands to man-made deserts. Lumbermen using fire and other destructive methods denuded the accessible redwood slopes that had flanked San Francisco Bay and the coast from Big Sur north to Crescent City. With an eye toward maximum quick profits in a highly speculative industry, *bonanza* wheat ranchers farmed the soil without crop rotation or fertilizers and, within ten years of first planting, rendered much land barren. By the 1870s, erosion from hydraulic mining, disturbed riverbeds, and watershed decline unleashed devastating floods on the Central Valley and elsewhere.

In towns and areas of dense farms, environmental alteration was nearly total. In the booming Mussel Slough country after 1870, for example, wild open lands were quickly subdivided, settled, fenced, and plowed in rectangular patterns. Wagon tracks and county roads marched out along the section lines, accentuating the geometric order being imposed on the land. In keeping with "efficient" land-management practices, natural watercourses and marshes were drained, filled, plowed over, or diverted to irrigation. Farmers with large plows and graders leveled the undulating land into the flat planes suitable for straight furrows, irrigation, and large farm machines. Wells were bored, and groundwater bubbled to the surface in artesian springs or was pumped by windmills and steam engines. By 1880, human culture had replaced nature as the principal determinant of landscape in the Mussel Slough area. Unable to survive, many of the remaining native species quickly vanished, their places taken by alien crops, weeds, ornamental plants, animals, and later even insects and birds. Like much of settled California in the last half of the nineteenth century, the Mussel Slough country had been transformed into a largely man-made world.

Bewitched by "progress," few Californians noticed these changes at first. Even fewer opposed them. Typically, local boosters celebrated them as the natural and inevitable byproducts of civilizing the wilderness, the value of which virtually no one questioned. Only a few prophets, such as the great naturalist John Muir, raised lonely voices against the assault on nature. Only occasionally, when environmental destruction impinged on other economic interests, was wider dissent aroused. Out of the few nineteenth-century environmental clashes, however, emerged important principles of scientific resource conservation and management in California.

JOHN MUIR AND EARLY WILDERNESS PRESERVATION

John Muir, circa 1912
This photograph of Muir was taken by W. E. Das-
sonville. *Courtesy of the Bancroft Library.*

In the late-nineteenth-century scramble for development and profit, most Californians
were indifferent to or hostile toward wilderness preservation. But a few dedicated writers, artists, and scientists who understood the spiritual and long-range economic value
of the wilderness wrote, lectured, and lobbied to save the state's unique natural landscapes. The growth after 1870 of irrigated agriculture and tourism—industries with a
stake in protecting mountain watersheds—converted some powerful allies among farm
and business groups. To promote irrigation, agriculture, tourism, and hence its freight
and passenger business, the Southern Pacific Company often furnished political lever-
age, financing, or leadership for resource-conservation and wilderness-preservation
movements.

Providing the inspiration for this activism was John Muir, a Scottish-born, Wisconsin-
bred naturalist. A promising young inventor and efficiency expert, Muir was almost
blinded by an industrial accident in 1867. Although he recovered, the trauma convinced
him to explore God's handiwork in nature instead of humanity's artificial creations.
After walking much of the way from the Midwest, Muir arrived in Yosemite Valley in
1868. While living there and on a Contra Costa County farm, Muir developed a worldwide reputation for his discovery of Yosemite's glacial origins and his writings champi-
oning wilderness preservation. Until his death in 1914 Muir dedicated himself to studying and protecting wilderness regions around the world. In terms of influence on
human thought and action, John Muir was perhaps the greatest of all Californians.

One of the foremost early ecologists, Muir was the father of modern environmental-

JOHN MUIR AND EARLY WILDERNESS PRESERVATION
(continued)

ism. He believed that humanity was selfish and arrogant in assuming that all nature had been created for its sole benefit. With machines that tore up the earth and disordered nature, "Lord Man," Muir felt, had usurped the power of God to determine which species died or lived. Instead, Muir maintained, nature existed for its own mysterious purposes, all beings were interrelated, and the long-term welfare of humanity depended on the preservation of nature's fullness down "to the smallest transmicroscopic creature that dwells upon our conceited eyes and knowledge." To the seeing eye, nature also provided insights into the rest of creation and divinity itself. "The clearest way into the Universe," he wrote, "is through a forest wilderness." Moreover, like Emerson and Thoreau before him, Muir maintained that contact with nature refreshes souls wearied by the conflict and superficiality of modern civilization. "Climb the mountains," he recommended. "Nature's peace will flow into you as the sunshine into trees." To Muir, preserving wilderness was thus as essential to human welfare as it was to maintaining natural ecological balances.

The high, rugged, and still-pristine peaks, meadows, and forests of the Sierra Nevada were the first objects of the preservationists' concern. The monoliths, meadows, and waterfalls of Yosemite Valley, first "discovered" by militiamen chasing Indians in the early 1850s, were quickly recognized as California's foremost landmarks. In 1864, when the federal government closed it to further private settlement and entrusted it to the care of the state, Yosemite Valley became the nation's first wilderness preserve. Encouraged by state mismanagement, however, poaching lumbermen, livestock herders, and farmers swarmed in anyway and were soon disfiguring the valley and surrounding areas. In the 1870s Muir and a few cohorts launched a crusade to save Yosemite.

Aided by eastern conservationist friends and Southern Pacific Company leaders, Muir finally overcame powerful vested interests who wanted to keep the Sierra open to exploitation. In 1890 he persuaded Congress to convert the territory surrounding the valley into a large national park for tougher protection. To encourage appreciation of wilderness, Muir and other San Francisco area intellectuals and business leaders founded the Sierra Club in 1892. In 1905 and 1906 Muir and the Sierra Club, again in league with the Southern Pacific, pushed bills narrowly through the legislature and Congress returning Yosemite Valley to federal control for inclusion in the national park.

In the 1890s and early 1900s preservationists and irrigators in the San Joaquin Valley, aided by the railroad, also secured the establishment of Sequoia National Park, the giant Sierra Forest Reserve, and national forests around Lake Tahoe. Nearly 200 miles of the Sierra Nevada had come under federal protection. A similar coalition pressed the state in 1902 to buy one of the few remaining stands of virgin redwoods in the Santa Cruz Mountains and to found Big Basin Redwoods Park, the beginning of the modern state park system. Although much of the California natural landscape was being despoiled or altered beyond recognition, at least a remnant was to remain a legacy to future generations. (RJO)

Especially significant was the uproar over hydraulic-mining debris. By the 1870s, miners armed with powerful water cannons had gouged out gigantic artificial canyons in the northern Sierra foothills. Billions of cubic yards of gravel and sand clogged valley riverbeds, reducing navigability and worsening the flood problems of Sacramento, Marysville, other river towns, and surrounding farmland. When they receded, the floods deposited an infertile layer of mining debris, often several feet thick, enough to ruin many farmers.

Hydraulic-mining devastation developed into one of the most explosive issues of the 1870s and 1880s. Aided by the Southern Pacific, valley people organized anti-debris associations, but the large mining companies were powerfully entrenched, with allies in the legislature and the courts. Anti-debris forces pushed a bill through the legislature in 1880 requiring hydraulic miners to catch debris behind dams built under state supervision, one of the first California laws aimed at controlling environmental destruction. Most mining companies, however, refused to comply and ignored valley court injunctions. When the state supreme court declared even this mild law unconstitutional on a minor point, farmers sued in U.S. Circuit Court in San Francisco. In January 1884 Judge Lorenzo Sawyer, of Mussel Slough fame, issued a permanent injunction against all discharge of debris into Sierra streams. "Hydraulicking" was dead. Mining companies closed down overnight, thriving towns emptied, and decay spread through the hydraulic regions. Valley people had established the important principle of governmental responsibility for prohibiting severe environmental damage, even if it meant an entire industry's destruction.

In the late nineteenth century, Californians also groped toward more enlightened policies to replenish depleted fisheries, control floods, and protect forests from fire, but most people, accustomed to exploiting resources at will, resented and ignored even the most innocuous conservation measures. Systematic, modern conservation had to await the Progressive era. Meanwhile, resource waste and environmental deterioration continued unabated.

SOCIAL AND POLITICAL CONFLICT

Society in gold rush California, although not rigid, had always been structured. As in the eastern United States, wealth, ethnicity, and family background divided Californians into classes of sharply differing status and opportunity. Upward mobility for the masses of poor miners, laborers, small farmers, and members of the lower middle class, while not totally closed, was slow and frustrating. Population turnover obscured social inequities. In a society composed mostly of transients, unsuccessful people skipped without notice from one temporary community to another, or simply returned home. But by the 1870s, as people settled down somewhat and families began replacing sojourners, glaring inequities became more apparent and politically explosive.

As cities matured, they grew more geographically and socially structured. During the 1870s San Francisco assumed the physical characteristics of an industrial city. Disparities in wealth and transportation innovations altered demographic arrangements, giving rise to specialized districts devoted to commerce, industry, entertainment, and residence. Wealthy citizens—the railroad, Comstock, and wheat kings—colonized the tops of hills made accessible by Andrew Halladie's cable cars after 1873. Middle-class families migrated west of downtown into pleasant new subdivisions served by streetcars.

Unable to afford new housing and transportation, the working-class majority was

Nob Hill Mansions
In 1878 Eadweard Muybridge photographed Collis P. Huntington's elegant home (*foreground*) and Charles Crocker's darker one behind it. The wall looming at the rear of the Crocker mansion is the famous "spite fence," built by the railroad king to isolate a stubborn neighbor who refused to sell his property. *Courtesy of Stanford University Libraries, Special Collections.*

caught in low-elevation pockets throughout the city, jammed into boardinghouses and small cottages, with little opportunity for upward mobility. The once-exclusive South-of-Market Street neighborhood developed into a factory and slum district, described by Rudyard Kipling as "a hopeless mass of small wooden houses, dust, street refuse, and children who play with empty kerosene tins." The contrast between such wretched poverty in the hollows and the ornate mansions rising atop Nob Hill aggravated social strife in San Francisco. Oakland, Sacramento, Los Angeles, and other cities also developed into stratified communities.

Restricted by prejudice to the bottom rung of the social ladder, Chinese, Mexican, African American, and some European immigrant minorities were pushed into the least desirable urban neighborhoods. Barred from business and employment opportunities, excluded from or segregated in schools, churches, and other majority-dominated institutions, and politically neutralized by gerrymandered ward boundaries and stringent voting requirements, minorities remained isolated from the mainstream.

California's major, urban, non-white minority groups had strikingly different experiences, however. During the railway era, especially in terminal cities such as Oakland and Los Angeles, stable and relatively high-wage railroad employment provided increased opportunity for African American men who worked as Pullman car waiters and porters. Beyond a small middle-class elite of railroad workers, skilled laborers, professionals, and small-business owners, however, most urban black people worked in low-paying service or industrial jobs. Although in the nineteenth century black people were too few in number and too dispersed to support large ethnic neighborhoods, they did, in communities such as Oakland, San Francisco, and Los Angeles, develop ethnic institutions in the form of newspapers, churches, and civil rights groups that began the long-term work of desegregating schools and other public facilities. Only later, after 1910, did large-scale migration of African Americans from the East and South and intensifying hostility toward black people by whites create large, dense ethnic neighborhoods such as the Watts district of Los Angeles.

On the other hand, large Chinese and Mexican districts emerged in many cities because of exclusionist pressures from the majority population, as well as the self-segregation normal within ethnic groups seeking to reestablish old-world social and cultural life. In the 1870s and 1880s, as hostility and violence toward the Chinese mounted in some rural areas, many immigrants retreated to the rapidly expanding "Chinatowns" in San

Francisco, Oakland, Sacramento, Los Angeles, and most other large towns. There, immigrants established community institutions, businesses, and recreations that gave them a measure of sustenance and protection. Since very few women had immigrated before 1882, when the Chinese were excluded from further entry into the country, the group was largely composed of men. It would be well into the twentieth century before normal gender ratios and family life could be recreated.

Especially in Los Angeles, Santa Barbara, and other southern California cities, where their populations were greater, Mexicans established *barrios*, within which thrived extended family networks, mutual aid associations, ethnic businesses, and Spanish-language and bilingual newspapers. Modernization and economic development brought by the railways generally passed the Mexicans by, however. In Los Angeles, for example, a city that was numerically dominated by *californios* and recent Mexican immigrants as late as 1880, the arrival of new industries and peoples drove Spanish-speaking persons from jobs, neighborhoods, and political influence that they had once controlled. Nevertheless, immigration continued from Mexico, though in small numbers, for the rest of the century, and the *barrio* grew in size and became ever more ethnically homogeneous and, in most respects, economically deprived. By the turn of the century, the extensive East Los Angeles Mexican neighborhood had already taken shape, and ethnic pride and self-defense movements had begun. When immigration from Mexico increased sharply after 1900, the newcomers found ethnic neighborhoods and institutions already in place.

Social stratification also ruled rural areas. Held for speculation or lease to wheat producers, fertile land, particularly with water rights, was scarce and expensive in most desirable, easily cultivated areas. High costs for land, fencing, irrigation facilities, orchard planting, mortgage interest, and other requirements for the new delicate crops raised farm building beyond the means of average people. Praised as the salvation of the small farmer, irrigation turned out to be a mixed blessing. Expensive to install and operate, water improvements gave an edge to those with capital by allowing them to raise more valuable fruit crops. However, as they became more dependent on water systems with limited storage capacity, irrigating farmers opened themselves up to greater loss during water shortages. Severe droughts during the 1870s and early 1880s pushed many farmers close to bankruptcy and forced others to abandon the land altogether, compounding tensions in areas such as Mussel Slough. As a final outrage, high railroad rates often ate into the profits farmers managed to make in bountiful years.

To prepare land and irrigation facilities and to plant and harvest grain and fruit, growers continued the gang-labor practices inherited from missions and ranchos. When the declining Indian population no longer met growing labor requirements by the 1860s, farmers turned to the oppressed and easily controlled Chinese, recent European immigrants, unemployed city workers, and children. Farm laborers roamed the countryside in large groups performing seasonal tasks for subsistence wages, camping in ragtag tent villages, and seldom putting down local roots or starting farms. By exploiting the economic distress and racial prejudice of the era, farmers became accustomed to making up for high irrigation and marketing costs by paying rock-bottom wages and assuming no responsibility for stable employment. After the 1890s, farmers augmented their labor supply with Japanese and Mexican immigrants. By 1900 California's "peculiar farm labor system" was firmly entrenched.

Because of high farm costs, public land

policies favoring speculators, and the growers' power to exploit low-paid laborers, immense landholdings dominated California for the rest of the nineteenth century. In 1872, of 27,000 agricultural holdings, the 122 persons who each owned more than 20,000 acres had amassed a combined six million acres, much more than the total of all other farms. The rise of irrigation and fruit culture caused some land to be subdivided. But most new growers were fairly well-to-do persons who were transferring capital from other farms or businesses, and some new large estates continued to be engrossed. Between 1870 and 1900 the average farm size decreased only from 500 to 400 acres. The California farm remained about twice as large as the national average. Geography, climate, and economic and social conditions conspired to prevent California from developing into an agrarian democracy.

Unstable farm prices, along with glaring social, economic, and political inequality, produced bitter rural conflict after the 1860s. Protesting farmers banded into spontaneous "clubs" to elect more sympathetic officials and secure better tax, land, fence, and mortgage laws, as well as regulation of railroads, wheat-trade monopolists, and other middlemen. In the early 1870s many affiliated with an emerging national movement, the Patrons of Husbandry, or Grange; a state Grange followed in 1873. By 1874 more than 13,500 farmers had flocked into California's 231 Grange locals.

EARLY LABOR MOVEMENTS AND THE "INDISPENSABLE ENEMY"

The gold rush, which attracted many skilled workers, coincided with increasing union activity among the nation's craftsmen. High labor demand in early pioneer years encouraged organizational efforts, but unions had only modest success. San Francisco typesetters, brewers, building tradesmen, musicians, and others combined to protect their interests and keep wages abreast of high living costs during the 1850s. Spontaneous strikes in the city and mining districts often succeeded temporarily, but an unstable economy and high turnover among workers constantly undermined union efforts.

Despite reversals, especially after 1855, when gold production and wages declined, craftsmen continued organizing. In the 1860s and 1870s, union agitation spread from San Francisco to industrial mining districts and emerging cities such as Oakland and Los Angeles. Although laborers periodically struck for higher wages, the principal statewide goal during the 1860s was the eight-hour day. In 1868, under pressure from unions, the legislature enacted an eight-hour law over employer opposition. Although workingmen rejoiced, the victory was more apparent than real. The law could not be enforced, especially during hard times when workers would agree to almost any employment conditions.

The "Terrible Seventies" decimated the early union movement. The first westbound trains, the Comstock boom collapse, and the nationwide Panic of 1873 had devastating consequences. Cheap goods arrived from all over the nation, driving California prices, wages, and production downward. While unemployment soared, thousands of new people flooded labor markets: released railroad-construction laborers, unemployed workers from eastern states and fading Nevada mines, and more Chinese immigrants (20,000 in 1876 alone). Neither unions nor the few organized charities could relieve the situation or meet increasing demands for aid. Some workers clung to their weakened craft unions, while a few affiliated with the national Knights of Labor, with little success. In short, the conditions that encouraged industry in California also undercut the position of labor.

Mounting working-class frustration vented

itself not only on employers but on California labor's "indispensable enemy"—the Chinese, who were, ironically, among the most exploited Californians. As in the mining era, white workers blamed the Chinese for unemployment and low wages and attacked them both politically and physically. Unions and "anti-coolie" clubs agitated for state and federal laws restricting the immigration and employment of Chinese. As early as 1871, a Los Angeles mob swarmed through the city's Chinatown and massacred a score of its residents.

Although outbursts occurred statewide, anti-Chinese sentiment climaxed in San Francisco in the summer of 1877, a season of national strikes and labor violence. A July 23 meeting of enraged workers ended with a cry of "On to Chinatown." Within hours, much of that district was in ruins or under siege. On subsequent days, mobs attacked firms that employed Chinese workers. Blaming the violence on malcontents, communists, and youthful hoodlums, Governor William Irwin called out the militia. Led by the venerable "lion of the vigilantes," William T. Coleman, respectable San Franciscans formed a Committee of Public Safety, which, armed with pick handles from Coleman's warehouse, restored order and preserved property.

Anti-Chinese Cartoon
This anti-Chinese cartoon by George Frederick Keller appeared in *The Wasp* on December 8, 1877. *Courtesy of the California State Library.*

THE WORKINGMEN'S PARTY OF CALIFORNIA

Out of San Francisco's depression and turmoil, the rabidly anti-Chinese Workingmen's Party of California (WPC) was born in September 1877. Party leaders argued that capitalists monopolized wealth and property, used political influence to keep workers subordinate, and employed cheap Chinese labor to enrich themselves. As a remedy, they recommended a workingmen's political movement to combat corporations and eject the

Chinese. They preached their gospel so effectively that the WPC mustered 10,000 members to march in San Francisco's 1877 Thanksgiving Day parade.

At the head of the column strode the WPC's new president, Denis Kearney, the young, self-educated Irish immigrant owner of a small, troubled wagon company. Traditional labor leaders dismissed Kearney as an opportunistic demagogue who was not to be taken seriously, but thousands thronged to his sandlot meetings. A natural orator, he appealed directly to working-class fears. Kearney proclaimed the dignity of labor, denounced railroad barons, landowners, bankers, and the "money power" in general, and called on workers to arm themselves against the common enemies—the Chinese and the corporation. Threats of violence and the concluding chant "The Chinese must go!" enlivened each speech.

Attracted by the party's social activities as much as by Kearney's tirades, workingmen quickly made the WPC a force in San Francisco and California affairs. Although the state and cities passed laws limiting freedom of assembly and expression and jailed Kearney and other leaders, the WPC made inroads among disenchanted laborers, lower-level white-collar workers, and small businessmen in San Francisco, Oakland, Los Angeles, and other towns. By 1878 the party had elected a state senator and local officials in Alameda County, members of the legislature and a mayor and a majority of the board of supervisors in San Francisco, and a scattering of local officials around the state. It also captured one-third of the seats in the Constitutional Convention of 1878–1879. WPC-dominated governments in San Francisco, Oakland, Los Angeles, and other centers adopted ordinances discriminating against the Chinese in housing, employment, and city services.

Despite some political victories and much notoriety, the WPC was a transitory phenomenon, more an emotional outlet for distress than a permanent influence. By 1880, internal dissension, the absence of a consistent reform program, and a brief economic revival had reduced its appeal. Members deserted and returned to more traditional unions and parties. A few leaders moved on to other labor-reform movements, but by 1885 even Kearney had abandoned political activism in favor of selling San Francisco real estate.

ANTI-RAILROAD POLITICS

Along with the Chinese, large corporations were a target for discontented groups in the 1870s. Although Californians actually suffered from many economic, social, political, and environmental problems, most visible were the growing monopolies over land, the wheat trade, and transportation. As the state's largest business, landowner, and em-

ployer of Chinese workers, with an annual income that dwarfed the entire state budget, the Central/Southern Pacific Railroad provided a convenient scapegoat. The company was not without guilt. Its owners were using the wealth they had derived from public construction subsidies to absorb or destroy competitors and enforce high transportation tariffs. To protect subsidies and privileges, the railroad employed a vigilant force of lawyers, lobbyists, and political bosses, and was not above using bribery and power politics. Although contemporary opponents and most later historians exaggerated its power and malevolence, the Central/Southern Pacific was a formidable foe, as the Mussel Slough squatters discovered.

In particular, discontented farmers, workers, and urban shippers in the 1870s charged that the monopoly's high freight tariffs discriminated against some regions, towns, and shippers, deprived producers of just profits, priced California out of the national market, and caused unemployment in many industries. Central/Southern Pacific officials countered that higher operating expenses over rugged and thinly populated terrain, not monopoly, raised tariffs higher than on eastern lines. Moreover, it was more efficient to charge lower rates on large shipments and long hauls and to award favorable terminal status only to some cities. In truth, the self-interested and contradictory rate demands of Californians would have been impossible for any railroad to reconcile. The furor was mostly raised by conflicting classes of shippers who sought only an advantage over competitors, not equal or lower overall rates.

The rate issue was complex, however, and failed to align everyone against the railroad. Although favored communities, farmers, and businesses, along with those who hoped to win rail service in the future, opposed railroad regulation or a general lowering of rates, the Grange and others agitated for state control of tariffs. In 1876, against strenuous lobbying by the railroad and its supporters, the legislature created an advisory railway commission. The weak body was ignored, however, and it was abolished within three years.

THE CONSTITUTION OF 1879

In 1878, continuing clamor by disaffected groups such as the WPC and the Grange pushed the legislature into calling a convention to revise the 1849 constitution to accommodate three decades of social change and to limit the power of corporations. The WPC shared the elected membership equally with Grangers and "nonpartisans" (primarily Democrats and Republicans). With such disparate groups present—including reformers and representatives of vested interests—conflict and confusion were inevitable. The delegates harangued each other for 157 days at Sacramento during late 1878 and early 1879 before finally hammering out a compromise constitution.

The question of regulating railroads and other corporations consumed the most energy. The new constitution declared railroads "subject to legislative control" and called for a railroad commission of three elected members with authority to fix maximum rates and prohibit railroads from discriminating among shippers. The document made intangible corporate assets (profits, franchises, and the like) subject to taxation, raised taxes on railroad and other corporate property, established a board of equalization to increase state revenues and stabilize tax rates among counties, transferred mortgage tax obligations from borrowers to lenders, and tightened banking regulations. The delegates also modernized the state's judicial system, reorganized and increased funding for the state's schools and university, and

sanctioned the eight-hour-day principle on public works. Concerning the Chinese, the constitution authorized the legislature to act against "dangerous or detrimental" aliens, forbade Chinese employment by corporations or on public works, and legalized residential segregation of the Chinese. In other matters, the convention ran into problems. Although the delegates debated ways to redistribute land, little could be done without violating private property rights. Many representatives, particularly land-owning farmers, vigorously blocked any land reforms. Characteristically, the all-male convention squashed a proposal to enfranchise women.

In the end, the convention produced one of the world's longest, most complex constitutions, more closely resembling a legal code than an organic law. The overly detailed compromise document satisfied almost no one. Corporate interests condemned its regulatory and taxation provisions as confiscatory and communistic. Protesting that the constitution did not resolve their grievances, disillusioned workers also called for its defeat. Somewhat appeased by promises of railroad rate control and more equitable taxation, farmers probably were responsible for the document's narrow passage in May 1879, by a majority of 11,000 out of 145,000 votes cast.

Whatever its shortcomings, the new constitution established important principles of state economic regulation, including supervision of public utilities such as railroads. The document also distributed the tax burden more widely, particularly by reducing the unfair share hitherto paid by farmers, and created the machinery for increasing state revenues. The state now possessed a stronger legal and fiscal framework for dealing more actively with the economic, scientific, and environmental problems of modernization.

Many of the constitution's most innovative

measures had little immediate effect, however. Like its predecessor, the new railroad commission was usually ignored. The legislature refused to finance it properly or to pay legal costs to enforce its edicts. Commission members frequently sympathized with railroads and approved their rate proposals, and by the mid-1880s many critics ridiculed the body as a tool of the Southern Pacific. Nevertheless, after 1880, because of more efficient operations and competition from the Santa Fe and other lines, overall rates on the Southern Pacific fell consistently for several decades. But many continued to denounce the railroad for charging excessive and discriminatory tariffs and exerting illegitimate political power. Litigation also delayed the constitution's provisions to tax corporate assets and equalize tax rates, and lenders simply raised interest rates to cover mortgage tax obligations. Complicating all these issues was a fundamental problem: the principle of corporate regulation was not yet fully accepted in American law.

CHINESE EXCLUSION

The new constitution did little to assuage the anti-Chinese movement. Broadly rooted in racism, suspicion of cultural differences, and economic rivalry, opposition toward the Chinese was not limited to a few radicals and labor leaders, but cut across socioeconomic, partisan, and even ethnic lines. Some of California's other oppressed ethnics—most notably African Americans—hostile toward Chinese religion and culture and fearful of economic competition with the numerous Asian immigrants, were among the most fervent supporters of anti-Chinese activities. For decades, "the Chinese question" remained an explosive issue that could not be ignored in contests for local and national office. During the 1870s the U.S. Supreme Court had

repeatedly struck down discriminatory state and local laws as violations of the U.S. Constitution, the Burlingame Treaty with China, or the Civil Rights Act of 1870. Anti-Chinese provisions of the new state constitution met similar fates. Each federal action in defense of the Chinese aroused indignation in the state. Perhaps out of concern for future elections, President Rutherford B. Hayes negotiated a treaty with China in 1880 allowing the United States to regulate immigration. Under the terms of that agreement Congress, pressured by its California members, enacted a bill in 1882 suspending the immigration and naturalization of Chinese for ten years.

The Exclusion Act of 1882 did not deport Chinese immigrants already in the country and therefore failed to satisfy many Californians, especially labor leaders. They organized boycotts of Chinese-made goods and agitated for expulsion. Into the twentieth century, whites continued to discriminate against, ridicule, beat, and occasionally lynch the Chinese with virtual impunity. Periodically, rioting mobs terrorized and burned their neighborhoods. Numerous rural communities rounded up and expelled the Chinese altogether. Pressure from California again influenced Congress in 1888 to strengthen the Exclusion Act to prohibit reentry by workers after visits to China and, in 1892, to extend its provisions for another ten years. By 1904 treaties and legislation had made exclusion permanent. Only during World War II, as a gesture to an ally, did the United States reopen its shores to Chinese immigrants.

CULTURE IN THE RAILROAD ERA

For several decades after 1865, California culture remained essentially derivative. Some progress was made in founding cultural institutions, best symbolized by the persistent, if fitful, expansion of colleges and public schools. Lagging behind, however, was the development of a regional culture, with aesthetic themes reflecting the state's distinctive landscape, peoples, and history. Second-generation Californians, following the lead of the gold rush pioneers, continued to mimic the cultural styles of the ancestral homelands they so much venerated, particularly the northeastern United States.

Developments in architecture were illustrative. While the houses and business buildings of ordinary people continued to be erected in the venerable New England frame tradition, the wealthy and middle classes, anxious to demonstrate their new respectability, copied the architectural fads of eastern trend-setters. Country estates and fashionable subdivisions in the railroad towns were built in a succession of increasingly elaborate (some would say gaudy) Victorian styles—for instance, Gothic Revival, Italianate, French Second Empire, Queen Anne, and Richardson Romanesque—each of which evoked distant places and bygone eras. At the same time, builders catering to their customers' conservative tastes shunned native stone and redwood, or disguised them with paint, stain, and other surfaces so that they could masquerade as standard eastern construction materials. For the most part, Californians lacked the maturity and sense of place and history that, beginning in the 1890s, would give rise to a creative regional architecture.

Reflecting the general population, some "carpetbagger" authors stayed for a few years, wrote briefly about their California experience, then wandered on. Such were Mark Twain and Bret Harte, who arrived in the twilight of the mining era, and produced nostalgic short stories about the humor and heroism of pioneer prospectors of the 1840s and 1850s or the fading miners and camps of the 1860s. Unable to support themselves by writing fiction, both turned to journalism, Harte as the first editor of *The Overland Monthly* (founded in 1868), Twain as an itinerant lecturer and newspaper reporter. The most significant event of Twain's three-year stay was the 1865 publication of his rollicking mining-camp story "The Celebrated Jumping Frog of Calaveras County," which established Twain's reputation as a frontier humorist and launched his literary career. Anxious for the state to repress its disorderly gold rush origins, many California critics rejected the stories of Twain and Harte. Twain (in 1867) and Harte (in 1871) returned to the East, where they were more appreciated and where better opportunities existed for professional writers.

Ina Coolbrith was the bright star of an otherwise lackluster poetry. Fleeing a troubled early life in southern California, Coolbrith resettled in San Francisco in the mid-1860s. A poet since childhood, she was immediately accepted into the city's growing literary community. Several years later, she became Harte's assistant editor at *The Overland Monthly*. As editor and later as librarian for the Oakland Public Library, one of the state's first and finest free circulation libraries, Coolbrith was for decades friend and patron to important California writers. Her own verse, which at first inclined toward eroticism and romantic love, turned later to celebrating California's hills, birds, and flowers. Coolbrith was honored by the legislature in 1915 as California's poet laureate.

The transformation of Ina Coolbrith's poetry suggested that, while California culture remained mostly imitative, distinctive regional themes had begun to sound before century's end. Some authors and artists discovered the spiritual and aesthetic potential in the state's magnificent landscapes. Joining John Muir in seeking beauty and meaning in unique natural surroundings, pioneer photographers such as Carleton E. Watkins and Eadweard Muybridge and painters such as Thomas Hill and the visiting Albert Bierstadt attempted to capture on film and canvas the spectacular scale and delicacy of Yosemite's cliffs, meadows, and waterfalls. The major figure of California's "nature school" of painting was William Keith, Muir's long-time friend and cohort in the wilderness-preservation crusade. For five decades before his death in 1911, Keith painted Yosemite Valley, the Sierra, and other California landscapes in a style that combined realistic attention to fine detail with the traditional romanticism of the Hudson River school he had emulated in his early years. Late-nineteenth-century California writers and artists stressed nature's fertility, harmony, and beauty and the imperative of achieving peaceful coexistence between the people and the land. Often, the Eden-like California landscape provided a contrasting background to the conflict and corruption of human society, a theme that became a hallmark of the state's culture in the twentieth century.

At the same time, railroad-era economic inequities and political corruption gave birth to a strong social-protest theme in California arts and letters. The tradition's founder, Henry George, arrived in San Francisco as a young man in 1858. While struggling to overcome grinding poverty, George worked as printer and reporter on various San Francisco, Sacramento, and Oakland newspapers and magazines and was already a well-known journalist by the time he published his 1868 *Overland Monthly* article questioning the benefits of railroad construction. By the early 1870s George was increasingly distressed by the inequality and poverty that appeared to be the price of industrial "progress." His first major work, *Our Land and Land Policy, National and State* (1871), condemned the monopoly in land fostered by railroad land grants, other federal and state laws, and ram-

pant speculation. As a remedy for the land monopoly and the unemployment that were smothering opportunities for ordinary people, George recommended confiscatory taxes on large land holdings. George's California experience also inspired his classic *Progress and Poverty* (1879), which advocated the single-tax theory, a simplistic cure for industrial evils that attracted a wide following outside the state. Like many contemporary cultural figures who attained fame, George soon left for greener pastures in the East, where he became a leading reformer and one of the most widely read and influential of California authors.

Others, however, took up Henry George's crusade against privilege. Journalist and short-story writer Ambrose Bierce produced cutting satire, particularly of the Southern Pacific's power. Illustrators such as *The Wasp*'s George Frederick Keller and the San Francisco *Examiner*'s Homer Davenport and James Swinnerton honed the acid political cartoon to a fine art. At the turn of the century, Edwin Markham's poem, "The Man with the Hoe" (1899), and Frank Norris's classic of naturalism, *The Octopus* (1901), attacked monopolies and defended the oppressed farmers. By the end of the nineteenth century, social protest had become an integral part of the California literary tradition.

Finally, in the last third of the nineteenth century, Californians began to reflect on the meaning of the state's history. As communities attained a measure of stability, beginning in the 1850s, local history first received attention. By the early twentieth century, more than 150 county histories alone had appeared. Typically written by amateur boosters and journalists, the local histories were usually little more than simple chronologies of major events and compilations of biographies of leading residents. In keeping with the intense ethnocentrism of the period,

SUGGESTIONS FOR FURTHER READING

Confrontation at Mussel Slough

Frank Norris, *The Octopus* (1901); Southern Pacific Company Land Records (California State Railroad Museum, Sacramento); Daniel K. Zumwalt Correspondence (Southern Pacific Land Company, San Francisco); Collis P. Huntington Papers (Syracuse University, Syracuse, New York); Collis P. Huntington Correspondence (Henry E. Huntington Biographical File, Huntington Library, San Marino, California), Settlers Grand League, *The Struggle of the Mussel Slough Settlers for Their Homes!* (1880), and *An Appeal to the People* (1880); Wallace Smith, *Garden of the Sun: A History of the San Joaquin Valley, 1772–1939* (1939); James L. Brown, *The Mussel Slough Tragedy* (1958); Richard L. Rollins, "The Mussel Slough Dispute: An Inquiry Based on the Census and Real Property Evidence" (M. A. thesis, California State University, Hayward, 1990); Barbara M. Bristow, "Mussel Slough Tragedy: Railroad Struggle or Land Gamble" (M.A. thesis, Fresno State College, 1971); William Clyde McKinney, "The Mussel Slough Episode: A Chapter in the Settlement of the San Joaquin Valley" (M.A. thesis, University of California, Berkeley, 1948); John A. Larimore, "Legal Questions Arising from the Mussel Slough Land Dispute," *Southern California Quarterly* (1976); Morton Rothstein, "Frank Norris and Popular Perceptions of the Market," *Agricultural History* (1982); Richard Maxwell Brown, "California Conflict and the American Dream," in Brown, *No Duty to Retreat: Violence and Values in American History and Society* (1991).

Nineteenth-Century Transportation and Communication, General

Rockwell D. Hunt, *Oxcart to Airplane* (1929); Oscar O. Winther, *Express and Stagecoach Days in California* (1936); W. Turrentine Jackson, *Wagon Roads West: A Study of Federal Surveys and Construction in the Trans-Mississippi West, 1846–1869* (1952); Edward Hungerford, *Wells Fargo: Advancing the American Frontier* (1949); LeRoy R. Hafen, *The Overland Mail, 1849–1869* (1926); Robert L. Thompson, *Wiring a Continent* (1947); Glenn D. Bradley, *The Story of the Pony Express* (1913); Jerry MacMullen, *Paddlewheel Days in California* (1944); Richard E. Lingenfelter, *Steamboats on the Colorado River, 1852–1916* (1978);

Thomas Frederick Howard, *Sierra Crossing: First Roads to California* (1998); A.C.W. Bethel, "The Golden Skein: California's Gold-Rush Network," in James J. Rawls and Richard J. Orsi, eds., *A Golden State: Mining and Economic Developement in Gold Rush California* (1999).

The Civil War in California

Milton H. Shutes, *Lincoln and California* (1943); Eugene W. Berwanger, *The Frontier Against Slavery* (1967); Benjamin F. Gilbert, "The Confederate Minority in California," *California Historical Society Quarterly* (1941), and "California and the Civil War: A Bibliography," *California Historical Society Quarterly* (1961); Leo P. Kibby, "Some Aspects of California's Military Problems During the Civil War," *Civil War History* (1959); Ann Casey, "Thomas Starr King and the Secession Movement," *Historical Society of Southern California Quarterly* (1961); Gerald Stanley, "Slavery and the Origins of the Republican Party in California," *Southern California Quarterly* (1978), and "The Slavery Issue and Election in California, 1860," *Mid-America* (1980); Robert Chandler, "The Press and Civil Liberties in California During the Civil War, 1861–1865" (Ph.D. dissertation, University of California, Riverside, 1978), "Friends in Time of Need: Republicans and Black Civil Rights in California During the Civil War Era," *Arizona and the West* (1982), and "Crushing Dissent: The Pacific Tests Lincoln's Policy of Suppression, 1862," *Civil War History* (1984); Ronald C. Woolsey, "The Politics of a Lost Cause: 'Seceshers' and Democrats in Southern California During the Civil War," *California History* (1990); Judson A. Grenier, *California Legacy: The James Alexander Watson-María Dolores Domínguez de Watson Family, 1820–1980* (1987).

Railway History, General

John F. Stover, *American Railroads* (1961); Robert E. Riegel, *The Story of the Western Railroads: From 1852 Through the Reign of the Giants* (1926); "Railroads in California and the Far West," special issue of *California History* (Spring 1991), especially Richard J. Orsi, "Railroads in the History of California and the Far West: An Introduction"; William Deverell, *Railroad Crossings: Californians and the Railroad, 1850–1910*

(1994); Ward McAfee, *California's Railroad Era, 1850–1911* (1973); Leslie L. Waters, *Steel Trails to Santa Fe* (1950); Keith L. Bryant, Jr., *History of the Atchison, Topeka & Santa Fe Railroad* (1976); Lloyd J. Mercer, *Railroads and Land Grant Policy: A Study of Government Intervention* (1982); Leslie E. Decker, *Railroads, Lands, and Politics: The Taxation of the Railroad Land Grants, 1864–1897* (1964); Julius Grodinsky, *Transcontinental Railway Strategy, 1869–1893: A Study of Businessmen* (1962); Franklyn Hoyt, "Railroad Development in Southern California, 1868–1900" (Ph.D. dissertation, University of Southern California, 1951); Lewis B. Leslie, "The Entrance of the Santa Fe Railroad into California," *Pacific Historical Review* (1939); Carlos A. Schwantes, *Railroad Signatures Across the Pacific Northwest* (1993).

The First Transcontinental Railway

George Kraus, *High Road to Promontory: Building the Central Pacific Across the High Sierra* (1969); Wesley S. Griswold, *A Work of Giants: Building the First Transcontinental Railroad* (1963); Robert West Howard, *The Great Iron Trail: The Story of the First Transcontinental Railroad* (1963); George Galloway, *The First Transcontinental Railroad* (1950); John Hoyt Williams, *A Great and Shining Road: The Epic Story of the Transcontinental Railroad* (1988); Harry J. Carman and Charles H. Mueller, "The Contract and Finance Company and the Central Pacific Railroad," *Mississippi Valley Historical Review* (1927); Theodore D. Judah, *A Practical Plan for Building the Pacific Railroad* (1857); Maury Klein, *Union Pacific: The Birth of a Railroad, 1862–1893* (1987); Robert G. Athearn, *Union Pacific Country* (1971); Alexander P. Saxton, "The Army of Canton in the High Sierra," *Pacific Historical Review* (1966); Ping Chiu, *Chinese Labor in California, 1850–1880: An Economic Study* (1963); Gunther Barth, *Bitter Strength: A History of the Chinese in the United States, 1850–1870* (1964); David Haward Bain, *Empire Express: Building the First Transcontinental Railroad* (1999).

Railway Leaders

Norman E. Tutorow, *Leland Stanford: Man of Many Careers* (1971); David Lavender, *The Great Persuader* [Collis P. Huntington] (1970); Oscar Lewis, *The Big Four* (1938); Carl I. Wheat, "A Sketch of the Life of Theodore D. Judah," *California Historical Society Quarterly* (1925); Helen Hinckley Jones, *Rails from the West: A Biography of Theodore D. Judah* (1969); Salvador A. Ramirez, ed., *The Octopus Speaks: The Colton Letters* (1992).

The Southern Pacific Company

Don L. Hofsommer, *The Southern Pacific, 1901–1985* (1986); Bill Yenne, *The History of the Southern Pacific* (1985); Stuart Daggett, *Chapters on the History of the Southern Pacific Company* (1922); Neill C. Wilson and Frank J. Taylor, *Southern Pacific: The Roaring Story of a Fighting Railroad* (1952); John H. Kemble, "The Big Four at Sea: The History of the Oriental and Occidental Steamship Company," *Huntington Library Quarterly* (1940); W. H. Hutchinson, "Southern Pacific: Myth and Reality," *California Historical Society Quarterly* (1969); Lewis B. Leslie, "A Transcontinental Railroad into California: Texas and Pacific Versus Southern Pacific, 1865–1885," *Pacific Historical Review* (1936).

The "Terrible Seventies"

Gertrude Atherton, *California, An Intimate History* (1914); Henry George, "What the Railroads Will Bring Us," *Overland Monthly* (1868); Earl Pomeroy, *The Pacific Slope: A History of California, Oregon, Washington, Idaho, Utah, and Nevada* (1965), pp. 83–190.

Cities

John W. Reps, *Cities of the American West: A History of Frontier Urban Planning* (1979); Beth Bagwell, *Oakland: The Story of a City* (1982); Remi A. Nadeau, *City-Makers: The Story of Southern California's First Boom, 1868–1876* (1965); Robert M. Fogelson, *Fragmented Metropolis: Los Angeles, 1850–1930* (1967); Andrew F. Rolle, *Los Angeles: From Pueblo to City of the Future* (1981); Robert W. Cherny and William Issel, *San Francisco: Presidio, Port and Pacific Metropolis* (1981) and *San Francisco, 1865–1932* (1986); Mel Scott, *The San Francisco Bay Area* (1959 and 1985); James E. Vance, Jr., *Geography and Urban Evolution in the San Francisco Bay Area* (1964); Charles Wollenberg, *Golden Gate Metropolis: Perspectives on Bay Area History* (1985); Richard Harold Smith, "Towns Along the Tracks: Railroad Strategy and Town Promotion in the San Joaquin Valley, California" (Ph.D. dissertation, University of California, Los Angeles, 1976); William A. Bullough, *The Blind Boss and His City: Christopher Augustine Buckley and Nineteenth-Century San Francisco* (1979); Rodman W. Paul, "After the Gold Rush: San Francisco and Portland," *Pacific Historical Review* (1982); William E. Mahan, "The Political Response to Urban Growth: Sacramento and Mayor Marshall R. Beard," *California History* (1990).

Business and Industry

Robert Glass Cleland and Osgood Hardy, *March of Industry* (1929); Ira B. Cross, *Financing an Empire: History of Banking in California* (4 vols., 1927); H. Brett Melendy, "One Hundred Years of the Redwood Lumber Industry, 1850–1950" (Ph.D. dissertation, Stanford University, 1952); David Lavender, *Nothing Seemed Impossible: William C. Ralston and Early San Francisco* (1975); Mary F. Stewart, *Adolph Sutro: A Biography* (1962); James J. Rawls and Richard J. Orsi, eds., *A Golden State: Mining and Economic Development in Gold Rush California* (1999); Daniel Meissner, "Bridging the Pacific: California and the China Flour Trade," *California History* (Winter 1997–98); Anthony Kirk, *Founded by the Bay: The History of the Macaulay Foundry, 1896–1996* (1996), and *A Flier in Oil: Adolph B. Spreckels and the Rise of the California Petroleum Industry* (2000).

Labor

Richard E. Lingenfelter, *The Hardrock Miners: A History of the Mining Labor Movement in the American West, 1863–1893* (1974); Mark Wyman, *Hard Rock Epic: Western Miners and the Industrial Revolution, 1860–1910* (1979); Cletus E. Daniel, *Bitter Harvest: A History of California Farmworkers, 1870–1941* (1981); Vardan Fuller, "The Supply of Agricultural Labor as a Factor in the Evolution of Farm Organization in California" (Ph.D. dissertation, University of California, Berkeley, 1939); Paul S. Taylor and Tom Vasey, "Historical Background of California Farm Labor," *Rural Sociology* (1936); Neil Shumsky, "San Francisco Workingmen Respond to the Modern City," *California Historical Quarterly* (1976).

Agriculture

Lawrence J. Jelinek, *Harvest Empire: A History of California Agriculture* (1982); Ann F. Scheuring, ed., *A Guidebook to California Agriculture* (1984); Claude B. Hutchison, ed., *California Agriculture* (1946); Gilbert C. Fite, "The Farmers' Frontier in California, 1850–1900," in Fite, ed., *The Farmers' Frontier, 1865–1900* (1966); Paul W. Gates, *California Ranchos and Farms, 1846–1862* (1967), and "Public Land Disposal in California," *Agricultural History* (1975), and *Land and Law in California: Essays on Land Policies* (1991); Rodman W. Paul, "The Beginnings of Agriculture in California: Innovation vs. Continuity," *California Historical Quarterly* (1973); W. W. Robinson, *Land in California* (1948); Ellen Liebman, *California Farmland: A History of Large Agricultural Landholdings* (1983); Gerald D. Nash, "Henry George Reexamined: William S. Chapman's Views on Land Speculation in Nineteenth-Century California," *Agricultural History* (1959); Theodore Saloutos, "The Immigrant in Pacific Coast Agriculture," *Agricultural History* (1975); Robert Glass Cleland, *The Cattle on a Thousand Hills: Southern California, 1850–1870* (1941); Vincent P. Carosso, *The California Wine Industry, 1830– 1895: A Study of the Formative Years* (1951); Joan M. Donohue, "Agoston Haraszthy: A Study in Creativity," *California Historical Society Quarterly* (1969); Rodman W. Paul, "The Wheat Trade Between California and the United Kingdom," *Mississippi Valley Historical Review* (1958); Morton Rothstein, "A British Firm on the American West Coast, 1869–1914," *Business History Review* (1963); Kenneth A. Smith, "California: The Wheat Decades" (Ph.D. dissertation, University of Southern California, 1969); Book Club of California, *Wheat in California* (1985); Harry M. Butterfield, *A History of Subtropical Fruits and Nuts in California* (1963); Minnie T. Mills, "Luther Calvin Tibbetts, Founder of the Navel Orange Industry of California," *Historical Society of Southern California Quarterly* (1943); Herbert J. Webber and Leon D. Batchelor, eds., *The Citrus Industry* (3 vols., 1943–1948); "Citrus in Southern California," special issue of *California History* (Spring 1995); John E. Baur, "California Crops That Failed," *California Historical Society Quarterly* (1966).

Agricultural Institutions

Clarke Chambers, *California Farm Organizations: A Historical Study of the Grange, the Farm Bureau, and the Associated Farmers, 1929–1941* (1952); Rahno Mac-Curdy, *A History of the California Fruit Growers' Exchange* (1925); H. E. Erdman, "The Development and Significance of California Cooperatives, 1900–1915," *Agricultural History* (1958); R. Louis Gentil-core, "Ontario, California, and the Agricultural Boom of the 1880s," *Agricultural History* (1960); Oscar O. Winther, "The Colony System of Southern California," *Agricultural History* (1953); Richard J. Orsi, "'The Octopus' Reconsidered: The Southern Pacific and Agricultural Modernization in California, 1865–1915," *California Historical Quarterly* (1975); Gerald D. Nash, *State Government and Economic Development: A History of Administrative Policies in California, 1849– 1933* (1964); Mansel G. Blackford, *The Politics of Business in California, 1890–1920* (1977); Ann Foley Scheuring, *Science and Service: A History of the Land Grand University and Agriculture in California* (1995).

Colleges and Universities

Verne A. Stadtman, *The University of California, 1868–1968* (1970); Gunther Barth, *California's Practical Period: A Cultural Context for the Emerging University, 1850s–1870s* (1994); Rockwell D. Hunt, *History of the University of the Pacific, 1851– 1951* (1951); Andrew F. Rolle, *Occidental College: The First Seventy-Five Years, 1887–1962* (1962) and *Occidental College: A Centennial History* (1986); John McGloin, S.J., *Jesuits by the Golden Gate* (1972); Gerald McKevitt, S.J., *The University of Santa Clara: A History, 1851–1977* (1979).

Social Structure

Kevin Starr and Richard J. Orsi, eds., *Rooted in Barbarous Soil: People, Culture, and Community in Gold Rush California* (2000); Warren Thompson, *Growth and Changes in California's Population* (1955); Peter R. Decker, *Fortunes and Failures: White-Collar Mobility in Nineteenth-Century San Francisco* (1978); Ralph Mann, *After the Gold Rush: Society in Grass Valley and Nevada City, California, 1849–1870* (1982), and "Frontier Opportunity and the New Social History," *Pacific Historical Review* (1984); Richard H. Peterson, *The Bonanza Kings: The Social Origins and Business Behavior of Western Mining Entrepreneurs* (1979); Paul S. Taylor, "Foundations of California Rural Society," *California Historical Society Quarterly* (1945); Barbara Laslett, "Social Change and the Family: Los Angeles California, 1850–1870," *American Sociological Review* (1977); Gregory Holmes, *Religion in the City of the Angels* (1978); Charles O. Slosser, "Social Mobility in Nineteenth-Century Los Angeles: 1880–1890" (Ph.D. dissertation, University of California at Los Angeles, 1978); Robert L. Griswold, *Family and Divorce in California, 1850–1890: Victorian Illusions and Everyday Realities* (1982).

Ethnic Groups

Sucheng Chan, "A People of Exceptional Character: Ethnic Diversity, Nativism, and Racism in the California Gold Rush," in *Rooted in Barbarous Soil: People, Culture, and Community in Gold Rush California*, Kevin Starr and Richard J. Orsi, eds., (2000); Glenna Matthews, "The Community Study: Ethnicity and Success in San Jose," *Journal of Interdisciplinary History* (1976); Leonard Pitt, *Decline of the Californios: A Social History of the Spanish-Speaking Californians, 1846–1890* (1966); Richard Griswold del Castillo, *The Los Angeles Barrio, 1850–1890: A Social History* (1979); Albert Camarillo, *Chicanos in a Changing Society: From Mexican Pueblos to American Barrios in Santa Barbara and Southern California, 1848–1930* (1979) and *Chicanos in California: A History of Mexican Americans in California* (1984); Dolores Hayden, "Biddy Mason's Los Angeles," *California History* (1989); Douglas H. Daniels, *Pioneer Urbanites: A Social and Cultural History of Black San Francisco* (1980); Sucheng Chan, *This Bittersweet Soil: The Chinese in California Agriculture, 1860–1910* (1986), *Asian Americans: An Interpretive History* (1991), and *Asian Californians* (1991); Roger Daniels, *Asian America: Chinese and Japanese in the United States Since 1850* (1988); Judy Yung, *Unbound Feet: A Social History of Chinese Women in San Francisco* (1995); Jeff Gillenkirk and

James Motlow, *Bitter Melon: Stories from the Last Rural Chinese Town in America* (1987); Yuji Ichioka, *The Issei: The World of the First Generation Japanese Immigrants, 1885–1924* (1988); "Japanese Americans in California," special issue of *California History* (Spring 1994); Mitchell B. Gelfand, "Jewish Economic and Residential Mobility in Early Los Angeles," *Western States Jewish Historical Quarterly* (1979); Robert A. Burchell, *The San Francisco Irish: 1848–1880* (1980); Charles M. Wollenberg, *All Deliberate Speed: Segregation and Exclusion in California Schools, 1855–1975* (1076); Robert W. Cherny, "Patterns of Toleration and Discrimination in San Francisco: The Civil War to World War I," *California History* (1994); Andrew Rolle, *The Immigrant Upraised* (1968).

Water, Resources, and Conservation

Donald J. Pisani, *From Family Farm to Agribusiness: The Irrigation Crusade in California, 1850–1931* (1984); William Kahrl, *The California Water Atlas* (1979); Frederick D. Kershner, "George Chaffey and the Irrigation Frontier," *Agricultural History* (1953); John A. Shaw, "Railroads, Irrigation, and Economic Growth: The San Joaquin Valley of California," *Explorations in Economic History* (1974); William L. Preston, *Vanishing Landscapes: Land and Life in the Tulare Lake Basin* (1981); Burton Gordon, *The Monterey Bay Area: Natural History and Cultural Imprints* (1977); Robert D. Kelley, *Gold vs. Grain: The Hydraulic Mining Controversy in California's Sacramento Valley* (1959), and "Taming the Sacramento: Hamiltonianism in Action," *Pacific Historical Review* (1965); Duane A. Smith, *Mining America: The Industry and the Environment, 1800–1980* (1987); Arthur F. McEvoy, *The Fisherman's Problem: Ecology and Law in the California Fisheries, 1850–1980* (1986).

John Muir and Wilderness Preservation

Frederick Turner, *Rediscovering America: John Muir in His Time and Ours* (1985); Sally M. Miller, ed., *John Muir: Life and Work* (1993), and *John Muir in Historical Perspective* (1999); Thurman Wilkins, *John Muir: Apostle of Nature* (1995); Linnie Marsh Wolfe, *Son of the Wilderness: The Life of John Muir* (1945); Michael P. Cohen, *The Pathless Way: John Muir and the American Wilderness* (1984), and *The History of the Sierra Club, 1892–1970* (1988); Holway R. Jones, *John Muir and the Sierra Club: The Battle for Yosemite* (1965);

Richard J. Orsi, "Wilderness Saint and Robber Baron: The Anomalous Partnership of John Muir and the Southern Pacific Company for the Preservation of Yosemite National Park," *The Pacific Historian* (1985); Douglas H. Strong, "The History of Sequoia National Park, 1876–1926," *Southern California Quarterly* (1966); Raymond H. Clary, *The Making of Golden Gate Park: The Early Years, 1865–1906* (1980); Michael L. Smith, *Pacific Visions: California Scientists and the Environment, 1850–1915* (1987).

Anti-Chinese Movements

Alexander P. Saxton, *The Indispensable Enemy: Labor and the Anti-Chinese Movement in California* (1971); Elmer C. Sandmeyer, *The Anti-Chinese Movement in California* (1938).

Workingmen's Party, Grange, and Political Protest

Spencer C. Olin, Jr., *California Politics, 1846– 1920: The Emerging Corporate State* (1981); R. Hal Williams, *The Democratic Party and California Politics, 1880–1896* (1973); Neil Larry Shumsky, *Evolution of Political Protest and the Workingmen's Party of California* (1992); Ralph Kauer, "The Workingmen's Party of California," *Pacific Historical Review* (1944); Henry George, *Our Land and Land Policy: National and State* (1871); Ezra S. Carr, *The Patrons of Husbandry on the Pacific Coast* (1875); Gerald L. Prescott, "Farm Gentry vs. the Grangers: Conflict in Rural America," *California Historical Quarterly* (1978); Rodman W. Paul, "The Great California Grain War: The Grangers Challenge the Wheat King," *Pacific Historical Review* (1958); John Ludeke, "No Fence Law of 1874: Victory for San Joaquin Valley Farmers," *California History* (1980); Ward M. McAfee, "Local Interests and Railroad Regulation in California During the Granger Decade," *Pacific Historical Review* (1968); Gerald D. Nash, "The California Railroad Commission, 1876–1911," *Southern California Quarterly* (1962); David B. Griffiths, "Anti-Monopoly Movements in California, 1873–1898," *Southern California Quarterly* (1970); Jack W. Bates, "The Southern Pacific Railroad in California Politics" (M.A. thesis, University of the Pacific, 1942); Ed Salzman and Ann Leigh Brown, *The Cartoon History of California Politics* (1978).

Constitution of 1879

Carl B. Swisher, *Motivation and Political Technique in the California Constitutional Convention, 1878–1879* (1930); E. B. Willis and P. K. Stockton, *Debates and Proceedings of the Constitutional Convention of the State of California* (1880); Dudley T. Moorehead, "Sectionalism and the California Constitution of 1879," *Pacific Historical Review* (1943).

Culture in the Railway Era

Kevin Starr and Richard J. Orsi, eds., *Rooted in Barbarous Soil: People, Culture, and Community in Gold Rush California* (2000); Kevin Starr, *Americans and the California Dream, 1850–1915* (1973); Franklin Walker, *San Francisco's Literary Frontier* (1939); Harold Kirker, *California's Architectural Frontier: Style and Tradition in the Nineteenth Century* (1960); Nigey Lennon, *Mark Twain in California* (1982); Ivan Benson, *Mark Twain's Western Years* (1938); Gary Scharnhorst, ed., *Bret Harte's California* (1990); David Wyatt, *The Fall to Eden: Landscapes and Imagination in California* (1986); "Landmarks of Early California Painting: Art in the Nineteenth Century," special issue of *California History* (Spring 1992), especially Anthony Kirk, "In a Golden Land So Far: The Rise of Art in Early California"; Eugen Neuhaus, *William Keith, The Man and the Artist* (1938); Charles A. Barker, *Henry George* (1955); John W. Caughey, *Hubert Howe Bancroft* (1946); Robert W. Righter, "Theodore Henry Hittell: California Historian," *Southern California Quarterly* (1966), and "Theodore H. Hittell and Hubert H. Bancroft," *California Historical Quarterly* (1971); Claude R. Petty, "John S. Hittell and the Gospel of California," *Pacific Historical Review* (1955); Earl Pomeroy, "Josiah Royce, Historian in Quest of Community," *Pacific Historical Review* (1971); Robert V. Hine, *Josiah Royce: From Grass Valley to Harvard* (1992).

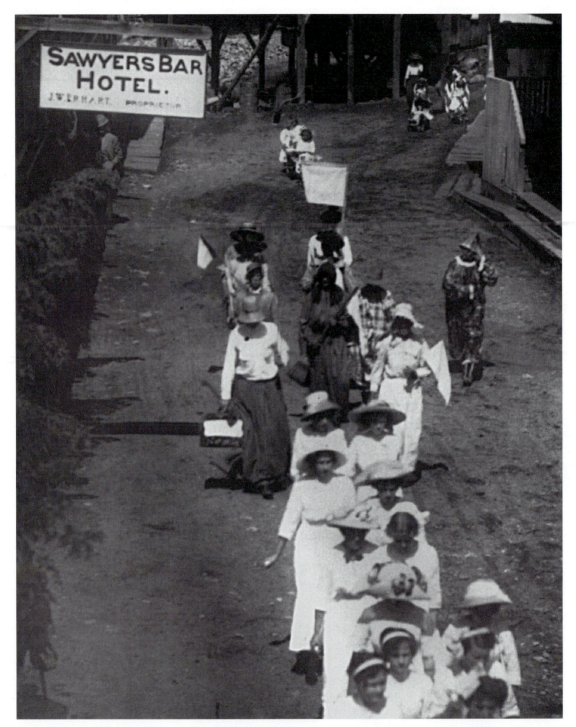

Suffragettes Marching, circa 1910, in the northern mining town of Sawyer's Bar, with Heckler in Clown Suit.
Progressive Era reforms were not the sole province of big-city professionals. Reform ideas and the controversy they
provoked spread into California's most remote communities. *Courtesy of James Rock, Klamath National Forest.*

PART SIX

CALIFORNIA AND THE NATION, 1880–1920

Much of the written history of California reinforces the late Carey McWilliams's assertion that the state has been "the great exception." In many ways, California was—and indeed is—unique. Yet it has also been intimately involved with the nation's history, even in the gold rush decades but particularly during the years that followed the Civil War and the completion of the transcontinental railway. Throughout the Civil War, most Californians remained essentially loyal to the Union, and by the time the railroad ended their isolation the state was a microcosm of the nation firmly planted on the Pacific Slope.

During subsequent decades California came to resemble the rest of the nation even more closely. Economic transformations, including the rise of industry and the emergence of new forms of corporate organization that accompanied it, paralleled changes occurring elsewhere. Throughout the last decades of the nineteenth century the state—like the nation—endured cyclic depressions, socioeconomic dislocations, and labor strife. The simultaneous process of urbanization accelerated the growth of San Francisco and spawned another instant city, Los Angeles. It also brought to the state problems of political tension and social adjustment similar to those experienced in longer-established cities.

Indeed, by the time Chris Buckley assumed his position as the "Blind Boss" of the Democratic party in San Francisco and California in 1882, the thirty-first state was no longer a frontier province but an important element in the nation's history. It experienced the growing pains of urbanization and industrialization and episodes such as the farmers' revolt that produced the Populist movement concurrently with the rest of the nation—not a decade or more later, as some have argued. Patterns of parallel historical development continued during the first decades of the twentieth century, as individuals calling themselves progressives sought to implement new social and political understandings that were compatible with economic and technological transformations in both the state and the nation.

EADWEARD MUYBRIDGE
Photographer of the City

In 1849 California began to attract practitioners of the art of photography, invented just a decade earlier. The first were itinerants who traveled the state making daguerreotype and tintype portraits and producing stereoscopic views, even in very remote regions. Later arrivals established studios, but they too remained wanderers. Carleton E. Watkins made some of the earliest images of Yosemite Valley, Alfred A. Hart documented the construction of the transcontinental railway, Adam Clark Vroman photographed the remains of deteriorating missions and Indian life in southern California and the Southwest, and Arnold Genthe recorded life in San Francisco's Chinatown before the earthquake of 1906. Among the most influential members of California's nineteenth-century photographic corps was "Helios," the eccentric English-born Eadweard James Muybridge.

Muybridge first pointed his camera northeastward across the city and beyond Yerba Buena Island to the Contra Costa ("opposite shore"). The Appraisers Building, the Montgomery Block, and other commercial establishments dominate the center of the photograph. California Street, with cable car tracks in place and St. Mary's Church at the right center, descends Nob Hill. In the lower left is Leland Stanford's stable, complete with mahogany stalls and crystal chandeliers, nestled against working-class residences.

The second view looks eastward across the roof of Stanford's mansion toward the busy waterfront. Grace Cathedral occupies the middle left on California Street, with the Wells Fargo building two blocks beyond. The ornate tower of the San Francisco Merchants' Exchange is seen in the center of the photograph; beyond it to the right is the Occidental Hotel. Smoke emerging from the the South-of-Market-Street districts testifies to a developing manufacturing economy.

EADWEARD MUYBRIDGE (continued)
Photographer of the City

Muybridge settled in San Francisco in 1855 when he was twenty-five years old and began his photographic career in 1867. He traveled into the field, often in his horse-drawn "Flying Studio," to make pictures of Yosemite, Alaska, Modoc War sites, and Central America. He also devised an ingenious system of cameras and trip-wires to settle Leland Stanford's wager that all four of a horse's hooves leave the ground simultaneously during its stride. During the 1880s, Muybridge's technique took him to the University of Pennsylvania where he conducted and published extensive studies of human and animal locomotion. His finding not only revolutionized artists' representation of moving people and animals but also laid the foundation for motion picture technology.

In 1894, poor health forced Muybridge to return to England where he died ten years later. Before he left San Francisco, however, he created a remarkable and informative historical document. In 1878 he poised his 18-by-24-inch glass-plate camera on the roof

William Ralston's Palace Hotel (*center*) on Market Street dwarfs the adjacent Grand Hotel to the right in the scene east-southeast of Nob Hill. Built in 1875 at a cost of $5 million, the seven-story Palace provided luxurious accommodations for 2,400 guests. Beyond Market Street are the city's factory tenement districts surrounding the once elegant Rincon Hill neighborhood and the mouth of China Basin.

Churches furnish landmarks in Muybridge's view to the southeast: Temple Emanu-El on Sutter Street with its Byzantine steeples (*left foreground*), the rear of St. Patrick's Church on Mission Street (*left center*), and Trinity Episcopal Church on Powell Street (*right center*). Beyond the city are more of China Basin and, in the distance, Mission Bay; both have been filled to provide more space for urban expansion.

EADWEARD MUYBRIDGE (continued)
Photographer of the City

of Mark Hopkins's mansion atop Nob Hill. From his vantage point, he made a series of thirteen photographs of the growing and diverse city. In Muybridge's panorama business establishments, factories, elegant houses, tenements, and hotels have replaced the ramshackle village on a mudflat that occupied the spot barely a generation before. Selections from his series provide a 180-degree view of the busiest, most densely populated half of the city. The virtual absence of people, animals, and vehicles in his images resulted from the extremely long exposures required by the wet plates used in his mammoth camera; only stationary objects could be recorded. (WAB)

A southerly view of the city records the extent of its growth and the variety of land use within its boundaries in 1878. To the left of center at Powell Street at Market is the Baldwin Hotel and Theater, built in 1872 at a cost of $2 million by Elias "Lucky" Baldwin but destroyed by fire in 1898. Just beyond the hotel are the twin chimneys of the U.S. Mint. The First Congregational Church on Mason Street occupies the center of the photograph. The foreground and background provide additional evidence of growing congestion and industrial development.

When Muybridge turned his camera to the southwest, he recorded evidence of urban maturity. Sherith Israel Synagogue stands at the center of his picture, and Market Street, making its way into still-unsettled hills, bisects it at the top. On the far side of Market, the Industrial Pavilion, an exhibition hall, nears completion with Woodward's Gardens, the city's most popular amusement park barely visible just beyond. Across Market from the Pavilion is the new City Hall; begun in 1872 and completed in 1897, it was destroyed by earthquake and fire in 1906. Many of the buildings seen in these selections suffered the same fate.

Photographs courtesy of the Cecil H. Greene Library, Department of Special Collections, Stanford University.

CHAPTER SIXTEEN

SAN FRANCISCO'S BLIND BOSS

During the final decades of the nineteenth century, dramatic change was everywhere apparent in the nation but nowhere more evident or tangible than in urban America. Revolutionary innovations in power, construction, and transportation technology transformed cities' landscapes; new residents—including migrants from rural America and immigrants from overseas—swelled and diversified their populations. Within a generation, the familiar walking city, often called "the village writ large," virtually disappeared, to be supplanted by an unfamiliar, potentially anonymous social and economic setting: the industrial city. Some things, however, changed little, among them the traditional understandings that provided the underpinnings for administering urban societies. In the political vacuum that ensued, uniquely American phenomena emerged: city bosses and their machines. In United States history, the exemplar of the process was William Marcy Tweed of New York City; in California it was Chris Buckley, the Blind Boss of San Francisco.

Before the sun's first rays penetrated San Francisco's morning fog on April 24, 1922, prominent men and women began to arrive at the stately home at 2220 Clay Street. Individually and in small groups they came: city officials, judges, physicians, attorneys, financiers, and socialites. They filed across the ornate portico and into a richly paneled parlor, paused to pay last respects before the open casket, and offered condolences to a grieving widow and her only son. Later, several hundred of the city's elite joined the funeral cortege to nearby Saint Dominic's Church where a cross-section of urban society had already assembled. Following a Requiem Mass, mourners accompanied the coffin to Holy Cross Cemetery for the interment. Some in the crowd were merely curious, but most were not. For, as the family priest observed in a brief eulogy, "His friends are legion."

Residents of San Francisco in 1922 could recall no more universal expression of grief or respect for a departed citizen. Yet the man being honored had neither held nor sought public office. Nor was he a member of the city's glittering social set or otherwise prominent in local affairs at the time of his death. Instead, he was Christopher Augustine Buckley, the son of Irish immigrants, known during the 1880s as the "Blind Boss of San Francisco." At the peak of his political

Christopher Augustine Buckley, the Blind Boss of San Francisco
Collection of William A. Bullough.

and even felonious crime. When he died, however, the same journals conferred only praise on him. Indeed, even Michel De Young's consistently hostile *Chronicle* lauded his charity, described his regime as "a kindly, just and generous dispensation" and concluded that "The passing of the great leader will be a tragedy to many who were aided by him in time of need."

The man who inspired such extremes of criticism and praise was born in New York City in 1845 and arrived in San Francisco with his parents in 1862. His father, John, a skilled stone mason, found employment in the numerous construction projects under way in the city during the 1860s. Young Chris secured his first job as a ticket-taker for the South Park and North Beach Street Railway Company, a horsecar line that wound its way from the Latin Quarter in the north end, traversed Montgomery Street's business and entertainment districts and adjacent residential areas, and terminated in the elite neighborhoods on Rincon Hill and in South Park. The months spent on the horsecars taught him much about the city and its varied population.

Like his young contemporaries in San Francisco, however, Chris was restless. In his memoirs, he recalled that

> it was the laudable ambition of aspiring youth [including himself] to secure a portfolio as a mixologist in one of the great saloons of the city, not so much for the sake of the salary but for the opportunity of meeting the great in their hours of relaxation and good humor, whereby connections were possible that often proved stepping stones to fortune.*

career, he was the major force in Democratic politics in the city. He made and unmade mayors, governors, and senators. He influenced state affairs and counseled a president on the distribution of federal patronage in California. He attracted the attention of Rudyard Kipling, Robert Louis Stevenson, and Ambrose Bierce, who vilified him as "what men call a crook" and worse. The local Chinese called him *maang paak gwai* (blind pale spirit), and the city's newspapers routinely accused him of bribery, corruption,

---

* Unless otherwise indicated, all quotations are from "The Reminiscences of Christopher A. Buckley," San Francisco *Bulletin* (31 August–9 October 1918, 23 December 1918–5 February 1919) and "Martin Kelly's Story," San Francisco *Bulletin* (1 September–26 November 1917).

Buckley made his first connections behind the elegant sixty-five-foot-long bar in The Snug Saloon, located in the basement of Tom Maguire's Opera House at the corner of Washington and Montgomery Streets. It was then the

> clearing house of all Bohemia, the favorite haunt of actors, artists, writers, journalists, and wits; of the great lawyers and other distinguished professionals; of stock brokers and financiers; of the beaux who existed in plenty.

There, the youth acquired not only his mixologist's portfolio, a "fine judgment of high-priced tobacco, a delicate taste for the rarest vintage, and a sincere love of good company," but also an introduction to his future profession—politics.

Tom Maguire and his partner, Tim McCarthy, provided early lessons, but Buckley's principal mentor was Republican boss Bill Higgins, a genial Irishman who controlled his party in San Francisco. To his young protégé Higgins imparted not partisan ideology or philosophy but more practical skills: organizing residents of waterfront boarding-houses, getting them to the polls on election days, and encouraging them to abide by the dictum "Vote early and vote often!" Buckley learned quickly, and Higgins soon came to regard him as a "handy man behind a ballot box." While acquiring his new knowledge at The Snug, he also made contacts that became important later in his career.

Despite The Snug's attractions, Buckley struck out on his own in 1866; with a partner he opened a saloon just around the corner from Maguire's establishment. But the enterprise did not flourish; disagreements with his partner and competition with better-known watering holes ended the venture, and early 1868 found Buckley back at The Snug, but in a new capacity. Maguire offered the twenty-two-year-old a partnership that he gladly accepted. Years later, Buckley recalled his reac-

tion: "I felt the dignity and the power of an independent prince."

Unfortunately, the triumph was only temporary. In 1864, William C. Ralston opened his Bank of California at California and Sansome Streets. He followed in 1869 with the luxurious California Theater on Bush Street and in 1870 with the magnificent Palace Hotel on Market Street. These and other developments shifted the focus of activity in San Francisco southward, away from the neighborhood of Maguire's Opera House and The Snug. In addition, in mid-1870 Ralston influenced state and city governments to approve a new street, one heading northwest from the intersection of Montgomery and Washington streets to North Beach. Thus, Maguire's enterprises were being threatened both economically and physically. Indeed, in 1871 the Opera House was razed to open the way for the new thoroughfare, Montgomery Boulevard (now Columbus Avenue).

But even earlier Chris Buckley had made his own decision to leave The Snug and San Francisco, and Maguire's declining fortunes were only part of the reason. Throughout the later 1860s, acute railroad fever gripped California, and towns competed with one another, seeking to become the Pacific terminus of the transcontinental route. Oakland vied with San Francisco in 1869 and won, while Vallejo challenged them both and lost. In 1870, rumors began to circulate, suggesting that the Big Four intended to confer a secondary prize on Vallejo, which had access to the interior by land and sea, the potential for a deep-water port, and far fewer fog problems than either of its rivals. The result was a land boom on the Carquinez Strait. By the spring of 1871, eager speculators flocked to the town, hoping to get rich. Among them were John and Christopher Buckley.

Neither father nor son invested in real estate. Instead, John Buckley plied his trade in the local building boom, and Chris did what

Maguire's Opera House
Maguire's Opera House stood at the corner of Washington and Montgomery streets until the city razed it to make way for a new thoroughfare, Montgomery Avenue (now Columbus Avenue) in 1871. At the lower right is the entrance to The Snug Saloon and a sign that proclaims "Buckley," confirming the Blind Boss's claim to partnership in the establishment while he was still in his twenties. *Courtesy of the Bancroft Library.*

he knew best: he and a partner opened the X-Change Saloon on the teeming waterfront. He then affiliated with the Solano County Republican Committee and helped to organize a volunteer fire unit, Engine Company No. Two, which dabbled in politics as often as it doused flames. In addition, federal positions at the Mare Island Navy Yard provided the younger Buckley with experience in the fine art of distributing patronage. He also may have helped to design the infamous "tapeworm ticket" described by another of Bill Higgins' protégés, Buckley's

contemporary and Republican counterpart, Martin Kelly:

> [It was] used in a general election in Vallejo and voted by a thousand or more employes [sic] of the navy yard. [It] was printed in "diamond" type, . . . the smallest size in use, only legible by the keen-eyed without a microscope, while the margin was cut down to almost nil. It was an air-tight, unscratchable ballot.

These were all valuable experiences for a budding young politico. Otherwise, however, the Vallejo interlude fell short of Buckley's expectations. The federal government curtailed activity at the Navy Yard and floods wiped out railroad links with Sacramento, which the Big Four decided not to rebuild. Then, in 1873, the railroad closed its repair yard in the town and transferred its corporate headquarters to San Francisco, bringing Vallejo's romance with the rails to an end. Land values and population declined as rapidly as they had risen, and in the spring Chris Buckley joined the exodus, leaving his partner with the X-Change Saloon and Solano County with a $6.75 bill for delinquent taxes.

Back in San Francisco, Buckley opened yet another saloon at the corner of Bush and Kearny Streets, near the California Theater. At about the same time, two significant changes occurred in his life. First, he became a Democrat and began close associations with Al Fritz, captain of the Gatling Gun Battery (A Company, 2nd Artillery Battalion of the state militia) and boss of the city Democratic party, and with Sam Rainey, master of Democratic politics in the city's volunteer fire companies. Second, he went blind. The affliction might have ended his political career, but he compensated by developing uncanny abilities that allowed him to memorize city ordinances, contracts, and other documents after having them read to him, to recognize individuals by voice or handclasp, and to resume conversations even following extended interruptions. Although his blindness was nearly complete by the mid-1870s, Buckley remained active in Democratic affairs throughout the decade and advanced through the ranks of the partisan organization.

After successful campaigns in 1875 and 1877, which included electing Andrew Jackson Bryant to two terms as mayor, dark days followed for Buckley and his allies. Denis Kearney's anti-Chinese tirades and economic demagoguery severely depleted both major parties as constituents defected to the Work-

ingmen's Party of California (WPC). The local Democracy, however, was hardest hit. Indeed, by the end of the 1870s "scarce a grease-spot was left to mark its place." Out of a voting power of about 22,000 it had dwindled away to less than 3,000, "a most pitiful faction at best." Desertions to the WPC resulted in a debacle in 1880; in that year's election, no San Francisco Democrat captured a city, county, or state office. The rout was complete, and a disenchanted Buckley left the city once again, this time "to take a long vacation in the southland, determined to let politics and politicians take care of themselves thereafter."

He was not finished with politics, however; nor were politicians finished with him. The disaster of 1880 convinced Democratic leaders that the party's revival in San Francisco demanded complete and immediate reorganization; by then, too, Buckley's familiarity with the city and political expertise were well established. In addition, popular issues, properly exploited, promised Democratic success in 1882. Internal divisions and returning prosperity reduced the appeal of the WPC, and prodigal Democrats were ripe to return to the fold. Anti-Chinese agitation continued, and demands for a federal exclusion law increased. Following the Mussel Slough tragedy and exposés of the Central Pacific's arrogant refusal to pay taxes since 1879, public clamor for regulation of "The Octopus" intensified. Strife between farmers and miners over hydraulic debris intensified, and renewed enforcement of the state's dormant Sunday-closing law provided yet another controversy that could breathe new life into the local Democracy.

For Buckley, fate also intervened. Martin Kelly recalled that in May 1881 the life of Al Fritz came to an end "in a strange and tragic way":

He was found dead in his own home, hung by the neck, with handcuffs on his wrists and his feet manacled. Fritz was an odd but not uncommon type of man. He was strong limbed and strong willed, affable, generous and magnetic in the ordinary contacts of life, but a holy terror when it came to a downright fight. . . . The passionate side of his nature was serious enough when he was cold sober. In drink he was dangerous to friend and foe alike. Because of numerous wild outbreaks when in his cups Fritz had been in the habit for some time, when he reached a certain point of intoxication, to drive home hurriedly in a hack and have his wife handcuff him and adjust an Oregon boot so that he might not stray off again to the cocktail route. . . . [A]ccording to the statement of Mrs. Fritz on the day of his death he had come home intoxicated. She had manacled him as usual and had gone out. When she returned he was dead.

Even though chains immobilized Fritz, a coroner's jury ruled that his demise was either an accident or suicide. Consequently, "there were strange stories whispered concerning the manner of his death" in San Francisco.

Among Fritz's friends and political allies, his death produced both sorrow and an unseemly scramble for his position in the party. In December 1881, however, Democratic leaders ended the competition. Eager to capitalize on opportunities presented by railroad controversy and other issues, they formed the Committee of Fifty on Reorganization, which enlisted Chris Buckley to revive the party. Success or failure in the "noble rescue work," he knew, depended on appropriate responses to conditions existing in the city.

Particularly important was the lawless, unregulated system of partisan activity typical of San Francisco and most other U.S. cities during the nineteenth century. Buckley observed that municipal politics was a "go-as-you-please affair." Martin Kelly was more specific:

To realize how the old-time boss of San Francisco rose to absolutism, . . . one must bear in mind that the early election laws of California bordered on the primitive. For instance, there was no enrollment of voters, no printed great register, during the first thirty years of the State's history. This enabled wagonloads of repeaters to swing around the circle from polling place to polling place. . . . All the crews of deepwater ships happening to be in the harbor on election day voted. . . . Once a boss [Buckley] voted the full crews of two visiting French men-of-war.

The real conduct of affairs was left exclusively to the political organizations— the State and county committees. Each party printed its own ballots. . . . [and] chose a different tint to prevent the inclination of unreasonable voters to scratch their tickets. The margins were left so small that it was a feat of penmanship to write in a new name. . . .

Up to the time of [the adoption of the Australian secret ballot in 1891], an ordinary voter . . . had no protection at all. He was seized upon by contending bands of political highbinders, who often waged severe battle over him in an effort to induce him to vote this or that rival ticket.

The law took no cognizance at all of primary elections. They were absolutely party affairs and arranged by the all-powerful county committees. These named the time, place and hours for holding primaries. The places as a rule were inconvenient, the hours short and impossible for [general] participation. . . . Thus were delegates chosen to conventions where candidates for high office were nominated and those of one party or the other elected at the polls.

The system, quite simply, meant that those who controlled partisan organizations also controlled nominating conventions and thereby determined voters' choices. False-bottom ballot boxes, polling places reached by rickety ladders, and bogus tickets helped to insure victory. If these devices were not sufficient, there were the parties' foot-soldiers who manned the polls, the "push," whom Buckley characterized as:

> the boys of the bejasus order, with the spring-bottom pants, who rivaled Orpheus on the concertina, who chanted that most moving of all songs, "Big Horse, I Love You," in one breath and unlimbered their awful battlecry in the next. . . .

With them around, municipal politics certainly was "not a branch of the Sunday school business."

There were other hazards as well. Since partisan organizations lacked legal definition:

> any group of cheap skates could assemble in a back room, create a sham party with a high sounding name, and claim to have four or five thousand voters. . . . With this for an asset, the head manipulators could sally forth and mace candidates of the regular parties out of large sums of money for nominations or endorsements. These were the famous "piece clubs" of long ago.

And, to further confuse an already chaotic situation:

> A general election day was also the occasion of a general riot and a general drunk. Saloons were opened all the previous night, and most of the electors showed up with a hold-over. All day long the saloons were wide open and liquor practically free.

Occasionally, miracles occurred; more than once, residents of city cemeteries turned out to exercise their franchise.

The obsolescence of municipal government also complicated matters. Like other American cities of the period, San Francisco had outgrown its political system. The Consolidation Act of 1856, a reasonably progressive city charter for its time, was designed for a community of some 30,000 residents. The organic law restricted municipal govern-

ment to a few basic functions. It granted limited authority to the mayor and vested real governmental power in a Board of Supervisors. The board, composed of a representative elected from each of the city's twelve wards, made most major decisions, awarded franchises to utility companies and others doing business in and with the city, and had the final word in employment and personnel matters.

After 1856, the city grew and changed dramatically, and each novel situation—such as new forms of power on street railways or growth in the school population—demanded a revision of the charter. This, in turn, usually required the consent of state legislators, a process that resulted in a maze of often-contradictory laws, amendments, and ordinances. Indeed, when the city codified the Consolidation Act twenty years after its adoption, the effort produced a volume of more than 250 pages, just 13 of them containing the original document.

Such conditions, of course, provided unethical politicos with rampant opportunity for manipulation, but they also affected the general populace. Municipal employees—from street cleaners to police to school teachers to department heads—found their jobs in jeopardy with every change of administration. Real needs in an expanding city—sanitation, public health facilities, new streets, and more—were neglected because of lack of authority or interest. Those in difficulty—fire victims, the ill, the aged, or the unemployed—found no official agencies to provide relief or assistance. At the other end of the scale—whether they sought licenses to operate, clarification of tax assessments, confirmation of real estate titles, or contracts with the city—members of the business community faced a maze of red tape and a wall of recalcitrant officials. An entrepreneur interested in transportation or utility franchises confronted an additional obstacle; state and city laws required the annual renegotiation of all such permits. In short, the Consolidation Act was inadequate for governing a growing, changing city.

During the 1870s, San Franciscans who recognized the defects of the 1856 act attempted on several occasions to ordain a new charter. They failed, however, and in 1880 an industrial city of 234,000 residents still functioned (or misfunctioned) under a governmental system devised for a relatively small town.

Buckley understood the city's problems, but he did not advocate changes in the laws. Instead, he responded in ways that benefited his party and himself. Following the appeal of the Committee of Fifty, he began by organizing forty-seven Democratic clubs in neighborhoods throughout the city. The clubs' principal functions were partisan: enrolling Democratic voters, selecting representatives to the party's County Committee, conducting primary elections to choose delegates to nominating conventions, and getting out the vote in general elections. Buckley ensured party loyalty by installing reliable followers—often called his "Lambs"—in the principal positions in each neighborhood and using able lieutenants such as Sam Rainey to oversee their general operation. In this way, he capitalized on the unregulated nature of partisan affairs in the city.

Without members (voters), however, even the most efficient organization could not succeed, and in his approach to this problem Buckley again demonstrated his understanding of the city and its people. He knew that club meetings held to debate party ideology would neither attract nor retain a constituency. He also recognized that the masses of voters to whom his party must appeal—principally members of the working classes—sought both sociability and recognition. Therefore, the clubs became social institutions where "Clam bakes, bull-head break-

Chris Buckley in Volunteer Fireman's Uniform
Volunteer fire companies were important components in the political life of nineteenth-century American cities. Here, probably in about 1875, Chris Buckley appears in the uniform of one of San Francisco's many fire-fighting units. *Collection of William A. Bullough.*

fasts, and the like, followed each other in perpetual succession." In addition, families of members took excursions across the bay to Oakland, and the young attended dances at club headquarters. Buckley also tried to provide "some kind of dignity" to his constituents by ensuring that each club had so many officers that "it was indeed an unlucky member who could not boast that he held down some kind of official station."

Buckley also recognized the more practical concerns of the urban masses. In the nineteenth-century city, few agencies existed to respond to the crises of everyday life, and here again the Democratic clubs took up the slack. They might provide a member with funds to tide his family over after a fire, with legal advice in a brush with the law, or with a decent wedding for a daughter or funeral for a parent. A club also was forced:

> to be an employment agency on the most wholesale scale possible. [It] had to explore every avenue and blind alley in search of an opportunity whereby a good fellow could gather in a few simoleons without overtaxing his strength.

When in power, the party could tap patronage jobs on the public payroll; otherwise, the task was more difficult. Nevertheless, "By hook or by crook, it was so managed that practically every member of the various clubs . . . had some occasion to be glad" of his affiliation with the rejuvenated Democracy.

The rebuilding effort required a great deal of money, which was "subscribed by various men of the highest character in the city." These were the "top-notchers—bankers, noted lawyers and other professionals, big men in the business world, captains of industry and the like." According to Buckley, their "sole impulses were party spirit . . . and a sincere hope for better government."

Actually, much more was involved—notably the potential for profit by doing business in or with the city. Economic opportunity abounded in growing nineteenth-century cities such as San Francisco, particularly in transportation and utility enterprises, as Martin Kelly observed:

> It was a most happy coincidence. . . . The people wanted better . . . facilities for the rapidly expanding city. The capitalists were falling over each other to get into the game. And we [politicians] were masters of the game. . . .
> [U]nder former laws, franchises of all

kinds were free gifts, given away by boards of supervisors. . . . No legal provision whatever existed for the sale of a franchise or for competitive bidding, or for participation by the public in the profits. . . . Often these franchises yielded millions to the beneficiaries. We, the bosses, were the distributors of these good things. When men of wealth came to us for gifts which meant golden fortunes for themselves, does any fool suppose that we didn't ask for a modest "cut"? Of course we did. Was it not equitable and just?

"Equitable and just" perhaps, but not always "modest." On one occasion, for example, Spring Valley Water Co. and California Electric Co. paid Buckley $125,000 for franchises to operate for a single year. No wonder a nostalgic Kelly reminisced in 1917: "Would that we had [the promoters] by the wind pipe again."

Not only utilities, but also printing companies, real estate interests, building contractors, and more paid willingly for the services that would expedite their projects and cut through the confusion at City Hall. Indeed, "it was surprising to see how universal was the desire among men of substance, firms and corporations, to get on the right side of politics." They made their way to Buckley's tiny office at the rear of his Alhambra Saloon on Bush Street to make appropriate contributions to the Democratic reorganization program. Willingness to invest substantial amounts on the mere promise of success confirmed the potential for profit in the city, confidence in Buckley, and his own self-evaluation: "I placed a stiff value on my services and always rated myself as a high-priced man."

As professionals, bosses such as Buckley retained part of the contributions in payment for their services. More money, however, was reserved to keep municipal officials cooperative, and more yet went into party coffers to fund the organization itself. It was an effective system based on conditions in the city. Neighborhood clubs responded to the needs of a vast constituency and provided a mass of loyal voters. Dependable lieutenants controlled the clubs for the County Committee, assuring a reliable delegation at municipal conventions that determined the voters' choices. And business interests furnished the financing in order to attain their own ends. Results of the election of 1882 demonstrated just how effective the system could be; the previously defunct Democrats swept nearly every city, county, and state office. Michel De Young's *Chronicle* summarized the consequences in a succinct headline: "Buckley Is Boss."

Subsequent victories at the polls—although not always so complete—and refinements in the machine allowed him to maintain his position for the remainder of the 1880s. The number of clubs increased as Democratic registrations warranted, and their functions changed in response to changing memberships. But the real key to success remained the same: only winning on election days allowed the machine to continue functioning.

For one thing, electing municipal officials such as police chief, school superintendent, or public health officer gave the Blind Boss's organization the patronage of those offices and jobs to distribute among the faithful. His father, for example, found a place in the street department and his nephew a position on the police force. The city and county had about 1,700 employees in the 1880s, providing the party faithful with ample opportunity to "gather in a few simoleons."

Victory also assured continued financial support. The charter provided that all actions of municipal government—including city ordinances, franchise and contract awards, and personnel decisions—receive approval of a majority ("Solid Seven") of the Board of Supervisors and of the mayor. Without a cooperative chief executive, a "Solid Nine" supervisors were imperative to override potential vetoes. Buckley managed to maintain one combination or the other during all but a single administration until 1890, but even then he controlled enough elected department heads to assure access to patronage and keep the machine afloat.

Some actions of Buckley boards benefited the city and its people. Employment was critical, as were expanded transportation and utility services and improvements to Golden Gate Park, the new City Hall, streets, sanitation, and other public facilities. In other instances, contracts or franchises were outright frauds. One contingent of real estate speculators, for example, formed a street railway company and applied for a permit to operate. When Mayor Edward B. Pond vetoed the project, a well-disciplined "Solid Nine" supervisors overrode him. Trolleys never ran on the proposed route, nor were they intended to. The sole purpose of the railway company was to increase land values in the vicinity of the mythical rails.

Whether projects were beneficial, fraudulent, or simply opportunistic, eager entrepreneurs paid the Blind Boss handsomely to expedite them. So too did candidates eager for political office, whose contributions usually involved pledges of patronage rather than cash. Through the clubs, Buckley controlled municipal nominating conventions that placed names on the party's tickets, and nomination was tantamount to election. In addition, local conventions—not the State Central Committee, which was "largely an ornamental body"—chose candidates for the legislature. Because the San Francisco delegation to state nominating conventions represented more than twenty-five percent of the population of California, the Blind Boss also influenced the selection of aspirants for governor, supreme court justice, and similar statewide offices and the general policies of his party. At the 1884 Democratic convention, he joined other anti-monopolists to banish pro-railroad Democrats from the organization. During the same year, he supported the judicial actions that upheld the state's Anti-Debris Act of 1880. Three years later, his help furthered George Hearst's ambition to become a U.S. Senator. When Stephen Mallory White of Los Angeles began his political career, he sought Buckley's assistance, and Washington Bartlett became mayor of San Francisco and governor of California with Buckley's support. The Blind Boss also used his influence to keep peace between "city" (San Francisco) and "hayseed" (the rest of the state) Democrats and avoid potentially disastrous controversies.

Despite constant allegations from hostile journalists, Buckley did not encourage the ambitions of political "hacks," incompetents, or mediocrities. Hacks and incompetents could not be trusted and could embarrass the party; mediocrities could not win. Therefore, he considered candidates carefully and not solely their contributions, tangible or otherwise, to the party and placed successful middle-echelon businessmen and professionals and other familiar, respected figures on Democratic tickets. He also recognized ethnic groups in the city, but despite editorial complaints about "too many O's and Mc's" on the tickets, his choices were not all Irish. Indeed, on occasion the Blind Boss promoted candidates with multiple appeals. Raphael Weill, for example, was a French Jew with important social connections who owned the popular White House dry goods chain; he served several terms on the board of education with sufficient distinction to have a city school named after him.

Shrewd intelligence, canny judgment, a sense of proportion, and intimate familiarity with the city and its people allowed the boss to sustain his authority through the 1880s and increase his personal wealth, frequently on the basis of information gleaned from political connections: "I had opportunities—certainties, you might say." Investments in real estate in San Francisco, Los Angeles, and elsewhere, in utility and railroad bonds, and in other ventures all proved highly profitable, and by the mid-1880s Buckley assumed the manners and demeanor of a polished gentleman, described by a political enemy in 1889:

> [A]ided by a sound and logical brain, he is no mean lawyer and can discuss decisions and quote authorities with the best of them. He rarely uses profane language and has acquired a suave and polished address, such as properly belongs to one of much travel and refinement. Always carefully dressed in the very extreme of fashion, with a lithe, erect person, he looks one full in the face with his large sightless orbs beneath his smooth and serene forehead, and seems to be all innocence and candor. He wears no beard and his dark mustache covers a firm mouth, and [he has] a face beaming with intelligence. . . . He speaks with a perfectly distinct and pleasant intonation and in a low tone. . . . He is quite youthful in appearance, and looks in fact, as he goes along the street, arm in arm with his companion [usually former prize fighter Alex Greggains], like a quiet, gentlemanly swell of about thirty-five.

It was an accurate portrayal, except that the Blind Boss was closer to forty-five years old at the time.

In 1886, Buckley sold the Alhambra Saloon and abandoned his tiny office there in favor of the elegant Manhattan Club on Nob Hill and more sophisticated companions. Simultaneously, he married a Boston socialite and purchased a large home in the exclusive, suburban Western Addition. About a year later, he acquired a country estate,

Ravenswood, in the Livermore Valley and began to spend much of his time there or on excursions abroad, prompting one Lamb, possibly Sam Rainey, to complain that:

> For the last year [the boss] has not paid as close attention to the minor details of politics as he should have. You hear a great deal of grumbling . . . that [he] does not pay as much attention to his old friends as he used to. The ward workers say they can't go and talk to him now.

For a political boss, such negligence could spell disaster. It became especially perilous late in the 1880s, for power and personal leadership made not only loyal friends but also persistent enemies. From 1886 onward, he was frequently in court responding to a variety of complaints. A pair of disappointed contractors, for example, initiated legal action that brought the boss before the state supreme court charged with contempt. In another instance, political rivals in southern California accused him of running a gambling operation in Los Angeles, at the very time that the Democratic state convention assembled there. In that action, Stephen Mallory White served as the boss's attorney, and he was acquitted. In numerous other cases, Buckley was cleared or charges were dismissed, but the episodes provided clear evidence of animosity toward him.

Power also produced malcontents within his own San Francisco organization. When he denied a nomination, he inevitably gained another foe ("soreheads," he called them). The Blind Boss, for example, enthusiastically supported the election of William T. Wallace to the superior court bench. Later, in 1890:

> the great jurist, . . . asked me to swing the San Francisco delegation [to the state convention] in his favor as candidate for Chief Justice. Without going into any details whatever, I didn't. . . . [He] became my unre-

lenting enemy, never for a moment forgetting the real or fancied wrong.

> Also, I had nominated and elected as State Senator an ambitious young man of wealth [Jeremiah Lynch]. When his term expired he wanted to climb higher. . . . He asked me to nominate him for member of Congress from his district. I couldn't. The organization had been pledged to another applicant.

Another sorehead was made, but not the only one:

> [A] clever young man from the northern part of the State [Barclay Henley], who had served two terms in Congress, likewise wished to climb higher. . . . [T]his person came to me and asked for my influence to elect him United States Senator. By all the rules of the game, another man was entitled to the high honor. . . . Thus another name was added to my ever-lengthening catalogue of enemies.
>
> And fourthly, a young man of affairs [Henry H. Scott], . . . asked me, in 1888, for the nomination for sheriff. But to have done this would have been an act of bad faith to another man and would have almost disrupted the Democratic organization. . . . [He], like the others, became a watchful enemy.

As the decade progressed, more disgruntled office-seekers added their names to the list of Buckley's antagonists, joined by disappointed entrepreneurs and by several ambitious younger Democrats on the way up. Among them was Gavin McNab, who wanted to assume the boss's mantle himself, and the wealthy James Duval Phelan who had his sights set on the mayor's office and the U.S. Senate. Buckley was a natural target for the barrages of Republican journals in San Francisco and throughout the state, and when William Randolph Hearst received the *Examiner* as a gift from his father in 1887, that Democratic daily joined the attack.

During the campaign of 1890, forces of opposition coalesced in the Reform Democracy, a faction of the boss's own party. In that election, San Francisco and California Democrats experienced a disaster equaling the debacle of 1880. Part of the problem was Buckley's lack of attention and mismanagement, but the split within the party also contributed to defeat. In addition, the political composition of the state had shifted, particularly after the "Boom of the '80s," which brought many midwestern Republican voters to southern California. Nevertheless, the blame was placed on the shoulders of the Blind Boss, and his now-organized enemies agreed with the conclusion of Stephen Mallory White: "Buckley must go."

While others licked their wounds after the defeat of 1890, the Blind Boss went abroad. In his absence, momentous events took shape. Reform Democrats assumed control of the San Francisco County Committee and, in alliance with Gavin McNab, dismantled the machine, including the clubs that had served Buckley and his constituents so well. At the same time, they mounted an investigation, ostensibly aimed at corruption in the city's delegation to the legislature. Soon, however, the true purpose became clear. In August 1891, Judge Wallace formed a grand jury to conduct an official probe. Instead of following the normal procedure—drawing from names submitted by all twelve of San Francisco's superior court judges—he halted the process after only a few names were extracted from the box, claiming that the slips were marked. Wallace then passed over the sheriff and coroner, whom the law said should impanel a jury under such circumstances, and appointed an elisor to complete the panel. The man chosen was Henry H. Scott.

The jurors that Scott selected and Wallace approved included nine members of the Reform Democracy. Barclay Henley served as

FAST IN THE FILTH OF THE PAST.

Unconvicted Felon Struggling to Escape From the Quagmire of His Own Crimes.

"Fast in the Filth of the Past"
By the end of the nineteenth century, the editorial cartoon had become a potent political weapon, and anything was fair game for the artist's pen, even the tragedy of blindness. In 1899, long after Buckley's political career was over, William Randolph Hearst's San Francisco *Examiner* continued to attack him at every opportunity. *Collection of William A. Bullough.*

the chairman of the jury, and he chose Jeremiah Lynch to head its committee investigating political abuses. In addition to the Reform Democrats, at least seven of the remaining ten jurors were active members of anti-boss (or anti-Buckley) clubs in the city. Still, after deliberating for two months and generating reams of editorial copy, the panel found only enough evidence to indict the boss on a single charge: accepting a bribe in a street railway scheme, at a time when he was abroad. The tactics were too blatant, and the California supreme court invalidated the indictment and the Wallace jury itself. Nevertheless, publicity related to the investigation discredited the Blind Boss and ended his political career. He did make several comeback attempts, notably in the municipal election of 1896, known as the "steam beer handicap." But the next thirty years he spent principally in San Francisco and "as a farmer in the beautiful Livermore Valley and always as a private citizen."

Buckley asserted that "After I retired from politics and devoted my mind entirely to business and investments, I learned for the first time what making money was," and his will validates the claim. Despite losing a six-story office building and an elegant home— neither of them insured—to the 1906 earthquake and fire, his estate totaled nearly $1 million—including treasury notes, railroad and utility bonds, and real estate holdings throughout California—and confirmed his persistent sympathetic instincts. Substantial bequests went to needy individuals and to organized charities that ranged from Catholic, Jewish, and Protestant orphanages to the San Francisco Association for the Blind. To his companion Alex Greggains, who was at his side when he died, he left $5,000.

That recipients of Chris Buckley's aid should attend his funeral presents no mystery. The presence of a host of political and business figures and even former enemies among the mourners, however, is more difficult to fathom. Perhaps passing years and nostalgia for an earlier, simpler age put his place in the history of the city in a different perspective. Or perhaps, even though, as Martin Kelly observed, "It is difficult to canonize a boss," many San Franciscans in 1922 were determined to try.

CHAPTER SEVENTEEN

BEGINNINGS OF MODERN CALIFORNIA

Although California's population increased at a slower rate than that of the nation at large during post–gold rush decades, its residents numbered 865,000 by 1880 and 1.5 million by 1900. The newcomers, along with the transcontinental railway, ended the state's seclusion from the rest of the nation. During the same decades, however, impressions of southern California as an alien frontier outpost, populated principally by outlaws, persisted. The opinion was uninformed, except in one sense: developments that bound the state to the nation before the 1880s occurred mainly in northern and central regions, leaving the south isolated and sparsely populated. During the turn-of-the-century decades, however, events integrated the entire state—not just a portion of it—with the nation and predicted southern California's ultimate rank among the most important and influential regions in the United States. At the same time, California men and women joined with other Americans in demanding change and reform.

SOUTHERN CALIFORNIA

When Chris Buckley arrived in San Francisco in 1862 and the city counted 56,000 inhabi-

tants, the entire population south of the Tehachapis barely surpassed 30,000. Mountain men and traders had visited southern California during the Hispanic periods, but few foreigners settled. Those who did, for all practical purposes, became californios themselves, and in 1846 a meager population of 1,200 made la ciudad (el pueblo until 1835) del río y valle de la reina de los ángeles de la porciúncula the largest settlement in the Mexican province. During the gold rush, the town was a way station for argonauts arriving by way of Mexico and southern overland routes; among them were a few individuals who gave Los Angeles and its environs an early reputation as a haven for outlaws (real and imagined) and made its calle de los negros one of the most notorious districts in the state.

Southern California's permanent residents hardly contributed to the region's notoriety. San Bernardino, settled by Mormons during the 1840s, was a stable farming community by the 1860s. Forty-Niner Elias J. ("Lucky") Baldwin invested in Los Angeles real estate and laid the foundation for one of the state's great fortunes. Along with future governor John G. Downey, Phineas Banning purchased part of the Domínguez rancho land and began to develop a port and the hamlet of San Pedro. A few rancheros prospered during the 1850s by selling beef to hungry gold-seekers, but the 1860s brought competitive southwestern cattle, declining local markets, severe droughts, uncertainty over land titles, and ruin to most. Not even increased demand sparked by the Civil War could save them, and their estates passed into the hands of *gringos:* sheepmen such as James Irvine in southern Los Angeles County, syndicates of wheat growers in the San Fernando Valley, vintners such as J. De Barth Shorb near San Gabriel, or speculators who carved rancho lands into plots to sell to farmers. Expansion continued, but relatively slowly. Los Angeles grew in population to 1,600 by 1850, 4,400 by 1860, and 5,700 by 1870. Only 2,300 people lived in San Diego in 1870, and just over 20,000 in all of the two huge counties.

The southern population remained heavily Hispanic, but most political and economic leaders were Americans, many of whom fell prey to the epidemic of railroad fever that infected the state during the 1850s. Hindsight makes the outcome of the resulting contest for rail connections and regional supremacy between Los Angeles and San Diego seem obvious, but as late as the 1860s it was not so apparent. Los Angeles remained an isolated village, located twenty miles from a mediocre port; by contrast, San Diego fronted a fine natural harbor and had superior access to the interior. Phineas Banning attempted to redress the imbalance by constructing a rail connection between Los Angeles and the coast, laying out the town of Wilmington, and improving the harbor. Still, many Angelenos conceded defeat, and most probably subscribed to the opinions expressed in an 1869 Los Angeles *Star* editorial:

> We are too far inland and have no reliable harbor in our country. We must be content to be the political and social capital of south California; we must be satisfied with our genial climate, our fruitful soil, our generous wines, our golden fruit, . . . [and] our cattle upon a thousand hills.

San Diego, the writer concluded, was destined to be the commercial center of the region.

San Diegans agreed. During the 1850s, when only a handful of settlers populated the place, owners of waterfront property urged Congress to adopt a southern route (favored by many in government) for a transcontinental railway and organized a local company to build a connecting link to the anticipated line. The Civil War and the Pacific Railway Act dashed their hopes, but peace revived them. Under the leadership of former Union general William S. Rosecrans, San Diegans entered into complex negotiations that eventually involved the federal government, John C. Frémont, Thomas A. Scott of the Pennsylvania Railroad, and the Central Pacific itself. In 1865, in collaboration with a syndicate of San Franciscans, they organized the Southern Pacific Railway Company to build a coastal route, but that firm fell under the control of the Big Four. Then, in 1871, Rosecrans and his San Diego associates formed the California Southern Coast Railway Company to link their city with the transcontinental rails. Neither their vigorous efforts nor those of less energetic Los Angeles rivals, however, determined the outcome of the competition.

During the 1870s, Los Angeles leaders such as John G. Downey became more optimistic about the town's future and eager to end its isolation. In 1872, they investigated possible ties with the Texas Pacific or Central Pacific, but Collis P. Huntington and his southern California agent, William P. Hyde,

Coronado Hotel and Balboa Park, San Diego
San Diego ultimately placed second in its rivalry with
Los Angeles during the 1870s and 1880s, but it, too,
became an important southern California city. Resorts
such as the luxurious Coronado Hotel *(top)*, built in
1887, introduced a thriving tourist industry. Economic
and cultural development continued, and by the early
1900s the city was ready to build beautiful Balboa Park
(left) to challenge San Francisco for the right to host
the Panama-Pacific Exposition of 1915. *Courtesy of the
Bancroft Library.*

actually dictated the course of events. Anxious to protect its monopoly in the state, the
Central Pacific was laying track for the Southern Pacific line, but not along the coast as
San Diegans had planned. Instead, the route
cut through the San Joaquin Valley and the
Mussel Slough country toward the two major
southeastern approaches to the state, Needles and Yuma. As the rails neared the
Tehachapis in 1876, Los Angeles interests resumed negotiations, and ultimately conceded to the corporation a $610,000 subsidy
from municipal funds, rights to Banning's
Los Angeles-San Pedro railway, and land for

a depot in the city. In return, the company built a fifty-mile link between the valley line and Los Angeles; its completion left San Diego isolated.

POPULATION: "THE ONE GREAT DESIDERATUM"

Until 1876, Los Angeles remained essentially a bucolic Hispanic *pueblo;* the rail connection began its transformation into a typical American city. Between 1870 and 1880, the population doubled to more than 11,000, while San Diego's increased by just 300 to 2,600. Other changes also became evident in the region. Cattlemen shifted from range-grazing to feed-lot operations, and vintners expanded their wine production. Louis Prévost and others organized the California Silk Association, and the California Cotton Growers and Manufacturers Association predicted things to come in the twentieth century when it planted 10,000 acres in cotton near Bakersfield and imported a community of black southerners to work the fields.

More promising than ill-fated experiments with silk and cotton was citrus production. Spanish padres had planted citrus crops in the region, but none was commercially important until the 1870s. Then it was discovered that the local climate and dry interior valley and coastal foothill soil could, with irrigation, provide ideal growing environments. Almost simultaneously, an orange variety called the Bahia navel (also known as the Washington navel because of the Department of Agriculture's role in its introduction) arrived from Brazil. In 1873, just two Bahia trees grew near Riverside; by the end of the 1880s, more than a million were producing throughout southern California. Earlier, in 1884, the state's oranges swept most of the prizes at an exhibition in New Or-

leans, and in 1886, 2,000 carloads of navels were shipped from the state.

Successful citrus agriculture, however, did not provide what southern California boosters regarded as "the one great desideratum" for their region's success—population—and during the 1870s they launched an aggressive advertising campaign to remedy the situation. Individual landowners traveled east to promote their tracts, but the Central Pacific, with its millions of acres to sell, took an early lead in the effort. Its land office commissioned numerous books and pamphlets touting southern California, where some of its available land was located. Charles Nordhoff's *California for Health, Pleasure and Residence* (1874) and B. C. Truman's *Homes and Happiness in the Golden State of California* (1883) typified the scores of widely distributed titles. The railroad also maintained emigrant cars and way stations to assist in relocation, offered credit arrangements for fares and land purchases, established employment agencies to lure prospective buyers and assist their settlement, and even provided translators for settlers recruited by agents in Europe. In addition, Californians formed statewide associations such as the California Immigrant Union and the Pacific Land Bureau to attract settlers, and the Los Angeles Board of Trade founded the Southern California Immigration Association to advertise their land as a "veritable sanitarium" offering health to the infirm and unlimited opportunity to the ambitious.

Results of their vigorous propaganda campaign disappointed Californians in general and southern Californians in particular. The population increased, but not at the dramatic rate that was both anticipated and deemed essential. Distance and cost inhibited response; with fertile land available at similar prices closer to home, easterners or midwesterners were reluctant to uproot families and undertake a long, expensive trip to California. Another problem involved competition; Oregon and other regions were more familiar, promoted themselves just as aggressively, and offered equally attractive inducements. Finally, the advertising campaign itself inhibited success: in graphic detail, booster literature depicted attributes of the life and land that southern Californians believed made their region "the greatest country on earth." But the arid landscape and peculiar agricultural systems described in the brochures seemed alien to many prospective migrants and not very conducive to permanent settlement.

THE "BOOM OF THE '80s"

External influences ultimately accomplished what local promoters could not achieve, and as usual the railroads were involved. During the 1880s, the Atchison, Topeka & Santa Fe extended its Arizona line to Needles, and it reached San Bernardino in 1885. The company then purchased several intrastate lines and entered Los Angeles in 1887, broke the monopoly of the Central Pacific (reorganized under Kentucky laws in 1884 and renamed the Southern Pacific) and precipitated a railroad rate war. The $125 fare between Kansas City and Los Angeles fell to half that, then to a fourth, then even lower, triggering the rather inaccurately named "Boom of the '80s" in southern California.

Boosters' promotional campaigns finally paid dividends. Thousands of farmers, health-seekers, and others who had read the literature and contemplated a visit or a move to the Golden State now seized the opportunity. Once in California, many skeptics changed their attitudes and decided to remain. Although Los Angeles was a small city, it did not appear backward. Permanent buildings, telephones, electric lights,

schools, and other amenities already were in place. Prosperous businesses and substantial homes lined broad streets, street railways provided transportation, and churches and civic associations functioned actively. The climate, too, lured settlers, as did apparently abundant land for towns and farms.

Potential profits also attracted a contingent of "boomers," promoters with experience on previous frontiers. Opportunists all, they acquired titles to land, planned towns, began construction of hotels and other impressive buildings, and opened sales offices. Picnics, barbecues, lavish entertainments, and extravagant publicity convinced customers to purchase lots in communities that often existed only on paper. Some were located in dry creek beds or on other worthless land, and titles frequently were shaky at best. Nevertheless, many of the boomers' communities did materialize, eventually to be absorbed into greater Los Angeles or to become cities in their own right. Before the excitement collapsed in 1889, it had produced sixty new towns covering almost 80,000 acres in southern California and had attracted the long-desired population: more than 50,000 in Los Angeles alone in 1890, 100,000 in 1900, and 300,000 in 1910.

Migrants to southern California created a society unlike the one that had evolved in the northern part of the state during the gold rush decades. Foreign-born residents were relatively few; in Los Angeles, for example, Europeans accounted for fifteen percent of the total population in 1890, Asians for about two percent, and Mexicans for less than one percent. American-born ethnic minorities were also small; black Americans and descendants of the *californios* and Indians each accounted for about two percent of the city's population. Age distribution and marital status closely resembled the national norm, as did the number of men for every

Downtown Los Angeles, circa 1905
Although the "Boom of the '80s" was brief, it began the process that made Los Angeles a bustling city by the turn of the century. The Hollenbeck Building stands at a busy intersection, surrounded by pedestrians and trolleys, which transported residents to Hollywood, Griffith Park, and other regions of the already-sprawling metropolis. *Courtesy of the Henry E. Huntington Library.*

100 women: 109 in 1890 and 97 in 1900. About a third of the new arrivals came from elsewhere in California, but whatever their origins, they brought with them strains of their conservative midwestern, Protestant, Republican tradition.

Thus, the "Boom of the '80s"—brief and misnamed though it was—introduced new elements into California history. Equally sig-

nificant, when the boom collapsed in 1889, it did not disable the southern California economy. Like profits, losses were often on paper; in *Millionaires of a Day*, T. S. Van Dyke's 1890 satire of the episode, for instance, a character observed: "I had half a million dollars wiped out in the crash, and what's worse, $500 of it was in cash." Individuals and syndicates new to the region absorbed much of the loss, and many of them departed. The more successful remained, however, and population continued to grow. Despite nationwide economic fluctuations, prosperity returned, not only in Los Angeles but also throughout the southern counties. Established banks and businesses survived the recession that followed 1889, and development persisted on a reasonably stable course.

THE FIRST OIL BOOM

While growers in the Central Valley increased operations to place California second only to Minnesota in wheat production by 1890 and San Francisco's manufacturing and commercial activity expanded, the southern California economy remained principally dependent on agriculture, real estate speculation, service industries, and retail trade. Recognition of this imbalance during the late 1870s and early 1880s prompted Los Angeles interests to form the Home Industry Protection League and the Society for the Promotion of Manufactures to encourage diversification. Editorials in major local newspapers—the *Times* and the *Herald*—also expressed concern and advocated investment in industry. But during the 1890s, Los Angeles lagged far behind San Francisco and even behind other comparable western cities in terms of manufacturing output, investment, and employment. The few existing industrial firms in Los Angeles and southern California in general usually were related to other economic activities such as agricultural processing, meat packing, fabricating household goods, and construction. Industrial development, especially production for export from the state, would await the new century.

Nevertheless, during the 1880s and 1890s southern California experienced the beginning of a *bonanza* that ultimately surpassed

gold in importance. Petroleum's presence was known in previous eras. Indians waterproofed boats and baskets and attached arrowheads with the tarry substance that oozed from the ground. Spaniards and Mexicans called it *brea* (tar) and used it to seal roofs. Padres at Missions San Fernando, Santa Barbara, and San Buenaventura distilled small quantities of lamp oil from it, as did Andrés Pico near San Fernando and others near Carpinteria. But petroleum had little commercial value until E. L. Drake perfected mass extraction technology and drilled the first well in the Oil Creek region of western Pennsylvania in 1859. During the following decade, Californians attempted to tap deposits throughout the state. R. S. Baker drilled in what is now central Los Angeles, and Phineas Banning's Pioneer Oil Company explored near Wilmington. In 1865, San Francisco capitalists organized the Union Mattole Oil Company to sink the state's first well at Petrolia in Humboldt County, and even earlier, in 1857, George S. Gilbert began a small operation refining crude oil that seeped from Sulphur Mountain on Rancho Ojai in Ventura County.

Only Gilbert's modest success received recognition, but it was sufficient to persuade Thomas A. Scott of the Pennsylvania Railroad to send Benjamin Silliman, the Yale University geologist who surveyed the Pennsylvania fields, to evaluate California's potential in 1864. Silliman's assessment, based principally on Gilbert's enthusiasm rather than objective investigation, predicted huge and immediate profits from petroleum in the state, and Scott responded by purchasing Rancho Ojai and several more properties—more than 250,000 acres. He also sent his young nephew Thomas R. Bard to oversee the operations and begin drilling in 1865. Local geology made drilling difficult and expensive, competition from eastern products drove prices down, wells produced only small amounts of poor quality crude, and Scott's California Petroleum Company encountered severe financial problems. In 1867 he divested himself of the project and placed his oil properties on the market as ranch lands. Scott was not the only loser: by the end of the 1860s, seventy companies capitalized at nearly $50 million had invested more than $1 million in sixty wells; they produced just 5,000 barrels of oil worth $10,000. One individual, however, did profit from the debacle. Thomas R. Bard deserted the oil business but remained in California to reap a fortune from the sale of his uncle's and his own lands.

BLACK GOLD

Others refused to abandon the quest during the 1870s and 1880s; Lloyd Tevis of Wells Fargo and state Senator Charles N. Felton, for example, incorporated the Pacific Coast Oil Company in 1878 to explore in the San Francisco Bay region. Most oil-seekers, however, were Pennsylvanians in partnerships and small companies who focused on southern California. Employing expertise gained in eastern fields, they located deposits, improved drilling and refining techniques, and built pipelines in anticipation of a *bonanza*. In 1883, Lyman Stewart and Wallace L. Hardison, moderately successful partners in Pennsylvania, joined the search in California.

Stewart and Hardison pooled their capital, and, with crews of Pennsylvanians, began drilling at Newhall in northeastern Los Angeles County, near the Ventura County line. During the next three years, they bought and leased additional land for exploration and moved into refining and marketing. The partners experienced modest success, but numerous dry holes and increased expenses

Early Oil Well
In 1877, Carleton E. Watkins photographed one of California's earliest oil-drilling rigs, Pico No. 4, near Newhall. The petroleum industry was then in its infancy and still something of a curiosity. *Courtesy of the Henry E. Huntington Library.*

kept them constantly overextended and deeply in debt, without the capital necessary to expand in the way that Stewart thought essential. To remedy the situation, they turned to the wealthiest man in Ventura County, Thomas R. Bard, who had returned to the oil business near Santa Paula and who, like Hardison, also had extensive interests in local citrus agriculture and real estate. In 1886, Bard, Stewart, and Hardison founded the Sespe Oil Company, which a year later produced 50,000 barrels of oil, about fifteen percent of the state's total output. By 1890, when they formed Union Oil Company of California, headquartered in Santa Paula, they were producing a fourth of the state's petroleum products. During the 1890s, Union continued to expand, established refineries at San Pedro and at Oleum on the Carquinez Strait, built tankers and pipelines to combat ruinous railroad rates, survived Standard Oil's takeover attempt, and developed oil resources in San Luis Obispo, Santa Barbara, Kern, and Los Angeles counties, as well as in the Ventura region. When Bard left the firm in 1900, Union ranked among the nation's major petroleum operations.

Union was the largest and most successful petroleum company in California by the 1890s, but it was not alone in the field. Pacific Coast Oil Company continued its operations in the Bay Area, and in 1892 Edward L. Doheny triggered a "backyard" oil boom in Los Angeles and laid the foundation for his Pan American Oil Company empire when he and a partner hand-dug a producing well near the La Brea Tar Pits. In 1900, Standard acquired control of Pacific Coast Oil and in 1906 renamed it Standard Oil of California. A year into the new century, San Joaquin Valley operators organized Associated Oil Company. In addition, both the Southern Pacific and Santa Fe railway companies became involved in California petroleum production as leasers of land and major shareholders in oil corporations.

Like gold mining, oil production rapidly became a corporate rather than an individual enterprise in the state, partially due to local conditions. Local operators were in constant combat with Standard Oil's campaign to expand its national monopoly by flooding the West with cheaper eastern products. California's geological formations demanded more difficult and deeper drilling,

greater expense, and unique equipment, much of it fabricated under Lyman Stewart's supervision in Union Oil Company shops. Making the state's asphaltum-based crude usable for lubricants and fuels also required more extensive refining than Pennsylvania's paraffin-based product, and many customers had to be convinced to use it at all. Even in the coal-starved West, railroads and industries were reluctant customers until oil companies themselves devised methods to convert locomotives and steam engines to burn oil. On the other hand, the asphalt residue of California refining, considered waste until the mid-1890s, proved to be an ideal base for paving material and was marketable nationwide. By 1900, the nation also stood on the threshold of the automobile age that would make gasoline, formerly a minor by-product of refining, the most profitable product of the petroleum industry.

THE FIGHT AGAINST MONOPOLY

California's politics, like its economic development, closely paralleled the national experience. From the 1870s on, the people and government of the United States experienced a period of adjustment to rapidly changing conditions that included the emergence of huge, monopolistic corporations to replace more traditional economic units. Defining relationships of those entities to the governments under which they existed proved to be a singular problem. In "Granger case" decisions such as *Munn* v. *Illinois* (1877), the U.S. Supreme Court upheld the principle of state regulation of corporate activity. But in subsequent decisions, perhaps influenced by social and economic Darwinism (more properly Spencerianism), the court reversed its interpretation. Despite the Interstate Commerce Commission, created in 1887, and the Sherman Antitrust Act, passed in 1890, the issue remained unresolved. In some parts of the nation, battles over corporate control involved farmers' demands for fair freight rates; elsewhere they focused on practices of such industrial giants as Standard Oil Company or the American Sugar Trust. In California, the conflict focused on the Southern Pacific and its transportation monopoly, its land policies, its evasion of taxes, and its influence in politics. Californians had expected great things of the railroad, but after the "Terrible 'Seventies" and the Mussel Slough affair they were disenchanted. To many, indeed, the railroad that was to save them became the "Octopus" that would strangle them, and they turned to government for help.

Provisions of the state constitution of 1879 that created a Railroad Commission with regulatory authority and permitted the assessment of intangible assets for taxation were sufficiently unique to inspire imitation and even attract the attention of Karl Marx. They also had a significant impact on political alignments within the state. Most Republicans were conservatives who opposed regulation, but a minority faction included individuals such as future senator Thomas R. Bard and former senator Cornelius Cole. Among Democrats, a small group of opponents to regulation included John P. Irish, editor of the Oakland *Times* and San Francisco *Alta California,* and Stephen J. Field, elevated to the U.S. Supreme Court in 1863 but still considered a California Democrat by himself and others. Party leaders from throughout the state comprised the antimonopoly majority led by Reginaldo Del Valle and Stephen Mallory White of Los Angeles County, Barclay Henley of Sonoma, and George Hearst and Chris Buckley of San Francisco.

During the early 1880s, the conflict involved taxation of the railroad more than its regulation by an impotent Railroad Commission. The company contested assessments made under the provisions of the Constitution of 1879, and its attorney, Creed Haymond, brought suit against several counties, including San Mateo and Santa Clara. When the cases reached federal courts in 1882 and 1883, Stephen J. Field upheld the railroad's position. The decision he wrote also set far-reaching precedents by defining a corporation as a legal "person" with Fourteenth Amendment rights identical to those of "the humblest citizen." Subsequently, Haymond proposed a compromise that, in effect, permitted the railroad to set its own tax rates. To Governor George Stoneman, the proposition was "humiliating," and in 1884 he called the legislature into special session. Every effort to enact stringent, enforceable measures to collect unpaid taxes failed miserably; pro-railroad Democratic senators voted with Republicans to defeat each proposed change in the law.

Majority Democrats reacted at the party's 1884 state convention in Stockton, where delegates adopted a strict antimonopoly platform, nominated only antimonopoly candidates for the impending election, read pro-railroad members out of the state party, and refused to support their bids for office. Finally, they denounced Field for his decisions and repudiated his aspirations for their party's presidential nomination. The action split the Democracy and produced more humiliation: Grover Cleveland won the presidency, but he lost in California—which sent only one Democrat, Barclay Henley, to Congress. Democrats elected Washington Bartlett to the governor's office but could not provide the legislative majority needed to prevent Leland Stanford's selection as U.S. Senator in 1885, and in San Francisco, Chris Buckley's machine barely held its own. Despite their losses, antimonopolists in the party continued to pin their hopes on the fight against the "Octopus." Henley wrote to White, "The fact is, that if we take no backward step—and stick to the principles of the Stockton convention we will win."

POLITICAL CHANGE IN THE 1890s

Henley was wrong. Democrats attributed their defeats to railroad manipulations, but other forces were involved. During the 1880s Californians became increasingly concerned with national issues that were divisive rather than unifying. Some in the state, for example, favored Grover Cleveland's tariff reduction policies, but commercial interests and many agrarians, regardless of party, feared the potential for increased foreign competition. As the monetary issue gained importance late in the decade, most Californians favored a return to silver coinage, but many others remained suspicious of possible inflationary consequences.

Also during the 1880s, the Santa Fe broke the Southern Pacific monopoly, mitigating Californians' most pressing grievances over rates and fares and prompting many Democrats—including Hearst and Buckley—to reject rigidly antimonopolist positions and make peace with ousted party members. Penetration by the Santa Fe had added consequences, not the least of them the arrival of the "tenderfoot vote." Migrants flocking to the state included thousands steeped in the orthodoxy of midwestern Republicanism. Moreover, they settled in southern California, where antagonism toward the railroad was less entrenched, and began to alter the state's political balance.

Most significantly, however, states could not regulate the practices of nationally organized corporations such as the Southern Pacific until policies changed at the federal level. This did not occur until the twentieth century, but during the 1890s, reform-minded Californians scored several significant victories. Although efforts to secure direct election of U.S. senators failed, in 1891 a bipartisan effort passed an Australian secret-ballot law. Two years later, the legislature sent Stephen M. White to the Senate to replace the deceased Stanford, enacted a Purity of Elections Law, and took steps to reduce corruption in franchise-granting and other municipal government functions. They also succeeded modestly in local battles with the railroad. The legislature overcame vigorous lobbying to pass the Railroad Reassessment Act of 1893, making it possible to collect $2.2 million in overdue taxes from the Southern Pacific, and, when the new century opened, state and federal governments had won two more important struggles: the fights for a publicly controlled port at Los Angeles and against a "Funding Bill" intended to refinance the railroad's debt to the nation.

THE FREE HARBOR FIGHT AND THE FUNDING BILL

Phineas Banning, who began port development at Wilmington-San Pedro, was also responsible for securing federal appropriations for inner-harbor improvements between 1870 and 1890. Without a breakwater, however, the port could not accommodate oceangoing vessels, and the Los Angeles Chamber of Commerce and other groups began a campaign for more federal assistance to complete the essential project. In 1890, the Corps of Engineers studied several potential harbor sites in the area, reported in favor of San Pedro, and recommended a federal expenditure of $4 million to build a breakwater there.

Angelenos rejoiced, but in 1892 Collis P.

Huntington became involved. He had purchased most of the Santa Monica waterfront for the Southern Pacific Company, and he pressured Congress and the administration for a second survey, which again favored San Pedro. Members of the Los Angeles Free Harbor League, formed to oppose spending public funds for a harbor controlled by Huntington, were therefore astonished to learn that an 1896 Rivers and Harbors Bill included a $2.0 million appropriation for a breakwater at Santa Monica. Los Angeles *Times* publisher Harrison Gray Otis led the campaign against the measure in California, and Senator Stephen M. White (known in the state as "Our Steve") brought his considerable oratorical skills to bear in Washington. Following a third study, which reiterated the results of the first two, Congress passed an amended bill and appropriated funds for San Pedro. Despite Huntington's delaying tactics, construction began in 1899 on the breakwater that made the Los Angeles-San Pedro Harbor one of the coast's major ports. Ultimately, it would accommodate two-thirds of California's maritime commerce and rank second among the nation's harbors and among the most important on the eastern Pacific Rim.

For Huntington and the Southern Pacific, defeat in the Free Harbor fight was significant, but simultaneous controversies over the Funding Bill were potentially more important. Government loans of $28 million, secured by six-percent bonds and payable in 1899, had financed the Big Four's construction of the Central Pacific. An 1878 federal law required that the Central Pacific set aside funds to retire the debt, but the company failed to comply. As the due date approached, Huntington sought means to have the payment delayed, perhaps permanently, and in 1896 used his influence to bring before Congress a measure that extended the

term of the loan to 100 years and reduced the interest rate to one percent.

Even Californians accustomed to Huntington's audacity were outraged. Adolph Sutro, elected mayor of San Francisco on the Populist ticket in 1894, mustered the city's resources against the measure. William Randolph Hearst collected 200,000 signatures opposing the bill and sent them to Washington, followed by *Examiner* satirist Ambrose Bierce and cartoonist Homer Davenport. Chris Buckley denounced the proposal, and legislators petitioned Congress against it. Huntington argued that paying the debt would bankrupt the Southern Pacific, but California lawmakers were unsympathetic; indeed, they urged the national government to foreclose and assume operation of the railroad. When Congress rejected the Funding Bill in January 1897, it did not precipitate the company's collapse. But the action was a blow against its unbridled corporate power, and Californians rejoiced in it.

AGRARIAN REVOLT

Californians' conflicts with the Southern Pacific were local manifestations of a national mood that spawned the Populist revolt of the 1890s. To protect themselves against the implications of an increasingly corporate economy, discontented members of the wage-earning classes formed a variety of associations: the reformist Noble Order of the Knights of Labor, the craft-oriented American Federation of Labor, and a few radical unions led by individuals such as Marxist Daniel DeLeon and socialist Eugene Debs. Even more emphatic expressions of dissatisfaction emanated from farmers, who seemed to be losing their time-honored place in American society.

Some agrarian problems resulted from overextension and overproduction, but other conditions were beyond farmers' control. As always, they were at the mercy of the elements. Railroads charged exorbitant freight rates and often controlled brokerages and warehouses to which farmers sold. The federal government seemed antagonistic; reciprocity treaties allowed cheap foreign produce into the country, while tariffs increased the prices of manufactured goods. Deflationary policies resulted in the demonetization of silver—the "Crime of 1873"—and the scarcity of silver in circulation forced payment of debts in "dear" money.

The nationwide Patrons of Husbandry, or Grange, was formed in the 1870s and influenced several states to pass laws controlling railroad practices. During the 1880s, however, federal courts consistently struck down regulatory legislation. Subsequently, the National Farmers' Alliance and numerous state and regional Alliances attempted to improve the situation through political action. They advocated nationalization of the means of transportation and communication, a monetary system based on paper currency and silver, and political changes including the Australian secret ballot, direct election of senators, and similar measures to give the public greater control over government. In some states, usually in concert with local Democratic parties, Alliance programs were moderately successful, but many goals required action at the national level, a necessity that produced the People's (Populist) Party.

At their first national convention in 1892, Populists drafted their Omaha Platform calling for unlimited coinage of silver, woman suffrage, the eight-hour day, public ownership of utilities, national banking and subtreasury systems, and other reforms. During the 1892 elections, Populists fused with traditional parties to capture several state governments and to send a substantial delegation to Congress. Four years later, the People's Party supported Democratic presidential candidate William Jennings Bryan against Republican William McKinley and suffered a resounding defeat that ended the agrarian revolt.

POPULISM IN CALIFORNIA

Californians participated in each phase of the agrarian revolt. Hard times returned to the state after the harsh winter of 1889–1890 decimated many crops. Commercial and other economic activity declined, and by 1890 nearly 25,000 unemployed people sought work in San Francisco alone. At the same time, hostility toward the railroad revived with a vengeance, but the only consequence of efforts to regulate the "Octopus" was that, according to Hearst's San Francisco *Examiner,* "legislators and [Railroad] Commissioners have gone on the [Southern Pacific] pay-roll." In fact, suspicious lawmakers attempted to abolish the commission in 1892 and 1893.

By then, many Californians had concluded that traditional politics could not represent their interests. Some were prepared to consider alternative economic systems and welcomed the 1888 publication of Edward Bellamy's *Looking Backward,* a utopian novel that described the peaceful evolution of a nationalized economy and democratic society of equals. Nationalist clubs sprang up across the nation and around the world, but nowhere with greater speed than in California. The first appeared in Oakland in 1889; a year later, the state's sixty-two clubs represented a third of the total in the nation. Strongest in southern California, the movement attracted 4,000 men and women from a spectrum of society representing everything from businessmen to socialists.

Despite members' enthusiasm, National-

WILLIAM RANDOLPH HEARST
California Journalist

William Randolph Hearst
Courtesy of the Bancroft Library.

Californians from the gold rush on have had a hunger for news exceeded only by their appetite for wealth. Early arrivals found two weeklies in operation: Sam Brannan's *California Star*, edited by Edward C. Kemble, and Robert Semple's *Californian*, founded in Monterey but merged with the *Star* in San Francisco in 1847. Two years later, the combination became the *Daily Alta California*. By 1860, scores of dailies and weeklies vied for readers in the city and in remote regions, from the *Trinity Journal* and *Shasta Record* in the north to the Los Angeles *Express* in the south. Still, month-old editions of eastern journals sold briskly at inflated prices.

Railroad and telegraph connections slaked the thirst for news, but only mass circulation dailies, beginning with the San Francisco *Examiner*, quenched it. George Hearst accepted the paper in payment of a debt in 1880, operated it to promote his senatorial ambitions until 1887, and then turned it over to his twenty-four-year-old son, recently expelled from Harvard. With family financial backing, William Randolph Hearst dispatched reporters, artists, and photographers to cover events across the nation and around the world, adopted modern printing technologies and a policy of "yellow journalism," and made the *Examiner* the "Monarch of the Dailies," with almost as many San Francisco readers as the *Call*, *Chronicle*, and *Bulletin* combined. Competitors appeared

---

WILLIAM RANDOLPH HEARST (continued)
California Journalist

throughout the state: the Oakland *Tribune*, the Sacramento *Bee*, the Fresno *Republican*, minor journals such as the Ventura *Democrat*, and major ones such as Harrison Gray Otis's Los Angeles *Times*. When necessary, Hearst bought local papers, including the Los Angeles *Examiner* and Oakland *Post-Enquirer*, to combat rivals, and by the early 1900s his California newspapers were the cornerstone of a publishing empire. They were not, however, the entire edifice.

In 1895, Hearst purchased the New York *Morning Journal* and entered that city's circulation wars as a rival of Joseph Pulitzer's *World*. He also employed popular writers such as Jack London, who reported the Russo-Japanese War of 1904–1905, and by the 1930s he controlled nearly twenty newspapers in a dozen cities, nine national magazines, and news agencies and publishing houses that not only informed and molded public opinion but also supported a vast ambition. They financed Hearst's spectacular spending on his grandiose castle at San Simeon and the European artworks and furnishings that filled it, on the advancement of the career of film actress Marion Davies, and on his own political aspirations. He represented New York in Congress for two terms (1903–1906), but his efforts to become mayor of New York City, governor of the Empire State, and Democratic nominee for president in 1904 and 1908 all failed.

Later reverses may have contributed to Hearst's shift to the political right. After the 1930s, rising production costs and proliferation of local dailies, radio, and television reduced the appeal of newspapers to readers and advertisers. The Hearst empire could escape neither the changes nor their implications; retrenchments, mergers, and diminished corporate and personal power were inevitable. Still, when William Randolph Hearst died in 1951, he left a $60 million estate to his wife and three sons and to a variety of charitable foundations. His legacy also included contributions to journalism in the state and the flamboyant career that inspired Orson Welles's 1940 film, *Citizen Kane*. (WAB)

---

ism's life was all but over by the end of 1890, when many of its adherents joined the Farmers' Alliance, organized at Santa Barbara. In California the Alliance attracted not only Nationalists, Grangers, disaffected farmers, antimonopolists, and currency reformers but also former Republican U.S. Senator Cornelius Cole and others like him. At their first state convention, at San José in 1890, leaders organized the California Farmers' Alliance and Industrial Union, with Ventura County rancher Marion Cannon as president, and adopted a platform that denounced monopoly and Wall Street and condemned politicians' subservience to the "money power." A year later, delegates representing 30,000 members from thirty-four counties met at Los Angeles, discarded previous policies of avoiding direct political action, and formed the People's Party of California.

The new party absorbed some Democrats such as Cannon and Thomas V. Cator, but it gained more followers from lifelong Republicans, especially southern Californians such as Cole and Stephen Bowers, editor of the Ventura *Observer.* In 1892, the party sent Cator and Cannon to the national Populist convention, adopted the Omaha platform, pledged support to presidential candidate James B. Weaver, and named candidates for statewide offices and Congress. Populist nominees often ran as Democrats, too, and when the votes were counted in 1892, Democrats had returned Grover Cleveland to office, and gained a majority in the state legislature. Eight Populists took seats in the assembly, and Marion Cannon went to Congress, but only a single People's Party candidate achieved victory without, like Cannon, running on the Democratic ticket as well.

In 1893, Populists in the legislature participated in enacting political reform measures and in sending Stephen M. White to Washington, and the 1894 election campaign was the party's high point in California. Populists gained strength in depressed rural counties in the north and in the Central Valley, helped to make antimonopolist Democrat James H. Budd governor, and elected Adolph Sutro mayor of San Francisco. These victories, however, resulted less from wide acceptance of the party's principles than from reaction to specific events, especially continuing depression and repressive government reaction to the Pullman Strike that spread to the state earlier in the year. By 1896, the year that pitted Bryan against McKinley and silver against gold, the California People's Party was in disarray, sundered by internal conflicts. By 1898, radicals in the party had de-

fected to socialism, moderates had returned to the Democratic or Republican fold, and even Cator was endorsing high tariffs and the gold standard.

The People's Party failed to implement sweeping reforms or to attain more modest goals such as limiting corporate power in politics. Indeed, through its active Political Bureau, headed by William F. Herrin after 1893, the Southern Pacific continued to influence election of legislators and a succession of sympathetic governors: Henry T. Gage (1898), George C. Pardee (1902), and James N. Gillett (1906). Nevertheless, Populism in California and the nation served an important purpose. It publicized a variety of social, political, and economic reform principles and set the stage for future change. Many measures considered radical when introduced by Populists became acceptable when embraced by progressives early in the twentieth century.

THE URBAN SCENE: PRELUDE TO PROGRESSIVISM

One inspiration for utopian schemes such as Nationalism—and perhaps for the Populist revolt as well—was dramatic change in American cities. Urban centers of the 1890s differed radically from familiar mid-century "walking cities," compact communities of about two and a half miles in radius and limited by topography, by the amount of time and energy residents could spend in the conduct of their activities, and by transportation dependent on muscle power. Walking city neighborhoods were heterogeneous and included people representing various socioeconomic and ethnic groups, as well as most social and economic activities. Political life also focused on the neighborhoods, called wards, where residents conducted elections to choose city officials and send representatives to city councils, school boards, and other governing bodies. In short, the walking city was simply "the village writ large," and most of its activities were conducted on a face-to-face basis.

San Francisco was a walking city of 35,000 when it adopted the Consolidation Act of 1856, but even when Chris Buckley arrived in 1862, change was already apparent. During the 1870s, real estate and transportation interests influenced the shift of urban activity southward toward Market Street, and industrial development altered not only physical configurations but also social and economic relationships. By the end of the decade, when San Francisco's population had reached 250,000 and pioneer photographer Eadweard Muybridge made his panorama of the city, the transformation was virtually complete. San Francisco was an industrial city. But some things had not changed—among them fundamental assumptions about municipal government. The Consolidation Act remained in force, but it was a patchwork of often contradictory amendments that produced the political anarchy that Martin Kelly and Chris Buckley described. Partisan arrangements remained those of the walking city, prompting Buckley's observation that "the vice of the old political system . . . was the lack of recognition and regulation by law."

This situation resembled conditions in other American cities, where obsolete charters contributed to municipal chaos and to the rise of bosses and machines. Efforts toward change in San Francisco also followed national patterns. In 1873, Mayor William Alvord proposed a revised city charter to modernize the city's government, eliminate political corruption, and minimize state intervention in municipal affairs. His attempt failed, as did four more recharter campaigns

before 1898. They did, however, establish the principles on which later reforms would be based: home rule, increased mayoral authority over personnel and fiscal matters, control of partisan activities, public ownership of utilities, and specified procedures for granting municipal contracts and franchises. Subsequent charter reformers added professionalism, efficiency, and nonpartisanship to the agenda, in keeping with the dictum, "The management of cities is not politics, it is business."

During the 1890s, inspired by reports of success elsewhere, the San Francisco recharter movement gained new momentum. In 1893, members of the city business elite formed the Merchants' Association and called for election of a Board of Freeholders to draft a new organic law. The document that the Freeholders produced in 1895, however, seemed to please no one but themselves and members of the Merchants' Association. The local Labor Council, teachers, and small businessmen objected to their exclusion from the board's deliberations. The Catholic Church denounced the influence of the American Protestant Association on sections related to public schools. Traditional politicians condemned the elimination of voting by wards, and one critic objected to making the mayor "a grand municipal mogul." In 1896, voters rejected the charter, but they did put wealthy businessman and recharter advocate James Duval Phelan in the mayor's office. Soon after his inauguration, he appointed another committee, larger and more representative of the population, to draft yet another new organic law.

The committee's document embodied the standard "good government" principles, and like its predecessor it encountered resistance. But by 1898 reformers had learned the rules of the political game. They appealed to the legislature for a law to allow

KAWEAH
The Quest for Utopia

Burnett G. Haskell
Well-educated and well-to-do, Burnett G. Haskell was one of many Californians who participated in efforts to create a perfect society in the nineteenth century. After graduating from law school, he studied radical doctrines ranging from Marx to Bakunin to Kropotkin, and his brainchild, the Kaweah colony, was among the state's first utopian experiments. It would not be the last. *Courtesy of the Bancroft Library.*

Radical transformations in society often inspire attempts to perfect it, to create a "utopia," and later decades of the nineteenth century—when rural-agrarian America became urban-industrial—produced utopian schemes ranging from doctrinaire Marxism to religious fundamentalism. For California, the short-lived Kaweah Co-operative Commonwealth epitomized the process.

In 1884, attorney-editor Burnett Haskell convinced San Francisco wage-earners' groups to establish a colony premised on absolute equality. The project required a marketable commodity for an economic base and land for a community, and leaders found

KAWEAH (continued)
The Quest for Utopia

Kaweah's Steam Tractor
Donations of money and material permitted
Kaweah to survive for a few short years. But the
fate of the colony's steam tractor predicted that of
the colony. Shortly after its acquisition, it crashed
through the bridge constructed to carry it across a
creek. *Courtesy of the Bancroft Library.*

both in Sierra Nevada tracts available under the Timber Act of 1878, a program like the
Homestead Act of 1862, with lumbering substituted for agriculture. Early in 1885,
Haskell and fifty-two associates filed claims on adjoining quarter-sections, to be deeded
to the community when titles were confirmed. Most were skilled craftsmen, but they in-
cluded professionals and a self-styled "capitalist," and diversity increased, according to
Haskell, eventually encompassing:

> temperance men and their opposites, churchmen and agnostics, . . . Darwinists, and spiritu-
> alists, bad poets and good, musicians, artists, prophets, and priests, . . . dress reform cranks
> and phonetic spelling fanatics, word purists and vegetarians.

Variety made Kaweah a "mad, mad world, and being so small its madness the more visible."

The colony's site was ideal: on the Kaweah River thirty miles from Visalia, with access to
the Southern Pacific Railway and the San Joaquin Valley. It would not support agriculture
or husbandry, but stands of virgin timber, deemed inaccessible by commercial interests,

---

KAWEAH (continued)
The Quest For Utopia

---

provided a potential harvest. In addition, spectacular beauty promised to emancipate human souls fettered by cities and factories. Indeed, the idyllic setting moved one observer to rhapsody: "Kaweah! embryonic regenerator of the sphere; Kaweah! where life is every day a picnic!" Despite its hyperbole, the comment underscored an evangelical strain present in most utopian ventures, secular or religious. Participants shared in the heady belief that they were, by their example, participating in the perfection of society.

Nevertheless, Kaweah life was not "every day a picnic." Hard work included hacking an eighteen-mile road out of granite with hand tools, felling trees and turning them into marketable lumber, and replacing tents with permanent buildings for families, a school, and community activities. While men toiled on the road and at the sawmill, women performed not only domestic chores but also tasks such as cutting and packing shingles for sale. All adults received equal pay in the form of "time checks" ranging in value from ten minutes (five cents) to 20,000 minutes ($100) and redeemable for goods and services, and all had equal voice in the General Meeting that governed the community.

Despite colonists' efforts, trouble plagued their paradise. Substantial donations arrived from as far away as New York, but financial problems persisted. Diversity among talented and opinionated residents—never more than 300—precipitated bickering and factionalism, exacerbated by what Haskell termed a "varied, vacillating, and truly democratic" government and by authoritarian leaders like himself. Outside the colony, innuendo disseminated by a press thriving on scandal fueled criticism. In addition, federal authorities, with no valid reason, refused to confirm colonists' claims, and in 1890 Congress dedicated the region that included Kaweah for Sequoia National Park, dooming the colony and prompting Haskell's final diary entry in 1892: "Oh, hell!"

Hindsight seems to validate assumptions that people such as Haskell and their efforts were naive, condemned to failure before they began; perhaps so. But they were also idealists whose ventures endorsed and implemented policies, such as women's equality, that would continue to challenge subsequent generations. (WAB)

---

charter issues to be decided at a special election, and they closed the polls two hours before sunset, in violation of state law. A minority of San Franciscans voted and approved the new charter by a slim margin.

Municipal reform took a different tack in Los Angeles, but it was an equally important prelude to progressivism. Despite the Free Harbor Fight, the city government remained subservient to special interests such as the railroads. In 1898, respected physician John Randolph Haynes organized a Direct Legislation League to campaign for reform. The league's proposed new charter failed in 1900, but during the following year civic leaders formed the Good Government

League to continue the effort. The driving force behind reform, however, remained Haynes, an exponent of direct public legislation and an advocate of "Christian socialism" blended with traditional political ideology. Haynes assembled a coalition of businessmen, labor leaders, socialists, Bellamyites, and other reformers to draft and support a charter based on the National Municipal League model. Opponents such as publisher Harrison Gray Otis of the Los Angeles *Times* ridiculed members of the Good Government League as "goo-goos," but in 1903 voters approved a new city charter.

In its principles of efficiency, expertise, and corporate management, the Los Angeles charter resembled those adopted in San Francisco and other cities during the same period. But it was also the first in any American city to include provisions (adopted from the Populists) for the initiative, referendum, and recall. Very quickly, Angelenos took advantage of their new authority; in 1904 they recalled a city councilman whose voting record identified him with the interests of the Southern Pacific and with Harrison Gray Otis. Simultaneously, Los Angeles *Express* publisher Edwin T. Earl employed Edward A. Dickson to write an exposé of remaining railroad influence in city government, and Dickson joined with other citizens in 1906 to form the Non-Partisan Committee of 100 to nominate a full slate of candidates for municipal office. All won, except the nominee for mayor. Three years later, however, a determined campaign very nearly made the winner, Arthur C. Harper, the first American mayor to be recalled from office; only timely resignation denied him the dubious honor.

PREPROGRESSIVE WOMEN

After the 1860s, families more frequently accompanied male migrants westward, and the gender imbalance that typified American California began to diminish throughout the state. Demographic patterns, however, made change most apparent in the cities, where social and economic potential attracted young women—and men, too—from the rural countryside. Urban life also exposed legal and traditional constraints on opportunity for women, and in American cities, including Los Angeles and San Francisco, they began to find the cohesiveness and collective voice needed to mount an assault on restrictive laws and policies. Although initial efforts did not always succeed, they marked important preludes to reform.

Despite a decade-long campaign dating from the organization of a statewide suffrage society in 1869 by Stockton editor Laura De-Force Gordon (later a state senatorial candidate and lawyer), the effort to include women's right to vote in the Constitution of 1879 foundered. It did, however, contain a provision that opened all legitimate businesses, professions, and occupations to their participation. Even so, less than five percent of Los Angeles or San Francisco businesses in the 1890s had female proprietors, most of whom were dressmakers, milliners, innkeepers, and the like. Women gained access to the legal profession when Gordon and Clara Shortridge Foltz of San José mustered support for a law eliminating gender barriers to admission to the bar in 1878 and sued to gain acceptance to Hastings College of Law in 1879. Still, few female lawyers practiced anywhere in nineteenth-century California. In medicine, however, they fared somewhat better. The University of California Medical School reluctantly admitted its first female student, Lucy Wanzer, in 1873, and the University of Southern California School of Medicine granted its first degree to a woman in 1888. By 1890, ten percent of Los Angeles physicians were women, as were ten percent of the students at Cooper Medical College in San Francisco. More were preparing for ca-

ANNA MORRISON REED
"The California Girl"

Anna Morrison Reed, The California Girl
Anna Morrison Reed went to wine regions to demonstrate support for the growers' fight against prohibitionists' Proposition 2. *From the Collection of John E. Keller.*

Anna Morrison Reed, born in Iowa in 1849 but known to contemporaries as "The California Girl," successfully combined a public career and motherhood—difficult for women in any age but doubly so in the later nineteenth century. As a lecturer, poet, and journalist, she entered public life, joining such notable Californians as novelist Gertrude Atherton and photographer Emma Freeman to set standards for a new generation of western women. As a wife and mother of five, she also epitomized the more traditional expectations for women of her time and social class. And throughout her seventy-two

ANNA MORRISON REED (continued)
"The California Girl"

years, she reaped the benefits of living in a West that was relatively tolerant of talented, creative women and evangelized her adopted state to readers in the East.

Four-year-old Anna arrived in California in the spring of 1852, accompanying her mother in search of her father, Guy Morrison, whose gold fever had lured him westward. They found him on the Feather River in a typical mining camp, where life was harsh and poverty, loneliness, poor health, and despair characterized the experience of most. Indeed, Morrison himself suffered recurrent ravages of malaria (then called "ague"), and by 1860 he was too physically debilitated to support his growing family. Then his eldest daughter Anna, barely into her teens, assumed that responsibility.

By lecturing throughout northern California—and taking a safe position on subjects such as "Temperance" and "A Women's Place"—she provided for herself and her family and, in the process, stepped into the public sphere where she remained until her death in 1921. After marriage to John Reed in 1872, she limited her lecture tours and for a time devoted her energies almost exclusively to raising her family in the vicinity of Ukiah.

John Reed's death in 1900, however, forced Anna once again to become a bread winner, and in 1904 she founded a new literary magazine, *The Northern Crown*, while serving as editor of the *Ukiah Times* and the *Sonoma County Independent* and involving herself in social and political issues. She campaigned energetically for women's rights, especially for passage of the state's equal suffrage amendment in 1911. Later, she denounced California's prohibition movement and in 1914 and 1916 lectured on behalf of the California Grape Growers' Association to defeat statewide initiatives to ban the sale and consumption of alcoholic beverages. Simultaneously, she remained active in the Pacific Coast Women's Press Association, which she and Mathilde Reinhart established in 1890, and in publishing. In addition to printing the literary magazine, her Northern Crown Printing Co. published volumes of her own poetry and that of others, including San Francisco's George Sterling. In 1918, Reed declared herself a candidate for the state assembly but lost her bid for the nomination. She had by then joined other California women who, as newly enfranchised citizens, sought to take their votes and their reform efforts one step further by running for public office.

When she died in 1921, Anna Morrison Reed left a legacy of energy and courage in the face of adversity and a defined course for later women to follow. Ever the opportunist, she carved out her own niche in a society in which most women were content to rely on men for their support and ideas. Always making her own decisions, sometimes unpopular ones, she endorsed temperance and opposed women's suffrage early on. Later, however, she resisted prohibition and actively supported women's right to vote and participate in the society that she and others like her had helped to create. (PCT) reers in medicine at the San Francisco Hospital for Children and Training School for Nurses, founded earlier as the Pacific Dispensary for Women and Children by Dr. Charlotte Amanda Brown.

By the 1880s, state normal schools at San José, Los Angeles, and Chico and programs at Claremont and Pomona colleges and the University of Southern California prepared women to teach. By 1900 they staffed almost all elementary classes in San Francisco and Los Angeles, but at salaries substantially lower than male counterparts received. In response to the discrepancy, Irish-born Kate Kennedy led San Francisco teachers in an "equal pay for equal work" campaign in 1874; it influenced legislation requiring that teachers be compensated solely on the basis of qualifications and performance. In practice the gender differential persisted, since few women held better paid secondary teaching positions or administrative posts in nineteenth-century California schools.

More women than ever entered the state's and the nation's urban work force during the turn-of-the-century decades, often as clerks, stenographers, and librarians, and in similar occupations that, like teaching, men had abandoned. A significant number also entered male-dominated trades such as photography and typography, but those who lacked skills or education took jobs where they could find them. In anti-union Los Angeles, they usually accepted whatever wages they were offered, but in San Francisco many became labor activists. They established the Ladies Assembly of the Knights of Labor in 1885, followed during the 1890s by unions including the Co-operative Shirtmakers of the Pacific Coast, Steam Laundry Workers, Glove Makers, and Bottle Caners. Women also joined previously all-male unions to advocate higher wages, shorter hours, and improved working conditions and to campaign

against their competitors, the Chinese, for unskilled jobs.

Both collectively and individually, California urban women focused their attention on issues of political and social reform. Chapters of the Women's Christian Temperance Union (WCTU) in Los Angeles, San Francisco, Sacramento, and other cities campaigned against saloons and vice and for the right to vote. In Los Angeles during the 1880s, women led by Caroline Severance founded the Friday Morning Club, which began as a social association but grew to 200 members who worked to expand kindergarten programs, improve education, mitigate the treatment of juvenile criminal offenders, and provide affordable housing for working women. By 1893, the Women's Parliament coordinated the efforts of Los Angeles clubwomen in support of a variety of reforms, including the suffrage campaign.

In 1890, journalists, writers, and publishers founded the Pacific Coast Women's Press Association (PCWPA), which not only advocated professional goals but also encouraged women to become active in social and political causes. Indeed, Charlotte Perkins Gilman recalled that membership in the PCWPA, WCTU, and other women's associations during her years in San Francisco contributed significantly to her development as a feminist and a writer. Other San Francisco women made important individual contributions. Phoebe Apperson Hearst, wife of George and mother of William Randolph, used her inherited fortune to support causes that included university scholarships for women, funding kindergartens, and founding the National Congress of Mothers. In 1878, Kate Douglas Wiggin moved from southern California to San Francisco where, with her German-born teacher Emma Marwedel, she established the state's first free kindergarten in the working-class South-of-

Market district. During the 1890s, New Zealand-born Donaldina Cameron began her forty-year career working among the Chinese of the city. Simultaneously, Mary Julia Workman began a career that would energize social service activites among Roman Catholic women in Los Angeles.

Thus, during the second half of the nineteenth century, women of various backgrounds in urban California engaged in activities that paralleled the settlement house movements, labor organization, and political, educational, and social reforms that counterparts pursued in older eastern cities. Their experiences introduced them to increased opportunities and also exposed legal and traditional barriers to their attainment. Responses both echoed the activism of Susan B. Anthony, Elizabeth Cady Stanton, and Jane Addams and predicted modern women's campaign to confirm their status as equal citizens of the state and nation that began with the progressive movement of the early 1900s and persisted through the remainder of the twentieth century.

CHAPTER EIGHTEEN

PROGRESSIVE CALIFORNIA

In *The Age of Reform,* Richard Hofstadter accurately assessed the breadth and diversity of the reform impulse that dominated the first two decades of twentieth-century United States history:

> Progressivism became nationwide and bipartisan, encompassing Democrats and Republicans, country and city, East, West, [North,] and South. A working coalition was formed between the old Bryan country and the newer reform movement in the cities.

National and state Progressive parties appeared, men and women from all strata of society enlisted in the crusade for "social justice," and Progressives borrowed freely from earlier reform programs, as Kansas editor William Allan White observed: they "caught the Populists in swimming and stole all of their clothes except for the frayed underdrawers of free silver." Despite their differences, individuals who called themselves progressives shared a common concern for the private exploitation of public resources—including human resources—and proposed comprehensive new policies to address the political, social, and economic problems confronting the modern nation.

ABRAHAM RUEF AND THE UNION LABOR PARTY

On the morning of April 18, 1906, a devastating earthquake rocked San Francisco. Followed by three days of fire, the cataclysm wrecked much of the city, left thousands homeless, and jolted residents out of their comfortable complacency. But the streets and buildings of San Francisco were not the only things in shambles. Despite a reform charter adopted in 1898, municipal government was in disarray; at the center of the chaos was Boss Abraham Ruef. Born in San Francisco in 1864 to middle-class French-Jewish parents, Ruef was ambitious and intelligent. In rapid order, he graduated from the University of California (1882) and Hastings College of Law (1883), passed the state bar examination (1886), and began a successful legal practice. Early political activities predicted a career as a reformer, but he fell under the wing of Chris Buckley's first mentor, Bill Higgins. When the old boss died, Ruef completed his apprenticeship under Martin Kelly and Phil Crimmins, and added an element of integrity to their machine. Then, in the Republican primaries of 1901, he attempted to strike out on his own, but the two professionals gave their protégé a sound thrashing at the polls.

Circumstances, however, gave Ruef a second chance. In the spring of 1901 the San Francisco Employers' Association, formed earlier to oppose unionism in the city, was embroiled in a bitter dispute with the Teamsters, the City Front Federation of waterfront workers, the local Labor Council, and other unions. A strike resulted and all but paralyzed the port. The association responded by locking out union workers, hiring strike-breakers, and convincing Mayor James Duval Phelan to assign city police to protect them. Before Governor Henry T. Gage intervened to end the strike in October, five were dead and wage-earners were disenchanted with Phelan and his Democratic party. Despite opposition by principal labor spokesmen, other leaders organized the Union Labor Party (ULP) to champion working-class interests.

Ruef had shown no previous interest in labor causes, but he used tested political skills to move swiftly into the leadership of the ULP. He engineered the nomination of his close friend and client Eugene Schmitz, president of the musicians' union, to run for mayor; during the November campaign the debonair Irish-German Catholic used his popularity in both society and labor circles to win. Schmitz triumphed again in 1903 and in 1905, when ULP nominees captured all eighteen seats on the Board of Supervisors. Then triumph turned to disaster.

From the time that Schmitz first took office, he and Ruef conducted a variety of highly profitable illicit activities: protecting the city's "French restaurants" (houses of prostitution above their first floors), selling favors to utility companies and other interests, and even using public funds to build a brothel known as the "Municipal Crib." The ULP supervisors elected in 1905 were political novices, but they were astute enough to know what was going on and demand a share of the profits. Despite Ruef's protests that he only accepted "fees" as a private attorney, he needed supervisors' votes and was forced to divide the substantial spoils received from Pacific Gas and Electric, United Street Railway Company, Spring Valley Water Company, and other firms. Worse yet, greedy supervisors began to freelance for individual opportunities (bribes), employing tactics that embarrassed even Ruef and Schmitz.

INDICTMENT AND TRIAL

Shortly after Schmitz's first inauguration, editor Fremont Older of the San Francisco *Bulletin* published a series of articles revealing conditions at City Hall, but response to his exposés was minimal. After the mayor's reelection in 1905, Older sought and received financial backing for an investigation from sugar heir Rudolph Spreckels and other businessmen and a promise of cooperation from the local district attorney. Next, he solicited help from President Theodore Roosevelt who provided the services of two of the government's finest investigators: Secret Service Chief William J. Burns and special prosecutor Francis J. Heney. After delays resulting from the earthquake and fire, Older and his allies struck.

In November 1906 a grand jury indicted Ruef and Schmitz for protecting vice operations in the city, but Heney and his fellow prosecutors were not satisfied. They wanted to convict givers of bribes as well as takers, corporate law breakers as well as corrupt politicians. Early in 1907 Burns trapped two supervisors by bribing them to vote for a phony city ordinance; he then convinced

"Atonement"
William Randolph Hearst made his opinion of both
Abe Ruef and the methods of the graft investigation
abundantly clear in the pages of the San Francisco *Examiner. Collection of William A. Bullough.*

returned to the courtroom, nearly killed Chief Prosecutor Heney with a pistol shot to the head, and later committed suicide in jail. In equally bizarre incidents, dynamite destroyed the front of a supervisor's home, and newly appointed police chief William J. Biggy disappeared from a police launch while on a night trip across the bay.

Despite such sensations, nationwide publicity, and the expenditure of substantial time and money, the prosecution failed. By the end of 1908, only Ruef and Schmitz had been convicted of anything; the verdict against the mayor required two trials and was eventually reversed on a technicality. Angered by Ruef's refusal to tailor testimony to their purposes, Heney and Hiram W. Johnson, who took charge following Heney's injury, reneged on promises of immunity and prosecuted him; he was found guilty of bribery and sentenced to fourteen years in San Quentin. None of the accused bribe givers was convicted, and in 1910 the case against the last defendant, Calhoun, was dropped.

By then, San Franciscans had tired of the entire affair. Business leaders who supported the investigation defected when the prosecution turned against members of their class, and in 1909 the voters elected a city administration committed to ending the trials. By 1912, Older was publishing Ruef's memoirs in the *Bulletin* and campaigning for his release. In 1915 Ruef was paroled and returned to San Francisco to manage his real estate interests. He was pardoned in 1920 and died in 1936, bankrupt and obscure. Schmitz turned to investments in oil and mines, but in 1915 he ran again for mayor and polled 35,000 votes. Even more incredibly, in 1917 he was elected to the first of several consecutive terms on the Board of Supervisors! When he died in 1928, he was buried with full civic honors and with Abe Ruef among his mourners.

them to confess what they knew in return for immunity. By the end of March 1907, the remaining supervisors had seized similar opportunities, and the grand jury returned sixty-five more indictments against Ruef, Schmitz, and officers of several utility companies.

Within a month, Ruef himself had confessed in exchange for immunity. By May his testimony resulted in twenty more indictments against the mayor, United Railway Company's president Patrick Calhoun and the firm's chief counsel Tirey L. Ford, and other business executives. During the subsequent prosecution, the longest of its kind in American history, hundreds of potential jurors were called and dismissed. One of them

THE LINCOLN–ROOSEVELT LEAGUE

Democrats might have brought organized progressivism to California early in the twentieth century, except for the ambition of William Randolph Hearst. For personal and political reasons, the publisher twice sabotaged Democratic gubernatorial candidates running on reform platforms. In 1902, Franklin K. Lane lost by a few thousand votes, as did Theodore Bell in 1906. With the backing of the publisher, a nominal Democrat, either could have won; instead, with support from railroad interests, victory went to George C. Pardee and James N. Gillett respectively. At the same time, the Southern Pacific became increasingly active in state politics, financing sympathetic candidates while continuing to charge "whatever the traffic will bear" for its services. Public indignation found expression in newspapers throughout the state, including all of San Francisco's major journals, Charles and James McClatchy's Sacramento *Bee,* Chester H. Rowell's Fresno *Republican,* Harrison Gray Otis's Los Angeles *Times,* Edwin T. Earl's Los Angeles *Express,* and many others. Their outspoken criticism and the publication of Frank Norris's *The Octopus* in 1901 added support to demands for reform.

In 1907 Earl sent Edward A. Dickson to Sacramento to cover the legislature for the *Express;* there, Dickson met Rowell, and the pair discovered that the Southern Pacific's manipulations and their own Republican party's subservience to the corporation were more endemic than either suspected. When Dickson returned to Los Angeles, he consulted with fellow members of the local Non-Partisan Committee and organized progressive "Lincoln Republicans." Rowell found substantial sympathy and support among associates in northern California and valley districts. Urged on by Dickson and Rowell, delegates from throughout the state convened in Oakland in August to form the League of Lincoln–Roosevelt Clubs, or Lincoln–Roosevelt League. These maverick Republicans were determined to recover their party from railroad control, to support progressive candidates in the 1908 elections, to send pro-Theodore Roosevelt delegates to the party's national convention, and to campaign for such reforms as direct primary elections, woman suffrage, and the direct election of U.S. senators.

The league could not control the California Republican party in 1908, but it did score victories, especially in contests for seats in the legislature. Its success resulted from effective grassroots efforts to establish Lincoln–Roosevelt clubs throughout the state, from growing disenchantment with the railroads and their policies, from revelations emanating from the Ruef trials, and from increasing public identification with the progressive policies of President Theodore Roosevelt and his administrations. Success in 1908 also permitted significant accomplishments in the legislature of 1909. Still outnumbered by "regulars," progressive legislators nevertheless managed to amend several railroad bills, to secure a preferential (but not binding) popular vote on U.S. senators, and to pass a direct primary law. By eliminating statewide nominating conventions, the direct primary law promised to reduce the influence of special interests in the selection of candidates, and it set the stage for subsequent progressive achievements.

HIRAM JOHNSON AND THE ELECTION OF 1910

Progressive Republicans realized that the new primary election law afforded an opportunity to gain control not only of their party but also of the state government if they placed electable candidates before the voters in 1910. The recognition that he received as graft-trial prosecutor made Francis J. Heney a logical choice to run for governor. But his outspoken attacks had alienated much of the business community, his recovery from the wound received in 1908 remained in doubt, and he was a registered Democrat. Therefore, progressive Republicans turned to Heney's replacement in the Ruef prosecution, Hiram W. Johnson.

Like many, if not most, progressive leaders in the state, Johnson was a native Californian and a successful professional. Born in Sacramento in 1866, he was the son of Grove L. Johnson, a conservative Republican who had been an assemblyman and who counted the railroads among the clients of his law firm. Hiram Johnson studied law in his father's office and joined him in practice in 1888. Gradually, however, father and son became politically and philosophically alienated, and in 1902 the younger man moved to San Francisco to establish his own practice, with clients ranging from business interests (but not the railroads) to organized labor. He subsequently gained statewide recognition through participation in the Ruef trials and from vociferous denunciations of corporate influence in politics and government. Indeed, because of his aggressive demands for reform, some Californians were calling him a "western Theodore Roosevelt."

Still, Johnson was not eager to seek the gubernatorial nomination; his practice prospered, and San Francisco suited him better than Sacramento. Only substantial pressure from associates—and perhaps recognition that the governorship might lead to the U.S. Senate—persuaded him, but once convinced he proved to be a formidable campaigner. He toured the state in a bright red Locomobile roadster, announcing his arrival in isolated communities with a cow bell, and spoke from the rumble seat of the car. Johnson armed himself with facts, and he used his data to document his condemnation of

Hiram Johnson
Courtesy of the Bancroft Library.

the railroads, their business practices, and their political influence. In the August primaries he won the Republican nomination, as did progressive candidates for most state offices. During the next months, he continued his vigorous campaign and captured the governor's office in November. But it was neither an easy victory nor a landslide; two other candidates campaigned on progressive issues and platforms. Democrat Theodore Bell won more than 150,000 votes and Socialist J. Stitt Wilson of Berkeley nearly 50,000. Only overwhelming strength in southern California raised Johnson's total to more than 177,000. No matter which candidate they voted for in 1910, however, nearly 380,000 Californians cast their ballots for progressivism and political change.

Hiram Johnson and other victorious progressives had formulated few specific programs before they were elected. They were agreed in their determination to end corruption and exploitation of public resources—including human resources—in California, but means to that end were not clearly defined. Therefore, in the interlude between his election and inauguration, Johnson sought advice from Theodore Roosevelt, from Governor Robert M. LaFollette of Wisconsin, and from Meyer Lissner and other leaders of the Lincoln–Roosevelt League throughout the state. When the new governor and his allies took office in 1911, they were prepared to act.

ECONOMIC REGULATION

Progressives in the 1911 legislature took swift action on the issues of railroad and utility regulation and unethical business practices in general. Early in the session, lawmakers received a measure drafted by Railroad Commissioner John M. Eshelman and introduced by Senator John W. Stetson of Alameda. The Stetson-Eshelman Act, which received unanimous legislative approval, increased the authority of the Railroad Commission and empowered it to fix both passenger and freight rates. Constitutional amendments designed to extend and reinforce the legislature's regulatory powers received popular approval at a special election in October. During the following month, the senate and assembly passed a Public Utilities Act without a dissenting vote. The law created a five-member Public Utility Commission (PUC), empowered the governor to appoint commissioners, and gave the agency authority over all public utilities, not just the railroads.

These and other measures enhanced previous legislation that supported the principle of economic regulation in the state. The Bank Act of 1909 had created a state superin-

tendent of banks to review and assess the soundness of financial institutions and to oversee savings and loan operations. A year later another law clarified revenue policies that had been embroiled in controversy since 1879. It authorized a state assessment on corporate incomes and turned property tax collection over to the counties, under the supervision of a state board of equalization.

Thus progressives accomplished in a few years what a generation of reformers since the 1870s had failed to achieve. But theirs was not an antibusiness program, as some opponents claimed. Many progressives were businessmen themselves, and financial and corporate interests contributed to drafting banking and taxation legislation. In fact, support for progressive policies was both statewide and universal, and representatives of even the largest businesses understood not only that regulation was inevitable but also that it could be profitable.

Regulation freed the railroads from rebate arrangements with oil and agricultural interests and from ruinous price wars with each other. Other enterprises benefited similarly. Indeed, during the early years of the PUC, utility companies brought competitors before the courts and the commission more often than they were sued by customers. In 1913, William F. Herrin—by then a Southern Pacific vice president—expressed the new attitude:

> There could be no more insidious or vicious practice than to favor one shipper or class of shippers at the expense of others. . . . Yet these vicious discriminations were frequent before they were abolished by the force of government regulation.

Except for a few reactionaries who denounced all forms of control as socialism or worse, businessmen found that regulation at state expense was congenial and that they could live with it more comfortably than with cutthroat competition among themselves.

California's program was not particularly unique in the early twentieth century. Much of it had been suggested by Populists and other nineteenth-century reformers, and Hiram Johnson solicited advice from progressive leaders elsewhere in the nation. Success in the state also depended on actions by the national government. Investigations conducted under authority of the federal Hepburn Act of 1906, for example, provided the information required to draft and pass the Stetson-Eshelman Act, and only the U.S. Supreme Court finally dissolved the troublesome corporate connection between the Southern Pacific and Union Pacific in 1913. Still, the principle of public regulation established during Johnson's first term was an important turning point in California history, and the governor contributed significantly to the transition. He participated in drafting bills, encouraged their passage, rallied popular support for progressive programs, and signed laws that most of his predecessors would have vetoed.

POLITICAL REFORM

Hiram Johnson and his allies believed that powerful partisan organizations, not California's form of government, were the principal causes of political corruption in the state. They were not the first, however, to reach this conclusion: in 1891 the legislature attempted to curb partisan influence by adopting the Australian secret ballot and followed in 1893 with a law to regulate campaign practices. In 1901 an amendment to regulate primary elections was adopted, but progressives were not satisfied.

Johnson's campaign platform proposed to draw "the people" more directly into public affairs and prescribed specific mechanisms for doing so: the initiative, referendum, and

recall. The initiative allowed voters to propose and approve laws and constitutional amendments, the referendum permitted a popular vote on existing legislation, and the recall provided for removal of elected officials. To place measures on the ballot, citizens would circulate petitions to gather a specified number of signatures, between five percent and eight percent of the vote in the previous election. Amendments providing for the "direct democracy" policies, as progressives liked to call the procedures, met with stubborn opposition from professional politicians and other vested interests. But in 1911 they received nearly unanimous legislative approval and, following Johnson's vigorous campaign on their behalf, overwhelming voter support.

Progressives attempted to reduce party influence even further with two additional policies: nonpartisanship and cross-filing. Legislation in 1911 and 1913 forbade party endorsement of candidates in primary elections and forbade partisan identification on ballots for nearly all state, county, and municipal offices. Only candidates for governor, lieutenant governor, the legislature, and a few state administrative posts were exempted. The 1913 legislature also created a California anomaly: the cross-filing system, which remained in effect until 1959. Cross-filing allowed candidates for state office to place their names, without stating their party affiliation, on primary election ballots of all parties. The practice extended the principle of nonpartisanship and struck at the legitimate purposes of party organizations. It also had some unusual, perhaps unanticipated results. By winning the primaries of both major parties, candidates could—and did—win office without facing constituencies in a general election, and name recognition gave incumbents a very distinct advantage.

Progressives regarded their efforts to "take the politics out of politics" with some satisfaction, but they neither increased popular participation nor curbed the influence of special interests. Californians did not hasten to implement the "direct democracy" offered by the initiative, referendum, or recall. As the number of voters increased, so did the number of signatures needed to qualify ballot measures, until they reached prohibitive levels. Later in the century, indeed, a multitude of highly organized and well-financed special interest groups, often in the guise of trade or professional associations and directed by skilled lobbyists, replaced the vital functions of partisan organizations as means of public influence on the political process.

Their suspicion of partisan politics and conviction that women's involvement would elevate political standards also influenced progressives to support a state suffrage amendment. California women had campaigned for the right to vote since they organized the first suffrage society in 1869, but without success. During the nineteenth century, a legislative committee dismissed their appeal in 1872, the Constitutional Convention denied their petition in 1878, the governor vetoed legislation to allow participation in local school board elections in 1891, and a popular vote rejected the same proposal in 1896. The drive for the vote revived during the progressive era with the formation of the Los Angeles Woman Suffrage League in 1901 and a statewide suffrage convention in 1904. Persistent argument subsequently persuaded enfranchised men that the vote was a woman citizen's right and disenfranchised women that it represented an opportunity to rectify inequities that inhibited them, and early in 1911 the legislature passed a suffrage amendment. Later in the year, despite opposition from men and women and meager support from the governor, it won popular approval—but by a margin of only 4,000 votes. Women subsequently cast their ballots,

but not consistently to promote feminist causes. Thus, like "direct democracy" policies, woman suffrage had less immediate impact than progressives anticipated; two generations later, however, male and female Californians would learn to use both effectively.

LABOR IN PROGRESSIVE CALIFORNIA

Before 1900, active labor organization in California had centered in San Francisco. Workers there had lost some ground since the 1880s, but they still earned more than the current national annual average wage of $425. To preserve their position, local unions formed the Representative Assembly of Trade and Labor Unions, the Coast Seamen's Association, the Federated Iron Trades Council, and other regional associations. In addition, increasing numbers of women in the work force, especially in the garment and service industries, joined unions to protect their interests. Simultaneously, employers banded together to combat unionism, and the erratic economy of the late nineteenth century gave them an advantage. Prosperity after the Panic of 1893, however, brought with it renewed worker activism and organization of the Building Trades Council and the City Front Federation.

The new century also revived employer resistance, led by the secret and well-funded Employers' Association of San Francisco. Consequently, conflict and strikes kept the city in turmoil for much of 1901, but no clear winners emerged from the episode. Mayor Phelan and Democrats lost labor support, and many workers joined the Union Labor Party. The Employers' Association failed to discredit unionism, but for wage-earners the result was mixed. They received no tangible benefits from their prolonged strikes, but they did preserve their right to

KATHERINE PHILIPS EDSON
AND EQUALITY FOR WOMEN

Published by Votes-for-Women Publishing Co., Wilson Bldg., 127 Montgomery St., San Francisco 217

A postcard published to promote votes for women included a poem:

> They said to him "We'll get your goat;"
> He said "It is the *System;*"
> With weapon of the *Woman's Vote*
> They shot; and never missed 'im.

Courtesy of the Bancroft Library.

Hiram Johnson's appointment of Katherine Philips Edson to the Bureau of Labor Statistics (BLS) in 1912 and to the newly created Industrial Welfare Commission (IWC) in 1913 broke with established tradition. To be sure, the constitution of 1849 protected married women's property rights, and beginning in the 1860s women launched a statewide feminist movement. Later in the century, Charlotte Perkins Gilman, Ellen Clark Sargent and others championed women's equality, and a few women were admit-

KATHERINE PHILIPS EDSON
AND EQUALITY FOR WOMEN (continued)

ted to the practice of law, medicine, and other professions. But as late as 1896, despite the example of Wyoming Territory and several states, voters rejected a suffrage amendment. When California became the sixth state, all of them in the West, to grant women the right to vote in 1911, it was a victory won without enthusiastic support from the governor or other progressive leaders. Nor did the appointments that Johnson conferred on Edson signal general approval of women in public life; indeed, Edson herself suspected that the governor was secretly amused by her efforts on behalf of women and workers. She could not be ignored, however.

With other women's club leaders, she had persuaded the Lincoln–Roosevelt League to make suffrage part of its platform and agitated successfully for the short ballot, pure food laws, civic improvements, and other reforms. She also campaigned for Johnson in 1910, supported his bid for the vice presidency in 1912, and, as a Labor Bureau member, lobbied for legislation to create the IWC and empower it to investigate and regulate wages and working conditions for women and children. Despite opposition from organized labor, business interests, and journals such as the Los Angeles *Times*, the commission received approval early in 1913. Edson knew, however, that regulatory agencies remained subject to legal challenge, and in 1914 she led a successful initiative drive for a constitutional amendment to protect their continued existence.

The *Times* sneered that Edson was a mere "female politician" who had "not yet learned to count," and resistance to the IWC and its objectives persisted. In addition, war in 1917 and 1918 and a 1923 U.S. Supreme Court decision (*Adkins* v. *Children's Hospital* judging a District of Columbia minimum-wage law unconstitutional) combined with economic fluctuations to undermine early successes. Still, when Edson stepped down from the IWC in 1931, her leadership had resulted in laws defining minimum wages and maximum hours for women and children in scores of California industries.

For a generation after Edson died in 1933, prejudice, depression, and another war provided powerful impediments to her principal cause: equality for women in public and private life. During the 1960s, however, her California successors gave strong support to adoption of the national equal rights amendment (ERA): "Equality under the law shall not be denied or abridged by the United States or any state on account of sex." Almost identical to an amendment drafted and placed before Congress in 1923, the ERA met determined opposition from women as well as men, and Congress endorsed it only in March 1972. The California assembly gave its approval a month later, followed by the state senate in November. But when time for ratification expired in 1982, the ERA remained three states short of the thirty-eight required. Late in 1983, Congress rejected a second version of the amendment, leaving the fundamental objective of Edson's life still unfulfilled. (WAB) organize, which they used effectively for the next ten years.

In southern California, unionism before 1900 mainly involved conflict between Harrison Gray Otis and employees of his Los Angeles *Times*. A union activist as a youth, by 1880 Otis was a determined foe of organized labor. He fought his battle alone until late in the nineteenth century, when the population, the number of employers, and union activity all increased in Los Angeles. Then the Merchants' and Manufacturers' Association (M&M), formed during the 1880s to promote commerce, joined the fight. Simultaneously, the American Federation of Labor (AFL) and other national unions sent their organizers to the city, and during the early 1900s strikes and lockouts became more frequent. With backing from Otis, publicity in the *Times*, and a municipal antipicketing law passed in 1910, M&M members resisted unionism with substantial success.

Where trade unionism was viable, even California's diluted brand of radicalism attracted few wage-earners. Jack London failed miserably as Socialist candidate for mayor of Oakland in 1901 and 1905. In Berkeley, hardly a working-class community, voters in 1911 chose a Socialist mayor, Methodist minister J. Stitt Wilson. A few Californians also supported Socialist Eugene Debs's presidential candidacies, and they sent an occasional Socialist to Congress or the state legislature. In Los Angeles, however, where employers defied unions and wages were thirty percent less than elsewhere in the state, socialism had greater appeal. Organization began during the 1880s under the leadership of millionaire real estate developer H. Gaylord Wilshire and continued during the 1890s under labor lawyer Job Harriman.

Harriman ran unsuccessfully for governor in 1898 and for vice-president on the Eugene Debs ticket in 1900. In May 1910, members of several unions went out on strike,

with support from the citywide Labor Council, the AFL, Socialists, and organized labor throughout the state. The strike spread, city officials enforced the antipicketing ordinance, and workers joined Socialists to form the Union Labor Political Club and nominate Harriman for mayor. On October 1, at the height of the strike, an explosion killed twenty employees in the Los Angeles Times Building.

Investigations led to union activists John J. and James B. McNamara, who denied both their guilt and union involvement in the bombing. Labor organizations across the nation raised funds and employed Clarence Darrow to defend the brothers against a suspected frame-up. At their trial in 1911, however, the McNamaras admitted guilt and were sentenced: John to life in prison and James to fifteen years. Public support for organized labor evaporated, union members quit in disgust, and antipicketing ordinances were passed throughout the state. At first, apparent persecution of the McNamaras increased Harriman's chances for election, but their confession doomed his candidacy and the Socialist party in Los Angeles. The episode also resulted in victory for Otis and opponents of organized labor in the city, where the "open-shop" principle prevailed until the 1930s.

Six years later, similar events had similar consequences in San Francisco. In 1916, the local Merchants' and Manufacturers' Association renewed its resistance to unionism. During the same year the Chamber of Commerce formed a "Law and Order Committee" with a million-dollar budget to break a longshoremen's strike for higher wages, and within a week strikers returned to work without pay increases. Almost simultaneously, San Franciscans held a "Preparedness Day" parade in response to the nation's potential involvement in World War I in Europe. As the procession moved along Market Street on July 22, a bomb blast killed ten people and maimed forty more. Days later, police arrested several union activists, including Tom Mooney and Warren K. Billings. Unlike the McNamaras, however, the accused San Franciscans maintained their innocence through a long and hysterical trial that bore little resemblance to a judicial proceeding. In January 1917 both were found guilty and sentenced: Mooney to death and Billings to life in prison.

Although Mooney's sentence was commuted, he remained behind bars despite appeals from around the world, evidence that contradicted much of the testimony against him, and proof that District Attorney Charles M. Fickert had encouraged perjury. Governor Culbert Olson finally pardoned Mooney in 1939, but as an immediate result of the affair, public and official hostility toward unionism reached unprecedented heights in California.

FEARS OF RADICALISM

As an attorney, Hiram Johnson defended organized labor, and as governor he appointed union leaders to positions in state government. But most progressives in California and elsewhere were less than enthusiastic supporters of the principle of labor organization. They could not, however, ignore either their working-class constituencies or their own commitment to the ideal of social justice. Associations such as the San Francisco Labor Council and the State Labor Federation had enthusiastically endorsed progressives' candidacies and proposed policies that the state government adopted. Among these were an Employer Liability Act to define responsibility for on-the-job injuries, an Industrial Accident Board to review cases, eight-hour and minimum-wage laws for women, an Industrial Welfare Commission to regulate working conditions

for women and children, and a state workers' insurance program. These and similar measures were long overdue departures from established tradition and demonstrated progressives' concern for the welfare of wage-earning Californians.

Many progressives, however, remained suspicious of organized labor. In 1911, for example, the legislature nearly approved a compulsory arbitration bill that was a step toward abolishing the right to strike. It also defeated a bill, introduced by Senator Anthony Caminetti and supported by other progressive Democrats, that would have limited the use of injunctions against strikes, forbidden employers' "black lists" and "yellow-dog" contracts, and legalized boycotts and peaceful picketing. Some progressives, in fact, exhibited no sympathy at all for striking workers and agreed with a remark attributed to James D. Phelan: "If they don't want to be clubbed, let them return to work." Several things influenced their attitudes. Some identified with employer interests; others rejected the notion of "class" in American society. More general was repulsion at events such as the Times Building bombing, but the fear of "radicalism" and its equation with working-class militancy was most significant in shaping their attitudes.

This aspect of the progressive disposition manifested itself quite early. When anarchist Emma Goldman appeared in San Francisco in 1908 and 1909, city and state authorities resorted to harassment and arrest to deny her a forum. Even more significant was the arrival of the radical Industrial Workers of the World (IWW or "Wobblies"). Founded in Chicago in 1905, the IWW began to make some progress among workers in the mines, forests, and fields of the West. In California in 1910 it had only 1,000 members in eleven locals, but that was enough to prompt Fresno, San Diego, and several other cities to pass laws outlawing the Wobblies' primary

JACK LONDON
Sometime Socialist

Jack London and his dog Rollo, circa 1885
Courtesy of the Bancroft Library.

Born in San Francisco in 1876, Jack London was the illegitimate child of spiritualist Flora Wellman and astrologer William Chaney. When Chaney denied his son and departed, Jack's mother married John London, a widower with five children, and joined a family that lived constantly on the brink of disaster. After the failure of an Oakland grocery store and a succession of farms in Alameda, San Mateo, and the Livermore Valley, the Londons returned to Oakland where Flora ran a boardinghouse and John did odd jobs. Jack contributed his meager income from a paper route and work in local canneries to the family's support. He attended school when he could and read voraciously, but by his fifteenth birthday he was well on his way to becoming a delinquent on the Oakland waterfront. To escape, in 1893 he signed on for a gruesome seal-hunting voyage to the Bering Sea and a year later he joined Jacob Coxey's army of unemployed workers marching to Washington. He made it as far as Chicago, drifted to Buffalo where he was jailed for vagrancy, and returned home to try his hand at writing. In 1897, he departed again—this time for the Klondike in search of gold.

JACK LONDON (continued)
Sometime Socialist

London's early experiences provided raw material for much of his writing: *The Cruise of the Dazzler* (1902), *The Call of the Wild* (1903), *The People of the Abyss* (1903), *The Road* (1907), *Martin Eden* (1909), *John Barleycorn* (1913), and more. They also influenced a philosophy that owed as much to Herbert Spencer and Friedrich Nietzche as it did to Karl Marx.

His ideas were confused and often contradictory. As a self-proclaimed socialist, he advocated the brotherhood and equality of man in lectures and writings, yet he was personally committed to notions of Anglo-Saxon superiority. He promoted the ideals of social responsibility and justice, but he understood life as a tooth-and-claw struggle that allowed only the fittest—those like himself—to survive. He championed the cause of the working classes, yet his associates were "The Crowd"—artists and intellectuals who populated an elite colony at Carmel. London defined success in materialistic rather than ideal terms. But when he achieved it as an author and journalist, he used its rewards for personal gratification, especially building the *Snark* for an ill-fated around-the-world voyage and his Beauty Ranch and Wolf House near Glen Ellen. He squandered his money, often unwisely and rarely to benefit wage-earners.

London's life, like his socialism, was a contradiction. He was obsessed with physical and mental fitness, but he abused his body and his mind by gorging on blood-rare meat and consuming prodigious quantities of alcohol and drugs to combat insomnia and ease pain. Indeed, his death at Beauty Ranch in 1916 resulted from an overdose of morphine; whether it was accidental or intentional remains uncertain. (WAB)

---

organizing tactic: making speeches and singing anticapitalist songs in public places. When IWW members tested the law in Fresno in 1910, they were jailed, doused with fire hoses, and threatened with lynching. Two years later in San Diego, Wobblies were denounced by a hostile press, confronted by a vigilance committee of armed businessmen, beaten brutally, and arrested. Two were killed while in jail, one of them kicked to death.

As governor, Hiram Johnson could not ignore such episodes. He ordered an investigation and appointed Sacramento merchant Harris Weinstock to direct it. No friend of labor, Weinstock nevertheless joined Fremont Older and Chester Rowell in challenging the legality of local anti-IWW laws (all were declared unconstitutional by state and federal courts) and condemning the actions of citizens and authorities in Fresno and San Diego. The Free Speech Fights, as they came to be known, did not, however, reduce hostility toward radicalism or end IWW activity in progressive California.

During the summer of 1913, 2,800 adults and children responded to recruiting literature from the Durst Hop Ranch near Wheatland, south of Marysville. When they arrived, they found that only 800 harvesters actually were needed, that housing and campsites (rented from Durst) were grossly inadequate, that sanitary facilities consisted of eight crude privies, that the only thing to drink in the scorching fields was "lemonade" (citric acid and water) purchased from Durst's cousin, and that a bonus promised for working through the harvest was a "hold-back" from wages to be paid at season's end. Among the workers were Wobblies who organized a meeting to protest conditions. Sheriff's deputies confronted the assembled workers, shots were fired, and five people were killed: two deputies, two workers, and the district attorney of Yuba County.

In the aftermath of the Wheatland riot, IWW members Blackie Ford and Herman Suhr were tracked down, convicted of second-degree murder because they had organized the protest, and imprisoned. In addition, the Commission on Immigration and Housing, established earlier in 1913, investigated living and working conditions of California farm laborers—nomads who existed almost invisibly on the fringes of society—and documented their universally appalling situation. The committee's report resulted in passage of the Labor Camp Act of 1915, but concern was not sufficiently sustained to overcome growers' resistance or to end the state's perennial farm labor problem. Nor did it lessen the progressive generation's suspicion of radicalism.

THE CRIMINAL SYNDICALISM ACT, 1919

Events in California—including Goldman's visit, the Free Speech Fights, Wobblies' presence at Wheatland, bombings in Los Angeles and San Francisco, and active Socialist Party agitation—increased fears of radicalism, however defined. Local attitudes also mirrored a national mood reinforced by involvement in World War I, by the Bolshevik revolution in Russia in 1917, and by hysteria generated by U.S. Attorney General A. Mitchell Palmer's "red raids" in the summer

of 1919. During the early twentieth century, more than twenty states enacted antiradical laws, but none was more energetically enforced than California's Criminal Syndicalism Act of 1919.

The vague statute made it illegal to promote "any doctrine or precept advocating . . . unlawful acts of violence . . . as a means of accomplishing a change in industrial ownership or control, or effecting any political change." Neither action nor encouragement of action was required for prosecution; mere advocacy of an ideology that accepted violence was sufficient. During the next five years, more than 500 individuals faced trial under the act; the first was fifty-two-year-old Oakland philanthropist and social worker Charlotte Anita Whitney, a descendant of prominent New England and California families. She was a pacifist who became a socialist in 1914, joined the Communist Labor Party in 1919, and was arrested for her activities shortly after the Criminal Syndicalism Act became law. Her trial in 1920 resulted in conviction and a sentence to fourteen years in the state penitentiary. While Whitney remained free on bail, Fremont Older and others supported a series of appeals and attorney John F. Neylan fought her case all the way to the U.S. Supreme Court, which in 1927 upheld both her conviction and the constitutionality of the California law. A month later, Governor Clement C. Young pardoned her, not because an injustice had been done but because sending a sixty-year-old woman to prison would create a martyr in the cause of radicalism. The law continued to function until 1968, when federal courts invalidated it.

RACE IN PROGRESSIVE CALIFORNIA

In most parts of the United States during the early twentieth century, African Americans were objects of hatred, discrimination, and even lynching; in 1915, attitudes toward them were confirmed symbolically in D. W. Griffith's film *The Birth of a Nation,* which glorified the Ku Klux Klan and which was regarded by many as "history." In California, the number of black people remained relatively small before World War I—about two percent of the population. They did experience discrimination in housing and employment, but they were sufficiently secure to form chapters of the National Association for the Advancement of Colored People (NAACP) and the Urban League, to protest showings of Griffith's film in Los Angeles and Oakland, and to host NAACP cofounder W. E. B. DuBois during his 1913 national tour. Black Californians were also politically active; in Los Angeles they helped to elect the state's first black legislator, Assemblyman Frederick M. Roberts, who served from 1919 to 1934.

During the first decades of the twentieth century, Spanish-speaking descendants of the *californios* were rapidly outnumbered by tens of thousands fleeing political and economic dislocations in Mexico and seeking employment in the United States. Although the number included members of the white-collar and professional classes, most found work only as menials and laborers. They settled in *barrios* in Los Angeles, Santa Barbara, San Diego, and other cities, or in *colonias* in agricultural regions, where they became the mainstay of the farm labor force. In Mexican communities, successive waves of immigrants preserved and reinforced elements of the native culture, especially their religion. They were barely tolerated in the state, but like African Americans, Chinese, and Indians, they were usually ignored rather than actively persecuted.

Such was not the case for Japanese migrants who arrived at the turn of the century, first from the Hawaiian Islands and then from Japan itself. By 1910, approxi-

mately 41,000 Japanese had settled in California and inherited the state's hostility toward Asians. Their small numbers mattered little; in 1906, a labor-sponsored Asiatic Exclusion League convinced the San Francisco Board of Education to combat the "yellow peril" by segregating the city's ninety-three Japanese schoolchildren. The incident resulted in a diplomatic crisis, intervention by President Roosevelt, and the "Gentlemen's Agreement" of 1907, by which Japan consented to limit migration to the United States.

This solution was neither permanent nor satisfactory to most Californians. Nor were labor leaders alone in their agitation for exclusion; James D. Phelan, Harrison Gray Otis, Chester Rowell, and Grove Johnson, among others, added their voices to the chorus. So, too, did members of all political parties (including Socialists), citizens of nearly every national origin, and small farm operators throughout the state. Although Japanese farm workers had joined with Mexicans in strikes in the fields as early as 1903, they were not content to remain laborers. They obtained land—often marginal tracts bought or leased from large growers—where they introduced rice, potatoes, and other crops to California agriculture. They became successful truck farmers, raising tomatoes, vegetables, and a variety of fresh produce. By 1910, Japanese farmers, most of them *issei* (first generation), owned about 17,000 acres, leased more than 80,000, and sharecropped another 60,000, putting them in direct competition with local small farmers.

Beginning in 1909 state Senator Anthony Caminetti and other legislators introduced a series of bills to restrict Japanese land ownership and to permit segregation in city schools and residential neighborhoods. The Los Angeles and San Francisco chambers of commerce, major growers who leased land to the Japanese, and a few editors argued that the "Gentlemen's Agreement" made restrictive legislation unnecessary and unwise. But only intervention by the Republican administration in Washington and pressure from business interests preparing for the Panama-Pacific Exposition scheduled for San Francisco in 1915 prevented the bills' passage. Early in 1913, however, the situation changed when Democrat Woodrow Wilson entered the White House. Wilson opposed anti-Japanese legislation and even sent Secretary of State William Jennings Bryan to present his views, quite ineffectively, in California. The state's Republicans felt little loyalty to the new president, and local Democrats were less than enthusiastic Wilsonians. Therefore, with Hiram Johnson's backing and only token Democratic opposition, the legislature passed the Alien Land Law of 1913 by votes of thirty-five to two in the senate and seventy-two to three in the assembly. The governor added his signature on May 19.

According to the law, "aliens ineligible to citizenship"—the same euphemism employed in discriminatory laws during the gold rush—could not purchase California land or lease it for more than three years. Legal loopholes remained, and Japanese took advantage of them by buying or leasing land in the name of their *nisei* (second generation) children or in partnership with whites. Still, most Californians believed with Hiram Johnson that the Alien Land Law had "laid [to rest], the ghost of the Japanese question." To make certain, farmers, organized labor, Native Sons of the Golden West, the American Legion, and other groups united behind a successful 1920 initiative campaign to make the law more restrictive.

WATER FOR THE CITIES: HETCH HETCHY AND OWENS VALLEY

Progressives at both state and national levels introduced important conservation policies, but they also differed on exactly what conservation meant. In 1910 the disagreement divided the U.S. Department of the Interior into opposing camps: utilitarians (who advocated conservation for use) aligned with Secretary Richard A. Ballinger and pure preservationists, represented by Chief Forester Gifford Pinchot. Pinchot's opposition to private exploitation of Alaskan coal and water resources led to his dismissal. In California, San Francisco's drive to obtain water from the Hetch Hetchy Valley on the Tuolumne River and Los Angeles's effort to tap the Owens River involved similar conflicts between utilitarian and preservationist philosophies, among other issues.

With no reliable source of water for a growing population, San Francisco relied on private contractors, especially the Spring Valley Water Company, to supply its needs. The charter of 1898 provided means to end the dependency through municipal ownership and, after considering several sites, Mayor James D. Phelan and city officials committed themselves in 1900 to Hetch Hetchy Valley. Because the area was within Yosemite National Park, San Francisco required congressional approval, but the city's application touched off a thirteen-year conflict between opposing factions of conservationists. The state's congressional delegation lobbied their House and Senate colleagues in favor of the project, but opposition was just as vigorous, especially from John Muir and the Sierra Club, which he founded in 1892. Preservationists denounced damming the valley, which they called a "miniature Yosemite," and argued that destroying it would deprive Californians of its natural benefits. Utilitarians argued that a lake would be just as beneficial and that San Francisco's dependence on private contractors placed the city in physical and political jeopardy; the 1906 fire and the Ruef trials had made that abundantly apparent.

Until 1913, however, neither side prevailed. Then Woodrow Wilson appointed Franklin K. Lane, former San Francisco city attorney, to the post of secretary of the interior. With Lane's backing, a measure introduced by Representative John E. Raker of Fresno provided the necessary congressional approval. Passage of the Raker Act in 1913 gave utilitarians a victory, and construction began immediately on a dam and a 200-mile aqueduct to deliver water to San Francisco. When it was completed in 1934, the Hetch Hetchy system supplied both water and hydroelectric power to residents of the city and other Bay Area communities.

If San Francisco was dry, Los Angeles was parched; water wars there pitted preservationists against utilitarians but utilitarians against one another. By the early twentieth century, population growth had created a water crisis in the city, and in 1904 former mayor and city engineer Fred Eaton suggested a solution: tapping the Owens River, 240 miles away on the eastern watershed of the Sierra. Eaton began buying land around Long Valley at the head of the Owens Valley as part of his private scheme to sell water to both local farmers and distant city dwellers. When a drought depleted Los Angeles reservoirs, Eaton enlisted the help of his friend, city engineer William Mulholland. Simultaneously, federal reclamation activities in the valley negated his original idea and, with Mulholland's support, he arranged to sell his holdings to Los Angeles. He also acted as the city's agent, buying additional land and water rights in the name of the municipality.

Both Eaton's activities and the city's involvement remained secret until July 1905, when the Los Angeles *Times* and its rival, the *Examiner*, published dramatically different treatments of the project. Harrison Gray Otis's *Times* enthusiastically detailed Eaton's plan and cataloged its benefits to the city. According to the *Examiner's* version, though, a syndicate of speculators—including Otis and Henry E. Huntington of the Pacific Electric Railway—had bought property in the dry San Fernando Valley and intended to use the Owens River scheme to increase its value at public expense. But these allegations did not deter local voters; in September 1905 they approved a bond issue and work on the project began. Mulholland supervised construction of the aqueduct system, which he designed to operate by siphoning action, virtually without pumping. Department of the Interior officials cooperated by including near-desert lands in the Sierra National Forest and preventing homestead and other claims from interfering with the aqueduct's right-of-way, and the first water entered the San Fernando Valley, recently annexed to Los Angeles, in 1913.

The Owens River project encountered opposition from preservationists, but the most vocal critics were utilitarians: residents of the valley who feared loss of their own water resources. They fought the aqueduct from the beginning, even resorting to sabotage and dynamite during the 1920s, and their fears—if not their tactics—were justified. Eaton's million dollar asking price for his Long Valley property prevented municipal acquisition. As a consequence, until 1941 water flowed directly from the river, not from the planned reservoir, into the aqueduct. By then, the crops and flocks of the region were disappearing. Subsequent enlargement of the project also threatened the Mono Lake ecosystem, but the Owens Valley system continued to expand to meet Los Angeles's constantly increasing need for water.

THE END OF AN ERA

Two events in 1906 marked the opening of the progressive era in California: the San Francisco earthquake and fire and the beginning of the Ruef graft trials. Two more in

1917 delineated the beginning of its demise: the nation's entry into World War I and Hiram Johnson's departure for the U.S. Senate.

The outbreak of war in Europe in August 1914 nudged a sluggish economy as demands for food and war materiel stimulated the state's industries and accelerated the pace of corporate organization. After the war ended in 1918, economic expansion continued into the 1920s. In the meantime, more than 150,000 Californians served in the military, the state's universities provided officer training programs, and the public furnished financial support through the purchase of Liberty Bonds. But war also disrupted the progressive movement.

Progressives rarely achieved consensus on the issue of foreign affairs, even before 1914, and during the period before the nation entered World War I they clashed over American relations with the European belligerents. Many Californians saw no connection between British or French interests and their own and supported efforts to form a League of Neutrals in order to maintain commerce with all warring powers. Progressives were also at odds over proposals to keep Americans from traveling into submarine zones on belligerent ships and over the preparedness policy advocated by the Woodrow Wilson administration. Like Hiram Johnson, who called preparedness "bunk" as late as 1917, they saw the heavy hands of munitions makers and bankers behind it. After the armistice was signed in 1918, they were equally unable to agree on the treaties negotiated in Paris and plans for a League of Nations. Thus the war and related issues fragmented the progressive movement and hastened its decline in both the state and the nation.

Hiram Johnson contributed to the same end, not only by his departure for the Senate in 1917 but also by his personality. He was self-centered, self-righteous, abrasive, ambitious, and, some say, messianic. By the end of his first term, he was regarded by many—perhaps including himself—as the embodiment of California progressivism. He was intolerant of disagreement and alienated former allies, including founders of the Lincoln–Roosevelt League, and his insistence on the formation of a California Progressive Party in 1913 added to the discord. When Francis J. Heney won the Republican nomination to run for the U.S. Senate in 1914, Johnson felt betrayed; Heney in turn accused Johnson of engineering his defeat when he lost the race to Democrat James D. Phelan. Nor did Johnson's 1914 reelection reduce problems. Johnson remained ambitious for a U.S. Senate seat. By cross-filing in the Republican and Progressive primaries, he won the office in 1916, but his tactics deepened divisions in reformers' ranks.

Earlier events also predicted strife. In the 1914 Republican primary, Helen K. Williams, publisher of *The Woman Citizen* magazine, became a candidate for lieutenant governor on a slate with John M. Frederick of Los Angeles to challenge the seemingly invincible incumbent. Two years later, she formed the Women's Republican Central Committee, an alternative to the party-sanctioned Women's Auxiliary of the Republican State Central Committee. In addition, when John M. Eshelman, Johnson's handpicked lieutenant governor, died early in 1916, Johnson was forced to placate progressives in southern California by filling the vacancy with William D. Stephens, whom he distrusted. The governor then refused to step down for two weeks after taking the oath as senator. Only the president's call to an emergency session of Congress forced his resignation; in the interim the fragile unity of California progressives eroded further.

As governor, Stephens compiled a modestly progressive record, but by 1917 cohesion was gone. Even Johnson was soon back in Republican ranks. The war dis-

The Ultimate Bungalow:
Greene and Greene's Gamble House, completed in Pasadena in 1908. *Photograph by Richard J. Orsi.*

tracted attention from issues of reform and produced bellicose patriotism and aggressive racism in the state. War was disillusioning, too, especially its failure to "make the world safe for democracy," and in its aftermath Hiram Johnson and many other progressives became rigid isolationists and irreconcilable foes of the League of Nations. But even earlier, most Californians had turned their energies to the economic development that characterized the 1920s.

California progressives' record was a mixed one. Their political reforms did not achieve all that they expected and, in some cases, had negative consequences. Despite their advocacy of social justice, they presented few programs to assist the state's growing minority population. Indeed, many were bigots, and most were extremely intolerant of dissent. Well-intended moral reforms to regulate gambling, alcohol, and prostitution often attacked symptoms of problems rather than causes. In the wake of

the passage of the Red Light Abatement Act in 1913, for example, 200 prostitutes gathered in the chapel of a San Francisco evangelist who had been one of its major supporters and asked what he proposed that they should now do to earn a living. On the positive side, progressives made drastic changes in the defined role of government. They agreed with the comment attributed to Abraham Lincoln that governments exist to do for the people what they cannot do for themselves, and they recognized that increasingly complex urban-industrial societies multiplied governments' responsibilities. To their credit, they acted on that recognition.

TURN-OF-THE-CENTURY CALIFORNIA CULTURE

Because the state's cultural development remained more imitative than innovative, Californians self-consciously sought something to call their own and in the process discovered (or "invented") and romanticized the region's Spanish and Indian heritage. Once assimilated into popular and promotional literature, prose and poetry, art and architecture, and even orange crate labels, the ideology persisted. It prompted mission restoration programs, renaming the mission trail (Highway 101) "El Camino Real," and marking it with miniature mission bells. It also inspired annual celebrations including the Ramona Pageant at Hemet, the Old Spanish Days Fiesta in Santa Barbara, and the ride of *los rancheros visitadores* through Ventura and Santa Barbara counties. Its most immediate and emphatic manifestation, however, appeared in the arts and architecture.

Residents of the state responded enthusiastically to New Yorker Helen Hunt Jackson's romance of early California, *Ramona*, in 1884, but within a year they had their own proponent of the Spanish-Indian heritage. Late in 1885, New England-born and Harvard-educated Charles Fletcher Lummis arrived at San Fernando after walking from Ohio to recover his health. He found employment with the Los Angeles *Times*, and a decade later he became editor of *Land of Sunshine* magazine, subsequently called *Out West*. In the interim, Lummis wrote for the *Times*, published *A Tramp across the Continent* (1892) and the *Spanish Pioneers* (1893), steeped himself in the lore of Spanish California, adopted the *charro* (Mexican cowboy) costume, and called himself "Don Carlos." In his role as editor, Lummis published his own work and that of like-minded writers of scholarly studies and fiction. He also became a cult figure and guru to a colony of artists and academics living along the Arroyo Seco near Pasadena in villas built of native stone and adobe, decorated with Indian artifacts (usually Hopi or Navajo), and filled with rough-hewn, "mission" furniture.

Despite his overt flamboyance, Lummis's

commitment to the West and its history ran deep, and he influenced the careers of numerous talented westerners. He published Mary Austin's first work and praised her *The Land of Little Rain* (1903), romances such as *Isidro* (1905) and *Santa Lucia* (1908), feminist novels including *A Woman of Genius* (1912), and extended essays such as *California, Land of Sun* (1914). He printed Jack London's early short stories, applauded Frank Norris's *McTeague* and *The Octopus*, and encouraged Robinson Jeffers, soon to be California's premier twentieth-century poet. Fresno-born painter Maynard Dixon likewise received Lummis's support before he focused his talent on the Southwest. To preserve the state's past, Lummis worked to establish The Southwest Museum, but when it opened in 1914 his health had begun to falter, as had his influence. To a generation maturing in a complex industrial society and about to become involved in a world war, his romantic vision of a simpler age no longer seemed appropriate. From his home on the Arroyo Seco, where he died in 1928, Don Carlos lamented the fading of his dream, but he could not stay the tide.

Turn-of-the-century California architects also responded to the rediscovered Spanish heritage and expressed it in Mission Revival designs for public buildings and in tile-roofed imitations of adobe villas. During the early 1900s Charles and Henry Greene of Pasadena introduced a more unique structure and style: the bungalow, combining beauty and utility in open patios, uncluttered interiors, and broad verandas with construction in native materials. Although the Greenes built for wealthy clients, imitators made the bungalow a favored residential style among all Californians. A different approach, however, resulted from the work of New Yorker Arthur Page Brown who arrived in San Francisco in 1889. Before he died seven years later at age thirty-six, Brown charted new directions by assimilating styles ranging from Classical to Mission Revival and integrating native materials with modern glass and steel. Brown's firm also provided employment and experience for individuals who continued to develop a local architectural tradition; they included New York-born Bernard Maybeck.

Maybeck served temporarily as professor of geometry and informally as professor of architecture at the University of California, but he lost the position in 1901 to another New Yorker, John Galen Howard. Subsequently, he designed Bay Area residences and evolved a personal approach that integrated traditional styles with natural materials, unpainted shingle exteriors with lightly-tinted accents, and living space with landscape in the Oriental manner. He also harmonized industrial products—steel, asbestos, and cast concrete—with past architectural traditions and natural elements, exemplified in his 1910 design for the Christian Science Church in Berkeley. His major contribution to public architecture is the sole survivor of the 1915 Panama-Pacific Exposition, the San Francisco Palace of Fine Arts, permanently rebuilt after the original temporary structure deteriorated. In addition, Maybeck taught and encouraged students, including Julia Morgan—the first woman to receive an engineering degree from the University of California (1894), the first to graduate in architecture from the Ecole des Beaux Arts in Paris (1902), and the first licensed to practice architecture in California (1904).

When Morgan established her own firm in San Francisco, she was a competent civil engineer who undertook and supervised projects such as rebuilding the fire-gutted Fairmont Hotel. But she was more. A master of architectural traditions, she expressed them in her Spanish treatment of buildings on the Mills College campus, in her application of Tudor Revival, Moorish, and Mediterranean elements to Piedmont residences, in the Renaissance design of the Oakland YMCA Building, in the Neo-Classical facade of a gymnasium on the U.C. campus, and in William Randolph Hearst's eclectic melange, La Cuesta Encantada, at San Simeon. To each style she added her own sense of line, form, mass, and proportion, and until she retired in 1950, she continued to work and to evolve new principles that produced unobtrusive exteriors blended with landscape and open, functional interiors bathed in light. Along with her teacher and friend Maybeck, Morgan was a major influence on the development of a recognizable California architectural esthetic. Ironically, the two innovators died within months of one another in 1957.

SUGGESTIONS FOR FURTHER READING

Politics and Reform

William A. Bullough, *The Blind Boss and His City: Christopher Augustine Buckley and Nineteenth-Century San Francisco* (1979), "The Steam Beer Handicap: Chris Buckley and the San Francisco Municipal Election of 1896," *California Historical Quarterly* (1975), and "Hannibal versus the Blind Boss: The Junta, Chris Buckley, and Democratic Reform Politics in San Francisco," *Pacific Historical Review* (1977); Alexander B. Callow, Jr., "San Francisco's Blind Boss," *Pacific Historical Review* (1956); R. Hal Williams, *The Democratic Party and California Politics, 1880–1896* (1973); Edith Dobie, *The Political Career of Stephen Mallory White* (1927); Walton Bean, *Boss Ruef's San Francisco* (1952); James P. Walsh, "Abe Ruef Was No Boss: Machine Politics, Reform, and San Francisco," *California Historical Quarterly* (1972); Spencer C. Olin, Jr., *California's Prodigal Sons: Hiram Johnson and the Progressives, 1911–1917* (1963); Tom Sitton, *John Randolph Haynes: California Progressive* (1992); Richard Coke Lower, *A Bloc of One: The Polit-*

ical Career of Hiram W. Johnson (1993); Mary A. Hill, Charlotte Perkins Gilman: The Making of a Radical Feminist (1980); George E. Mowry, The California Progressives (1951); William Deverell and Tom Sitton (eds.), California Progressivism Revisited (1994); Norris C. Hundley, Jr. "Katherine Philips Edson and the Fight for the California Minimum Wage, 1912–1923," Pacific Historical Review (1960); Jacqueline R. Braitman, "A California Stateswoman: The Public Career of Katherine Philips Edson," California History (1986); Joan M. Jensen and Gloria Ricci Lothrop, California Women: A History (1987); Martin J. Schiesl, "Progressive Reform in Los Angeles under Mayor Alexander, 1909–1913," California Historical Quarterly (1975); Herbert P. LePore, "Prelude to Prejudice: Hiram Johnson, Woodrow Wilson, and the California Alien Land Controversy of 1913," Southern California Quarterly (1979).

Labor and Radicalism

David F. Selvin, A Place in the Sun: A History of California Labor (1981); Ira B. Cross, A History of the Labor Movement in California (1935); Grace H. Stimson, Rise of the Labor Movement in Los Angeles (1955); Louis B. and Richard S. Perry, A History of the Los Angeles Labor Movement (1963); Robert E. L. Knight, Industrial Relations in the San Francisco Bay Area 1900–1918 (1960); Carey McWilliams, Factories in the Fields (1939); Donald J. Pisani, From the Family Farm to Agribusiness (1984); Carleton H. Parker, "The Wheatland Riot and What Lay Back of It," The Survey (1914); Alexander Saxton, The Indispensable Enemy: Labor and the Anti-Chinese Movement (1971) and "San Francisco Labor and the Populist and Progressive Insurgencies," Pacific Historical Review (1965); Arnold Berwick, The Abraham Lincoln of the Sea: A Biography of Andrew Furuseth (1993); Ronald Genini, "Industrial Workers of the World and Their Fresno Free-Speech Fight, 1910–1911," California Historical Quarterly (1974); Richard H. Frost, The Mooney Case (1968); W. W. Robinson, Bombs and Bribery: Story of the McNamara and Darrow Trials (1969); Woodrow C. Whitten, Criminal Syndicalism and the Law in California, 1919–1927 (1969); Howard Quint, "Gaylord Wilshire and Socialism's First Congressional Campaign;" Pacific Historical Review (1957); Mary Ann Irwin, "'Going about Doing Good': The Politics of Benevolence, Welfare and Gender in San Francisco,

1850–1880," Pacific Historical Review (1999); Jacqueline R. Braitman, "A California Stateswoman: The Public Career of Katherine Philips Edson," California History (1986); Gayle Gullett, "Women Progressives and the Politics of Americanization in California, 1915–1920," Pacific Historical Review (1995); R.J. Chandler, "In the Van—Spiritualism as a Catalyst for the California Women's Suffrage Movement," California History (1994); Woodrow C. Whitten, "The Trial of Charlotte Anita Whitney," Pacific Historical Review (1946); Lisa Rubens, "The Patrician Radical: Charlotte Anita Whitney," California History (1986); Joyce M. Dicks, "Repression in the Progressive Era: Emma Goldman in San Francisco, 1908–1909" (M.A. thesis, California State University, Hayward, 1984); Michael E. Engh, S.J., "Mary Julia Workman, the Catholic Conscience of Los Angeles," California History (1993); William B. Friedricks, "Capital and Labor in Los Angeles: Henry E. Huntington vs. Organized Labor, 1900–1920," Pacific Historical Review (1990); Burnette G. Haskell, "How Kaweah Fell," San Francisco Examiner (29 November 1891) and "Kaweah: How and Why the Colony Died," Out West (September 1902); Robert V. Hine, California's Utopian Colonies (1953) and California Utopianism: Contemplations of Eden (1981); William Carey Jones, "The Kaweah Experiment in Co-operation," Quarterly Journal of Economics (October 1891); Paul Kagan, New World Utopias: A Photographic History of the Search for Community (1975); Ruth R. Lewis, "Kaweah: An Experiment in Co-operative Colonization," Pacific Historical Review (November 1948); Daniel Cornford (ed.), Working People of California (1995).

Southern California

Glenn S. Dumke, The Boom of the 'Eighties in Southern California (1944); Robert R. Fogelson, The Fragmented Metropolis: Los Angeles, 1850–1930 (1967); Clarence H. Matson, Building a World Gateway: The Story of the Los Angeles Harbor (1945); Andrew Rolle, Los Angeles: From Pueblo to City of the Future (1981); Carey McWilliams, Southern California Country (1946); W. H. Hutchinson, Oil, Land and Politics: The California Career of Thomas R. Bard (1965); Gerald T. White, Scientists in Conflict: The Beginning of the Oil Industry in California (1968); John E. Baur, Health Seekers of Southern California (1944); Richard Griswold del Castillo, The Los Angeles Barrio (1979); Kevin

Starr, *Material Dreams: Southern California Through the 1920s* (1990).

Water and the Cities

Abraham Hoffman, *Vision or Villainy: Origins of the Los Angeles-Owens Valley Water Controversy* (1981); William L. Kahrl, "The Politics of California Water: Owens Valley and the Los Angeles Aqueduct," *California Historical Quarterly* (1976) and *Water and Power: The Conflict over Los Angeles's Water Supply in the Owens Valley* (1982); Holway R. Jones, *John Muir and the Sierra Club: The Fight for Yosemite* (1965); Kendrick A. Clements, "Politics and the Park: San Francisco's Fight for Hetch Hetchy, 1908–1913," *Pacific Historical Review* (1979).

Culture and Society

W. A. Swanberg, *Citizen Hearst* (1961); Sandra Sizer Frankiel, *California's Spiritual Frontiers: Religious Alternatives to Anglo-Protestantism, 1850–1910* (1988); Richard B. Rice, "The California Press and American Neutrality, 1914–1917" (Ph.D. thesis, University of California, Berkeley, 1957); Arnold Genthe and Will Irwin, *Pictures of Old Chinatown* (1909); Peter E. Palmquist, *Carleton E. Watkins: Photographer of the American West* (1983) and *Shadowcatchers: Women in California Photography Before 1901* (1990); Robert B. Haas, *Muybridge: Man in Motion* (1976); William A. Bullough, "Eadweard Muybridge and the Old San Francisco Mint: Archival Photographs as Historical Documents" *California History* (1989); and "History through the Lens: The Photographs of John Calvin Brewster, 1874–1909" Ventura County Historical Society *Quarterly* (1995); Donald J. Pisani, *From the Family Farm to Agribusiness* (1984); Andrew Sinclair, *Jack: A Biography of Jack London* (1977); Joan London, *Jack London and His Times: An Unconventional Biography* (1939); Robert V. Hine, *Josiah Royce: From Grass Valley to Harvard* (1992); Harold S. Kirker, *California's Architectural Frontier* (1960) and *Old Forms on a New Land: California Architecture in Perspective* (1991); Sara Holmes Boutelle, *Julia Morgan, Architect* (1988); Sally B. Woodbridge, *California Architecture* (1988); Robert Winter, *The California Bungalow* (1980); Robert C. Pavlic, "'Something a Little Different': La Cuesta Encantada's Architectural Precedents and Cultural Prototypes," *California History* (1992/93); Albert Shumate, *A San Francisco Scandal: The California of George Gordon* (1994); Robert W. Cherny, "City Commercial, City Beautiful, City Practical—The San Francisco Visions of William C. Ralston, James D. Phelan, and Michael O'Shaughnessy," *California History* (1994); James P. Walsh and Timothy O'Keefe, *Legacy of a Native Son: James Duval Phelan and Villa Montalvo* (1994); Michael L. Smith, *Pacific Visions: California Scientists and the Environment: 1850–1915* (1988); Franklin Walker, *A Literary History of Southern California* (1950); Karen S. Langlois, "A Fresh Voice from the West: Mary Austin, California, and American Literary Magazines, 1892–1910," *California History* (1990); Pauline C. Thompson, "A California Girl: The Life and Times of Anna Morrison Reed, 1849–1921" (M.A. thesis, California State University, Hayward, 1993); Gerald D. Nash, *A. P. Giannini and the Bank of America* (1992); Felice A. Bonadio, *A.P. Giannini: Banker of America* (1994); Ted Orland, *Man and Yosemite: A Photographer's View of the Early Years* (1985).

"The Migrant Mother"
In her famous work, "The Migrant Mother," photographer Dorothea Lange captured the suffering endured by many newcomers who were seeking California's "promised land" during the Great Depression. *Courtesy of the Library of Congress.*

PART SEVEN

CALIFORNIA BETWEEN THE WARS, 1920–1940

As modern California emerged from the progressive era and World War I, an important economic transformation and dramatic population change were under way. New thriving industries in oil and the making of motion pictures turned Los Angeles into a booming manufacturing city just as a new migration brought hundreds of thousands of residents to the region. To keep the boom going, southern California boosters successfully reached out for distant water and hydroelectric power supplies. The decade after World War I was one of rapid economic development, marked by the evolution of modern, large-scale business organizations and the pervasive influence of the automobile. Many of the new migrants were conservative midwestern Protestant Republicans who strengthened the political base for the fundamentalist, nativist, and prohibition movements that characterized the 1920s. They flocked to hear the evangelist Aimee Semple McPherson, who, in spite of her own tumultuous personal life, understood and comforted them.

When the boom of the 1920s went bust in the 1930s, few were more devastated than the migrants of the 1920s, whose dreams were shattered by the collapse. Sister Aimee led them in fending for themselves and in helping others when state and local assistance proved inadequate. And although Towsendites, the Technocracy movement, the Utopians, and Upton Sinclair all had ready answers to the economic disaster, it was the New Deal that had the greatest impact on the state, as the administration of President Franklin D. Roosevelt attempted to pull the nation out of the worst depression it had ever known. The New Deal's programs were designed to provide relief for the unemployed and stimulate the economy. They involved the state in huge public construction projects and a myriad of smaller works involving actors, writers, artists, and musicians. At the same time, the New Deal threw the weight of the federal government behind labor's long-time demand for the right to organize and bargain collectively with employers, making the decade one of the most important in California labor history. The 1930s ended with the state's businesses and agriculture struggling out of the depression as a new world war began.

CHAPTER NINETEEN

SUPER SISTER: AIMEE SEMPLE McPHERSON IN LOS ANGELES

In the late 1920s Carl Sandburg made the laconic observation that "God once took the country by Maine as the handle, gave it a good shake, and all the loose nuts and bolts rolled down to southern California." Many Americans probably shared this view, regarding Los Angeles in particular as a haven for faddists, fanatics, and fakes. The scene of sometimes scandalous Hollywood goings-on and a refuge for countless religious cults, the city has had more than its fair share of flamboyant personalities, but few can compare with Aimee Semple McPherson, evangelist supreme. From her arrival in Los Angeles in 1918 to her death in 1944, "Sister Aimee" preached her novel brand of religious revivalism to literally millions and had a remarkable impact on the city. Mrs. McPherson made the front pages of the major Los Angeles newspapers on an average of three times a week for nearly ten years, and appeared almost as frequently in the rest of the nation's press. One columnist called her "the most original, exciting, and newsworthy space-getter in the land." Aimee's experiences in Los Angeles also tell us a great deal about the people of Los Angeles and the times.

After years of traveling the country as an itinerant revivalist preacher, Aimee Semple McPherson arrived in Los Angeles in December 1918 with her mother and two children and, she enjoyed saying later, "one hundred dollars and a tambourine." From these humble beginnings she managed, in the next five years, to build a huge 5,300-seat temple, organize her own Church of the Foursquare Gospel, and found the first religious radio station in the United States. She attracted a congregation of 10,000, estimated to be the largest in the world, and established branch churches, called "Lighthouses," all over the country and overseas. Her congregation was organized into departments that provided music, players for dramatizations of her sermons, community services of all kinds, and missionaries who spread the Foursquare Gospel throughout the world.

"Sister," as she was known to her followers, became a major influence in the life of the city. She had a shrewd instinct for publicity and adopted attention-getting methods, such as scattering leaflets announcing her services from an airplane. Her sermons were vaudeville-style theatrical productions, sneered at by her critics as "supernatural whoopee." But even her detractors had to agree that she put on "the best show in town." An honorary member of the police department, honorary battalion chief of the fire department, and member of the Chamber of Commerce, she was constantly in the news. Then, one day in May 1926, Aimee Semple McPherson disappeared.

During that spring the thirty-five-year-old Aimee had begun regular excursions to swim at Ocean Park beach. On May 18, accompanied by her secretary, Emma Schaffer, she drove to the shore, changed clothes at the hotel where she kept a room, rented an umbrella tent, and splashed into the Pacific, having sent the timid, tight-lipped Emma on an errand. On returning, Emma waited nearly an hour for Mrs. McPherson to come in from the sea. At last, thoroughly frightened, she called Aimee's mother to report her daughter's disappearance. By nightfall the news had flashed through the city. Newspaper "extras" blanketed the area, Aimee's mother publicly announced her daughter had drowned, and thousands crowded Angelus Temple and Ocean Park beach in a state of shock. For the next three days "Sister's" faithful followers, joined by droves of curious onlookers, watched and prayed while police, lifeguards, and divers sought the evangelist's body, and searching airplanes flew back and forth over the ocean.

Who was this person who could create such a commotion? One of Aimee Semple McPherson's favorite sermons was "The Story of My Life," and she told it with a riveting eloquence that always held her audiences spellbound. Born on October 9, 1890, on a farm in Ontario, Canada, she was the daughter of Mildred and James Kennedy. Her mother, eventually known to millions as

Minnie or "Ma Kennedy," had long been active in the Salvation Army and dedicated Aimee to that cause. The child demonstrated a strong will, a flair for the dramatic, and unusual leadership qualities. When teased at school one day about her Salvation Army background, she quickly took charge of the situation and soon had the other children following her around the schoolyard in a Salvation Army parade. A natural actress, she loved to be the center of attention and delighted in starring roles in school plays.

As a teenager, Aimee's interest in dancing, movies, and ragtime music brought her into conflict with her mother. Minnie's world had no place for such frivolities, and many a stormy scene resulted. James Kennedy, some thirty years older than his wife, was more tolerant, but the domineering Minnie usually prevailed. When a new Pentecostal mission came to town and the seventeen-year-old Aimee expressed an interest in attending its meetings, her mother would not allow it. Minnie frowned on speaking in tongues and other physical manifestations of the power of the Spirit, the hallmark of the Pentecostalists. "Shouters" and "Holy Rollers," she called them. But Aimee persuaded her father to take her to the mission, and on her first visit she was captivated by the handsome preacher.

Robert Semple, a tall, dark-haired young man with intense blue eyes, had a dramatic style that held enormous attraction for Aimee. She began sneaking away from school to attend his meetings and one day "fell under the Power" in an exciting conversion experience. Before long she realized that she was in love with Robert, and he with her. After a brief courtship they were married in the summer of 1908 and lived for a short time in Stratford, Ontario. Although they were poor, Aimee was supremely happy. She adored Robert, reveled in her position as the preacher's wife, and perhaps for the only time in her life willingly submitted to the will of another. Robert spoke often of going to China as an evangelist, and Aimee shared his enthusiasm. In 1910, after several months of work as evangelists in Chicago missions, they financed their voyage to Hong Kong through collections taken at farewell meetings with Robert's parishioners. But the excitement and novelty of missionary work among the Chinese soon turned to disaster. Within a year Robert fell critically ill, probably of typhoid fever, and died soon afterward, leaving Aimee alone in Hong Kong, penniless and pregnant. A month after Robert's death she gave birth to a daughter, Roberta, and six weeks later, in January 1911, Aimee and her baby were on their way back to America.

Lonely and dispirited, she drifted aimlessly among east coast missions until she married Harold McPherson, a grocery clerk. This marriage, which she later admitted had been an effort to provide a home for Roberta, was not a happy one, and Aimee became seriously depressed. Even the birth of a son, Rolf Kennedy McPherson, failed to revive her spirits. Her condition worsened until she found herself near death following an operation. At this point, she was fond of telling her audiences, she heard a nurse say, "She's going," and then God called her to go out and "preach the Word."

> Just before losing consciousness, as I hovered between life and death, came the voice of my Lord, so loud that it startled me: "Now-will-you-go?" And I knew it was "Go," one way or the other. . . . And with my little remaining strength, I managed to gasp: "Yes—Lord—I'll—go."

Then "the Lord poured such strength into me that within a few days I was able to be up and go home." Within a short time she was on her way to Canada, leaving McPherson behind.

Aimee joined her parents in Canada in the summer of 1915 and spent the next few months attending a Pentecostal camp meeting nearby. One day, when asked to preach at Mount Forest, a small local town, she set out to conduct the first revival meeting of her new career.

Despite the eagerness with which Aimee prepared her first sermon she found herself facing only a handful of people—and a great many empty chairs. When the next night brought the same scant audience, she set out to fill the hall. Picking up a chair, she strode down the main street to the center of town, put her chair down, and stood on it. Arms outstretched, eyes closed, and standing motionless, she began to pray. Curious passersby stopped and stared at her, and soon a crowd gathered. All at once Aimee snapped open her eyes, jumped down, and shouted, "Quick! Follow me!" Snatching up her chair, she raced back to the meeting hall and through the doors with the crowd at her heels. "Shut the doors; don't let anyone out," she ordered the ushers and launched into her sermon. The crowd loved it. "From that day to this," she would later tell her congregations, "I've always preached to crowds."

With her first "offering," as she called the money collected at her meetings, she bought a tent and went from town to town holding revival meetings. As her career progressed she bought bigger tents to hold hundreds of people, and a touring car on which she painted, "Jesus Is Coming Soon—Get Ready" and "Where Will You Spend Eternity?" Traveling from New York to Florida and back, she preached to whites and blacks, often together. She became an expert at pitching tents in the wind, driving stakes with a heavy maul. She founded a small religious magazine, *The Bridal Call*, and sold subscriptions at her meetings, forming a network of helpers wherever she went. In the face of frequent harassment she preached a message of love and joy, and she always preached to crowds.

Harold McPherson joined Aimee for a time as her business manager, but detested the itinerant life. They separated again in 1917 and were divorced in 1921, but without Harold a notorious lack of business sense was nearly Aimee's undoing. She collected large sums of money at her meetings but could never seem to manage them. At last she turned to her mother for help, forming a stormy partnership that took them both to the pinnacle of success. Minnie Kennedy joined the caravan in Florida in the winter of 1917 and soon had their financial affairs in order. Aimee had proved she could bring in a great deal of money; blessed with a fine instinct for business, Minnie proved they could hang on to it.

In 1918 the caravan traveled north again, and in New York little Roberta was stricken with the deadly influenza that was then sweeping the country. Frightened by the near loss of her daughter, Aimee decided to take her family west to a more healthful climate. She headed for Los Angeles in a large touring car with her mother, the two children, and a woman companion. Aimee, who did the driving, probably was the first woman to drive across the United States, a considerable accomplishment in an era when roads were likely to be horse-and-buggy trails, often flooded, or almost nonexistent and tires were in constant need of repair. Towns were few and far between, and at times they crossed vast empty stretches with the aid of a compass. Often they had to clear boulders and fallen trees from the road in order to pass. Sometimes in mud to the hub caps, sometimes in snow, the three women and two children made their lonely way from New York through the southwest to California, holding revival meetings in the towns and camping out between settlements. Through it all Aimee remained cheerfully undaunted, a pillar of strength to her family.

Aimee Semple McPherson, Mother, and Daughter
Aimee Semple McPherson *(center)* with her mother *(left)* and daughter in the early 1920s. *Courtesy of the Los Angeles Public Library.*

It was an experience many of her followers could identify with, and they never tired of hearing her tell it in her dramatic way.

Aimee and her family arrived in Los Angeles shortly before Christmas, 1918. Already famous, she was immediately invited to preach to a local congregation. Aimee had recognized that people were tired of the Calvinist style of preaching and of being told they were damned and destined for hell, so instead adopted an affectionate, anecdotal style, preaching an emotional, charismatic revivalism that emphasized love and hope. Aware that her followers longed for a cheerful, positive religion she would say, "Who cares about old Hell, friends? Let's forget about Hell. Lift up your hearts. What we are interested in, yes Lord, is *Heaven* and how to get *there*." As one writer later commented, "Calvin must have turned over in his grave."

Aimee achieved instantaneous success in Los Angeles, and she shrewdly observed that it could last. A steady stream of God-fearing midwesterners flowing into southern California promised her a constantly growing audience, and she decided to put down roots. By 1921 she had such a large and devoted Los Angeles following that when she mentioned wistfully in her sermons her family's need for a home, they quickly volunteered to build her one. "The house that God built," as Aimee called it, was her first piece of property, and it made her aware that if she wanted anything, all she had to do was ask for it.

From 1916 to 1921 Aimee became famous for her successful faith-healing. She never claimed credit for her astonishing cures, however, saying her followers were cured by Christ through their own faith. Always a secondary part of her service, healing nevertheless stole the show when she held a revival in San Diego in the summer of 1921. For years the sick had congregated in the beautiful little seaside city, hoping to return to health in its balmy climate (and giving it an astonishingly high death and suicide rate). When Aimee appeared there, they swarmed around her in such numbers that she finally consented to hold a special meeting in Balboa Park devoted to healing only. Nearly 15,000 people jammed the place, requiring special squads of police to manage the crowd, while the sick and disabled "fell over one another in their rush to the platform—in chairs, in litters, in wheelbarrows, or staggering on foot." For two days Aimee administered to them, "laying on hands" and

praying fervently, as countless miraculous "cures" amazed onlookers. Overnight she became a sensation, and the local press dubbed her the "Miracle Woman." Until 1923 Aimee devoted much of her time to faith-healing sessions, but eventually she began to deemphasize them. Never comfortable with that which she could not control, she believed that the cures were really the work of God and that she was merely His instrument.

At about this time Aimee had begun to enunciate the basic tenets of her religious beliefs more clearly. She called her theology the Foursquare Gospel—belief in the literal infallibility of the Bible, conversion, physical healing through faith, and the return of Christ to earth. Yet she remained essentially an itinerant preacher; she had no real church of her own, just thousands of passionately devoted followers held together by her little magazine, now called *The Foursquare Monthly*, and by the power of her personality. She began to dream of building her own auditorium or tabernacle, where her people could be organized into a more permanent denomination and where they might become a permanent source of income enabling her at last to give up the itinerant life. They had built her a house, why shouldn't they build her a church? The design for a great temple began forming in her mind.

With $5,000 her mother had managed to save through tight-fisted management, Aimee bought a pie-shaped piece of property across from Echo Park, where the trolley lines met in the fastest-growing section of Los Angeles, and ordered the foundations begun for her tabernacle. Then she set out on another of her frequent whirlwind tours of the country to raise money for the building. Using every enticement at her command, she accumulated the funds that kept

Aimee and Converts
A regular feature of Sister Aimee's services included individuals possessed with "the spirit" clapping, shouting, and flopping on the floor. Many, overcome with emotion, had to be assisted by her helpers. *Courtesy of the Bancroft Library.*

construction going. When not out raising funds, she was on the site leading volunteer workers in prayer and directing the design and construction of what she now called Angelus Temple.

Almost unnoticed by Angelenos in the building boom of the times, the structure rose during 1922 at Echo Park. On January 1, 1923, Aimee formally dedicated the tem-ple to the cause of worldwide evangelism. To architects the structure was a monstrosity, but to Aimee and her followers it was glorious—a huge white building shaped like a wedge of cake, with a large stage at the point and several sections (including two spacious balconies) fanning out from the stage. Along the sides of the temple were stained-glass windows designed by Aimee, and the ceiling

Angelus Temple
Angelus Temple in the 1920s, topped by radio towers. Aimee's radio station was so powerful that she was frequently in trouble with the FCC over interference with the signals of other local stations. *Courtesy of the Los Angeles Public Library.*

was a large shallow dome painted sky blue and speckled with glass stars. The modern stage lighting rivaled that of most theaters, and adjoining the temple a large luxurious home, known as the "parsonage," housed Aimee and her family. The entire project cost more than a million dollars.

Construction of Angelus Temple was a turning point for Aimee. Her prodigious energies could now be concentrated in one location, and the results were remarkable. She organized her followers into the Church of the Foursquare Gospel with twenty-four departments. Temple workers manned telephones around the clock, to minister to the troubled and lonely; the City Sisters baby-sat, distributed food to the needy, and tended

the sick; the Brotherhood helped ex-convicts find jobs. The Children's Church, the Bible School, and an evening school for working-men reached other members of the congregation, while teams of the faithful prayed twenty-four hours a day, year after year, in a Tower of Prayer. Everyone who joined the Foursquare Gospel Association had something to do, even if only typing for the *Monthly* or ushering at services. In return, Aimee gave her people the sense of purpose and personal importance they craved in the complex, impersonal society of Los Angeles in the 1920s. And she gave them a good time as well.

With the assistance of Thompson Eade, a former vaudeville performer, Aimee wrote, produced, and starred in lavishly staged "il-lustrated" sermons. Each one featured a large choir and orchestra, dozens of actors costumed by the Western Costume Corporation (which also supplied all the major movie studios), and Aimee, engulfed in flowers. Writing for Harper's magazine, Sarah Comstock described a visit to the temple:

> . . . in this unique house of worship called Angelus Temple in the city of Los Angeles the Almighty occupies a secondary position. He plays an important part in the drama to be sure but the center stage is taken and held by Mrs. McPherson. It is in her praise that the band blares, that flowers are piled high, that applause splits the air. It is to see her and hear her that throngs travel, crushed in the aisles of electric cars, thrust, elbow, and bruise one another as they shove at the doors of her Temple. . . . Over the great lower floor and two balconies attendants are hurrying to seat the mob, a full hour before the entrance of the star. Men and women stand against the wall, they sit upon the steps of the aisles, and still, when the final whistle blows, there are thousands turned away, thousands who stand for two, three, four hours on the street in the nearby park, to listen to the concert and the inspired utterances as they scream themselves forth from the loud-speaker outside the building. . . . Aimee Semple McPherson is staging, month after month and even year after year, the most perennially successful show in the United States.

In 1924 Temple members raised $75,000 to build a powerful radio station, and thereafter Aimee's services were broadcast each night to thousands of listeners over station KFSG (Kall-Four-Square-Gospel), the third radio station in Los Angeles. She became the first woman to hold a broadcaster's license from the Federal Communications Commission. By the end of 1925 Sister was at the peak of her success. She had the largest Christian congregation in the world; its con-

tributions made her a millionaire. She was a power in Los Angeles and a national figure, often called the "world's greatest evangelist." In the three years since the dedication of Angelus Temple, she had made it the center of a network that spanned the globe. She had survived the animosity of rival preachers who saw their parishioners drifting away to Angelus Temple, and the sneers of her detractors who called her services "a sensuous debauch served up in the name of religion." She had also survived petty politics and factionalism within her organization resulting from her success and Minnie's heavy-handed control of church funds. But beneath her ebullient, vivacious surface she was not altogether happy.

Day after day Aimee made the monotonous walk from house to temple and back again. She preached as often as twenty times a week, taught Bible classes, presided at weddings, baptisms, and funerals, attended meetings of the church board, and prepared her sermons. At the height of her success she was experiencing the loneliness of the star. She had no really close friend and her dream-come-true, Angelus Temple, was beginning to seem like a prison. It was then that the voice of Kenneth Ormiston, her radio engineer, took on new meaning for her. Each night when she broadcast her sermons, she talked to Ormiston by telephone from the stage while the choir sang or some other group performed. He would advise her how the program was going over the radio and would give her encouragement and support. "You have done splendidly tonight," he would say, or "Your voice sounds as if you are tired tonight, Mrs. McPherson." More and more she began to feel he was the only one in the world who cared about her as a person, and their conversations became more personal. Soon they were spending time alone together in the broadcasting studio of the temple.

Massed Choirs at Angelus Temple
An example of Aimee Semple McPherson's showmanship is the way the stage at Angelus Temple is filled with the massed choirs during one of her services. *Courtesy of the Los Angeles Public Library.*

Minnie Kennedy was frightened by this turn of events. A shrewd bargainer, domineering, undiplomatic, and sharp-tongued, she had relentlessly fought her way to economic security. The Echo Park Association had been incorporated to hold all she had managed to retain of the prodigious sums Aimee could raise at her meetings. The temple, the parsonage, and all other church properties were mortgage-free, and belonged to Minnie and Aimee. Thousands of dollars were taken in weekly, and Minnie reveled in this financial success. ("Only quiet money tonight, folks," Aimee would sometimes say during a collection. "Sister has a headache.") Now this security was threatened. The acoustics in the temple were so fine that, even with the choir singing, some of Aimee's giggling telephone conversations

with Ormiston (a married man) had been overheard in the balcony. People were beginning to ask questions. Worried about a possible scandal, Minnie scolded and nagged Aimee about her indiscretion.

Then one day, in January 1926, Kenneth Ormiston quit his job at Angelus Temple and dropped from sight. At about the same time, Aimee left Los Angeles to tour the Holy Land. A few weeks later Minnie heard a rumor that Ormiston had joined Aimee in Europe and, terrified, she cabled this news to her daughter. Soon afterward, Ormiston casually appeared at the temple "to advise on the radio operation" and then drifted off again. When Aimee returned she settled into her old routine, and Minnie heaved a sigh of relief. All seemed well—except that Aimee took to staying in a hotel at the beach in order, she said, to avoid the noise and dust from construction of the new five-story Bible College next door. And she began to demand more money. Under strong pressure from Aimee, Minnie finally agreed that the collection taken on the first Sunday of each month, usually several thousand dollars, would go directly to her, without being counted and with no questions asked. Aimee pocketed the money, and, as the weather warmed, began to go for a regular swim at the beach—until she disappeared that day in May.

For five weeks Minnie tried to carry on the work of the temple, but she was tormented by secret suspicions as to why Aimee had vanished, and by a press openly suspicious about the absence of her body. Swarms of journalists investigated Aimee's disappearance as the two great rival Los Angeles newspapers, the *Times* and Hearst's *Examiner*, competed for scoops. Reporters dug out Ormiston's name and spread rumors that Aimee had run off with him or that her disappearance was another publicity stunt. Hoping to offset these allegations, Minnie offered a $25,000 reward for the safe return of her daughter.

On June 20, some 14,000 attended a memorial service for Aimee. Three days later, and five weeks after her disappearance, she suddenly surfaced in the small Mexican border town of Agua Prieta near Tucson, Arizona, with a dramatic story of having escaped from kidnappers. She was immediately taken across the border to a hospital in neighboring Douglas, Arizona, where Los Angeles police interviewed her and reporters mobbed her. She told them that two men and a woman had seized her on May 18 through a ruse—asking her to administer to a sick baby—and that two of them had held her in a shack in the desert until her escape. She estimated she had wandered fifteen or

twenty miles in the scorching heat before finding help in Agua Prieta. The next day Minnie and the two children arrived for a tearful reunion while the world hummed with the news.

On June 26 Sister returned by train to Los Angeles, where her reception surpassed any seen before in that city. No foreign monarch, no president, no national hero had ever evoked such an outpouring of people and emotion. Airplanes rained rose petals from the air, city police carried her regally from the train station to her automobile in a sedan chair, and youngsters flung down a carpet of flowers in her path. Perhaps a hundred thousand people lined the streets for the triumphal cavalcade to her home. Within minutes of her arrival at Angelus Temple, she was on stage, recounting the story of her kidnapping to her nearly hysterical followers.

Exciting and dramatic, the story lacked but one thing—credibility. From the moment Sister Aimee met police investigators and the press in Arizona, they began asking questions that made their skepticism clear. They demanded to know why she had not immediately asked for water after wandering miles across the hot desert, why her clothes showed no signs of perspiration, why her shoes were not scuffed. They wanted explanations for reports that she had been seen more than once since her disappearance in a car resembling one belonging to Kenneth Ormiston, who had also seemingly dropped out of sight. Further doubt was cast on her story by failure to locate the shack she claimed had been her prison for weeks. To her dismay, Sister found the attention of the investigation focused more on the veracity of her statements than on the apprehension of the kidnappers. By the time she met her followers at Angelus Temple following her return to Los Angeles she was heaping scorn on her doubters and demanding that authorities redouble their efforts to find the criminals.

Had Aimee Semple McPherson left the matter where it was and turned away the reporters who hounded her every step, the affair might have eventually died from lack of interest. But, staking everything on the credibility of her story, she embarked on another tour of the country, demanding vindication from an increasingly skeptical public. In the process she set into motion a chain of events that resulted in sensational court hearings and the tarnishing of her image. When it was all over, Sister Aimee was no longer Mrs. McPherson the great evangelist. To the world she was just "Aimee."

Her demand for vindication and pressure from her competing clergy as well as the Chamber of Commerce finally goaded the district attorney, Asa Keyes, to action. A Los Angeles grand jury was called to look into the case, and Aimee made a dramatic appearance before it. It found "insufficient evidence to warrant an indictment," meaning her story was unconvincing. Aimee, however, claimed she had been vindicated and seemed to want the matter laid to rest. But aggressive reporters, not willing to let a good story die, continued to dig into the case until at last they unearthed evidence that Kenneth Ormiston had spent ten days at the little resort town of Carmel-by-the-Sea, near Monterey, with a woman whom residents identified as Mrs. McPherson. Experts identified the woman's handwriting on grocery slips as Aimee's, and the case became a sensation again. The sleepy village of Carmel, with its sand streets, artsy atmosphere, and reclusive citizenry, was immediately overrun by newspapermen asking questions and sightseers looking for the "love cottage," while Aimee's rival evangelists demanded a new inquiry. The grand jury was

called into session again, and strange things began to happen. A woman grand juror took the damaging grocery slips into the rest room and they disappeared; secret files of the police also vanished; the prosecuting attorney and chief investigator were removed from the case; and when members of the grand jury tried to cover up their destruction of evidence they were dismissed in disgrace.

Meanwhile the case went on. A woman appeared, claiming to be the one seen in Carmel with Ormiston, only to be exposed by reporters as perpetrating a hoax in which she claimed Aimee had participated (a claim she later retracted). In September, Aimee, Minnie, and Ormiston were indicted for corruption of public morals, obstruction of justice, and conspiracy to manufacture evidence. At the preliminary hearing another parade of witnesses spewed forth testimony filling the pages of the press and the airwaves, and the hearings drew such prominent journalists as H. L. Mencken. In the face of all this, Aimee used her formidable talents of mimicry and eloquence to ridicule the prosecutors and their witnesses in her sermons and broadcasts. The grand jury hearings became a spectacle and the talk of the town. On November 3, after six exhausting weeks, the presiding judge wearily ordered Aimee and her codefendants to stand trial in January 1927. City editors gleefully contemplated a long one.

During November and December, however, the prosecutor's case crumbled; key witnesses recanted their testimony, and the district attorney declared that with "so many contradictions and inconsistencies," the case could not be prosecuted with any reasonable hope of success. In January, to the frustration of editors, reporters, and a sensation-hungry public, the case was dismissed. Through it all Aimee's story was the only one that did not change.

It was not surprising, as Carey McWilliams later wrote, that the controversial story of Aimee's disappearance became "one of the great news stories of the decade":

> It contained . . . all the right ingredients: sex, mystery, underworld characters, kidnappers, the ocean, hot desert sands, an escape, and a thrilling finale. It was a story made for the period, a period that invested the trivial with a special halo, that magnified the insipid, that pursued cheap sensationalism with avidity and passion. While admittedly quite a story, the "kidnapping" of Sister Aimee became invested with the proportions of a myth and the dimensions of a saga in the great vacuum of the age.

The end of the kidnap case did not take Aimee Semple McPherson out of the headlines, however. For the next ten years major Los Angeles newspapers assigned reporters to cover Aimee, her family, and temple activities full-time. Minnie and Aimee were, each in her own way, masters at using the press for publicity, while the press had learned how to use the Angelus Temple to sell newspapers. It was a convenient relationship, and one that lasted into the mid-1930s.

Aimee returned from a "vindication" tour in 1927 to be faced with a rebellion that erupted into an angry dispute with her mother. She set out to break free once and for all from Minnie's domination, bluntly informing her mother that she was going to take over control of all the business affairs of the temple. Minnie fought this vigorously, maintaining for anyone to hear that Aimee had absolutely no business sense and would ruin the sound financial position of the church. But Aimee won out, threatening to resign as pastor if she did not have her way. Reluctantly, Minnie retired with a settlement that assured her an income of $10,000 a year. After church reorganization gave Aimee absolute control of all its religious and business affairs, she embarked on a program designed

The Glamorous Aimee
By the 1930s the "glamorous" Aimee had appeared. She loved fine clothes and rarely appeared without a corsage pinned to her dress. Her followers took great pride in her chic appearance. *Courtesy of the Los Angeles Public Library.*

to give the lie to her mother's public disdain for her business talents.

Unfortunately, Minnie had been right. Aimee had no business sense, and her managers involved her in one fiasco after another; one was a proposal to sell burial plots in a "Blessed Hope Memorial Park" cemetery, the closer the plot to Aimee's, the higher the price. "Buy a Grave and Go Up with Aimee," was reportedly the slogan. A particularly disastrous undertaking involved organizing a movie company, with Aimee to star in an extravagant religious production. One after another these schemes collapsed, leaving Aimee with a myriad of lawsuits for breach of contract on her hands and a steady stream of court appearances. Noting that Aimee had appeared in court one morning in a natty wool suit and that afternoon in a chic silk suit, a newspaper aptly headlined the story "Life Is Just One Suit After Another."

Aimee's stylish wardrobe accompanied other manifestations of an effort to upgrade her appearance under the glare of the public spotlight. In her early years in Los Angeles she had adopted as her normal public attire a blue cape over a white dress that resembled a nurse's uniform, prompting one reporter to describe her as "robust and motherly." Gradually, however, she had shed the motherly image and developed into a glamorous figure, slim and elegantly dressed. This and other changes brought her into conflict again with her mother when Minnie returned to the Temple to try to salvage the business organization. Minnie disapproved of Aimee's new look and seeming tolerance of modernism. Aimee, for her part, probably disagreed with half the Pentacostalists of America, for she was trying to bring fundamentalism into the twentieth century. Nine months after Minnie's return she entered the hospital with a broken nose received in one last violent argument with Aimee, who then went into seclusion, reportedly suffering from a mysterious illness that was making her blind. But Minnie, whose venomous tongue was hereafter turned on her daughter, maliciously informed the press that Aimee had had a face-lift.

Since physical "rejuvenation" was considered outrageously worldly in Aimee's church, Minnie's charge added fuel to an already blazing fire of dissension. Aimee's business dealings and her autocratic and se-

cret control of church finances led to another schism. A number of her Lighthouses seceded, one of their leaders forced a grand jury hearing into her finances, and the episode produced more negative publicity. In 1930 Aimee's iron constitution finally gave way, and she suffered a nervous breakdown. By 1931 she had recovered sufficiently to elope with David Hutton, who sang in the choir and had been giving her singing lessons. But two years later they separated and in 1934 quietly obtained a divorce.

Despite her personal problems, Aimee found time to throw her great energy into alleviating the distress of the Great Depression. Los Angeles teemed with retired farmers and tradespeople who had been ruined by the collapse of the economy after 1929. State, county, and city relief funds were pitifully inadequate to deal with the suffering as the Depression deepened; by 1931 there were 200,000 unemployed in Los Angeles alone. For most of the early 1930s Aimee's followers were everywhere in the Los Angeles area, giving aid and sustenance to the victims of the Depression. In November 1931 she opened her first "soup kitchen," serving meals to all who came. Soon she opened another, which served 5,000 persons a day, and when the school system could no longer serve hot lunches to its pupils, Aimee did. Her City Sisters cared for people all over the Los Angeles basin. She enlisted the police and fire departments to distribute clothing to the destitute. She established a free medical and dental clinic, staffed by dozens of volunteer doctors and dentists, and a school to train practical nurses, especially in the care of the malnourished young and elderly. She cajoled and pressured ranchers, meatpackers, business groups, and grocers into contributing to her effort by donating supplies, and she talked truckers into delivering them free of charge. She even persuaded the federal government to open an unused army camp east of Los Angeles, where 25,000 unemployed could live and grow their own food.

The huge relief effort, and her personal troubles, took their toll on Aimee. She was frequently ill and periodically went on a tour or a cruise to regain her health, only to become embroiled in another crisis on her return. All the while, she continued to design, organize, and produce sermons that surpassed most of the spectacles offered in local theaters. But by the mid-1930s she was also becoming obsessed with a fear that others were conspiring to take control of Angelus Temple and church affairs away from her, a fear that drove her into her last great conflict—this time with her daughter, Roberta, and another evangelist, Rheba Crawford. The conflict eventually led to Aimee's dismissing both Roberta and Rheba in a messy disagreement that, as usual, landed in court. In 1937 Roberta won a libel suit against Aimee's attorney, and Aimee, who had no heart for further legal maneuvering, settled with Rheba out of court. This left the disheartened Aimee with only her son, Rolf, as her steadying force in temple affairs.

After this episode Aimee Semple McPherson faded from the headlines. By then both she and the press seemed to agree that the public had become satiated with her antics. Besides, world affairs were pushing the frivolous from the front pages. The vacuum filled by Aimee and those like her was now occupied by concerns such as the Spanish Civil War, Japan's attack on China, and the mounting fear of Hitler. Aimee quietly rebuilt her church, expanding the number of Lighthouses nationwide, while her son, Rolf, took over its business management. When World War II came, she made numerous appearances to conduct revival meetings for servicemen and to sell war bonds. In late September 1944, she traveled with Rolf to hold a revival meeting in Oakland, where she filled the auditorium with 10,000 enthusiastic people. The next morning Rolf found her near death in her bed, sleeping pills spilled around her. By midmorning she was dead. Doctors reported that the barbiturates she had taken had probably led to loss of memory, confusion, and an accidental overdose. Sister's last front-page headline, "Aimee Is Dead," appeared in the newspapers on September 27, as Rolf hurried to Los Angeles to arrange her funeral. The temple overflowed with grief-stricken followers wailing and praying in disbelief, while newspapers printed long obituaries struggling to explain her life.

Fifty thousand mourners filed past the bronze casket where Aimee lay dressed in her temple uniform, with a Bible bound in white satin clasped in her hands. The temple was so filled with flowers that five carloads could not even be unloaded, and, when Rolf cried out for a rededication to carry on her work, her people surged to their feet, hands upraised in the gesture of joy she had taught them. Aimee Semple McPherson was buried on Sunrise Slope at Forest Lawn Memorial Park on her fifty-fourth birthday, October 9, 1944.

Through her long, sensational career, many of Aimee's contemporaries shrugged her off as one of the "loose nuts" who had rolled down to southern California. To them, she symbolized the frivolous and trivial aspects of the times, while to her devoted followers, and those who benefited from her depression-era relief work, she represented hope and a cheerful, active religious faith.

From the vantage point of history, the story of Aimee Semple McPherson's life can be viewed not only as the story of a colorful, dynamic personality, but as the story of a colorful, dynamic age propelled, like Aimee, by a restless and capricious energy. Aimee's venturesome coast-to-coast drive across primitive roads in 1918 was the precursor of an historic, and equally speculative, automobile migration that brought hundreds of thousands of new residents to California in the 1920s and 1930s. Her lavish productions in the extravagant Angelus Temple paralleled increasingly lavish Hollywood productions, as the movie industry prospered and expanded. Her establishment of the first religious radio station occurred at the beginning of a great radio age centered in southern California. The ease with which she attracted huge crowds and dominated news-

paper headlines testified to the cultural vacuity of the period. Yet when times turned suddenly dark and challenging she, like most of her fellow Californians, turned her energy to coping with depression and supporting the war effort. Aimee's death less than a year before the end of World War II coincided closely with the end of an era and the beginning of another, for California was soon to emerge into a new age, never to be the same again.

CHAPTER TWENTY

PROSPERITY AND THE RISE OF SOUTHERN CALIFORNIA

When Aimee Semple McPherson drove her battered Oldsmobile into Los Angeles, enormous changes were under way in California. In the next decade nearly two million Americans followed her west, two-thirds of them settling south of the Tehachapis. By 1930 the state's population center had shifted to southern California, Los Angeles had emerged as the dominant city of the west, and the region symbolized California as an Eden—an image that persists. Only later would come an awareness of the cost of such growth.

Important social and economic changes accompanied the rise of southern California. Dynamic leaders of the area successfully acquired the crucial water and power resources that fueled a huge real estate boom; reliance on the automobile for transportation promoted creation of the "decentralized" city and doomed mass rail transit; the rise of the garment, food-processing, oil, auto, and tire industries made Los Angeles a major manufacturing center; and the nature of the migration of the 1920s—primarily rural midwesterners seeking their personal Eden—

produced a new and different society. Meanwhile, urban competition for federal military facilities created what historian Roger Lotchin has called the "metropolitan-military complex"—the foundation of the post–World War II military-industrial complex.

WATER AND POWER FOR GROWTH

From 1880 to 1920 there developed in the south what Kevin Starr calls a kind of "Southern California Raj—an orchestration of business, financial, political and governmental power, all of it controlled by one oligarchy." It was this private elite that had the vision and power to acquire for southern California, and especially Los Angeles, the resources permitting the spectacular growth of the region. In the 1920s this meant extension of the Owens Valley aqueduct to the Mono Lake watershed (completed in 1941), the development of the Imperial Valley and, particularly, the Boulder Canyon Project.

The Salton Sink, 150 miles southeast of Los Angeles, is part of a large arid basin, much of it below sea level. Over the ages, silt-laden flooding by the Colorado River resulted in a thick layer of fertile soil and created a great potential for agriculture that required only available water to be tapped. In 1859 Dr. Oliver Wozencraft proposed diverting Colorado River water to the area by gravity flow through the Alamo River, an old channel of the Colorado running into the sink south of the border with Mexico. Wozencraft's plan did not materialize, but it attracted another entrepreneur, Charles R. Rockwood, who in 1896 incorporated the California Development Company to carry it out. Rockwood enlisted the support of George Chaffey, whose reputation and financial backing brought national attention to the project. By 1900 settlers were pouring into the area, by then given the attractive name of Imperial Valley. Chaffey cut into the Colorado River north of the border and, under an agreement with the Mexican government, turned water from the river into the Alamo. In June 1901 the first water arrived, and, over the next eight months, 400 miles of canals and laterals were built and 100,000 acres were prepared for cultivation.

Unfortunately, the California Development Company made its diversions from the river without adequately protecting against high flood levels. In 1905 an extremely heavy runoff broke through the headgates, turning the entire flow of the Colorado into the Alamo and other old river channels. For sixteen months the river emptied into the Salton Sink, creating the Salton Sea at the north end of the Imperial Valley, submerging the tracks of the Southern Pacific's New Orleans line, and flooding towns and hundreds of farms. The California Development Company went bankrupt trying to control the river, and its assets were eventually taken over by the Southern Pacific Company. Dumping millions of tons of rock into the half-mile-wide break, the railroad finally

stopped the flow in February 1907, and the development of the valley resumed. After 1917 a newly formed Imperial Irrigation District, with the financial assistance of the Southern Pacific, took over the California Development Company facilities from the railroad. By 1920 there were 425,000 acres under cultivation in the valley.

The directors of the Imperial Irrigation District, however, were never very happy with the Alamo facilities. To control the flow of water into the intake canal and prevent flooding, they had to erect an expensive weir in the Colorado River below Yuma and remove it each winter. The requirement of delivering water at cheap prices to Mexican land also caused continuing problems for the district. Not surprisingly, by 1920 there was a growing demand for an all-American canal on the California side of the border. Phil Swing, the energetic counsel of the district, became the foremost advocate of this project.

At the same time, Arthur Powell Davis, director of the U.S. Reclamation Service, began a vigorous campaign to control the Colorado River to prevent flooding and to store water for irrigation. In 1919 Davis and Swing joined forces to urge congressional approval of development of the lower Colorado River by construction of a high dam at Boulder Canyon and an all-American canal to the Imperial Valley. There was immediate opposition from representatives of the upper Colorado states, who feared that the project would inhibit irrigation projects in their own states. Their legitimate fears led Congress to establish a commission to negotiate a treaty among the states involved, under a little-used section of the Constitution. The commission, consisting of one representative from each interested state and under the chairmanship of Secretary of Commerce Herbert Hoover, met in 1921 and 1922 and hammered out the Colorado

River Compact, an extraordinary agreement whereby the watershed of the river was divided into an upper basin (Wyoming, Colorado, Utah, and New Mexico) and a lower basin (Arizona, California, and Nevada) with the average annual flow of the river, some fifteen million acre-feet, divided between them.

Meanwhile, Phil Swing, now a congressman, and Senator Hiram Johnson introduced legislation in 1922 calling for construction of the All-American Canal and a dam at Boulder Canyon. When Arizona refused to ratify the Colorado River Compact, the Swing-Johnson bill was amended to provide for congressional approval of the compact when ratified by only six states, provided California was one of them, and agreed to limit its use of lower-basin water to 4.4 million acre-feet per year. The California legislature adopted this self-limiting legislation and on December 21, 1928, President Calvin Coolidge signed the Boulder Canyon Project Act into law.

Much of the support for the Swing-Johnson Act had come from Los Angeles officials, who hoped to alleviate a threatening power shortage and were concerned about their perennial need for an expanded water supply. Studies had shown that a large storage reservoir at Boulder Canyon would allow water to be delivered economically to the Los Angeles region. The Metropolitan Water District (MWD) embracing Los Angeles and many surrounding communities was created for this purpose. The district began planning for construction of Parker Dam, halfway between Needles and Blyth on the Colorado River, and for a great aqueduct to bring water 242 miles to Lake Mathews for distribution to the cities and irrigation districts it served. In 1931 voters in the district approved a $220 million bond issue for construction of the dam and aqueduct, despite the depression's adverse effect on municipal bond sales. In 1933 construction finally

began, after the Reconstruction Finance Corporation, established by Congress to stimulate business activity, agreed to buy the bonds. In 1941 the completed system delivered its first water. The 80-mile-long All-American Canal to the Imperial Valley was also completed in 1941, and a 125-mile extension to the Coachella Valley was finished in 1948.

The Boulder Canyon (Hoover) Dam and Colorado River Aqueduct were not built without a major battle over whether disposal of the electric power from Hoover and Parker dams would be through public or private systems. The conflict ended in a compromise, with Colorado River electricity distributed jointly by the publicly owned MWD and Los Angeles Bureau of Power and Light and by the private Southern California Edison utility.

CALIFORNIA AND THE AUTOMOBILE

One of the largest migrations in the history of the United States, the movement to California in the 1920s also uniquely demonstrated the impact of the automobile on American life. The motor car was generally regarded as a rich man's toy until the 1920s, when Henry Ford's assembly-line methods brought the price of his Model T down to $280. Automobile ownership increased from seven million to twenty-three million in the United States between 1919 and 1929. Well suited to the automobile, California registered two million of the vehicles in 1929, more cars per person than in any other state.

The impact of widespread automobile use on California cities was enormous, stimulating suburban home development, dispersing business areas and overwhelming local rail transit systems. In southern California it led to the emergence of Los Angeles as the first modern decentralized American city. The 1930 census revealed a southern California population of nearly three million, while from 1920 to 1930 the population of Los Angeles grew from 576,000 to 1,238,000, the fruit of three decades of boosterism. As one observer commented: "Los Angeles has not grown; it has been conjured into existence."

Drawn by the promise of a better, easier life, midwestern farmers, bankers, and merchants abandoned declining rural midwestern towns for southern California, where the explosive growth in the oil, movie, and manufacturing industries—and the migration itself—stimulated property values and created new job opportunities. Legions of real estate salespersons greeted the thousands of new arrivals with open arms, producing a boom reminiscent of that of the 1880s while city planners approved thirty to forty subdivisions

Downtown Los Angeles, circa 1929
Downtown Seventh Street in Los Angeles, in about 1929, decorated for a Shriner's convention. Note the automobile traffic and Pacific Electric cars. Auto congestion contributed to the financial decline of the Pacific Electric and its eventual replacement with bus lines. *Courtesy of the Huntington Library.*

a week. No longer bound to electric car lines because of the automobile, people gravitated toward the new subdivisions, which spread over the region like spilled milk, the emphasis always on the separate single-family home rather than the eastern-style row houses. Between March 1923 and March 1924 over 125,000 homes were built in Los Angeles county alone.

By 1924 heavy speculation fueled the boom. Excursion buses lined Los Angeles streets to take sightseers out to new subdivisions for "a free ride and a free lunch." High-powered salespeople made their deals with hard-to-crack prospects in special "closing booths." Developers organized country clubs, golf clubs, swimming clubs, hunting clubs, lake clubs, trout clubs, and beach clubs to promote sales, and hired Hollywood stars to attract customers. The speculative bubble collapsed in 1925, but the persistent arrival of thousands of new migrants and continuing home construction softened the blow. Indeed, the level of real estate activity remained high until the end of the decade, as countless acres of the famous "California bungalows" spread across the landscape.

But suburban residents driving their cars to work and shop in the downtown business district of Los Angeles created traffic jams that hurt business and ruined rail transit schedules. By the mid-1920s both the Pacific Electric and the Los Angeles Railway were losing money and lacked the capital to establish separate rights of way or to expand service to new suburban areas. The city, therefore, dealt with the problem by measures easing automobile congestion—traffic controls and wider streets. At the same time the motor truck made possible the dispersal of business and manufacturing industries to suburban areas. In the long run, this decision to depend on the automobile for transportation doomed the rail transit systems and established the pattern of development of the typical modern city. By 1930 over half

HENRY EDWARDS HUNTINGTON AND THE "BIG RED CARS"

Henry Huntington at the doors of his library, 1920s
Courtesy of the Huntington Library.

Southern California captivated Henry Edwards Huntington during a visit in 1892. The nephew of Southern Pacific president Collis P. Huntington had learned the intricacies of railroading and was en route from the East to San Francisco and a new position as his uncle's watchdog over Pacific Coast operations. Collis hoped that the appointment, and Henry's arranged marriage to a distant relative, would perpetuate family control of the transportation empire. It was not to be, however. Collis died in 1900, and Edward H. Harriman of the Union Pacific bought controlling interest in the Southern Pacific.

Henry divested himself of most of his Southern Pacific stock and San Francisco property, bought Rancho San Marino near Pasadena, and moved personal and business activities south in 1901. Long intrigued by the investment potential of electric streetcars, Huntington quickly purchased scores of street railway companies in the region. Within a few years, in partnership with the Southern Pacific, he had consolidated these into the Pacific Electric Railway, the largest interurban system in the nation, serving the entire

HENRY EDWARDS HUNTINGTON AND THE "BIG RED CARS" (continued)

Los Angeles basin. Converting all of the company's track to standard railroad gauge allowed his "Big Red Cars" to move both goods and people efficiently among forty cities within a radius of nearly as many miles. It was an impressive achievement that made Huntington wealthy, but not on the basis of fares or freights. He made shrewd land investments in regions soon to be penetrated by his lines, subdivided the property into housing tracts and shopping districts, and subsidized the Pacific Electric's often red-ink operation with his real estate profits.

In 1910 Henry Huntington sold his share of the railway to the Southern Pacific and devoted himself to managing the rare books, manuscripts, and paintings he was collecting at his San Marino ranch. Before he died in 1927, he had donated the estate, his magnificent collection, and much of his personal wealth to endow the Huntington Library and Art Gallery. "The Huntington" became immediately renowned as one of the state's outstanding art museums and a mecca for the world's literary and historical scholars. For decades after the Pacific Electric's sale and Huntington's death, the railway provided dependable, inexpensive transportation throughout the Los Angeles area. With routes that predicted the freeway rights of way of later years, the Pacific Electric facilitated the region's phenomenal growth between 1910 and 1930. As late as 1945, despite growing competition from buses and private automobiles, the "Big Red Cars" still carried more than 100 million passengers annually.

In the next decade, however, Californians' love affair with the automobile made the Pacific Electric obsolete. Rubber, auto, bus, petroleum, and other interests allegedly conspired to buy out and shut down the railway, but by the 1950s its days were numbered in any case. As automobile registration soared, streetcar passengers decreased. One by one, Pacific Electric routes ceased operation. In 1961, the last "Big Red Car" made its run on the Los Angeles-Long Beach line. Since then, neither Los Angeles nor any other California city has managed to devise a mass-transit system approaching Huntington's in reliability and economy. (WAB)

the residents of Los Angeles lived in detached single family homes—three times the number of any other major American city— yet the city was one of the major manufacturing areas of the country.

In the north, the automobile had a similar effect on metropolitan development, particularly in the East Bay communities in Alameda and Contra Costa counties and in the peninsula south of San Francisco. Ironi-

cally, as the state grew, traffic congestion in the new suburban areas led to the freeway era after World War II, and freeway congestion in the 1980s produced a revival of interest in mass rail transit.

The increase in automobile ownership also prompted important highway construction by the state. The California State Automobile Association and the Automobile Club of southern California, with many

HOW DO YOU SAY M-O-T-E-L? A CALIFORNIA ORIGINAL

A modern motorist can scarcely imagine highways without glitzy façades and neon signs beckoning *VACANCY;* mispronouncing *M-O-T-E-L* is unthinkable. Yet before December 1925, when the Milestone Motel designed by Pasadena architect Arthur S. Heineman opened on Pacific Coast Highway near San Luis Obispo, neither circumstance was impossible. To early customers, operators—and even newspapers such as the Los Angeles *Times*—had to explain facilities and that "motel" rhymed with "hotel."

During the 1920s, when Californians began their passionate love affair with Henry Ford's "Tin Lizzies" and more exotic machines, any excursion more ambitious than a one-day outing could become an unpredictable adventure. Overnight accommodations consisted of traditional hotels in downtown districts, occasional "auto camps," or whatever travelers might improvise by the roadside. Hotels could be inconvenient, auto camps rustic, and tent camping downright primitive. Thus, Heineman's innovation responded to immediate needs of an increasingly mobile populace. But it did more. Original plans projected a series of motels situated, like the Spanish missions, "a day's journey apart" along the coastal highway. That enterprise never materialized, but the Milestone Motel not only prospered but also introduced a word, copyrighted by Heineman, to Americans' vocabulary and an institution to the national landscape.

The Milestone Motel, circa 1930
Courtesy of the San Luis Obispo Historical Museum.

Motels had distinct advantages over traditional hotels. They were less formal, and roadside locations eliminated searches through unfamiliar city streets for a resting place. Cars waited at the traveler's door, ready to resume journeys without bothersome treks from hotels to parking garages several blocks away. Laundry and eating facilities on the premises added convenience, and the Milestone, like many of its successors, provided the oil changes and other ministrations that early vehicles frequently demanded.

Heineman's fusion of architecture and advertising also established a permanent standard. To attract customers, the Milestone Motel's highly visible front emulated the bell tower of Mission Santa Barbara sixty miles to the south; a less pretentious version of mission design guided hungry sojourners to the restaurant. Behind the Spanish Revival veneer, adequate guest bungalows were far less spacious or elegant than the highway vista suggested.

Over decades, motel design responded to changing architectural vogues, but Heineman's pioneer pattern—elaborate façades fronting modest accommodations—not only persisted but also became ubiquitous phenomena flanking the highways of California, the nation, and the world. Despite their proliferation, lexicographers did not deem them sufficiently significant to warrant including the word "motel" in dictionaries until 1950. (WAB)

The Milestone Motel, circa 1994
Photograph by William A. Bullough.

wealthy and influential members, joined the construction industry to promote a system of roads covering the entire state. With politicians acutely aware of the new "highway lobby," the state embarked on a major program of highway construction financed by a large bond issue and a gasoline tax. Gas stations, hotels, motor courts, orange juice stands, and other auto-related businesses sprang up along the new roads. New crossroads towns appeared, while new highways snaked into even the remote parts of the state.

Widespread auto ownership stimulated tourism and recreation. As a new federal highway program tied the country together in the 1920s, touring became a popular national pastime and the lure of California's climate, natural beauty, and exciting cities attracted many to the Golden State, some with an eye to future settlement. Vacation centers such as Lake Tahoe in the north and Big Bear and Lake Arrowhead in the south led the way in resort development, and the state began to develop an extensive system of beaches and parks, now within reach of the average family. The automobile also contributed to the revolution in morals of the 1920s. In 1919 hardly ten percent of American automobiles were enclosed, but by 1927 more than eighty-two percent were, leading Pasadena's police chief to report that "the greatest menace now facing the morals of Pasadena youth is the coupe and the sedan."

OIL

New developments in the oil industry contributed to the popularity of the automobile and to a stronger economy, especially in southern California. The industry also illustrated a phenomenon typical of the period—integration and consolidation of business structures. By 1911, when John D. Rockefeller's Standard Oil trust was dis-solved by the U.S. Supreme Court, the newly independent Standard Oil Company of California had already become, with Union Oil, one of the state's major producers and refiners. Associated and, to a lesser degree, Shell and General Petroleum were also emerging as leading companies.

Several new fields opened at this time, among them the highly productive Coyote Hills and Baldwin Hills fields near Los Angeles. In the San Joaquin Valley, the Kern River, Sunset, and Midway fields expanded rapidly, stimulated by western railroads' switch from coal to oil as a fuel and the United States' entry into World War I. Wartime conditions also increased emphasis on gasoline refining, for which California's crude oil, with its naturally high content of iso-octane hydrocarbons, was particularly suited.

The wartime stimulus proved to be but a prelude to the golden years of the 1920s, when phenomenal fields of high-gravity oil were discovered in the Los Angeles basin. Standard Oil discovered the first field at Huntington Beach in 1920. The next year Union Oil opened the Santa Fe Springs field, and Shell tapped the fantastically rich Signal Hill site. Within three years California crude oil production rose from 105 million to 264 million barrels per year. Additional fields at Dominguez Hills, Torrance, Whittier, and Wilmington, along with coastline drilling from Huntington Beach to Santa Barbara, kept California the first-ranked state in oil production until the 1930s.

A frenzy of speculation in oil stocks accompanied this oil boom and led to the Julian scandal. Chauncey C. Julian was an oil-field worker who bought oil leases, adopted a polished appearance, and mounted an advertising campaign aimed at small investors that, within a few months, produced $11 million from 40,000 subscribers, presumably to develop Julian's holdings. In 1924 the high-living speculator

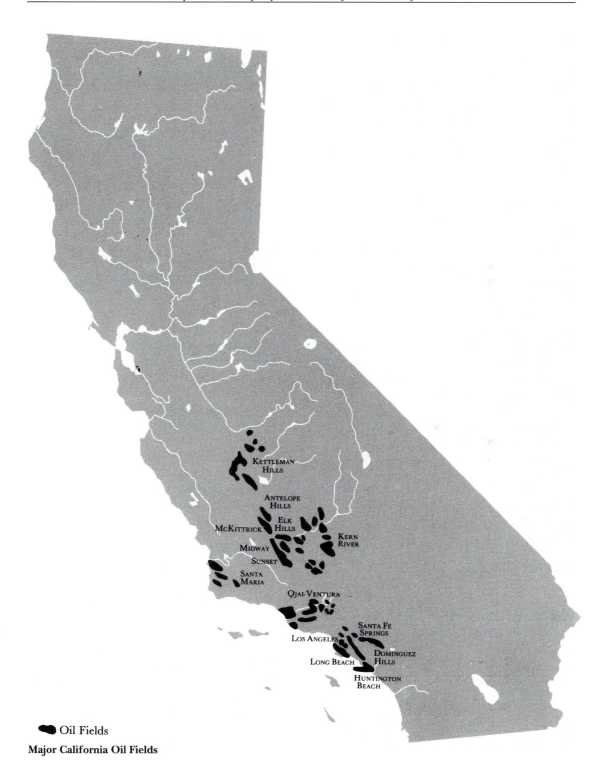

Major California Oil Fields

sold out to a couple of smooth-talking operators, S. C. Lewis and Jack Bennett, who proceeded to issue nearly five million shares of unauthorized stock in the Julian Petroleum Company and to organize stock pools attracting some of the most prominent businessmen in the region. In 1927 the overcapitalization became known, the bubble collapsed, and thousands of small investors were ruined.

The oil boom of the 1920s promoted restructuring of the industry. At first, hundreds of small companies, along with the large, produced a tidal wave of oil, overwhelming refineries and storage facilities. By 1925, however, fifty-seven refineries processed some 186 million barrels of oil per year, and by 1928 the larger companies had tank farms capable of storing more than 340 million barrels of oil, nearly a two-year supply. The flood of oil also depressed world prices, accelerating the trend toward consolidation through mergers and purchase. By 1930 an oligopolistic industry had emerged, dominated by a handful of integrated companies—Standard, Union, Shell, Tidewater-Associated, General Petroleum, Richfield, and the Texas Company—that could stabilize prices well above those of the newly opened Texas and Oklahoma fields.

GAS AND HYDROELECTRIC POWER

The use of natural gas (an important by-product of the search for oil) for heat and power evolved slowly in the 1920s. The huge expansion of oil production in the decade meant a similar increase of natural gas, but consumption was only a tiny fraction of modern-day use, and natural gas remained only on the threshold of becoming a major energy source.

It was a different story with hydroelectricity. In 1893 there were only four hydroelectric plants, two of them in southern Califor-

nia, producing power for commercial purposes in the United States. Thirty years later California far outdistanced any other state in the production of hydroelectric energy. Major problems had to be solved along the way: huge dams and power plants had to be built, often in remote mountain areas, to store sufficient water to run turbines year-round, and means had to be found to transmit the electricity to the areas of use. There was little thought at the time of the environmental consequences.

Development of electrical utilities required large amounts of capital, and, as in the oil industry, a few well-financed corporations merged with and absorbed smaller companies to dominate the field. The merger of San Francisco Gas and Electric with California Central Gas and Electric in 1905 created Pacific Gas and Electric (PG&E), destined to be the state's largest utility. By additional acquisitions it had grown by 1930 to serve thirty-eight northern and central California counties. The second-largest consolidated utility was Southern California Edison, which by 1928 served two million people in southern California outside of San Diego and Los Angeles. Only a few municipally owned systems were formed in the progressive era; the largest was Los Angeles's Bureau of Power and Light, which distributed electricity throughout the city from facilities connected with the Owens Valley project.

The generation, distribution, and marketing of hydroelectric power by municipalities led to serious conflict between advocates of publicly owned facilities and private enterprises. Ironically, in Los Angeles, that bastion of free enterprise and the open shop, ideology succumbed to the need for cheap power, and the city joined the fight to include hydroelectric power production and distribution in the Boulder Canyon project. At the same time, the major private utilities fought to restrict government competition. Los Angeles obtained the power it needed for continued growth in 1930, when the Secretary of the Interior approved a contract allocating thirty-six percent of the Boulder Canyon dam power to the Metropolitan Water District and gave the district first call on unused power to pump water through the Colorado Aqueduct. In addition, two of the four generating units at Parker Dam belonged to the MWD. An important consequence of the development of these resources was that Los Angeles controlled enough water and power to coerce surrounding communities to annex to the city in order to obtain the resources necessary for their own growth.

THE MOVIES

No other industry had as great an impact on the world's view of California as the motion picture industry. From 1896 to 1946 movies were the most popular form of mass entertainment in America, and between 1916 and 1946 moviemaking was the biggest industry in southern California. With tens of thousands of employees and payrolls in the hundreds of millions of dollars, it had an enormous impact on the state.

For several years after 1900 companies such as Biograph, Vitagraph, and Edison produced a multitude of one-reel movies, twelve to fifteen minutes in length. They soon were used primarily by storefront theaters, which charged a nickel admission, in working-class neighborhoods. These "nickelodeon" theaters provided a brief, cheap, and convenient form of entertainment for workers working a normal eleven- or twelve-hour day, six days a week.

As nickelodeons grew in number, enterprising individuals established distribution exchanges to provide them with new films, while others began to build strings of movie houses. In 1908, however, Thomas A. Edison

and other moviemakers organized the Motion Picture Patents Company, known as the "movie trust," and, by pooling camera and projector patents, attempted to monopolize all phases of the industry. Instead, the Edison trust drove independent distributors and theater owners into the production field. A group of companies in the hands of new movie "moguls" emerged to dominate the industry, and the trust failed. For the most part foreign-born Jewish immigrants who had started life in America dealing in clothing, furs, rags, or jewelry, the movie moguls included William Fox, Adolph Zukor, Samuel Goldwyn, Louis B. Mayer, Marcus Loew, and Jesse L. Lasky. Together they built a new integrated industry around a few major studios: Paramount, Fox (later 20th-Century Fox), Metro-Goldwyn-Mayer, Universal, Columbia, Warner Brothers, and RKO (Radio-Keith-Orpheum). In the process they centered the industry in southern California.

There is an old story that the independent motion-picture companies pioneered moviemaking in California to escape from movie-trust subpoena servers. Actually, most of the state's first movies were produced by movie-trust companies. One such firm, Essanay, which made 375 Bronco Billy westerns, joined Charlie Chaplin's and other companies to produce films at Niles, near San Francisco, between 1910 and 1916 before moving south. Southern California's climate, however, proved ideal for making movies and its open shop labor policy provided a ready supply of cheap labor. Moreover, the Los Angeles area boasted a variety of terrain that could pass for almost anywhere else in the world: deserts, snowy mountains, ocean, and islands were all just a short trip from the studio. By 1914 more than seventy firms were producing films in the region. Most of these studios were located in and around the community of Hollywood on the western outskirts of Los Angeles, transforming this village of transplanted Kansans into the motion-picture capital of the world.

Major advances in moviemaking accompanied the move west. The short one-reel films of the early 1900s gave way to the "feature" film several reels long, and production techniques changed dramatically, too. Probably the foremost filmmaker of the early 1900s was Edwin S. Porter, who produced the classic *The Great Train Robbery* in 1903. In this and other films Porter explored a wide range of now-familiar techniques, including the use of dissolves to move from one image to another, multiple shots of the same scene, side lighting, and close-ups. Twelve years later David W. Griffith, in a brilliant display of the possibilities of the new medium, used all the techniques pioneered by Porter to tell a compelling story of the South during Reconstruction in *The Birth of a Nation,* the first great feature film. A huge success, the film also had unfortunate social consequences; based on a novel that lauded the Ku Klux Klan, it treated blacks as an inferior race and impressed negative stereotypes of the ex-slaves on American minds.

With development of the feature film, moviemakers reached out to a whole new audience—the growing American middle class. Simultaneously, the "star" system developed when moviegoers adopted favorites among the heretofore anonymous actors and actresses. By 1916 Charlie Chaplin could demand and receive a salary of $10,000 a week from Mack Sennett's Keystone Company, and star-struck youngsters and gawking tourists flocked to Hollywood.

In addition to would-be stars, Hollywood also attracted talented writers, directors, and artists, many of them women. In fact, it probably offered more opportunity for women than most places in the 1920s. Anita Loos,

June Mathis, and Frances Marion were leading scriptwriters; Lois Weber was a well-known director and independent producer; and a number of other women, including Elinor Glynn and Dorothy Arzner, were successful film directors. In addition, the studios employed thousands of cameramen and film editors as well as carpenters, electricians, and painters who built and maintained movie sets in scores of locations in and around the area.

Integration of the movie industry was completed in the 1920s when the major studios developed their own theater chains. Loew's Theaters (with its MGM production subsidiary), Zukor's Paramount studio, Fox, and RKO all built lavish motion-picture palaces to exhibit their films. A growing number of middle- and upper-class Americans were attracted to the movies with the construction of these lush theaters, some so richly appointed it was said to be worth the price of admission just to use the restroom.

With some justification, older Hollywood residents were apprehensive about the arrival of the movie colony. The scandalous conduct of some of the stars and a series of risqué movies led to threats of censorship. In 1922 industry representatives persuaded Postmaster General Will H. Hays to leave President Harding's cabinet for a $150,000-a-year position as "movie czar," after which the Hays Office issued a code of ethics and plan for self-regulation of the movies that effectively recovered public support.

In 1927 Warner Brothers, one of the smaller studios, revolutionized the industry with its production of *The Jazz Singer,* the first talking picture. As with the early silent films, the new talking pictures developed with free-ranging ideas, experimentation, and iconoclasm. The Marx Brothers movie *Duck Soup* (1933) has been called "as thorough a satire on politics and patriotism as any film before *Dr. Strangelove.*" Similarly, Mae West's *She Done Him Wrong* (1933) represented a daring departure from accepted sex roles for women.

Sex continued to be portrayed openly in some films, leading the Catholic Church to organize the Legion of Decency and threaten to boycott such films. Seriously hurt by the depression and losing millions, Hollywood agreed to stronger self-regulation and in 1934 organized the Breen Office to oversee a new code of ethics. For the rest of the 1930s, with few exceptions, Hollywood produced a series of glamorous and appealing escapist—and noncontroversial—movies. Comedies, mysteries, westerns, lavish musicals, pictures based on classic literary works, and films featuring child stars reinforced traditional values and were big moneymakers in a new "golden age" that lasted until the rise of television after World War II.

Hollywood attracted many well-known American writers, as well as a large number of well-known European refugees from Hitler's Germany, whose contribution to a cultural awakening in southern California was impressive. Some were critical of the Hollywood culture in spite of the fact that they wrote for the movies. Nathanael West's *Day of the Locust* and F. Scott Fitzgerald's *The Last Tycoon* are examples of this disillusionment. However, California's premier writer of the era, Robinson Jeffers, rejected the Hollywood scene and left southern California for the central coast region, where he wrote moody poetry.

AGRIBUSINESS

The new business structure of the 1920s was especially apparent in agriculture, and California became the nation's foremost example of industrialized farming; by 1930 "facto-

ries in the fields" had replaced the traditional family farm. Industrialized and corporate farms, processors, shippers, and bankers dominated the state's agriculture. Closely allied with the scientific community through the University of California College of Agriculture, they exerted their political strength through the powerful California Farm Bureau Federation, formed in 1919. Land ownership became increasingly concentrated; by the 1930s only four percent of the state's farms controlled sixty-two percent of all farmland. Farming in California had become agribusiness.

The development of the Tejón Ranch Company is one example among many. Like so many other large holdings, the Tejón operation was based on several large Mexican land grants—in this case, those of Edward F. Beale. As a young officer with Commodore Stockton, Beale had entered California in 1846, aided in the rescue of General Kearny at San Pascual and served as the state's first Superintendent of Indian Affairs in the 1850s. His holdings, acquired mostly in the 1860s, included the Liebra, Alamos y Agua Caliente, Castaic, and Tejón grants, totaling 221,838 acres. By his death in 1893 Beale had purchased an additional 100,000 acres. In 1912 his son, Truxton, sold these holdings for $3 million to a group of Los Angeles capitalists headed by Harry Chandler, and the Tejón Ranch Company, a modern corporate farm, became one of the state's largest producers of livestock, alfalfa, fruit, and potatoes.

Another agricultural giant grew out of the incorporation in 1903 of the Kern County Land Company, which assumed control of 350,000 acres of Kern County land from James Ben Ali Haggin and his associates. This company developed into one of the largest and most successful corporate farming operations in the world. Miller and Lux,

ROBINSON JEFFERS
Poet of the Coast

Robinson Jeffers
Photo by Edward Weston. Courtesy of the Bancroft Library.

When asked what characterized great poetry, Robinson Jeffers observed that "permanent things, or things forever renewed, like the grass and human passions, are the materials for poetry." From an early age Jeffers had learned to love and respect the natural environment, but as he matured he became deeply disillusioned with humanity. In powerful, violent, and often controversial poems he extolled nature while portraying the dark side of human passions. His long narrative poems—such as *Tamar, Roan Stallion, The Women of Big Sur, Cawdor,* and *Thurso's Landing*—described rape, incest, murder, and insanity against the ruggedly majestic background of the central California coast.

Jeffers was a transplanted Pennsylvanian who emerged as California's master poet in the 1920s. He had come to California in 1903 at the age of sixteen, when his father, an austere Presbyterian college professor and Old Testament scholar, moved his family to Highland Park in southern California in hopes of improving his health. Young Robinson had spent much of his youth studying the classics under the stern eye of his father and had attended a different European boarding school each year in his early teens. Accord-

ROBINSON JEFFERS (continued)
Poet of the Coast

ingly, when he enrolled in Occidental College, a Presbyterian school in Highland Park, he was immediately accorded junior status. At Occidental, Jeffers enjoyed the usual student activities and wrote poetry for the student magazine, which he edited in his senior year.

An important element in Jeffers's emergence as a major poet was his marriage to Una Kuster in 1913. They met in 1905, when Robin (as he was known to friends and family) attended the University of Southern California after graduating from Occidental. At twenty, Una was two years his senior and had been married to Theodore Kuster for three years. For the next seven years their love affair dominated Robinson's life as he studied medicine at USC and forestry at the University of Washington, and led a bohemian life at Hermosa Beach, writing poetry and roaming the nearby coast and mountains. Una's husband filed for divorce in 1912, and the next year Robin and Una married, moved to Carmel, and began a new life together.

Living on the dramatic coast of the Big Sur country, Jeffers absorbed the environment around him. Long walks with Una, and later with their twin sons, along the beach or through the mountains that plunged to the shore filled him with images he used in his poetry. He built their home, Tor House, and a retreat for Una called Hawk Tower on a point overlooking the ocean near Carmel. He hauled stones up from the beach and set them in mortar himself, while he framed his day's writing in his mind. His disciplined routine was jealously guarded by Una, whose wide-ranging intellect complemented his own.

Jeffers's first two books of poems had been in the traditional mode, but after moving to Carmel he began to experiment with unconventional styles, producing the long narrative poems whose rhythms have been likened to those of the sea. But the controversial subject matter of these poems was unacceptable to publishers, leading Jeffers to use his own funds to publish *Tamar* in 1924. Favorable reviews of the book marked him as a major literary figure, and the publication of *Roan Stallion, Tamar, and Other Poems* the next year began a long, successful career, with Jeffers publishing important work almost annually for the next fifteen years. During and after World War II, in poems such as *The Double Axe,* he spoke out vigorously against war and the threat of atomic weapons, warning of the very extinction of humankind. In 1946 he demonstrated another facet of his talent, writing a new stage version of *Medea* for his friend Judith Anderson, whose performance in the title role made the play a Broadway success that was repeated abroad.

The fire that Una kindled in Robinson Jeffers died with her death from cancer in 1950. In the next dozen years he produced only one major work and lived what he regarded as a "rudderless" existence until his own death at seventy-five in 1962. (RBR) the Newhall Land and Farming Company, the Irvine Company, and Standard Oil Company of California, among many others, were similarly involved in large-scale corporate farming by the 1920s.

Concentration of land ownership, or horizontal integration, encouraged vertical integration, in which a company operated not only vast acreages of farmland but also food-processing, distribution, and marketing enterprises. In 1916, for example, Mark J. Fontana organized four large packing companies into the California Packing Company, making it the largest canning company in the world. The company bought and farmed thousands of acres of land and contracted with hundreds of independent growers for their fruits and vegetables. CalPack then processed and shipped these crops to its nationwide network of warehouses for marketing under its Del Monte label, establishing a relationship between food processors and growers that characterizes California agriculture to this day. Joseph DiGiorgio, an Italian immigrant, achieved similar success with the organization of a vertically integrated company, the DiGiorgio Corporation, dealing primarily in fruit and wines, and marketing canned goods under the S&W label.

For decades the citrus industry dominated California agriculture, but an expanding market for fruits and vegetables after World War I made California agriculture more diversified. By the end of the 1920s the state was producing such a variety of crops that it was in a class by itself. With some 200 commercial crops, compared to twelve or fifteen in most farming states, California dominated national production in such products as vegetables, fruits, nuts, and poultry. In the 1920s the marketing of these specialty crops was more and more "rationalized" through the development of exchanges patterned after the pioneering California Fruit Grower's Exchange ("Sunkist").

Growers of walnuts, almonds, dates, figs, and raisins, among many other crops, all organized "co-ops" designed to assure orderly, profitable marketing.

The spectacular growth of specialty crops tended to overshadow other important changes in the state's agriculture, including the rapid development of two major staple crops, rice and cotton. In the 1920s scientific farming and irrigation combined to transform the San Joaquin Valley into a new cotton kingdom where growers achieved yields three times those of the traditional cotton-growing areas of the country, making California one of the top cotton-producing states in the nation. Similarly, rice culture, introduced by Japanese farmers in 1900, became an important Sacramento Valley farm crop in the 1920s. Rice producers, like cotton growers, achieved the highest yields in the nation, and the state soon ranked third in national production.

Only the wine-making industry failed to share in the boom of the 1920s, since prohibition curtailed production drastically. However, sales of table grapes to eastern buyers rose phenomenally, and by 1925 the sale of grapes for home wine-making and illegal "commercial" production enabled growers to survive and recapture their dominant position in the American wine industry when prohibition was repealed in 1933.

The University of California's College of Agriculture made important contributions to specialty crop and business farming. University scientists made increased yields, scientific business methods, and farm mechanization their first priority. Seeing the business farms as their primary clientele, institutional research became oriented to the agribusiness community. At the same time, the California Farm Bureau Federation, with offices at the College of Agriculture, exerted exceptional political influence on behalf of corporate farmers.

FARM LABOR

Political influence helped farmers manage another fundamental element of successful large-scale specialty agriculture in California—a ready supply of cheap harvest labor. Almost all farmers hired help at harvest time, but most small farmers used neighbors or local high school students; the employer-employee relationship in such cases was not exploitative. On the other hand, large-scale farm operations had always depended on a supply of migrant labor that could be hired at the lowest cost for the shortest possible time. They sought an oversupply, to guarantee that their crops would be harvested on time and to keep wages down. Also, fewer and fewer growers employed most of the migratory labor force. By 1935, for example, one-tenth of California's growers hired three-fourths of the harvest labor and, incidentally, controlled one-half the production of specialty crops.

To ensure the labor supply they needed, California growers organized labor bureaus or exchanges in the 1920s. Growers in each agricultural district banded together to estimate their harvest labor needs, set wage rates, and establish an organization to provide the workers. Pressure from growers and processors, who supplied funds for these exchanges, made sure that the agreed-on rates were adhered to. In effect, farm workers were hired by the local industry, not by individual growers, and consequently were even less able to bargain for higher wages. The system reduced labor costs by as much as thirty percent in some areas.

The main source of farm labor also changed drastically during the decade. Japanese had made up a large part of the farm labor force after 1900, but they tended to move as quickly as possible from farm-labor status to producer status, competing with whites. After 1915 they were replaced by Mexican nationals and Mexican Americans, who were the first to use the automobile in creating a mobile labor force.

Working conditions in the fields remained poor. Growers took little responsibility for decent treatment of harvest workers and used their political influence to prevent government action on the laborers' behalf. They were joined in this by processors, canners, teamsters, railroads, utilities, and all others who had a stake in the profits of business farmers. Consequently, the 1920s were a ten-year lull in public efforts to promote better working and living conditions for farm labor. Thousands of workers thus continued to live in unsanitary conditions in tent villages or automobiles and to work exceedingly long hours for low pay. It was a situation ripe for trouble when the depression of the 1930s revived the spirit of unionism.

OTHER INDUSTRIES

The impact of population growth and the trend toward consolidation, efficiency, and order affected other industries as well. Amadeo P. Giannini, who founded the Bank of Italy in San Francisco in 1904 as a bank "for the little fella," salvaged the bank's assets from the San Francisco fire in 1906, and within days reopened for business. In the next two decades Giannini acquired additional banking interests in New York and Italy and pioneered the concept of branch banking—particularly in California's booming agricultural regions, where by 1927 the Bank of Italy held mortgages on one of every eleven farms. In 1930 the Giannini bank holdings were merged to form the Bank of America, which in 1945 became the largest bank in the world. In Los Angeles, Joseph Sartori formed another giant, the Security Pacific Bank, by merging the First National Bank of Los Angeles with Security National Bank.

Population growth, the aggressive development of water and electricity, and cheap labor attracted a number of major national industries to southern California. In 1919 Goodyear Tire and Rubber Company established the first branch plant in the West in Los Angeles, where its huge water needs could be met. Firestone, B. F. Goodrich, and U.S. Rubber Company soon followed, making Los Angeles the nation's second-largest tire manufacturer. In 1927–1928 the first automobile assembly plants in California were opened in Los Angeles by Willys-Overland Motor Company and Ford. In the same decade Owens-Illinois Glass Company, Swift & Company, Procter and Gamble, Bethlehem Steel, U.S. Steel, and many other firms located major branch plants in Los Angeles. The city moved from twenty-eighth among manufacturing centers in the United States in 1919 to ninth place by 1930, surpassing San Francisco, while California was ranked eighth among the states in value of manufactured products.

THE DECLINE OF ORGANIZED LABOR

A marked decline in the power and influence of organized labor accompanied postwar economic expansion. As the nation entered a period of "red-baiting," many Americans found it relatively easy to apply the "radical" label to unions, and, seizing this opportunity, California employer associations mounted aggressive campaigns to establish the open shop throughout the state. In southern California the Merchants and Manufacturers Association redoubled efforts to prevent unions from gaining a foothold in the area. By 1929 the Los Angeles *Times* proudly ran a month-long series of articles titled "The Forty-Year War for a Free City," which attributed the "phenomenal" growth of southern California industry to employer success in maintaining the open shop.

In the north, the battle between organized labor and employers quickly resumed when World War I ended. By 1921 the longshoreman's and seafarer's unions had been demolished, the former replaced by new company unions under company-controlled foremen, and the Building Trades Council had been overpowered by San Francisco employers. San Francisco's Industrial Association successfully instituted an area-wide open shop in the following years. It set up a system for hiring and training nonunion labor, denied employers of union labor access to building materials, and pressured banks to deny these employers credit. Lacking public support, union membership and influence declined in California, as it did in the rest of the country. The criminal syndicalism law enacted in California in 1919 was one of the chief weapons of antiunion forces in this period. It was successfully used to eliminate the IWW as a factor in agricultural labor and to intimidate all labor organizations in the postwar decade. The period ended with the state's labor organizations weaker than they had been since the 1870s.

URBAN RIVALRY AND THE MILITARY

While business and labor clashed over unionization they generally cooperated to promote uban growth and development. The dramatic expansion of southern California sparked an intense rivalry between cities for urbanization. Local businesses, labor, and government came together to promote growth, and many of the public projects of the 1920s and 1930s such as the great municipal water projects, bridges, transit systems and "worlds fairs" of the era were a part of this competition.

This community of interest also applied to efforts to obtain a steady flow of federal funds into cities through the favorable location of military facilities. Accordingly, throughout the 1920s and 1930s California cities particularly San Diego, Los Angeles, San Francisco, Vallejo, and Alameda vied with each other to attract military bases. In 1919, for example the United States Navy created the Pacific Fleet and began the search for its home base—kicking off a bidding war eventually won by San Diego, despite the general agreement that San Francisco was the "strategic center" of the west coast. San Diego simply outbid, and politically outmaneuvered, all others. Subsequently, the Navy poured millions of dollars annually into the San Diego economy.

Similarly, southern California successfully attracted Army Air Force bases, particularly March Field, developing close economic and personal ties with the Army. Air Force and Navy installations and the research and experimentation they stimulated were important considerations in the decisions of such aircraft manufacturing companies as Douglas, Lockheed, and Consolidated to locate in southern California—laying the foundation for the area's domination of the aerospace industry after World War II. By 1941, California cities had developed a civil-military partnership of enormous and continuing significance.

A CHANGING SOCIETY

In a comment on American society in the 1920s, historian Lawrence Levine once noted, "The central paradox of American history . . . has been a belief in progress coupled with a dread of change; an urge toward the inevitable future combined with a longing for the irretrievable past." The diversified, explosive, paradoxical society emerging in California in the 1920s bears this out. Like most Americans, Californians embraced the automobile, the movies, the radio, and other products of the new technology. Many were fascinated by the new moral standards, "flappers," and "modernist" religious teachings. Yet a great many rejected any form of radi-

calism or labor organization, and feared ethnic minorities. They supported prohibition, religious fundamentalism, and the nativism of the Ku Klux Klan. At the same time, they tried to retain the sense of identity, community, and morality they had left behind. For a great many people, Aimee Semple McPherson and those like her filled this need.

THE NEW FREEDOM OF WOMEN

For white, middle-class women in particular, the 1920s was an era of new freedom. They entered colleges in vastly greater numbers, went to work in the business world whether they needed to or not, discarded at least half the volume of clothing worn by their mothers, smoked, drank, and drove automobiles. Demanding for themselves the same social freedoms men enjoyed, women in the 1920s laid the foundation of modern society. In California their prominence in sports and aviation, in the new sportswear industry, and in public service bespoke their new status. For example, by 1930 almost thirty percent of female American airplane pilots were Californians, and Louise Thaden, who moved to California in 1926, had set women's records for altitude, speed, and endurance. In 1928, she won the first National Women's Air Derby.

Women also made modest progress in control of reproduction. State law made performing an abortion a felony, but by 1930 it was seldom enforced and illegal abortions were generally available. Also, while public discussion of birth control was almost nonexistent, thousands of California women were receiving advice on contraception in clinics established by the American Birth Control League and from private, non-Catholic physicians. Moreover, they increasingly demanded "companionate" marriages and less subordinate family roles.

While no grand cause such as the suffrage movement united California women in the

1920s, they were active and effective through innumerable clubs and organizations promoting specific issues. Few were elected to public office—San Francisco's Florence Prag Kahn was California's lone female representative in Congress, replacing her husband after his death—but those with money got results. Backed by chocolate heiress Myra Hershey and others, Arti Mason Carter, for example, inaugurated the "Symphonies Under the Stars" series in a location that became the Hollywood Bowl. To preserve the site, Mrs. Carter personally halted the earth-moving equipment about to begin development of the area for another purpose. Other southern California women philanthropists, including Estelle Doheny, Mabel Beckman, and Ellen Browning Scripps, also contributed significant sums to education and the arts throughout the period.

THE ROLE OF RELIGION

Aimee Semple McPherson was the most famous of many faith healers, spiritualists, health faddists, and cult leaders who played to the emotional needs of southern Californians and gave Los Angeles a reputation for being peculiarly hospitable to unorthodox ideas and bizarre behavior. The population of the south differed markedly from that of the older, more cosmopolitan north. Probably no more than one-fourth of the residents of Los Angeles in the 1920s had been born there—newcomers were always in the majority. Many, like earlier migrants, were health-seekers, but the majority were rural midwesterners fleeing the cold winters, stifling summers, and drudgery of farm life. Rootless, they sought a sense of community, flocked to newly organized State Societies, and attended annual state picnics where they hobnobbed with folks from "back home." Paradoxically, H. L. Mencken could call Los Angeles in the 1920s "Double Dubuque," a

hundred midwestern towns laid end to end, while others were calling the 1920s in Los Angeles the "Golden Age of Crackpotism."

Religion had always been a large part of the midwestern migrants' lives, perhaps their only entertainment, but they had left the stern life of the Old Testament behind. In Los Angeles, Aimee Semple McPherson offered them a more upbeat religion in a form that could compete with the entertainment of Hollywood. She understood their loneliness and bewilderment, their love of fantasy, and their dreams. Substituting a gospel of love for the gospel of fear, she preached salvation in the here-and-now and stressed God's grace rather than the pessimistic doctrines of her rivals who believed in original sin. Filling her sermons with humor, she entertained them, offered them hope, and helped thousands of "nobodies," as Kevin Starr has noted, "become somebodies in Los Angeles." A young Anthony Quinn became her interpreter when she held services in the Mexican American community. Enraptured, he spent years playing the saxophone in her orchestra. Through her radio station, KFSG, her melodious voice became the most recognizable in the West. Simply put, through the 1920s Aimee Semple McPherson symbolized the hopes of thousands of Californians.

Sister Aimee was not the first woman evangelist to attract attention in the region. The Theosophical Society, which followed various Buddhist and Brahman theories, produced two earlier evangelists. As early as 1900 Katherine Tingley, also known as the Purple Mother, built an enclave at Point Loma near San Diego. From a ninety-room, high-domed building of Moorish-Egyptian style, the flamboyant revivalist autocratically ruled her church membership, which included Spot, a dog whom she believed to be the reincarnation of one of her former husbands. Another theosophist, Annie Besant, established a colony on a large tract of land in the Ojai Valley, where she brought the spiritualist Krishnamurti as the "new messiah." Besant made Ojai an important center of the theosophic movement until her death in 1933.

But Aimee Semple McPherson was in a class by herself. At her death in 1944, her Church of the Foursquare Gospel counted 410 churches in North America, 200 missions, 29,000 members, and assets of $2,800,000. In 1992, under her son Rolfe's leadership it had grown to over 25,000 churches worldwide, with 1,700,000 members and a fund balance of $357,335,000.

PROHIBITION

California ratified the Eighteenth (Prohibition) Amendment in 1919 after a bitter campaign between "wets" and "drys." Once prohibition was the law of the land, California, like every other state, found it a nightmare to enforce. The Volstead Act, which went into effect on January 17, 1920, instituted federal enforcement of prohibition but left state and local enforcement open. In 1920 California's Anti-Saloon League pushed the Harris Act, providing for state enforcement, through a legislature dominated by rural and southern representatives. The wets, however, defeated the bill in a referendum, revealing that no major city in the state had a dry majority, and two more years passed before legislation was adopted to put state officers nominally behind the enforcement of prohibition. Even then the state effort was not overwhelming; in 1929 it spent only $1,767 for the purpose. At the local level twenty-six counties and fifty-six cities and towns had "little Volstead" ordinances by January 1922, motivated mainly by the revenue produced by fines levied on violators. By then, though, it was also obvious that some cities, especially San Francisco and Sacramento, were going to stay, as one witness said, "hilariously wet." San Francisco's Board of Supervisors, in fact, refused to permit assignment of city and county officers to prohibition enforcement. In the south, with many thousands of rural midwestern newcomers, prohibition had much greater support. Even so, Los Angeles did not adopt prohibition under local option before the Volstead Act took effect, and the wets there were a large majority.

Throughout the country the enforcement of the Volstead Act's prohibition on the manufacture or sale of any beverage containing more than one-half of one percent alcohol proved to be impossible and California, with its 1,200-mile coastline, was a rum-runner's paradise. The chief sources of illegal alcohol were ships that sailed down the coast from Vancouver, British Columbia, where large export houses did a big business with thirsting Americans. By 1926 smuggling liquor from Canada had become a major industry; southern California alone illegally imported an estimated 150,000 cases of scotch whiskey valued at $10 million per year. Canadian exporters, with agents in most coast cities, took orders and arranged for deliveries to a variety of bootleggers. Some big operators owned ships carrying up to 10,000 cases, speedboats to run liquor ashore, and a fleet of trucks and converted passenger cars for distribution on land. Smaller operators simply bought "over the rail" from the Canadian supply ships thirty miles or more offshore and ran the goods ashore in speedboats. Hijackers, meanwhile, raced with police to intercept the speedboats as they came ashore at places such as Oxnard, Summerland, Seal Beach, Santa Barbara, and coastal inlets around San Francisco.

Although many groups publicly defended prohibition as a return to traditional, sober morality, large numbers of individuals defied the law. There is no way of knowing how many illicit stills existed in California, but a measure of sorts is the fact that, in 1927 alone, prohibition agents seized 185 distilleries and 572 stills from basements, garages, canyons, stables, dairies, and tents. The government, however, simply did not have the resources to enforce the law effectively. For California's drys, therefore, the prohibition experience was a long, sorry tale of failure.

ETHNIC MINORITIES IN THE 1920s

Many of the same people who supported prohibition also supported the nativist movement of the 1920s, which took the form of a revived Ku Klux Klan and agitation against racial and ethnic minorities. The Japanese continued to be the chief target of nativists in California. Despite the 1907 Gentlemen's Agreement and the Webb Alien-Land Law of 1913, there were some 72,000 Japanese in California in 1920, and they were heavily entrenched in important segments of agriculture. Shrewd and efficient businesspeople as well as excellent farmers, they elicited intense resentment from white farmers and were vilified in the press, which caused further efforts to restrict their immigration. After World War I the Joint Immigration Committee, formed by V. S. McClatchy, editor of the Sacramento *Bee,* and leaders of the American Legion, Native Sons of the Golden West, and other patriotic or nativist groups, aggressively led this effort. In 1920 voters overwhelmingly approved an initiative strengthening the Webb Act by providing that alien Japanese could not even lease land temporarily or invest in any company owning real property in the state. In 1924 California representatives successfully persuaded Congress to end the Gentlemen's Agreement as part of the Immigration Act of 1924. This ended Japanese immigration and substantially changed the character of the Japanese American population. By World War II, two-thirds were Nisei—American-born citizens.

After 1920 thousands of Mexican immigrants entered California, drawn by the needs of agribusiness for mobile harvest labor as well as by the booming manufacturing, food-processing, garment, and construction industries of southern California. This led to proposals to restrict Mexican immigration by putting Mexico on the quota system established by the Immigration Act of 1924. Fearful growers reacted by importing Filipino field workers to ensure a plentiful supply of harvest labor, introducing another target for nativist groups. The decade ended with Mexicans comprising nearly eighty percent of the California farm labor force and more than 20,000 Filipinos making up the balance. Meanwhile a growing community of Mexican Americans and Mexican immigrants settled in East Los Angeles. White discrimination (Los Angeles was ninety percent white in the 1920s) limited employment opportunities, pay, and housing, but Latinos developed a stable community based on work, religion and family. Women led the way in creating associations among Mexican Americans such as El Club Anachuac and La Sociedad Montezuma for young women and men and La Sociedad Mutualista Mexicana, an interbarrio, interorganizational coordinating agency, all reinforcing the inward focus of the community. By 1930, the Mexican population of Los Angeles had tripled to over 97,000 and was one of the largest urban concentrations of Mexicans outside of Mexico City.

The African American population of California remained relatively small after World War I, generally no more than two to three percent of the population of San Francisco or Los Angeles. Two wage-earner families were typical with over half the working-age women employed. Most black men found work with the railroads or as laborers while women rarely found employment other than as domestics. By 1930 the African American community had concentrated in Watts in Los

Angeles and, to a lesser extent, in West Oakland in the north. As with the Mexican American population, African American women were leaders in the formation of organizations promoting equal opportunity for blacks. Frances Albrier, for example, educated at Howard University and the University of California in the early 1920s, galvanized local black middle-class women in Berkeley and Oakland to work against racial discrimination in jobs and housing. In Los Angeles, Charlotta Bass edited the *California Eagle* and spent many years in a variety of African American organizations combatting increasing discrimination as the black community grew—to nearly 40,000 by 1930.

African American immigration, however, was not the chief cause of the revival of the Ku Klux Klan in the state. Rather, Klan membership, which increased considerably in the decade after World War I, seemed more related to the drive for prohibition and the xenophobia of the times. Klan "klaverns" appeared in San Francisco, Oakland, Sacramento, Fresno, and other San Joaquin Valley towns, but the Klan's real strength was in Los Angeles and the surrounding communities, where at one time Klan members controlled the city of Anaheim. Closely allied with fundamentalist church groups, Klan members were most active in Anti-Saloon League drives to promote the enforcement of prohibition. Since many Americans associated the use of alcohol with foreign Catholic immigrants, the prohibitionist and nativist sentiments of Klansmen were linked. It might be noted, however, that while the growth of the Klan reflected the national experience, there was much less violence associated with its actions in California than elsewhere.

ONE-PARTY GOVERNMENT

Politics in the 1920s reflected California's paradoxical society. The influx of midwestern Republicans to southern California, the increased power of large-scale business, the peculiarities of cross-filing, and the emotional issue of prohibition all combined to make the state solidly Republican. The Democratic party, already diminished by the progressive crusade, split so badly on the issue of prohibition that it nearly disappeared. Between 1920 and 1930 Democrats won only 25 of the 555 contests for partisan office in the state, and not one Democrat won a statewide executive office. The Democratic decline led essentially to one-party government throughout the 1920s, with most important political contests taking place between the conservative and progressive wings of the Republican party or along sectional lines. Regardless of which faction controlled state government, its policies and actions reflected the decade's prevailing business ideology, with its emphasis on corporate organization, efficiency, and order.

When Hiram Johnson left California in 1917, the break-up of the Progressive party followed and most of its members drifted back into the Republican fold. Moreover, Johnson's successor, William D. Stephens, represented much of the conservatism of the southern counties. He was an ardent prohibitionist, expressed antiunion sentiments, supported the anti-Japanese initiative of 1920, and played an active role in passage of the Criminal Syndicalism Act of 1919—which may be understandable, since the governor's mansion was bombed while he was in it.

On the other hand, Stephens did manage to hold the progressive coalition together well enough to be elected governor in 1918 and to attain a number of pragmatic progressive goals. State regulation of business was expanded, and he supported conservation, public development of water and power resources, and a $40 million bond issue to build a modern highway system. Perhaps his most important contribution was in the area of fiscal policy and management. To meet the growing role of government in public af-

Whittier Boulevard, 1928
California highway development in the 1920s was the envy of the nation. This 1928 photo of Whittier Boulevard as it cuts through Los Angeles County orange groves shows the concrete roadway, with curbs, typical of highway construction of the period. *Courtesy of the California Department of Transportation.*

fairs, Stephens successfully sought a fifty percent increase in the biennial state budget in 1921 and a thirty-five percent increase in corporation taxes to pay for it. At the same time, he consolidated dozens of independent state agencies into five major departments and installed a modern budgeting and accounting system.

In 1922 Stephens sought reelection on his record as a pragmatic business-manager politician, but he fell victim to the emotional, conservative appeal of Friend W. Richardson, publisher of the Berkeley *Gazette* and incumbent state treasurer. Richardson aggressively attacked the Stephens budget increases and called for a massive reduction in state expenditures, decisively defeating the incumbent governor in the Republican primary—which was tantamount to election.

Friend Richardson proved to be all he said he would be. The old-guard Republicans swept back into power with his election, and in 1923 he submitted—and the conservative legislature adopted—a budget that slashed expenditures for education, social welfare, and a host of state services. In addition, Richardson vetoed a large number of spending bills and supported the antiunion proposals of employer organizations.

The conservatism of Richardson's administration led to the formation of the Progressive Voters League, which orchestrated the election of many progressives in 1924 and produced a stand-off between the two Republican factions in the legislature. Richardson gave no ground, even when the League attempted to force substantial increases in the 1925 budget. The governor, in fact, vetoed more than half the bills passed by the legislature in 1925, a record that still stands.

The Progressive Voters League challenged Richardson in the gubernatorial primary of 1926 with Lieutenant Governor C. C. Young, a former teacher and businessman. Young's progressive platform called for continued government reorganization, highway development, conservation, forest preservation, tax reform, and development of water and hydroelectric resources. Successfully defusing Richardson's campaign rhetoric on economy in government, he narrowly defeated the governor in the primary and was easily elected in the general election.

With Young as governor, progressives made important gains, including support for conservation and parks, the first state old-age pension law in the country, and aid to the blind, physically handicapped, and needy. Although his personality was rather

bland, Young has been regarded as one of the ablest of California's governors, and his administration's record supports the contention of some historians that progressivism remained quite alive in the state despite the conservatism of the times.

Reapportionment was an important factor in the election of 1926. The census of 1920 indicated that southern California deserved increased representation, but the legislature failed to pass reapportionment bills in 1921, 1923, and 1925. Southerners attempted to force the issue with an initiative creating a reapportionment commission, but northern and rural interests countered with another initiative that proposed what they called the "federal plan." Under this plan, the assembly remained apportioned on a basis of population, but the state senate was apportioned by counties, with no county having more than one senator and no senator representing more than three counties. The federal plan initiative carried, while the commission initiative was defeated. The result was nearly forty years of underrepresentation for urban counties, especially in southern California, where by 1965 the Los Angeles County state senator represented 450 times as many people as the senator representing Mono, Inyo, and Alpine counties. A peculiar alliance of urban business and agribusiness interests successfully defeated efforts to return the state senate to population-based apportionment until the 1964 U.S. Supreme Court "one man, one vote" ruling in *Reynolds* v. *Simms* forced the change.

C. C. Young probably would have been reelected in 1930, had the prohibition issue not caused confusion in the Republican primary campaign. Whereas Young supported prohibition, his chief opponent appeared to be the "soaking wet" James ("Sunny Jim") Rolph, Jr., long-time mayor of San Francisco. But former governor Richardson then persuaded Los Angeles district attorney Buron

Fitts, a crusading dry, to enter the race and Young and Fitts split the dry vote. Rolph won the nomination, and he was elected governor in November. This was Richardson's revenge for his own defeat by Young in 1926.

In Rolph, the state got one of its least competent governors in one of its most critical times of need. With the misery of the Great Depression descending on the state, Rolph suggested that the best way to deal with it was for everyone to take a vacation to stimulate the economy through spending—advice he followed by going fishing. Rolph's administration, however, belongs to the story of the Great Depression in California.

CHAPTER TWENTY-ONE

THE DEPRESSION DECADE

The Great Depression brought a terrifying worldwide economic collapse that shook the faith of millions of Americans. In 1932 the nation reacted by turning to new political leadership, electing Franklin Delano Roosevelt as president. Although many flirted with more radical solutions than the new president offered, Roosevelt's New Deal dominated the 1930s and changed the role of the federal government in American society. It restructured federal-state relationships, bringing the federal government into the lives of citizens through relief, social security, and federal tax programs. It took over the burden of relief from the states, pumped huge quantities of money into the economy through public works projects, adopted legislation strengthening organized labor, and dramatically changed the political life of the nation. The depression and the New Deal had a profound effect on California.

THE IMPACT OF THE DEPRESSION

The good times of the 1920s came to an end with the great stock market crash of October 1929. That blinding flash of disaster started the long, grinding decline of the American economy, the worst business contraction and deflation the world has known. By 1932 national income had declined by fifty percent; per capita production of goods and commodities fell to the rate of 1889; housing construction barely reached fifteen percent of the 1929 rate; and nearly 15 million workers, almost a third of the nation's work force, were unemployed. Millions roamed the country, frightened and perplexed by the calamity.

One of the myths of the Great Depression pictures California as a balmy paradise of orange groves and Hollywood fantasy somehow shielded from the economic disaster. In reality, modern business and agriculture, the automobile, radio, and hundreds of other connections had tied the state so closely to the rest of the nation that there could be no escaping the universal economic collapse. Moreover, some of the state's chief products—specialty crops, tourism, and movies—made the state particularly vulnerable to the contraction of national income after 1929.

California therefore felt the full impact of

Sacramento "Hooverville"
Unemployed workers who had lost their homes lived in shantytowns made of salvaged boxes, boards, tin, and tar paper. Usually called "Hoovervilles" to mock President Hoover's failure to ease the depression, they appeared on the outskirts of most sizable towns—in this case, Sacramento. *Courtesy of the Bancroft Library.*

the depression. Its agricultural revenues, $750 million in 1929, fell to $327 million in 1932, and its rural areas were suddenly poverty-stricken; also in 1932 the oil industry produced 200,000 more barrels of oil a day than it could sell, leading to thousands of layoffs. Developers and real estate firms, construction companies, and savings and loan associations—the high flyers of the 1920s—crumbled, revealing a sad picture of fraud, embezzlement, and other forms of financial chicanery that spelled ruin for thousands. Even the movies, propped up temporarily by the introduction of the "talkies," eventually went down with the other industries, losing $83 million in 1932 and another $40 million in 1933.

Southern California—with an unusually high percentage of the work force in service occupations, a large number of lower-middle-class white-collar workers, and the highest proportion of elderly people in the nation—was devastated. Thousands of midwestern migrants living on savings and investments were wiped out by the financial crash; older persons were the first to be "disemployed" as the new manufacturing industries of the region laid off thousands. With one-fifth of its population on relief (at $16.20 per month per family) Los Angeles County's public welfare costs had increased tenfold. No wonder city officials welcomed the aid of Aimee Semple McPherson's commissary and her Foursquare Brothers and Sisters. Even in affluent Santa Barbara, unemployment was severe and relief resources quickly evaporated.

In the north, the work force of San Francisco, still home of the state's largest corporations, included a high percentage of salaried white-collar employees, yet the city's unemployment rate approached twenty-five percent in 1932 and remained there for several years. In Sacramento the state government, with 1,250,000 people on relief by 1932, faced a huge increase in delinquent taxes and a drastic reduction of revenues.

The human toll of the depression was incalculable. Thousands of formerly secure people were reduced to selling apples or pencils on street corners. Some rushed out at street intersections to clean auto windshields, hoping for a tip from the driver. Others just sat in whatever shelter they could find, lived off pitiful relief payments of a few cents a day, and waited, giving a strange kind of stillness to their communities. Those with jobs often worked only two or three days at reduced wages, yet frequently supported more and more relatives who had lost jobs and homes. For African Americans, Hispanics and Asians, massive unemployment meant increased discrimination. Women activists such as Frances Albrier fought this through local organizations, often in alliance with white women's groups such as the League of Women Voters. Unions, however, generally did not admit blacks or take up their cause. Others, particularly Mexican American women, built self-help community organizations to meet the crisis.

Under a barrage of front-page newspaper stories covering the nation's economic collapse and the shady dealings of prominent California businessmen—especially when the Richfield Oil Company went bankrupt in 1932 and its officers were indicted for conspiracy and grand theft—the people's faith in the business community, Herbert Hoover's business-oriented presidency, and, for some, the whole economic system, was shattered. In the process, a large segment of the voting public was radicalized, ready to consider the most unorthodox proposals for their betterment. And in California there were plenty to chose from.

THE PROBLEM OF RELIEF

Relief of the unemployed was the most urgent problem of the early 1930s. Until the end of his presidency, Herbert Hoover clung to the belief that the federal government had no responsibility to help individual citizens; the burden of relief, he felt, belonged to state and local agencies. At the county level, California had always provided some form of aid for the "indigent poor," and in times of economic crisis the unemployed had been included in these programs or employed by the state on expanded public works projects. Private charities and church groups also performed an important role in caring for the poor. The depression, however, simply overwhelmed the existing system, and the number of homeless and unemployed skyrocketed. The state was forced to divert increasing amounts of funds to counties and municipalities for relief and to a greatly expanded public works program. In 1931 the State Unemployment Commission was established to coordinate unemployment relief.

Transient and homeless men and women were a major problem—a far more serious one, a 1931 Census Bureau report noted, than in eastern states. Wandering families and unattached men, women, boys, and girls entered the state at a rate approaching 1,000 a day. To aid them, the State Unemployment Commission recommended the use of state labor camps, and in 1931–1932 twenty-eight forestry camps and two highway camps were established to house and feed transient and homeless men while they cleared firebreaks and built campground facilities and roads in

DOROTHEA LANGE
The Photographer and the Migrant Mother

Dorothea Lange: The Photographer
Courtesy of the Oakland Museum.

On a rainy March day in 1936, in a farm workers' camp near Nipomo, Dorothea Lange focused her camera on a woman and several children in their canvas shelter. The images that she produced were among the scores already taken for the California Rural Rehabilitation Administration and the hundreds to be made for the federal Farm Security Administration (FSA) program documenting rural America in the 1930s. An established San Francisco photographer, recently married to University of California economist and political activist Paul S. Taylor, Lange joined the FSA at the request of the director of its Historical Division, Roy Stryker. With her husband, she toured the state making photographs and writing descriptions, especially of dust-bowl migrants from the drought-ravaged South and Southwest. At Nipomo, Lange's subject was Florence Thompson, a thirty-two-year-old widow and mother of six, who had just sold her automobile tires in order to feed her children. Frost had destroyed the local pea crop, and there was no work for her or hundreds of other pickers.

To the public, Thompson became known as the "Migrant Mother," a symbol of the trials of the Great Depression; the title given to Lange's photograph (see p. 378) could not have been more fitting. After the women's brief encounter, the photographer continued in the profession that eventually brought her recognition, including a Guggenheim Fellowship and exhibitions of her work at the New York Museum of Modern Art and elsewhere. But the Migrant Mother remained obscure and anonymous, even to Lange. She followed the crops until the 1940s, when she settled in Modesto and bore four more children. For a time, the proud woman objected to appearances of the photograph depicting her early poverty, but during the 1970s, widowed again and in poor health, she publicly associated herself with the famous image. She hoped that she might

DOROTHEA LANGE (continued)
The Photographer and the Migrant Mother

receive some compensation for its repeated use, but she was disappointed. As property of the federal government, it is in the public domain, and no royalties have ever been paid for its publication. Thompson, however, did receive recognition and the opportunity to tell her moving story on national television.

Dorothea Lange died of cancer in 1965, and Florence Thompson succumbed to the same disease in 1983. Despite vast differences in their lives, both women made contributions to California. Lange's is tangible: a photographic record, housed in the Library of Congress and the Oakland Museum, that documented and influenced a crucial period in state and national history. Thompson's is less immediately apparent: her toil, and that of thousands like her, which allowed California agriculture to flourish even during the depths of the Great Depression. (WAB)

state parks and national forests. But state expenditures for relief and public works soon exhausted the $30 million surplus Governor Rolph had inherited, and by 1933 he was sadly contemplating a $9.5 million deficit. With the nation's financial system foundering and almost all the banks closed, Californians, like most other Americans, looked to their new president for help when he took office in March 1933.

Help came quickly. Roosevelt had none of Hoover's reservations about the role of the federal government in relief; within a hundred days of Roosevelt's inauguration, Congress had adopted a wide range of legislation attacking the problems of relief for the unemployed and economic recovery and reform. The Federal Emergency Relief Administration (FERA) provided matching funds to the states for relief, to be administered by a quickly established State Emergency Relief Administration. Opposed to simple handouts, New Dealers then instituted a program of work relief through the Civil Works Administration (CWA), which in 1933–1934

employed more than 150,000 Californians building airports, bridges, roads, schools, and other public structures. At the same time, the Civilian Conservation Corps (CCC) put thousands of unmarried, unemployed young men between the ages of eighteen and twenty-five to work in forest and soil conservation programs not unlike the forestry camps set up by the state in 1931. By 1935 federal expenditures for relief in California amounted to $285 million.

A new phase of federal relief activity in the state began in 1935, when Congress established the Works Progress Administration (WPA) to supersede the FERA and CWA and to concentrate relief activity in public works projects. For the rest of the decade, hardly a school, post office, city hall, bridge, or road was built without WPA funds. Through the Federal Writers Project, the WPA also engaged unemployed writers and historians in research projects such as producing county histories. The Farm Security Administration put photographers such as Dorothea Lange to work recording the impact of the depression on farm families, creating a priceless heritage of documentary photographs. Unemployed actors and musicians, through the Federal Theatre Project, presented plays and musicals throughout the country, paying special attention to rural communities unused to such fare. And more than 200 Federal Arts Project muralists covered California public buildings with New Deal art, a unique style of painting heavily influenced by the Mexican muralist Diego Rivera. Ironically, California's New Deal art expressed a kind of cultural nationalism stressing the strengths of American society and the middle-class values promoted by Roosevelt's New Deal. It was, as one analyst observed, an art form that "affirmed traditional American values in the visual style of a Mexican Marxist."

LARGE-SCALE PUBLIC WORKS

New Dealers saw public works not only as a way to provide unemployment relief but also as a means to promote economic recovery through stimulation of the construction industry. Accordingly, vast sums of money were allocated to large-scale construction projects, often contracted to private industry through a variety of federal agencies. Many important municipal improvement projects, such as Orange County's development of Newport Harbor, were financed by the Public Works Administration (PWA), an agency set up to manage such large undertakings. Meanwhile, the Reconstruction Finance Corporation (RFC) provided loans for construction of such large projects as the Oakland-San Francisco Bay Bridge. Even these ventures, however, were surpassed by the Bureau of Reclamation's Colorado River and Central Valley projects.

The works comprising the Colorado River Project made it a stupendous enterprise: the world's largest and highest dam at Black Canyon; the world's largest and longest aqueduct, carrying Colorado River water to

The Golden Gate Bridge
The Golden Gate Bridge was one of the engineering marvels of the 1930s. Construction of the span claimed the lives of ten workmen, despite elaborate safety nets strung beneath. In 1939–1940, completion of the Golden Gate Bridge and the San Francisco–Oakland Bay Bridge was celebrated with the Golden Gate International Exposition on Treasure Island. *Courtesy of the Bancroft Library.*

the Los Angeles basin; and the All-American Canal to the Imperial Valley. While the RFC bought more than $200 million worth of Metropolitan Water District (MWD) bonds to finance the aqueduct, the Bureau of Reclamation financed the rest. The most spectacular of the works proved to be the great dam on the Colorado. Begun during the presidency of Herbert Hoover, it was called Boulder Dam during the New Deal era, then officially named Hoover Dam in 1947.

Approval of the contract in 1930 for sale of the electricity the dam would generate led Congress to appropriate the first funds for the project. In April 1931 the contract for construction was awarded to a syndicate of firms incorporated as the Six Companies, with Henry J. Kaiser as chairman of the board and Frank Crowe as superintendent of construction. Crowe emerged as the driving force in the actual building of the dam.

The job required enormous facilities: a complete air-conditioned model city (Boulder City, Nevada) built near the site to house the workers, and four by-pass tunnels, each a mile long and 50 feet in diameter, carved in the canyon walls before the riverbed could be cleared. The dam itself, 660 feet thick at the bottom and 45 feet thick at the top, stood 1,282 feet high. When completed, it created Lake Mead, holding 32 million acre-feet of water. And with profits of more than $10 million from this enterprise, the Six Companies moved on to sink the towers for the Golden Gate Bridge, work on the Oakland-San Francisco Bay Bridge, and complete the Grand Coulee and Bonneville dams on the Columbia River before taking on major defense work during World War II.

The building of the Golden Gate Bridge was one of the magnificent technological achievements of this age of public works. Financed by Marin and San Francisco county bond issues, the bridge was begun in 1933 and completed in 1937. It was one of the outstanding engineering achievements of the time, given the difficulties of construction in the narrow opening to the bay and the swift currents and tides, and it was, for a time, the longest suspension bridge in the world. Construction of the Oakland-San Francisco Bay Bridge, built at the same time within the calm confines of the bay, proceeded more quickly and was finished in 1936. San Francisco civic leaders hoped that the two great bridges would revive the city's position as the business and population center of the Bay Area, but ironically they accelerated population dispersal and contributed to San Francisco's relative decline in following years.

THE CENTRAL VALLEY PROJECT

The depression and New Deal financing also finally broke the opposition to another gigantic California undertaking, the Central Valley Project (CVP). For decades the idea of transporting the abundant waters of the Sacramento Valley to the arid San Joaquin had intrigued agriculturists. Many others saw in the proposal the opportunity to control Sacramento River flooding, to improve navigation of the river, and to generate hydroelectric power. In 1919 Colonel Robert Bradford Marshall, chief hydrographer of the U.S. Geological Survey, suggested a complex plan for the transfer of Sacramento River water south through two large canals. Subsequent legislation and initiative measures designed to implement this scheme were defeated through the efforts of the Pacific Gas and Electric Company (PG&E) and other utilities that feared the plan's provision for publicly produced power. Nevertheless, Marshall's proposal generated twelve years of intensive study that finally led to a new plan compiled by the state engineer, Edward Hyatt, in 1931. The deepening depression, however, made state financing unlikely, despite Governor Rolph's support.

Luckily for CVP advocates, the most pressing political issue in 1933 was taxation. Lobbyists for the major corporate taxpayers—particularly oil, railroad, and utility interests—were so involved in the issue that they paid scant attention to the Central Valley Project bill, ably promoted by State Senator John B. McColl of Redding. Much to their surprise, McColl's bill was adopted that year and signed by the governor. The act authorized a $170 million revenue bond issue to finance the CVP and included provision for public distribution of publicly generated power, an obvious effort to attract New Deal money to the plan. The PG&E reacted by backing a referendum to kill the act but lost narrowly in December 1933.

Few people really expected the state to pay for the Central Valley Project. In 1935 President Roosevelt and Secretary of the Interior Harold Ickes decided to make the CVP a Bureau of Reclamation project and funds were allocated to the Bureau to start work; two years later Congress officially assigned the CVP to the Bureau of Reclamation. Construction began in February 1937 and continued into the 1950s. As it stands today, the CVP is one of the most complex and massive water transfer systems ever built.

The chief components of the initial system were Shasta and Keswick dams on the Sacramento River, Friant Dam on the San Joaquin River, and the Delta-Mendota, Friant-Kern, and Madera canals. Shasta Dam at the time of construction was second only to Hoover Dam in size. It impounds the waters of the Sacramento, Pit, and McCloud rivers just north of Redding, creating the $4\frac{1}{2}$ million acre-foot Lake Shasta. Water from the lake flows south to the Sacramento-San Joaquin Delta and then is lifted to the huge Delta-Mendota Canal, which carries it 117 miles south into the San Joaquin Valley. Friant Dam impounds the waters of the San Joaquin River east of Fresno for distribution south to the Bakersfield area by the Friant-Kern Canal and north by the Madera Canal. Well over 700,000 acres of San Joaquin Valley land came under irrigation with construction of this project. Since completion of the initial plan, the waters of other rivers have been integrated into the system, bringing many thousands of additional acres into production. For example, the Trinity River, which normally flows to the coast, is impounded by Trinity and Lewiston dams, most of its waters diverted through tunnels to the Sacramento Valley via Whiskeytown Dam and Reservoir. Construction of Folsom and Nimbus dams added the American River to the system, and construction of the New Melones Dam added the Stanislaus River. Completion of the $2\frac{1}{2}$ million acre-foot San Luis Reservoir west of Los Banos, which stores winter runoff for release to the west side of the San Joaquin Valley, increased the capacity of the CVP even further.

Controversy accompanied this burst of large-scale public works construction, especially over distribution of the electric power the system produced and over Bureau of Reclamation policies limiting the amount of land that could be irrigated with subsidized water to 160 acres. Nevertheless, the state and federal governments spent hundreds of millions of dollars creating thousands of jobs, relieving the impact of the depression on the state, and endearing the New Deal to many Californians.

DEPRESSION POLITICS

The liberal deficit-spending policies of the New Deal were offset by the tight-fisted conservatism of California's Republican governors. While Governor Rolph supported the expenditure for relief payments of the $30 million surplus he inherited from Governor Young and approved the forestry and highway work-relief camps recommended by the State Unemployment Commission, his 1933–1935 budget of $258 million was $24 million less than the 1931–1933 budget and did little to relieve depression suffering. Having cultivated a glad-handing "smile with Sunny Jim" political image, he found it difficult to deal seriously with the depression and offended even his friends by condoning violence against striking farm workers and publicly approving the lynching of two kidnap-murder suspects in San José in 1933. He died suddenly in June 1934, after embarking on a strenuous reelection campaign against the advice of his doctors. Rolph's successor, Lieutenant Governor Frank E. Merriam, seemed to be cut from the same conservative cloth and very likely would have been replaced by a Democrat that year, had Upton Sinclair not appeared on the political scene.

THE SINCLAIR EPISODE

The Democrats had every reason to expect a return to power in 1934. The depression had discredited Republican policies; Democratic voter registration had rebounded from a three-to-one disadvantage to equality with Republican voters; and the party itself had come into the hands of leaders with close ties to the immensely popular Roosevelt administration. Instrumental in the Democratic revival was William Gibbs McAdoo, Secretary of the Treasury under Woodrow Wilson and long a major figure in national Democratic affairs, who came to southern California in 1922. In 1932, he won the party's nomination for the U.S. Senate and led the state

delegation to the national presidential nominating convention where he played a prominent role in switching the California delegation's allegiance to Roosevelt, assuring the latter's nomination. In the ensuing election Roosevelt won the presidency, McAdoo was elected to the Senate, and the party made substantial gains in the state's congressional and legislative representation. The time seemed ripe for the Democrats to win the governorship in 1934.

The party, however, was divided. Northerners backed Justus Wardell, a San Francisco magazine publisher, while southerners backed McAdoo's old friend George Creel, a federal relief administrator in California. Both were moderate to conservative Democrats, and, in supporting them, party leaders ignored the depression's radicalizing of hundreds of thousands of normally moderate middle-class voters. Failure to reckon with this churning, dissident force proved disastrous when Upton Sinclair took up their cause with his End Poverty in California (EPIC) program.

Sinclair was a progressive-era muckraker, wrote *The Jungle* and dozens of other controversial books, and had been the Socialist party candidate for governor in 1926 and 1930. Far more attuned to the misery caused by the depression than Democratic party leaders, he published a pamphlet in 1933 outlining a program of action to end poverty in California—from which the EPIC movement sprang. That fall he changed his registration to Democrat and announced his candidacy for the party's nomination for governor by publishing a book entitled *I, Governor of California and How I Ended Poverty: A True Story of the Future*, in which he set forth his ideas in detail.

Desperate victims of the depression eagerly embraced Sinclair's program. An End Poverty League was formed to coordinate the activities of more than 2,000 EPIC clubs that were formed all over the state. More than 330,000 new Democrats were registered by Sinclair's supporters—among them one former Republican, Edmund G. (Pat) Brown of San Francisco. An almost fanatical fervor imbued their campaign—not surprisingly, since Sinclair's proposals were a radical departure from the party's past platforms.

The EPIC program contained many attractive features, including repeal of the sales tax, shifting the burden of taxation to the wealthy and corporations, and a $50-a-month pension for aged, blind, and needy people over the age of sixty. The most controversial proposal, however, was Sinclair's plan for unemployment relief through a program he called "production-for-use." This scheme called for the state to acquire idle factories and agricultural land where the unemployed would be put to work in a system of cooperative self-help and in which the exchange of goods was facilitated by issuing a state scrip. A $300 million bond issue would enable the state to purchase the necessary properties. The production-for-use proposal appealed to a huge middle class experiencing real poverty for the first time. Their support turned Sinclair's campaign into a crusade that won him the Democratic gubernatorial nomination with more than fifty-two percent of the vote in a large field of candidates. EPIC-backed Sheridan Downey, a Sacramento lawyer and a spellbinding orator, won the nomination for lieutenant governor, becoming the other half of a team newspapers dubbed "Uppie and Downey."

Party leaders, on the other hand, deserted Sinclair in the general election campaign, influencing Roosevelt's decision not to endorse him—a fatal blow to Sinclair's chances. The campaign itself has been called the most bizarre in California history, its central issue becoming Sinclair himself.

For thirty years Sinclair had attacked established social institutions in his writings, and as a socialist he had consistently denounced the capitalist system. Thin, bespectacled, and mild-mannered, he was easily perceived as weak and naive, and he became the target of a vicious campaign based on fear and ridicule. Excerpts from his writings were taken out of context to depict him as an atheist, an advocate of free love, and a communist. Cartoonists pictured him as a wild-eyed fanatic, and EPIC became "Easy Pickings in California." The movie industry ground out fake "newsreels" showing thousands of unemployed migrating to the state anticipating Sinclair's election, and Sinclair was accused of deliberately attracting hoboes and relief chiselers to the state. Newspaper stories, often fabricated, and editorial cartoons ridiculed the new society held out in the EPIC program. The campaign against Sinclair has been called the first modern "media" campaign—a precursor of politics in the age of television.

In contrast to Sinclair, Governor Merriam, who had easily won the Republican nomination, projected an image of reason and moderation. Although he had called out the National Guard to deal with the waterfront strike in San Francisco in July 1934, he now came out in favor of collective bargaining and a shorter work week and let it be known that he would cooperate with Roosevelt's New Deal programs. Leaving the vituperative personal attacks on Sinclair to others, Merriam presented himself as a moderate, pragmatic reformer.

All of these tactics were effective and Merriam easily won election as governor. Sinclair retired again from politics to write the story of the EPIC campaign in a book titled *I, Candidate for Governor and How I Got Licked.* The EPIC organization disintegrated rapidly, and the Democratic party began another long struggle to rebuild cohesion and unity. In retrospect, the mass support for Upton Sinclair's quixotic movement is a measure of the seriousness of the depression and the structural weakness of the state's post-progressive political system. The election denied the Democrats the state house at a time when Democrats were sweeping into power all over the nation. When they did come to power in California in 1938, the reform impulse had passed.

MERRIAM'S "PRAGMATIC CONSERVATISM"

Governor Frank Merriam has long been regarded by historians as a do-nothing conservative who held his state still as the New Deal marched by. But Merriam's conservative rhetoric must be contrasted with his moderate to liberal actions; then, as Jackson Putnam has noted, he "can be viewed as the governor who brought the New Deal to California, hesitatingly perhaps, on tiptoe, and a little shamefacedly, but he brought it nevertheless." In a performance Putnam calls "pragmatic conservatism," Merriam led California as far into the New Deal as his party would let him, using political skills he had developed in sixteen years as an assemblyman, speaker of the assembly, state senator, lieutenant governor, and chairman of the Republican state central committee.

Calling for "social justice without socialism" Merriam promoted establishment of the State Emergency Relief Administration (which qualified the state for federal relief funds), approved federal takeover of the Central Valley Project, and backed a pension law that brought the state additional federal funds under the Social Security Act of 1935. Merriam "unabashedly" secured a state income tax, higher taxes on inheritances, banks, and corporations, and a liberalized

sales tax that exempted groceries, fuel, and prescription drugs, to finance other social legislation. But opening the state to the grant-in-aid programs of the New Deal was as far as he could go, and after 1937 he generally resisted liberal social legislation.

While Merriam was governor, the Democrats sought to recover from the debacle of 1934. The party regulars remained in disarray, but the "radical" wing coalesced around Culbert Olson, who had been elected as Los Angeles County's state senator in 1934 with EPIC backing, and had emerged as the leading proponent of Democratic reform proposals in the legislature. Olson announced his candidacy for the Democratic gubernatorial nomination in September 1937, running on a liberal platform that included a modified production-for-use program, increased welfare and pension payments, progressive taxation, slum clearance, low-cost housing, public ownership of public utilities, and support for organized labor. In a deal of questionable legality he secured labor support with a commitment to pardon Tom Mooney as his first act in office. Mooney had spent nearly twenty-two years in prison, convicted on perjured testimony of the 1916 Preparedness Day parade bombing in San Francisco. Labor's support proved decisive, and Olson won the nomination in the 1938 primary.

Democratic prospects for the general election of 1938 were excellent. The New Deal was still popular and Olson obtained the president's endorsement. Democrats were at last united and Olson's "New Deal for California" slogan attracted wide support among Republicans as well. Governor Merriam, on the other hand, was in deep trouble. His cooperation with the Roosevelt administration had offended conservatives in his party, and his 1935 proposal to impose oil and mineral severance taxes and liquor taxes had offended powerful business interests in the state, whose wholehearted support he required. As expected, Olson was elected in November 1938, bringing the first Democratic administration to the state in the twentieth century. It was not a Democratic sweep, however, as the Republicans regained control of the rural-dominated state senate and the Democratic majority in the assembly was reduced. Nevertheless, Olson's victory was the result of a well-run, well-financed, enthusiastic campaign, in which support from the Roosevelt administration, a high voter turnout, the failure of Republican "red scare" tactics, and Olson's evasion of a commitment on a controversial pension plan initiative were all factors.

UTOPIAN SCHEMES AND THE PENSION MOVEMENT

Hard times produced a wide variety of self-help organizations that received financial aid from New Deal agencies. In addition, radical and sometimes utopian schemes to provide for the elderly and unemployed proliferated in depression California. One popular early movement was Technocracy, which proposed to replace the existing monetary system with an energy system whose basic units were called "ergs." It attracted wide support in 1932, but collapsed within months. Similarly, the Utopian Society, which offered a vague "new economic order," found favor in 1933 and by 1934 claimed a membership of 500,000. The society's heavy emphasis on social activities led one observer to call it a "colossal Lonesome Club."

In many respects, the social movements of the 1930s substituted economic cults for the popular religious cults of the 1920s, and Upton Sinclair was unique in directing their energies into a mass political movement. The old-age pension phenomenon was quite different. Whereas the social and

utopian reformers were dealing in dreams of the perfect society, the pension movement leaders were promoting specific legislation and were highly political. Of all the economic movements of the decade, pension plans attracted the widest support and caused the biggest headaches for politicians. By the mid-1930s, Jackson Putnam has observed, "it was virtually raining pension plans." While California's 1929 Old Age Security Act was the first mandatory state pension plan in the nation, the depression made it sadly inadequate. Pension requirements (essentially one had to be a propertyless indigent with no support from relatives) seemed degrading, yet a growing number of older people were faced with the prospect of permanent unemployment. Sinclair was one of the first to appeal to this group when he proposed a $50-a-month pension and a ten-year reduction in the age of eligibility. His primary victory in 1934 was partly the result of their support, but he probably lost much of that support in the fall election by rejecting the Townsend plan, which by then had become surprisingly popular.

The Townsend plan was the product, borrowed from various sources, of an unsuccessful Long Beach physician and sometime real estate promoter, Francis E. Townsend. In 1934 Townsend, with a realtor named R. Earl Clements, formed an organization called Old Age Revolving Pensions. Their proposal called for Congress to adopt a national sales tax in order to provide all persons over sixty years of age with a $200-per-month annuity on the condition that it be spent within the following month. The organization's newspaper, *The Townsend Weekly*, soon had a circulation of more than 100,000, oldsters flocked to join Townsend clubs all over the state and nation, and the Townsend plan became a factor in politics from 1934 on. However, when the Townsend party was formed in 1936 and became involved in right-wing opposition to Roosevelt, the organization went into decline. At the same time, adoption of the Social Security Act by Congress sapped the movement of much of its strength.

The most sensational of the pension plans was one that came to be called "Ham and Eggs" when one of its supporters shouted out, "We want our ham and eggs." It began in 1936 as the brainchild of an unscrupulous radio personality and promoter, Robert Noble, who was ousted and replaced in 1937 by the even shadier Allen brothers, Willis and Lawrence. By 1938 the Allens had an organization in full swing, boosting their program under the slogan "Thirty Dollars Every Thursday." The plan called for the state to issue thirty $1 pieces of scrip every Thursday to all unemployed persons over the age of fifty; the scrip would then circulate like money. Every Thursday a holder of scrip was to put a 2-cent stamp on the back of the scrip dollar. At the end of the year (fifty-two weeks) the state would redeem the scrip for a dollar and supposedly thus collect 4 cents per scrip dollar for administrative expenses of the program. Picking up where Sinclair and Townsend had left off, the Allens by 1938 had gathered more than a million supporters. That year, Thirty Dollars Every Thursday qualified as an initiative measure and was an important issue in the general election. Merriam endorsed the plan; Olson equivocated. Narrowly defeated in 1938, the measure qualified again as an initiative in 1939. Olson, now governor, came out against it, set the election for late in the year, and aided in organizing opposition to the measure as economically unsound: the measure lost decisively. The Allens and their plan faded from public view, but not before they brought into their company George McLain, an organizational genius who would dominate old-age pension politics for years thereafter.

The Townsend and "Ham and Eggs" movements had much in common: attractive plans, leaders who were skilled propagandists, autocratic organizations that nevertheless offered important psychological and emotional returns to their supporters, and political clout. They played an important role in forging California's elderly into a potent and highly vocal political interest group that put the state in the forefront in the treatment of those currently called "senior citizens."

OLSON'S "NEW DEAL FOR CALIFORNIA"

Democratic expectations were unduly high when Olson took office in January 1939, and his administration proved to be a study in frustration. He failed to achieve passage of almost all of his principal reform proposals and so offended the legislature that it stripped the lieutenant governor of his committee-appointing powers, replaced a pro-Olson assembly speaker with a conservative Democrat, and forced Olson to seek relief funds in driblets from special sessions.

Nevertheless, Olson had his successes. His pardon of Tom Mooney momentarily made him the most famous governor in the United States. He achieved significant humanitarian reforms in the state's mental-health and parole systems. He vigorously protected civil liberties and minority groups, raised the standards of living conditions for migrant labor, and took satisfaction in the appointment of liberals to numerous judgeships. Ironically, the outbreak of World War II made Olson's reform program essentially irrelevant, and American entry into the war led him to cooperate, against his better judgment, in one of the most tragic events of the period—the removal and incarceration of Japanese Americans in 1942.

THE REVIVAL OF LABOR

The depression and the New Deal ushered in a whole new era for organized labor in California, one characterized by a new militancy and radical leadership that eventually overturned the open-shop policy. In 1932 one of four workers in San Francisco and one of three in Los Angeles was out of work. In some fields, such as the building trades, unemployment ran as high as fifty percent. Workers scavenged at restaurants and produce markets, assisted charitable organizations in return for food, or sought public relief. Employers, on the other hand, saw layoffs, the reduction of wages, longer hours, and the "speed-up" as ways to maintain profits and stay in business.

On the waterfront, particularly in San Francisco, these conditions were most troublesome. There the employer-controlled "blue-book" union operated its own closed shop. Hiring was accomplished by the degrading "shape-up," whereby longshoremen assembled each morning on the dock and company-controlled foremen selected men for the day's work, generally picking those who would kick back part of their wages or who were compliant participants in the speed-up. Others might get "casual" work for a day or two per week, in a system that fostered inequality in work distribution and discrimination against pro-union workers.

The adoption of the National Industrial Recovery Act (NIRA) as the New Deal's program for business recovery inspired organized labor to challenge this system. Section 7(a) of the NIRA for the first time guaranteed by law the right to organize and to bargain collectively with employers. An unprecedented era of union formation and

strikes followed. When the U.S. Supreme Court declared the NIRA unconstitutional in 1935, Congress quickly passed the Wagner Act, which maintained labor's guarantees and established the National Labor Relations Board (NLRB) to oversee their implementation. Employers, however, refused to comply until court decisions upheld it, and sometimes encouraged defiance of the law even then.

Confrontation in the maritime industry came in 1934. That spring, membership in the International Longshoremen's Association (ILA) rose dramatically all along the Pacific coast from Seattle to San Diego, and its members, in a test of strength, successfully challenged the "blue-book" union on the Matson Company docks in San Francisco. Then, joining forces with other reviving maritime unions, the longshoremen demanded shorter hours, higher pay, and an end to the shape-up. They also called for a union-controlled hiring hall and coastwide bargaining. Led by San Francisco's Industrial Association, the shipping companies refused to deal with the union, which they said was in the hands of communists. Nor would they consider coastwide bargaining or what they called the "un-American" closed shop.

On May 9, 1934, the longshoremen went out on strike and were joined by unions representing sailors, masters and mates, marine engineers and firemen, and stewards. A total of 3,500 men quit work, paralyzing Pacific coast shipping. In June the Industrial Association negotiated an agreement with conservative eastern leaders of the ILA to end the strike, only to have it voted down by the union rank and file. The strikers then established a Joint Maritime Strike Committee and elected Harry Bridges, the longshoreman who had emerged as the militants' leader, as its chairman. Waterfront employers in San Francisco, however, were deter-

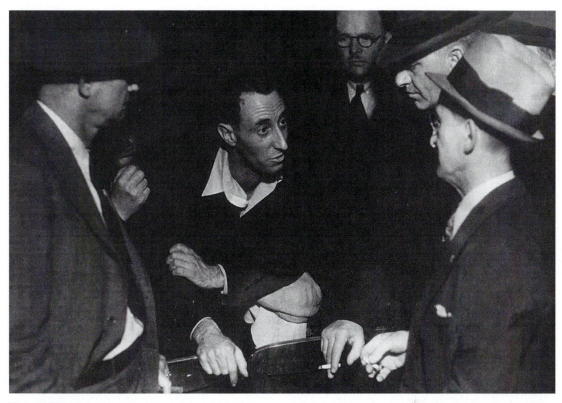

Harry Bridges
The longshoremen's and general strike of 1934 produced, in Harry Bridges, one of California's most imaginative and innovative labor leaders. Born in Australia, Bridges migrated to California as a seafarer and became a key figure in winning the strikes of 1934, expanding the union inland, developing the areawide contract eliminating racism in union membership, and adapting in later years to containerization. Accused of being a Communist party member, he was harassed with attempts to deport him for twenty years. *Courtesy of the Bancroft Library.*

mined to open the port and on July 3 forced the issue by sending a fleet of trucks under police escort from Pier 38. A two-day battle ensued, ending on July 5, a day that became known as "Bloody Thursday," with scores of injuries and two longshoremen dead. That night Governor Merriam called out the National Guard to patrol San Francisco's docks.

Bloody Thursday evoked massive sympathy for the strikers, and in the following days San Francisco unions voted overwhelmingly for a general strike to protest that day's violence. On July 16 tens of thousands of workers left their jobs, and the city fell silent in a display of labor solidarity that shocked and frightened the people of the state. Four days later the general strike ended when strikers and employers agreed to arbitration of the longshoremen's dispute, and employers agreed to recognize and bargain with other maritime unions. On July 31 the maritime strike ended, and on October 12 the National Longshoremen's Board's arbitration decision was handed down.

The decision was a substantial victory for Harry Bridges' longshoremen. It provided for recognition of the ILA as bargaining agent for the workers, and called for coast-wide bargaining, jointly operated hiring halls with union-selected dispatchers to guarantee fair distribution of the work, a six-hour work day, and a substantial wage increase. It did away with the hated shape-up and established the basic structure of a hiring system for longshoremen that is still in existence. By early 1935 the other maritime unions had negotiated their own settlements with employers.

The success of the young militants under Harry Bridges next led them to protect their flanks by organizing the poorly paid, local warehousemen. In what has been called "the march inland" that led to a major strike in 1936–1937, Bridges's group brought almost all Bay Area warehousemen into a union affiliated with the ILA. In 1937, they were brought together in the International Longshoremen's and Warehousemen's Union (ILWU) when the ILA broke away from the American Federation of Labor (AFL).

The great maritime and San Francisco general strikes of 1934 were symbolic of labor's rush to organize and were an inspiration to others. Older unions took on new life, and new unions sprang up among a host of previously unorganized workers; union membership in California tripled between 1933 and 1938. But labor on the march was not always invincible, and the open shop gave way slowly. In San Francisco the Employers Council, formed in 1938, ultimately replaced the Industrial Association and asserted the right of employers to bargain collectively. In 1938 the council negotiated a landmark contract with the ILWU, in which Bridges accepted a multiemployer agreement covering an expanded geographical area. Other unions and employers adopted this concept, and within a short time most Bay Area workers were covered by such contracts. The regional, multiemployer, union contract is standard in the state today.

THE OPEN SHOP IN LOS ANGELES

As might be expected, Los Angeles put up an even stiffer defense of the open shop. As workers flocked to join unions following adoption of the NIRA, the Merchants and Manufacturers Association (M&M) and the Los Angeles *Times* swung into action, pressuring employers not to deal with outside unions or comply with Section 7(a). The M&M mounted a vast propaganda campaign, pouring hundreds of thousands of dollars contributed by local businesses into the effort, organized Southern Californians, Inc., as a steering committee, and formed numerous front organizations such as The Neutral Thousands (TNT) and Women of the Pacific to undertake strikebreaking activities. Its tactics—use of spies, blacklists, tear gas, and toughs—earned it the condemnation of the La Follette Committee, a subcommittee of the U.S. Senate Committee on Education and Labor, for its violation of basic civil rights. The M&M's campaign effectively slowed labor's drive to organize the unorganized, but could not stop it. From 1934 to 1939 unions increased their economic power and successfully eroded the open shop in southern California until they claimed more than half the Los Angeles work force. In that period the auto, tire, movie, oil refining, and airplane industries were organized, and union membership shot from 33,000 to more than 200,000. In July 1939 Los Angeles mayor Fletcher Bowron noted that "even the most conservative manufacturers have come to realize that . . . the effort to maintain the open shop is a lost cause."

Several important factors explain Los Angeles's long defense of the open shop: only one-fifth of total employment in the city was in manufacturing in the 1930s; the largely unorganized service and trade industries constituted nearly sixty-eight percent of the work force. Furthermore, Los Angeles was a regional market, typically a small-plant town with few industries dominated by any one employer. And the nature of the state and city economy—dependent on extractive industries such as oil and agriculture and on the businesses associated with them—made organization of their workers especially difficult. Only the stimulus of the New Deal, the development of branch plants in Los Angeles by national corporations accustomed to dealing with unions, and the industrialization of the area when World War II began finally broke down the barriers to unionism.

Conflict within the union movement itself produced a great deal of the agitation and violence of the 1930s. Militant labor leaders such as Harry Bridges fervently believed in organization along industrial lines, while older AFL leaders clung to organization by craft or job task. In 1935 the AFL reluctantly set up the Committee for Industrial Organization (CIO) under the aggressive John L. Lewis, head of the United Mine Workers, to undertake industrial organization. Lewis successfully organized the auto, steel, and rubber industries in bitter campaigns and attracted others committed to the principle of industrywide organization. In 1937 the ILWU and several maritime unions affiliated with the CIO. But AFL leaders became increasingly unhappy with radical influences in the CIO, several of whose unions were heavily infiltrated by communists, and with CIO political activities. Attempts to discipline CIO unions finally led to their expulsion and the establishment of the independent Congress of Industrial Organizations in 1938. Consequently, work stoppages of the later 1930s often stemmed from disputes between rival AFL and CIO unions. Never-

theless, as the period closed, employer-employee relations had been irrevocably transformed.

AGRICULTURAL LABOR

No such transformation took place in agriculture, due to the nature of California farming, the composition of the farm labor force, and the successful organization of growers to resist unionization. The depression found the state with an agricultural work force, perhaps three-fourths Mexicans and one-fourth Filipinos, that conveniently appeared at harvest time, worked for low wages, and then disappeared to live on relief during the off season in communities on the outskirts of cities such as Fresno and Los Angeles. During the depression, these urban areas could no longer afford this relief, harvest labor, relief cycle and started a program of "voluntary" repatriation, frequently forcing Mexicans and Mexican Americans to accept one-way tickets to Mexico City. By 1937 probably 150,000 Mexicans had left California, while the same period saw Mexican immigration to the United States fall from an annual rate of more than 50,000 to less than 8,000.

Forced repatriation of Mexican Americans in the 1930s was supported by agricultural interests because of the Mexicans' participation in efforts to organize farm worker unions and in a number of spontaneous strikes for higher wages. Such activities attracted the attention of the Communist party, which formed the Trade Union Unity League (TUUL) and entered the agricultural field with the TUUL-affiliated Cannery and Agricultural Workers Industrial Union (CAWIU). In 1933–1934 CAWIU-led strikes in California accounted for more than half the farm strikes in the nation, and three-fourths of them won wage increases for farm workers. Nearly 15,000 workers were involved in the 1933 San Joaquin Valley cotton

JOHN STEINBECK
Galahad of the Long Valley

John Steinbeck
Courtesy of the Bancroft Library.

Signs in Salinas, in the surrounding 100-mile Long Valley, and around Monterey pro-claim that "This Is John Steinbeck Country," but it was not always so. Indeed, the author once observed that residents of Salinas, where he was born in 1902, "want no part of me except in a pine box." Time, recognition, and awards including the 1962 Nobel Prize, however, altered opinion before he died in 1968.

Steinbeck's youth in the Long Valley profoundly affected his life and career. Work in the fields, packing sheds, and processing plants of the region provided the settings, characters, and sympathies that appeared in some of his finest novels. His parents intro-duced him to literature and music and on his ninth birthday gave him Thomas Malory's *Morte d' Arthur.* The book engendered a lifelong fascination with the ideas of knight-hood, chivalry, and the heroic quest, and perhaps confirmed his decision to write. Stein-beck pursued that ambition during high school and Stanford University years, but with-out success. He therefore supported himself with odd jobs while he embarked on his own quest, completion of his first book, *Cup of Gold,* published in 1928. Not until the 1935 publication of *Tortilla Flat,* a novel based on *paisano* life on the Monterey Peninsula, however, did he achieve recognition: the annual Commonwealth Club Award for the best book on a California subject. A year later, *In Dubious Battle* captured the same prize.

JOHN STEINBECK (continued)
Galahad of the Long Valley

Despite its social commentary and overtones of the Arthurian legend, *Tortilla Flat* could be read as humor. *In Dubious Battle* could not. It related the bitter, violent, and tragic depression-era conflict between growers and communist-led farm workers, with little sympathy for growers or their tactics. In the Salinas Valley, it also branded the author as a subversive, a position apparently confirmed in 1939 by the Pulitzer Prize–winning narrative of dust-bowl migrants, *The Grapes of Wrath*. Steinbeck's neighbors condemned his work as "trash," full of "lust, sex, and vile words!" and as a political, moral, and economic threat. Local libraries would not stock his books; his mother could not even give them away.

Passing years and fame apparently heal even the deepest wounds, and in 1968 the author's ashes were welcomed back and interred—not in a pine box—in his beloved Long Valley. In Salinas, in the Victorian home where he spent his boyhood, tourists buy gourmet delicacies, books, and souvenirs, and profits from sales are distributed among local charities serving farm workers and their families. The Galahad in John Steinbeck would certainly have understood and probably enjoyed the irony. (WAB and PJB)

---

strike, making it the largest in the history of American agriculture. Two years later John Steinbeck used the strike as the basis for a short, but powerful, novel entitled *In Dubious Battle*. Communist leadership provided a convenient excuse for growers to use intimidation and violence in dealing with farm workers, and grower political pressure eventually resulted in the arrest and conviction of CAWIU leaders under the state's criminal syndicalism law. This, along with a shift in Communist party strategy away from organizing their own unions to infiltrating mainstream unions, destroyed the CAWIU.

Mexican Americans and Mexican immigrants dominated most of the successors to CAWIU which often included a number of women in leadership roles. In southern California, for example, the Confederación de Uniones de Campesinos y Obreros Mexicanos (CUCOM) led several successful strikes for higher wages and better conditions in the mid-1930s. By 1938 attempts to organize agricultural labor centered on the United Cannery, Agricultural, Packing and Allied Workers of America (UCAPAWA) of the newly formed Congress of Industrial Organizations (CIO). Initially successful in California, the Dust Bowl migration, grower resistance, and harassment of alleged Communist organizers weakened it after World War II. UCAPAWA, however, was exceptional in successfully organizing both urban and rural Mexican workers and in the number of its women leaders—including the dynamic Louisa Moreno, one of its chief organizers. Moreno was also a founder, with Josephine Fierro de Bright among others, of El Congreso de Pueblos de Habla Española (Congress of Spanish Speaking Peoples), an important civil rights organization that grew out of the labor movement. Fierro de Bright, another charismatic Chicana, also brought significant financial support to the Congress through her husband, screen writer John Bright.

The most important organization to develop out of the reaction of growers and farm communities to the strikes of 1933–1934 was the Associated Farmers of California. Ostensibly representing growers and processors, but actually a front for a cross-section of California business interests, the Associated Farmers was financed by contributions from San Francisco's Industrial Association, Southern Californians, Inc., PG&E, Southern Pacific, Holly Sugar Corporation, and the Spreckels Investment Company, among others. From its inception the Associated Farmers played a dominant role in suppressing farm labor organizing activities. It formed what amounted to a private vigilante army of men (who were often deputized by local sheriffs) that protected strikebreakers, disrupted mass meetings, and attacked pickets. It successfully pushed for antipicketing ordinances in agricultural areas and in general made violent resistance to unionization a deliberate policy. It was responsible, said the La Follette Committee, for "the most flagrant and violent infringement of civil liberties." Others labeled its actions "farm fascism."

Whatever their methods, California growers effectively prevented farm labor organization. Even in the late 1930s, when UCA-PAWA organizers entered the fields with the support of the Olson administration, they could not overcome the antiunion climate engendered by the Associated Farmers and its allies. Meanwhile, the AFL had abandoned the effort, believing the "one big agricultural union" idea was a pipe dream.

THE "OKIES"

A dramatic change in the makeup of California's harvest labor force contributed to the failure to organize farm labor. Between 1935 and 1939 nearly 300,000 southwesterners migrated to California. Most of them came from the lower Plains states, notably Oklahoma, Arkansas, Missouri, and Texas but were generally dubbed "Okies." A variety of factors accounted for this migration. Years of drought had made their small farms unprofitable, especially when the depression hit. The New Deal Agricultural Adjustment Act (AAA) programs that paid farmers not to plant grain or cotton allowed landowners to evict tenant farmers. Mechanization made larger holdings more efficient, eliminating other tenant farmers. The great dust storms of the mid-1930s ruined large areas for farming. Poverty-stricken, "blowed out," and "tractored out," the Okies moved their families west.

California was a logical destination, given the image of the state created by years of boosterism. Moreover, favorable reports from friends and relatives of good wages picking cotton and fruit encouraged the move west and transportation was easy (by automobile on Route 66). Like the migrants of the 1920s, nearly half settled in metropolitan areas, primarily Los Angeles, where they were quickly absorbed. The rest, however, turned north to the San Joaquin Valley where they sought work in the complex, industrialized agricultural system. Ineligible for relief for a year because they were new to the state, they accepted the low wages that the Mexican work force would not, and in a short time almost completely displaced the Mexicans as California's harvest laborers. When the Okies became eligible for unemployment relief, the state relief administration under Governor Merriam cut off relief payments if work was available in an agricultural harvest, forcing them into the old relief, harvest labor, relief cycle that essentially subsidized low farm wages.

Important distinctions between the Okies and traditional harvest labor were not only that the migrants were white Anglo-Saxon Protestants but also that they sought permanence. They settled in Central Valley towns, sent their children to local schools, and registered to vote. Their poverty could not be ignored. Living in shocking conditions in tent camps along irrigation ditches, they exposed the exploitation of farm labor in California's peculiar agricultural system and became a highly visible burden in local communities, particularly in the San Joaquin Valley. In 1939 their plight became a national scandal with the publication of John Steinbeck's *The Grapes of Wrath* and Carey McWilliams's *Factories in the Field.*

Grower satisfaction with the Okies was short-lived. The flood of migrants in 1937 had created an embarrassing oversupply of labor, and the squalor of their camps reflected on the industry. In 1938 it became apparent that the Okies were politically embarrassing as well. They were Democrats, supported Culbert Olson, and displayed firm loyalty to the New Deal. They also disrupted the strong Republican hold on rural communities, a fact that led to the formation of the California Citizen's Association (CCA), which, like the Associated Farmers, fronted for banking, oil, railroad, real estate, and insurance interests allied with the agribusiness community. The CCA, determined to attack the New Deal and Olson through the migrants, launched a publicity campaign that, as Walter Stein has pointed out, went a long way toward creating a popular view of the Okie in California as a "degenerate, degraded loser in the American struggle for survival." By 1939 the CCA campaign had engendered widespread antagonism toward the migrants and their sympathizers, who were subjected to much harassment and discrimination. Olson's appointment of Carey McWilliams to head the Division of Immigration and Housing indicated his concern for this situation, but it also angered the conser-

vative bloc in the legislature, which began a running battle with the blunt McWilliams. The latter, however, effectively used his position to publicize the shameful conditions of California's migrant labor force.

Organized labor might well have expected to capitalize on the disappointment and anger of the Okies at their treatment. But they brought with them such a strong individualism and antiradical patriotism that proletarian rhetoric about collectivism and class struggle was lost on them. When the CIO established UCAPAWA in 1937, it got nowhere with the new migrants. Ironically, then, the ideologies of the Okies led them to sympathize with farm owners and they frequently appeared among the ranks of strikebreakers. Their arrival actually impeded the union movement in agriculture and contributed to lowering the already insufferable standard of living for farm workers.

In the long run the inhospitality of Californians contributed to the creation of what historian James Gregory calls an "Okie subculture," defined by notions of personal toughness, economic justice, racism, and Americanism—a group identity reinforced by their "country" music. It was a subculture that had considerable political and cultural impact on California, including a militant racism. When World War II nearly quadrupled California's African American population, blacks met resistance everywhere, but it was the Okies who found them most difficult to accept. The result was tension and violence. Moreover, while nominally Democrats, the Okies moved away from California's more liberal Democratic Party and developed a kind of populistic conservatism expressed by George Wallace thirty years later.

World War II dramatically ended the poverty of the depression and altered the Okie experience in California. After 1939 the migrants, joined by 600,000 more southwesterners, drifted rapidly into the war industries developing in urban areas, while an army of Mexicans, the *braceros*, replaced them in the fields. Those who remained in agriculture were better paid, experienced greater acceptance, and developed greater self-esteem. The war ended the depression era in California, but the influence of the Okie subculture remained, as the continued popularity of religious radio stations and country music attest.

THE CULTURAL SCENE BETWEEN THE WARS

The good times and expanding economy of the 1920s brought increased support for the arts, while the automobile age promoted an orientation toward the outdoors that was reflected in architecture and leisure activities. San Francisco maintained its role as the state's cultural leader in this period. Construction of the de Young Museum in Golden Gate Park and the Palace of the Legion of Honor provided the city with two outstanding and popular art galleries by the mid-1920s. At the same time, plans proceeded for construction of the War Memorial Opera House, which, when completed in 1932, became the nation's first municipal opera house. City taxes supported not only the opera company but also the excellent San Francisco Symphony, established in 1911. Attracting outstanding conductors such as Alfred Hertz and Pierre Monteux, the symphony earned a reputation as one of the best in the nation.

Los Angeles, meanwhile, developed its cultural institutions, despite the fact that many migrants of the 1920s preferred Aimee Semple McPherson to the opera. In 1919 William Andrews Clark, Jr., endowed the Los Angeles Philharmonic Orchestra, which in 1921 began its famous series of summer evening "Concerts Under the Stars" in the Hollywood Bowl. The Huntington Library and Art Gallery was rapidly becoming a world-renowed institution, especially with its acquisition of Thomas Gainsborough's painting *Blue Boy*. Establishment of the Otis Art Institute in the home of Harrison Gray Otis and the Chouinard Art Institute gave Los Angeles an important start in the visual arts. Most important was the arrival in the 1930s of thousands of European intellectuals fleeing the spread of Hitler's Nazi regime. Bringing "high culture" primarily to southern California, where many worked in the movie industry, their homes became cultural "salons" for lively discussion. The famous novelist, Thomas Mann, the playwright Bertold Brecht, composer Arnold Schoenberg, conductors Otto Klemperer and Bruno Walter, as well as numerous well-known artists and actors, were a part of this migration that continued through the war years and contributed immensely to what historian Gerald Nash calls the subsequent "cultural explosion" of the region.

Architecture between the wars reflected and encouraged a trend toward outdoor living, notably in southern California, where Richard Neutra—like Frank Lloyd Wright a student of Chicago's Louis Sullivan—introduced "functionalism." An Austrian immigrant, Neutra pioneered the "art moderne" style and opened houses to the light through the use of glass. Wright and Neutra both subscribed to the concept that "form follows function," and their homes, with extensive use of glass, rock work, and split-level design, contributed significantly to the evolution of the modern California ranch-style house. In northern California "form follows function" was also the creed of Irving F. Morrow, consulting architect on San Francisco's Golden Gate Bridge in the mid-1930s. A modernist, considered by many to be radically ahead of his day, Morrow combined beauty with simplicity. For the bridge, he designed functionally graceful arching lamps over the roadway, insisted on a rail with open balusters so motorists and pedestrians could see through to the magnificent view all around, emphasized the height of the portals by having them diminish in width as they rose upward, and designed a vertical facet motif that he used subtly on the piers and braces. Most daring of his innovations was to paint the bridge "international orange." Noting that fog made San Francisco gray and colorless much of the year, Morrow criticized local architecture for ignoring this problem and itself remaining colorless. By chosing a full polychrome beginning with red-orange and culminating in a pure metallic gold on the monumental towers, he truly, as well as symbolically, created a "Golden Gate."

Another bright addition to the 1930s was the exuberantly cheerful musical style known as "swing," which Californians helped to launch. In 1935, when Benny Goodman brought his first "big band" to Los Angeles at the end of an unsuccessful cross-country tour, southern California youth gave him such an enthusiastic reception at the Palomar Ballroom that, as one observer noted, "the swing era was born." Goodman became known as the "King of Swing" and in 1936 organized the first integrated big band when he added black pianist Teddy Wilson and vibraphone player Lionel Hampton to his group. For the next two decades California hotels and ballrooms were especially popular bookings for the swing bands of Goodman, Glenn Miller, the Dorsey Brothers, Duke Ellington, and others.

Musicians, artists, writers, historians, and actors and actresses were frequently found on the roles of the New Deal's varied programs. The WPA artists covered the walls of public buildings with murals that only now are attracting the attention they deserve as works of art. Dorothea Lange did some of her most powerful work as a photographer for the Farm Security Administration; her photographic documentations of the depression's effect on farm workers became classic works in the world of photography. Popular fiction often reflected the anxieties of the depression years, producing a number of bleak novels of despair such as James M. Cain's *Double Indemnity* and Raymond Chandler's *The Big Sleep.*

Compassion for California's agricultural workers produced equally powerful literature, such as John Steinbeck's *The Grapes of Wrath* which was quickly made into a successful movie starring Henry Fonda. Carey McWilliams joined Steinbeck in exposing the plight of migrant farm workers with publication of *Factories in the Field* (1939), a well-researched study of the state's agricultural system. The Colorado-born McWilliams migrated to California and worked for the Los Angeles *Times* in the 1920s, attended law school in his spare hours, and joined a prestigious law firm. But he devoted much of his time to researching and writing on California themes, and most of his works on these topics were published in the 1940s. *North From Mexico* (1949) was a sympathetic account of the difficulties endured by Mexican migrants. *California: The Great Exception* (1946) developed the theme of the uniqueness of the state and has influenced the thinking of writers to this day, while his *Southern California Country* (1949, republished as *Southern California: An Island on the Land* in 1973) remains one of the best surveys of that region. McWilliams left the state in 1953 to become editor of *The Nation.* Another side to California's agriculture, ranching and the huge cattle-feeding business, is delightfully captured in Robert Easton's *The Happy Man,* published during the war and reissued in 1993.

Other fine writers made California and the West their themes. University of California professor George R. Stewart published

Ordeal by Hunger (1936), a gripping account of the Donner party disaster, while at San Francisco State, Walter Van Tilburg Clark was writing *The Ox-Bow Incident*, published in 1940. The San Joaquin Valley was the locale for much of the writing of William Saroyan, whose heartwarming accounts of his boyhood in Fresno's Armenian community appeared in *My Name Is Aram* (1940). Two of Saroyan's best works, *The Time of Your Life* (1939) and *The Human Comedy* (1943), were made into movies. Saroyan's work, especially *The Time of Your Life*, which deals with the foibles of some down-and-out San Francisco waterfront characters, revealed a refreshingly positive view of human nature. In contrast to Saroyan, the era also produced Robinson Jeffers, who took a gloomy view of his fellow man.

Thus the "roaring '20s" and the Great Depression, two strikingly different decades, produced some of the most moving and contradictory literature in the state's history. The essential innocence and optimism of Saroyan's view of life generally pervaded the era despite the hardships of the depression, while the somber view of Jeffers played a disturbing subdominant theme, warning of the dark destructive side of human nature.

San Francisco's Golden Gate International Exposition of 1939–1940, held on a large man-made island attached to Yerba Buena Island in San Francisco Bay, embodied the optimistic view. Commemorating completion of the Golden Gate and Bay bridges, the "Treasure Island" world's fair dazzled visitors with exhibits of the latest technological developments, such as television, and entertained them with everything from "swing" to opera. Ironically, the fair opened in the darkening shadow of war. Upon its closing, Treasure Island became a major facility of the U.S. Navy during World War II.

SUGGESTIONS FOR FURTHER READING

Aimee Semple McPherson

Robert Bahr, *Least of All the Saints: The Story of Aimee Semple McPherson* (1979); Lately Thomas, *Storming Heaven: The Lives and Turmoils of Minnie Kennedy and Aimee Semple McPherson* (1970); Nancy Barr Mavity, *Sister Aimee* (1931); Aimee Semple McPherson, *In the Service of the King: The Story of My Life* (1972); William McLoughlin, "Aimee Semple McPherson: Your Sister in the King's Glad Service," *Journal of Popular Culture* (1968); Sarah Comstock, "Aimee Semple McPherson: Prima Donna of Revivalism," *Harper's* (1927); David L. Clark, "Miracles for a Dime: From Chautauqua Tent to Radio Station with Sister Aimee," *California History* (1978–1979); Gloria Ricci Lothrop, "West of Eden: Pioneer Media Evangelist Aimee Semple McPherson in Los Angeles," *Journal of the West* (1988); Daniel M. Epstein, *Sister Aimee: The Life of Aimee Semple McPherson* (1993).

Agriculture, Power and a Maturing Economy

Ann Scheuring (ed.), *A Guidebook to California Agriculture* (1982); Donald J. Pisani, *From the Family Farm to Agribusiness*, (1984); Gilbert G. Gonzales, "Labor and Community: The Camps of Mexican Citrus Pickers in Southern California," *Western Historical Quarterly* (August, 1991); Paul W. Gates, "Corporation Farming in California," in Ray Allen Billington (ed.), *People of the Plains and Mountains: Essays in the History of the West Dedicated to Everett Dick* (1973); Norris Hundley, *Water and the West: The Colorado River Compact and the Politics of Water in the American West* (1975); Philip L. Fradkin, *A River No More: The Colorado River and the West* (1981); Joseph E. Stevens, *Hoover Dam*, (1988); Frank Waters, *The Colorado* (1946); Nelson S. Van Valen, "A Neglected Aspect of the Owens River Aqueduct Story: The Inception of the Los Angeles Municipal Electric System," *Southern California Quarterly* (1977); Jules Tygiel, *The Great Los Angeles Swindle* (1994); R. G. Cleland and Osgood Hardy, *The March of Industry* (1929); Joe S. Bain, *Economics of the Pacific Coast Petroleum Industry (1944–1947);* Marquis James, *The Biography of a Bank: The Story of the Bank of America* (1954); Thomas Schatz, *Hollywood Genres: Formulas, Filmmaking and the Studio System* (1981); Carl Beauchamp, *Without Lying Down: Frances Marion and the Powerful Women of Early Hollywood* (1997); Robert Sklar, *Movie-Made America: A Cultural History of American Movies* (1975); Ben M. Hall, *The Best Remaining Seats: The Story of the Golden Age of the Movie Palace* (1961); Gregory D. Black, *Hollywood Censored: Morality Codes, Catholics, and the Movies* (1994); Frank Walsh, *Sin and Censorship: The Catholic Church and the Motion Picture Industry* (1996); Neal Gabler, *An Empire of Their Own: How the Jews Invented Hollywood,* (1989); Tina Balio, *Grand Design: Hollywood as a Modern Business Enterprise, 1930–1939* (1995); Roger W. Lotchin, *Fortress California 1910–1961; From Warfare to Welfare,* (1992), and "The Darwinian City: The Politics of Urbanization in San Francisco Between the World Wars," *Pacific Historical Review* (August, 1979).

1920s Labor and Politics

Louis B. and Richard S. Perry, *A History of the Los Angeles Labor Movement, 1911–1941* (1963); Los Angeles *Times, The Forty-Years War for a Free City: A History of the Open Shop in Los Angeles* (1929); Edwin Layton, "The Better America Federation: A Case Study of Superpatriots," *Pacific Historical Review* (1961); Russell M. Posner, "The Progressive Voters' League, 1923–1926," *California Historical Society Quarterly* (1957); Jackson K. Putnam, *Modern California Politics* (1984).

The Depression and Public Works

Frank L. Kidner, *California Business Cycles* (1946); Paul N. Woolf, *Economic Trends in California, 1929–1934* (1935); Leonard Leader, *Los Angeles and the Great Depression,* (1991); William H. Mullins, *The Depression and the Urban West Coast, 1929–1933: Los Angeles, San Francisco, Seattle and Portland* (1991); Irving G. Hendrick, "The Impact of the Great Depression on Public School Support

in California," *Southern California Quarterly* (1972); James Leiby, "State Welfare Administration in California, 1930–1945," *Southern California Quarterly* (1973); Robert L. Pritchard, "Orange County During the Depressed Thirties: A Study in Twentieth Century California Local History," *Southern California Quarterly* (1968); Loren B. Chan, "California During the Early 1930s—The Administration of Governor James Rolph, Jr., 1931–1934," *Southern California Quarterly* (1981); James T. Patterson, "The New Deal in the West," *Pacific Historical Review* (1969); Marlene Park and Gerald E. Markowitz, *Democratic Vistas: Post Offices and Public Art in the New Deal* (1984); Anthony W. Lee, *Painting on the Left: Diego Rivera, Radical Politics, and San Francisco's Public Murals* (1999); Stephen M. Gelber, "Working to Prosperity: California's New Deal Murals," *California History* (1979); Jerre Mangione, *The Dream and the Deal: The Federal Writers Project, 1935–1943* (1971); Mary Montgomery and Marion Clawson, *History of Legislation and Policy Formation of the Central Valley Project* (1946); Marion Clawson, *The Effect of the Central Valley Project on the Agricultural and Industrial Economy and on the Social Character of California* (1945); Clayton R. Koppes, "Public Water, Private Land: Origins of the Acreage Limitation Controversy, 1933–1953," *Pacific Historical Review* (1978); Paul S. Taylor, "Excess Land Law: Pressure versus Principle," *California Law Review* (1959); Carl D. Thompson, *Confessions of the Power Trust* (1932).

1930s Panaceas, Labor, and Politics

Jackson K. Putnam, *Old Age Politics in California* (1970); Abraham Holtzman, *The Townsend Movement: A Political Study* (1963); Robert E. Burke, *Olson's New Deal for California* (1953); Greg Mitchell, *The Campaign of the Century: Upton Sinclair's Race for Governor of California and the Birth of Media Politics* (1992); Carey McWilliams, *Factories in the Field* (1939); Abraham Hoffman, *Unwanted Mexican-Americans in the Great Depression* (1974); Francisco E. Balderrama, *In Defense of La Raza: The Los Angeles Mexican Consulate and the Mexican Community, 1929 to 1936* (1982); Francisco Balderrama and Raymond Rodriguez, *Decade of Betrayal: Mexican Repatriation in the 1930s* (1995); Camille Guerin Gonzales, *Mexican Workers and American*

Dreams: Immigration Repatriation, and California Farm Labor, 1900–1939 (1994); Devra Weber, *Dark Sweat, White Gold: California Farm Workers, Cotton and the New Deal* (1994); Eiichiro Azuma, "Racial struggle, Immigrant Nationalism, and Ethnic Identity: Japanesse and Filipinos in the California Delta," *Pacific Historical Review* (1998); K. Scott Wong and Sucheng Chan (eds.), *Claiming America: Constructing Chinese American Identities During the Exclusion Era* (1998); Mario T. Garcia, *Mexican Americans: Leadership, Ideology, and Identity, 1930–1960* (1989); Mike Quinn, *The Big Strike* (1949); Charles P. Larrowe, *Harry Bridges: The Rise and Fall of Radical Labor in the United States* (1972); Harvey Schwartz, "Union Expansion and Labor Solidarity: Longshoremen, Warehousemen and Teamsters, 1933–1937," *New Labor Review* (1978), and *The March Inland: Origins of the ILWU Warehouse Division* (1978); Lawrence M. Kahn, "Unions and Internal Labor Markets: The Case of the San Francisco Longshoremen," *Labor History* (1980); Bruce Nelson, *Workers on the Waterfront*, (1988); Paul Taylor and Dorothea Lange, *American Exodus* (1939, 1969); Walter J. Stein, *California and the Dust Bowl Migration* (1973); James N. Gregory, *American Exodus: The Dust Bowl Migration and Okie Culture in California* (1989); David Selvin, *Sky Full of Storm* (1966).

A Changing Society

Carey McWilliams, *Southern California: An Island on the Land* (1973); Kevin Starr, *Material Dreams: Southern California Through the 1920s*, (1990); and *Endangered Dreams: The Great Depression in California* (1995); John D. Weaver, *Los Angeles: The Enormous Village, 1781–1981* (1980); Bruce Henstell, *Sunshine and Wealth: Los Angeles in the Twenties and Thirties* (1984); Norman M. Klein and Martin J. Scheisl (eds.), *Los Angeles and the Memory of Many Hopes: 20th Century Los Angeles, Power, Promotion, and Social Conflict* (1990); Ricardo Romo, *East Los Angeles: History of a Barrio* (1983); Douglas Monroy, *Rebirth: Mexican Los Angeles from the Great Migration to the Great Depression* (1999); Ellen Carol DuBois and Vicki L. Ruiz (eds.), *Unequal Sisters: A Multicultural Reader in U.S. Women's History* (1990); David G. Gut-

tiérrez, *Wall and Mirrors: Mexican Americans, Mexican Immigrants and the Politics of Ethnicity* (1995); Joan M. Jensen and Gloria Ricci Lothrop, *California Women: A History* (1987); W. W. Robinson, "The Southern California Real Estate Boom of the Twenties," *Southern California Quarterly* (1942); Ashleigh E. Brilliant, "Some Aspects of Motorization in Southern California, 1919–1929," *Southern California Quarterly* (1965); Mark S. Foster, "The Model T, the Hard Sell, and Los Angeles' Urban Growth: The Decentralization of Los Angeles During the 1920s," *Pacific Historical Review* (1975); Scott Bottles, *Los Angeles and the Automobile* (1987); Gilman M. Ostrander, *The Prohibition Movement in California, 1848–1933* (1957); John R. Meers, "The California Wine and Grape Industry and Prohibition," *California Historical Society Quarterly* (1967); Wendell E. Harman, "The Bootlegger Era in Southern California," *Southern California Quarterly* (1955); Kenneth D. Rose, "'Dry' Los Angeles and Its Liquor Problems in 1924," *Southern California Quarterly* (1987); Richard Melching, "The Activities of the Ku Klux Klan in Anaheim, California, 1923–1925," *Southern California Quarterly* (1974).

Culture Between the Wars

Lawrence Clark Powell, *Robinson Jeffers: The Man and His Work* (1940); Melba Berry Bennett, *The Stonemason of Tor House: The Life and Work of Robinson Jeffers* (1966); Lawrence Lee and Barry Gifford, *Saroyan: A Biography* (1998); Gerald Haslam, *Many Californias: Literature from the Golden State* (1992), *Voices of a Place: Social and Literary Essays from the Other California* (1987), and "Literary California," *California History* (Winter, 1989); Harold Kirker, *Old Forms on a New Land: California Architecture in Perspective* (1991); David Wyatt, *The Fall into Eden: Landscape and Imagination in California* (1986); Michael Davidson, *The San Francisco Renaissance: Poetics and Community at Mid-Century* (1989); Patricia Carpenter and Paul Totah, *The San Francisco Fair: Treasure Island, 1939–1940* (1989); David Fine, "Down and Out in Los Angeles: John Fante's *Ask the Dust*," *The Californians* (Sept/Oct, 1991); K.D. Kurutz and Gary F. Kurutz, *California Calls You: The Art of Promoting the Golden State, 1870–1940* (2000).

Dorothea Lange and John Steinbeck

Milton Meltzer, *Dorothea Lange: A Photographer's Life* (1978); Therese T. Hayman, *Celebrating a Collection: The Work of Dorothea Lange* (1978); John Steinbeck, *The Acts of King Arthur and His Noble Knights* (1976); Nelson Valjean, *John Steinbeck, The Errant Knight* (1975); John Steinbeck, *The Grapes of Wrath* (1939); Jay Parini, *John Steinbeck* (1995).

Woman in Vegetable Garden
The evacuees produced a good deal of their own food in vegetable gardens such as this one at Manzanar. *Courtesy of the Bancroft Library.*

PART EIGHT

WORLD WAR II AND POSTWAR EXPANSION

World War II proved to be an important watershed for California, setting the stage for extraordinary growth and prosperity in the postwar years. At the same time, the war brought the culmination of one hundred years of anti-Asian racism in the state, with the forced removal of Japanese Americans, two-thirds of whom were U.S. citizens, and their detention in America's version of the era's concentration camps. The experiences of the Uchida and Wakatsuki families described in Chapter 22 illustrate the consequences of unjustified questioning of loyalty, as well as the power of racial bias. The narrative of the Wakatsuki family's experiences is based on the book *Farewell to Manzanar* (1973) by Jeanne Wakatsuki Houston and James D. Houston. The Uchida family's story is based on the book *Desert Exile: The Uprooting of a Japanese-American Family* (1982) by Yoshiko Uchida. Their stories have important ramifications for other minorities, particularly for the Hispanic and African American populations, which grew rapidly in the postwar period, and for the history of racial relations in the state.

The war also lifted the state out of the depression and set in motion the development of what came to be called "high-technology" industries. California dominated this field, particularly the aerospace industry, and soaked up a huge proportion of the federal government's expeditures for research, development, and production of sophisticated military hardware and space vehicles. Wartime economic development also began a new migration to California that rivaled the state's growth rate of past decades, while total population leaped from 6,900,000 in 1940 to 15,650,000 in 1960. The strains of such expansion were apparent everywhere, but especially in schools, housing, transportation, and recreation.

The postwar years also saw the development of an often vicious anticommunist movement when American relations with the Soviet Union deteriorated into the Cold War. California had its own version of anticommunist "witch hunting" in this period, which affected state politics for years to come. Meanwhile, the state's economic and social growth attracted more and more national attention, its politicians became national figures, and its affluent society set the pace for the rest of the nation.

CHAPTER TWENTY-TWO

A QUESTION OF LOYALTY

Japan's attack on Pearl Harbor, December 7, 1941, played directly into California's long history of hostility toward minorities, especially Asians, and created a war hysteria that brought down on Japanese Americans the full force of that legacy. Organizations such as the California Joint Immigration Committee, successor to the old Asiatic Exclusion League, and the Native Sons of the Golden West, loudly questioned the loyalty of all persons of Japanese ancestry and demanded their removal from the state, a proposal endorsed by politicians and public alike. The resulting removal and detention of Japanese Americans such as the Wakatsuki and Uchida families, however, was such an extreme reaction that in the long run it was an important turning point in the relations of Caucasians and Asians in California.

Tall and lean, Ko Wakatsuki stood proudly at the helm of his trawler, the *Nereid*, while his two older sons, William and Woodrow, readied it to join the fishing fleet heading out of San Pedro harbor. It was a beautiful December day, and on shore his wife, Riku, and two of his daughters joined a handful of other women to watch the familiar procession of white boats gather, turn seaward, and begin to sail into the distance.

Ko had reason to be satisfied. A good wife and ten children, some of them married and starting families of their own, looked to him as the head of the family. Flamboyant and autocratic, he appeared the classic Japanese patriarch. At fifty-four he had been in the United States for thirty-five years, always longing to send word back to Japan that "Wakatsuki Ko has made it big in America."* Now he was the proud owner of two fishing boats, one a $25,000 trawler. In spite of the fact that as an Issei (a first-generation Japanese immigrant) he was denied the right to become a citizen or own land, he was pleased that his children, as Nisei (American-born, second-generation Japanese), were citizens and unhampered by the discriminatory laws aimed at his generation.

---

*Adapted from *Farewell to Manzanar* by James D. and Jeanne Wakatsuki Houston. Copyright (c) 1973 by James D. Houston. Reprinted by permission of Houghton Mifflin Company. All rights reserved.

On shore, the women lingered, watching the boats even after they could no longer see the men on board. Then, strangely, the white specks on the horizon began to grow larger, and the women realized that the boats were returning. But why? they asked. The sky was cloudless. Had there been an accident? Suddenly a man ran down from the nearby cannery, waving his arms and shouting, "The Japanese have bombed Pearl Harbor!" The women looked at each other in puzzlement, calling to him as he rushed by, "What is Pearl Harbor?" But he passed before they got an answer.

Until this time Ko and Riku had lived with their younger children at Ocean Park near Los Angeles, but now they moved to Terminal Island in San Pedro harbor to be with their older children and the Japanese community there. Fear and confusion reigned, especially for the Issei, as the country they had chosen plunged into war with their homeland. They were now enemy aliens, and the near-hysteria on the west coast filled them with anxiety. Two weeks later the FBI came for Ko Wakatsuki, as they came for most Japanese with commercial fishing licenses, and took him away. His family did not see him again for almost a year, and two months passed before they even learned where he had been taken—Fort Lincoln, North Dakota, an all-male internment camp for enemy aliens. Meanwhile the family had moved again. The U.S. Navy, with a major base on Terminal Island and reacting to rumors of sabotage and espionage, gave the Japanese American families on the island forty-eight hours to leave. Drawn together by the two older boys, Bill and Woody, the Wakatsukis were soon huddled in rented housing in Los Angeles, wondering what would happen next.

On the same December day that Ko Wakatsuki's boat strangely returned to shore, the gentlemanly Dwight Takasai Uchida proudly took his wife and two grown daughters to the Japanese Independent Congregational Church in Oakland, as he did every Sunday. Uchida, too, could take pride in his life in America. After working his way through Doshisha University in Kyoto, where he was converted to Christianity and given the name Dwight, he had come to America in 1906 at age twenty-two. Precise, punctual, and quietly efficient, he became successful in business and in 1917 obtained a position in the San Francisco branch of Mitsui & Co., one of Japan's largest export-import firms. That same year he married Iku Umegaki, a fellow graduate of Doshisha University, in a union arranged by faculty members who had known them both. Now, at age fifty-seven, he had retired from his position as assistant manager at Mitsui. One daughter, Keiko (Kay), had graduated from Mills College, and the other, Yoshiko (Yo), was a senior at the University of California at Berkeley. Ordinarily, church services were followed by the entertainment of friends for dinner at the Uchidas' Berkeley home, but this Sunday was an exception. The family had just sat down to a simple lunch when suddenly the radio blared forth the terrible news. Pearl Harbor had been bombed by Japan! Distressed and frightened, the family nevertheless dismissed the bombing as the work of fanatics, and Yo went off to the campus to study for finals. There, her friends all agreed it was incredible that Japan would attack the United States.

That very afternoon, however, the FBI came for Dwight Uchida—as they had come for Ko Wakatsuki and many other leaders of the Japanese American community—and took him away for questioning. It was a week before his wife and daughters knew where he had been taken, and nearly six months before he was allowed to rejoin them. The three women were left to assume duties and responsibilities they had never dreamed they could or should have, at a time when rumors and war hysteria filled them with apprehension.

Probably no group in America watched the deterioration of relations between the United States and Japan with more apprehension than the Japanese minority—hardly more than one percent of California's population. When war came, they were powerless and vulnerable. Since their arrival in California in the 1890s, they had been subjected to the same hostility and discrimination that the Chinese had suffered before them. They were denied the right to become naturalized citizens, to own land, or to control property through corporations. Social indignities were heaped upon them. Attempts were made to force their children into segregated schools, and restrictive covenants denied them housing of their choice. They were denied service in commercial establishments, forced into segregated facilities in public places, and had to endure harassment and physical abuse. All the while they were the focus of a persistent campaign in the California press warning of the "yellow peril," an irrational fantasy of Oriental conquest of western America.

Denied access to American society, the Issei, like most other immigrant groups, developed their own subculture. Applying the labor-intensive methods of their homeland, they eventually dominated important segments of California agriculture and played an important role in the state's advance in specialty crops. Perhaps half were employed in farming by 1920, while the rest organized small businesses that catered largely to the "little Tokyos" emerging in urban centers. Shrewd, thrifty, and hard-working, they familiarized themselves with American institutions and the English language. They retained what ties they could with family in Japan and with Japanese tradition, through

Japanese-language newspapers and social clubs. In America, the Issei created a social order in which age, sex, and generation determined status, in which relationships and conduct were governed by precise rules, and in which group solidarity was more important than the individual.

Most of their children, the Nisei, were born in the 1920s and 1930s and, like most children of immigrants, developed a measure of social distance from their parents. Relatively few in number, they attended integrated schools and were as a group unusually successful students. Their close contact with American culture led them to identify with their white contemporaries, to resist parental control, and to challenge their parents' cultural orientation to Japan. Yet the Nisei were not completely Americanized, nor were they a threat to group solidarity. They were too young and economically dependent on the Issei-dominated community. Family discipline was still strong enough to force most of them to attend Japanese-language classes after school and to participate in Japanese cultural activities. Moreover, the general public's acceptance of the racist views behind the "yellow peril" propaganda of the period placed significant social barriers in the way of the Nisei's assimilation and led to widespread economic discrimination against them. For example, after Kay Uchida graduated from Mills College with a major in child development, she could find work only as a glorified nursemaid and had to take her meals in her employers' kitchen. American in culture, the Nisei had no place in American social or economic life.

Life in America proved even more difficult for a subgroup of the Nisei, the Kibei, who, while born in the United States and thus American citizens, had been sent to Japan to be educated. On returning to the United States, they had much less in common with their Americanized brothers and sisters, found the English language a barrier, and were more oriented to the customs and social arrangements of their parents. Like the Issei, they remained close to the "little Tokyos" subculture, where their ability with the Japanese language and more traditional attitudes reinforced group solidarity.

The Wakatsukis joined a close-knit Japanese American community in Los Angeles when they moved from Terminal Island and watched panic grip the state as rumors of a Japanese invasion spread, fed by the amazing successes of Japan's military and naval forces in the Pacific. Within six months Japan overran French Indochina, Singapore, the Dutch East Indies, the Philippines, the major Pacific island chains, and American bases at Wake and Guam. By the middle of 1942 its forces threatened India and Australia. In California, cities were blacked out at night, civil-defense forces were organized, and plans to repel an invasion were hastily prepared. Air-raid sirens wailed frequent false alarms, and reports circulated that Japanese ships and planes were approaching.

Attention quickly turned to the Japanese American population, concentrated on the west coast, and the old anti-Asian prejudices rapidly intensified. Stereotypical views of the Japanese as sly, devious, unassimilable, and dangerous were aired in the press and on radio. The Japanese Americans were said to have systematically settled near sensitive military installations in order to conduct espionage and sabotage. Charges were made that Japanese workers in Hawaii had cut arrows pointing to Pearl Harbor in the sugarcane fields on Oahu and that Japanese American fishermen such as Ko Wakatsuki were fueling Japanese submarines at sea. Public opinion was further inflamed by newspaper columnists and radio commentators who proposed that Japanese Americans be removed from California and even that Nisei

be stripped of their citizenship. More and more Japanese Americans kept to themselves as word spread that they might be forced to leave their homes and even their state.

As the weeks passed, the situation worsened; important political figures, including Los Angeles mayor Fletcher Bowron and state attorney general Earl Warren, began to join the anti-Asian forces in calling for removal of all persons of Japanese ancestry from the "war zone." It was impossible to tell the loyal from the disloyal, they said, so all should go. Then in February 1942 came the news that President Roosevelt had signed Executive Order 9066 authorizing the army to remove any person, alien or citizen, from military areas if required by military necessity. Some sort of removal appeared imminent, and how to react to it became a matter of serious debate among the Japanese Americans. Most concluded that only a cooperative attitude would prove their loyalty.

With their father gone, the elder Wakatsuki children devoted their efforts to holding the family together and finding housing in the same district so they might not be separated. Other than that, they could only say to one another *shikata ga nai* ("it cannot be helped," "it must be done"), a Japanese phrase of resignation to enduring something difficult but unavoidable.

In Berkeley, the Uchida women tried to go on living normally like other Americans, buying defense bonds and signing up for civil defense work. At the same time, letters from Dwight, now imprisoned in an army internment camp in Missoula, Montana, grew more and more anxious about reports of a mass evacuation and begged for news. They could not give him information they did not have, but they began to prepare for a forced move, packing up books and household goods. Already, an 8:00 P.M. to 6:00 A.M. curfew and a five-mile travel limit had been im-

WESTERN DEFENSE COMMAND AND FOURTH ARMY
WARTIME CIVIL CONTROL ADMINISTRATION
Presidio of San Francisco, California
May 3, 1942

INSTRUCTIONS
TO ALL PERSONS OF
JAPANESE
ANCESTRY
Living in the Following Area:

All of the County of San Mateo, State of California.

Pursuant to the provisions of Civilian Exclusion Order No. 35, this Headquarters, dated May 3, 1942, all persons of Japanese ancestry, both alien and non-alien, will be evacuated from the above area by 12 o'clock noon, P. W. T., Saturday, May 9, 1942.

No Japanese person living in the above area will be permitted to change residence after 12 o'clock noon, P. W. T., Sunday, May 3, 1942, without obtaining special permission from the representative of the Commanding General, Northern California Sector, at the Civil Control Station located at:

Masonic Temple Building,
100 North Ellsworth Street,
San Mateo, California.

Such permits will only be granted for the purpose of uniting members of a family, or in cases of grave emergency.

The Civil Control Station is equipped to assist the Japanese population affected by this evacuation in the following ways:

1. Give advice and instructions on the evacuation.
2. Provide services with respect to the management, leasing, sale, storage or other disposition of most kinds of property, such as real estate, business and professional equipment, household goods, boats, automobiles and livestock.
3. Provide temporary residence elsewhere for all Japanese in family groups.
4. Transport persons and a limited amount of clothing and equipment to their new residence.

The Following Instructions Must Be Observed:

1. A responsible member of each family, preferably the head of the family, or the person in whose name most of the property is held, and each individual living alone, will report to the Civil Control Station to receive further instructions. This must be done between 8:00 A. M. and 5:00 P. M. on Monday, May 4, 1942, or between 8:00 A. M. and 5:00 P. M. on Tuesday, May 5, 1942.
2. Evacuees must carry with them on departure for the Assembly Center, the following property:
   (a) Bedding and linens (no mattress) for each member of the family;
   (b) Toilet articles for each member of the family;
   (c) Extra clothing for each member of the family;
   (d) Sufficient knives, forks, spoons, plates, bowls and cups for each member of the family;
   (e) Essential personal effects for each member of the family.

All items carried will be securely packaged, tied and plainly marked with the name of the owner and numbered in accordance with instructions obtained at the Civil Control Station. The size and number of packages is limited to that which can be carried by the individual or family group.

3. No pets of any kind will be permitted.
4. No personal items and no household goods will be shipped to the Assembly Center.
5. The United States Government through its agencies will provide for the storage, at the sole risk of the owner, of the more substantial household items, such as iceboxes, washing machines, pianos and other heavy furniture. Cooking utensils and other small items will be accepted for storage if crated, packed and plainly marked with the name and address of the owner. Only one name and address will be used by a given family.
6. Each family, and individual living alone, will be furnished transportation to the Assembly Center or will be authorized to travel by private automobile in a supervised group. All instructions pertaining to the movement will be obtained at the Civil Control Station.

**Go to the Civil Control Station between the hours of 8:00 A. M. and 5:00 P. M.,
Monday, May 4, 1942, or between the hours of 8:00 A. M. and 5:00 P. M.,
Tuesday, May 5, 1942, to receive further instructions.**

J. L. DeWITT
Lieutenant General, U. S. Army
Commanding

SEE CIVILIAN EXCLUSION ORDER NO. 35.

Exclusion Order
Copy of WCCA Exclusion Order, 1942. *Courtesy of the Bancroft Library.*

posed on all Japanese Americans, while their radios, binoculars, cameras, and firearms had been designated contraband to be turned in to local police. The Uchida girls' box cameras remained in the Berkeley police station for the rest of the war.

Early in March, General John L. DeWitt, commander of the Western Defense Command, began to exercise the authority delegated to him under Executive Order 9066 with a proclamation dividing Washington, Oregon, California, and Arizona into military areas. Military Area No. 1, roughly the western half of these states, was prohibited to enemy aliens and any person of Japanese ancestry. DeWitt's proclamation actually encouraged the Japanese to move out of Military Area No. 1 voluntarily, but few did so; lack of funds and the hostility of Americans in inland areas severely limited their mobility. Reports from those who did attempt to move voluntarily told of migrants being clapped into jail and harassed by vigilante groups. Finally, effective March 29, DeWitt issued another proclamation prohibiting all Japanese Americans from leaving Military Area No 1. Evacuation had been put in the hands of Colonel Karl Bendetsen, one of the early and most insistent advocates of removal, who was now appointed to head the Wartime Civilian Control Administration (WCCA) under DeWitt's command.

Bendetsen's plan was relatively simple. He divided the west coast into 108 "exclusion areas," each containing approximately 1,000 persons of Japanese ancestry, and established a civil control station for each area. The plan included a program to remove these persons, first to assembly centers and then to inland camps for detention. The assembly centers were racetracks, exhibition centers, and fairgrounds, although some 20,000 persons were moved directly to two of the inland camps, called "relocation centers" and administered

by a new civilian agency, the War Relocation Authority (WRA). On March 30, 1942, three and a half months after the attack on Pearl Harbor, the WCCA issued the first civilian exclusion order, and the forced removal of Japanese Americans from their homes began.

For weeks the Uchidas had watched pressures mount for their forced removal, anxious over the hysteria and racism in the statements of the press, public officials, and the military. Now they helplessly packed their belongings and awaited the exclusion order for their area. Even then they were shocked when it came. On April 21 the newspapers announced: "Japs Given Evacuation Orders Here." Numbly, they read that Berkeley's 1,319 Japanese aliens and citizens would be evacuated to Tanforan racetrack, south of San Francisco, by May 1. Ten days' notice! Kay, as the oldest citizen, assumed the position of head of the family, reported to the local Civil Control Station for registration, and returned with identification tags for all their belongings. From then on the Uchidas were just family no. 13453. Frantically, they tried to pack and dispose of possessions accumulated over fifteen years. Many years later Yo remembered their plight:

> We surveyed with desperation the vast array of dishes, lacquerware, silverware, pots and pans, books, paintings, porcelain and pottery, furniture, linens, rugs, records, curtains, garden tools, cleaning equipment, and clothing that filled our house. . . . We sold things we should have kept and packed away foolish trifles we should have discarded. . . . desperate as the deadline approached. Our only thought was to get the house emptied in time, for we knew the Army would not wait.*

---

*All quotations concerning the Uchida family are taken from Yoshiko Uchida, *Desert Exile: The Uprooting of a Japanese-American Family* (Seattle: University of Washington Press, 1982).

The piano, a few pieces of furniture, boxes of books, and some other possessions were stored with friends and neighbors, while larger pieces such as beds, mattresses, and rugs were put in commercial storage. The Uchidas had been told to bring only what they could carry, but also to bring their own bedding, dishes, and eating utensils, so these were bundled into a large canvas bag into which they stuffed what would not fit into the two suitcases apiece they planned to carry. Then, after one last night in their now-barren house, the Uchidas reported with suitcases and by now enormous, bulging bag to the Civil Control Station, where they were unnerved by the sight of armed soldiers in charge of the place. Depressed and angry, they boarded buses and were driven across the bay to the Tanforan racetrack, the Assembly Center for Bay Area Japanese Americans. There, behind barbed-wire fences punctuated by tall guard towers, they were assigned to Barracks 18, Apartment 40, a hastily renovated horse stall in a long stable. Linoleum had been laid over the manure-soaked floorboards, but the smell remained. The partition between the stalls had been whitewashed, but it ended a foot or more below the roof, providing little privacy for the various families housed in the stable's twenty-five stalls. This twenty-by-eighteen-foot "apartment" became the Uchidas' new home for the next five months. As she stood in the long line for meals, Yoshiko Uchida was overwhelmed by feelings of degradation, humiliation, and longing for her Berkeley home.

Life in an army-run assembly center— there were thirteen in California—was truly traumatic for the internees. The women found the lack of privacy in latrines and showers especially humiliating, and some took to covering their faces with newspapers when using the open facilities. The army, un-equipped to provide living quarters for women and children, made little attempt to meet their needs. Laundry had to be done by hand, and hot water was gone by early morning. Some women arose at 3:00 or 4:00 A.M. to do their washing. Food was generally bad and skimpy (on the day of their arrival, the Uchidas were greeted with two sausages, a baked potato, and some unbuttered bread for dinner), leading to constant illness and physical complaints.

Above all, it was communal living, with only semiprivate sleeping quarters. There was no way or place to be alone, no way to avoid others or escape the constant noise. For those with young children and teen-agers, the close quarters, mess-hall eating, and lack of activity put severe strains on family ties. Children no longer ate with their parents, and they roamed the racetrack in search of something to do. The barracks and stalls carried every conversation two or three families away. Discipline broke down under such conditions, yet for many the family unit was crucial to survival. More than one resident remarked that only the stabilizing influence of the family enabled them to cope with life in the center.

For the Uchidas, living at Tanforan was at least brightened by the return of Dwight as head of the family; after five months in the army's Missoula, Montana, camp for "dangerous enemy aliens" (including an eighty-two-year-old and a man who, four days before his detention, had been operated on for stomach cancer), Dwight was released on parole. After all, he had been retired from Mitsui & Co. for two years, had an impressive record of public service and was well recommended by many prominent Bay Area friends. With his return, the Uchida "home" once again became a social center for their many friends. Dwight spent long evenings recounting to them (and the neighbors listening over the partition) his experiences in Missoula and his efforts there to organize community activities, promote church services, and build morale.

The internees had to create a whole new community behind the barbed wire at Tanforan, an experience being repeated at other centers in Washington, Oregon, and California. Food, medical, and postal services were established, an educational system organized, and recreation provided for. Within a few weeks local mess halls serving sections of the camp replaced the huge grandstand mess hall, evacuee chefs took over the cooking, and meals improved. Kay and Yo Uchida became involved in building a school system, Kay heading up a nursery-school program, where, for the first time, she could practice the profession she had trained for in college. Yo was soon teaching second grade (at a salary of $16 a month) and marveling that, by the end of June, forty percent of the internees were either teaching or attending school.

The need for recreation was obvious, and the internees swamped programs established to fill their leisure time. They organized 110 softball teams, and the racetrack grandstand was regularly filled with spectators. Musical theater, art classes, music lessons, hobby-shop programs, Saturday night dances, and talent shows attracted hundreds of participants. Many internees turned to gardening and gradually transformed the center's appearance with vegetable and flower gardens and a small parklike area. Within the barracks, scrap lumber and materials obtained from catalogue sales converted the horse stalls into modest living quarters with window curtains, shelves, tables, and chairs.

The great effort the evacuees at Tanforan put into making their incarceration bearable was tinged with irony; they all knew that they would eventually have to move again. As they made their horse stalls and barracks into

"homes," many residents, fearful of the unknown, became reluctant to leave. Finally, in late August the word came: they would be moved between September 15 and 20.

As September progressed the Uchidas began packing again. Dwight dismantled the scrap-lumber tables and chairs to make packing boxes and suitcases. Then, on September 16, the Uchidas and the other residents of their mess-hall unit were registered, counted, and marched between two rows of armed soldiers to a train pulled up at a racetrack siding. That night, with curtains drawn, their train left Tanforan—destination: the Topaz Relocation Center in Utah.

In Los Angeles, in the meantime, the Wakatsukis watched the initial sympathy of whites for their difficult situation erode, as FBI raids picked up more and more Issei men and rumors of Japanese American sabotage and espionage flared in the press. By March the evacuation was a certainty, and the Wakatsukis were resigned to it. At least, the older children said, they would be under government protection and away from the growing hatred in the war zone. When the order came, the Wakatsukis met at the Los Angeles Buddhist Church designated as their pick-up point.

It was a scene they would long remember. Old people leaned in confusion on the young. Small children hung wide-eyed on their mothers' skirts, while their older brothers and sisters struggled with the mass of suitcases, duffel bags, and enormous bulging bundles. Confused, bewildered, and frightened, they clung together in little family groups. For many besides the Wakatsukis, "Papa," the family head, had already departed, snatched from their midst for "questioning" only to disappear without notice. Here and there, lonely individuals appeared, no family to absorb and comfort them.

Behind them lay the shattered remains of

Manzanar Camp
Manzanar Relocation Center was located east of the Sierra Nevada in the high desert region of the Owens Valley. *Courtesy of the Bancroft Library.*

their lives as free people. Furniture worth hundreds of dollars had been sold to second-hand dealers for five or ten dollars. Homes, farms, and businesses acquired through years of hard work and frugality had been sold for pennies on the dollar, or left in the care of friends. For the youngsters, there was the puzzling, unanswered question of why they had suddenly been pulled out of school—in many cases, just as they were about to graduate.

Under the watchful eyes of armed soldiers, the Wakatsukis registered, received

identification tags to attach to their clothing, and were herded to trucks and buses where they heaped their belongings in great piles with numbered tags matching those they wore. When they boarded the bus the order was given to close the window curtains. The buses then rolled through the city and into the countryside as the passengers talked in low voices, played cards, or dozed. Late in the day the curtains were drawn to reveal a harsh desertlike terrain, where wind-blown dust and sand yellowed the sky and turned the sun red. The passengers found them-

Crowded Barracks at Manzanar
At Manzanar and other relocation centers, evacuees had to put up with a minimum of space and privacy. *Courtesy of the Bancroft Library.*

selves approaching the camp that, for many, was to be their home for more than three years. At last the buses drove through a large gate in a high barbed-wire fence where soldiers watched from towers spaced at intervals around the compound. Rows of black tar-paper barracks came into view, and a number of waiting people gathered around looking for friends and relatives among the new arrivals. The passengers sat frozen in apprehensive silence as their vehicle eased to a stop. Finally, Jeanne, the youngest Wakatsuki, threw open a window, leaned out, and cried, "Hey, this whole bus is full of Wakatsukis!" and suddenly tension-relieving laughter rocked the bus.

They had arrived at Manzanar, in the high-desert Owens Valley east of the Sierra, one of the two camps that served as assembly centers before conversion to relocation centers. Here, in this isolated area subject to extreme temperatures of near 0°F in winter and more than 100°F in summer, the army

was constructing row upon row of flimsy barracks—single-thickness pine plank walls covered with tar paper, with gaping cracks and knotholes in walls and floors through which the wind carried clouds of dust. Each building was divided into six units measuring sixteen by twenty feet, with one bare light bulb hanging from above and one oil stove for heat. Open ceilings were an invitation to the lively young boys to climb into the rafters and spy on their neighbors.

The Wakatsukis were assigned two of these units for the twelve in the immediate family. Woody and Bill and their wives, with Woody's baby, took one unit, which they partitioned with a blanket. Riku, her mother, and the five youngest children were crammed into the other. Eleanor, the recently married oldest daughter, and her husband were assigned another one-room unit with six strangers—another couple, like themselves recently married, and a third couple with two teenage boys.

Family in Mess Hall, Manzanar
Mess-hall meals made it difficult to maintain traditional family life. *Courtesy of the Bancroft Library.*

With the camp still under construction, problems abounded. Lack of refrigeration spoiled food so frequently that the "Manzanar runs" became a condition of life. The latrines were shocking to a people whose cultural traditions placed so much emphasis on personal privacy. The wash basin was a long metal trough on a concrete slab, with hot and cold water spigots at intervals. In the same room, twelve toilets were arranged in two rows of six, back-to-back without partitions. At one end of the room was a bank of open showers. The women in particular were appalled at these facilities and devised countless schemes to affect a bit of privacy. One woman had a huge cardboard carton she set up around one of the toilet bowls when her turn came. Even standing, her head barely appeared over the top. She was kind enough to lend it to Riku.

The cold wind off the Sierra rolled up clouds of sand and dust, which poured through the gaping cracks and knotholes in the barracks walls. The new arrivals woke up after their first night with hair and eyebrows covered with a fine powder as though a dirty flour had been sifted over them while they slept. Woody's first priority was to set the younger boys to work nailing tin-can lids over the knotholes and stuffing the cracks with paper. Few were prepared for the cold. Riku had lived in eastern Washington and knew how cold the April winds could be, so the Wakatsukis had all arrived with warm overcoats, but like the other residents they lacked sufficient cold-weather clothing. The army issued surplus World War I woolen clothing, almost all of it too big, and the evacuees shuffled about in their loose trousers, as Jeanne remembered, like "a band of Charlie Chaplins marooned in the California desert."

Even when the food improved, the mess-hall eating was resented, especially by the Issei. They saw the rapid disintegration of their families as their children chose to eat with friends, often hopping from one mess hall to another in search of the best food. Crowded tables made it almost impossible for families to eat together in the cafeteria-style meal system, while the oldest, the sick, and the disabled had food brought to them on trays in their cubicles. Family living was replaced by communal living, and the barracks became mere sleeping quarters. In the daytime the camp population circulated in the open, seeming to Jeanne like "10,000 people on an endless promenade inside the square mile of barbed wire."

In September 1942, Ko Wakatsuki was paroled from Fort Lincoln and sent to Manzanar; his return was a shock to his family. Limping because his feet had been frostbitten in the −30°F weather of North Dakota, he seemed to have aged ten years. Morose and humiliated by his imprisonment and the imputation of disloyalty, he moved in with Riku and the six others in her cubicle. He refused to leave the room and took to drink, making a kind of brandy in a little homemade still. Frequently in a rage, he was a man without a home, a job, or any control over his life—a powerlessness all shared.

For months, anger and humiliation festered in the camp, dividing friends, families, and age groups. Because Japanese-language newspapers were prohibited, rumors filled the communications vacuum, particularly for the Issei. Yet the mess-hall bells rang day after day, calling meetings to demand better food or higher wages (the top pay for evacuee professionals was $19 a month, while Caucasian personnel received $150 to $200 a month), to look into charges of corruption, to plan revolt, to urge common sense, to seek repatriation to Japan, or to prove their loyalty.

Above all, the meetings focused on those Nisei in the Japanese American Citizen's League (JACL) who had been early arrivals and had obtained the best jobs in the camp's administration, or who had most loudly advocated the policy of cooperating with the evacuation as a way of "proving our loyalty," or who looked on the Issei as a declining class that should relinquish its leadership position to the next generation. Rumors flew through the camp that those who were most cooperative with the administration were really *inu*, the Japanese word for "dog"—that is, informers or even traitors. Many Issei willingly believed this, as did many of the Kibei, who were culturally closer to their parents than other Nisei and embittered by their exclusion from the developing relocation program. The JACL, they believed, was destroying the group solidarity that had enabled the Japanese to survive so long in America, a view that even many Nisei came to accept as their detention continued. That fall the Issei and Kibei gradually regained power in the community, and the most prominent members of the JACL were isolated as *inu*. Passions boiled over on December 5, when Fred Tayama, Manzanar's representative to a JACL convention in Salt Lake City, was severely beaten. When a popular Kibei was jailed as a suspected assailant, the community rose to demand his release in what came to be called the "Manzanar Revolt." Thousands of evacuees marched to the administration area, while others attacked the hospital looking for Tayama and other *inu* to "finish the job" the assailant had started. In the ensuing melee, some guards opened fire on the crowd. One young man was killed, and several were wounded; one of them died the next day. But order was finally restored.

The next great issue to strain the community was the loyalty oath controversy. In February 1943 the WRA sent around a questionnaire designed to speed up the clearance process for relocation of evacuees to eastern communities; everyone over the age of seventeen was supposed to fill it out. At the same time, the army was organizing an all-Nisei infantry group and was seeking volunteers from the camps. It was thought that the questionnaire could serve both purposes, so it included two questions originally intended only for Nisei of draft age:

27.nAre you willing to serve in the armed forces of the United States on combat duty, wherever ordered?

28.nWill you swear unqualified allegiance to the United States of America and faithfully defend the United States from any or all attack by foreign or domestic forces, and forswear any form of allegiance or obedience to the Japanese emperor, or to any other foreign government, power or organization?

Naively, administrators thought this would provide the means to weed out "disloyals," who would be sent to one center—Tule Lake, California.

The camp was again thrown into an uproar. Question 28 was absurd for the Issei, who were prohibited by law from becoming American citizens. For the Nisei a "yes" answer could be said to imply that some form of allegiance to Japan had in fact existed. The question was eventually rewritten to read:

28.nWill you swear to abide by the laws of the United States and to take no action which would in any way interfere with the war effort of the United States?

Issei could more easily respond affirmatively to this revised question, but a great deal of confusion and resentment had already been generated. Moreover, the two questions increased the tension between Issei and Nisei, as did the call for volunteers for the all-Nisei army unit. Ko and Woody Wakatsuki carried on a running argument for weeks, then reached a compromise—Woody would answer "yes, yes" but would not volunteer. Meanwhile, embittered elements in the community organized a movement to promote "no, no" answers and exerted pressure

for a mass refusal to cooperate. This debate finally forced Ko Wakatsuki out of his self-imposed isolation. There had never been any question that he would answer "yes, yes" on the questionnaire. If he had any future, he reasoned, it was in the United States, in spite of what he had endured. He was infuriated at the attempt to bully the whole block into a "no, no" vote. Cleaned up and sober, he attended the mess-hall meeting called by the protest organizers and spoke his mind. Murmurs of *inu* passed through the audience until one man actually spoke it aloud. Ko attacked, and the two scuffled, rolling out of the room, where they were finally pulled apart. That night Ko sat up late drinking tea and tearfully singing songs in Japanese, but he no longer remained shut up in the barracks. He had taken his stand.

For all the conflict and pain it caused, the loyalty questionnaire did succeed in speeding up the relocation process. By the spring of 1943 a substantial number of evacuees had relocated, relieving the congestion at the camp. Riku, who had taken a job as a camp dietitian, got the family moved to new quarters that doubled their space. There, a new pattern of life evolved and lasted until the end of the war. Woody and Bill sheetrocked the walls and ceilings. They laid linoleum on the floors and built furniture, shelves, and cabinets from scrap lumber. The barracks became livable. Ko drank much less and puttered outside much more. Like most older Issei men he did not take a job at the camp. Instead, he pruned and cared for the trees in an abandoned apple and pear orchard next to the camp, built and maintained a rock garden around the barracks entrance, painted watercolor landscapes, and hiked to the streams at the foot of the nearby mountains for wood to carve. His resigned manner (*shikata ga nai*) seemed to typify the dominant mood of camp life.

Manzanar essentially became another small American town in this period—the largest, in fact, between Reno and Los Angeles—with schools, churches, police and fire departments, Boy Scouts, softball leagues, and other usual community activities. The younger children were engrossed in schoolwork and recreational activities, while the older ones took jobs. Woody clerked in the community co-op, while Bill led a dance band called the Jive Bombers, which played the current big-band repertoire. That fall Woody was finally drafted, and the next spring Bill and his wife and five more Wakatsuki children relocated to New Jersey, having found jobs in a frozen-food plant there.

Ko and Riku, her mother, and the three youngest children were the only Wakatsukis who remained at Manzanar in 1945. By then the government was urging people to leave. The Supreme Court in late 1944 had finally ruled that their detention was unconstitutional, the army exclusion orders of 1942 had been rescinded and the announcement made that the camp would be closed by the end of the year. Still the Wakatsukis, like so many others, remained. Where would they go? What would they do on the "outside"? Rumor had it that those returning to their former homes had been received with hostility. Even when the war ended in August 1945, a fearful paralysis still gripped thousands in the camp. Ko decided to wait until the government forced him out. With no home, no job, and no word of his boats, he had nothing to look forward to.

That summer the schools at Manzanar closed for good, and the farm operation shut down. Crops were harvested and not replaced; equipment was sold off. The government announced that those who did not leave the camp voluntarily would be assigned dates and taken by bus to the destination of their choice. In October the Wakatsukis learned they were at last scheduled to leave,

and Ko, in one last gesture of defiance, went to the nearby town of Lone Pine and bought a car, determined to leave in style. When the day to leave arrived, the Wakatsukis were able to reject the government buses and drive away with dignity from what had been their prison home. Later that afternoon they arrived in Long Beach where they began the long road back in vacated defense-worker housing.

No record was left of Ko's boats. Moreover, the silver, furniture, and other possessions for which Riku had paid storage fees while the family was held at Manzanar had "unaccountably" been stolen from the warehouse. Riku went back to work in the local cannery, while Ko went from one occupation to another, trying to make his own way independently. Finally, some six years after leaving Manzanar, he took up farming in the Santa Clara Valley near San José. For the rest of his life he was the proud producer of premium strawberries.

While the Wakatsukis were struggling to survive at Manzanar, the old, crowded, and heavily guarded train carrying the Uchidas and 500 others from Tanforan to Topaz sped eastward. As the train departed they stole one last look out of the sides of the drawn curtains, "unutterably saddened" by this furtive peek at all that had meant home to them.

At Delta, Utah, they were transferred to buses for the final leg of their journey into the heart of the barren Sevier Desert, south of the Great Salt Lake. There the vegetation disappeared, and "dry skeletal greasewood" replaced trees and grass. Finally Topaz appeared—"rows and rows of squat, tar-papered barracks sitting sullenly in the white chalky sand." The one-mile-square camp contained forty-two blocks of twelve barracks, each block with a mess hall, latrine, washroom, and laundry. Overnight the army

Topaz Relocation Center
The dust begins to roll across Topaz Relocation Center, located in one of the most isolated sections of the West. As in almost all War Relocation Authority photographs, the barbed-wire fences and guard towers do not appear. *Courtesy of the Bancroft Library.*

had created a city of 8,000, the fifth-largest in Utah, in a desolate wasteland. Army bulldozers had turned the old lake bed into a mass of loose sand; each step sent up swirls of dust. The Uchidas were greeted by friends who "looked like pieces of flour-dusted pastry" and escorted to their new home. Like the Wakatsukis at Manzanar, they were appalled by their new home: a room of twenty by eighteen feet, with four metal army cots, no ceiling, a bare light bulb hanging from the rafters, and a stove not yet installed. Ribbons of powdery dust streamed in through knotholes in walls and floors. A quick inspection by Yo and Kay revealed toilets without seats, no hot water, and no electricity in the latrine or laundry room. In despair they unpacked, sickened by the thought that they were in a concentration camp.

The next morning there was ice in the tea kettle they kept in their room, a reminder that at 4,600 feet in the desert of central Utah, extremes of weather would be com-

mon. Temperatures often began below freezing in the morning, only to rise into the eighties and nineties in the afternoon. Severe dust storms periodically engulfed the camp, the wind reaching furious proportions, churning the dust and blasting it through every opening. Visibility might be no more than five to ten feet, and when Yo was caught in the first of these sudden storms after their arrival, her hair, eyebrows, and eyelashes were turned a chalky white. As winter deepened, temperatures approached 0°F, there were coal shortages, and hot water was available only from 7:00 P.M. to 9:00 P.M. each day. Yo and Kay caught a succession of colds, and upset stomachs and diarrhea afflicted the whole camp for weeks at a time. Not until mid-November were ceilings installed and sheetrock applied to barracks walls, at last making them habitable.

One day Yo Uchida visited the barracks of a Caucasian teacher who, with her husband and child, lived in the administration compound. They occupied one-half of a barracks (three evacuee families were assigned to an equal amount of space), and had carpeted floors, a fully equipped kitchen, separate bedrooms, and a living room. Yo returned to the cubicle she shared with the rest of her family "filled with envy, longing, and resentment."

Despite their despondency, the Uchidas, following Dwight's example, devoted themselves to public service. Kay became involved in planning a nursery-school system for the camp, while Yo got a job teaching in one of the two elementary schools. Classes at first were held in unfinished, completely bare barracks—no supplies, no equipment, no blackboards, no heat; the teachers noted angrily that work still went ahead on the barbed wire fence and guard towers around the camp. Because of the cold, class time was shifted to the afternoon, when the sun provided some warmth, but dust storms were more frequent later in the day and disrupted classes. When the head of the elementary schools reprimanded Yo and the other teachers for dismissing classes during one particularly bad storm, he touched off a near mass resignation. Because of his arrogant and insensitive attitude toward the internees, he was replaced. Finally, a succession of dust storms, rain squalls, and snow, with temperatures under 10°F, forced a closing of the schools in mid-November. They reopened only after sheetrock walls, ceilings, stoves, and a minimum of basic equipment had been installed.

Meanwhile, Dwight and Iku once again made their home a gathering place for their friends and spent countless hours befriending and counseling old and young alike in an effort to counteract the deterioration of family ties caused by camp life. Because of his prominent business background, Dwight soon became involved in camp business affairs. From the beginning he was chairman

of the board of directors of the Consumers Cooperative and president of the Cooperative Congress, which operated such services as the canteen, barber shop, radio repair shop, movie houses, and dry-goods store. Within a few months he was also on the camp's judicial commission and its arbitration committee and had been asked to run for city manager. He enjoyed being busy and helping people adjust to camp life, as well as participating in camp social affairs. He was always happy, for example, to sing his "Song of Topaz," an adaptation of his "Missoula Camp Song" that seemed to delight his Issei friends.

At Christmas many evacuees were touched to receive gifts from strangers all over the United States in response to an appeal from the American Friends Service Committee. Still, Yo and Kay were miserable in the bleak concentration camp and by the end of December were determined to relocate. Many of their friends had relocated or gone to school somewhere in the East, and the young women's sense of imprisonment was stifling. Yo eagerly followed the efforts of educators to get colleges and universities across the country to accept students from the camps, despite the fact that the army and navy often refused to continue their training or research programs at institutions enrolling Japanese Americans.

Growing controversy within the camp created additional anxiety in the Uchida family. Malcontents began to harass Dwight about the operation of the cooperative. In addition, he often attended meetings of Issei and Nisei until late at night, trying to conciliate and arbitrate the differences of contending factions. In February 1943 the loyalty questionnaire triggered even greater anger and bitterness. A pro-Japan faction arose, made up primarily of tough, arrogant Kibei and Issei who began to intimidate those trying to be cooperative. The head of the art school

Evacuees at Fence
Over 700,000 Californians served in the armed forces in World War II and made the difficult adjustment to peacetime after 1945. Among them were thousands of young Japanese Americans whose families spent the war in American concentration camps. Here evacuees watch Nisei volunteers depart from Topaz Relocation Center for Army service. Army personnel seldom acknowledged the contradiction of soliciting volunteers and drafting Japanese Americans for military service from families held behind barbed wire. *Courtesy of the Bancroft Library.*

was beaten one night, and on another occasion a church minister was assaulted by masked men wielding lead pipes. Dwight was accosted by two men from the pro-Japan faction and denounced as "obsequious" to the white administrative staff. The anger in the camp was kept boiling when a soldier shot and killed a sixty-three-year-old man near the fence surrounding the camp. The guard claimed the old man had tried to crawl under the fence and get away, but the evidence indicated otherwise.

Relief for the Uchidas came in the summer of 1943. In May, Kay got word that she had been appointed as an assistant in a nursery school run by Mount Holyoke College and could spend the summer at a Quaker study center in Pennsylvania. Shortly thereafter, Yo received a full graduate scholarship to Smith College and an opportunity to spend the summer with friends in Connecticut before school began. By the end of May both daughters were on their way east.

Not long after Yo and Kay departed, a

stink bomb was thrown into the Uchidas' room, and the threat led the camp administration to arrange the relocation of Dwight and Iku to Salt Lake City; by the summer of 1943, the Uchidas were once again on the "outside." They eventually joined their daughters in New York where Dwight, having lost all his Mitsui retirement benefits, began his long road back as a packer in the shipping department of a church organization. When he returned to California after the war, Dwight found work in a dry-cleaning business owned by a friend. Once a prominent business executive, he remained there until his second retirement, still the generous, community-spirited person he had always been.

Like the great majority of Japanese Americans incarcerated during World War II, the Wakatsukis and Uchidas lived through their ordeal with determination and dignity. The fathers, Dwight Uchida and Ko Wakatsuki, each in his own way, seemed determined to survive—to prove the rightness of his decision, made long before, to make America his home. And despite the painful lack of privacy, the personal loss, and the humiliation of having their loyalty questioned, the two mothers struggled successfully to make homes for their families out of horse stalls and flimsy tar-paper barracks. Forcibly removed to the most desolate regions of the country, the families clung to cultural traditions that gave them the strength of spirit and the endurance to prove their loyalty to the United States. This was their contribution to the war effort, and to all Americans.

CHAPTER TWENTY-THREE

WORLD WAR II: THE BEGINNING OF A NEW ERA

The Wakatsukis and the Uchidas returned to a California far different from the one they left in 1942. The outbreak of World War II in 1939 brought the economic recovery Franklin D. Roosevelt's New Dealers had struggled to achieve since 1933, as war orders lifted the depression. Then, America's entry into the war following Japan's attack on Pearl Harbor turned the nation's economy to war production on a scale that profoundly affected the state's economy. By 1945, as historian Gerald Nash has pointed out, the war had speeded up the development of the west and ushered in the "post-industrial" era, in the process changing California from a resource-based, dependent section into the "pace-setter for the nation." The need of war industries for workers also triggered another wave of migration that soon made California the most populous state in the Union, faced with the serious social consequences of such growth.

WAR IN EUROPE

When Hitler's troops marched into Poland in September 1939, Californians on the whole were engaged in the production of goods unrelated to war. Agriculture, mining, fishing, textiles, metalworking, and making furniture and movies still comprised much of their economy, along with tourism and real estate development. On the other hand, the state had a significant potential for war work. Its oil, aircraft, shipbuilding, auto, and tire industries—as well as its amazingly productive agricultural system—were capable of rapid expansion and conversion to military use. In addition, California's wide variety of terrain was well adapted to training troops for battle almost anywhere in the world, and major bases at San Diego and Mare Island in San Francisco Bay facilitated a rapid naval expansion.

The war brought a flood of war orders and military spending to California. With institution of the military draft in 1940, the army expanded its already substantial training facilities, such as Fort Ord near Monterey and Camp Roberts near Paso Robles. The marine corps began to construct a major west coast base at Camp Pendleton near Oceanside, which proved to be ideal for training in amphibious warfare; and, as relations with Japan deteriorated, the navy expanded its California facilities as well.

One of the first California industries to feel the impact of the war was shipbuilding, a result of Germany's frighteningly successful submarine war on British shipping. Hunting in "wolf packs," German U-boats sank hundreds of thousands of tons of Allied shipping early in the war, threatening Britain's survival. By 1941 orders for transports had revived private shipbuilding in Los Angeles and the San Francisco Bay Area. Similarly, steel, chemicals, textiles, machine tools, and agricultural products all began to respond to the war's stimulus, while the state's young aircraft industry nearly quintupled in size. Tremendous change was therefore well under way by the end of 1941, as employment expanded, wages rose, and thousands of workers made the shift from service-related jobs to production work. The depression was over.

THE IMPACT OF PEARL HARBOR

If the impact of the war in Europe on California was surprising, the effect of Pearl Harbor was phenomenal. United as they had hardly ever been in war, Americans turned their nation into an awesome war production machine; and, because of the nature of the war, California assumed a key role. World War II was far-flung, with major battlefields in western Europe, the Soviet Union, Africa, and the western Pacific islands. The need for planes and ships to move personnel and equipment seemed limitless. In the Pacific, island-hopping tactics made amphibious warfare essential, and the attack on Pearl Harbor and the battles of the Coral Sea and Midway in 1942 demonstrated that the naval war would be dominated by aircraft carriers. Moreover, modern warfare required the development and use of highly technical communications and electronic equipment. Cali-

fornia possessed the industries necessary to meet these needs and had long-standing close relations with both the Army and the Navy. Consequently, the federal government poured some 40 billion dollars into California—more than ten percent of the nation's wartime expenditures.

The state's geography and location also affected its contribution to the war effort. Its deserts proved ideal for training the tank corps that went into action in North Africa in 1942. Its beaches provided the training ground for thousands of soldiers and marines sent ashore on Pacific islands. Its climate permitted year-round training of Air Force personnel. A huge expansion of military training facilities followed Pearl Harbor. Fort Ord became a city of 50,000. The navy took over Treasure Island in San Francisco Bay and vastly expanded its other facilities in the Bay Area, as well as at San Diego and the Terminal Island installation in Los Angeles. Air Force bases up and down the state were expanded, and many new ones were established. March Field, McClellan, Mather, Travis, and George air force bases became major establishments. Naturally, California became the staging area and depot for the war against Japan. Ships, planes, tanks, trucks, personnel, and incredible amounts of food and matériel were all funneled through the state to Pacific battlegrounds. Almost all the troops sent to the Pacific were processed through huge staging facilities such as Camp Stoneman near Pittsburg and Antioch, while navy and marine corps personnel made their way to assignments in Pacific war areas through California.

Meanwhile the state's chief ports, San Francisco, Los Angeles, and Oakland, hummed with activity. Strikes were a thing of the past as longshoremen and military personnel worked night and day. It could be dangerous work and led to one of the state's worst wartime tragedies, at Port Chicago on

Suisun Bay east of San Francisco. There, on the night of July 17, 1944, a ship that had been fully loaded with ammunition from the nearby naval ordnance depot exploded with a tremendous blast, killing 323 people, demolishing 350 nearby homes, and breaking windows thirty-five miles away.

THE RISE OF THE AIRCRAFT INDUSTRY

One of the most spectacular effects of the war was to turn aircraft construction in California into a giant industry that became a critical part of the state's postwar economy. Until the war, several factors made the state's fledgling aircraft industry weak and unstable. Almost from the first, airplane manufacturers were dependent for their survival on a wildly fluctuating government demand for military aircraft. Moreover, a rapidly changing technology made for a high rate of obsolescence and unusually high engineering costs, compounding the problems caused by an extremely long design-manufacturing cycle. Consequently, the industry developed, one might say, with its share of ups and downs.

California's airframe industry (motors were built in the East and Midwest and shipped to California assembly plants) began as early as 1912 when Glenn Martin formed a company in southern California, followed soon after by the Loghead and Christofferson companies near San Francisco. Their production was negligible, however, and even World War I, during which Martin moved to the East, did not stimulate much growth. In fact, most California aircraft companies failed in the postwar depression, when the government dumped wartime planes on the market.

A turning point came in 1920, when Martin's chief engineer, Donald Douglas, formed his own company and located in southern California. The region had several attrac-

tions: the climate permitted year-round testing and minimal building maintenance, investment capital was available, it was a nonunion area with lower wages, and nearby military airfields were an attraction. Douglas was soon building planes for the army and navy and, in 1924, scored a major success when he built the single-engine biplanes that made the first round-the-world flight. In 1926 he organized the Douglas Aircraft Company, the first to succeed in California. That same year Allan and Malcolm Loghead (whose original company had gone out of business in 1921) joined with John K. Northrup to form the Lockheed Aircraft Company, a phonetic spelling of the name being deemed necessary to eliminate mispronunciations. A year later, the firm Claude Ryan had organized in San Diego achieved fame by building Charles Lindbergh's *Spirit of St. Louis*, the first airplane to fly nonstop from New York to Paris.

Douglas, Ryan, and Lockheed all designed passenger planes, since government mail contracts promoted the development of commercial air travel, but military construction remained basic to their survival. Between 1927 and 1937, for example, ninety-one percent of Douglas's sales were military. In 1935, though, the company introduced the DC-3, one of the most successful commercial aircraft ever built. Valued for its economy of operation and stability in flight, the DC-3 captured ninety-five percent of the passenger airline business by 1939. This was a growing business, too, despite the depression. New major airline companies—United, Trans-World (TWA), and Pan American—had developed through mergers in the late 1920s and early 1930s and were rapidly expanding the air-travel business. Favorable conditions attracted other aircraft manufacturers to California. In 1935 Consolidated Aircraft Corporation moved from Buffalo, New York, to San Diego, and in 1936 North

PORT CHICAGO AND THE MARE ISLAND MUTINY

On the night of July 17, 1944, while sailors loaded munitions aboard the *E. A. Bryan* and the *Quinalt Victory*, a massive explosion jolted U.S. Naval Magazine Port Chicago (now part of Concord Naval Weapons Depot) on Suisun Bay. The blast atomized the *Bryan*, broke the *Quinalt* in half, demolished the naval base, damaged the adjacent town, and killed 320 men. More than 200 of the dead were black seamen from segregated units commanded by white officers, standard policy in U.S. armed services during World War II. After reassignment to Mare Island Naval Depot near Vallejo, survivors received orders to resume loading munitions. Most—including some commended for courage in response to the Port Chicago tragedy—refused, citing lack of training, dangerous conditions, and sheer terror; fifty eventually faced mutiny charges and court martial.

The trial at Treasure Island Naval Station lasted thirty-three days; Admiral Hugo S. Osterhaus presided over a seven-member board that acted as judge and jury; Lieutenant Gerald E. Veltman headed a six-officer defense team; and Lieutenant-Commander James F. Coakley, later Alameda County District Attorney, acted as chief prosecutor. Throughout the proceedings, Veltman challenged the prosecution on the validity of the mutiny charge, the admissibility of evidence, Coakley's harassment of defendants, and additional points, all without success. Defendants' testimony revealed that officers organized munitions-loading contests between their crews, bet on results (and punished them if they lost), condoned other hazardous procedures, and exhibited blatant racism. Despite the complexity of the case, its fifty defendants, and its 1,400-page transcript, the trial board reached a verdict on October 24 during its lunch break; it found all of the accused guilty and sentenced each to fifteen years in prison and a dishonorable discharge. Subsequent appeals involving Thurgood Marshall, who attended the trial and filed a brief for the NAACP Legal Defense Fund, Secretary of the Navy James Forrestal, First Lady Eleanor Roosevelt, and future presidential candidate Captain Harold Stassen resulted in penalty reductions. In January 1946, sentences were set aside, and the seamen returned to active duty.

The defense did not make segregation a major issue at the trial. Nevertheless, the Port Chicago incident and others like it—on Guam in 1944 and at the Port Hueneme, California, Construction Battalion (Seabee) base in 1945—focused embarrassing attention on rampant Jim Crowism in the Navy and provoked criticism. In response, the Navy began to eliminate segregationist policies, starting with Great Lakes Naval Training Center in September 1944 and followed by all training facilities and duty assignments. In February 1946, the Navy Secretary ordered an end to racial discrimination, well before Harry S. Truman's presidential decree desegregated all branches of the military in July 1948.

The "mutineers," about a dozen of whom survive, eventually were discharged from the service "under conditions less than honorable," but lives went on, despite convictions that stained their records and deprived them of veterans' benefits. During the summer of 1991, California Congressmen Pete Stark and Ron Dellums sponsored legislation authorizing the Secretary of the Navy to reexamine the cases; early in 1994, the Navy upheld its original decision. (WAB)

American Aviation moved to Los Angeles from the East. By 1939 more than half the aircraft workers in the nation were employed by southern California firms.

The expansion of the state's aircraft industry after Pearl Harbor is one of the extraordinary events of the war years. A massive infusion of federal funds, some $10 billion, increased employment from 20,000 in 1939 to 280,000 by 1944. When President Roosevelt called for production of 50,000 planes per year at the start of the war, people scoffed, but the industry built nearly 100,000 planes in 1943 alone. Lockheed, which built 37 planes in 1937, produced more than 18,000 between 1941 and 1945. Concentrated in Los Angeles, Orange, and San Diego counties, the giant new industry became the base of the aerospace industry that developed after the war.

SHIPBUILDING

California's shipbuilding industry, traditionally centered in the San Francisco Bay region, underwent a similar expansion. Employment in state shipyards soared from 4,000 to 260,000 as the federal government poured more than $5 billion into the state for ships of all kinds. Private and navy yards in Sausalito, Vallejo, Alameda, Oakland, and San Francisco built hundreds of transport, cargo, amphibious, and naval craft in a huge burst of activity. Most impressive was the creation of a great new facility at Richmond by the ubiquitous Henry J. Kaiser. This shipyard relied on all the techniques of management, engineering, design, and construction technology that Kaiser had developed in his years of directing the construction of such massive projects as Hoover Dam, and the venture brought assembly-line methods to the shipbuilding industry. Amazing production records were achieved at Richmond. The yard built one-fourth of all the Liberty ships

produced in the United States during the war, and, by prefabricating huge sections, ships were built in record time. When the war began, these rugged, dependable freighters took nearly 250 days to construct. Kaiser brought the time down to twenty-five days and set a record of eight days with construction of the *Robert E. Perry*. The Kaiser shipyard was responsible for a soaring increase in Richmond's population, from 20,000 to more than 100,000, causing serious housing problems; Kaiser took the lead in constructing low-cost housing to relieve the strain of such growth. He also pioneered the concept of prepaid health care by organizing the Kaiser Foundation Health Plan for his workers.

Anxious for a ready supply of steel for his wartime industries, Kaiser also orchestrated the establishment of the state's first integrated blast furnace and steel-rolling mill at Fontana, fifty miles east of Los Angeles. With a capacity of 700,000 tons per year when completed in 1942, the Fontana plant increased the state's steel production by seventy percent. At the same time, Bethlehem Steel and U.S. Steel plants in the San Francisco area were substantially expanded, and the dependence of the state's war industries on steel shipped from distant eastern plants was significantly reduced.

OTHER WAR INDUSTRIES AND AGRICULTURE

Conversion of California industry to war production was thoroughgoing. Oil production increased by fifty percent between 1941 and 1945, as the state produced most of the high-test aviation fuel and fuel oils necessary for the war against Japan. The state's rubber industry developed plants to produce synthetic rubber when Japan overran Southeast Asia and shut off America's supplies of natural rubber. Surprisingly, synthetic rubber

Richmond Shipyard at Night
At Henry J. Kaiser's Richmond shipyard, whole sections of ships that had been prefabricated on shore were lifted onto the ways by huge cranes, which worked around the clock like great mechanical spiders. The production of Liberty ships at Richmond was an important factor in winning the fight against Hitler's submarine "wolfpacks" during World War II. *Courtesy of the Bancroft Library.*

proved to have qualities superior to natural rubber for many important uses and became a permanent industry in the state. Many other state industries were converted to war production—from radios to electronic devices such as radar and sonar; from furniture to plywood subchasers and torpedo boats; from autos to tanks. Thousands of new plants produced amphibious craft, airplane parts, munitions, and electrical equipment. Heavy industry became a major part of the California economy, tripling the industrial labor force.

Increased prosperity and population growth, plus government purchases for troops being trained in California and for shipment overseas gave most types of agriculture a mighty boost. Dairy products, fruits,

nuts, vegetables, cotton, and livestock all increased two to three times in value, and the overall value of agricultural products rose from $623 million in 1939 to $1.75 billion in 1945. California's position as the leading agricultural state in the Union was solidified in the process.

The chief wartime problem in agriculture was a shortage of harvest labor. More than 700,000 Californians entered military service, the booming war industries soaked up the Okies, and the removal and detention of the state's Japanese all left California growers with a sudden, drastic labor shortage. Convicts, high-school students, housewives, and prisoners of war were pressed into service to bring in the crops until grower complaints finally persuaded the federal government to arrange a harvest labor importation program with Mexico in 1942. Under this program, the United States agreed to provide transportation, health care, decent housing, a minimum wage, and unemployment pay in case of a work shortage to Mexicans who would sign up to work in California's fields, far supassing benefits available to domestic agricultural workers. This arrangement was the origin of the *bracero* program, which reached a modest peak of 26,000 workers in 1944 and which in the postwar years became a major factor in the state's harvest labor picture.

SCIENCE

When the war came, California had developed one of the nation's foremost scientific communities in its institutions of higher education. The California Institute of Technology, Stanford University, and the University of California, especially at Berkeley and Los Angeles, had faculties and laboratories that constituted a significant scientific resource. Turned to military work, they made important contributions to the war effort, developing, for example, rocket-assist systems for aircraft and new torpedoes that homed in on sounds emanating from their targets. In addition, most campuses of the state's universities carried on sizable officer- and specialist-training programs for the various branches of the armed forces.

Most important, however, was the role of the University of California in developing the atomic bomb. During the 1930s Berkeley professor of physics Ernest O. Lawrence developed the cyclotron, or atom smasher, and synthesized new elements and isotopes, such as neptunium, uranium 235, and plutonium, that were important in nuclear research. His achievements attracted bright young scientists to Berkeley—among them J. Robert Oppenheimer—whose work put the university

in the forefront of atomic science. In 1942, fearful that German scientists might be developing an atomic bomb, the U.S. government embarked on an urgent, top-secret program for the same purpose—the Manhattan Project. The government recruited the free world's best minds for the project and—at a laboratory in Los Alamos, New Mexico, managed by the university—teams of scientists under Oppenheimer's leadership finally made the first atomic bomb. Use of the bomb on the Japanese cities of Hiroshima and Nagasaki in August 1945 ended World War II and ushered in a whole new age for the world.

WOMEN IN THE WAR

The bombing of Pearl Harbor created a unity and commitment to war lacking before 1941, and after the initial shock, fear, and chagrin of the attack, Californians turned to the task of winning the war. Thousands changed occupations, leaving low-paying jobs for work in shipyards, airplane assembly plants, and hundreds of other war-related industries, while the makeup of the labor force changed markedly. Women went to work in large numbers, taking over production jobs heretofore dominated by men, and moved into types of employment that had rarely accepted them before. "Rosie the Riveter" became an important symbol of this change.

The war proved to be an important turning point for California women. As men entered the armed forces, employment opportunities for women were greatly expanded, and many gained experience in managing family finances and property as well. Six million women entered the nation's work force during the war, a large percentage of them attracted to jobs in California shipyards and especially aircraft plants, where women made up over forty percent of the work force. Many more took jobs as chemists, en-

Women Aircraft Workers
Women workers assemble aircraft fuselage sections in a Los Angeles area plant during World War II. The war produced a major shift of women into industrial jobs. While often displaced by returning veterans when the war ended, many women gained a self-confidence through their war work that affected postwar society. *Courtesy of the Los Angeles Public Library.*

gineers, railroad workers, lawyers, and journalists and in expanding service industries such as banking, retail sales, and education. Barriers that had always denied women access to a wide range of employment were destroyed. For the first time, women enjoyed occupational mobility and many moved to higher-paying war-related jobs. African American women in particular benefited from the opportunity to leave low-paying jobs and the number in domestic service declined from fifty-five percent to forty percent. Early in the war employers often refused to employ blacks in war work and unions would not admit them to membership. But by organizing to get help from the federal Fair Employment Practices Committee, African American men and women forced significant changes. By 1944 blacks were over seven percent of the war industries work force. In the process African American women workers became leaders in securing state funds for child-care services and the adoption of the state's first Fair Employment Practices Commission.

While there was a severe labor shortage in war industries, there was also a high turnover rate. Lack of housing, food services, and transportation placed unique pressures on women workers, many of whom tried to continue traditional responsibilities as homemakers and mothers. These problems contributed to turnover rates of 100 percent and higher per year in some plants. Moreover, when the war ended many women workers were displaced by returning veterans.

There is another side to the impact of the war on the home front. In 1991 Robert and Jane Easton published *Love and War*, a touching glimpse into the loneliness, fear, and bravery of those left behind as well as of those going off to war. In the wartime letters of one couple, *Love and War* is a reminder that millions of wives, mothers, sisters, and girlfriends made their own contributions, raising families and just being "home" to the nearly 15 million men and women in the armed services during World War II. It is also a highly personal record of the impact of such a catastrophe on the individual caught up in the whirlwind of total war.

REMOVAL OF THE JAPANESE AMERICANS

The removal of Japanese Americans such as the Wakatsukis and Uchidas from the West Coast and their detention in concentration camps has been called "our worst wartime mistake," a blunder resulting from fear, confusion, and racial prejudice. The bombing of Pearl Harbor found Lieutenant General John L. DeWitt in charge of the Fourth Army and Western Defense Command in San Francisco. A supply specialist with almost no combat experience, he was near retirement and determined not to suffer the fate of his Hawaii contemporary, Lieutenant General Walter C. Short, whose career ended with his failure to prepare an adequate defense of Pearl Harbor. But DeWitt almost immediately came under pressure to act decisively, as the bombing ignited anti-Japanese sentiment and a growing movement to solve the "problem" of the Japanese Americans by removing them. Few opposed such action, and even representatives of the Japanese American Citizen's League (JACL) concluded that to resist would only reinforce the pervasive stereotype of the Japanese as disloyal.

Although at first opposed to removal, DeWitt, under pressure from the army's Provost Marshal General, Allen W. Gullion, and the chief of the Aliens Division, Karl R. Bendetsen, finally agreed, recommending on February 14, 1942, that "Japanese and other subversive persons" be removed from the coast. In a much-quoted statement, he noted that "the very fact that no sabotage has taken place to date is a disturbing and continuing indication that such an action will be taken."

DeWitt's certification that removal was a military necessity was quickly followed by presidential approval of Executive Order 9066, which authorized the secretary of war to prescribe military areas from which any and all persons could be excluded. The secretary delegated this authority to General DeWitt, whose March removal order placed almost all west coast residents of Japanese ancestry in assembly centers by June 1942. Ironically, any threat of Japanese attack, real or imagined, had disappeared by then because of Japan's losses in the naval battles of the Coral Sea in May and at Midway in June. Still, the evacuation continued, seemingly having taken on a life of its own. In the next few months the evacuees were transferred to ten "relocation centers" spread from eastern California to Arkansas. In a critical decision, the War Relocation Authority (WRA) set up to administer these centers, made relocation, or dispersal, of the Japanese Americans its primary objective.

Within two years, more than a quarter of the evacuees, mostly young Nisei like the Uchidas' and the Wakatsukis' children, had been granted "indefinite leave" to midwest and east coast communities. The program ended only when the U.S. Supreme Court, in the *Endo* case, ruled that detention of Japanese American citizens in the camps was unconstitutional. But when the war ended in August 1945, nearly one-third of the evacuees (about 44,000) remained in the camps, many of them still frightened by the lingering hostility in California to their return. A large number of them had to be evicted when the camps closed at the end of the year.

CONSEQUENCES OF THE EVACUATION

The removal of the Japanese Americans from the West Coast in 1942 raised fundamental questions of civil rights, since two–thirds of the evacuees were citizens. In a series of cases, the *Hirabayashi, Korematsu,* and *Endo* cases, the U.S. Supreme Court handed down decisions upholding the removal that trouble many legal scholars and historians to this day. In the *Hirabayashi* (1943) and *Korematsu* (1944) cases, the Court refused to question the judgment of military officials on the existence of a military necessity (despite the evidence that DeWitt's orders were based on prejudiced racial views), thus condoning restriction of the liberties of Japanese American citizens solely on the basis of race. In a famous dissent, Justice Frank Murphy stated that the exclusion orders had gone "over the very brink of constitutional power . . . into the ugly abyss of racism." Al-

though the Court decided in the *Endo* case that detention of citizens in the relocation centers was unconstitutional, it evaded the question of whether the government had exceeded its war powers in the evacuation.

The precedents established in these decisions have been the most troubling. As Justice Robert Jackson wrote in his *Korematsu* case dissent:

> Much is said of the danger to liberty from the Army program for deporting and detaining these citizens of Japanese extraction. But a judicial construction of the due process clause that will sustain this order is a far more subtle blow to liberty. . . . The principle then lies about like a loaded weapon ready for the hand of any authority that can bring forward a plausible claim of an urgent need.

Forty years later Fred Korematsu's conviction for violating the evacuation order was vacated in the U.S. District Court of San Francisco; Judge Marilyn Hall Patel stated that the evacuation and internment had been "based upon unsubstantiated facts, distortions and misrepresentations of at least one military commander whose views were affected by racism." Using the Freedom of Information Act, Korematsu's attorneys demonstrated that the government had suppressed evidence that a "military necessity" no longer existed when the evacuation took place. Gordon Hirabayashi's conviction was reversed on similar grounds in 1987.

The removal of Japanese Americans in 1942 also illustrated the convenience of bureaucratic euphemisms to cover embarrassing administrative actions. The forced removal of 112,000 people, two-thirds of them citizens, because of their race became an "evacuation." What amounted to concentration camps, American-style, became "relocation centers," and the Nisei, American citizens, became, in army communications, "non-aliens."

The economic cost of the removal also was never resolved. Forced from their homes and businesses, often with only hours' notice, Japanese Americans disposed of property at fire-sale rates, left possessions and property in the hands of unreliable friends or acquaintances, and frequently, like the Wakatsukis, were robbed of everything while locked up in WRA camps. Their losses were estimated by the San Francisco Federal Reserve Bank at $400 million, yet Congress denied them disaster grants or long-term, low-interest loans to aid in their economic rehabilitation. Not until 1948 was the Japanese American Evacuation Claims Act adopted by Congress, and even then claims were limited to $2,500 each. Congress appropriated only $38 million dollars to settle all claims, less than 10 cents on the dollar. Many years later, in 1980, Congress established the Commission on Wartime Relocation and Internment of Civilians, which once again took up the matter of compensation for economic loss resulting from the evacuation. The Commission reported in 1982 that the removal had been a "grave injustice" resulting from "race prejudice, war hysteria and a failure of political leadership," but it took another six years before Congress approved compensation for the wrong. In 1988 President Reagan issued a formal apology to Japanese Americans and signed legislation granting each surviving internee $20,000. It took another year and a half for Congress to fund these grants.

Finally, there is probably no measure of the human cost of the relocation. Who can measure its effect on Ko Wakatsuki and his family? The great majority of Japanese Americans accepted it and cooperated, like the Wakatsukis and Uchidas, in the spirit of *shikata ga nai* and in the hope that their loyalty to the United States would be proven.

But the sense of loss, invasion of privacy, destruction of family, and humiliation was suppressed, not to surface until many years later. Only when their children and grandchildren, influenced by the civil rights movement of the 1960s, began to question why the removal was not resisted did Nisei begin to express themselves: Jeanne Wakatsuki Huston wrote *Farewell to Manzanar* nearly thirty years after the fact, and Yoshiko Uchida wrote *Desert Exile* twenty years after her removal to Tanforan and Topaz.

In spite of their wartime removal and internment, Japanese Americans have had substantial success in postwar America. Japanese Americans as a group have a higher education rate and lower crime and juvenile delinquency rates than any other ethnic group in America; opportunities for employment, especially in white-collar jobs, are much improved. By 1970 the median family income of Japanese Americans exceeded the national average by $3,000 per year. Californians have also elected Japanese Americans to the state legislature and Congress, a further sign that perhaps the prewar prejudices are fading away.

Several factors contributed to this progress. The war record of the 105th Battalion and the 442nd Regimental Combat Team, segregated Nisei infantry units, was sensational, contributing, as JACL leaders had hoped, to widespread public respect and acceptance. A reawakened concern for civil liberties in the 1950s and 1960s focused attention on the injustice of 1942, and perhaps a feeling of national guilt over the horrifying atomic bombing of Hiroshima (Ko Wakatsuki's hometown) and Nagasaki contributed to the decline of anti-Asian prejudice. Changing political conditions and the American occupation of Japan diluted the strains of prejudice. Reacting to the new national mood, in 1952 Congress at long last removed the prohibition against naturalization that had made Ko Wakatsuki and Dwight Uchida enemy aliens.

OTHER MINORITIES AND THE WAR

Two million new residents arrived in California from 1941 to 1945, and for the first time a significant percentage of them were African Americans. Shipyard work, especially in Los Angeles, Oakland, and Richmond, attracted southern blacks in large numbers, as did new military installations. In 1940 African Americans were 1.8 percent of the California population, a figure that nearly quadrupled during the war. Until World War II blacks had generally escaped serious racial oppression in California; their numbers were small, and other racial groups, most notably Asians, were the chief targets of discrimination. But their increasing numbers during the war generated increased hostility. Housing discrimination in particular meant the formation of small ghettos in Los Angeles, San Francisco, Oakland, and Richmond, beginning a cycle of rising black population, rising white racism, discrimination in housing and employment, and the ghettoization of significant parts of the state's major cities. From 1945 on, as war production wound down, whites moved out of war industries to peacetime jobs, leaving African Americans more highly concentrated in the soon-to-be-closed war plants. When the war ended and plants closed, blacks found themselves out in the cold. The good peacetime jobs were filled and they were again at the bottom of the hiring list. Unemployment pay and welfare became the chief refuge for a great many. The foundation for the explosive Watts riots of the 1960s may well have been laid during World War II.

Racial conflict was pronounced in Los Angeles, where war work, educational opportunity, and other benefits attracted a sizable Mexican migration. Mexicans, like African Americans, were subjected to discrimination in housing and employment and were limited to residence in the *barrios* of East Los Angeles. In the early 1940s many Mexican American youths adopted a distinctive style of dress—long coats with wide lapels; pants with extremely pegged cuffs, full-draped at the knees and pleated at the waist; and long, well-greased hair. They came to be called "zoot-suiters" and "pachucos." Newly arrived war workers from the South and Southwest and military personnel, mostly sailors, in Los Angeles found the "zooters" offensive. In the summer of 1943, violence erupted in which carloads of sailors, encouraged by crowds of other Anglos, ran down zoot-suiters and stripped and beat them. In retaliation, groups of "pachucos" beat up unwary sailors on the streets of the city. It was a nasty reminder of the state's record of racial contention and called attention to the serious problems Hispanics faced in California. The Office of the Coordinator of Inter-American Affairs (CIAA) under Nelson Rockefeller subsequently devloped the most comprehensive program to deal with Hispanic problems devised during the war.

Nevertheless, the experience of Mexican American servicemen and war workers brought, for many, a determination to move into the mainstream of American society. The war enabled large numbers of Chicano workers to move from unskilled to semiskilled and skilled labor jobs. In 1930 8 percent of males were in semiskilled positions; in 1950 the number was 21.6 percent. Similarly, in 1930, 13.6 percent of Chicano women workers held clerical positions; in 1950, 23.7 percent were so employed. A growing Mexican American middle class resulted that developed new community organizations and set the stage for participation in the civil rights movement of the 1960s.

Ironically, while Japanese Americans were forcibly removed from California and detained, conditions improved for other Asians after Pearl Harbor. Chinese, Filipinos, and Asian Indians, whose native lands were now allies of the United States, experienced greater acceptance and found increased job opportunities in fields previously closed to them. Chinese, in particular, began a movement into professional and technical positions that continues today. One-third of Chinese professionals, for example, are women. This was translated into action with removal of immigration quotas, the end of laws barring naturalization, and elimination of other prewar restrictions. The Immigration Act of 1965, in fact, led to the immigration of over a million Asians in the 1970s and 1980s.

COMMUNITY PROBLEMS

Wartime migration meant that population growth was heavily concentrated in parts of the state where aircraft and shipbuilding predominated and where the largest military installations were located. San Diego's aircraft and naval facilities produced a population increase from 203,000 in 1940 to 362,000 by the end of the war. Shipbuilding nearly quadrupled the populations of both Vallejo and Richmond. Towns near air force bases, army training camps, and major processing centers experienced similar growth, and with it came difficult local community problems.

A shortage of housing plagued the state's cities during the war years. Material and labor shortages caused by the war substantially reduced construction. Yet the needs of new migrants for shelter were pressing. Some companies built low-cost, dormitory-style, barracks-like buildings near new war plants, providing minimal housing for their workers. Thousands of low-cost units were built by the National Housing Authority (NHA) and many large tracts of single-family working-class homes were constructed by private builders under Federal Housing Authority (FHA) programs. The government, however, made little effort to prevent racial segregation in the allocation of housing by local officials. Consequently, the wartime federal housing program accelerated the creation of ethnic "ghettos," particularly in the shipyard cities of Oakland and Richmond. Elsewhere, prefabricated houses and trailers helped to ease the shortage, but supply never caught up with demand and the war years were characterized by the crowding of two and three families into single-family homes and apartments. The wartime migration also stretched related municipal services such as sewers, water, gas, electricity, and telephones to the limit, while almost all highway construction was essentially suspended and street repairs indefinitely delayed. One congressional investigator called the conditions in Richmond the "worst in the country."

California's reputation for a superior public school system suffered because of wartime population growth. In 1940 Richmond's schools had 3,000 students. In 1943 they had 35,000. Unable to adapt immediately to such rapidly swelling student populations, schools were forced onto double-session schedules with half their students attending a morning session and half an afternoon session. Although parents expressed concern that the quality of education would suffer, the practice seemed permanent in some metropolitan areas as the educational system faced even greater population growth after the war.

Waiting in lines to board crowded buses and streetcars, or at the local meat counter, became a part of daily life in wartime California. Grocery store shelves were quickly depleted of scarce items and most Californians had their first experience of rationing. A variety of necessities, such as meat, dairy products, sugar, and gasoline, were subject to rationing, and the ration-coupon book became an important household item. Thousands of families planted backyard vegetable gardens at the government's urging to "grow your own for victory." For the highly mobile Californians, the rationing of gasoline involved the greatest sacrifice and curtailed travel sharply. Although a black market in gasoline ration stamps arose, the vast majority of Californians saw adherence to the rules as a part of the war effort and, through carpooling and careful planning, managed their transportation needs on their allotted share.

Californians not directly employed in war work found other ways to contribute to the war effort. Hollywood actors and actresses, including a latter-day politician named Ronald Reagan, made training and propaganda films for the government, while others worked for the Red Cross and the United Services Organization (USO). The USO was perhaps most fondly remembered by World War II veterans for its canteens, which offered refreshments and dancing with local volunteer girls. At the Hollywood canteen a volunteer dancing partner might turn out to be a famous movie star!

Civil defense was another field in which Californians could show their support for the war. Volunteer "block wardens" inspected their territories for blackout violators, while other citizens joined aircraft-spotting units. Long after any real threat of a Japanese attack had passed, if one ever existed, such activities continued to give thousands of people a sense of contributing to the war effort.

PREPARING FOR PEACE

The year 1944 marked the beginning of the end of World War II. Soviet armies, which had stopped Hilter's invasion of Russia at Stalingrad in 1943, began their relentless march from the east on the Third Reich.

The Americans and British, under General Dwight D. Eisenhower, crossed the English Channel in June to begin the march on Germany from the west, and, in October, American troops landed in the Philippines. By then there was little doubt about the outcome of the war—Allied victory was only a matter of time—and thoughts turned to preparations for peace.

In San Francisco a momentous meeting took place in April 1945, when representatives of forty-six nations met to establish the United Nations. Meanwhile, planning began for winding down the tremendous war production machine the United States had created. In California, orders for tanks, ships, aircraft, and other war matériel were gradually reduced, with an accompanying decline in related industries. Shipyard and aircraft workers were laid off, and there developed a growing concern that the war would be followed by a serious economic recession, as World War I had been.

Those who feared a recession, however, overlooked some important facts. In a very real sense, the war years had returned the nation to prosperity. In California personal income rose during this period from $3 billion to $13 billion. Although individual spending increased with rising incomes, increases in savings had also been considerable; liquid assets of Californians rose from $4.5 billion to $15.25 billion during the war. Thus the war ended with a huge, pent-up buying power. Moreover, the state's population grew nearly thirty percent during the war, creating a growing demand for consumer goods, housing, and services. Finally, the Servicemen's Readjustment Act of 1944 (the GI Bill of Rights) proved to be not only an effective buffer to unemployment for millions of men and women returning to civilian life, but also an important stimulus to the economy. The act provided veterans with low-interest loans for farm and home purchases and paid the full educational costs of veterans returning to school. Millions of veterans thus enrolled in colleges all over the nation to complete baccalaureate and graduate degrees. The impact on state university systems was enormous, more than tripling the wartime enrollment.

Careful analysis revealed that California had developed, under the hothouse stimulus of the war, a complex, modern, technological economy with enormous potential for the future. The war years, then, provided the economic base that was to make the state the "pace-setter" in the development of the high-technology society of the late twentieth century.

THE WARREN ADMINISTRATIONS

Suspension of partisan politics generally accompanied the war. To no one's surprise, the popular Republican attorney general Earl Warren easily defeated Culbert Olson for the governorship in 1942 and went on to establish one of the state's most notable records in that office. Warren has often been compared to Hiram Johnson (whom he greatly admired) because he dominated the political arena of his era in the same fashion. Like Johnson, he had an uncanny ability to appeal to a broad range of voters, and he never lost a bid for state office.

Born in Los Angeles in 1891, Warren supported Johnson's progressivism as a young man, earned a law degree from the University of California's Boalt School of Law in 1914, served in the army during World War I, and, after a short stint of private law practice, was elected district attorney for Alameda County in 1926, where he built a solid reputation and emerged as an important Republican party figure. As chairman of the Republican State Central Committee, he played a key role in establishing the California Republican Assembly (CRA). The CRA

Earl Warren
Earl Warren spent almost his entire adult life in public service and is remembered as one of California's most admired and successful governors. As Chief Justice of the U.S. Supreme Court after 1953, he led the Court into a period of judicial activism that made the "Warren Court" one of the most significant in the body's history. *Courtesy of the California State Library.*

was formed in 1934 as an informal organization representing local Republican voters' groups which could perform functions, such as pre-primary endorsements, that were prohibited to the regular party apparatus by the state election code. It became a vital mechanism that helped Republicans remain in power in California for twenty-five years after the Democrats became the state's majority party.

In 1938 Warren won election as state attorney general—the only Republican elected to statewide office that year. With the attack on

Pearl Harbor, he became one of the leading politicians calling for the removal of Japanese, whether citizens or not, from the state. His election as governor in 1942 signified his emergence as the midcentury's preeminent practitioner of California's unique style of politics, which was a legacy of progressivism. Distrustful of political parties and fearful of bossism, California progressives, through nonpartisanship, cross-filing, and a stringent elections code, had succeeded in weakening parties to the point of impotence. Candidates campaigned independently of their party; party affiliation was played down; emphasis was on the individual, not the party and its platform; incumbency was a huge advantage under cross-filing, since the incumbent led the list of candidates on primary ballots without mention of party affiliation.

To all of these features of California politics, Earl Warren pioneered the added practice of hiring public relations firms to manage his political campaigns. In his 1942 campaign for governor he had the help of Clem Whitaker and Leone Baxter, whose firm, Campaigns, Inc., used advertising techniques to manage political campaigns and became the prototype of present-day campaign organizations. By 1946 Warren had so mastered progressive-style politics that, by cross-filing, he captured the nomination of the Democrats as well as the Republicans, the only person ever to win both major party nominations for governor. In 1950 he became the only California governor to be elected to a third term.

In national politics Warren accepted the Republican's nomination for the vice presidency as Thomas E. Dewey's running mate in 1948. When President Harry Truman's famous "give-em hell Harry" whistle-stop campaign produced the political upset of the century, Earl Warren suffered his one and only election defeat. He remained prominent in national Republican party affairs, however, and in 1952 was instrumental in Eisenhower's nomination. After the latter's election as president, Eisenhower promised Warren appointment to the next opening on the Supreme Court, the position the Californian had long coveted; it was only by chance that the first vacancy turned out to be the position of chief justice, from which Warren led the Court into epoch-making decisions in the fields of civil and individual rights.

Warren's talent and personality made him perhaps the best governor California has ever had. Warren proposed, and obtained, significant reductions in taxes, yet managed to build a substantial surplus in the state treasury as a "rainy-day fund" for potential postwar problems. As the war came to a close, he promoted planning for demobilization and reconversion to a peacetime economy, persuading the legislature to authorize special state construction projects to provide jobs for returning veterans.

Throughout his career, Warren was a typical progressive. Nonideological on the issues, he preferred a scientific approach. He regularly appointed boards and commissions to study specific problems and based his legislative proposals on their recommendations. He respected the independence of the legislature, but effectively lobbied its members. Ninety percent of his legislative proposals were adopted in one form or another.

Probably not a highly imaginative or innovative leader, Warren took great pride in the modernization and upgrading of the state's Public Health Service, Mental Health Department, and Department of Corrections; in the expansion of workmen's compensation and unemployment benefits; and in a program of aid to families with dependent children (AFDC). He strongly supported the state's systems of higher education and promoted important state expenditures for highways, housing, and public schools.

Critics of Earl Warren often characterized him as enigmatic, as failing to crusade for progressive legislation, and as a stand-still politician. They also criticized him for not curbing the power of lobbyist Artie Samish, the self-styled "governor of the legislature." Others thought that his budgets were too high, that he sponsored unnecessary taxes, or that he meddled too much in social issues. It was in the last field, actually, that Warren's record was mixed. For several years he sought legislation for a social security type of medical health insurance plan, only to lose to the California Medical Association lobby, which employed Whitaker and Baxter against him. He also unsuccessfully called for the establishment of a commission on political and economic equality to protect the rights of California's expanding ethnic minorities. Not until he wrote his memoirs, published after his death, did he express regret for the role he played in the removal and detention of the state's Japanese in 1942. In the economic field, his long battle with utility interests, especially PG&E, over public distribution of Central Valley Project power from Shasta Dam, ended in a compromise generally regarded as favorable to the utility.

Warren served California as governor in a period of booming growth and prosperity and enjoyed nearly universal press support. These advantages, along with his ability to cover the political middle of the road and mastery of progressive-style politics, made him the state's most successful politician since Hiram Johnson.

CHAPTER TWENTY-FOUR

AMAZING GROWTH: CALIFORNIA AFTER WORLD WAR II

Dancing in the streets with an elation, fervor, and relief that young Americans of today may never experience, Californians celebrated V-E (victory in Europe) Day in May 1945, when Germany surrendered to Allied forces in Berlin. The following August they celebrated V-J Day, when Japan surrendered after the atomic bombing of Hiroshima and Nagasaki, and World War II came to an end. In their joy, few gauged the meaning of the use of atomic weapons, or anticipated that relations between the United States and the Soviet Union would soon deteriorate.

Like the gold rush, World War II stands as one of the major turning points in California history. It began another era of migration and population increase that made California the most populous state in the Union and ushered in a period of amazing growth and development. By 1970 California had become such an economic force that, if regarded as an independent nation (as some say Californians are inclined to do), it ranked seventh in the world; only the United States itself, the Soviet Union, Great Britain, France, West Germany, and Japan had a higher gross national product. With this great growth, Californians established a way of life that became the envy of the world. To many, the state seemed on the cutting edge of American civilization, with an economy pushed by World War II to the forefront of the post-industrial society of the future.

THE GREAT MIGRATION

When World War II ended, California was in the early stages of a population explosion that rivaled its rate of growth in the 1920s and in sheer numbers was nearly overwhelming. Between 1940 and 1970 the state grew by 13 million persons. The increase in the state's population alone exceeded the total population of any other state except New York. In 1962, California surpassed New York as the nation's most populous state. Nearly two-thirds of the growth of the 1940s and 1950s represented migration from other states, and the pattern of settlement mirrored that of the 1920s; the great majority of migrants headed for southern California.

The population of the counties south of the Tehachapis, 3.5 million in 1940, grew to 5.5 million by 1950 and to 9 million in 1960. Moreover, ninety percent of Californians lived in what were officially classified as metropolitan areas, making it not only the nation's most populous state but also the most urbanized.

Gay men and lesbians were an important new element in the migration to California. Many had come to the state during the war in the service and found greater acceptance, especially in Los Angeles and San Fancisco. With the war's end they returned and developed distinct communities in both cities, increasingly coming "out of the closet," fighting for gay civil rights, and forming effective political pressure groups. By the 1970s gay men and women were well established in the civil rights movement and in Califiornia politics.

Most of the state's new residents came for the old reasons—climate and economic opportunity. Among the first arrivals were veterans who had trained in California or, when passing through the state on the way to military action, liked what they saw and returned to stay. More than 300,000 servicemen and women from other states elected to receive their discharges in California. They were followed by a huge number who took advantage of the loan and educational benefits of the GI Bill of Rights to leave the colder climates of the East for a new start in the Golden State. Young, productive, highly skilled, and eager for success, they gave the state a transfusion of new blood and great energy. On the other hand, the influx intensified the problems caused by wartime growth.

THE HOUSING BOOM

The postwar population explosion made the wartime housing shortages pale by compari-

son. An incredible demand for single-family dwellings arose, and the construction industry scrambled to meet it. Home builders had developed mass production techniques during the war that soon covered the landscape with "tract" homes. These were homes of almost identical plan built by crews moving from one site to the next, one laying foundations and basic plumbing, another framing, the next roofing, another finishing interiors, and a final crew painting and cleaning up. Prefabrication of large sections speeded the process even more. An amazing record of construction, along with handsome profits for home builders and tract developers, resulted. The uniformity and boxy style of postwar housing elicited a good deal of humor, since it was frequently difficult to tell one home from another, but these houses were home to two-thirds of California's new residents, many of whom had never owned property before. For most, the opportunity was simply too good to pass up. Veterans' loans often made it possible to purchase a home for no money down and monthly payments that, as one said, "made any kind of rent seem like extortion."

Fueled by the great migration, the housing boom pushed into agricultural areas surrounding the state's urban centers. Rural communities suddenly swelled to the size of major cities. In the south, Los Angeles and Orange counties and portions of Ventura, Riverside, and San Bernardino counties rapidly changed from agricultural to residential in character. In the north, the peninsula counties south of San Francisco, along with San José and the East Bay counties of Alameda and Contra Costa, grew nearly as rapidly.

The sprawling tract-housing suburbs eventually evolved into modern "subdivisions," as counties and cities struggled to gain control over the process, imposing stricter standards on real estate developers. Larger lots, better streets and drainage systems, sidewalks, and even parks and schools became normal requirements. The California ranch-style house that was popularized by the architect Cliff May and others also evolved at this time and became almost universal in the subdivisions of the 1950s and 1960s. Larger, usually one-story, shake-roofed, and more expensive, the ranch-style homes were also built by mass production methods, but with modest variations in design to avoid the regimented look of earlier tract homes. Developers now sold what they called "California living," the concept of a leisurely, self-indulgent style of life emphasizing the outdoor patio, barbecue, and swimming pool as integral parts of the home.

The rise of suburban California brought a new set of problems. Developers of subdivisions and shopping centers gobbled up some 3 million acres of the best agricultural land in the state. Farmland in the path of residential development skyrocketed in value. Property taxes followed suit, forcing growers to sell out to the developers; southern California saw a substantial shift of the citrus industry to the San Joaquin Valley as a result. Mass production of housing also far outstripped the ability of most communities to provide essential services for the new residents. Water, gas, electric, and sewage-treatment facilities were often insufficient. A year's wait for telephone service was not uncommon. Special districts, financed from a portion of the county property tax, usually provided most other services such as flood control, air-pollution control, and even mosquito abatement. Today there are some 6,000 special districts in the state, ranging from tiny zones allocated for cemeteries and some 1,000 school districts to the Bay Area Rapid Transit District and the South Coast Air Quality Management District.

Perhaps the most serious consequence of the suburban housing boom was the decline of the inner city, as a substantial number of whites from the core cities migrated to the new "bedroom" communities. Lack of economic opportunity and discrimination combined to leave the poor and ethnic minorities behind, a process begun during the war. The continued heavy migration of African Americans to California, therefore, led to their concentration in sections such as Hunters Point and the Western Addition in San Francisco, portions of Oakland and Richmond in the East Bay, and Watts and sections of Los Angeles vacated by the Japanese in 1942. In San Diego and Los Angeles, the swelling Mexican population was similarly confined to inner-city barrios. Inferior housing, high unemployment, dependence on welfare, de facto segregation of schools, frustration, and a high crime rate in these areas can all be traced to the pattern of postwar housing development and the efforts of real estate operators, through restrictive covenants and other forms of discrimination, to limit access to new housing to whites.

The postwar construction boom was not confined to housing. Population growth generated a major expansion of state and federal government services that required enlarged public building programs. New state and federal office buildings, courthouses, and correctional facilities met pressing needs throughout the state. In Sacramento the new Capitol Mall and the expansion of the Capitol Office Building reflected this development. In the metropolitan areas, height restrictions were removed or relaxed, and high-rise commercial buildings and office towers rapidly changed the skyline. The most dramatic change took place in downtown San Francisco, where a soaring new skyline dwarfed such famous landmarks as the Ferry Building. However, it was the great postwar housing boom that created the most serious problems in other areas.

TRANSPORTATION

One such field was transportation. "California living" meant mobility, among other things, and mobility meant the automobile. Since the 1920s it had become clear that Californians were determined to solve their transportation problems with the automobile. The postwar years saw no change, even though the housing boom and suburban development put a severe strain on existing highways. Very soon after the end of the war, pressure mounted for the construction of limited-access highways to facilitate the commute from suburban bedroom communities to downtown workplaces, resulting, eventually, in the legislature's enactment of the Collier-Burns Act of 1947.

An extraordinary piece of legislation, the Collier-Burns Act committed the state to a huge construction program of some 12,500 miles of freeways and expressways. It established a state gasoline tax of 7 cents per gallon, which would be deposited not in the state's general fund, but in a special gas-tax fund available only for construction and maintenance of the highway system. In the 1950s federal highway programs provided another important source of funding for the state's ambitious plan, including ninety percent of the funds for interstate freeways and half the funds for other federal highways in the state. By the end of the 1950s California spent $1 million a day on freeway construction, and the state's highway system was the most sophisticated one in the nation. Freeways encircled and plunged through the heart of all the great metropolitan centers of the state, promoting continued suburbanization. Los Angeles in particular became identified with the freeway age; one famous four-level interchange became known as "the mixmaster." Registration figures reflected this dependence on the automobile. By 1970 there were nearly 12 million autos registered

in California, twice the number in any other state.

Reliance on the automobile spawned a culture particularly associated with California. Satellite shopping centers easily accessible by car became the norm. Drive-in fast-food restaurants, movies, and shops of all kinds became common. Motel construction became a major industry, even in the downtown hotel sections of the cities. Trucking became a major industry, moving ninety percent of the goods distributed in the state in 1970 and boasting an $8 billion payroll.

What some have called California's love affair with the auto also meant the demise of the fine electric rail transit systems that had been so important to growth in earlier eras. The Pacific Electric in Los Angeles and the Key System in the San Francisco Bay Area were allowed to die, their routes eventually converted to bus service. The Key System's two rail lines on the lower deck of the Bay Bridge became just two more auto lanes. Moreover, elimination of the Pacific Electric and Key System lines made a return to electric rail transit more difficult and expensive in later years, even when oil and gasoline shortages loomed ominously in the 1970s. Los Angeles, for example, did not begin construction of a subway along Wilshire Boulevard until the mid-1980s.

In the north, business and construction industry interests successfully led a drive to create such a system for the Bay Area through formation of the Bay Area Rapid Transit District (BART). Completion of the ultramodern system in 1974 marked the first electric rail transit system to be built in the United States in twenty-five years. But BART was criticized as too expensive to truly be a mass-transit system and as a skeletal track layout designed mainly to tie the East Bay suburbs to downtown San Francisco and Oakland. Critics argued that it would not

become a mass-transit system without a considerable expansion of track and subsidized fares. Meanwhile, the vast majority of Bay Area commuters continued to travel to work by auto.

Freeway construction also produced criticism. Bureaucratic planners rarely took account of the social cost of building freeways through communities, wiping out large sections of housing, razing historic landmarks, and destroying neighborhood cohesion. On occasion, therefore, they encountered groups of irate citizens who successfully blocked their plans. In the north, San Franciscans forced a halt to construction of the half-completed Embarcadero Freeway, and a proposed freeway through Golden Gate Park was stopped. Citizens of both Laguna Beach and Pasadena rose up to stop proposed freeways that would have destroyed the attractive qualities of their communities. Similarly, conservationists blocked plans for a freeway through the heart of the redwoods of the north coast. On the whole, however, these were minor obstacles to the juggernaut set in motion by the Collier-Burns Act. The vulnerability of the freeway systems developed in these years was tragically demonstrated by the collapse of major segments in the Loma Prieta earthquake near San Francisco in 1989 and the Northridge earthquake near Los Angeles in 1994.

The Coming of the Freeways
The Hollywood Freeway, looking east to Los Angeles Civic Center, 1956 *(upper left)*. The Bayshore Freeway entering San Francisco from the south, 1955 *(upper right)*. Looking southeast along the Santa Ana Freeway, as subdivisions encroach on orange groves, 1955 *(lower left)*. The Nimitz Freeway, which opens southern Alameda county agricultural lands to subdivisions, 1959 *(lower right)*. *Courtesy of the California Department of Transportation.*

EDUCATION

To a much greater extent than in earlier periods, the postwar migrants were productive young people—especially when it came to babies. The postwar "baby boom," coupled with the migration itself, put immense pressure on school facilities, forcing schools in suburban areas onto double and even triple sessions and creating a serious shortage of teachers. School construction proceeded at a feverish pace, with local tax and bond issues for expansion of facilities constantly before the voters. Inadequate calculation of future needs became apparent, however, when departure of the baby-boom students in the 1970s left school districts with expensive, vacant facilities on their hands.

In the field of higher education, the number of veterans attending California colleges and universities forced a similar expansion in the 1950s, which continued as the baby-boom students reached college age in the 1960s and the proportion of high-school graduates who went on to college jumped to fifty percent. Not until the mid-1970s did college enrollments level off. In this period California led the nation in the development of essentially free public higher education. More than 100 two-year junior colleges, or community colleges, financed largely through local property taxes, were established in the state by 1975. Their numbers grew so rapidly that concern arose about their proper function in the overall structure of higher education in the state, leading in 1948 to a special study of the question under the direction of Joseph Strayer. The resulting report limited these two-year institutions to offering the first two years of academic instruction leading to the baccalaureate degree and to two-year occupational curriculums.

In the same period the public state colleges expanded their role from primarily

WALT DISNEY
Last of the Movie Moguls

Walt Disney Gets Advice from Mickey Mouse
Courtesy of the Los Angeles Public Library.

It is a tribute to a particular quality of perseverance that when Walt Disney died in 1966 at age sixty-five he was called "the last of the movie moguls." There is also a certain irony in the fact that of all the Hollywood studios, Walt Disney Productions was the strongest and most profitable of the postwar era and that it reached such status by relegating animated film production to a sideline and embracing the new medium of television.

Oddly enough, Walt Disney had no great ability as an artist, but he had a sure feel for the cinematic tastes of the average American, an eye for technological innovation, and organizational ability. When he came to Hollywood in 1923, he had had some experience in making animated short films in Kansas City and, lacking other work, began to

WALT DISNEY (continued)

Last of the Movie Moguls

produce cartoons. His almost legendary success in animated shorts (he won all but two of the Academy Awards in this field from 1932 to 1942) revealed his strengths. He had remarkable ability as a story editor, attracted the best animators available, gave them the finest equipment, sent them to school to perfect their talents, and quickly adopted major technological advances as they appeared. In 1927 he introduced the Mickey Mouse series, based on his experiences as a boy on a Kansas farm and his observations of pet field mice he had kept in his animation studio in Kansas City.

With production of *Steamboat Willie* in 1928, Disney introduced sound to the cartoon field, and, as early as 1931, he produced an animated short in color. Two years later his *Three Little Pigs* was a sensational hit, and Disney had become a significant figure in Hollywood, although his studio was by no means considered a major one. By then, he had also started work on his first full-length animated feature, *Snow White*, which consumed most of his annual profits, required him to expand his staff from 150 to 750, and took five years to complete. *Snow White* was released in 1937 and became another box-office sensation, encouraging Disney to embark on a series of expensive animated cartoon features that included *Bambi, Pinocchio,* and *Fantasia.* The outbreak of World War II, however, cut off his foreign sales and reduced his profits by nearly forty-five percent. Only government contracts for propaganda and military training films enabled the studio to survive the war years.

In the late 1940s Disney pointed the company in new directions: reduced emphasis on expensive animated films, increased production of live-action, family-oriented movies, a series of nature films, and construction of Disneyland, an idea he had clung to since 1930. It proved to be a formula for the stable prosperity he had always sought. His live-action feature films dominated the family movie market just when the old major studios deserted it for "adult" films or left it to television. Unlike the old major studios, Disney was unafraid of television and in 1954 entered the field himself, hosting programs first on ABC and later on NBC. The "Mickey Mouse Club," "The Wonderful World of Disney," and "Disneyland" TV shows were really designed to promote his newest venture, Disneyland, the revolutionary amusement park opened in Anaheim in 1955. Its phenomenal success made the Disney organization the most profitable Hollywood studio and the only one that did not sell off its library of films to television or rely on independent producers for its product. Walt Disney, who had been more or less "tolerated" by the moguls of the prewar era, sat on the top of the heap in 1965. He also left a business organization that could go on smoothly without him—a classic example of modern entrepreneurial success. (RBR) teacher training institutions to four-year liberal arts colleges granting baccalaureate and master's degrees in all major fields. At the same time, new state colleges appeared throughout the state in response to the rising student demand and increasing population, while the older state colleges embarked on major programs of expansion.

Meanwhile, the University of California also grew rapidly. It poured funds into the development of the University of California at Los Angeles (UCLA), making that campus an institution rivaling Berkeley. It also acquired the old Santa Barbara State College, made "general" campuses out of its specialized agricultural units at Davis and Riverside, and established new campuses at San Diego, Irvine, and Santa Cruz. By 1960 the student population of these public systems numbered in the hundreds of thousands.

Rivalry for state budgetary support, particularly between the state colleges and the university, eventually led to the formation of a commission in the 1950s whose recommendations were embodied in the state's Higher Education Act of 1960—a pioneering effort to resolve the conflicts by differentiating the functions of the three main segments of public higher education. The act designated the University of California system as the state's primary research and professional training institution, with only the top 12.5 percent of high-school graduates eligible for direct admission. The act also organized the state colleges into one system with a governing board of trustees in some respects similar to the University's Board of Regents. The institutions in this new system became primarily undergraduate, liberal arts, baccalaureate-degree-granting institutions, with graduate training generally limited to the master's-degree level. In special circumstances the Ph.D. could be granted in conjunction with a cooperating department of the University of California system—a rarely used arrangement. High school graduates in the top one-third of their class would be eligible for direct admission to any state college. In the 1970s the state college system became the California State University. The act meanwhile accepted the Strayer Report's definition of the functions of community colleges, whose students, on successfully completing the two-year academic track, could transfer to either a state college or a UC campus.

The Strayer Report and the Higher Education Act of 1960 made California a model for several other states that faced a similar problem of competing segments within a public system of higher education. They also served to maintain strong popular support for free public higher education through generous budget allocations, until the administration of Governor Ronald Reagan. Hundreds of thousands of graduates of California colleges helped make the state a leader in the modern industrial world. Many superb private institutions, such as Stanford University and the California Institute of Technology, also contributed to this record. The state's high per capita income and its advanced industrial society are closely related to the quality of its system of higher education.

RECREATION

Migrants to California have always been attracted by the state's magnificent landscape and excellent system of beaches and parks, as well as by the Yosemite, Sequoia, Kings Canyon, and Lassen national parks, various national monuments, and extensive national forests. It is not surprising, therefore, that the postwar population growth put great pressure on these recreational areas. In 1970 Forest Service records revealed that the annual 14 million visitor days of 1940 had grown to 60 million. The state thus undertook a large expansion program of its parks system, while local communities struggled, in the face of escalating land values, to develop urban park sites. As might be expected, the increased number of trailers, campers, backpackers, sightseers, and off-road vehicles brought increased litter, water pollution, and noise to California's scenic areas, giving an important impetus to the environmental movement.

The great demand for recreational outlets also attracted profit-oriented businesses. The creation and fantastic success of Disneyland near Anaheim led to similar amusement park and entertainment facilities in other metropolitan areas. The popularity of travel trailers, motor homes, and other recreational vehicles (RVs) led to the development of private summer camps. Boise-Cascade, Fibreboard, and other corporations, for example, were active in building RV and summer homesites in mountain areas (with mixed results). The giant entertainment conglomerate Music Corporation of America (MCA) entered the field by taking over the Yosemite Park and Curry Company.

Unfortunately, in such arrangements, interest in making money often took precedence over such considerations as preservation of the environment, as seemed to be the case in early proposals by MCA to build high-rise visitor facilities at Yosemite and a tram from the floor of Yosemite Valley to Glacier Point. And the crush of public park users, plus a concern for personal security, produced, in later years, organizations with names such as American Trails and Thousand Trails that catered to RV owners and campers who wanted guaranteed, secure campsites in parklike settings and could afford, for a considerable fee, to join these organizations.

POSTWAR ECONOMIC GROWTH

A short period of economic decline followed the end of the war in 1945; it was not as serious as expected, since population growth served to lessen the impact of the conversion to a peacetime economy.

Nationwide, GI Bill loans to veterans took up much of the slack, and the unmet demand for consumer goods of the war years provided a quick stimulus to business. In California the surge in population created a whole new range of jobs in home construction, real estate and financial services, highway construction, and auto-related industries and services. It quickly became evident that the war had promoted substantial diversification in the state's economy, which had been centered on agriculture, oil, movies, and tourism. After the war these remained important industries, but the state now produced for national markets in such fields as electronics, footwear, clothing, and frozen foods. Moreover, its growth encouraged national companies to open branch plants in California, producing such items as technical instruments, autos, tires and tubes, chemicals, and cosmetics in smaller cities such as San José, Stockton, and Sacramento.

THE DEFENSE AND AEROSPACE INDUSTRIES

Ironically, California's peacetime economy was dominated by industries that grew out of war and international tension. The spirit of common interest and cooperation that had characterized Soviet-American relations during the war was quickly replaced by mutual distrust and confrontation, culminating in the Soviet blockade of Berlin in 1948. The American government adopted a policy of containment of Soviet expansionism and entered the Cold War, a long period of military spending that lasted until the breakup of the Soviet Union in the 1990s. In 1950 the Cold War intensified as the United States moved to defend South Korea against invasion from North Korea. In the meantime, technology had changed the nature of military equipment drastically. Development of jet engines and rockets put the emphasis on supersonic aircraft, missiles, and sophisticated electronic devices. In 1957, when the Soviet Union placed the first man-made satellite in orbit around the earth in space (Sputnik), Americans reacted with another great technological effort: in 1961 President John F. Kennedy set the national goal of placing a man on the moon.

Mind-boggling sums were involved in the nation's defense and space programs, and for a variety of reasons California dominated the industries they gave rise to. The wartime development of giant aircraft manufacturing firms provided a superb manufacturing base for the production of modern weapons. Companies such as Douglas, Lockheed, and North American, for example, easily converted to the missiles era. The state's scientific establishment was without parallel in the country; the California Institute of Technology, Stanford University, and the University of California at Berkeley possessed faculty and research laboratories that C. P. Snow called the greatest collection of scientific talent in the world. The state continued to attract many of the specialists and technicians necessary to the modern defense industry, and the defense and scientific establishment easily adjusted to the needs of the new era. Thus federal funds poured into California's defense and space industries, turning California's prewar "metropolitan-military complex" into the foremost "military-industrial complex" in the country. It was the political and economic power of this combination that President Eisenhower warned of in a famous speech upon leaving the presidency.

Southern California became the nation's foremost center of planning, research, and manufacturing in this new aerospace industry in the 1950s. The region's economy soon centered on the production of intercontinental ballistic missiles (ICBMs) and other

missiles, supersonic and other jet aircraft (military and commercial), and space equipment. Douglas, Lockheed, and North American were joined by Rocketdyne, Aerospace Corporation, and Litton Industries, among others, as defense and aerospace contractors. By 1960 the industry employed seventy percent of San Diego's manufacturing workers and sixty percent of those in Los Angeles and Orange counties. Twenty-five percent of the nation's defense expenditures and forty-two percent of Defense Department research contracts went to California firms. In the 1960s, after the National Aeronautics and Space Administration (NASA) was organized, the agency spent fifty percent of its funds in California. Most of the components of the Apollo space craft that landed men on the moon were made in the state.

The extent to which California dominated the nation's huge aerospace industry meant that the industry dominated the state's economy during much of the 1950s and 1960s, making the state especially vulnerable to political decisions regarding the federal defense budget. Significant cuts in defense spending in the late 1950s, and again in 1968 and 1973, led to hard times in southern California and some south San Francisco Bay communities that had become dependent on defense employment. Unlike the victims of other recessions, the unemployed this time were relatively highly paid technicians and engineers—white-collar professionals to whom unemployment was a new, and bad, experience. Numerous bankruptcies accompanied these recessions, and even Douglas and North American were forced into mergers to survive. Lockheed eventually needed a government loan to continue to operate.

By the 1970s the aerospace industry no longer dominated the state economy to the same extent, although California companies continued to dominate the industry. Cutbacks in defense spending, conclusion of the moon-landing program, population growth, and continued economic diversification all contributed to a more balanced, stable economy. A major aspect of this diversification was the emergence of yet another "high-technology" industry, pioneered and dominated by Californians and centered on the research, development, and manufacture of computers, semiconductors, communications equipment, and related materials such as computer software. Because the companies involved in this new industry were concentrated in the Santa Clara Valley near San José, that region came to be called Silicon Valley.

THE NEW HOLLYWOOD

For various reasons, the motion-picture industry, southern California's leading prewar business, had the hardest adjustment to make after the war. The federal government immediately pressed antitrust suits that in 1948 forced the major studios to divest themselves of their profitable theater chains. At the same time, costs of production increased because of higher taxes and the rise of independent producers, directors, and stars. Unlike the arrangement under the old contract system, independents demanded, and got, a percentage of the studio's gross profits on their films; they also often produced their own films, renting studio space and facilities for this purpose. Meanwhile, talented foreign producers and directors from Sweden, Japan, France, and Italy were challenging Hollywood's domination of the moviemaking field with films of exceptional quality that sold well in the United States. The studios themselves joined the trend toward producing movies "on location" all over the world, and some even sold off the old Hollywood studio lots where they had once constructed elaborate sets. The prewar studio system was no longer economical.

However, it was the introduction of television after the war that most seriously challenged Hollywood's dominant position in the entertainment field. Television shows not only siphoned off movie patrons but also changed public tastes to more realistic material than offered in the formula films Hollywood had come to depend on. It took several years for the Los Angeles-based movie industry to adapt to the challenge of television. One of the first film directors to do so was Walt Disney, but others also successfully merged their products, producing shows for television along with their traditional movie work. By the end of the 1950s, Hollywood had developed a television production and transmission industry rivaling New York's, the early leader in the field. With a growing recording industry as well, Los Angeles had once again become a leading center of the mass entertainment industry.

On another level, World War II made Hollywood a major cultural force, with worldwide influence. The stimulating influence of European emigrés also expanded the cultural influence of southern California. The result was the transformation of Los Angeles from a regional cultural center to one of national and international importance.

POSTWAR POLITICS AND THE ANTICOMMUNIST CRUSADE

The Cold War and the Korean War affected politics as well as the economy, touching off a new wave of "red scares" and intolerance. Anticommunist activity, the search for "un-American" attitudes and actions, became a surefire formula for political success. Throughout the nation Republicans seized the opportunity to charge the incumbent Democrats with softness on communism, and in the early 1950s Senator Joseph McCarthy of Wisconsin rose to prominence in this role. Flamboyant and reckless in his charges of communist infiltration of the government, McCarthy contributed to the development of a near-hysterical fear of communism and gave the name "McCarthyism" to unsubstantiated, guilt-by-association accusations.

In California, Richard M. Nixon emerged as the foremost practitioner of the new "red-scare" tactics. Nixon first came to public attention in 1948, when he ran successfully for Congress against the incumbent Democrat Jerry Voorhis with a campaign that questioned Voorhis's loyalty and implied his association with subversive forces. As a congressman Nixon achieved national prominence in 1949 through service on the House Un-American Activities Committee (HUAC), especially with his dogged questioning and investigation of Alger Hiss, a former official of the U.S. State Department. Hiss's conviction for perjury as a result of the committee's investigations established Nixon's reputation as an anticommunist. The following year he defeated Congresswoman Helen Gahagan Douglas, actress wife of movie star Melvyn Douglas, for election to the U.S. Senate. Again his campaign relied heavily on tried-and-true red-scare tactics, associating Mrs. Douglas with subversive groups by innuendo and by constant references to his opponent as "the Pink Lady." In 1952 Nixon parlayed his anticommunist reputation into election as vice president of the United States, when the more liberal Eisenhower wing of the party sought unity with the conservative faction.

HUAC had its counterpart in California. In 1947 the state senate established its own Un-American Activities Committee, chaired by state senator Jack B. Tenney, whose only other claim to fame was composing the song "Mexicali Rose." Tenney became a heavy-handed anticommunist and used the committee to bully witnesses, make unsubstantiated charges of disloyalty, and ruin the reputations and careers of a significant number of accused individuals. That same year HUAC held hearings in Hollywood leading to sensational charges against a number of well-known movie scriptwriters. Dalton Trumbo, and others became known as the "Hollywood Ten" when they were indicted for refusing to answer the question "Are you now or have you ever been a member of the Communist Party?" on the grounds that it violated their First Amendment rights. The incident provoked an emotional conflict within the movie industry and led to the blacklisting of hundreds of writers, actors and actresses, directors, and producers.

Tenney's activities also sparked one of the most unfortunate episodes of the anticommunist era. In 1949 University of California officials, fearful of a threatened Tenney committee investigation of the university, recommended adoption of a loyalty oath for all its employees, which the Board of Regents approved. The oath sparked a disruptive controversy, since most faculty members regarded it as both a violation of academic freedom and unconstitutional. Governor Warren attempted to get the Regents to rescind the oath, but he was opposed by John Francis Neylan, the erstwhile defender of Charlotte Anita Whitney in the 1920s, and by Regent Amadeo P. Giannini, who claimed that "flags would fly in the Kremlin" if Warren succeeded. In 1950, badly split, the Regents fired forty-six nonsigning faculty members for insubordination, bringing on the university the condemnation of the prestigious American Association of University Professors (AAUP).

The dispute then moved to the courts where, in April 1951, the district court ruled in *Tolman* v. *Underhill* (the Secretary of the Regents) that the oath was a violation of tenure and unconstitutional. Led by Neylan, and over Warren's objections, the Regents appealed the decision. More than a year and a half later, the California supreme court invalidated the oath and ordered the dismissed faculty reinstated. The court, however, based its decision on the narrow grounds that the state had preempted the field when it adopted the Levering Act in 1950 requiring an anticommunist oath of all state employees. Ironically, after 1953 Earl Warren led the U.S. Supreme Court in a series of decisions that eventually prompted the state supreme court, in 1967, to declare even the Levering Act unconstitutional—a measure of revenge for Warren's treatment by the Board of Regents.

Meanwhile, the Tenney committee had become an embarrassment and was abolished in 1949, when Tenney injudiciously alleged that some members of the legislature were "tainted with communism." It was replaced shortly, however, with another state senate Committee on Un-American Activities under the chairmanship of Hugh Burns, who managed to keep the committee's activities lower-keyed. This committee was abolished in the 1970s, when members discovered that the committee staff had been compiling files of personal information on other state senators. By this time the near-hysterical anticommunism that fueled these activities had substantially subsided, leaving a trail of shattered friendships and careers and reputations ruined by innuendo and unproved association. Like the relocation of the Japanese Americans in 1942, it was an indication of the power of mass hysteria.

GOODWIN KNIGHT MOVES LEFT

Earl Warren left the governorship in 1953 for the U.S. Supreme Court, having established a remarkable record for holding the state in the political middle of the road in wartime and through a time of extreme pressure from right-wing elements within his own party after the war. Warren successfully fenced out extremists of both the right and the left, preventing a polarization of the state's people that might threaten to drive moderates to each end of the political spectrum, a potential threat to the democratic process itself. The effectiveness of Warren's moderate political stance was not lost on his successor, Lieutenant Governor Goodwin J. ("Goody") Knight.

A lawyer, businessman, radio commentator, and popular after-dinner speaker, Knight had been elected lieutenant governor with the rare personal endorsement of Warren in 1946. Once elected, however, Knight lined up with the conservative wing of the Republican party and opposed Warren on such matters as medical insurance, fair employment legislation, and the oath controversy. He even toyed with the idea of opposing Warren in 1950, but thought better of it and ran for reelection as lieutenant governor instead; he cross-filed and became the only person to win the nomination of both Democrats and Republicans for the office. His patience was rewarded when Warren was appointed chief justice of the U.S. Supreme Court.

As governor, Knight shrewdly moved left to the political center to pick up Warren's following. He backed Warren-like programs in mental health, increases in unemployment benefits, workmen's compensation, old-age pensions, and child-care centers. Most important, he vigorously opposed so-called right-to-work legislation, which organized labor simply considered union busting. As a result, Knight was reelected governor in 1954 with labor's backing. In fact, he had so successfully adopted Warren's political style that he almost won the Democratic nomination for governor, having cross-filed in the primaries.

Knight thus proved an effective successor to Warren, but after 1954 he served in the context of a serious power struggle for con-

JACK KEROUAC
King of the Beats

Jack Kerouac
Courtesy of the Bancroft Library.

The Beat Generation, whom San Francisco *Chronicle* columnist Herb Caen dubbed the "beatniks," represented the "lost generation" of World War II and, for some, a new romantic movement in postwar literature. Reacting to parents' seeming obsession with security, the beatniks dismissed the adult world as a kind of modern hell. They could not accept the legacy of atomic war, wars of containment, or the Cold War. The world of their fathers was, to them, an "organization man" existence, a stultifying nine-to-five work day, an accumulation of material goods, and life in a suburban sameness, where boredom, divorce, and the stifling of creativity and self-dependence awaited them. The Beats rejected it all.

The heroes of Beat Generation writers refused to enter the "phony" competitive world or accept their parents' middle-class "realism." Instead, they projected childhood visions of innocence as the ideal, looked inward to the self, instead of to institutions, for strength, and placed their faith in their own emotions and sensations rather than in conventional responses. For some, this meant a life that disparaged regular employment, material goods, and the usual forms of communication; it also included experimenta-

JACK KEROUAC (continued)
King of the Beats

tion with mind-expanding drugs in an effort to heighten sensations of mind and body, which they regarded as all-important.

Jack Kerouac has been called the "king of the Beats." He gave them their name and, in a series of novels that included *On the Road, Dharma Bums, A Visit to Cody, The Subterraneans*, and *Big Sur*, best described their desperate and often frenetic search for alternatives to middle-class life in America. *On the Road* (1957) is Kerouac's best-known book. With its focus on the migrant hero and the lure of California, it can be considered a work in the tradition of Jack London's *The Road* and John Steinbeck's *The Grapes of Wrath*, yet for Kerouac life on the road could also be a form of rebellion against the suburban nothingness of the older generation.

Kerouac's books are essentially a chronicle of the Beat scene, especially the doings of the group of poets and writers—including Allen Ginsberg, Michael McClure, John Clellan Holmes, and Lawrence Ferlinghetti—who collected in and around San Francisco in the 1940s and 1950s. They also provide a valuable running commentary on Beat behavior and the anxiety of those coming of age during and after World War II.

Beginning with *On the Road,* Kerouac adopted a style he called "spontaneous prose," an attempt to imitate the conversational style of Neal Cassady, who was the inspiration for much of his writing and perhaps one of the most zealous of the Beats. Spontaneous prose was intended to be representative of the nature of the Beat search for an alternative to modern society and was likened to the spontaneous creativity of jazz musicians. The style was picked up, in modified form, by successors of the Beats such as Ken Kesey in his *One Flew Over the Cuckoo's Nest.*

Although critics complained that Kerouac made no effort to analyze and really understand the experiences he was recording, he was able to project a vivid sense that his world was "vibrating apart," and he spoke for many young people who returned from wartime experiences to find themselves unable to communicate with parents or community. But unlike other new romanticists, Kerouac never reconciled himself with the realities of American life in the postwar era, nor did the central characters of his novels, who followed a path to ultimate loneliness prophetic of Kerouac's death in 1969, at the age of forty-seven, from the effects of alcohol and drug use. (RBR)

trol of the Republican party in California between Vice President Richard Nixon and William F. Knowland, the state's senior U.S. Senator (he was the Senate majority leader and later minority whip), who were ambitious and powerful adversaries. When he approached reelection in 1958, Goodwin Knight was squeezed between the two like a California orange, leading to his retirement from politics, disaster for the state's Republican party, and a Democratic revival in California politics.

CALIFORNIA CULTURE IN TRANSITION

California has been a promised land for many Americans since the time of the gold rush, as periodic migrations to the state attest. After World War II people began to regard the Golden State as the symbol of a new culture and a harbinger of the nation's future. California lifestyles were the subject of countless magazine articles, Hollywood movies, and television shows, inspiring a national interest in leisure living and informality. Still, the postwar period was essentially transitional, tinged with some of the innocence and naiveté of the prewar years. Swing, jazz, and the upbeat big-band music of the 1930s carried on into the 1950s, and while the new sound of rock 'n' roll had emerged from the nation's black ghettos, it absorbed country and western styles (and bore little relation to the "acid rock" and "heavy metal" of later generations). The sophisticated jazz quartet of Dave Brubeck, who was born and raised in Concord, California, topped popular music charts of the era, and the Monterey Jazz Festival emerged as one of the major national events in the world of popular music.

In the 1920s and 1930s writers, artists and other social critics rebelled against the popular view of urban and suburban culture. This was reflected in the movie industry with the film noir cycle of the mid-1940s and early 1950s. Based on popular fiction of the 1930s films such as *Double Indemnity*, *The Blue Dahlia*, and *The Postman Always Rings Twice* were urban stories of violent crime and powerless protagonists trapped in a threatening world—the city. Location shooting in Los Angeles created a dark and existential mood that belied the Los Angeles Dream of southern California boosters.

Nevertheless, Hollywood's wholesome, noncontroversial movies of the 1930s carried on into the 1950s and 1960s, particularly through the Disney organization's popular hits such as *Mary Poppins* and *The Absent-Minded Professor*. Television programming in Los Angeles, as in New York, was essentially family-oriented, the top programs being comedies such as *I Love Lucy* and shows built around the transfer to television of popular Hollywood radio personalities such as Jack Benny and Bob Hope. California culture, therefore, reflected the postwar emphasis on rebuilding lives dislocated by the war, on family formation, and on the pursuit of material well-being.

The postwar years in California, like the 1920s, were a prosperous time for a rapidly growing middle class with increased leisure time. The state's recreation industry blossomed with a whole range of activities including skiing, surfing, boating, hiking, and camping that required investment in recreational paraphernalia from tents to wet suits, and the home swimming pool became a "must" for many suburbanites. Spectator sports attracted large crowds, and college students created huge cheering sections of carefree merrymakers at their games.

In architecture, the housing boom of the postwar years brought the California ranch-style house to its ultimate popularity. With its low profile, gently sloping roof, wide overhang, and split-level design, the modern ranch house had much in common with its antecedent, the Mexican rancho home, if for different reasons. The ground-hugging silhouette of the rancho home resulted from the difficulty of building more than one story with adobe bricks without foundations, and the need to fit the site with little excavation. The low-pitched roof reflected the mild climate of the region, while wide roof overhangs protected the vulnerable adobe walls from the weather. The low profile of the postwar ranch house derived from the Mexican model but conformed to modern principles, popularized by Frank Lloyd Wright,

Cliff May, and others, that the house be designed as part of the site. The low eaves and wide overhang protected large glass walls, and the ground-level floors promoted the unity of indoor and outdoor space. Like the Mexican rancho home, the modern ranch house concentrated family life in an outdoor patio. Since World War II the California ranch house, with innumerable variations, has dominated western residential architecture.

The postwar years also spurred southern California's cultural awakening. The new arrivals were well educated, sophisticated, and affluent, including a much higher proportion of professionally trained people than in previous migrations to the state. With strong interests in scientific and intellectual pursuits, and heavily influenced by the large contingent of European writers, artists and musicians who had migrated to California upon fleeing Hitler's Germany, they demanded increased attention to the arts. Their influence was reflected in the 1960s and 1970s with the energetic development of museums, art institutes, and facilities for the performing arts as well as in the growing cultural influence of Los Angeles.

Meanwhile, California universities produced a number of good writers in the period. Wallace Stegner at Stanford published *Mormon Country* (1942) and *Big Rock Candy Mountain* (1943). George R. Stewart at Berkeley turned natural phenomena into vivid novels with *Storm* (1941) and *Fire* (1948). At the same time William Everson, who taught periodically at the University of California at Santa Cruz, emerged as California's best poet since Robinson Jeffers. The uniformity and conformity of the war years and postwar culture provoked the rebellion of a small but vocal group of poets and writers in the 1940s and 1950s who called themselves the Beat Generation. Rejecting traditional forms they protested in writing and lifestyle what they regarded as the stultifying effect of the postwar suburban culture. Led by poet Allen Ginsberg and writer Jack Kerouac (see page 502), the Beats paved the way for a harsher, more cynical California literature in the late 1950s. But most Californians chose to ignore the warnings of the disenchanted and the specter of nuclear war by immersing themselves in comfort and a sense of well-being that characterized the 1950s but failed to survive the 1960s.

SUGGESTIONS FOR FURTHER READING

World War II and Japanese Americans

Jeanne Wakatsuki Houston and James D. Houston, *Farewell to Manzanar* (1973); Yoshiko Uchida, *Desert Exile: The Uprooting of a Japanese-American Family* (1982), and "Topaz, City of Dust," *Utah Historical Quarterly* (1980); Sandra C. Taylor, *Jewel of the Desert: Japanese American Internment at Topaz* (1993); Kim Kodami Hill, *Topaz Moon: Chiura Obata's Art of the Internment* (2000); John Moddell (ed.), *The Kikuchi Diary* (1973); Edison Uno, *Japanese Americans: The Untold Story* (1971); Michi Weglyn, *Years of Infamy: The Untold Story of America's Concentration Camps* (1976); Bill Hosokawa, *Nisei: The Quiet Americans* (1969); Harry H. L. Kitano, *Japanese Americans: Evo-* *lution of a Subculture* (1969); Audrie Gardner and Anne Loftis, *The Great Betrayal: The Evacuation of the Japanese Americans During World War II* (1969); Arthur Hansen and Betty Mitson, *Voices Long Silent* (1977); Leonard J. Arrington, *The Price of Prejudice: The Japanese American Relocation Center in Utah in World War II* (1962); Roger Daniels, *Concentration Camps USA: Japanese Americans and World War II* (1971); Richard Nishimoto, *Inside an American Concentration Camp* (1995); Ansel Adams, *Born Free and Equal: The Story of Manzanar* (1944); Peter Irons, *Justice at War: The Story of the Japanese American Internment* (1983) and *Justice Delayed: The Record of the Japanese American Internment Cases* (1989); U.S. Commission on Wartime Relocation and Internment of

Civilians, *Personal Justice Denied* (1983); John Tateishi, *And Justice for All: An Oral History of the Japanese American Detention Camps* (1984); Dillon S. Myer, *Uprooted Americans* (1971); Lawson Fusao Inada (ed.), *Only What We Could Carry: The Japanese American Internment Experience* (2000); Leonard Broom and John I. Kitsuse, *The Managed Casualty: The Japanese American Family in World War II* (1956); Valerie Matsumoto, "Redefining Expectations: Nisei Women in the 1930s," *California History* (1994); Yuji Ichioka, *The Issei: The World of the First Generation Japanese Immigrants* (1988); Stetson Conn, Rose Engleman, and Byron Fairchild, *Guarding the United States and Its Outposts* (1964); Jacobus Ten Broek, Edward N. Barnhard, and Floyd W. Matson, *Prejudice, War and the Constitution* (1954); Kevin A. Leonard, "'Is This What We Fought For': Japanese Americans and Racism in California, The Impact of World War II," *Western Historical Quarterly* (November, 1990); Stephen Fox, *The Unknown Internment: An Oral History of Italian American Relocation During World War II* (1990).

Economic Impact of the War

Richard White, *It's Your Misfortune and None of My Own: A History of the American West* (1991); Paul Rhode, "The Nash Thesis Revisited: An Economic Historian's View," *Pacific Historical Review* (August, 1994); Gerald D. Nash, *The American West Transformed: The Impact of the Second World War* (1985) and *World War II and the West* (1990); William A. Schoneberger, and Paul Sonnenburg, *California Wings* (1987); John B. Rae, *Climb to Greatness: The American Aircraft Industry, 1920–1960* (1968); William G. Cunningham, *The Aircraft Industry, A Study in Industrial Location* (1951); Arlene Elliott, "The Rise of Aeronautics in California, 1849–1940," *Southern California Quarterly* (1970); Mark S. Foster, *Henry J. Kaiser: Builder in the Modern American West* (1989); Katherine Archibald, *Wartime Shipyard: A Study in Social Disunity* (1947); Charles Wollenberg, *Marinship at War: Shipbuilding and Social Change in Wartime Sausalito* (1990); Marilyn S. Johnson, *The Second Gold Rush: Oakland and the East Bay in World War II* (1993); Shirley Ann Wilson Moore, *To Place Our Dead: The African American Community in Richmond, California, 1910–1963* (2000); Arthur C. Verge, *Paradise Transformed: Los Angeles During the Second World War* (1993); Wytze Gorter and George

H. Hildebrand, *The Pacific Coast Maritime Shipping Industry, 1930–1948* (1952, 1954); David L. Clark, *The Aerospace Industry as the Primary Factor in the Industrial Development of Southern California* (1976); Clayton R. Koppes, *JPL and the American Space Program: A History of the Jet Propulsion Laboratory* (1982); James L. Clayton, "Defense Spending: Key to California's Growth," *Western Political Quarterly* (1962); Roger Lotchin, *Fortress California, 1910–1961: From Warfare to Welfare* (1992) and *The Way We Really Were: The Golden State in the Second Great War* (2000).

Problems of Growth

Warren S. Thompson, *Growth and Changes in California's Population* (1955); Marilyn S. Johnson, "Urban Arsenals: War Housing and Social Change in Richmond and Oakland," *Pacific Historical Review* (August, 1991); Mel Scott, *The San Francisco Bay Area: A Metropolis in Perspective* (1959); John Anson Ford, *Thirty Explosive Years in Los Angeles* (1961); Scott L. Bottles, *Los Angeles and the Automobile: The Making of a Modern City* (1987); Winston W. Crouch and Beatrice Dinerman, *Southern California Metropolis: A Study in Development of Government for a Metropolitan Area* (1964).

Politics and Politicians

Edward G. White, *Earl Warren: A Public Life* (1982); Richard B. Harvey, "Governor Earl Warren of California: A Study in Non-Partisan Republican Politics," *California Historical Society Quarterly* (1967); Robert J. Pitchell, "The Influence of Professional Campaign Management Firms in Partisan Elections in California," *Western Political Quarterly* (1958); Lester Velie, "The Secret Boss of California," *Colliers* (1949); Arthur H. Samish and Bob Thomas, *The Secret Boss of California* (1971); Robert L. Pritchard, "California Un-American Activities Investigation: Subversion on the Right?" *California Historical Society Quarterly* (1970); Edward L. Barrett, Jr., *The Tenney Committee* (1961); Gordon Kahn, *Hollywood on Trial* (1948); David P. Gardner, *The California Oath Controversy* (1967); Paul Bullock, "Richard Nixon's 1946 Campaign Against Jerry Voorhis," *Southern California Quarterly* (1973); Paul Bullock, *Jerry Voorhis: The Idealist as Politician* (1978); Ingrid W. Scobie, "Helen Gahagan Douglas and Her 1950 Senate Race with Richard M. Nixon," *Southern California Quarterly*

(1976); James A. Fisher, "The Political Development of the Black Community in California, 1850–1950," *California Historical Society Quarterly* (1971).

Culture and Society

Robert and Jane Easton, *Love and War: Pearl Harbor Through V-J Day* (1991); Robert L. Allen, *The Port Chicago Mutiny: The Story of the Largest Mass Mutiny Trial in U.S. Naval History* (1989); Charles Wollenberg, "Black vs. Navy Blue: The Mare Island Mutiny Court Martial," *California History* (1979); A. Russell Buchanan, *Black Americans in World War II* (1972); Robert A. Hipkiss, *Jack Kerouac: Prophet of the New Romanticism* (1976); Thomas Parkinson (ed.), *A Casebook on the Beats* (1961); Dennis McNally, *Desolate Angel: Jack Kerouac, the Beat Generation, and America* (1980); John A. Maynard, *Venice West: The Beat Generation in Southern California* (1991); John Russell Taylor, *Strangers in Paradise: The Hollywood Emigrés, 1933–1950* (1983); Gregory Black, *The Catholic Crusade Against the Movies, 1940–1975* (1998); Lawrence Clark Powell, *The Creative Literature of the Golden State* (1971); Gerald Haslam, *The Other California: The Great Central Valley in Life and Letters* (1990); Ted Gioia, *West Coast Jazz: Modern Jazz in California, 1945–1960* (1992); Gary Giddins, *Bing Crosby: A Pocket Full of Dreams—The Early Years, 1903–1940* (2001); David Gebhard et al., *A Guide to Architecture in San Francisco and Northern California* (1973); David Gebhard and Robert Winter, *A Guide to Architecture in Los Angeles and Southern California* (1977); Irving Hendrick, *California Education: A Brief History* (1980); John Margolies, *The End of the Road: Vanishing Highway Architecture in America* (1981).

Police and Student Protester, San Francisco State College, 1968
The 1960s, which began in optimism, ended in pessimism and upheaval. Local, national, and international issues increasingly divided Californians into hostile camps. *Courtesy of Stephen Shames/Visions.*

PART NINE

THE 1960s AND AFTER

Historian Jackson K. Putnam has observed that the legacy of turn-of-the-century progressives to Californians included a nonpartisan, nonideological political tradition that, despite the excesses of lobbyists such as Artie Samish, remained essentially free of major corruption. In addition, the progressive heritage that Putnam calls "neoprogressivism" forced officeholders to govern, rather than substituting inflated ideological rhetoric for leadership, and to practice political pragmatism, rather than engaging in extremist posturings. Finally, the progressives' legacy insured a "sustained political activism" in response to the social and economic demands of California constituencies. These three elements—nonideological pragmatism, moderation, and activism—informed the politics of the state and served Californians well until they were replaced by the contrasting political styles that characterized the régimes of Ronald Reagan, Jerry Brown, and George Deukmejian.

The transformations, however, were not wholly local phenomena. The election of John Fitzgerald Kennedy to the presidency in 1960 brought a note of cautious optimism to both California and the nation. Kennedy's victory was a narrow one, and a majority of Californians gave their votes to native (if not always favorite) son, Richard Milhous Nixon. Still, there was something appealing and reassuring about the young, energetic president-elect, his "New Frontier," and his inaugural challenge: "Ask not what your country can do for you; ask what you can do for your country."

The hopeful mood gradually evaporated as recurrent international crises punctured the calm: the Bay of Pigs incident, the Cuban missile crisis, and escalating involvement in Vietnam. Domestically, an erratic economy continued to sputter, racial tensions persisted, and the assassinations of John Kennedy in 1963 and of Robert Kennedy and Martin Luther King, Jr. in 1968 shocked the nation. Incumbent President Lyndon B. Johnson refused to seek reelection, and Americans sent Richard Nixon to the White House, hoping for better things.

To some degree, they were rewarded. Nixon reestablished diplomatic relations with mainland China, and détente replaced previous aggressive policies in relations with the Soviet Union. Involvement in Vietnam also terminated. But domestic affairs were less promising. Persistent controversy derailed Nixon's promise to "bring us together again," and the economy continued to falter. Racial tensions did not diminish, and the protracted Watergate scandal—lasting from the spring of 1972 until the summer of 1974—resulted in the first presidential resignation in history and undermined confidence in government.

Californians' reactions to events of the 1960s, 1970s, and 1980s made the state a virtual microcosm of the nation. They began the period by electing Edmund G. ("Pat") Brown to the governor's office in 1958, replaced him with Ronald Reagan in 1966, and then turned to Edmund G. "Jerry" Brown, Jr. in 1974 and George Deukmejian in 1982. Voters' choices mirrored changing moods, shifting from optimistic liberalism to hesitant conservatism to something else that defied definition and sundered the state's neoprogressive political tradition, perhaps permanently.

CHAPTER TWENTY-FIVE

PROLOGUES TO VIOLENCE: GENESIS OF A GHETTO

Before an audience seeking relief from stuffy homes on the warm evening of August 11, 1965, a piece of street theater began to unfold when a California Highway Patrolman made an arrest in the Watts district of preponderantly black south-central Los Angeles. Principal players were Officer Lee Minikus, who was white, and twenty-year-old Marquette Frye, stopped for drinking and speeding in his mother's car, who was black. The drama tilted toward tragedy as Frye's mood shifted from jocular to belligerent, his family and friends appeared on the scene, officers reinforced Minikus, and rumors of police brutality flew through the neighborhood. More people spilled into the streets, igniting a tragic six days of violence, destruction, and looting.

The episode stunned most Californians—including some black Californians. They were well aware of violence that accompanied the struggle for civil rights in the South, but they remained generally oblivious to "palm-tree ghettos" and discrimination in their own communities. After all, they thought, the state had neither Jim Crow laws nor Bull Connors, black Californians participated in the bounties of the state, and during the postwar era they were represented in its government. In the assembly sat W. Byron Rumford (elected in 1948), F. Douglass Ferrell and Mervyn Dymally (1962), and Willie F. Brown (1964). They would be joined in 1966 by Yvonne Brathwaite Burke, Bill Green, and John Miller, and in 1962 Augustus Hawkins, an assemblyman since 1940, was elected to the U.S. House of Representatives. State laws mandated equal opportunity in housing and employment, and the appearance of African American neighborhoods, mostly of single family residences, did not typify the stereotype of a ghetto. Consequently, Californians persisted in the comfortable assumption that the state's racial climate was unique; indeed, even after violence began in Watts, Police Chief William Parker commented—and probably believed—that "Los Angeles is quiet as far as race problems are concerned." Awareness of the history of the Los Angeles ghetto and of Watts itself would have disabused Parker and other Californians of their complacency.

Recent usage in the United States has made the Italian word *ghetto* virtually synonymous with African Americans and slums. (Usage of the Spanish *barrio*, originally a city ward or district, has undergone an analogous evolution.) Ghetto actually translates as "foun-

511

dry"—literally "jet"—and it apparently was first applied with a meaning similar to present connotations to *Il Campo del Ghetto Nuovo,* an armory district in sixteenth century Venice to which Jews were restricted. Residence in ghettos usually involves some element of constraint or coercion, but it has not always been based on ethnicity or race. In U.S. history, the impetus has been social, economic, and cultural and occasionally even voluntary; Italians in San Francisco, Chicago, and other American cities, for example, maintained the old-world tradition of *campanilismo:* residing within sight of one's church steeple.

Ghettos in the United States have been home to all sorts of people: Jews on the Lower East Side of New York in the late nineteenth century and Poles in the Hamtramck district of Detroit in the twentieth century, for instance. Nor has ghetto consistently meant slum; witness late nineteenth and early twentieth century Harlem. The assumption that ghettos are populated exclusively by members of a single ethnic group has not invariably been the case in the American experience and requires qualification. Residents of common ethnicity rarely composed more than half of a district's population. Most frequently, a third might constitute the dominant element, giving the region its character, flavor, or even aroma—making it a "Little Italy" or "Over the Rhine," while a majority consisted of diverse groups sharing socioeconomic status rather than ethnic origins. Principal exceptions to the pattern in U.S. history have been African Americans and, in California history, the Chinese.

For most residents of American ghettos, escape routes existed; taking advantage of them was often difficult but possible. But most black people—even accomplished black people—persistently found exits either narrow or blocked, which is ironic. During the late nineteenth and early twentieth cen-

turies, European immigrants regarded learning English and acquiring citizenship as primary tickets to escape. For African Americans, who already had both, they mattered little.

Before the Civil War, black people comprised no more than four percent of the population of any northern city. Between 1865 and the early twentieth century, they began to move to cities, but principally in the South. During World War I, the pattern began to change when an estimated half-million left the rural South for the urban North. This process continued during the 1930s and accelerated dramatically during World War II, when California experienced its first major influx of black residents.

During the same period, a team of scholars led by Swedish sociologist Gunnar Myrdal published *The American Dilemma* (1944), a study of race relations in the nation. Among other things, the book observed that just over two percent of all African Americans lived west of the Mississippi River. But what it did not record was even more important. More than twenty-five percent of all western black people at the time—120,000—lived in just one place, Los Angeles, making it the fourteenth-largest African American urban concentration in the nation. This was a serious oversight in 1944; it was infinitely more significant in 1965 when it was the sixth largest and Watts exploded.

By the time of Myrdal's study, the history of what Lawrence B. de Graaf perceptively called "The City of the Black Angels" already spanned more than 150 years. Although more than half of the original *pobladores* of 1781, including founders of the prominent Pico and Tapia families, were of some African ancestry, during the Mexican Period intermarriage and assimilation all but eliminated black *californios* as a distinct, identifiable group. The Mexican-American War and gold discovery brought a few black migrants

Dining-car waiters on a Southern Pacific Railroad train, Los Angeles Union Station, ca. 1940s. It was the promise of employment, such as in the burgeoning railroad business, that lured migrating African Americans to Los Angeles from states in the East and South in the late nineteenth and early twentieth centuries. Along with merchants, professionals, and skilled workers, railroad porters and waiters were part of an elite group of relatively well-paid people who settled in Los Angeles, founded middle-class families, acquired property in numerous neighborhoods, and provided leadership for the growing black community. Relatively good housing, economic opportunity, and relations with other groups in the city generated a mood of optimism among Los Angeles African Americans through the 1920s. *Security Pacific Collection, Los Angeles Public Library.*

to the *pueblo*, but the majority of them, like other argonauts, continued on to the mining districts. During the same period, the most notorious street in Los Angeles was known as *calle de los negros*, but *negros* did not mean black people. It was instead a colloquial reference to "people of darkness," outcasts or criminals; only later-arriving Americans translated it to "Nigger Alley."

The earliest black migrants who settled in Los Angeles included former slave Biddy Mason, who won her freedom in 1856. Em-

ployed by black physician John Strother Griffin, she established herself as a midwife and nurse, using skills in folk medicine probably learned on the plantation and perhaps from Mexican *curanderas* in Los Angeles. She later bought property on Spring Street to provide a home for herself and her children and during the 1880s sold part of her land for $1500 and built a commercial building on another parcel. In the interim, she influenced the establishment of the First African Methodist Episcopal Church (sometimes paying its minister from her own funds) and became known and respected for her charity to people of all races. Robert Owens, who supported Mason's bid for freedom, was a freedman who arrived from Texas in 1850, established a thriving livestock business, employed a dozen *vaqueros,* and invested profitably in downtown and suburban real estate. Indeed, Owens' son Charles married Mason's daughter Ellen to begin something of a permanent dynasty. Mason's employer, Dr. Griffin, and several partners formed a water company that in 1868 contracted for the city's business and later became part of the municipal water system for a reported price of $2 million.

During the 1860s and 1870s a few more black people settled in the town and began, in collaboration with earlier arrivals, to develop a stable community; many of their descendants became—and some remain—political and social leaders among the city's African Americans. Despite the apparent successes, however, the number of black residents of Los Angeles was persistently small during the remainder of the nineteenth century; in 1880, a total city population of 11,000 included just 102. Another influx came with the "Boom of the '80s," lured by the same booster propaganda and railroad rate wars that attracted white migrants to southern California. The city's population in 1890 included almost 1,300 African Americans, and more than 2,000 in 1900—still only two to three percent of the total.

Most black migrants to Los Angeles before 1900 arrived from elsewhere in California or the Midwest, not directly from the rural South, and they came for about the same reasons as others: jobs, land, homes, and the climate. A Georgia lawyer, for example, called the area God's country and encouraged family and friends to join him. Some were part of the "health rush"—including a group that established a sanitar-

ium near Duarte. Some also arrived with substantial capital—such as the Kansas congregation that brought funds to build homes and a church. Indeed, they closely resembled other turn-of-the-century migrants to southern California. But at the same time, they began to establish the first identifiable black district in the city. In the downtown region along First and Second streets, they lived in individual homes, apartments, or boarding houses, usually bought or rented from African American owners such as the Masons and Owens.

A rigidly defined ghetto did not yet exist, however; black people lived throughout the city from the late nineteenth century into the 1920s. During the early twentieth century, also, they formed a cohesive community centered on organizations such as the Afro-American Protective Association and their churches. In 1879, the oldest still-published black newspaper in the state, *The California Eagle,* appeared. White people provided encouragement and support—even the rabidly anti-Chinese and anti-Mexican Los Angeles *Times.* Laborers, skilled craftsmen, and service workers found reasonably steady employment—although usually at lower wages than whites—and African American professionals—attorneys and physicians—served white clients as well as their own people. Others succeeded in businesses such as real estate, most notably the numerous descendants of Biddy Mason and Robert Owens, who remained leaders among local African Americans.

Between the 1880s and the 1920s, black Angelenos felt quite optimistic about their future, an outlook that persisted as their population increased to 7,600 in 1910 and almost 16,000 in 1920, between two and three percent of the city's total. In 1913, cofounder of the National Association for the Advancement of Colored People (NAACP) William E. B. DuBois visited Los Angeles and wrote in the organization's journal, *The Crisis,* that in the city, "[African Americans] are without doubt the most beautifully housed group of colored people in the United States. They are full of push and energy and are used to working together." He also described a business community that included "a splendid merchant tailor shop with a large stock of goods," "a contractor who was putting up some of the best buildings in the city," and "physicians, lawyers and dentists with offices in first-class buildings." In 1915, like their counterparts in Oakland and other communities, members of the city's NAACP chapter joined with church groups and social organizations in a vigorous protest against screenings of D. W. Griffith's film *The Birth of a Nation,* and in 1918, they collaborated with white voters to elect the state's first African American assemblyman, Frederick M. Roberts, publisher of the Los Angeles newspaper *The New Age.*

Despite their confidence and hope for the future, the 1920s brought several significant changes. For one thing, by 1925, more than half of all African American newcomers were arriving directly from the rural South. Since the black proportion of the population remained stable at around three percent, this might not have made much difference except for another influence: the mood of the nation following World War I. The 1920s was a decade of intense nativism and xenophobia (fear of strangers) in the United States, especially after the Bolshevik Revolution in Russia in 1917. Attitudes were revealed in several ways: the 1919 "red raids" on alleged communist organizations sanctioned by U.S. Attorney General A. Mitchell Palmer, restrictive Immigration Quota Acts based on the 1880 census that excluded the "new immigration" from southern and eastern Europe, overt public and official expressions of anti-semitism, racial violence in eastern and midwestern cities, and lynchings in the South.

Most illustrative, perhaps, was a resurgence of the Ku Klux Klan. In contrast to its southern, principally rural ancestor during the Reconstruction Period after the Civil War, the 1920s incarnation attracted a membership that was at least half northern and urban. Surviving records of California Klaverns confirm a minimum of 15,000 members in the Los Angeles region and another 8,000 in the San Francisco Bay Area. Because the Klan was, at least in theory, a secret society, how many more joined its ranks will likely remain unknown.

African Americans in southern California did not escape the xenophobic tide. Before the mid-1920s, ability to buy property or pay rent constituted the main limitation on black residence. White residents who wanted to take advantage of the "bungalow boom" and head for suburbs such as the San Fernando Valley were eager to sell, so homes were available to black people who could afford them—and many could. Indeed, approximately one-third of all black families in Los Angeles in 1930 owned or were buying their homes, about the same proportion as whites. But during the 1920s, white resistance became the controlling dynamic, and it delineated the origin of the Los Angeles ghetto, subsequently to become a slum. Until that decade, white sellers or black buyers who violated *de facto* boundaries encountered occasional violence, but it was sporadic, private, and unorganized. Later resistance became both public and well-organized, and results became evident as early as 1925. One black enclave was located downtown between Central Avenue and Spring Street and First and Fourteenth streets— near the present Civic Center complex. This was the area of early black settlement, but by the mid-1920s it housed many times its original population, and it was deteriorating. Another neighborhood, along West Jefferson Boulevard, near the campus of the Univer-

Ralph Bunche (right) in Los Angeles, 1926. In many ways, the life of Ralph Bunche (1904–1971) illustrated the promise that early Los Angeles held out to African Americans. Like so many of his fellow Angelenos, Bunche was a native of the Middle West (Detroit) and had migrated as a child with his family to Los Angeles, where he was reared and educated. Graduating from UCLA in 1927, he went on to Harvard University, where he earned a doctorate. A professor of government at Howard University in Washington, D.C., Bunche in 1941 began a long, distinguished career as a diplomat for the United States government and United Nations. For his service as leader of the U.N.'s Palestine Commission, he was awarded the Nobel Peace Prize in 1950, the first African American to be so honored. The Los Angeles black community fostered other leaders, some of whom served ethnic causes such as civil rights, others of whom had distinguished careers in the broader society in education, government service, the professions, and sports and entertainment. *Security Pacific Collection, Los Angeles Public Library.*

sity of Southern California, was home to African American professionals and business people. By 1925, more than seventy-five percent of the city's African American population lived in these areas and a smaller downtown enclave near the railroad depot, and most were finding it difficult to live anywhere else.

Restrictive covenants based on race contributed significantly to their problem.

These were provisions written into deeds that prohibited sale, lease, or rental of property to nonwhites under penalty of fine or, less frequently, loss of property. Before the 1920s, covenants were generally ineffective; white people who wanted to move to the suburbs ignored them and courts rarely upheld them. Indeed, judicial decisions had favored black plaintiffs who were denied the right to purchase property and brought suit. But in

1919, the case of *Los Angeles Investment Co.* vs. *Albert Gary* set a new precedent. The state supreme court decided that alienation (sale, rental, or lease) of property could not be legally restricted on the basis of race, but use (residence or occupancy) could be. In short, black people could buy, rent, or lease property, but they could not occupy it. The Gary case left loopholes that were closed by later court decisions and legislation, and covenants remained in force until the state supreme court declared them unconstitutional in 1948. By then, however, the Los Angeles ghetto was an established fact, and "private understandings" and similar devices continued to circumvent the court's decision and later fair housing legislation, limiting the access of even affluent African Americans to decent housing.

Other forms of discrimination accompanied residential segregation during and after the 1920s and complicated matters. Restaurants, hotels, theaters, clothing stores, and other businesses refused black patronage. Public facilities—swimming pools, parks, and playgrounds—were restricted by law or intimidation, effectively circumscribing black social life. Discrimination in employment—as often the product of union policies as of employers' practices—had similarly negative results. African American wage-earners secured jobs mainly as menials of various sorts: porters, laborers, janitors, waiters, maids, and servants. By the 1930s, few occupied the upper ranks even in those occupations. Hotels, for instance, employed numerous black bell "boys," but rarely a black bell captain. Industrial employment was generally scarce in Los Angeles, and whites monopolized most of the available jobs. Sales and clerical opportunities were likewise limited; in 1930, the city's retail sales force exceeded 11,000 but included fewer than thirty African Americans representing just 0.2 percent of the city's salespeople,

when their proportion of the population was 3.1 percent.

By the end of the 1920s, then, even when property was available outside the ghetto, few black residents of Los Angeles could afford it, and lines around restricted areas hardened. The city's African American population grew, but living space to accommodate it did not expand commensurately. Congestion and deterioration inevitably resulted. White-owned businesses moved out of black districts, leaving empty buildings behind. Absentee landlords subdivided properties into apartments, increasing congestion, and the city itself ignored the districts, resulting in poor sanitation and street maintenance, inadequate schools, limited utility and transportation services, and accelerated decline.

Even African Americans who had the means to flee the ghettos for the suburbs were frustrated. A black attorney attempted an upscale "country club" type development at Huntington Beach in 1925, but it mysteriously burned to the ground before completion. During the same decade, the city of Santa Monica denied a permit for a bath house and amusement center to black applicants and closed a dance hall. Black investors who purchased a country club in Corona and its patrons were so intimidated that it failed. In Manhattan Beach, Klan pressure on city government resulted in the condemnation of waterfront property owned by black families since 1911 and a prohibition against their using the beach. And in the San Gabriel Valley, Booker T. Washington, Jr. fought a protracted court battle to keep his home. Thus, poverty and rural origins were not the sole motives behind discrimination.

Since the late nineteenth century, black people had been moving a few miles south of Los Angeles to the semirural, working-class community of Watts, which has its own unique history. Originally part of *El Rancho*

Baptist ministers meeting, Pleasant Hill Baptist Church, Los Angeles, 1930. As was true elsewhere in the country, churches and their ministers were an important focal point in the lives of Los Angeles African Americans, not only for their religious services but also because they served as leaders in ethnic improvement programs, civil rights activities, and community organization. *Security Pacific Collection, Los Angeles Public Library.*

Tajuato, a large grant confirmed by the Land Commission of 1851, it was reduced significantly by encounters with lawyers, tax assessors, and squatters when the grant holder died in the late 1870s. His will distributed the remainder among numerous heirs, most of whom sold their small parcels to speculators who divided the land into lots to sell for $25—"a dollar down and a dollar a week"— principally to railroad workers recruited from Mexico. In 1907, Hispanic, black, and white residents incorporated the town, and almost simultaneously, the Pacific Electric Railway Company acquired a parcel of land from an early investor and established "Watts Station," which accelerated settlement.

During World War I, migrants from the rural South gave Watts a larger black population, and by the mid-1920s—while Italian immigrant Simon Rodia was at work on his tribute to his adopted country, "Watts Tow-

ers"—the town was ready to elect an African American mayor when it became part of the city of Los Angeles in 1926. Two influences seem to explain annexation—one external, the other internal. The Ku Klux Klan may have backed the move to prevent the election of a black town government. Watts residents, however, had more pragmatic concerns. Growth made the community desperate for water for homes and farms, and annexation meant access to the city's Owens Valley water system. Other towns followed the same course during the period, but annexation had special long-range implications for Watts. It provided access to water, but it also eliminated political autonomy and insured that the community would become a black enclave in a white city—just another "palm-tree ghetto." Other California cities— such as Compton, Richmond, and Oakland—retained political autonomy, and their black populations ultimately were able to exercise substantial authority and control. But that would not be the case for Watts.

The depression decade of the 1930s witnessed a slight decrease in the rate of white migration to Los Angeles and a slight increase in the rate of black migration. At the same time, industries began to locate on the fringes of Watts to tap the abundant and cheap labor supply. But until World War II, the community remained mixed, both racially and residentially. Whites, blacks, and Hispanics lived in the district—although not in equal proportions—and members of each group lived in housing ranging from decrepit to substantial.

The war years brought dramatic changes in both the number of black people in Los Angeles and their proportion of the population that are recorded in census data.

Los Angeles Population, 1890–1970

	Total	African Amer.	% African Amer.
1890	50,395	1,258	2.5
1900	102,479	2,131	2.1
1910	319,198	7,599	2.4
1920	576,673	15,579	2.7
1930	1,238,048	38,898	3.1
1940	1,515,428	63,774	4.2
1950	1,967,919	171,209	8.7
1960	2,480,859	334,916	13.5
1970	2,813,441	503,606	17.9
1980	2,966,850	505,210	17.0
1990	3,485,398	478,674	13.6

Data are compiled from several sources, including U.S. Census abstracts, which are not entirely consistent. The decline between 1980 and 1990 is not explained.

Between 1890 and 1930, the African American population of Los Angeles grew steadily, but the proportion did not change appreciably. When their numbers doubled or even tripled in a decade, so did the total population. During the 1920s and 1930s, however, more than 20,000 arrived each decade and

the situation became critical; inability to disperse into a proportionately larger area of the city resulted in accelerated congestion and deterioration in regions where black people could live—including the Watts district. During the World War II decade, the black population nearly tripled and its proportion more than doubled, and during the 1950s, both gross and proportional increases nearly doubled once more.

Rather ironically, Japanese relocation ameliorated conditions for African Americans in Los Angeles slightly during the war years, when the abandoned area known as "Little Tokyo" became part of the center-city ghetto. But available space could not absorb the mass migration, and newcomers competed for space with Mexican migrants and crowded into established black communities such as Watts. To ease the pressure for housing during the war years, the federal government constructed "interracial" projects that rapidly became overcrowded and all black. They were not the rat and roach infested high-rise tenements that typify facilities in regions such as New York City's Bedford-Stuyvesant, but animal and insect pests would arrive soon enough—and so, too, would varieties of human vermin.

Nevertheless, anomalies persisted in African American districts of Los Angeles, even into the 1960s. In Watts itself, some turn-of-the-century $25 lots remained vacant, while as many as six residences crowded others. Some neighborhoods maintained an air of middle-class respectability, while adjacent blocks, according to a black journalist, would "make Sodom . . . look like a Sunday School picnic." Many residents continued to make modest livings, and creativity persisted in music, art, and theater among some, but hopelessness and stark poverty characterized the lives of most inhabitants of the community.

As early as the 1940s, severe physical and

social deterioration in Watts was apparent, observed, and documented. A federal study conducted during the war commented on conditions that included lack of quality and integration in schools, inability of black youth to take advantage of facilities such as the city's junior college system, lack of leadership and employment opportunity, and conflict within the community and between the community and the police. In 1947, a city planning commission investigation called Watts "an obsolescent area in which all of the social and physical weaknesses of urban living are to be found." It identified inadequate recreational facilities, deteriorating streets, decaying private and public buildings, ineffective public transportation, limited shopping facilities, and high disease, death, and delinquency rates. Another study two years later in 1949 was a dismal echo of its predecessors.

By 1960, increased congestion had rendered conditions worse. Urban renewal programs had demolished some neighborhoods, displaced their residents, and relocated them to other already-congested areas where they could afford housing. The freeway system "balkanized" black districts, creating unanticipated difficulties. For people with automobiles, freeways can increase mobility and opportunity; for those without reliable cars or access to public transportation, they can be "Berlin Walls" that preclude both. By 1960 also, about sixty percent of the population of Watts was under age twenty-five, and forty percent of those between eighteen and twenty-five years of age had no job at all; most of the remainder were underemployed.

The state did not neglect conditions entirely, although it frequently responded tardily. To combat continued discrimination in hiring and compensation, Governor Earl Warren in 1946 proposed a Fair Employment Practices Law, but reluctant legislators delayed its passage until 1949. In 1963 law-makers passed the Rumford Fair Housing Act, but a referendum on the 1964 ballot—Proposition 14—repealed the law by a two-to-one margin that Pat Brown appropriately called "a vote for bigotry." The state supreme court reinstated the Rumford Act in 1965, and the U.S. Supreme Court upheld its decision in 1967, but by then Watts had exploded. Ironically, black and white people in Los Angeles managed to live together before the 1920s—even in the same neighborhoods—at least amicably, if not in total harmony. Subsequently, however, Watts and similar districts in other California cities became "palm-tree ghettos" where social and economic conditions contradicted overt resemblances to "typical" neighborhoods of homes surrounded by lawns. In reality, Los Angeles was as racially segregated as almost any city in the South in 1960 and less segregated than only two cities in the North: Cleveland and Chicago.

Thus, by August 11, 1965, when Marquette Frye was arrested on Avalon Boulevard near 116th Street, a powder keg of accumulated frustration was primed to explode. Even the climate that Wednesday evening magnified the potential. The temperature had dropped out of the eighties into the seventies, pleasant enough to attract an audience to the streets to witness the unfolding outdoor drama; spectators, in turn, provided a fertile field for misunderstanding. Tales of police brutality, often embellished in the telling, spread rapidly and drew people from blocks away to the scene. Scant prior contact between white officers—or white society in general—and residents of the ghetto provided neither side with a basis for understanding, and lack of communication added to immediate tensions. Since only sergeants' car radios could communicate with one another, patrolmen receiving "officer needs help" calls from their headquarters responded without clear knowledge of conditions, plunged into the apparent chaos,

Angelenos celebrating the return of jazz musician Lionel Hampton, outside the Alabam Club, ca. 1954. The relatively open environment of early-twentieth-century Los Angeles, particularly its movie, radio, and recording industries, nurtured the talents of numerous black artists and entertainers. As a child, Lionel Hampton migrated with his family from Alabama in 1927. In Los Angeles, he attended the University of Southern California and played with the Benny Goodman Quartet. Eventually starting his own orchestra, Hampton moved on to New York and international acclaim as one of the country's greatest jazz artists. *Security Pacific Collection, Los Angeles Public Library.*

assumed the worst, and reacted—or overreacted—accordingly. Many officers, in fact, never heard an order to withdraw, issued to reduce the provocation of their presence. The police department activated its Emergency Control Center (E.C.C.) on Thursday, but inaccurate information and frequently overloaded radio frequencies hampered its effectiveness. In combination with limited prior preparation and riot training and inadequate manpower and equipment, faulty communication inhibited ap-

propriate official responses from the episode's beginning to its end. Rather ironically, however, one form of communication was all too effective; televised reports of locales being burned or looted turned them into beacons, attracting potential participants.

Through Wednesday night and into early Thursday morning, random violence sputtered sporadically, especially in the vicinity of Avalon Boulevard and Imperial Highway, where groups of African Americans—mostly young—stoned police, randomly attacked white drivers passing through the area (traffic was not diverted), and clashed with television crews, who reportedly encouraged some incidents. Simultaneously, community leaders attempted to defuse the increasingly volatile situation, and local residents, such as the couple who gave first aid to County Supervisor Kenneth Hahn, assisted, protected, and even rescued white people caught in attacks. Meanwhile, at a police headquarters press conference, Chief William Parker expressed his probably sincere conviction that problems were isolated and attributable to a few "agitators" who advocated civil disobedience.

Members of the African American community knew better on both counts, and their leaders scheduled a meeting at Athens Park on Thursday afternoon to avert an escalation of violence. Even the weather, however, seemed to conspire against them; southern California's notorious Santa Ana wind began to blow from the desert, and by eight o'clock on Thursday morning thermometers approached eighty degrees. By 1:30 in the afternoon, when Congressman Augustus Hawkins, County Supervisor Kenneth Hahn, clergymen of several denominations, and delegates from the police, sheriff and fire departments and the district attorney's office, the NAACP, and several social service agencies convened, they registered nearly ninety. The assembly hoped to organize teams of peacemakers to contact neighborhood gangs quietly in an effort to prevent another night of violence, but the unanticipated presence of television crews and dozens of citizens determined to voice their grievances subverted the plan. Most residents who spoke recited litanies of accumulated frustration not related to the immediate issue, and only one speaker, a young man with no apparent political affiliation, condoned violence. Marquette Frye's mother,

Rena, free on bail after her arrest for obstructing an officer, begged officials "to help me and to help others in this community to calm the situation down so that we will not have a riot tonight."

Toward that goal, leaders who attended the meeting requested that police presence in Watts be limited to African American officers in civilian clothes to remove the most obvious provocation and scheduled a second meeting for seven o'clock at the Bel-Vue Presbyterian Church. They also secured an agreement from CBS affiliate KNXT-TV to provide time for a local minister to explain matters and appeal for peace and met privately with several gang leaders to solicit their cooperation. Unfortunately, peacemakers' efforts foundered. Deputy Police Chief Roger Murdock, acting for severely ill Chief Parker, rejected petitions to assign black officers to the district, although police did limit their initial presence on Thursday evening to routine patrols. Appeals to the Businessmen, Slausons, Gladiators, and other neighborhood gangs that could be contacted fell, for the most part, on deaf ears, and their members were joining the fray by nightfall. The minister's plea for peace aired at 5:45 P.M.—just before the local news—and reached few viewers; the regular broadcast that followed—whose audiences were substantial—provided no coverage of the Athens Park meeting, except for the single incendiary speaker.

Although only a few random incidents occurred during the early afternoon on Thursday, by 7:00 P.M., the time scheduled for the second meeting of local leaders (which never took place), crowds had assembled at numerous points along Avalon Boulevard. Residents futilely appealed to authorities to block the street and then attempted to divert traffic themselves, for which some were arrested. By 8:00 P.M., after an abortive proposal of a street dance on Imperial Highway as a distraction, automobiles came under attack. Fires erupted—cars at first, but later stores—and fire units that responded to alarms provided additional targets. Shortly before midnight, police officials declined an offer of assistance from Colonel Robert L. Quick, California National Guard liaison to the Los Angeles Police Department, despite increased attacks on property and looting of liquor stores and pawn shops. Early on Friday morning—ironically the thirteenth—Lieutenant Governor Glenn Anderson (Governor Pat Brown was in Greece) was advised that the situation was under control and that the National Guard was not needed—despite a score of burned cars and seventy-six buildings looted or destroyed during the night—and he left Los Angeles for a University of California Board of Regents meeting in Berkeley. Mayor Sam Yorty departed almost simultaneously for a speaking engagement in San Francisco. Before noon, however, Chief Parker realized that he was not dealing with just a handful of troublemakers, changed his mind, and appealed formally for state assistance.

When Lieutenant Governor Anderson finally received the request, he vacillated, fretting about procedures for activating the National Guard. In the meantime, circumstances changed rapidly and drastically. Violence spread over a far greater area, not only into central Watts along 103rd Street (known as "Charcoal Alley") and north along Central Avenue and Broadway in the immediate vicinity of earlier outbursts, but also several miles northwest to the region beyond the University of Southern California and the Los Angeles Coliseum. At the same time, the number of participants swelled dramatically. Either as participants or as members of an exuberant audience applauding and encouraging players on center stage, people of all ages and both sexes joined the predominantly young

males who originally assaulted police, firefighters, vehicles, and property. By Friday night, the expanded perimeter and increased numbers overwhelmed local law enforcement agencies, still dispatching individual patrol cars manned by standard two-officer complement to scenes of violence.

Deteriorating conditions late in the day and intensified sniper attacks on police and fire units prompted officials to relax restraints on officers' use of their firearms. By early evening, the first units of the National Guard, some of whom had received riot training, began to assemble, but indecision over their precise function delayed deployment until 11:00 P.M., when they began to sweep the streets of Watts and establish road blocks in an effort to contain the riot. In the meantime, Oak Park Hospital at Broadway and Manchester, where medical staff and administrators grappled with a constant flow of casualties, came under attack. And the first fatality occurred, probably the result of a ricocheting bullet; before violence abated early on Saturday morning, when entire blocks were ablaze or in ashes, more than a dozen were dead.

At dawn on Saturday, smoke hung over much of the Los Angeles Basin, buildings flamed and smoldered, and debris, including scorched hulks that had been vehicles, littered riot zone streets. Following a brief early morning reprieve, burning and looting resumed, and among the first to go was a Safeway store on Imperial Highway. From across the highway, an exhausted minister who had participated in the Athens Park meeting guarded the building with a rifle through the night and fell asleep briefly at around 9:00 A.M.; when he awoke, he saw the market and an adjacent shopping center engulfed in flames. Before noon, more than fifty structures were torched, looted, or both.

National Guard reinforcements arrived

steadily from Friday on, some flown from northern California or diverted from annual training duty at Camp Roberts near Paso Robles. Because they lacked adequate maps and information, some convoys located their assigned destinations only with difficulty; one even lost its way for several hours in the freeway system maze. Nevertheless, about 13,000 guardsmen were on duty by Saturday night. Faulty intelligence and communications and jammed E.C.C. facilities continued to hamper operations, contributed to the spread of rumors, and resulted in confrontations, especially at roadblocks established to contain the disturbance and enforce a curfew that Governor Pat Brown ordered when he returned to the United States. Some drivers defied roadblocks, but most problems occurred when citizens who were ignorant of the curfew approached barricades manned by young troops made tense by rumors of incidents at other posts. Mistakes and misunderstandings on both sides resulted in serious injuries and several more deaths. Still, the show of force began to have its effect in areas such as Watts itself, where troops were present in strength and highly visible.

To the north of Watts, however, conditions were far less promising. Along Central Avenue new fires flared in aged, flimsy buildings and defied attempts to douse them. At the perimeter of the riot zone, on Washington Boulevard near Central Avenue, just blocks from downtown Los Angeles, waves of looters systematically stripped a major department store throughout the day, despite 200 arrests made at the scene. Until National Guard officers assigned teams of riflemen to each fire unit, snipers forestalled assaults on new fires along Broadway, the last major area torched during the week of violence. The E.E.C. continued to receive sporadic reports of new outbursts and "shots fired" through Monday morning, but the situation was sufficiently stable to allow Governor Brown to tour the region on Sunday—to a less-than-enthusiastic reception from residents. By Monday morning, businesses began to re-open, where any residue of them remained, and on Tuesday morning, authorities ended the curfew. A week later, on August 23, the last of the National Guard troops pulled out and returned to their home armories.

During the tumultuous week, flare-ups occurred in other southern California communities, but they remained relatively confined, minor incidents as a result of cooperation between their residents and officials. But before turmoil subsided in Los Angeles, it involved at least 10,000 local people, approximately 13,000 National Guard troops, the California Highway Patrol, and law-enforcement officers from several other jurisdictions. More than thirty were dead, all but three of them black. Inconsistent record-keeping places the number of seriously injured (those who received medical treatment) in some doubt; assessments range from 849 to 1,309. Arrests numbered nearly 4,000; courts completed preliminary processing of the majority of them during a single week. Estimates of property damage (principally to white-owned business establishments) approximated $40 million. Despite the extent of devastation that some described as resembling a war zone, it was not universal. Many structures stood unscathed in the midst of chaos. In some cases, residents saved homes from flames by dousing them with garden hoses or by maintaining a constant vigil, sometimes armed, over them. Some businesses also survived, not only those owned by African Americans but also a few where white owners had gained the respect of black neighbors who, in several cases, protected establishments from impending assault. And the tide of violence simply flowed around some neighborhoods, bypassing them entirely.

Following the riot, the state-sponsored

The Philanthropic Matrons, Los Angeles, ca. 1955. Women's groups, often associated with the churches, assumed many responsibilities of community organization for black residents of Los Angeles. The Philanthropic Matrons sponsored charities and community improvement. *Security Pacific Collection, Los Angeles Public Library.*

McCone Commission report, *Violence in a City—An End or a Beginning?* and other investigations identified numerous contributors to the explosion, including immediate issues such as controversy over the repeal of Proposition 14 and frustration over political impotence. But little else was original—except in magnitude. New studies reiterated inequities and conditions that had been observed and documented twenty years earlier but had grown worse over time: congestion that resulted in decaying neighborhoods, severe underemployment, police harassment, limited opportunity made worse by inadequate education, increased poverty and dependency, functional illiteracy, and general discrimination that characterized the experience of many black Californians of all classes. African American industrial workers still received less pay than their white counterparts, despite the state's Division of Fair Employment Practices. Professional organizations excluded black men and women from membership; the Los Angeles Bar Association, for example, did not drop its color barrier until 1950, and it was among the first.

Violence in Watts drew belated attention to conditions and awakened Californians to grim realities. Neither city, state, nor nation, however, responded in anything resembling an expeditious or consistent manner. Federal "Great Society" programs, initiated during Lyndon Baines Johnson's presidency to promote academic and vocational education and increase employment opportunity, were promising and benefited at least some urban African Americans, but with a price. Talented black men and women entered the middle class, moved out of Watts and other ghettos, and diminished the leadership pool that remained. White Californians like their counterparts throughout the nation— apparently assumed that the policies continued to function effectively. In reality, controversy over war in Vietnam and priorities of subsequent administrations relegated domestic issues, such as inner cities and their residents, to secondary status. Consequently, circumstances improved little for most residents of places such as south-central Los Angeles and worsened for many of them. A quarter of a century after the 1965 Watts Riots, the scenario of violence was replayed under disturbingly similar circumstances but with even more devastating consequences. By that time, new ingredients rendered the volatile atmosphere even more explosive: increased single-parent families and an ongoing economic recession that contributed to poverty and declining social services, organized street gangs battling for turf, persistent and ubiquitous drug trafficking, proliferation of firearms, and enclaves of Asians and Hispanics competing for space and opportunity.

CHAPTER TWENTY-SIX

DREAMS DEFERRED: THE 1960s

When Californians elected Edmund G. ("Pat") Brown to the governor's office in 1958, they not only expressed an optimistic view of their future but also broke with a longstanding historical tradition. Brown was only the second Democratic governor since the 1890s, and voters gave a majority in the legislature to boot. The significance of the event, however, was not exclusively partisan or historical.

Brown was a political heir to the ebullient, expansive optimism of the California progressivism of Hiram Johnson and Earl Warren, and a disciple of the concerned liberalism of Franklin Delano Roosevelt and the New Deal. He also was the only member of his party holding statewide elected office in 1958 and therefore the Democrats' logical choice to run for governor. Republicans, by contrast, had several potential candidates, each with a substantial following: incumbent governor Goodwin Knight and two conservatives, U.S. Senator William F. Knowland and Vice President Richard M. Nixon, both of whom had their sights set on the presidency. After acrimonious and divisive intraparty disputes, Republicans settled on Knowland as their candidate, but in the 1958 election Californians settled overwhelmingly on Pat Brown.

THE ELECTION OF 1958

When Earl Warren accepted nomination to the U.S. Supreme Court in 1953, his mantle fell on Lieutenant Governor Goodwin Knight, who won the governorship in his own right in 1954. Although Knight began his tenure as a conservative Republican, he soon adopted Warren's policies of moderation and pragmatic nonpartisanship. His support for labor, social programs, and resource management established him as a popular governor in the progressive tradition and gave him a broad, bipartisan constituency. As a candidate for reelection, however, Knight discovered that popularity was not an unmitigated asset, especially where powerful and ambitious rivals within his own party were concerned. Foremost among the governor's competitors were U.S. Senator William F. Knowland and Vice President Richard M. Nixon. Both hoped to succeed Dwight D. Eisenhower in the White House in 1960, and both considered winning the California governorship an important step in that direction.

In addition, Nixon disliked Knight both personally and politically—especially after

1956 when the governor refused to endorse his bid for a second term as vice president. But Knowland made the first intraparty assault on the incumbent by announcing in 1957 that he would seek the Republican nomination for governor. Simultaneously, it became clear that Knowland enjoyed the support of the right wing of his party (including many of Nixon's backers) and that Knight would be denied access to campaign funds if he chose to wage a primary fight. The governor understood the precariousness of his position, dropped out of the gubernatorial contest, and announced his candidacy for Knowland's U.S. Senate seat, which he subsequently lost to Democrat Clair Engle.

The falling out among Republicans pleased California Democrats, who recognized an unusual potential for victory. They had begun to prepare for such an opportunity in 1953 when, twenty years after the founding of the California Republican Assembly (CRA), they took belated steps to overcome their weaknesses and founded the California Democratic Council (CDC). An outgrowth of the informal, liberal-oriented Adlai Stevenson Clubs of 1952, the CDC was designed to coordinate campaigns and other partisan activities. After 1954, under the direction of Palo Alto journalist Alan Cranston, the organization became increasingly effective. Also in 1952, a voter referendum modified the state's cross-filing law and increased Democrats' opportunities by requiring candidates to designate party affiliation on primary ballots. Previously, cross-filing favored incumbents (usually Republicans) by listing them first on ballots, without party identification. The new requirement gave Democrats at least an equal chance in their own primary elections. During the 1950s, they won often enough to reduce traditional Republican majorities in the legislature.

THE FIRST GOVERNOR BROWN

In addition to partisan rejuvenation and changes in election laws, Democrats had a third asset in 1958: unified support for one candidate for the governor's office, Edmund G. ("Pat") Brown, a second-generation Californian whose Irish and German ancestors arrived in the state during the 1850s. Joseph and Bridget Brown from County Tipperary established themselves in San Francisco while August and Augusta Schuckman from the province of Westphalia settled in the Sacramento Valley near the town of Williams. Both couples raised families and prospered modestly, and in 1896 their paths crossed. Apparently dissatisfied with country life, the Schuckman's daughter, eighteen-year-old Ida, left home and family, like the young rural Americans epitomized by the heroine of Theodore Dreiser's *Sister Carrie*, to seek her fortune in the city. In San Francisco, she met the Browns' son Edmund Joseph, a budding businessman with a taste for derby hats and tailored clothes and a determination to succeed.

Ida was an attractive, proper German Protestant with an affinity for books and a keen interest in ideas. Edmund was a bright, burly, boisterous, and dapper Irish Catholic with the gift of the blarney, and a love of people and poetry. Despite obvious differences, the couple began "keeping company" soon after their introduction, and within a year they married and established residence with Edmund's parents. During the following decade Brown's business interests grew, and the couple moved to their own apartment on Central Avenue where the first of their four children was born and christened Edmund Gerald in 1905. All of the children were raised in their father's church, and both parents exposed them to literature, music, and poetry at home. As soon as they were old enough, Edmund and his brother Harold worked in their father's businesses, and at Fremont Grammar School during World War I the oldest son acquired his nickname. He closed a Liberty Bond drive speech with Patrick Henry's stirring "Give me liberty or give death"; for the rest of his life, he would be "Pat."

Young Pat Brown inherited personal characteristics from both of his parents. He was gregarious, eager, bright, ambitious, and athletic. At Lowell High School, he stood out as a quick student with an inquiring mind, a solid basketball player, an enthusiastic cheerleader, a holder of twelve offices in student government, and an accomplished debater. But when he graduated, he had no firm career plans. Family finances did not permit following friends across the bay to the university at Berkeley, and experience in his father's marginal businesses convinced him that the life of a small-time entrepreneur was not for him. But he continued to work for his father, enrolled as a night student in a local law school, and worked part-time for blind attorney Milton Schmitt. In 1927, Brown completed his law course, passed the state bar examination, and took a permanent position in Schmitt's office. A year later, Schmitt died and left his practice to his protégé.

Pursuit of the law, however, did not consume all of Brown's youthful energy; he also pursued Bernice Layne, daughter of a San Francisco police captain. His infatuation with her began while both were students at Lowell, but his suit languished until he completed his legal studies and she received her degree and teaching credential from the University of California, both in 1927. During their subsequent courtship, Brown made his first bid for public office as a Republican candidate for the assembly in 1928. With a campaign staff composed principally of friends and family members, he waged a creditable canvass, but inexperience de-

feated him. He then returned to his expanding law practice, in partnership with his brother Harold, and in 1929 he and Bernice eloped.

Marriage failed to diminish Pat's political ambition, but the Great Depression sweeping the land during the early 1930s prompted him to question his partisan affiliation. In 1931, his friend, labor lawyer Matt Tobriner, reacted to the Hoover administration's lack of response to the economic collapse by renouncing his Republicanism, registering as a Democrat, and proclaiming support for Franklin Delano Roosevelt's presidential candidacy. In 1934, as conditions worsened in California and Republican Governor Frank Merriam seemed little inclined to address them, Brown too changed his registration to Democrat and became a confirmed New Dealer, active in the Democratic organization and a member of the party's county committee. Brown shared Tobriner's commitment to the plight of the poor, unemployed, and aged during the Depression, but he was equally interested in other matters: political reform to clean up local government and law enforcement and to end the influence of lobbyists in Sacramento.

To that end—and against advice from Bernice and his parents—Brown embarked on a second quest for office in 1939 by challenging twenty-two-year incumbent San Francisco District Attorney Matthew Brady. Pat feared that gambling at his father's Padre Club in the Tenderloin might become a campaign issue, but Brady demolished the young reformer at the polls without even mentioning the place. Four years later, however, the outcome was different when Brown again campaigned for Brady's office, using the slogan "Crack down on crime, elect Brown this time." With the support of major local newspapers, he won a decisive victory that astonished professional politicians and gamblers who had given 5 to 1 odds against him. They were not surprised when he won again in 1947 or when, with Governor Earl Warren's support, he became state attorney general in an otherwise Republican sweep in 1950.

Warren's political backing was not his sole contribution to Brown, however. As district attorney for Alameda County in the 1930s, he made the office honest, efficient, and vigorous in the prosecution and conviction of lawbreakers. During the 1940s, Brown studied Warren's methods and, applying what he learned, transformed his own outmoded and historically corrupt San Francisco department into an aggressive agency that warred against political corruption, vice, gambling, and juvenile delinquency. He also opposed efforts to deport labor leader Harry Bridges, denounced Japanese relocation during World War II on moral and constitutional grounds, and supported efforts to provide decent housing for thousands of African Americans who migrated west to work in war industries. As district attorney of San Francisco County and as attorney general of California, Brown's policies built the reputation and broad support that made him governor in 1958.

In a vigorous campaign for himself and his party's candidates, Brown stressed confidence in the future, articulated his philosophy of "responsible liberalism," condemned his opponent's negative conservatism, and stressed labor issues. Knowland had earned a reputation as a supporter of the "open shop," "right-to-work" laws, and other anti-union policies, and he reiterated his position as candidate for governor. In contrast, Brown established himself as a friend of labor when, as attorney general, he forced a change in the title of Proposition 18 on the 1958 ballot from "Right-to-Work" to "Employer and Employee Relations," an action

that confirmed his prolabor reputation. Californians responded to this issue, to Brown's personal charm, and to his optimism with an overwhelming majority of their votes. In addition, they elected Democrats to every statewide office except secretary of state, a strongly Democratic delegation to Congress, and a Democratic majority in both houses of the state legislature. They also soundly rejected antilabor Proposition 18.

THE CALIFORNIA WATER PLAN

Brown's inauguration in 1959 began four years of governmental activism unmatched since the regime of Hiram Johnson. Among the first Brown administration's major accomplishments, adoption of the California Water Plan (CWP) stands high. The CWP represented the first comprehensive effort to cope with a problem that had persisted since the gold rush era and was becoming more acute as population grew and shifted in the twentieth century. Cities such as San Francisco, Los Angeles, and San Diego tapped distant sources for water supplies, and farmers throughout the state established irrigation districts with elaborate delivery systems. State and federal governments funded major water projects, and localities dammed streams to create reservoirs. But, with the exception of the Central Valley and Colorado River projects, little coordination existed among programs until 1960.

Although planning for the new state plumbing project began during the Warren administration, opposition proved insurmountable. By the late 1950s, however, the need for action was urgent and apparent. Almost half of the state's population lived south of the Tehachapis where less than ten percent of its water resources were located. The new governor pressed both water experts and legislators for a comprehensive water plan and an $11 billion bond issue to finance it. Again, opposition was intense and vocal. Agribusiness interests objected to proposed federal collaboration on the project, since it would mean extension of the despised 160-acre limit on irrigation. Northern Californians envisioned their water flowing south, while some southerners considered the plan an incentive to accelerated growth, added pollution, and increased congestion. Conservationists objected in principle to damming more rivers, and fiscal conservatives condemned another major expenditure. Others in the state suspected that money for water projects would be siphoned from programs such as education.

The governor responded to critics with characteristic energy. First, he appealed to Congress for an exemption from the 160-acre limit; when that failed, he suggested an exclusively state-sponsored program with modified limits, a proposal of dubious legality or feasibility. In response to regional conflicts, he resorted to diplomacy emphasizing mutual benefits: jobs, progress, and an end to historic sectional controversy. Similarly, he identified himself as a conservationist and stressed the environmental controls that would be part of his proposal. Finally, he reduced his request for an initial bond issue from $11 billion to $1.75 billion and embarked on an extensive television campaign to win support.

Voters approved both the California Water Plan and the bond measure in November 1960, and work began in 1961 with the Oroville Dam on the Feather River. It was completed in l968 and is capable of storing more than 3.5 million acre-feet of water. The system has subsequently been expanded to include additional dams and aqueducts to deliver water throughout the San Joaquin Valley and to southern California. One later component of the CWP, however, remains

Governor Pat Brown with Assemblyman William Byron Rumford
Governor Pat Brown (*right*) with Assemblyman William Byron Rumford. *Courtesy of the Bancroft Library.*

highly controversial: the often-proposed but still unbuilt peripheral canal around the Sacramento–San Joaquin Delta.

CIVIL RIGHTS AND MINORITIES

Civil rights constituted another concern of the first Brown administration. In 1960, 600,000 African Americans comprised six percent of the state's population. Most of them had settled in cities to take advantage of opportunity for industrial employment, but they continued to experience economic prejudice. In response to both local conditions and a civil-rights movement gaining nationwide momentum, the 1959 legislature enacted a law forbidding discrimination in the workplace and created the Division of Fair Employment Practices to enforce its provisions on employers and unions alike. The same legislature passed the Unruh Civil Rights Act to ban discrimination in business dealings (including real estate transactions), in access to restaurants and other public accommodations, and in occupancy of publicly funded housing facilities.

The laws fell short of ensuring equal opportunity to black Californians, and they were resented and resisted by many employers, unions, businesses, and real estate interests. They also ignored a major impediment to social and economic progress—inadequate educational opportunity. Like other states outside the American South, California responded tardily to the implications of the U.S. Supreme Court's 1954 *Brown* v. *Board of Education of Topeka* decision, which required desegregation of public schools. Still, the 1959 actions and the Rumford Fair Housing Law of 1963, named for black assemblyman William Byron Rumford, placed the state in the vanguard of the drive for equal rights for African Americans.

California took less specific action on behalf of members of other ethnic minority groups. Japanese Americans found hostility toward them somewhat diminished by the 1960s. But even though Congress had authorized compensation for lost property and the return of confiscated bank accounts as early as 1948, collecting was painfully difficult, and neither state nor federal governments moved to expedite it. In 1952, the state supreme court did nullify the Alien Land Act of 1913, and during the same year federal action eliminated the "aliens ineligible for citizenship" prohibition from naturalization policies. Also, during World War II, Congress had rescinded the Chinese Exclusion Act as insulting to citizens of an Allied power. For the most part, however, Japanese, Chinese, Filipinos, and other Asians in California were left to their own devices through the early 1960s, as were the state's Hispanic

Americans, who numbered nearly 1.5 million by 1960 and included both descendants of the *californios* and more recent arrivals from the Southwest, Mexico, and elsewhere.

By the 1950s, most Hispanic Americans in California were not farm workers but resided in urban *barrios*. They occasionally gained notoriety, as in the "Zoot Suit" riots in Los Angeles in 1943, but they were generally overlooked and ignored. Most of them were poorly housed and underemployed, with a high rate of functional illiteracy, a low level of secondary school enrollment, and a high school completion record lower still. During the later 1950s, they began to find their political voice, principally through the Mexican-American Political Association (MAPA). Formed in 1959, MAPA supported the presidential campaign of John F. Kennedy in 1960 and the election of Los Angeles City Councilman Edward R. Roybal to Congress in 1962. Nevertheless, Hispanic Californians remained seriously underrepresented in the state's agencies through most of the decade, and few of their children reaped the benefits of the federal Elementary and Secondary Education Act or the state's Miller-Unruh Reading Act, both passed in 1965 to enhance basic educational accomplishment.

If Hispanics in California were barely audible in politics during the period, Indians were virtually mute. Indeed, never had an individual of discernible Native American heritage held either elective or appointive office in the government. Throughout the early twentieth century, their numbers continued their historic pattern of decline, but during the postwar decades they began to increase again, reaching 75,000 by 1965. Most, however, were recent migrants, not descendants of members of local tribes. The vast majority (about ninety percent) lived in cities, interspersed with the general population, especially after the 1950s when the U.S. Bureau of Indian Affairs (BIA) accelerated its policy

Indians on Alcatraz
In 1969, Indians representing several tribes stood before an altered
sign proclaiming Alcatraz Island to be "United *Indian* Property."
AP/Wide World Photos.

of "terminating" federal supervision and support of reservations, and Congress passed Public Law 280 to give the states jurisdiction over their Indian residents.

California considered Indian affairs to be a BIA function and resented the new responsibility and its potential cost. Early in the century, the state had removed legal and civil distinctions between Indians and other citizens and assured them equal access to public education and other services, but changes in federal law presented novel problems. Beginning in 1953, a state senate Interim Committee on Indian Affairs con-

ducted investigations and found that most California Indians opposed termination and the inadequate compensation that the federal government offered as a substitute for reservations. The committee also attempted to formulate responsive policies. In 1961 the Brown administration created the Advisory Committee on Indian Affairs (ACIA), which made additional studies documenting most Indians' abject poverty and limited education but produced few tangible improvements. More effective were private initiatives. White sympathizers founded the Sequoia League in 1901 to protect the interests of displaced Cupeños in San Diego County, and as early as 1919, when they formed the Mission Indian Federation, Native Californians united to preserve their culture and to advocate education. During the 1960s they established the American Indian Historical Association and the California Indian Education Association, which promoted the addition of Native American studies programs to college curricula. They also organized political action groups, including Indians of All Tribes (IAT), which occupied Alcatraz Island in San Francisco Bay from 1969 to 1971.

Alcatraz was an abandoned federal penitentiary, deserted until 300 IAT men, women, and children settled on "The Rock" in 1969. They demanded that the site be given to their association for an Indian cultural and medical research center, but they did not achieve their objectives. Instead, the Indians were evicted, and the island currently remains federal property under the jurisdiction of the National Park Service. The demonstration did, however, result in a state Indian Assistance Program in 1970 and in increased political activism on the part of Indians in California.

REFORMS IN POLITICS AND GOVERNMENT

Under the leadership of Jesse M. Unruh, first as Chairman of the Assembly Ways and Means Committee and later as speaker of the assembly, legislators during Pat Brown's first administration grappled with immediate and longstanding problems in state politics and government. Cross-filing had been modified earlier in the 1950s; it was abolished entirely in 1959. So too was California's "federal plan" of allocating state senators on the basis of counties. The 1927 policy resulted in gross overrepresentation for residents of rural regions and equally blatant underrepresentation for those in cities, but

in 1964 the U.S. Supreme Court declared such systems unconstitutional in its "one man, one vote" ruling (*Reynolds v. Sims*). California responded when the legislature mandated districts based on population, even if this resulted in combining as many as three small counties or dividing larger ones. Results were dramatic and important. Los Angeles County, which historically had sent just one senator to Sacramento, suddenly had thirteen, and the seven counties south of the Tehachapis saw their representation in the state senate increase from seven to a more equitable twenty-one. Simultaneously, Brown and Unruh seized an overdue opportunity to alter procedures of state government substantially.

For more than a century, California government has functioned (critics say malfunctioned) under the Constitution of 1879. Over the years, the document was amended nearly 350 times and increased more than fourfold in volume. By 1960 the organic laws of only two states (Alabama and Louisiana) and one nation (India) were longer; few were as complex. The amendment process was difficult and time-consuming, requiring approval by two-thirds of each house of the legislature and the voters. In addition, efforts to make even minor changes usually encountered determined opposition from vested interests. Governors William D. Stephens (1917–1923) and Clement C. Young (1927–1931) and legislative commissions during the 1940s and 1950s had attempted revision, but confusion and obsolescence remained the state constitution's principal distinctions. Finally, legislation in 1962 authorized the formation of a sixty-member Constitutional Revision Commission that operated until 1974.

The Commission's efforts produced significant results, including a fifty percent reduction in the Constitution's length. Over ten years, the body also wisely presented proposed changes to the voters a few at a time, and seventy-five percent of them received approval. Among the few additions were sections to guarantee that the rights of Californians would not be diminished as a result of interpretations of the U.S. Bill of Rights and to protect the property rights of aliens in the state. In addition, the commission reduced percentages of voters needed to qualify ballot initiatives, increased requirements for appointments to the bench, and expanded city and county authority over local affairs. Other changes made it possible to govern more efficiently; they abolished the 120-day limit on legislative sessions, the separate budgetary session, and the $500 ceiling on legislators' salaries, and they authorized the governor, with legislative consent, to reorganize and streamline the executive bureaucracy.

With Brown's backing, Unruh guided through the legislature additional reforms that eliminated some obsolete executive agencies, consolidated others to increase the scope of their authority, and created new ones to deal with current issues and problems. The legislature itself also underwent thorough reorganization. Measures sponsored by Unruh and others established year-round sessions, increased compensation to make service in the legislature more attractive, and streamlined the procedures of the legislature and its staff. Critics denounced the creation of a "supergovernment" in Sacramento, but the reforms of the 1960s made California's government a model of professionalism and efficiency and won national recognition and awards for Jesse Unruh.

SCHOOLS AND SOCIETY

As it did in the rest of the nation, the Soviet Union's successful *Sputnik* launch in 1957 precipitated a sweeping assessment of public education in California. Responses included the adoption in 1960 of the Master Plan for Higher Education to coordinate and define responsibilities of the three levels of postsecondary education serving the state: community colleges, the state colleges (operating as virtually autonomous campuses until 1963), and the University of California. To upgrade the quality of instruction in public schools, the legislature approved the Fisher Act of 1961, requiring students to major in academic subjects, rather than education, to qualify for California teaching credentials. In addition, the state increased its level of funding for public schools at all levels and for programs ranging from advanced scientific and technical training to teaching basic skills.

Like the drives for efficiency in government and educational improvement, other actions of the first Brown administration recalled elements of progressivism, especially the commitment to social and economic justice, to concerns for the environment, and to the use of public authority to attain desired ends. By the end of 1962, the legislature had raised levels of unemployment, disability, and workmen's compensation payments and set up the Office of Consumer Affairs and the State Economic Development Agency. Within the next few years, it enacted the most stringent air quality control laws in the nation and established an Air Quality Control Board to oversee their implementation.

Such policies were expensive, as were paying interest on CWP bonds, raising legislators' salaries, funding schools and mental health programs, improving the highway system, and similar activities. Brown had inherited a treasury deficit, since the Knight administration had depleted Earl Warren's "rainy-day fund." Eliminating the red ink while financing both new and established programs required larger budgets ($2.2 billion in 1959 and more in each successive year) and increased taxes. But Californians hardly protested. Tax increases had not been levied for several years, and the new rates generally conformed to population growth, inflation, increased standards of living, and expanded levels of government service. Furthermore, during Brown's first term Californians were confident in the future of their state, in its economy, and in its leadership.

THE ELECTION OF 1962

Although Pat Brown was an eminently successful first-term governor, he did experience setbacks for both his programs and his political reputation. Throughout much of his career, for example, he had been an energetic advocate of minimum-wage laws. Despite vigorous efforts as governor to establish $1.25 as the minimum for the state, opposition by agricultural and other interests prevented the proposal's success. Brown had been an equally staunch opponent of capital punishment, but he was stymied in his attempts to eliminate the practice in California. Although he granted a stay in the celebrated Caryl Chessman case, Chessman ultimately went to the gas chamber in 1960; he was one of thirty-two prisoners executed during Brown's two-term tenure. During the same year, events at the Democratic National Convention tarnished Brown's image as a master politician. A badly splintered California delegation refused to follow the governor in supporting the candidacy of John F. Kennedy, probably costing Kennedy the 36,000 votes by which he lost California—and very nearly the presidency.

Despite such reverses, Brown's record and his popularity made him a strong candidate for reelection in 1962, a position made stronger by his opponent Richard Nixon. Still smarting from defeat in the 1960 presidential race, Nixon had little real interest in being governor of California; he only sought the office in order to renew his quest for the White House. He was unfamiliar with state issues and resorted to accusing Brown of being "soft on communism" and ineffective in preventing radicalism in the state. Voters were not impressed by these tactics; they returned Brown to office by another wide margin. Nixon responded with a speech blaming the press for his defeat and promising journalists that they would not have him "to kick around any more."

The Democratic victory was not as complete as it had been in 1958, however. The party's legislative majority diminished slightly, the delegation to Washington included more Republicans, such as Senator Thomas Kuchel, and the ultraconservative Max Rafferty became State Superintendent of Public Instruction. Nevertheless, prospects for a successful second term seemed auspicious to Pat Brown and to Californians in general.

Shortly after the election, a symbolic event seemed to confirm popular confidence in Brown. On November 24, 1962, a huge counter straddling the Oakland–San Francisco Bay Bridge ticked over to 17,393,134 and proclaimed the state's status as the most populous in the nation. The count was based solely on estimates and projections and was not official. Indeed, both New York state and the U.S. Census Bureau disputed the figure, and only the 1970 federal census ultimately confirmed California's number one ranking. Later generations would be less enthusiastic about the benefits of numbers, but at the moment residents of the state remained disciples of the nineteenth-century booster who asserted that "population is the one great desideratum" for progress. Among the newcomers were professionals and highly skilled technicians attracted by burgeoning aerospace and other industries and the apparent economic potential that they offered. It did not seem to matter to Californians in 1962 that the in-

California First Days
In December 1962, the New York *Times* drew national attention to Pat Brown's claim that California was the most populous state in the nation when it published a photograph of the overjoyed governor celebrating with a contingent of "mountain men" from Amador County. *AP/Wide World Photos.*

flux also included even larger numbers of African Americans from the rural South, Mexican Americans from the Southwest, and displaced blue-collar workers from throughout the nation. The future seemed to have space in it for any number of people of all kinds. If bigger was better, Californians assumed, biggest must be best. An elated Governor Brown gave state employees a holiday on December 31 and set aside four "California First Days" for celebration. Equally enthusiastic residents of towns from Truckee to San Diego took advantage of the opportunity.

Early in Brown's second term, the legislature confirmed its own optimism by enacting the Rumford Fair Housing Law to forbid racial discrimination in real estate transactions, but it was not long before events made

it clear that the public mood was changing. Property owners contested the Rumford Law in the courts, and in November 1964—in what an outraged Brown called "a vote for bigotry"—Californians approved Proposition 14 to repeal the law by a two-to-one margin. Even though the state supreme court subsequently overturned the repeal, the "white backlash" that it represented was a portent of difficult times to come.

THE POLITICS OF CONFRONTATION

In the aftermath of the 1965 Watts Riots that stunned Californians, militant and radical political-action groups rapidly emerged, notably the Black Panther Party founded in Oakland in 1966 in reaction to local conditions and to Stokely Carmichael's nationwide "Black Power" movement. Articulate leaders—Huey P. Newton, Bobby Seale, and *Soul on Ice* author Eldridge Cleaver—attracted young African American men and women with a mixture of Marxist-Maoist rhetoric and advocacy of resistance to police and other symbols of white authority. The issue of armed resistance became synonymous with the Panthers and could provide dramatic evidence of their existence. During a 1967 debate on a gun control measure aimed principally at radical groups, a contingent of party members, some armed and in uniform, entered the Capitol in Sacramento to observe the proceedings. No violence ensued, but later in 1967 and 1968 clashes with police resulted in the wounding and arrest of both Newton and Cleaver and the death and injury of several officers. Newton's protracted trials for manslaughter ended without conviction, and he subsequently assumed leadership of a Panther Party more dedicated to social programs and prison reform than the ideology of armed defense. In 1968, while Cleaver was the Peace and Freedom Party candidate for president, the state revoked his 1966 parole on a previous assault conviction; he chose exile in Algeria rather than return to prison and continued to preach armed insurrection. In 1973, Seale lost his bid to become the first black mayor of Oakland.

By the end of the 1960s, the Black Panther Party itself was splintered, and the remaining radical faction was embroiled in power struggles with separatist organizations such as Ron Karenga's US, a conflict that ended with blacks killing blacks in a Los Angeles incident allegedly provoked by the FBI. At issue were ideological and political questions, especially control over black studies programs and the Black Student Union at UCLA. The result, however, was a devastating blow to support for US, for the Panthers, and for black militant groups in general. A final episode in 1970 had the same effect. At Marin County Court House in San Rafael, an abortive and tragic attempt to free George Jackson and the "Soledad Brothers" from custody ended in death for both blacks and whites and capped a decade of racial confrontation in California.

The turmoil of the 1960s produced at least two positive results for black Californians. It made whites more sensitive—if not more sympathetic—to their presence, and it stimulated increased participation in traditional politics. In 1970, black votes helped to send Ronald Dellums to Congress and Wilson Riles to the office of superintendent of public instruction. Two years later, Yvonne Burke joined Dellums in Washington, Mervyn Dymally became lieutenant governor, and more black legislators appeared in Sacramento. Black officials also became more numerous in state, county, and municipal governments. Their emergence was impressive; it was not matched, however, by improved conditions for many of their constituents.

HISPANIC CALIFORNIANS IN THE 1960s

For California's largest ethnic minority, Hispanics, the 1960s experience was generally similar to that of black residents of the state. Middle-class Hispanic citizens began to find their political voice in the Mexican-American Political Association (MAPA) founded in 1960, but it produced few immediate results. Nor did MALDEF, the Mexican American Legal Defense and Education Fund established in 1968. Younger Hispanics, perhaps inspired by the Panthers and other black organizations, therefore formed the militant Brown Berets and the culture-oriented La Raza (the people) to give cohesiveness and substance to their cause. They also identified themselves—and distanced themselves from older generations of Mexican Americans, often derided as *tío tacos* or *pochos*—with the label *chicano*. Despite substantial effort, commitment, and a large voting population that included many citizens of recent Mexican ancestry, tangible accomplishment and political recognition proved elusive.

Two fundamental conditions precluded success. One involved the long-established Hispanic tradition in California, reinforced and diversified periodically by new migrations (both legal and illegal) north across the border from Mexico and from other Latin American countries. An apparently cohesive community was actually thus divided, but not only by national origin. According to Ralph Guzmán, the state's largest Hispanic group included "Americans of Mexican Ancestry," who placed little emphasis on their cultural heritage; "Mexican Americans," who regarded its positive and negative implications with ambivalence; and "Chicanos," who were militantly committed to its preservation as a distinct entity. The term *chicano,* chosen by younger activists to express ethnic solidarity, also illustrates differences, especially among generations. Probably derived from *chico* (child), which Anglos in California once employed much as southern whites used "boy" to refer to black men, it had decidedly derogatory overtones before the 1960s. Even established Mexican Californians habitually referred to temporary, unsophisticated, and generally unwelcome migrant field workers in the state as *chicanos*. Gradually, however, the term acquired a modicum of respectability, at first in *corridos* (folk ballads) such as "*Yo soy chicano*" about heading north to look for work. Finally, during the 1960s, it became the term used to express cultural and political unity. A second barrier to cohesive achievement, however, remains and involves a phenomenon that Leonard Pitt has called "the schizoid heritage" resulting from persistent and general failures—on the part of Anglos and Hispanics alike—to distinguish between the "romance" of California's rich Hispanic tradition and the reality of existing conditions in the state's urban *barrios* and rural *colonias*.

Paradoxically, the smaller agricultural component (about twenty percent in 1960) in the state's Hispanic population drew greatest public attention and, in some cases, support during the decade. Since late in the nineteenth century, floating subcultures with minimal access to the benefits of society, even to education for their children, provided the labor needed for the state's "factories in the fields." Over the generations, the migrant work force consisted of various ethnic groups: whites, Asians, Filipinos, Hindus, Punjabis, and others. Periodically, it made its presence known through strikes and incidents such as the Wheatland Riot of 1913 and the violence of the 1930s. From World War II on, however, California's fields became the province of Hispanics, many of them relatively recent arrivals from Mexico; most residents of the state remained comfortably oblivious to their presence until 1965.

The situation began to change in 1964 when Congress refused to renew Public Law 78, the *bracero* law that had kept local farm laborers' wages depressed ever since 1951. Ten months after Congress acted, workers in the grape fields near Delano in the southern San Joaquin Valley went out on strike against DiGiorgio and Schenley interests and thirty other growers, demanding higher pay, improved working conditions, and recognition of their right to organize. The AFL-CIO–sponsored Agricultural Workers Organizing Committee (AWOC) initiated the walkout in September 1965, and it was quickly joined by the National Farm Workers Association (NFWA) headed by César Chavez.

Chavez spent his youth and his early adult life as a migrant farm worker, and he experienced the handicaps of that life, including a formal education that consisted of about eight years in forty different schools. He was, however, a devout man concerned about the plight of his fellow workers, and during the later 1950s he committed his energies to community and social service among them, especially through NFWA. Unlike AWOC, neither NFWA nor Chavez was oriented toward traditional organized labor goals, and Chavez himself was highly skeptical of the effectiveness of strikes by agricultural workers. Nevertheless, he threw his own and his association's support behind the AWOC strike at Delano. It was at first an uneasy alliance between a mainly Filipino, labor-oriented AWOC and a principally Mexican American NFWA dedicated to community service and civil rights. Still, the coalition led to the United Farm Workers Organizing Committee (UFWOC) and ultimately to the AFL-CIO–chartered United Farm Workers of America (UFWA).

Unity made it possible to win the strike at Delano. Through the winter of 1965, growers hired strikebreakers and armed guards to combat UFWOC efforts to stay organized.

CÉSAR CHAVEZ AND "LA CAUSA":

The Union as a Social Movement

A new era in farm labor relations began in California when César Chavez organized the National Farm Workers Association in 1962. For decades employers had successfully beaten down attempts to organize their workers. In Chavez they encountered a unique, charismatic leader who turned the organization of a farm labor union into a social movement involving ethnic minorities, church leaders of many faiths, student activists, and the whole spectrum of civil-rights and antipoverty forces of the 1960s and 1970s. Through the use of militant but nonviolent tactics, Chavez built his union into the United Farm Workers of America (UFWA), affiliated with the AFL-CIO and the first to survive and win important contracts from California growers. And his success had much to do with passage of the historic Agricultural Labor Relations Act of 1975.

Born and raised on an Arizona farm, César Chavez came to California in 1938 after his father lost his land in the depression. The family joined the ranks of migrant farm labor, enduring that era's disgraceful working conditions and low pay (at one point the entire family earned only 20 cents a day picking peas). In 1944 César joined the navy; he returned to farm work after the war. In 1952 he became an organizer for the Community Services Organization (CSO) and a national director in 1958. Four years later he left the CSO and, with his wife Helen working ten hours a day in the fields to support the family, he set out to establish a union that would bring social justice to farm labor.

Building on his CSO experience, his own deeply held religious beliefs, and his commitment to Gandhian nonviolent tactics, Chavez introduced a new concept of union or-

César Chavez
AP/Wide World Photos.

CÉSAR CHAVEZ AND "LA CAUSA":

The Union as a Social Movement (continued)

ganization. His union supplied a wide range of social services, including credit unions, co-ops, death benefit programs, and assistance in dealing with government agencies from schools to welfare offices; in the process it built a loyal following. Emphasis on Mexican cultural and religious values made union meetings a religious experience, with Mass and prayer a part of the agenda. Chavez recruited the support of students, civil-rights leaders, clergymen, and liberal Democrats, turning the union movement into a broadly based social movement with national support and the motto "La Causa."

When he joined the Delano grape strike in 1965, Chavez mobilized supporters for a nationwide boycott of table grapes and organized a dramatic, highly publicized, 300-mile march on Sacramento, placing enormous pressure on growers. Within two years the major grape growers had signed contracts with Chavez's union. In the 1970s, when growers refused to renew contracts and shielded themselves from the UFWA with "sweet-heart" contracts with the Teamsters, Chavez made the boycott international and even obtained an audience with Pope Paul VI, strengthening church support for "La Causa." Frequently, too, he adopted the fast as a tactic to reinforce his emphasis on nonviolence, attracting national publicity and support (Robert Kennedy attended the Mass at which Chavez ended his first fast in 1968) and eliciting from his followers a fervent rededication to the movement.

César Chavez's ability to blend community service, religious and cultural experiences, and Gandhi's nonviolent principles with the traditional drive to unionize and bargain collectively for better wages, working conditions, and benefits has been the key to the survival of the UFWA. By the time Chavez died in April 1993, however, union membership among farm workers had declined precipitously; only about ten percent are currently organized. (RBR)

The strikers received support from the AFL-CIO, but they also encountered vigorous and often violent opposition from Teamsters, who were determined to control the fields. Finally, following a twenty-four-day march of nearly 300 miles from Delano to Sacramento, Chavez and his allies won their first concessions. In June 1966, Schenley Industries announced its willingness to negotiate a contract. Soon after, DiGiorgio Corporation authorized elections at its Delano site; field workers chose UFWOC to represent them, and shed workers and drivers selected the Teamsters. Although the outcome re-quired further arbitration, the precedent had been set, and the organizational effort spread southward to the Imperial Valley, involved a nationwide boycott of table grapes, and finally resulted in the negotiation of additional UFWOC contracts with growers in the Coachella Valley and throughout the state.

During the early 1970s, the UFWOC campaign expanded to other regions of California, especially the Salinas Valley and again faced vigorous opposition. Teamsters attacked picket lines with baseball bats and tire irons, killing two UFWA members. In 1970 growers' associations secured injunctions to limit union activity, and in 1972 they spent millions on Proposition 22, designed to curtail farm workers' rights to organize and negotiate. But by then the UFWA had gained substantial public support, and the measure lost by 1.3 million votes. Shortly after the election, growers suffered another blow; the state supreme court invalidated previously granted antiunion injunctions. Only in 1975, however, would another Governor Brown sponsor legislation to create a state Agricultural Labor Relations Board and give workers in the fields the protections enjoyed by their counterparts in industry.

STUDENTS IN REVOLT

Events of the 1960s made it apparent that the "silent generation" of college students—those who barely reacted to the Tenney Committee or the McCarthy witch-hunts of the 1950s—had departed from California's and the nation's campuses. When the House Un-American Activities Committee met in San Francisco City Hall in 1960, hundreds of students excluded from its sessions occupied the building until they were dispersed by police clubs and firehoses. Brief and isolated as it was, the incident rang like Thomas Jefferson's "fire-bell in the night," predicting more serious confrontations to come.

The University of California at Berkeley soon became a volatile flash point for student dissent. During the 1960s, civil rights activism increased on campus, a vocal "ban-the-bomb" movement emerged, protests against U.S. involvement in Southeast Asia increased, and representatives of various unconventional and radical political philosophies took to the streets. As Berkeley students became more outspoken, the university administration and Board of Regents restricted on-campus political activity,

despite a 1963 U.S. Supreme Court decision defining such policies as contrary to the First Amendment. In response, Berkeley students united behind philosophy student Mario Savio in the Free Speech Movement (FSM) in 1964. When the university disciplined several students for violating its policies, the FSM occupied Sproul Hall in what members believed to be a legitimate gesture of civil disobedience. Instead, their action provoked a confrontation with police who were ordered into action by Governor Brown. More than 700 students were arrested and nearly 600 were tried and found guilty of trespassing, resisting arrest, or both. The results severely shocked California parents, taxpayers, and especially students. Philosopher Savio had not explained that engaging in even legitimate civil disobedience has a price; Henry David Thoreau, after all, went to jail for the principle, and Socrates paid for it with his life.

Within a month, the university rescinded its ban on political activities, but the change did not bring calm. Instead, for five more years campus-related disruptions occurred with disconcerting regularity. As was the case throughout the nation, opposition to involvement in Southeast Asia, reaction against ROTC programs and the draft, spreading "ban-the-bomb" sentiments, an increasingly militant civil-rights movement, and a feminist cause gathering momentum perpetuated confrontation. By the end of 1965, destructive violence and systematic "trashing" of property were integral elements of campus protest, especially as Students for a Democratic Society (SDS), the Youth International movement ("Yippies"), drug-oriented "hippies" or "flower children," and politically radical organizations became involved. Official responses simultaneously increased in aggressiveness and violence and often included armed riot police equipped with Mace, tear gas, and attack dogs.

Mario Savio at FSM Rally
During the fall of 1964, students, various other members of the University of California community in Berkeley, and representatives of the news media attended rallies supporting the Free Speech Movement. Here, they crowd around the decorated Christmas tree on Sproul Plaza—with their signs, cameras, and even baby strollers—to hear Mario Savio speak. *UPI/Bettmann Newsphotos.*

Similar incidents spread outward from Berkeley. Late in 1967, an antidraft protest attempted to close the induction center at Oakland and ended in a prolonged riot. A year later, across the bay at San Francisco State College, a strike supporting black studies programs and other causes degenerated into weeks of disruption, destruction, and violence. Stanford University experienced a major confrontation in 1969, and the same year brought the "People's Park" incident, the National Guard, helicopters spraying tear gas over Berkeley, and one student fatality. A second student died during a demonstration on the university's Santa Barbara campus in February 1970.

The killing of four students by National Guardsmen at Kent State University in Ohio in May 1970 and other fatalities in the state dampened enthusiasm for espousing radical causes in the streets. So, too, did the get-tough policies of new Governor Ronald Reagan, the dismissal of President Clark Kerr of the University of California, and the appointment of S. I. Hayakawa to restore order at San Francisco State. Equally important was the demise of causes. Opposition to the war in Vietnam made its point, and involvement diminished in the early 1970s. The movement for racial equality made slow but observable progress. In 1971 the Twenty-sixth Amendment gave eighteen-year-olds

ERIC HOFFER
Uncommon Common Man

One evening in September 1967, a burly California longshoreman appeared on prime-time television to discuss his philosophy of life in an hour-long interview. When the program ended, CBS switchboards across the country were immediately swamped with calls, telegrams began pouring in, and, as the week progressed, letters arrived in almost unprecedented numbers. Sixty-five-year-old Eric Hoffer—ex-hobo, ex-migrant worker, ex-prospector, member of the ILWU, unschooled and self-taught, yet author of four internationally admired philosophical books—had become an overnight American celebrity. Intensely charismatic and completely natural, Hoffer had captivated his audience as he laughed, frowned, perspired, and pounded his fist while expressing his very positive views of life in America. His certainty served as a powerful antidote to the uncertainty Americans felt in the mid-1960s, as their cherished beliefs in their country's power abroad and their institutions at home were being challenged on all sides. As his interviewer, Eric Sevareid, said later, Hoffer had redefined the old truths about America and shown why they remained alive and well.

Behind Hoffer's persuasiveness lay a rare authenticity that grew out of the unusual circumstances of his life. While growing up, he had not been indoctrinated into a structured belief system—religious, political, or social; he had not had to think a certain way because he was told to, nor had he had to live a certain way because it was expected of him. Born with a remarkable intellect, he had enjoyed a remarkable freedom to make of his life what he would.

An only child, born to German immigrant parents in 1902, Eric taught himself to read in both English and German at the age of five. Two years later his mother died, and Eric went suddenly blind. For the next eight years he was cared for by a large motherly

Eric Hoffer
UPI/Bettmann Newsphotos.

ERIC HOFFER
Uncommon Common Man (continued)

German woman named Martha, who made him feel wonderfully important and clever. "If I am anything," he said in later years, "it is because of Martha." At fifteen his eyesight returned unexpectedly and, fearing that his blindness would recur, he began to read voraciously. Apparently holding the same belief, his father made no effort to put him in school or prepare him for a job. When his father died in 1920, leaving him only a few hundred dollars, the eighteen-year-old Eric decided to go to California, which he had heard was a paradise for the poor. Since he had never had experience outside the home, never attended school, or played with other children, California became the shaper of his experience and the furnace in which he forged his thought.

Hoffer worked at odd jobs in Los Angeles throughout the 1920s, living in a cheap room on Skid Row where he spent all his spare time reading and writing ideas in notebooks. During the 1930s he became a migrant farm worker, following crops from southern to northern California during the harvest season. During the winters he prospected for gold, tried his hand at writing, and studied until his education would have been the envy of many a college student. Meanwhile, he was being educated by his fellow migrant workers, with whom he lived in close proximity and in whom he became intensely interested. Out of this experience grew his theory that it is the misfits who make history because, due to their insecurity, they become "true believers," attaching themselves to dogmatic leaders and supporting "holy" causes. California, he later said, is one of the best places in the world to study true believers because nearly everyone there is a transplant and insecure. He published his first book, *The True Believer,* in 1951 and it became widely admired in intellectual circles.

Meanwhile, he had joined San Francisco's ILWU in 1941. It was the first steady job of his life and one he held until retirement in 1967. On the waterfront he engaged his fellow longshoremen in intense discussions, listening to their stories and ideas and captivating them with his philosophical observations. Deeply impressed by the "common man," Hoffer became convinced that America is unique because it has been shaped by its masses, who are "the most skilled and competent population the world has ever known."

During the next forty years Hoffer published eight books dealing with the role of the masses in history, the problem of change in human society, and, in essays and aphorisms, thoughts on the human condition. He became a special lecturer at the University of California at Berkeley, wrote a syndicated column, served as a member of the President's Commission on the Causes and Prevention of Violence, and was awarded the Presidential Medal of Freedom, the highest civilian award in the nation. Despite success and fame, Hoffer held steadfastly to his simple way of life. He continued loading ships with his fellow longshoremen until he was sixty-five. He never owned a suit and, until his death in 1983, remained in his small apartment on the waterfront, reading and writing and taking long daily walks on the streets of his beloved San Francisco. (EWR) the right to vote, making conventional politics more attractive than confrontation. For example, Tom Hayden—a founder of Students for a Democratic Society in 1962 and one of the "Chicago Seven" convicted of conspiring to disrupt the 1968 Democratic Convention—attempted to win the Democratic nomination for U.S. Senator (1976), espoused consumer rights through his Campaign for Economic Democracy, received appointments to serve on state commissions, and won a seat in the assembly in 1982. For Hayden and others like him, the radicalism of the l960s became the common sense of the 1970s.

THE 1960s: AN ASSESSMENT

Neither California nor the nation would be quite the same after the 1960s. On the one hand, the activism of the period persisted as a fact of political life, not only for the young and radical but also for citizens of all ages and persuasions. Teach-ins and similar activities focused on contemporary issues to heighten awareness among a generation of students and even their parents, who became increasingly vocal in expressing discontent with the quality of life in California and about an array of concerns ranging from environmental pollution and exploitation to suburban sprawl and urban blight to ineffective public education and hazardous thermonuclear power plants.

California women exemplified the renewed political vigor and its limitations. Generations of them recognized that the state had compiled a comparatively positive record on feminist issues prior to the 1960s. But many also came to understand that modest progress was, in fact, a two-edged sword that bred complacency and allowed remaining serious inequities to be ignored. After establishment of the National Council on the Status of Women in 1961, for instance,

California was only the forty-fourth state to follow suit, and took three years to do it. Political leaders—including some women—assumed that favorable conditions made a local version superfluous. Similarly, when a 1964 federal law required equal pay for equal work, Californians presumed that it would make little difference, since similar state legislation had been on the books since 1949. In reality, the third of California's work force that was female still earned nearly forty percent less than their male counterparts.

Armed with statistics from the Women's Bureau of the U.S. Labor Department, and perhaps energized by the spirit of the decade, leaders of moderate women's groups from throughout the state convinced a reluctant legislature to approve and a less-than-enthusiastic governor to appoint a state Commission on the Status of Women in 1964. After conducting systematic research, the commission in 1967 presented its findings and recommendations to the governor; they extended far beyond evidence of inequitable compensation to include more controversial issues such as child care, abortion, divorce and property law reform, and access to education, as well as a score of proposals for legislation. It was not Pat Brown who received the report, however, but Ronald Reagan, who was significantly less sympathetic to feminist causes than his lukewarm predecessor. Response was therefore minimal, but women had laid a firm and positive foundation for subsequent achievements.

On the other hand, campus disruptions had both immediate and long-range negative consequences. Student unrest reduced public confidence in and support for institutions of higher learning and severely diminished the reputation of one of the nation's finest universities. Simultaneously, conflict in the cities and the fields shattered the optimistic mood that had put Pat Brown in the governor's office in 1958 and 1962. Changes in federal spending priorities, inflation, and rising taxes resulted in a faltering economy and reduced confidence still further. Nor was extremism entirely put to rest. On the right, the John Birch Society remained active, vocal, and politically influential. On the left, frustrated militants resorted to terrorism. The Symbionese Liberation Army assassinated Oakland Superintendent of Schools Marcus Foster and kidnaped heiress Patricia Hearst in 1974, committed a series of bank robberies and other crimes, and ended its existence in a fiery Los Angeles shoot-out in 1975.

The controversies of the 1960s also undermined unity among Democrats. Members of the party remained generally agreed in support of civil rights legislation and social programs, but the war in Vietnam remained deeply divisive. It split the party during the 1964 elections and allowed Republican song-and-dance man George Murphy to capture a seat in the U.S. Senate. It also sundered the California Democratic Council, precipitated the dismissal of its president, Simon Cassady, and rendered the organization virtually useless in Pat Brown's bid for a third term in 1966. Brown lost additional backing because his responses to the occupation of Sproul Hall and other campus disturbances were too lenient for some, too harsh for others.

In sharp contrast to Democrats' disarray in 1966, Republicans were united. During the 1966 primary campaigns, most abided by the party's "Eleventh Commandment" to speak no ill of fellow Republicans. And after moderate Republican Mayor George Christopher of San Francisco lost his bid for the gubernatorial nomination, the party rallied to support a single candidate: actor-turned-politician Ronald Reagan.

CHAPTER TWENTY-SEVEN

ERAS OF LIMITS: RONALD REAGAN, JERRY BROWN, AND AFTER

Jerry Brown summarized his view of government's role in society with the phrase "era of limits"; with only modest alteration, the concept could be applied to the public mood that put his predecessor Ronald Reagan into office. By the mid-1960s the expansive optimism that made Pat Brown appealing had evaporated. The fabric of California's society was unraveling, and the state's economy, which had promised an improved quality of life for all, staggered erratically. Universities and colleges, the pride of many Californians, were plagued by often-violent discord. And the cost of maintaining the ship of state on an even fiscal keel continued to escalate. Reaction to these developments was the cautious conservatism that made Reagan governor in 1966. Eight years later, public attitudes had changed little, and Californians opted not for a return to the enthusiastic progressive-style leadership of the first governor Brown, but for the unique (some say incomprehensible) mixture of philosophies espoused by the second.

THE RISE OF RONALD REAGAN

Born in Illinois in 1911, Ronald Reagan matured in the midwestern heartland. After college, he worked for several years as a radio announcer in Iowa before leaving for Hollywood in 1937 to begin a twenty-year career as a movie actor, principally in Westerns. A politically active college student, he later served as president of the Screen Actors' Guild (SAG). As a young adult, Reagan was a Democrat with liberal tendencies, but he began a conversion to conservatism following a World War II stint in the military. He was a militant supporter of SAG's effort to purge suspected communists from its ranks during the later 1940s and a Democratic supporter of Dwight Eisenhower in the 1950s. Simultaneously, he found lucrative employment as a public relations executive for General Electric Company, and in 1960 he backed Richard Nixon's campaign for the presidency, still as a Democrat. Finally, he became a Republican and campaigned actively for his new party's presidential candidate, Barry Goldwater, in 1964.

Thus, even though Ronald Reagan had not held public office, he was hardly a political neophyte when he decided to run for governor in 1966. During years of making speeches and hosting television shows for General Electric, he honed his version of conservatism and distilled it to a few adaptable points: the virtues of free enterprise, the inequities of taxation, and the dangers of big government. Earlier campaign experiences also made it as clear to him as to Jesse Unruh that "money is the mother's milk of politics," and he surrounded himself with the "Friends of Ronald Reagan," wealthy backers who included both Hollywood personalities and successful business people. In 1965 they began to provide the financial nourishment essential to a quest for the governor's mansion and even the White House. Reagan understood, too, that chance did not produce election victories and employed Spencer-Roberts & Associates to make his first bid for office in 1966 a polished and professional performance.

For Democrats, the 1966 campaign was anything but polished and professional. Pat Brown ran on his record, but his progressivism no longer appealed to the electorate. Indeed, conservative Mayor Sam Yorty of Los Angeles took nearly a million votes from him in the primary contest. Brown had no backing from the CDC, the liberal wing of his party refused its support, and organized labor defected, alienated by the incumbent's housing and jobs policies for African Americans. Reagan, on the other hand, used access to the media, especially television, to attack Brown's record. He held the governor responsible for "the mess at Berkeley" and for urban disturbances, assailed his stance on the Rumford Fair Housing Act and Proposition 14, and blamed him for increased budgets and tax burdens. Reagan also defused charges of extremism by insisting that support for him meant acceptance of his ideas, not his acceptance of the ideas of right-wing groups such as the John Birch Society. Throughout the campaign, he repeated versions of his set speech defending free enterprise and political morality, attacking lib-

Ronald Reagan's Midnight Inauguration
Ronald Reagan grasped the reins of gubernatorial authority as soon as possible after his election. Very shortly after midnight on January 2, 1967, he took the oath of office in the rotunda of the Capitol Building in Sacramento. His hand rested on Junípero Serra's centuries-old Bible, held by state senate chaplain Wilbur Choy. *UPI/Bettman Newsphotos.*

erals as dangerous extremists, and promising reductions in taxes, budgets, and the scope of government. Reagan's message was congenial to Californians in 1966; they made him governor by a margin of almost a million votes, elected Republicans to nearly every statewide office, and substantially reduced Democratic majorities in the legislature.

REAGAN IN POWER: THE FIRST TERM

Like politicians before and after him, Ronald Reagan quickly learned that ideologies are more readily articulated as a candidate than implemented as an officeholder. Although his "creative society" program faced hostile majorities of 21 to 19 in the state senate and 42 to 38 in the assembly, he believed that they could be enacted with support from conservative Democrats. But he discovered that many programs requiring state expenditures were mandated by law or tied to federal policies on which the state depended. He also found that many Californians, his own constituents among them, had vested interests in perpetuating and even expanding costly programs. Finally, inflation and an economy weakened by periodic recession made it impossible to "squeeze and cut and trim" spending across the board. Instead, just six months after his inauguration, he "bit the bullet" and approved the largest budget (more than $5 billion) and the greatest tax increase (almost $1 billion) in the state's history. There were, however, areas in which cuts might be made with substantial popular support: higher education, mental-health programs, and welfare.

Reagan acted on his promise to "clean up the mess at Berkeley" by backing the dismissal of President Clark Kerr early in 1967. Despite increased enrollments and inflated costs, the governor also reduced support for the university and state colleges by thirty percent, triple his promised ten percent across-the-board cut. In addition, he advocated an end to the historic policy of tuition-free higher education on grounds that paying tuition would make students more responsible and more likely to sit in classes than demonstrations. A new regime at Berkeley did not end disturbances there and the legislature and Regents rejected tuition hikes as rank anti-intellectualism, but most Californians regarded the "crackdowns" as long overdue.

Changes in mental-health and welfare programs were equally problematical. Since the 1950s California had developed a mental-health program regarded as the most progressive in the nation. It institutionalized only the most seriously ill patients and treated others as outpatients in communities. Failing to recognize that hospitalized patients were severely disturbed and required more, not less, professional care, Reagan reduced state mental health personnel by more than 2,500, closed hospitals, and abolished many outpatient clinics. He rescinded some of the cuts in 1969, but most of his constituents supported his policies. They also sanctioned his campaign to eliminate "welfare cheaters" from assistance rolls. He approved reductions in MediCal payments to low-income Californians, an action later reversed by the courts, and he vetoed legislation to tie levels of state welfare payments to increases in Social Security benefits. Only legislative opposition and potential conflict with federal Department of Health, Education and Welfare (HEW) policies prevented him from making deeper cuts.

Reagan's first-term record was similarly mixed on other issues. Legislation providing more severe penalties for violent crimes received approval, but promises to repeal the Rumford Act could not be kept. His veto of plans to dam the Feather and Eel rivers (motivated by economic not environmental considerations) won grudging approval from conservationists. But despite all efforts to "squeeze and cut and trim," the state budget approached a record $7 billion by the end of his first term.

In 1968 Reagan sought the Republican presidential nomination and lost to the well-organized, well-financed primary campaign of Richard M. Nixon, but the contest had some positive results for the governor. It put a Republican in the White House and gave Reagan a national forum that he exploited effectively. In California, it yielded modest

Republican majorities in the legislature, but that was a mixed blessing; the governor could no longer blame failure to fulfill campaign promises on "a few willful Democrats." The election was less promising for Democrats, but they did send Alan Cranston to the U.S. Senate to replace Thomas Kuchel.

THE ELECTION OF 1970

Although Reagan's first term disappointed many, particularly fiscal conservatives, his potential for reelection in 1970 was excellent. Responsibility for failure to achieve fiscal reform goals could be shifted to the legislature and to his opponent in the race, former assembly speaker Jesse Unruh, since the small Republican majority elected in 1968 was neither sufficiently large nor sufficiently united (it could not even agree on a nominee for a speaker) to overcome Democratic opposition. In addition, Reagan could remind voters that despite increasing budgets, the rate of their growth had diminished during his first term. Unruh attempted to discredit Reagan's leadership and stressed his failures to keep the promises of 1966, but it was an uphill battle. The incumbent was a superb campaigner, well financed, and capable of skillful use of the media. Although Unruh's campaign was respectable, it received only token support from a still-divided CDC. Moreover, his reputation as "Big Daddy" or "Boss" of Democratic politics proved impossible to overcome, and Reagan won by a margin of a half-million votes.

But the 1970 victory was personal rather than partisan. Reagan campaigned actively for Republican candidates for statewide office, the legislature, and Congress, and they won all but two statewide offices: Wilson Riles became superintendent of public instruction and Edmund G. Brown, Jr. secretary of state. In legislative contests, however, the governor was less effective; Democrats won a majority of two in the senate and six in

the assembly, and their margins would increase in 1972. Their majority in the congressional delegation also increased; even Reagan's long-time associate George Murphy forfeited his U.S. Senate seat to Democrat John Tunney. Overall, the governor and his party had lost more than they gained.

THE SECOND REAGAN ADMINISTRATION

Reagan began his second term by a vetoing a reapportionment bill and leaving the matter to the courts, further antagonizing already-hostile Democratic lawmakers and reducing their inclination to cooperate on issues held over from his first term, especially welfare and tax reform. To Reagan, welfare reform meant drastic reductions in the number of recipients, but the number of Californians on public assistance increased during the 1960s and early 1970s. The governor proposed more stringent standards for welfare eligibility and a "work-fare" program to force the able-bodied from relief rolls, policies that could not produce significant savings. Nearly ninety percent of assistance recipients were aged, disabled, or children; many programs were tied to federally mandated payment levels; and the economy remained too weak to support a work-fare system in the private sector. Reagan was stalemated by a recalcitrant legislature until he turned to new assembly speaker, Los Angeles Democrat Robert Moretti. Their compromise, the California Welfare Reform Act of 1971, gave the governor several points by tightening requirements for participation in the Aid to Families with Dependent Children (AFDC) program, by including work-fare policies, and by attempting to reduce MediCal costs through a prepaid insurance scheme. But the law did not include the governor's principal objectives: reduced benefit levels and an absolute ceiling on welfare spending.

Rising welfare costs contributed to the

problem of tax reform, but they were not the sole impediment. Inflation accompanied an erratic economy, the budget approached $7 billion in 1971, despite Reagan's vetoes, and the governor had to retreat from his opposition to income tax withholding. He believed that "taxes should hurt" and that withholding diminished pain. Nevertheless, he signed a bill requiring tax deductions from paychecks, a policy that increased annual revenue by an estimated $100 million. The governor also turned to Moretti once more for help with school finance problems. In *Serrano* v. *Priest* (1971), the state supreme court ruled that using property taxes to finance schools was unconstitutional, placing an additional burden on the state. The Reagan-Moretti tax bill of 1972 responded by raising sales taxes to six percent and increasing levels of corporate taxation, which produced sufficient revenues to offset homeowners' exemptions and other tax relief measures and even created a treasury surplus. But it did not permanently alleviate the problem of financing schools or deal with Californians' major complaint: property taxes.

Efforts to limit property taxes have a long history in the state, including the "dollar-limit" in Chris Buckley's San Francisco. But during the 1960s, inflation increased both property values and assessments, making the problem particularly acute. Los Angeles County Assessor Philip Watson responded with a one percent property tax limitation proposal that qualified as a ballot initiative in 1968. Although the measure failed, it did prompt the legislature to enact a general reduction and special reductions for senior citizens. Voters defeated a second Watson initiative in 1972, but this one influenced passage of the Reagan-Moretti tax bill. Legislative action, however, neither resolved the issue nor enhanced Reagan's reputation as a tax-reformer. Therefore, in 1973 he introduced an initiative of his own, Proposition 1.

Proposition 1 did not focus on property taxes. Instead, it was a constitutional amendment to prohibit legislatures from raising tax rates above a stipulated percentage of Californians' cumulative income. Opponents convinced voters that the measure would transfer fiscal responsibility to local agencies and ultimately result in higher property taxes. Length and complexity, moreover, forced Reagan to admit that he did not fully understand the proposal himself, thereby contributing to its defeat.

Thus, after two terms Ronald Reagan's record as governor was mixed. Reductions in taxes and budgets proved to be impossible, and from 1967 on both increased faster than the population or the cost of living. The rate of increase in government spending declined somewhat, but Reagan's last budget in 1974 exceeded $10 billion. Nor was it possible to implement "creative society" principles designed to transfer responsibility for social programs to local communities and the private sector. Democratic legislators were less than cooperative, but the governor himself lacked the skills or experience required to deal effectively with lawmakers, even Republicans. Moreover, most policies that he championed were negative, requiring reduction or elimination of programs without alternative proposals. On the other hand, even though Reagan's environmental attitudes angered conservationists, he did sign into law measures to establish the most stringent standards for air and water quality in the nation and to require environmental impact studies for public works projects. And despite his failure to cut budgets and taxes, he retained a positive public image when he stepped down in 1974.

Indeed, even though he announced before the 1970 election that he would not seek a third term, he might have been re-elected. He remained popular, and the state constitution placed no limit on a governor's tenure. But his decision was a sound one. Only three previous California governors had been elected twice and only one, Earl Warren, three times. Equally important was Watergate, a scandal that discredited politicians in general and Republicans in particular; even Reagan could not entirely escape its tarnish.

THE SECOND GOVERNOR BROWN

In contrast, Edmund G. ("Jerry") Brown, Jr. projected the precise image needed to counter popular mistrust of politicians. Born in San Francisco in 1938, he attended Catholic schools, but more than religion prompted the choice. Behavior that made him the "Terror of Magellan Street" to neighbors indicated that he needed the discipline of parochial education. Intelligent, energetic, and inquisitive, he led friends into mischief, impressed them with four-letter words learned from his father's cohorts, and allegedly lit a fire under a playmate's feet to discover how Indians burned their captives. Indeed, many doubted that he would last one term in a Catholic school, but he surprised them.

He was an excellent student who incessantly raised questions, especially about religion, and participated in social activities, all the while contemplating his future. By the time he graduated from St. Ignatius High School in 1955, he had decided to attend the Sacred Heart Novitiate at Los Gatos to study for the priesthood. After a year spent at Santa Clara University, he entered the seminary and enthusiastically began the required fifteen years of study. Rigor, discipline, and periods of silent meditation appealed to him, but by his second year at the novitiate, doubts intruded on his thoughts; during his third year, uncertainty overwhelmed conviction and, after securing release from his vows, he left the seminary early in 1960, his future as unsure as ever.

He considered medicine, but at the University of California, where the governor ex-

pedited his admission, Jerry demonstrated a dismal aptitude for prerequisite science courses. Public service offered possibilities, but years of observing the workings of politics left him with distaste for the profession. The law was another option, but he remained unsure and graduated from Berkeley in 1961 with a degree in classics.

Seminary and university years did not lead Jerry Brown to a career, but they did influence him. The novitiate taught him about humility and the dignity of physical labor. When he arrived in Berkeley, waves of student dissent had not yet crested. He participated in discussions of lunch counter sit-ins in the South, implications of segregation in California, the menace of a nuclear arms race, the morality of capital punishment, and other issues. He also journeyed to the Sacramento Valley with Dorothy Day's Catholic Workers' Group to experience farm laborers' problems and to Hunter's Point in San Francisco to learn about life in an urban ghetto.

Finally, Pat Brown sent his son to Judge Matt Tobriner who persuaded Jerry to study law at Yale University Law School and wrote a letter supporting his application. In the fall of 1961 Brown arrived in New Haven to embrace his studies and political activism. In the spring of 1962, he traveled to Mississippi to participate in the desegregation movement, but when he and his companions arrived, they discovered the accuracy of reports of dogs, clubs, and water hoses being used to intimidate "agitators" and began to doubt their own wisdom. To insure a modicum of safety, Brown visited Governor Ross Barnett, who immediately contacted his California counterpart, warning that Jerry could be in danger and horrifying Brown's parents. When their son contacted them, after several marches and covert civil-rights conferences, he announced his impending return to Yale; Mississippi had been terrifying and unforgettable.

During Jerry's years at Yale, where he received his law degree in 1964, the Bay of Pigs crisis and the assassination of John Kennedy numbed the country, the civil-rights movement expanded, conflict in Vietnam escalated, and student protests against racism and war began to rock the nation's campuses. An outspoken opponent of U.S. involvement in Vietnam, in 1968 Jerry helped to organize antiwar candidate Eugene McCarthy's California campaign for the Democratic presidential nomination and served as a McCarthy delegate to the party's convention in Chicago. There his distaste for traditional politics returned as party leaders subverted every peace plank proposed for the national platform and Mayor Richard Daley's Chicago police attacked peace demonstrators outside the convention hall.

But the experience did not end Jerry's political involvement. In the Coachella Valley, he marched with César Chavez to support the United Farm Workers. He also campaigned for and won a seat on the Los Angeles Community College Board. The only liberal member of the board, Brown accomplished little during his tenure, but he did enliven meetings with suggestions that a campus be named for Martin Luther King, Jr., that the board protest the deaths of four students at Kent State University in Ohio, and that money be spent on academic programs rather than physical education facilities. And in 1970 he decided to run for statewide office.

The position he sought was innocuous: California Secretary of State, held almost unchallenged by two men—Frank Jordan, father and son—since 1911. After the younger Jordan died in 1970, however, Brown faced stiff opposition. But primary campaign coffers filled by Pat Brown's supporters and a scandal surrounding his opponent's performance in the state senate gave him a decisive victory and the nomination. In November,

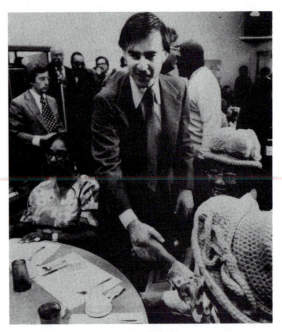

Jerry Brown Campaigning, 1974
During the 1974 gubernatorial race, Jerry Brown sought and won the votes of a cross-section of the California populace, including residents of Watts. *AP/Wide World Photos.*

he conducted another vigorous and well-financed campaign that capitalized on the public mood by promising to revitalize the office and use it to reform campaign practices in the state. He won again, one of only two Democrats to capture statewide positions, and by 1974 he was ready to make a bid for his father's former office.

THE ELECTION OF 1974

Jerry Brown ran for governor on his record as secretary of state. In 1972, he used the office to oppose Proposition 22, an initiative measure restricting union organizing activity among agricultural workers; he revealed that qualifying signatures had been fraudulently obtained and attempted to disqualify the measure. Because Governor Reagan refused to act, it remained on the ballot, but Brown's exposure contributed to its defeat. He also proposed, promoted, and enforced political campaign disclosure laws, and in 1974 he sponsored an initiative to create a Fair Campaign Practices Commission, control campaign funding, and require full disclosure of candidates' assets and spending. Brown's office also discovered and publicized Richard Nixon's manipulation of records related to a donation of vice presidential papers in order to secure a tax deduction of dubious legality. Thus, he entered the gubernatorial race as a champion of organized labor and political integrity.

Brown had another asset in his familiar name, especially since he had held himself aloof from traditional partisan politics and its practitioners. Still, he clearly understood the importance of media exposure, particularly the importance of television as a molder of opinion. His adviser and publicist Tom Quinn ensured not only that Brown retained his name recognition but also that his official actions received wide, frequent, and favorable coverage. Quinn managed the vigorous 1974 primary campaign in which Brown appeared often on television and in print to stress his record and his uniqueness as a politician, and the tactics were effective. In winning the nomination, he overcame a pair of seasoned, familiar Democrats: Speaker of the Assembly Robert Moretti and San Francisco Mayor Joseph Alioto.

With Lieutenant Governor Ed Reinecke under indictment for perjury in the Watergate investigations, Republicans chose State Controller Houston Flournoy as their candidate. Although he was personally attractive, he was relatively unknown and Brown initially underestimated him. Relying on his reputation as a political reformer and champion of labor, on the aftermath of Watergate, and on Gerald Ford's controversial pardon of Richard Nixon to ensure victory, Brown

conducted a dull, low-keyed campaign. It was short on specifics and long on abstractions about a "new spirit" in politics, and it was a mistake. After trailing badly in early opinion polls, Flournoy recovered and lost to Brown by just 178,694 votes or 2.9 percent of the total.

In general, however, Democrats did well in 1974. Mervyn Dymally, an African American state senator, became lieutenant governor, and most statewide offices went to Democrats, including March Fong Eu as secretary of state and Wilson Riles as state superintendent of public instruction for a second term. The party also established solid majorities in both houses of the legislature and increased its control over the congressional delegation. Thus, the new governor had substantial potential support for his programs, if he had any to offer.

NEW BLOOD AND FARM LABOR

Historically, political appointees in California and the nation have been middle-aged white males, successful in business or the professions. The new governor departed from tradition by appointing numerous young men and women from a wide variety of backgrounds to his staff, to regulatory and licensing bodies, and to important positions in numerous state departments and agencies. Brown's adviser Tom Quinn, for example, chaired the Air Resources Board, while Richard Maullin headed the Energy Development and Conservation Commission, and former radical Tom Hayden served on two different bodies. For the first time members of minority groups also found places in the higher echelons of state government, notably the first African American justice of the state supreme court Wiley Manuel, Secretary of Health, Education and Welfare Mario Obledo, and Regent of the University of California Vilma S. Martinez. Brown appointed more than 1,500 women to positions in state government during his two terms in office.

Compared with most other states, California has a generally positive record on feminist issues. The state protected the property rights of married women in its first constitution in 1849, granted women the right to vote in 1911, and ratified the ill-fated Equal Rights Amendment (ERA) almost immediately after its official proposal in 1972. By that time, a majority of women in the state held jobs outside their homes, but few held leadership positions in business and the professions and fewer still in politics or government. In 1918, the first three women served in the assembly, in 1967 Treasurer Ivy Baker Priest became the first woman elected to statewide office, and in 1976 voters sent the first woman, Rose Vuich, to the state senate. California women occasionally served in Congress and, like Anna Morrison Reed and Katherine Philips Edson, on state commissions, but never in proportion to their numbers.

Brown attempted to modify the situation. The legislature rejected his effort to place actress Jane Fonda on the California Arts Council. More important and successful—but hardly less controversial—was the nomination of his Berkeley classmate Rose Elizabeth Bird first to head the Department of Agriculture and, in 1977, to be chief justice of the state supreme court. Brown also placed women in charge of several departments usually led by men (Transportation and Corrections among them) and supported the creation of a seventeen-member Commission on the Status of Women to advise him and the legislature. Perhaps as a result of the governor's actions, women also became more visible in local government, including Mayors Janet Gray Hayes of San José, Dianne Feinstein of San Francisco, and Maureen O'Connor of San Diego. Winning elective office at the state level remains difficult, however. In 1984, Secretary of State March

Fong Eu, elected in 1974, was only the second woman to hold statewide elected office, and as late as 1985 the 120-member state legislature included only 15 women. In 1990, however, another Brown, Kathleen, became state treasurer, and Dianne Feinstein and Barbara Boxer won seats in the U.S. Senate.

Brown's appointment policies represented a major break with historical tradition in California; his actions on behalf of farm labor went even further. During the early 1970s Brown had marched with César Chávez and the migrant workers of the UFW, and in 1974, as secretary of state, he had worked to disqualify a growers' ballot initiative to curtail union activity. His sympathies were clear, and in one of his first acts as governor he collaborated with Rose Bird to draft the Agricultural Labor Relations Act of 1975. Passage of the law was an unprecedented action for both the state and the nation. The right of farm workers to organize unions had never been recognized, not even by the National Labor Relations Act (the Wagner Act) of the New Deal era. In California, previous administrations' efforts to deal with the issue had been thwarted by powerful agribusiness interests. But in a remarkably short time Jerry Brown accomplished the seemingly impossible.

The act of 1975 protected farm workers' rights to organize, to bargain collectively, and to select their bargaining agents by secret ballot. It allowed them to use labor's traditional weapons—picketing, strikes, and boycotts—in disputes with employers, and it protected growers' interests by specifying conditions under which such tactics could be employed. It also set up a five-member Agricultural Labor Relations Board (ALRB) to supervise elections, decide cases of alleged unfairness, and oversee general enforcement of the law's provisions. Many growers resisted the policy on principle and objected to individuals appointed to the board. Funding also provided a major problem. During its first few months in operation, the ALRB supervised nearly 200 elections in California's fields, and the unexpected level of activity depleted its original $1.3 million budget. When the agency appealed for additional funds, the legislature refused the request, and the ALRB ceased its work in April 1976. To defuse the threat of the UFW's Proposition 14, an initiative to reconstitute the board with additional authority, lawmakers subsequently approved funds to continue the ALRB's existence. The action made Proposition 14 unnecessary, the UFW withdrew active support, and the measure died.

"SMALL IS BEAUTIFUL"

Appointing women and members of minority groups to office and using government authority to uphold the interest of farm workers placed Jerry Brown in California's liberal-progressive political tradition. Categorizing other actions and policies, many of them derived from *Small Is Beautiful* by British economist E. F. Schumacher, is more difficult. Schumacher argued that contraction of production and consumption, rather than expansion, provides the soundest basis for a humane society, and Brown adopted this philosophy as his own. It formed the basis for his "era of limits" concept, and he applied it to issues ranging from conservation of the environment to the state's fiscal policies.

Brown was committed to preserving California's natural setting and its resources and to ending their exploitation. Of particular concern in the 1970s was an ever-increasing demand for energy, and the governor created the Office of Appropriate Technology (OAT) to explore energy sources other than fossil fuels and natural gas and areas of economic development compatible with environmental preservation. To ensure energetic pursuit of his policies, he appointed conservationists to head not only the OAT but also the Air Resources Board, the Energy Development and Conservation Commission, and other environmental agencies. He also created the California Conservation Corps to provide a work force for wilderness and urban improvement projects and to alleviate the problem of youth unemployment. For personal, political, and ideological reasons, he advocated stringent controls on nuclear power development, supported a ballot initiative to create the California Coastal Commission, proposed increases in the state's protected parklands, and joined the movement to save the Pacific whales. On both fiscal and philosophical grounds, he opposed construction of the New Melones Dam and fought efforts to rescind the 160-acre limitation on irrigation from water projects involving federal funds.

Naturalists and others concerned about the quality of life in California applauded Brown's policies. Their admiration diminished, however, when he made it clear that "small is beautiful" and "era of limits" ideologies applied to them as well as to industry and government, reversed himself on the 160-acre issue, recommended construction of a peripheral canal around the Sacramento–San Joaquin Delta, opened negotiations for an Alaskan pipeline oil terminal at Long Beach, and denied adequate funding to agencies responsible for implementing his environmental programs.

Brown also lost support in other quarters. While running for office, he repeatedly denounced government policies that sent "dollars chasing a problem." But numerous tangible issues involving Californians' quality of life demanded additional expenditures. Reagan economies and persistent inflation left colleges and universities severely underfinanced and with programs in jeopardy. Mental hospitals were badly understaffed, and over a two-year period 139 patients died, many as a result of inadequate care. As the

economy slowed, unemployment increased and along with it the number of recipients of public assistance. The MediCal insurance program proved to be ineffective and was discredited by scandals and frauds. Numerous state agencies and departments remained understaffed by demoralized employees whose workloads increased as their salaries fell further behind the rising cost of living. As it became apparent that these and other problems would need to be "chased" by dollars, Brown adhered to promises that taxes would not increase during his tenure and that the growth of the state budget would not surpass the rate of inflation. The 1975–1976 budget of $11.3 billion was just five percent higher than the previous year's; each subsequent budget was equally austere.

The governor's adamant refusal to approve appropriations to deal with pressing problems in the state, despite an ever-growing treasury surplus, precipitated constant confrontation with legislators—especially with members of his own party such as speakers Leo McCarthy and Willie Brown. Indeed, his conflicts with lawmakers were even more deep-rooted and persistent than Ronald Reagan's. Brown exacerbated the situation by failing to propose alternatives other than "small is beautiful" rhetoric such as admonishing underpaid public school teachers to live on their "psychic income." Criticism, however, could spur the governor into at least the semblance of action. When the Los Angeles *Times* denounced his inattention to serious unemployment problems, Brown announced a major public works program—a sewer project that would produce more than 30,000 jobs and improve water quality and waste disposal. The measure had broad appeal, especially since it would cost state taxpayers nothing; federal funds already allocated for the project, illegally impounded during Richard Nixon's presidency, became available in 1975. Brown also authorized attorney James Lorenz to devise a jobs program. But when conservatives criticized Lorenz's proposal as "socialism," the governor demanded his resignation and dismissed him without implementing any concrete unemployment reduction policy.

Despite such conflicts, Brown maintained his public image as both a fiscal conservative and a concerned, humane leader. He was able to "squeeze and cut and trim" more effectively than his predecessor, but without acquiring a reputation for "recycled Reaganism." Brown managed, as he confided to aides, to "move left and right at the same time," to "have a flurry of activity" when occasion demanded, and to use the media as effectively as Reagan.

THE ERA OF POSSIBILITIES AND THE ELECTION OF 1978

Jerry Brown had presidential ambitions, and in 1976 and 1980 he actively sought his party's nomination. Although he bemused many Californians and amused others, he attracted a substantial nationwide following. His appointments and support for farm labor were unprecedented, and his budgetary policies contradicted the traditional image of the

IBM Plant Development, San José, 1954–1984
During the post–World War II decades, California became a mecca for high-tech industries, with International Business Machines (IBM) among the leaders in the migration. In 1954, IBM purchased farmland for a plant site (*top*) adjacent to Highway 101 south of San José. A decade later (*center*) other industries had joined IBM in the fields and orchards. By 1984, agriculture had virtually diappeared from the area, replaced by industrial, commercial, and residential development (*bottom*). *Courtesy of International Business Machines, Inc.*

spendthrift Democrat, as did his residence in a rented Sacramento apartment and travel in a spartan sedan. By 1980, also, he had acquired a reputation as a tax-reformer, defender of the environment, and proponent of nuclear regulation. In addition, the governor's personal life added to the image of uniqueness; he was frequently seen in the company of singer Linda Ronstadt, and he often meditated at Zen centers in the state. Despite Brown's image and appeal and victories in several primary elections, his party denied him the presidential nomination in 1976 and again in 1980. After the 1980 convention, however, he began to publish a national newsletter promoting his brand of politics and possibly preparing for a third presidential bid, but in 1992, his "maverick" candidacy fared no better than its predecessors.

Despite his aspirations, Brown had a state to govern, and when he returned to California after the 1976 primaries he found it increasingly difficult to maintain his balance on the liberal-conservative tightrope. Conflict with the legislature on spending persisted, and it came to include other issues. The governor had vowed to veto any bill reinstating the death penalty, declared unconstitutional by the state supreme court, and he kept his promise in 1977. Legislators promptly and decisively overturned his veto. Brown further antagonized law-and-order advocates by supporting legislation to decriminalize moderate use of marijuana and sex acts between consenting adults and by his appointments to law enforcement and judicial posts.

Equally hostile was a business community at odds with the implications of the "era of limits" philosophy and other Brown policies. Sponsorship of the Agricultural Labor Relations Act alienated agribusiness interests, and appointing individuals sympathetic to farm workers to the ALRB made matters worse. Naming liberals and conservationists to serve on state regulatory and licensing

agencies drew fire from utility, timber, and other industries. And environmental policies, such as opposition to the New Melones Dam and to nuclear plants, made enemies in the camps of both business and labor. In short, it seemed that California government under Jerry Brown was hostile to business and not conducive to economic growth. Evidence usually used to substantiate the argument—a Dun & Bradstreet report ranking the state among the lowest in terms of favorable business climate and Dow Chemical Company's decision against building a plant near Sacramento—was effective, if not subjected to close scrutiny. The Dun & Bradstreet survey was based on 1974 data, gathered when Ronald Reagan was governor, and the Dow withdrawal involved failure to obtain local, not state, permits.

Nevertheless, the governor reacted to mounting criticism by beginning to speak of an "era of possibilities" rather than an "era of limits" and by launching another "flurry of activity" that included a highly publicized "California Means Business" campaign. Brown journeyed to Japan, Canada, Mexico, and England, and to various states to tout the advantages of doing business in California. He also capitalized on the impending first flight of the space shuttle *Enterprise,* scheduled for August 1977. In July, he attended a symposium at NASA-Ames Laboratory in Sunnyvale in "Silicon Valley," the center of high-technology research and development in Santa Clara County. There he stressed the state's leadership in the aerospace and electronics industries and became a convert to Gerald O'Neill's ideas of space colonization. Later, he installed astronaut Russell Schweikart, on leave from NASA, as his science and technology adviser, suggested that the state launch its own satellite, and proposed a $6 million space institute at the University of California. To further enhance his image, Brown appointed growers to the ALRB, named business people to several important state agencies, and made it clear that henceforth, when the environment and jobs came into conflict in California, jobs would receive priority.

Brown's flirtation with space colonization prompted Chicago columnist Mike Royko to dub him "Governor Moonbeam," but by the time of the 1978 elections he had mended numerous political fences, and he handily defeated his opponent, state Attorney General Evelle Younger. Voters approved an initiative reinstating the death penalty, dealing a blow to the governor, and the Democratic advantage in the legislature decreased. The vote also implied a minor backlash; Republican Mike Curb replaced Mervyn Dymally as lieutenant governor, and George Deuk-majian thwarted Yvonne Burke's bid to become attorney general. On the other hand, Lionel Wilson became Oakland's first African American mayor in 1978 and would win again in 1982 and 1986, and Wilson Riles retained the superintendency of public instruction. In 1976, Tom Bradley had been reelected mayor of Los Angeles, an office that he would hold until he stepped down in 1992.

For Californians of all political persuasions, however, tragedy rapidly replaced election post-mortems. On November 28, 1978, San Francisco Board of Supervisors President Dianne Feinstein announced that law-and-order advocate and former supervisor Dan White had assassinated Mayor George Moscone and Supervisor Harvey Milk. White—apparently angered by the mayor's refusal to rescind his resignation from the board and by Milk's advocacy of gay rights — smuggled a pistol into City Hall and killed them both. To complete Moscone's term, the board chose Feinstein, who was elected in her own right in 1979 and 1983. In the meantime, a jury convicted White of voluntary manslaughter rather than murder in May 1979; less than two years after his equally controversial parole in January 1984, he committed suicide.

Tom Bradley, Mayor of Los Angeles
Before he was elected the first black mayor of Los Angeles in 1973, Tom Bradley served on the city's police force and city council. He subsequently won reelection to consecutive terms and remained in office when he lost the race for governor in 1982. He participated in organizing the highly successful Olympic Games in Los Angeles in 1984. *Courtesy of the Bancroft Library.*

THE TAX REVOLT OF 1978

The real issue in 1978 was not Brown, capital punishment, political parties, or race; it was property taxes. Voters made this clear during the primary elections earlier in the year, when they gave almost 2 to 1 approval to the Jarvis-Gann Amendment, Proposition 13. The conditions that prompted Philip Watson's tax initiatives in 1968 and 1972 and Ronald Reagan's Proposition 1 in 1973 worsened during Jerry Brown's administrations. Inflation pushed prices and incomes upward and wage-earners into higher tax brackets, creating a treasury surplus. Property values increased dramatically, and property assessments and tax bills inevitably followed. Re-

Celebrating Proposition 13
Los Angeles supporters of Proposition 13 celebrate the impending victory of the initiative to "Save the American Dream" for Californians. *AP/Wide World Photos.*

publicans proposed tying income tax brackets to cost-of-living increases ("indexing"), but the governor opposed the idea until 1979. New initiatives to limit taxation levels, especially on property, appeared on ballots but failed, and by the end of the decade Californians were more adamant than ever about the need for reform.

The tax revolt of 1978 should not be construed as a grassroots movement, however. One of its nominal leaders, Utah-born Howard Jarvis, migrated to California during the 1930s, formed a manufacturing firm, lost it during World War II, became director of the Los Angeles Association of Apartment Owners, and in 1977 joined Paul Gann, a depression era migrant from Arkansas, to form the United Organization of Taxpayers (UOT). A year later they introduced their property tax limitation amendment. Like earlier versions, the Jarvis-Gann proposal would

limit taxes to one percent of assessed value, but it went further. It would apply to both residential and business property, use 1975 values as the basis for assessment, restrict assessment increases to two percent a year, forbid reassessment except in cases of sale or improvement, and require a two-thirds popular vote for local governments to institute new taxes. The measure had tremendous appeal, and the Butcher-Forde Consulting Agency, hired by UOT to manage a $2.5 million campaign, easily gathered the signatures needed to place it on the ballot as Proposition 13.

The governor and most officeholders opposed the initiative, arguing that it would benefit owners of rental and business properties more than homeowners and severely deplete resources and services, lead to dismissal of many public employees, and damage an already struggling educational system. Democrats offered an alternative, the

Behr Bill, which would provide tax relief to residential property only and which Brown supported during the primary campaign. His eventual opponent in the gubernatorial race, Evelle Younger, championed Proposition 13 just as consistently, and when results were in, public opinion was clear. Democrats named Brown to run for governor, Republicans chose Younger, and voters of both parties overwhelmingly endorsed the Jarvis-Gann Amendment.

Jerry Brown conveniently discovered that Proposition 13 was entirely compatible with his own "small is beautiful" and "era of limits" ideologies. Well before the general election, the governor began to implement the new law in what he called "a humane way." Immediately after the June primaries, he opened negotiations with legislative leaders to explore methods for distributing a $35 million treasury surplus—termed "obscene" by Jarvis—to local and county governments as "bail-out" funds. The governor also used his executive authority to halt state hiring and to freeze state employees' salaries, and he created a special commission headed by retired legislative analyst Alan Post to study Proposition 13's implications and recommend appropriate responses. Brown's well-publicized "flurry of activity" rebuilt his reputation as a fiscal conservative and helped to ensure his reelection.

Brown spent much of his second term combating a crop-threatening Mediterranean fruit fly infestation, dealing with problems caused by Proposition 13, running for the presidential nomination, and feuding with Democratic legislators. His stand against cost-of-living increases for welfare recipients brought him into conflict with assembly Speaker Leo McCarthy. Since federal law mandated adjustments in welfare payments, the governor compromised on that issue, but when he vetoed pay raises for state workers, the legislature responded with one of three humiliating overrides in as many weeks.

Brown's inability to lead his own party in his own state certainly contributed to defeat in the presidential primaries of 1980. Also contributing was a conviction among Democratic voters nationwide that, as one of his aides phrased it, "Jerry has a whim of iron."

Brown also discovered that the tax revolt did not end in 1978; on local election ballots in 1979 appeared yet another initiative sponsored by Paul Gann. Designated Proposition 4, or "The Spirit of 13," the measure tied all government spending to rates of inflation and population growth. Although Proposition 4 succeeded by a 3 to 1 margin, Jarvis's Proposition 9 failed miserably in 1980. Called "Jarvis II" ("Jaws II" by its opponents), the initiative would have cut state tax rates by fifty percent, but the extremity of the proposal and Jarvis's own intemperate speeches in its support were too much even for California tax warriors.

ENERGY CRISIS AND RESPONSE

Like their nineteenth-century predecessors, twentieth-century Californians often assumed that their resources were infinite; events of the 1970s proved them wrong. During and after World War II, sources of petroleum, natural gas, and hydroelectric power remained constant or diminished, while demands on them increased annually. Consequences became all too apparent in 1973 when the Organization of Oil Exporting Countries (OPEC) declared an embargo on oil shipments to the United States and initiated regular price increases that raised the cost of imported crude oil more than tenfold by 1980. Gasoline prices escalated, impatient drivers waited in long lines at pumps, and governments attempted to allocate supplies equitably. OPEC policies also had devastating effects on plastic, chemical, fertilizer, power, and other petroleum-dependent industries in the state and on the economy in general.

Residents and businesses in California, which had been an oil exporter, relied on petroleum products to fill over half of their energy needs, on natural gas for about a third, and on hydroelectric power and other sources for the remainder, and they considered the situation critical. Oil companies reopened abandoned fields and explored for additional sources, especially beneath coastal waters. Environmentalists opposed offshore drilling, but federal support allowed the industry to sink new wells in the sea. Similar controversy surrounded proposals for terminals at Point Conception to import and store liquid natural gas and at Long Beach to receive oil from the Alaskan Pipeline; although both projects won approval, expense and danger prevented construction and operation. None of the expedients could, in any case, eliminate dependence on foreign products, and alternate sources of energy remained essential. Public agencies such as the OAT and the University of California, private interests such as PG&E, and individuals searched for substitutes. Proposals ranged from tapping solar and geothermal sources to harnessing the wind and tides to burning refuse and methane gas from garbage dumps to generate electricity. The greatest expenditure of money and research, however, focused on the most controversial possibility: nuclear fission.

In 1957, well before the 1970s crisis, the experimental Vallecitos generating plant began operation near Livermore, but its construction on an earthquake fault subsequently forced its closure. PG&E opened its problem-ridden Humboldt Bay facility in 1963 but was denied approval for another at Bodega Bay in 1964. Southern California Edison Company's huge station at San Onofre near San Diego went online in 1968, and PG&E began construction at Diablo Canyon near San Luis Obispo in 1969. These early nuclear generation plants encountered little sustained opposition, except from vocal environmentalists. By the 1970s, however, information generated by the federal Atomic Energy Commission (AEC), the Nuclear Regulatory Commission (NRC), and the California Energy Commission (CEC) formed in 1975, increased awareness of potential hazards and heightened public concern. Nevertheless, the Rancho Seco plant near Sacramento began operation in 1975, and in 1976 Californians defeated Proposition 15, the Nuclear Safeguards Initiative, by a wide margin.

Although the CEC disapproved San Diego Gas & Electric Company's 1976 request to build a nuclear plant in the Riverside County desert, the real catalyst for resistance was the near-disaster at Three Mile Island, Pennsylvania, in 1979; in California, the major target for opposition was the PG&E facility under construction at Diablo Canyon. Organizations such as the Abalone Alliance fought PG&E in the courts, and the NRC and the CEC demanded major design changes and reinforcement against possible earthquake damage. Despite the company's claim that the plant would save millions of barrels of oil annually and provide cheap power, when it began operation in 1985, its cost surpassed $2 billion, most of which would be paid by customers. Clearly, nuclear power would not immediately provide an inexpensive source of abundant energy. Some early alternatives,

Alternative Energy Sources
The energy crisis of the 1970s prompted an intensified search for alternatives to petroleum, especially in the field of renewable resources. Pacific Gas & Electric Company built geothermal generating plants near Geyserville in Sonoma County (*top left*) and constructed windmill "farms" on Altamont Pass in Alameda County (*top right*). PG&E's most controversial effort was and remains the Diablo Canyon nuclear generating plant on the coast near San Luis Obispo (*bottom*). *Courtesy of Pacific Gas & Electric Company.*

however, began to show promise, including cogeneration: using wasted industrial heat and energy to generate electricity. Regulatory agencies and industry, including power and construction companies, took steps to increase energy efficiency and reduce waste. The crisis of the 1970s also influenced consumers to demand energy-efficient products, including homes and automobiles, and rising costs forced them to slow their demands on energy supplies.

AFTER THIRTEEN

Jerry Brown did not seek a third term in 1982; he ran instead for the U.S. Senate and lost to Republican Mayor Pete Wilson of San Diego. The governor's race pitted two southern Californians against one another: Democratic Mayor Tom Bradley of Los Angeles, previously a captain on the city's police force, and Republican Attorney General George Deukmejian, formerly a state senator from Long Beach. Although Deukmejian carefully avoided the issue of race during his campaign, it probably contributed to his narrow victory as voters turned out to defeat both Proposition 15, a gun control initiative, and Bradley. Running on a "back-to-basics" platform, William Honig captured the nonpartisan superintendency of public instruction, and Democrats increased their majorities in the assembly and senate.

The administration and the legislature that took office in 1983 confronted for the first time the long-term effects of Proposition 13. The most dire predictions by the measure's opponents—massive layoffs in the public sector, drastically reduced or eliminated services, and rapidly deteriorating roads, parks, and buildings—did not immediately materialize, but the "obscene" surplus was gone, the state confronted a deficit, and local governments clamored for help. Recession continued, high unemployment persisted, and homeowners still shouldered a disproportionate share of

the revenue burden. Public facilities showed the result of deferred maintenance, and inflation assured higher costs for repairs or replacements. As agencies at all levels struggled for survival and turned to Sacramento, Deukmejian and the legislature deadlocked over the state's own unbalanced budget. Implications of the situation were nowhere clearer than in California's once-envied educational programs. In the spring of 1983, the San José School District declared bankruptcy, trustees of the state college and university systems increased students' costs substantially, and community colleges imposed tradition-shattering "fees" (the state constitution prohibits "tuition"). In the meantime, the economy continued to stagger, industries in Silicon Valley and elsewhere, following the lead of the General Motors plant in Fremont, closed their doors, and smaller businesses failed with alarming frequency.

During the second year of the new governor's term, however, the economy began to stabilize and the rate of inflation slowed, resulting in increases in the state's treasury balance and decreases in unemployment. In 1984, for example, the idle General Motors facility at Fremont reopened after federal approval of a joint venture, New United Motors Manufacturing, Inc. (NUMMI) involving Toyota of Japan. William Honig simultaneously drafted a comprehensive educational reform program and, with the governor's enthusiastic support, campaigned for public and legislative backing. Also in 1984, despite Deukmejian's opposition, voters approved a lottery plan intended to provide funding for education. In the interim, the governor showed little of his predecessors' inclination to block spending on important public programs. In addition to increased support for schools from primary grades through the universities, he approved funds for construction of new highways (some relegated to limbo through two previous administrations) and renovation of old ones, overdue salary increases for state employees, and other purposes. Deukmejian's version of fiscal conservatism contrasted sharply with both Ronald Reagan's and Jerry Brown's; so did his low-key approach to the office of governor. But he could not entirely avoid controversy.

Although environmentalists applauded his toxic waste elimination program, his support for a peripheral canal and offshore drilling and opposition to policies of the California Coastal Commission and similar agencies angered them. His vetoes of welfare legislation produced hostility in another sector, and he could not divorce himself entirely from his supporters' efforts to block the reconfirmation of Rose Bird and other Jerry Brown appointees to the state judiciary. Nevertheless, by the mid-1980s both the governor and other Californians believed that they had reason for renewed confidence and optimism, and Deukmejian won a second term in 1986.

ANOTHER BOOM OF THE EIGHTIES

Former governor Ronald Reagan won election to the presidency in 1980 with an agenda that included a huge reduction in federal income tax rates (especially on high incomes), severe cutbacks in government spending on social programs, sharp reduction of much government regulation of business, and a massive increase in military spending. A Congress dominated by conservative Democrats and Republicans acquiesced, producing booming prosperity for business. Critics, however, labeled the period an "era of greed" as the rich got richer and a seemingly shrinking American middle class threatened to create a two-tiered society— one rich and one poor.

President Reagan's huge increases in spending for military programs dramatically revived California's economy, given the state's continued role in the nation's defense and aerospace industries. By the mid-1980s twenty percent of Defense Department expenditures went to California companies, while both the Department of Energy and NASA spent a third of their funds in the state. Vast sums poured particularly into the region surrounding Los Angeles, by this time the largest manufacturing center in the United States and the foremost complex of aerospace industries in the world.

Los Angeles continued to develop as a magnet for business and migrants. A majority of the state's largest companies were centered in the Los Angeles area, where cumulative income surpassed that of all but three other states. The region accounted for one-eighth of the total gross domestic product (GDP) of the United States and a large majority of the state's population growth. Simultaneously, Los Angeles had a growing impact on American popular culture as the state came to dominate the nation's film and television industry. By the 1990s Californina produced ninety percent of all prime-time television programs and three-fourths of all feature film and video productions in the nation. At the same time, revolutionary changes in computer and telecommunications technology bolstered high-technology industries of northern California's Santa Clara Valley, soon to be known as Silicon Valley, and placed it, as one participant said, "at the center of the technology world." By 1991, *Time* magazine reported, the valley had "three times the number of jobs and twice the number of electronic firms with sales of $5 million or more" as the nation's next largest high-technology region.

Governor Deukmejian capitalized on the good times of the 1980s to win reelection in 1986 by promising little more than to hold down new government spending, to improve the climate for business in the state, and to fight crime. He left office having done that, but not much more. In the process he proved to be far more conservative than expected, given his previous record during many years in the legislature and as state attorney general. Indeed, confrontations between an ideologue of the Republican right in the governor's office and a legislature controlled by Democrats characterized Deukmejian's second term. Each year brought bitter conflict over the state budget. The legislature frequently refused to approve important Deukmejian appointments, and the governor used his line-item veto authority to slash programs approved by the legislature, especially social and environmental programs. Republicans in the legislature united to prevent the two-thirds vote necessary to override the governor's vetoes.

Deukmejian lived up to his pledge never to approve a new tax, for the most part approving only limited increases in existing levies. But as the economy revived in the mid-1980s, state revenues rose to such levels that he could approve increases in state spending on existing programs (particularly for prison construction and education) and, in 1987, a $1 billion rebate to taxpayers. Still, his resistance to new spending of any kind led critics to claim that he had put the state "on hold" for eight years as simply a "caretaker" governor. Deukmejian's greatest impact was in the area of criminal justice. An adamant proponent of punishment, not rehabilitation, as the fundamental purpose of the criminal justice system, he had authored, as a state senator, the bill that restored the death penalty in California and legislation mandating tough sentences for commission of a crime with a gun. As state attorney general he had reduced the department's environmental protection unit in order to strengthen the criminal division and conducted an ongoing feud with Rose Bird, the liberal chief justice of the state supreme court. As governor he capitalized on public concerns about crime to push through the legislature a 250 percent increase in state prison capacity and a 310 percent increase in the budget of the Department of Corrections. As a result, between 1984-1994 California's

prison population tripled. Moreover, when Rose Bird and two other Jerry Brown appointees to the supreme court failed to win reconfirmation in 1986, Deukmejian was able to reshape the state's judicial system entirely by the time he left office in 1991, appointing a majority of the court and three-fourths of the state judiciary overall, with most of the new judges carefully selected to reflect the governor's views. The state supreme court accordingly took a decided turn to the right, approving death sentences where they had been denied before. Even so, while the overall crime rate in the state had declined, as Deukmejian left office violent crime was increasing at an appalling rate and became a major political issue in the 1990s.

HIGH-TECH REVOLUTION

The high-tech revolution that created Silicon Valley in Santa Clara County and ultimately affected all of California occurred in two phases. The first began during the 1920s, when Stanford University professor Frederick Terman encouraged formation of local electronics enterprises to rival those centered on Harvard and MIT. Development progressed slowly until World War II, when former Stanford students William Hewlett and David Packard entered the field. Not until after the war, however, did the nascent electronics revolution begin to approach reality. In 1956, William Schockley of Stanford described the principle of the transistor, a tiny device that replaced tubes and wired circuits in electronic systems to reduce their size and had potential applications ranging from personal radios to missile guidance systems. Three years later, Jack Kilby of Texas Instruments and Robert Noyce of Fairchild Semiconductor in Silicon Valley achieved a breakthrough of astonishing potential: the silicon microchip. A single minuscule chip could incorporate thousands of circuits capable of storing an incredible volume of information in memory, executing multitudes of commands, and performing tasks as sophisticated as navigation in space and as mundane as telling time or imitating musical instruments. So tiny are the chips and so universal their applications that, once production consistency was achieved, they made transistor-based systems virtually obsolete. New firms such as Apple rapidly proliferated, joining established giants—Intel, Fairchild, National Semiconductor, and IBM—not only in Silicon Valley but also south to San José and east across the bay. The industry's characteristics—its products' diminutive size, its presumed environmental friendliness, and its ability to conduct research, development, marketing, and manufacturing at widely separated sites—promoted unprecedented geographic mobility. By the early 1970s facilities appeared throughout the state, frequently lured by concessions offered by eager small towns and suburban communities.

The second phase in the process resulted from the technological development of the first and provided the catalysts for the real revolution: the personal computer (PC) and software to accompany it. In 1976 Steve Jobs and Steve Wozniak formed Apple Computer Company and began to market their Apple II. A year later, Bill Gates and Paul Allen founded Microsoft in Seattle, and Tandy Corporation placed the TRS-80 PC in its Radio Shack stores. IBM entered the field in 1981 with its PC, powered by Microsoft's disk operating system and, in the following year, its revolutionary Windows. Subsequent developments were nothing short of explosive. Dozens of clones of the IBM product appeared on the market almost immediately. Apple's Macintosh appeared to compete with the IBM version, and continuing research produced refinements that made software more sophisticated and hardware more efficient and less costly. By the end of the 1980s, PCs became commonplace in businesses,

homes, classrooms, and libraries across the nation. By late 2000 an estimated sixty-two percent (up from thirty-seven percent in 1997) of all U.S. households had a least one PC, and of those fifty-two percent had Internet access. In addition, spin-offs from original applications of microchip technology, ranging from cellular telephones to genetic research to an impending "information super highway" made all of California, not just Silicon Valley, a major international center of the high-tech revolution. Perhaps the most remarkable evolution of the process was the birth of an entirely new industry: biotechnology. From the earliest firms—notably Genentech, founded in 1976, Chiron and Cetus in Silicon Valley, and Amgen in Thousand Oaks—scores of smaller companies have spun off to conduct research and development and make amazing breakthroughs in pharmaceuticals, biology, and genetics.

Implications of the new technology range far beyond anything that early scientists and engineers could have envisioned. To most observers it initially seemed to promise unlimited benefits: expanding employment and economic opportunities, accelerating advancement in fields sych as communications and medicine, proliferating varieties of consumer conveniences, and expanding horizons in education. By the mid-1980s, however, less sanguine commentators—Ian Rienecke and Theodore Roszak among them—expressed serious reservations. As acids and other toxins used in high-tech manufacturing seeped into water tables and wells and the potential for accidental release of deadly gases into the atmosphere became apparent, environmentalists denounced the industry's "clean" reputation as illusory. Law enforcement agencies found the new technology a mixed blessing. It could fascillitate identifications and the collection of data, but it also spawned new varieties of crime that included counterfeiting, industrial espionage, and the theft of highly portable and easily disposable chips and other components.

Most important, perhaps, critics' warnings that the job obsolescence and other dislocations associated with the previous century's industrialization could recur proved valid as the high-tech revolution reshaped a large sector of the work force. A few highly paid and upwardly mobile individuals in management, research and development, and marketing contrasted sharply with thousands of semi-skilled workers—often female members of ethnic minority groups who did routine production and assembly jobs in settings that have been likened to sanitized versions of nineteenth-century sweatshops. In addition, a national economic recession, magnified in California by reductions in federal spending in defense and aerospace industries and impending military base closures, precipitated top-to-bottom layoffs—euphemistically called "downsizing"—in what many assumed would be an ever-expanding industry. Foreign and domestic competition compounded problems. It forced firms to cut costs by shifting assembly operations of established products to other states and to Mexico, Taiwan, Shanghai, and other overseas sites, while keeping only cutting-edge research and production facilities in the state. Indeed, between the mid-1980s and mid-1990s, the number of high-tech jobs in the state fell by fifteen percent.

CULTURAL MATURITY AND DIVERSITY

The 1960s and 1970s brought maturity, diversity, and national recognition to California culture. California artists, centered mainly in southern parts of the state, participated in such movements as pop art, op art, and the geometric hard-edge school that reduced painting to the essentials of color and design. Some innovation and tradition to achieve unique results; printmaker Ed Ruscha, for example, focused on the commonplace to produce works reminiscent of the earlier "Ashcan" school of painting. Cristo, on the

other hand, discarded tradition entirely to build his nylon "Running Fence" from the Marin hills to the Pacific and, in 1991, to scatter nearly 3,000 blue and yellow umbrellas along the Tejon Pass.

Musicians also contributed: Dave Brubeck's influence on jazz persisted, southern California's Beach Boys and their "surfin' sound" set trends in popular music, and Joan Baez added a serious political dimension to the folk-music revival of the 1960s. Classical music likewise achieved new vigor and popularity. The Los Angeles Philharmonic Orchestra attained greater prominence under the baton of maestro Zubin Mehta, while Seiji Ozawa and Edo de Waart advanced the development of the San Francisco Symphony Orchestra. A series of conductors—notably innovative African American Calvin Simmons, whose death in 1982 ended a brilliant career at age thirty-two—breathed new life into the Oakland Symphony. In addition, public and private funds provided permanent quarters for performing artists. Los Angeles identified itself among the cultural centers of the West with the 1967 opening of its Music Center complex and the Dorothy Chandler Pavilion. San Jose completed its Community Center in 1972, Oakland refurbished the Art Deco Paramount Theater in 1973, and performances began in San Francisco's Louise M. Davies Symphony Hall in 1980.

At the same time, Californians provided facilities to house art, historical documents, and scientific exhibits. During the 1960s, the Los Angeles County Museum modernized its buildings and added the Page Museum devoted to prehistoric animal life. Late in 1986 the Los Angeles County Museum of Art opened the Robert O. Anderson Building; almost simultaneously, the Museum of Contemporary Art presented its first exhibit of work by practicing artists. In 1969, the new Oakland Museum began to establish its reputation as a leading collector and exhibitor of the state's

JEFE ROJAS

The Vaqueros' Homer

In 1987 writer Gerald Haslam introduced his readers to a unique *californio*. Born in Pasadena in 1896, Arnold R. *"Jefe"* ("Chief") Rojas was descended from Sephardic Jews who fled Spain and the Inquisition during the sixteenth century and from Yaqui and Mayo Indians. More immediate ancestors, however, migrated from Mexico to California during the Spanish period. After his parents died, he lived in an orphanage until he was twelve; then ambition to become a *vaquero* (and avoid a life picking fruit) led to escape and a stint as a novice rider on a ranch near Cholame, east of Paso Robles. He later made his way to the San Joaquin Valley where concerns such as Miller and Lux, Inc., and the Tejón Ranch Company ran immense herds on spreads comprised of thousands of acres. In the valley, Rojas recalled, he "found the miracle of his youth, great ranches, horses to ride, and matchless story-tellers turning back in retrospect the pages of their adventurous lives." For a quarter-century, Rojas learned the skills that made his mentors expert at riding horses and managing cattle and the lore and legend of an already-vanishing breed. In 1935 he settled near Bakersfield and established his own stable—the BAR-O, "because I had to borrow everything"—where services included horse dentistry.

Jefe **Rojas: The Vaqueros' Homer**
Courtesy of Chuck Hitchcock, Shafter, California.

JEFE ROJAS
The Vaqueros' Homer (continued)

Despite formal education limited to two or three years, Rojas' keen mind and curiosity led him through works by Alexander Dumas, Miguel de Cervantes, Rudyard Kipling, Robert Louis Stevenson, O. Henry, and Jack London. Also intriguing to him were the *chismes* (literally "bits of gossip") handed down from one generation of *vaqueros* to the next, which he collected and published. His first volume, *California Vaqueros*, appeared in 1953; when *The Lore of the California Vaquero* followed in 1958 and *The Last of the Vaqueros* in 1960, a reviewer declared that the "vaquero has found his Homer!"

Rojas' work husbands fading fragments of California's past: the experiences of *paisano, gringo,* Indian, and occasional black vaqueros, the alternating drudgery and excitement of their lives, the idiosyncrasies of the animals that they handled, and the re-collections of contemporaries and *los viejos* (oldtimers). Vignettes recount episodes involving individuals such as cattle baron Henry Miller and cattlewoman Mae Arnold, describe brands unique to the valley and arcane implements of the horsemen's trade, trace the history of horses and riding, and preserve scraps of *el español que no está escrito,* the unwritten idiom peculiar to the time and place. Rojas also distinguishes between southwestern *vaqueros* and Plains cowboys; in the process, his lively pen demolishes Hollywood's romanticized versions, with their low slung pistols, flashy outfits, and swaggering manners.

From his first book in 1953 to his last—*Vaqueros and Buckaroos*—in 1979, *Jefe* Rojas demonstrated obvious pride in his Mexican heritage, beginning years before its expression became fashionable or politicized. When he died in September 1988, he left a singular legacy to the history of California culture: vivid sketches of a past that might otherwise be lost and forgotten. (WAB)

---

art work and historical artifacts. Five years later, the public gained access to major private collections: the Norton Simon Museum in Pasadena and the J. Paul Getty Museum near Malibu, which would open a truly outstanding new facility in 1997. The 1981 completion of the California Railroad Museum in Sacramento, built collaboratively by the state and the Railroad and Locomotive Historical Society, and the 1984 opening of the Monterey Bay Aquarium on Cannery Row, endowed by the family of electronics magnate David Packard, marked additional milestones.

Most Californians believed culture in the state to be alive and well, but not all agreed. Dissenters included young writers who fol-

lowed in the tradition of William Saroyan, John Steinbeck, and Nathanael West, with work expressing pessimism about the so-called "California Dream." Ken Kesey's disturbing *One Flew Over the Cuckoo's Nest* (1962), set in a psychiatric hospital, reflected disenchantment with society's enforcement of arbitrary norms, and Richard Brautigan's *Trout Fishing in America* (1967), with wit and sometimes-biting irony, denounced the demise of both the environment and the values of rural-agrarian society. Joan Didion's essays in *Slouching Towards Bethlehem* (1968) and novels such as *A Book of Common Prayer* (1977) expressed nostalgia for a California that might have been. Simultaneously, established writers continued to produce fine literature, such as Wallace Stegner's Pulitzer Prize-winning novel *Angle of Repose* (1971), and younger authors contributed to the diversity; Gerald Haslam based essays and short stories, later collected in *Snapshots* (1985), *Voices of a Place* (1987), and *Coming of Age in California* (1990), on the "other California" of the Central Valley and the "Okie" culture.

Writers also drew upon ethnic experiences. In 1965 Luis Valdez's *El Teatro Campesino*, first located in Delano and later in San Juan Bautista, dramatized both the cultural pride and bitter experiences of farm workers; his audience expanded with *El Teatro's* 1976 European tour and the 1978 appearance of his play *Zoot Suit* based on the 1942 Sleep Lagoon killings in Los Angeles. In 1959, Jose Villareal published *Pocho*, a novel illuminating cultural conflicts that confronted Mexican migrants and their children, and Maxine Hong Kingman pursued analogous themes in *The Woman Warrior* (1976) and *China Men* (1980). In *Yellow Back Radio Broke Down* (1969) and

The Last Days of Louisiana Red (1974), novelist Ishmael Reed challenged established literary canons and tenets of current African American politics.

If attributes of California and national disenchanted some, they alienated many young people from a society in which commericalism and materialism seemed to predict inevitable repression and involvement in militaristic ventures like the war in Vietnam. By the mid-1960s, colonies of dissenters—called "hippies," "flower children," or the "love generation"—appeared throughout the nation, the largest in San Francisco's Haight-Ashbury district where they hoped to establish a community based on love, peace, and individualism. In a sense, hippies followed in the state's utopian tradition, but unlike their predecessors they lacked a cohesive philosophy on which to found their "Age of Aquarius." Instead, they vacillated among ideologies that ranged from astrology to Zen Buddhism and too readily accepted the advice of gurus like Harvard professor Timithy

Los Angeles Civic and Music Center
Courtesy of Security Pacific National Bank Collection, Los Angeles Public Library.

Leary to "tune in, turn on, and drop out." Substituting chemicals, especially marijuana and the hallucinogenic LSD (lysergic acid diethylamide) for reality transformed the counterculture into a drug culture, often with tragic consequences, including health problems, antosocial behavior, psychosis, and even drug-induced suicide.

Theodore Roszak assessed hippies' efforts to create a new society in *The Making of a Counterculture* (1969), but little otherwise marks their passage, except perhaps altered musical tastes. The laid-back "surfin' sound" of the Beach Boys gave way to the hard-driven, amplified, strobe-lit "acid rock" of groups such as the Jefferson Airplane, featuring vocalist Grace Slick, and the Grateful Dead. Indeed, music marked both the apogee and the perigee of the movement. Following the 1967 "be-ins" and "summer of love" in San Francisco, an estimated 300,000 gathered for a free Rolling Stone concert at Altamont Speedway east of Livermore late in 1969. During the performance, several people were severely beaten and one was killed. The "flower children" never quite recovered; by the mid-1970s "yuppies" (young urban professionals), not hippies, occupied the gentrified Haight-Ashbury, which became stop on the itineraries of curious tourists.

SUGGESTIONS FOR FURTHER READING

Los Angeles and the Watts Riots

Nathan Cohen, ed., *The Los Angeles Riots: A Socio-Psychological Study* (1970); Lawrence B. DeGraaf, "The City of the Black Angels: Emergence of the Los Angeles Ghetto, 1890–1930" and Joseph Boskin and Victor Pilson, M.D., "The Los Angeles Riot of 1965: A medical Profile of an Urban Crisis," *Pacific Historical Review* (1970); Dolores Hayden, "Biddy Mason's Los Angeles, 1865–1891," *California History* (1989); Bruce M. Tyler, *From Harlem to Hollywood: The Struggle for Racial and Cultural Democracy, 1920–1943* (1992); Jerry Cohen and William S. Murphy, *Burn, Baby, Burn! The Los Angeles Race Riot, August 1965* (1966); Robert Conot, *Rivers of Blood, Years of Darkness* (1967); John A. McCone and others, *Violence in the City—An End or a Beginning?* (1965); Paul Bullock, *Watts: The Aftermath* (1970); Gilbert Osofsky, *Harlem: The Making of a Ghetto* (1963); Kenneth T. Jackson, *The Ku Klux Klan in the City, 1915–1930* (1967); Mike Davis, *City of Quartz* (1991).

Politics and Politicians

H. Brett Melendy and B. F. Gilbert, *The Governors of California: From Peter H. Burnett to Edmund G. Brown* (1965); Ed Salzman, Jerry Brown: *High Priest and Low Politician* (1967); J. D. Lorenz, *Jerry Brown: The Man on the White Horse* (1978); John C. Bollens and G. Robert Williams, *Jerry Brown in a Plain Brown Wrapper* (1978); Roger Rapoport, California Dreaming: *The Odyssey of* *Pat and Jerry Brown* (1982); Jackson K. Putnam, *Modern California Politics* (1984); and "The Pattern of California Politics," *Pacific Historical Review* (February 1992); John H. Culver and John C. Syer, *Power and Politics in California* (1980); Lou Cannon, *Ronnie and Jessie: A Political Odyssey* (1969); Bill Boyarsky, *Ronald Reagan: His Life and Rise to the Presidency* (1981); Edmund G. Brown and Bill Brown, *Ronald Reagan: The Political Chameleon* (1976); Lou Cannon, "The Reagan Years: An Evaluation of the Governor Californians Won't Soon Forget," *California Journal* (1974); Totton J. Anderson and Eugene C. Lee, "The 1962 Election in California," *Western Political Quarterly* (1963); Garin Burbank, "Speaker Moretti, Governor Reagan, and the Search for Tax Reform In California, 1970–1972," *Pacific Historical Review* (1992); T. J. Anderson and Charles G. Bell, "The 1970 Election in California," *Western Political Quarterly* (1971); Maureen S. Fitzgerald, "California's Future under Proposition 13," *California Journal* (1980); James W. Guthrie, "Proposition 13 and the Future of California's Schools," *Phi Delta Kappan* (1975); Gayle B. Montgomery and James W. Johnson, *One Step from the White House: The Rise and Fall of Senator William F. Knowland* (1998); John Jacobs, *A Rage for Justice: The Passion and Politics of Phillip Burton* (1995).

Race and Radicalism

Roger Dabiels and Spencer C. Olin, Jr. eds., *Racism in California: A Reader on the History of Oppression* (1972); Raymond E. Wolfinger and Fred E. Green-stein, "The Repeal of Fair Housing in California: An Analysis of Referendum Voting," *American Political Science Review* (1968); Charles Wollenberg, *All Deliberate Speed: Segregation and Exclusion in California Schools, 1855–1975* (1977); Philip S. Foner, ed., *The Black Panthers* (1970); Bobby Seale, *Seize the Time: The Story of the Black Panther Party and Huey P. Newton* (1970); Steve Talbot, *"Free Alcatraz: The Culture of Native American Liberation,"* *Journal of Ethnic Studies* (1975); Ralph Guzman, *The Political Socialization of Mexican American People* (1976); Albert Camarillo, *Chicanos in California* (1984); Peter Matthiessen, *Sal Si Puedes: Cesar Chavez and the Farm Workers* (1975); William Barlow and Peter Shapiro, *An End to Silence: The San Francisco State Student Movement in the 60s* (1971); Seymour M. Lipset and Sheldon S. Wolin, eds., *The Berkley Student Revolt* (1965); William M. Rorabaugh, *Berkley at War: the 1960s* (1989); David L. Goines, *The Free Speech Movement:Coming of Age in the 1960s* (1993); Gerard J. De Groot, *"The Limits of Moral Protest and Participatory Democracy: The Vietnam Day Committee,"* *The Pacific Review* (1995); Raphael J. Sonenshein, *Politics in Black and White: Race and Power in Los Angeles* (1993); Sara Davidson, *Loose Change: Three Women of the Sixties* (1997); Rebecca C. Lowen, *Creating the Cold War University: The Transformation of Stanford* (1997); Delores N. McBroome, *Parallel Communities: African Americans in California's East Bay, 1850–1963* (1997).

Water, Energy Crises, and the Environment

David Potter, *People of Plenty: Economic Abundance and the American Character* (1964); Raymond Vernon, *The Oil Crisis* (1976); California Energy Commission, *Energy for Tomorrow: Challenges and opportunities for California* (1981); Stephen Anderson and others, *California Energy: The Economic Factors* (1976); Joseph Castrovinci, "Nuclear Power: Arguments for the Defense," *San Francisco Business* (1979); Hal Rubin, "Guide to Nuclear Power in California," *California Journal* (1979); E. A. Engelbert and A. F. Scheuring, eds., *Competition for California Water* (1982); Douglas Strong, *Tahoe: An Environmental History* (1984); William L. Kahrl, *Water and Power* (1982); David R. Brower, *For the Earth's Sake: the Life and Times of David Brower* (1990); James C. Williams, *Energy and the Making of Modern California* (1997); Gray Brechin, *Imperial San Francisco: The Environmental Costs of City-Building on the Pacific Basin* (1991).

The High-Tech Revolution

Dirk Hanson, *The New Alchemists: Silicon Valley and the Microelectronics Revolution* (1982); T. R. Reid, *The Chip* (1985); Ian Rienecke, *Electronic Illusions: A Skeptic's View of Our Electronic Future* (1984); Theodore Roszak, *The Cult of Information: The Folklore of Computers and the True Art of Thinking* (1986); Moira johnson, "Silicon Valley," *National Geographic* (October, 1982); Everett M. Rogers and Judith K. Larsen, *Silicon Valley Fever: Growth of High-Technology Culture* (1984); Charles Wollenberg, "The Godfather of Silicon Valley," in *Golden Gate Metropolis: Perspectives on Bay Area History* (1985); T. R. Reid, *The Chip* (1984); Paul Frieberger and Michael Swayne, *Fire in the Valley: The Making of the Personal Computer* (1984); Fred Guterl, "Reinventing the PC," *Discover* (September 1995); Gene Smarte and Andrew Reinhart, "15 Years of Bits, Bytes, and Other Great Moments," *Byte* (September 1990).

Culture and Society

Nancy Newhall, *Ansel Adams: The Eloquent Light* (1963); Ansel Adams and Mary Street Alinder, *Ansel Adams: An Autobiography* (1985); Jonathan Spaulding, "The National Scene and the Social Good: The Artistic Education of Ansel Adams," *Pacific Historical Review* (1991); Irving G. Hendrick, *California Education: A Brief History* (1980); Landon Y. Jones, *Great Expectations: America and the Baby Boom Generation* (1980); Howard S. Becker, ed., *Culture and Civility in San Francisco* (1971); Gene Anthony, *The Summer of Love* (1980); Theodore Roszak, *The Making of a Counterculture* (1969); and *The Voice of the Earth* (1992); Joan Didion, *Slouching Toward Bethlehem* (1968); Mark R. Winchell, *Joan Didion* (1980); Gerald Haslam, *Voices of a Place: Social and Literary Essays from the Other California* (1987) and *Snapshots: Glimpses of the Other California* (1985); Wallace Stegner and Richard W. Etulain, *Conversations with Wallace Stegner on Western History and Literature* (1983); Tom Gioia, *West Coast Jazz: Modern Jazz in California, 1945–1960* (1994); James J, Rawls, "Vision and Revisions," *Wilson Quarterly* (1980); Barbara Rose, "Los Angeles: The Second City," *Art in America* (1966); Christopher Rand, *Los Angeles: The Ultimate City* (1967); Richard F. Pourade, *City of the Dream: The History of San Diego* (1977); Raymond F. Dasmann, *The Destruction of California* (1965); Norman Giller, *The 1981 Olympics Handbook* (1984); Los Angeles Times Co., *The Los Angeles Times Book of the 1984 Olympics* (1985).

Carmel Highlands, South of Point Lobos State Park
Preserving the beauty of such sublime stretches of coast proved to be one of the most ambitious, as well as frustrating, of California's environmental efforts. *Photograph by William A. Bullough.*

PART TEN

ENVIRONMENT AND SOCIETY: CRISIS IN THE MOST POPULOUS STATE

For California, the twenty-first century dawned amid clouds of doubt. California has become the most materially successful of American states. Since the 1860s, despite periodic setbacks, California's population has grown more consistently than that of other states, doubling about every twenty years. In 1968 it passed the twenty-million mark, by 1990 the thirty-million mark, and by 2000, the state pushed thirty-five million. By 2000 more than one-tenth of all residents of the United States were Californians. In slightly more than one and a half centuries, the state had developed from a remote, thinly settled colonial frontier into the nation's most productive and heterogeneous region. Its varied economy is led by an agricultural system unrivaled in technology and organization, as well as yield and diversity. Its cities have grown large, complex, and affluent, and its advanced high-technology industries have set standards for modern development around the globe. California enjoys, on the average, one of the highest standards of living in the nation. Its total output of agriculture, industry, and services is outstripped by only a handful of the world's nations, one of which is the United States itself.

After decades of soaring growth in the state since the 1930s, the 1960s complex new problems were slowing California's momentum for the first time. Aerospace and computer industries languished with the end of the Vietnam War and the Cold War and a resulting reduction in national defense spending. Because of inflation and higher operating costs, along with rising foreign competition, other major businesses, particularly manufacturers of computers, automobiles, tires, steel, and related products, cut back production, closed factories altogether, or shifted operations to other states or countries. Birth and immigration rates also declined precipitously in the 1970s, threatening many California industries whose major markets had historically depended on population growth: building, road, and utility construction; processing of lumber and building materials; and education and other service industries. Other parts of the United States, especially the South and Southwest, increasingly outbid California for new migrants and industries. Immigration, especially from other countries, revived by the mid-1980s and soared in the 1990s. But for many, the Golden State had lost its luster.

California also showed the strains of overdevelopment. As at the end of the gold rush era, uncontrolled exploitation had depleted the resource base of many activities. After several decades of post–World War II boom, most of California's remaining resources—forests, petroleum and natural gas, farmland, scenery, open space, electricity, water, and even the air itself—approached exhaustion. Like the overused older states to the east, much of the state was congested, littered, polluted, and disfigured. Californians were destroying the unique natural heritage that had caused so much of their success. Smog, traffic jams, urban sprawl, overcrowded parks, and polluted water were only the most obvious manifestations of profound environmental transformations. In a region such as California, where resources and populations were out of kilter, each new thrust of economic development or population growth further upset natural balances. Nature proved too intricate, interrelated, and unpredictable, and human knowledge too limited.

Issues other than the environment also perplexed Californians after 1970. Dramatic social and cultural changes swept the state, aggravating some old problems, raising new ones, and precipitating debate and conflict. New immigration patterns—particularly a sharp decline in migration from within the United States and a corresponding increase in people coming legally and illegally from other countries—transformed California into a region populated primarily by an aggregate of ethnic minorities, especially Hispanic and Asian. As this was occurring, the growing assertiveness of minorities collided with aggressive efforts by some earlier arrivals to reassert their control, and even the different ethnic groups themselves vied against each other for economic opportunity, cultural dominance, and living space. At the same time, California women were in the vanguard of a nationwide movement to win equality with men, while others struggled just as fervently to preserve traditional gender roles and family systems. Rising crime and drug abuse, unsettling changes in moral and cultural values, crises in public education, the rapid deterioration of public roads, buildings, parks, and libraries in the wake of Proposition 13, and natural disasters born of drought, fire, and earthquake, all added to the ferment. In the face of these challenges, the state and local governments, increasingly financially strapped, hamstrung by partisan bickering, and drained of leadership by term limits for officeholders, were apparently no longer capable of dealing effectively with major policy questions.

When, in the early and mid-1990s and again in the early 2000s, economic recessions struck the state, bringing with them soaring unemployment, poverty, and depriving state and local government of tax funds, California's long-term difficulties reached crisis proportions. Growing ever more diverse economically and culturally, Californians appeared to be fragmenting into self-interested regional, economic, and cultural groups with scant recognition of wider community needs and divided bitterly over how to resolve their problems.

Along with the challenge of building a better balance between people and nature, social, economic, cultural, and political issues cast shadows over the state's bright future and muted the carefree optimism that had usually characterized its people. More than any other part of the United States, California has been acclaimed as the new paradise on earth. It remains, however, an elusive Eden.

CHAPTER TWENTY-EIGHT

THE DELTA AND THE PERIPHERAL CANAL: CALIFORNIA'S ENVIRONMENTAL CRISIS IN MICROCOSM

By the early twenty-first century, California's environmental management systems had grown gargantuan, yet resources were increasingly strained and natural conditions disordered. Controversies erupted over resource supplies and environmental policies. Urbanites battled with country people, farmers with industrialists, loggers with intellectuals and scientists, northerners with southerners, and the federal government with state and local agencies. Also, a rising environmental ethic clashed with the entrenched belief that development equaled progress. Most sections became embroiled in environmental controversy, but none more so than the Sacramento-San Joaquin River Delta. The Delta exemplified the drastic rearrangement of natural conditions and the Byzantine conflicts associated with modern development in the state. The Delta, with its proposed Peripheral Canal, was a microcosm of California's environmental crisis.

The geographical heart of California beats in the Delta. Formed by the intermingling of the Sacramento and San Joaquin rivers, the Delta before 1848 was a region of meandering streams, sloughs, and tule marshes encompassing more than one thousand square miles. The Delta was a natural reservoir, collecting half the state's freshwater runoff before discharging it into San Francisco Bay to the west. Half the Delta was at or below sea level, protected from flooding by natural levees along the riverbanks. No point rose higher than ten feet above the water. Ocean tides washed three-fifths of the Delta, so that much of the region had salty water some of the time. But heavy outflows from inland streams kept the sea at bay, and most waterways were fresh most of the time. Ground water was also fresh.

Since 1848, large-scale water developments have centered in the Delta. By the late twentieth century the Delta's exported water sustained the farms, cities, and industries of two-thirds of the state's people. Delta residents and industries also draw their water directly from local rivers and wells. The region has become a farming area in its own right, and its major channels carry oceangoing ships to inland ports at Sacramento and Stockton. Attracted by nearby shipping lanes and abundant water, giant refineries and factories line the Carquinez Strait and Suisun Bay at the western end of the Delta, while bay area suburbs encroach from the west and southwest. Despite development, enough original marshland remains to shelter migratory waterbirds on the Pacific Flyway, and nearly half the state's anadromous trout, salmon, and striped bass still swim up Delta streams to reach freshwater spawning grounds. Boating, fishing, hunting, and camping are mainstays of the local economy. Like much of California, the Delta has become a land of multiple uses.

It is also a fragile land. All the Delta's functions require a constant outpouring of fresh water from the interior to meet the irrigation, industrial, and municipal needs of local and distant people, to scour channels and prevent siltation, to cleanse waterways and maintain their oxygen levels, but most of all to keep the salty ocean from invading from the west. Moreover, fresh water from the Delta maintains the purity of Suisun Bay, the Carquinez Strait, and San Francisco Bay.

The Delta's freshwater supply, however, is exactly what is most unreliable. The freshwater-saltwater boundary fluctuates naturally, each day advancing eastward on high tides and retreating westward on low tides. Before the last century's developments, the average saltwater line lay across the strait or Suisun Bay. But in summer and in drought years, it struck far into the heart of the Delta; in winter and in wet years, it fell back, occasionally into San Francisco Bay. Freshwater discharge through the Delta also varies greatly according to rainfall. During the wet year of 1974, for example, forty million acre-feet of runoff flowed through the Delta, compared to only two million acre-feet in 1977, one of the driest years on record. Thus, even the natural extremes of saltwater intrusion into the Delta were enormous, from day to day, season to season, and year to year. But in the last century, diversions for upstream irrigation and freshwater exports away from the

Delta started a relentless march of the saltwater line inland, creating one of California's most serious environmental crises.

The tangled history of the Delta water crisis stretches back to the first settlement of the interior during the gold rush. When steamers began plying the rivers between San Francisco and inland ports, adventurous pioneers settled on higher Delta riverbanks, cut down trees growing on natural levees and islands, and opened stations to sell firewood to the riverboats. The soil was rich, water was close at hand, and passing riverboats offered ready access to urban markets. As early as 1851, settlers were building levees of peat and tule sod blocks to enclose artificial, below-sea-level "islands." When the water evaporated or was pumped out, farmers built houses and raised corn, wheat, cattle, vegetables, and orchard crops. Reclamation was slow and grueling, but crop yields and profits were large.

By the early twentieth century, one thousand miles of levees had created sixty large agricultural islands. Steamboat and farm towns such as Isleton, Walnut Grove, Rio Vista, and the Chinese community of Locke developed, some below water level. Virtually the entire natural structure of the Delta had been replaced by a man-made world of farms, towns, canals, boat channels, irrigation works, and flood-control projects, all shielded behind the intricate levee system. By the mid-twentieth century, Delta farms each year produced hundreds of millions of dollars in crops from deep soils and inexpensive water.

Even while Delta settlers were wresting land from the tides, new problems threatened their labors. As human activities grew dependent on the delicate environmental balance, that balance became ever shakier. Eroding rapidly after their trees had been cut down, natural banks and levees offered

Delta Channel and Reclaimed Farmland, 1961
Aerial photographs capture the extent to which geometric, man-made patterns dominate the Delta behind the protective levees. Remnants of original channels and marshes are still in evidence in some artificial waterways. *Courtesy of the California Department of Water Resources.*

less flood protection. Composed of spongy peat, the settlers' own low dikes soon began to cave in. Waters repeatedly poured over the hard-won islands, destroyed farms, threatened towns, and ruined residents. Then from the 1860s to the 1880s hydraulic mining debris from the Sierra foothills choked the Delta, permanently narrowing and raising channel beds as much as fifteen feet. With the flood threat greatly worsened, settlers piled their levees higher, and the re-

claimed land fell farther below water levels, making it more vulnerable to inundation. This combat with nature continues today. Porous and sinking, the aging levees break down regularly under the buffeting of winter rains, winds, and waves, sometimes flooding thousands of acres. Much of the decaying levee network must be rebuilt soon if Delta settlement is to continue.

As difficult as the fight against unwanted water has been, growing freshwater short-

Salt-encrusted Delta Cabbage Field
Soil-salt buildup, caused by excessive or improper irrigation and poor drainage, threatens hundreds of thousands of California's most productive acres, including large stretches of the Imperial and San Joaquin valleys and especially the Delta. In this Delta cabbage field, salt encrusts the surface and stunts the plants. *Courtesy of the California Department of Water Resources.*

ages have been more ominous. Channelizing larger streams for navigation and flood control and converting tens of thousands of acres of tule marshes into farms have greatly reduced the Delta's capacity to store fresh water and withstand the invading saltwater tides. By the early twentieth century, increasing local demand for fresh water for irrigation, cities, and sugar and petroleum refineries in the western Delta further taxed the

supply. Even more significant were declining freshwater flows from upstream. As the San Joaquin and Sacramento valleys boomed in the late nineteenth and early twentieth centuries, irrigation projects and cities there sucked up ever more water, leaving less to find its way to the Delta. After 1920, San Francisco and Oakland dammed major tributaries of the San Joaquin and imported their water directly by aqueduct, bypassing the river and the Delta. The volume and velocity of Delta rivers thus declined dramatically in the first three decades of the twentieth century, especially during dry summer months.

By 1920, the mean saltwater line was moving eastward. At first, the encroaching sea polluted the industrial and municipal supplies of the western Delta, but eventually it threatened inner Delta irrigation works. Overdrafts on wells began to draw salt water into underground basins as well. Salt water is a greater hazard to the Delta than to other regions. Lying below water level and lacking natural drainage, its soils cannot be easily drained or leached of accumulated salts that stunt or destroy crops. The area's refineries also required much salt-free water to operate efficiently. When droughts in the 1920s reduced freshwater outflows to a trickle, the region stood on the brink of ecological disaster.

Mark Twain, a former Californian, reputedly once quipped that "whiskey is for drinking—water is for fighting over." That certainly became true in the Delta. Led by the urban and industrial western Delta, the region struck back to defend its water supply. As early as 1915, leaders spoke out against uncontrolled upstream diversions, but salt water crept in farther, polluting wells and intakes, clogging refinery pipes, destroying piers, and encrusting farmlands with salt. During the drought of 1920 the Delta water systems neared collapse. When upstream interests refused to reduce their drafts of river water, Delta water users joined the city of Antioch in suing to prevent upstream irrigation districts, private land and water companies, and individual irrigators from diverting Sacramento River water further. Such early defensive efforts brought only legal disaster. The state supreme court in 1922 ruled that upstream diverters had vested rights to river water, that Delta users had no right to the

preservation of water quality, and that there was no legal requirement that valuable water be "wasted" to flush the Delta. This decision, and others in the 1920s and 1930s, undercut virtually all the region's legal protections against saltwater intrusion.

During the 1920s, recurrent drought, the likelihood of future water shortages, and the Delta water conflict finally forced California to adopt comprehensive water planning. Different interests disagreed vehemently over alternative solutions, however. Faced with dividing scarce water resources, regions and economic groups usually pursued narrow interests with little regard for the overall welfare. To escape litigation and regulation of their water use, Sacramento Valley diverters campaigned for a barrier or dam across the western Delta to keep out salt water. Although some western Delta industries and Bay Area cities at first supported this plan because it might assure their own water supply, the inner Delta strenuously objected that such a barrier would raise water levels and flood its farms and towns. Delta agricultural interests demanded that the state firmly establish their legal right to enough freshwater flow to hold back the salt, a concept opposed vigorously by upstream users. Inland shipping and coastal fishing interests joined in fighting the saltwater barrier because it would impede ships and spawning fish from reaching the interior. Some scientists also predicted that the entire Delta region behind the barrier, flushed by neither tides nor freshwater outflows, would become hopelessly polluted.

State and federal water experts favored instead the building of large upstream dams in the northern Sacramento Valley to store excess winter water, channel it into canals to irrigate the interior, and release it in summer into the rivers to flush salt from the Delta. This plan was supported most vigorously by the San Joaquin Valley, which by the 1920s was running short of local water for agriculture and longed to import water from northern streams and the Delta. Southern California strongly opposed all these schemes. Geographically isolated and developing its own water supply from the Owens Valley and Colorado River, that region objected to spending general state funds to benefit residents north of the Tehachapis. For decades, northern Californians had ignored southern needs; now they could solve their own water problems. By the early 1930s, the onset of comprehensive statewide water planning had exposed the differences among California interests and precipitated intense interregional rivalries. From then on, the consensus on water would be narrow, and most major decisions would provoke bitter controversy.

In 1931, after a decade of study, state water agencies finished designing the Central Valley Project (CVP), the most ambitious water-redistribution plan in California history to date. The plan proposed: (1) to build Shasta Dam on the northern Sacramento River to store water for irrigation, flood control, navigation, and Delta flushing; (2) to modify natural channels to carry purer and more abundant Sacramento River water into the San Joaquin portion of the Delta; (3) to install giant pumps to raise water from the southern Delta into gravity canals down the west side of the San Joaquin Valley; and (4) to construct the Contra Costa Conduit to supply the salt-plagued western Delta with fresh water from farther east. To placate the inner Delta and southern California and to improve chances for passage, the costly saltwater barrier was dropped.

After acrimonious debate, the legislature passed the Central Valley Project bill in 1933. Enemies, particularly southern California and private power companies that objected to the inexpensive public electricity the project would generate, forced the bill into a

referendum later that year; it passed by the narrow margin of 35,000 out of a total of 900,000 votes cast. San Franciscans endorsed the measure two to one, while Angelenos rejected it by about the same proportion. As it turned out, in the mid-1930s, the impoverished state manipulated the federal government into building and operating the CVP, which began delivering water to cities and farms in the 1940s.

The Central Valley Project revolutionized the Delta waterscape. Developed when water science was still in its infancy, the CVP suffered from incomplete information and faulty engineering. Although it stabilized the flow of the Sacramento River for the purpose of flood control and exported much water south to open up new farmland in the San Joaquin Valley, the project compounded, rather than resolved, most of the Delta's environmental problems. The San Joaquin River, the site of the intakes for the canals moving the water toward the south, had far less outflow than the Sacramento and was more naturally prone to saltwater intrusion. CVP pumps sucked up so much fresh water from the southern Delta, especially during dry summer months, that some channels reversed direction of flow, drawing salt water from San Francisco Bay even farther into the Delta. Cross-Delta channels from the Sacramento River failed to carry enough fresh water to flush the southern Delta, and the pumps occasionally sent a river of salty water southward to pollute soils and water supplies in the San Joaquin Valley. Overall, the CVP upset the natural water balances of the Delta and worsened saline and other forms of pollution.

Delta interests complained but found scant relief. Although the original state plan had listed saltwater control as a responsibility of the CVP, federal authorization laws failed to mention it. When appealing for support in the late 1930s and early 1940s, the federal

Bureau of Reclamation promised to release water from Shasta Dam to maintain the Delta's water purity. Once the project was operating, however, the bureau insisted it had no legal obligation to use Shasta water to maintain Delta water quality beyond what was needed to assure the quality of water exported south. Increasingly, federal and state experts viewed releasing fresh water to flush the Delta and bay as a waste of valuable resources that could be used to stimulate development elsewhere. The Bureau of Reclamation's position that as a federal agency it was not bound by state laws, including water standards, was generally upheld by federal courts, and during drought, the CVP refused to cooperate with the state to maintain Delta water quality. By the 1950s Delta water rights had eroded still further.

New developments caused California to reassess its water policies in the 1950s. A fierce postwar boom taxed available water resources, especially in southern California. About half of the state's people now inhabited a region with less than one percent of the state's natural stream flow. At the same time, the long-simmering feud with Arizona over the Colorado River Compact imperiled California's share of the river's water. In *Arizona* v. *California* (1963) the U.S. Supreme Court ordered California to relinquish half of its Colorado entitlement when the Central Arizona Project was to be completed in the late 1980s.

Facing soaring demand and shrinking resources, the state found itself with little power over water storage and distribution. Major facilities were in the hands of local districts or, in the case of the Central Valley and Colorado River projects, the federal government. Not only did the Bureau of Reclamation ignore state policies, but there also loomed the danger that the federal government would start enforcing the so-called

"160-acre principle," the provision in the 1902 National Reclamation Act prohibiting any landowner from receiving subsidized water for more than 160 acres. If applied to the CVP, the Imperial Irrigation District, and other federally aided water projects, the principle would force the sale and subdivision of some of California's most valuable land. Naturally, agribusiness opposed the 160-acre rule and delayed its enforcement in California. Many landowners, however, refused to accept federal water and urged the state to provide cheap, state-subsidized water so that they could safely irrigate their large holdings without the 160-acre limitation.

Pressed by many interests, in the 1950s the state embarked on its own daring water program to satisfy its needs through the mid-twenty-first century. The California Water Plan (CWP) envisioned a network of dozens of reservoirs, pumping stations, and electrical generating plants, linked by thousands of miles of aqueducts and pipelines. The CWP's central objective was to impound the runoff of Sacramento River tributaries, to transport the water through a north-south artery to irrigate the dry western and southern San Joaquin Valley, and then to pump it over the Tehachapi Mountains into southern California. Along the way, shorter aqueducts were to carry water over the Coast Range to quench the future thirsts of growing seaside cities from San Francisco Bay to San Diego. The plan was so monumental that its completion would require six decades and cost more than $13 billion in 1950 dollars.

As with the CVP, the Delta was at the CWP's heart. Water from the Sacramento, particularly from the proposed Oroville Dam on the Feather River, had to be transferred into the San Joaquin basin. State engineers planned to rebuild additional channels so that the pure water could be moved across the Delta without being adulterated with salt and pollutants. A large pumping plant in the south Delta west of Stockton would lift the water into the California Aqueduct for its journey to the southern part of the state. The CWP made it clear that, by the 1950s, state as well as federal water planners saw the Delta primarily as, in the words of one state Department of Water Resources engineer, "a natural pool to which the surplus water of the northern part of the state can be funneled and from which the water can be pumped and transported to the water-short areas in the central and southern parts." The needs of the Delta and the San Francisco Bay area were a low and fading priority.

Predictably, the CWP sparked immediate controversy. By the late 1950s the state's feuding interests had shifted stands somewhat, but had lost none of their emotion on the water question. The plan contained no guarantees of Delta water quality. Repeatedly stung by saltwater intrusion, invasion of its water supply by rival regions, and broken government promises, the Delta even more adamantly opposed additional water exports. The Bay Area had once led the way in large water developments and had favored the CVP. Some Bay Area communities now stood to gain supplies of state-funded water, but many were beginning to appreciate that the bay's health was closely related to Delta water purity, feared the growing political strength of the southern counties, and saw the CWP as a southern raid on northern resources. Most residents of northern and central districts agreed. Once the pipeline to the south was opened, they asked, what was to keep southerners from tapping more northern streams. Northern interests, including cities and large farms, solidly opposed the CWP.

The primary projected recipients of CWP water—agribusiness in the San Joaquin Valley and communities south of the Teha-

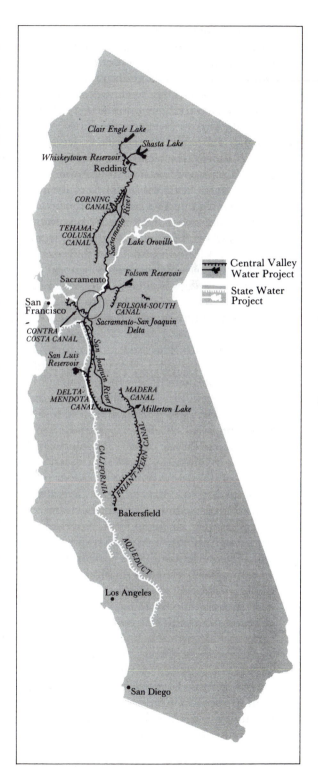

California Water Projects

chapis—strongly supported the plan. Southern California, once the principal opponent of large-scale state water projects, had done a complete about-face. The south now favored using state funds to import water to meet its future needs and compensate for possible losses to Arizona. The only major reservation was raised by the Metropolitan Water District, the mammoth agency that supplied water to most southern communities, which protested that the CWP did not permanently guarantee southern rights to northern water. So vehement were its objections that it threatened to move independently to seize the water of the north coast's Eel River, much as the city of Los Angeles had once acquired the Owens River, and to pipe it over the mountains to southern counties. The legislature, however, amended the California Water Project plan to prohibit the state from reneging on its promises to the south, and the Metropolitan and most other southern districts then campaigned for passage of the plan.

In the late 1950s and early 1960s, California groups divided over the issue according to the plan's effects on their own economic interests. The state's few environmentalists raised lonely warnings of dangers for the entire state from additional large water-transfer systems. Not many listened, even among the CWP's opponents. As late as 1960, Californians were still caught up in their historic boosterism. This battle over Delta water was waged primarily along economic and regional lines.

At the urging of Governor Pat Brown, who insisted that the CWP was essential to prosperity and growth, the legislature in 1959 passed the Burns-Porter Act, calling for a referendum to approve $1.75 billion in bonds for the central transfer system from Oroville Dam to southern California. The 1960 referendum was a classic north-south struggle over water. Reflecting its growing population

and political power, southern California won, though narrowly. Southern California overwhelmingly passed the measure; every northern county voted it down, except for Butte County, proposed site of the Oroville Dam.

With its regions polarized, California embarked on the construction of the most elaborate plumbing system in history. Oroville Dam, then the world's tallest, first trapped Feather River water in 1967. Delta channels were reconstructed and pumping plants were in place the next year. In 1973 the first northern water heaved over the Tehachapis into southern reservoirs. By 1975 the project annually exported two million acre-feet from the Delta. Existing contracts bound it to deliver nearly 4.25 million acre-feet in the year 2016. By then, additional dams, aqueducts, and pumps were to be operating.

By the end of the 1970s, some benefits of the CWP were already apparent. New water transformed thousands of acres of unfarmed, grazing, or oil land, especially in the western and southern San Joaquin Valley, into large-scale, modern, irrigated vineyards, orchards, cotton fields, and rice bogs, primarily on land owned by the Southern Pacific Company, multinational oil firms, and agricultural corporations. Cities also benefited. East San Francisco Bay and Santa Clara Valley towns used the water to reduce overdependence on groundwater and to purge underground aquifers of intruding salt water. In southern California, although all the water was not yet needed, it promised to make up for future losses of Colorado River entitlements. In fact, by the mid-1970s, the CWP was producing a surplus, particularly below the Tehachapis. Most unneeded supplies were resold to large San Joaquin irrigators, at below-market-value prices subsidized by urban water users.

The CWP also helped California to survive the severe drought of 1975 to 1977 with little

California's Longest "River"
The California Aqueduct follows the foothill contours of the Antelope Valley near Palmdale, carrying northern water on its 500-mile journey to the southern California metropolis. By the 1970s California had become the only state whose longest "river" was man-made. *Courtesy of the California Department of Water Resources.*

lasting economic damage. The new distribution system allowed the state to shift water to areas of dire need. Cities and farms drew from state aqueducts when their own supplies ran dry. Southern California voluntarily relinquished most of its entitlement and temporarily increased imports from the Colorado, leaving water for drought assistance to the north.

Nevertheless, the CWP compounded the problems begun by the federal Central Valley Project. The state's pumps removed more fresh water, while rebuilt channels failed to coax enough additional Sacramento water into the southern Delta to compensate. Salt water struck deeper and more often into the Delta. In dry seasons even the water pumped southward became heavily polluted. By the 1970s, freshwater flows from the interior had declined, and exports increased, to the point that the Delta could no longer relinquish water without adulterating it. Pollution and flow disturbance also decimated fish populations in the Delta, bay, and offshore waters. Even before its initial phase was fully operating, it was clear that without radical changes the state project could not increase its output.

Tampering with natural water flows was causing other complex problems. Transferring large amounts of water from one watershed to another not only produces shortages in the region of origin, but it taxes the drainage capacity in the region of delivery. Prolonged or improper irrigation concentrates crop-killing salts in soils, especially those with poor drainage. By the early 1970s scientists warned that hundreds of thousands of acres of once-fertile land in the San Joaquin and Imperial valleys, the Delta, and elsewhere were poisoned by salt and might have to be abandoned.

At present, the most common method of combating salt accumulation is to install underground drainpipes and ditches to carry it away. Although used in the San Joaquin Valley, this method merely transfers the problem elsewhere. Saturated with deadly salts, herbicides, pesticides, manure, nitrates, and a multitude of other chemicals, agricultural waste water seeps from the soils, trickles down farm drainage ditches, pours into natural rivers, and eventually penetrates underground basins. The only natural drain for much of its valley, the San Joaquin River had itself become a major source of Delta pollution and a threat to the purity of export water by the 1970s. To a considerable extent, the CVP and the CWP continually recycled contaminated water between the Delta and the valley, exacerbating the environmental problems of both regions.

Once again, water experts proposed still more powerful technologies to alter natural conditions. So strained were the water resources of the Delta, bay, and valleys, however, that all solutions carried the potential for even worse disaster. To deal with soil-salt buildup and wastewater disposal, for example, state and federal water agencies proposed building concrete-lined drains paralleling the major streams. Such a project for the San Joaquin basin had been contemplated for decades, but high costs and controversy over its location and operation repeatedly delayed it. Under pressure from customers and other water agencies, in the late 1960s the Bureau of Reclamation finally began constructing a 300-mile-long open sewer intended to capture wastewater from the valley and empty it directly into the west Delta or San Francisco Bay, but in response to environmental concerns, Congress instituted a requirement that this and other similar drains meet state water quality standards. By the early 1980s the northern unit, or San Luis Drain, neared completion, but protests erupted from communities near the proposed outlets. No one, apparently, relished playing host to deadly pollution from a region of 15,000 square miles.

Although protests blocked completion of its outlet to the Delta or bay, in 1975 a segment of the San Luis Drain began discharging water saturated with toxic salts, lead, boron, arsenic, mercury, pesticides, and especially selenium into the ponds of the Kesterson Wildlife Refuge west of Merced. Soon fish and frogs were wiped out, water birds died and their young were born deformed, and the polluted water was killing livestock and seeping into groundwater basins. Local farmers and water districts

joined the U.S. Geological Survey and Fish and Wildlife Service in condemning the drain. In fact, by this time, evidence was building that Kesterson was only one of many sites severely polluted with selenium and other irrigation wastes in the San Joaquin Valley and other areas of California and the West. Early in 1985, the legislature moved to ban agricultural wastewater dumping in the Delta, and the state Water Resources Control Board ordered the Bureau of Reclamation to clean up the refuge or close it and the drain. In March 1985, Secretary of the Interior Donald Hodel, pressed by lawsuits and the threat that the polluted refuge might violate the federal Migratory Bird Treaty Act, suddenly ordered the refuge and drain closed and Central Valley Project water shut off to parts of the western San Joaquin Valley, threatening growers there with bankruptcy. Only when a plan was worked out by environmentalists and western valley irrigation districts to impound and reclaim agricultural wastewater did the Department of the Interior resume irrigation water deliveries to the region. As late as the mid-1990s, although Kesterson Wildlife Refuge had been partially filled in and some clean-up of agricultural waste toxins had been performed, the site had yet to be completely rehabilitated. However, in order to seal off the area, the Department of the Interior had purchased 10,000 acres of uncontaminated surrounding land, which held out the hope that in the distant future a major wildlife refuge might result. The problem of irrigation-induced selenium pollution remains a severe and growing threat to western agriculture.

In the decades after 1960, federal and state water experts sought ways to move additional northern water for export through the Delta without polluting that water with water from the San Joaquin River or the sea. Eventually, they settled on what came to be known as the Peripheral Canal. First suggested to the state by the Bureau of Reclamation in 1963, the proposed addition to the CWP was a concrete trough forty-three miles long and more than one hundred yards wide. The canal would intercept the Sacramento River south of Sacramento, carry the clean water around the eastern and southern edges of the Delta, and deliver it directly into the barrels of the export pumps. Initially the canal would annually transport about 700,000 acre-feet of water directly southward, bypassing the Delta, but its future potential was enormous. The canal would be capable of diverting more than half of the Sacramento's flow in wet years, all of it in dry seasons.

At first glance, the Peripheral Canal appeared to satisfy several needs. The volume of the CWP could be greatly increased without endangering the purity of the export water. The state also proposed to release ten percent of the canal's water into Delta channels to reduce saltwater intrusion, refresh the decaying waterways of the inner Delta, and maintain a healthier environment for fish, birds, boaters, and hunters. All this could be accomplished, it was maintained, without injuring the Delta or San Francisco Bay. Indeed, proponents argued, the canal would save those regions. Although only superficially studied, the Peripheral Canal became an immediate favorite of some parties to the Delta water dispute, including state and federal water agencies, southern water users, the state Department of Fish and Game, and even at first some environmentalists. In 1965 the California Department of Water Resources quietly approved the canal, which was scheduled for completion in 1975. The Delta's baffling water problems seemed about to be resolved.

At first, the canal attracted little public attention. Into the early 1970s, planning progressed behind the scenes for a joint federal-state facility to serve both the CVP and the CWP. The state tried to convince the federal government to pay for the canal, yet allow the state to control its operation. Federal agencies increasingly disagreed over the canal's environmental effects and its high cost, however, and the Bureau of Reclamation reaffirmed that it would not relinquish control over Delta water to the state. Inheriting Pat Brown's commitment to deliver more water to southern counties, Ronald Reagan's administration vigorously pushed the project and, when it failed to secure federal assistance, announced in 1971 that California would build the canal alone.

As more information surfaced about the project's likely effects, however, the Peripheral Canal became the most controversial water proposal in California history. Virtually from the beginning, Delta interests, led by Contra Costa County, attacked the canal because the plan still failed to protect Delta water rights specifically. The canal could reduce the flow of the Sacramento River enormously and greatly increase saltwater intrusion, a possibility that even state water planners admitted. By this time, Delta water could not be exploited further to satisfy the needs of some people without injuring the interests of others. If the canal were built, Delta waterways might have to be abandoned for recreation, irrigation, and municipal water. In 1969, local Delta water agencies adopted a resolution condemning the Peripheral Canal, and regional representatives assailed the canal before public hearings, in Congress, and in the legislature.

Despite vehement Delta opposition, the ultimate completion of the canal seemed inevitable, given the south's growing population and influence, the enthusiasm of the Reagan administration, and the state's tradition of meeting water needs with large-scale transfers. However, the canal question had

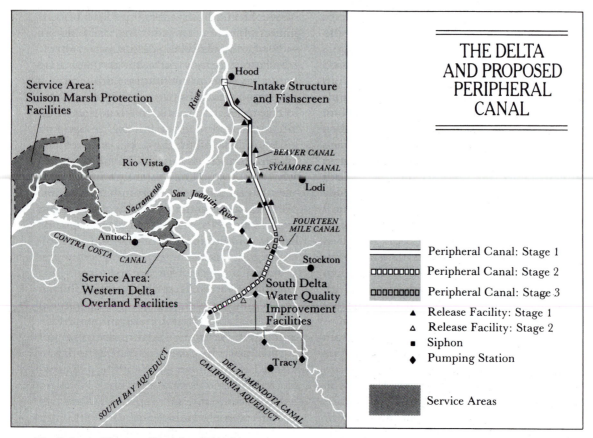

The Delta and Proposed Peripheral Canal

become broadly regional. Since it would open the gate to exporting theoretically unlimited amounts of northern water, even from streams beyond the Sacramento basin, a canal around the Delta was an ominous threat that unified the region. By the early 1970s northern and central newspapers, local governments, business and farm groups, and political leaders rallied to defend the Delta.

At first the conflict over the canal, like previous water battles, was between competing economic and regional interests. The rise of environmentalism, however, added a new dimension to the conflict. Supported by growing public dismay at environmental de-

terioration, environmentalists stressed that for long-range human, economic, biological, and spiritual welfare, plant and animal life, water systems that support them, and entire habitats must be maintained. After 1960, new environmental values spread widely, membership in environmental organizations soared, and campaigns began to curb destructive practices. To environmentalists, the Peripheral Canal epitomized abuse of nature on a grand scale. They charged that the project would reduce the Delta to a reeking cesspool and injure San Francisco Bay, the Sacramento and San Joaquin valleys, and inevitably the ocean. The canal, they warned, would also pave the way for the destruction of the north-coast rivers and other surviving wilderness areas, and encourage more growth in southern California, where air, space, land, and drainage resources were already strained.

In contrast to opponents of earlier large-scale water projects, environmentalists in the early 1970s were for the first time questioning the theoretical bases of California water development. Such massive rearrangements of nature, the Sierra Club maintained in a 1970 report on the CWP, erred in assuming that economic use of water is "proper," while maintaining natural flows and habitats is "waste." "Such systems," the club concluded, "are devised with inadequate understanding of their overall consequences and with little regard for the emerging land-use ethic, which recognizes that man must, for his own survival, place himself in better balance with his total environment." Future water needs, environmentalists countered, should be met by conservation, wastewater reclamation, and location of necessary developments nearer to water supplies.

In the early 1970s, environmentalists and northern California leaders forged an anti-canal alliance that cut across political parties and economic ideologies. Economic interests shifted to environmental arguments, which aroused more public opposition to the canal. Although the new environmental philosophy made inroads into southern California, its center was in the north, which had a stronger tradition of supporting resource conservation and wilderness preservation.

Opponents of the canal turned to legal action to delay its planning. They were assisted by passage of a 1970 federal act that required the builders of large projects to complete detailed environmental-impact studies. Canal enemies filed lawsuits in the 1970s, charging federal and state authorities with failing to conduct proper environmental studies, and won a victory when courts ordered the state

to file environmental-impact reports on its Delta pumping plants and the Peripheral Canal. These lawsuits delayed the construction of the canal, the San Luis Drain, and other major water projects. In addition, the lawsuits, along with the studies they provoked, armed the canal's enemies with scientific ammunition and gave them vital time to organize and to win broader public support.

Many of the studies concluded that the canal would indeed aggravate water problems, and respected scientists joined a growing number of governmental agencies in criticizing the canal. The federal Environmental Protection Agency and U.S. Geological Survey questioned the accuracy of initial state surveys, predicted that the canal would harm San Francisco Bay, and warned against hasty construction. Charged with determining and enforcing water quality standards under new federal and state laws, the California Water Resources Control Board, in its 1971 Delta Decision, determined that large-scale water transfers had dangerous side effects, and, as a result, it raised the water purity standards that projects such as the canal had to meet. In a blow to canal supporters, the board called for "a balanced program for water development and [environmental] protection."

Legal, scientific, and bureaucratic victories encouraged increased political action. On the offensive in Congress and the legislature, the canal's opponents in the 1970s raised public concern, stalled federal participation, and thwarted the Reagan administration's moves for immediate state approval. State and federal agencies increasingly disagreed on the canal's likely environmental effects. The Water Resources Control Board criticized the state's 1974 environmental-impact report and raised doubts about the canal and large water transfers in general, while the departments of Water Resources and Fish and Game defended the canal as the only environmentally safe way to increase CWP water flow.

Finally, in late 1974, as Governor Reagan was leaving office, and only one year before construction was to have begun, the state Senate's Natural Resources Committee reported to the legislature that the environmental effects of the canal were uncertain, federal cooperation was unlikely, and the entire project was "premature." Jerry Brown's administration delayed the planning schedule for the canal one year to study alternatives. By 1975 anti-canal forces seemed victorious; they had raised new issues, forced water projects to meet more stringent environmental standards, and delayed the canal by at least a decade. For the first time, environmental factors had intervened in state water policy and politics.

Jerry Brown's inauguration as governor in January 1975 promised a sharp departure from tradition. In contrast to his two predecessors, who had aligned with water-development interests and southern California, Brown, in his campaign and early official statements, heralded a new "era of limits" and preached such heresy as austerity and conservation of resources, and he was initially supported by environmentalists. Although the new governor called on citizens for restraint, pressure to move more water south was strong and conflicts over water policy remained intense. For the next three years, state water agencies gathered evidence about the canal and alternatives to it. Experts considered desalinization, wastewater reclamation, enlarging existing Delta channels, mandatory water conservation, groundwater management, and building new reservoirs. Most proposed solutions were dismissed as technically, economically, or politically unworkable.

What was clear was that water interests were hopelessly polarized. Southern California and San Joaquin Valley agribusiness demanded great increases in imports from the north and the installation of a large Peripheral Canal, not only to compensate for future losses of Colorado River supplies but to irrigate more acreage and expand suburban tracts. Their extreme spokesmen opposed all measures restricting water use, requiring conservation or groundwater management, or protecting water quality in the Delta, San Francisco Bay, or northern rivers. The latter could cut southern imports during drought and make it difficult to tap additional northern water in the future. Bay Area and Delta residents and most environmentalists insisted that water moving south had to use natural Delta channels in order to assure their water quality. The canal's opponents also insisted on legal protection for their water rights, water quality, and north-coast rivers. Some rejected all additional water exports.

The severe 1975-1977 drought, like previous shortages, gave impetus to water developments such as the Peripheral Canal. When Delta water standards became difficult to maintain by 1976, conflict again erupted between the state and the Bureau of Reclamation. The bureau refused to furnish water to flush the Delta. To prevent serious saline intrusion, the state was forced to increase its releases and to cut deliveries to some CWP users. To avoid having their supplies reduced, some San Joaquin Valley buyers of state water sued to prevent the state from "wasting" water to maintain Delta water quality. Although the state prevailed, such events confirmed to canal critics that the south lacked any commitment to protecting northern pools and streams. Despite state water releases, salt water invaded the Delta as never before, polluting the region's supplies and threatening to flow freely into export pumps. By late 1977, state officials feared that much of the state's water supply would be destroyed, perhaps for years. The crisis convinced state water experts that only the Peripheral Canal would allow more water to be shipped south and give the state flexibility to meet such emergencies.

Pressure from agribusiness, the south, and his own advisers converted Governor Brown into a canal advocate, although he worked for a compromise to avoid another divisive water battle. Brown's plan envisioned building the canal and expensive companion facilities, while at the same time guaranteeing Delta water quality and assuring releases to flush the Delta. It was to take effect only if the federal government agreed to abide by Delta water standards and to protect the north-coast streams as wild and scenic rivers. In February 1978, however, the plan was killed in the legislature by an unlikely combination of northerners who feared the environmental safeguards were weak and southern extremists who wanted even more water. In early 1978 heavy rains began to fall, but divisions over water remained deep.

Undaunted, the Brown administration reintroduced the canal package in 1979 with two important changes. Insistence on federal cooperation was dropped, and protections for Delta water quality and preservation of north-coast rivers were to be strengthened by amendments to the state constitution. Senate Bill (SB) 200 had the sometimes reluctant support of southern water agencies, southern San Joaquin agribusiness, southern land-development firms, and the state Chamber of Commerce. Because of the proposed constitutional changes, some northerners and environmentalists also initially supported the plan as the lesser of evils. Prodded by Brown and state agencies, the divergent interests, few of which were completely satisfied, narrowly pushed the multi-

billion-dollar plan for the canal and associated additions to the CWP through the legislature in early July 1980. A constitutional amendment protecting the Delta and north-coast rivers also passed. Although voters approved it as Proposition 8 in November, it was not to take effect unless the canal bill also became law.

SB200 sat on Brown's desk for nearly two weeks after passage, prompting speculation that he might be having second thoughts. On July 18, two days before it would have become law without his signature, the governor announced his decision in a tense, uncharacteristically long television address. "We can have water with problems," he told Californians, "or we can have problems without water." Stressing that the state's future hinged on shipping more water south, that the Peripheral Canal was the best method, and that the proposed constitutional amendment would protect northern waterways, Brown dramatically signed the bill. In what even he must have realized was empty rhetoric, the governor proclaimed an end to the era of growth without conservation in California and declared that "today we show we're one state working together to ensure our prosperity." Apparently, Brown preferred "water with problems."

Problems, he would have. The governor and other canal proponents had not reckoned on the intensity of feeling over water and environment. The canal's enactment galvanized northerners and environmentalists as never before. Opposition hardened further in August, when the farm lobby squashed a companion bill that would have required areas receiving canal water to enact water conservation and groundwater management plans. Northern community leaders, governments, and environmental organizations easily collected 840,000 signatures, more than double the required number, on

Wind Gap Pumping Plant on the California State Water Project
One of several such plants near Bakersfield, at the foot of the San Joaquin Valley, the Wind Gap Pumping Plant helps to hoist northern water 2,000 feet over the Tehachapi Mountains. The soaring cost of electricity to power such vast facilities was a telling argument used by Peripheral Canal opponents to win support among some southern Californians. *Courtesy of the California Department of Water Resources.*

petitions calling a referendum on SB200, the first time in thirty years that a legislative act had been forced to a referendum. Canal backers, especially the Los Angeles *Times*, pressed the governor to call a special election coinciding with southern municipal elections in June 1981, which would have greatly increased the turnout, and thus the power, of southern voters. Brown refused,

and the referendum was left for the next statewide election in June 1982. The stage was set for a classic confrontation over water and environment.

Proposition 9, the Peripheral Canal referendum, was one of the most bizarre in U.S. history. Early opinion polls disclosed the obvious: southern counties strongly favored the canal; northern counties strongly opposed it; and because of the preponderance of southern voters, the measure was likely to win comfortably. Tasting victory, canal promoters fell back on the traditional booster arguments: prosperity depended on continued economic and population growth, and hence on water transfers; southern taps were running dry, and more northern water was imperative to the well-being of the region and state. Defenders praised the canal as an environmental marvel that could channel huge amounts of water south, while improving the water quality of the Delta and San Francisco Bay. Playing on fresh memories of the 1975-1977 drought, defenders raised the specter of even worse shortages if the canal were not dug. The canal, its publicists emphasized, was "the missing link" in the California Water Project. Completing the chain was inevitable, and long overdue.

Opponents stressed the familiar environmental and economic dangers that had concerned northerners for more than a decade. Critics protested, moreover, that the proposed environmental protections were meaningless. The federal government would not cooperate, and southern water imperialists would be able to overturn any environmental protections at will. Hearkening back to Los Angeles's "rape" of the Owens Valley in the early twentieth century, anti-canal propaganda predicted the same fate for the north. In appealing for southern support, the canal's foes cited studies showing that projected southern population growth and water shortages were exaggerated. Building the canal when it was not needed would saddle southern households with high water and energy bills, while the extra water would go, as it presently did, at cheap rates to San Joaquin farmers. The canal, urban southern voters were told, was one of the biggest boondoggles for agribusiness in the state's history, at the expense of urban consumers.

Even modest water conservation, particularly reducing waste of irrigation water by farmers, could produce more water than the canal, at little or no cost. Such arguments issued not only from northerners and environmentalists, but also from some southern consumer organizations and anti-canal water officials.

Through 1981 and into 1982, the controversy over Proposition 9 grew increasingly bitter. Exaggerations and inflammatory statements were common on all sides. A few northern extremists hinted that, as it had earlier in the Owens Valley, vigilante violence would erupt if the canal were constructed. Southern water agencies predicted that their region would revert to desert without the canal. Northern fears appeared justified by the extreme statements of some canal supporters. One spokesman for Kern County agribusiness, for example, when asked by a reporter how far water development should go, replied on statewide television that "we won't rest until not a drop of California water flows down to the sea." As the campaign continued, southern support for the canal held steady, perhaps weakening slightly, while northerners became even more vehemently opposed.

Although local politicians of all parties generally lined up with their regions, statewide leaders scrambled over each other to get out of the crossfire. Democratic Governor Brown anticipated running for the U.S. Senate in 1982. Astounded by the fury he had helped to unleash, Brown quickly disassociated himself from his own controversial project, with the excuse that he was too busy fighting crime. Lieutenant Governor Mike Curb, the conservative southern Republican who was angling to replace Brown as governor, began as a supporter, but midway in the battle he inexplicably condemned the canal as too expensive and deserted to the opposition. Heaped with abuse from his region and traditional backers, Curb spent the rest of the campaign trying to rationalize or back away from his new position. Their vacillation on the canal issue helped defeat both Brown and Curb in 1982.

Even more unexpected were defections by some of the canal's most ardent agribusiness friends. Although most large southern farmers and organizations, realizing that compromise with other interests was politically necessary, strongly supported the bill, some criticized it as too environmentally restrictive. Determined that the needs of agricultural users of CWP water should take precedence over the water quality of the Delta and bay, and that north-coast rivers must be left "free" only to flow south, the California Farm Bureau, the California Cattlemen's Association, and a handful of farm giants such as J. G. Boswell and the Salyer Land Company announced that they would oppose Proposition 9 and trust that a canal could be built someday without environmental safeguards. Canal supporters such as state Senator Reuben Ayala, the bill's author, criticized the bureau's greed and insensitivity to legitimate northern environmental concerns. The Farm Bureau stood firm in its defection, however, and Boswell and Salyer donated $4 million to the anti-canal war chest. As the campaign drew to a close, Ayala lamented that, because of bewildering political, sectional, and interest-group alignments, "conventional water development in California is in a state of chaos."

On June 8, 1982, the voters delivered a fitting climax to one of the most divisive and expensive political struggles in California history. More than $6 million had been spent in the campaign, the great majority by canal foes. Citizens voted down Proposition 9 by a sixty-two to thirty-eight percent margin. Election results disclosed extreme regional divisions over water and the environment. Only eight counties, all in the south, approved the canal. Fifty counties, including two southern ones, Santa Barbara and San Luis Obispo, where environmentalist sentiment ran strong, rejected it. Turnout in the south was unusually low, and the measure carried only sixty percent of the vote, much less than predicted. Some southerners agreed that the canal and further water transfers were environmentally unsound or too costly. Throughout the north, where voters flocked to the polls, the vote against the canal *averaged* ninety percent. The northern defeat of Proposition 9 was one of the most nearly unanimous votes on a major question in United States history.

The first rejection of a big water project at the polls since the 1880s, the 1982 referendum on Proposition 9 was a thumping blow to interests that favored water transfers and environmental manipulation to foster development. Former governor Pat Brown, a fitting representative of that group, called the results "a tragedy" and predicted "water shortage in years ahead." The California Farm Bureau simultaneously rejoiced at the defeat of the measure (and with it the constitutional amendment protecting north-coast rivers) and announced a campaign to enlarge Shasta Dam, tap the waters of the Eel River, and build a new Peripheral Canal. "Make no mistake about it," the bureau advised, "California desperately needs new water development." Northerners and environmentalists, on the other hand, agreed with Sunne McPeak, Contra Costa County supervisor and anti-canal leader, who pronounced the issue to be "virtually laid to rest." Northern glee was perhaps best expressed at a canal wake in the tiny Delta town of Locke, by one man who staggered down the street singing a tune adapted from the *The Wizard of Oz*: "Ding dong, the ditch is dead, the wicked ditch is dead." After a century of combat, California's water war was just beginning.

What the future holds is impossible to predict. The Delta water crisis and the struggle over the Peripheral Canal illustrate both the achievements and the contradictions of California water development. The canal controversy shook the values and institutions that had always guided water development, although it failed to topple them. Water policy in California has moved somewhat away from waste, casual intrusions into nature, and appropriation of one region's resources by another, and toward conservation, higher environmental standards, and greater respect for nature's balance. State and federal laws, administrative practices, and court rulings since the late 1960s reflect these new directions. Soaring energy prices and interest rates have also made large-scale water developments less likely in the future. As a result, management of existing resources is replacing development of new supplies as the focus of California water planning. Nevertheless, the dilemma of scarce water resources and increasing demand persists, along with sharp division over how to resolve it. As of the early 2000s, California's major policy question remained enmired in confusion and stalemate.

The peripheral canal idea is not dead. During the 1984 legislative session, Governor George Deukmejian, who had over his long political career supported agribusiness and southern California water developers, pressed the legislature to enact a cheaper "compromise" plan to send more Delta water south by building at least a partial canal. When the predictable furor erupted and Democrats in the legislature seemed about to maneuver the issue back onto the ballot in 1986, when Deukmejian would be up for reelection, the governor hastily withdrew his proposal. Into the early 2000s, building a peripheral canal around the Delta remained an important goal of water planners, particularly in the state Department of Water Resources and southern water agencies, and the idea came up occasionally in documents and hearings. Cal-Fed, a new combined state and federal water planning agency charged with finding solutions to the water problems of the Delta–San Francisco Bay region and the state at large, worked quietly behind the scenes for acceptance of such a waterway. Anxious to avoid provoking another public controversy, however, proponents avoided using the inflammatory phrase "peripheral canal," substituting instead bureaucratic euphemisms such as "cross-Delta transfer facility." As the official *California Water Atlas* concluded, "that compromise which is essential for resolving the problems of the Delta has yet to be found."

CHAPTER TWENTY-NINE

CALIFORNIA: EDEN OR WASTELAND?

THE "NOT SO GOLDEN STATE"

By the 1960s many of California's natural systems, like the Delta, were troubled. The state's population had tripled since World War II, and the new residents did not spread evenly across the landscape. Affluent, skilled, and searching for a gentle climate, most flocked to the coastal cities, moved to suburbs—where land and houses were cheaper—and commuted to work in private automobiles. By the mid-1960s, eighty percent of Californians inhabited the largest metropolitan areas; more than half lived in southern counties.

By the same time, while most Californians rejoiced in their state's growth, a few lamented the destruction of its unique natural heritage. One of the earliest indictments of environmental decay was *California Going, Going . . .* (1962), a booklet published by California Tomorrow, a nonprofit educational group of concerned writers, business people, and government leaders dedicated to "greater public awareness of the problems we face in maintaining a beautiful and productive California." Read and discussed around the state, the pamphlet helped ignite California's environmental crusade.

California Tomorrow warned that environmental changes had accelerated since the 1940s. With rampant and unplanned population growth consuming alarming amounts of land, California was running out of space, causing congestion and straining other finite resources such as air, water, forests, and wilderness. In the 1940s, for example, smoke from orchard smudge pots clouded the Los Angeles air on a few winter days. Twenty years later, homes, factories, automobiles, and power stations belched 12,500 tons of contaminants per day into the air, eighty percent of them from petroleum products, and the city had become a notorious smog capital. By then, air pollution suffocated all California cities, at least sometimes, impairing the health of two of every five persons.

The new Californians were also wasting their waterways. The San Joaquin-Sacramento River Delta's crisis was symptomatic of statewide disaster. Sewage had made San Francisco Bay waters and the ocean outside the Golden Gate unhealthy for public use.

Two Views of Downtown Los Angeles
Two views of the same portion of downtown Los Angeles in the mid-1950s—on a clear day and on a smoggy day—illustrate the blanket of air pollution that has blighted the city, and other California urban areas, since World War II.
Courtesy of California Air Resources Control Board.

One hundred industries, several cities, and untold numbers of ships dumped pollutants into Los Angeles harbor, which had little freshwater flushing, and by the 1960s virtually all marine life had vanished from the harbor. Some inland streams were so polluted, according to California Tomorrow, that in summer their flow was "in reality almost entirely sewage effluent." Particularly ominous were the thousands of new chemicals, of unknown hazard, that were making their way, perhaps permanently, into the water and the food chain. What's more, the growing population was "swallowing in huge gulps" the state's dwindling pure water. With most pure river water already impounded, the gap between demand and supply of fresh water in the 1960s exceeded what it had been before the building of the Central Valley Project.

The California Tomorrow study regretted that a "friendly invasion" of urbanites thirsting after the open space had ignited a "recreation explosion" that threatened wilderness with "general desecration." Beaches were increasingly crowded, cluttered, and closed to the public by developers. Offshore oil-drilling platforms loomed on the horizon of the Santa Barbara Channel. Fleets of off-road vehicles invaded the deserts, littering and guttering the fragile sandy floor. Lumber companies clear-cut trees to feed the booming construction market, while forests disappeared, soil eroded, and watersheds weakened. No area was safe, no matter how remote. Samples of Sierra snows at 14,000 feet yielded traces of lead and other air pollutants.

California Tomorrow found that little was being done to control growth or reduce the harmful effects of environmental mayhem. Despite the efforts of well-meaning individuals and local governments, funds were short and regulations weak, and powerful development groups blocked more effective mea-

sures. As a result, natural conditions deteriorated more rapidly than solutions could be applied. In most areas, the worst was yet to come.

In the 1960s, scientists, scholars, writers, artists, journalists, and government officials joined California Tomorrow in warning of impending environmental Armageddon and in building public outrage. In contrast to California Tomorrow, which emphasized the economic problems caused by natural destruction, the angrier environmental critics, like those who would later attack the Peripheral Canal, rejected the materialistic, pro-development values that for so long had ruled the state. In *The Destruction of California* (1965), biologist Raymond F. Dasmann reserved special scorn for those Californians who were intent on building a world no one would want to inhabit: "those who have looked so long into the blast furnaces of civilization that they can no longer appreciate a sunset—those to whom growth is progress and progress is good, regardless of its direction—those to whom money is the single standard against which all else must be measured." Greed and ignorance, Dasmann lamented, had turned California into the "not so golden state."

TWENTIETH-CENTURY CONSERVATION

Modern California environmentalism evolved from a vigorous tradition of conservation. Absorbed in conventional economic matters, most Californians of the nineteenth and early twentieth centuries were apathetic or hostile toward conservationism. An important minority dissented, however, and the state generated some of the earliest American conservation movements at the turn of the century. Its beauty attracted writers, artists, photographers, scientists, and others likely to be captivated by nature and concerned about environmental destruction. The University of California, Stanford, and smaller colleges acted as important organizing forces, providing funds, facilities, and experts to foster conservation movements. Bay Area citizens were particularly receptive to conservation ideas. There, where the state's people and organizations centered, appreciation of hills, water, and forests was an important theme of regional culture. The Bay Area furnished leaders, such as John Muir, as well as funds and issues for early California conservationism. After Muir's death in 1914, the Sierra Club he had founded helped keep alive a strong minority tradition of resource conservation and wilderness preservation.

The Sierra Club was not alone. After the 1880s, smaller groups sprang up to prevent the desecration of state landmarks and watersheds. Sometimes, they succeeded. Sequoia National Park (1890) and Big Basin Redwoods State Park (1902) grew from local preservationist movements. Particularly significant was the Save the Redwoods League, founded in 1918 by San Francisco area naturalists and business people to buy redwood groves for donation to the state as state parks. At the same time, other groups promoted more efficient resource use.

At first, the Sierra Club and other organizations embraced two somewhat contradictory philosophies: utilitarianism and preservationism. On the one hand, they supported utilitarian conservation movements to reduce waste and exploit resources efficiently for long-range development. On the other, they worked to preserve remnants of wilderness as examples to present and future generations of the beauty, serenity, and spirituality that communion with nature offers. Conservationists also tried to broaden public appreciation of wilderness, improve tourist facilities, and increase the recreational use of the parks. In days when population was small, the parks were remote, and an opti-

mistic faith in human progress prevailed, such contradictory goals seemed attainable. Only occasionally, as in the Hetch Hetchy case, did conservationists seriously differ among themselves or with dominant economic values.

In part because of this, railroads, lumber companies, and other California businesses with an interest in orderly growth often supported conservationism. Alliances with powerful groups brought conservationists notable victories. By the 1950s such coalitions had worked with government and private interests to create state agencies to manage resources, including the Board of Forestry (1905), Conservation Commission (1911), and Water Commission (1913). They had also set aside federal and state recreation and wilderness areas, administered by the National Park Service (1916) and the State Division of Beaches and Parks (1927). By the 1950s the state park system encompassed more than one hundred units, including more than 75,000 acres of redwood forest. Other federal lands were under various levels of protection by the U.S. Forest Service and the Bureau of Land Management. Large urban parks, such as Golden Gate Park in San Francisco, the East Bay Regional Parks system across the bay from the city, Griffith Park in Los Angeles, and Balboa Park in San Diego, attempted to preserve natural settings in the midst of modern cities.

FROM CONSERVATION TO ENVIRONMENTALISM: THE 1960s

The growing postwar environmental crisis forced a reassessment of traditional conservationism. The old strategy of exploiting resources more efficiently, while shielding small fragments of wilderness, could not cope with rampant growth, and conservation and wilderness preservation suffered from conflicting goals and interests. Resource exploitation and recreation, no matter how well planned, clashed with wilderness preservation. In and around wilderness parks, the proliferating roads, campgrounds, and visitor businesses—along with continued mining, grazing, and logging—jeopardized precisely the natural ecosystems that were being saved. In resource and harvesting programs, such as private, state, and national forests, businesses often dominated policy, environmental standards were lax, and public lands deteriorated. Even well-run conservation programs, however, broke down under increased postwar use. Saving bits of pristine nature had not worked, and the wilderness appeared about to be lost forever. A new urgency gripped the conservation movement. "What we save in the next few years," David Brower, executive director of the Sierra Club, warned in 1960, "is all that will ever be saved."

By the 1960s changing scientific views were also leading conservationists in new directions. The new science emphasized the interrelationships of nature's parts, the importance of protecting all species to maintain genetic diversity, and the capacity for human-induced environmental changes to spread dangerously in many directions. Civilization, it was now thought, could survive only if it reestablished a harmony between people and environment. To accomplish this, the totality of nature must be preserved, not just isolated species or habitats, and further tampering must cease. This reassessment of humankind's relationship to nature called into question conventional forms of technological progress, as well as practices in water development, land use, and wildlife management that conservationists had once condoned.

Conservationism had thus evolved into modern environmentalism—noted for its emphasis on preservation of the environment as a whole, criticism of unrestrained economic and technological growth, apocalyptic concern for the future if environmental harmony is not restored, and refusal to compromise. The "ecology movement" appealed particularly to an expanding group of young, affluent, idealistic, and highly educated professionals who read widely, traveled, and appreciated wilderness. Ecology proved perhaps the most popular and enduring of the idealistic crusades of the 1960s. Concern for a common natural world cut across class, regional, gender, ethnic, and political lines.

Sensational incidents such as the 1969 Santa Barbara oil spill dramatized the grave ecological crisis and popularized environmentalism. Ignoring the objections of Santa Barbara Channel communities, the federal government in 1968 sold offshore drilling rights in a fragile area to a consortium of petroleum companies headed by Union Oil and also waived existing safety regulations to allow drilling without the installation of casings to protect wells from breaks. On January 28, 1969, a Union well sprang underwater gas and oil leaks, and within days, a giant oil slick covered six hundred square miles of ocean. Black, sticky, reeking oil sloshed across dozens of miles of treasured beaches and tidal pools. In subsequent months, thousands of oil-soaked shore birds and sea mammals died horrible deaths. Damage to boats and beachfront property ran to untold millions of dollars. By the time the spill was controlled, more than a year later, it had developed into one of the worst ecological disasters in American history.

Public outrage at such tragedies curtailed oil drilling in sensitive coastal areas, tightened federal and state environmental regulations, and increased the membership and treasuries of ecology groups. By the early 1970s, public opinion polls disclosed that a majority of the state's people supported environmentalist ideas and programs. Hitherto restricted to a social and intellectual elite, environmentalism had become a popular movement. The movement flourished particularly in the San Francisco area; by 1970 that region was home to one hundred environmental organizations, many of which fought against the Peripheral Canal. During the 1960s and 1970s, however, the ecology movement became increasingly statewide.

California's growing environmental organizations devised new tactics. Taking advantage of the movement's popularity, they modernized operations, organized broad membership drives, and undertook action on new fronts. The Sierra Club's membership, for example, swelled from 15,000 in 1960 to 30,000 in 1965 and to 150,000 in 1974. Although still devoted to wilderness preservation, environmental organizations increasingly acted as adversaries to business and government and moved into new policy areas: land use, water and air quality, population, agriculture, chemical pollution, and nuclear energy. A few paid professionals led a growing army of volunteers, often women, in projects that took on the intensity of crusades. The organizations raised large sums of money, employed modern media advertising, hired skilled attorneys to plead class-action cases, and became master gadflies and lobbyists.

Significantly, environmentalists increasingly involved themselves in electoral politics. They backed or opposed candidates for office on the basis of their stands on environmental issues. Militant ecologists themselves captured elective and appointed offices at the local, state, and national levels, dramatically changing the composition of officialdom. Whereas past political leaders had generally aligned with pro-development groups, the newcomers enacted new environmental laws and enforced old ones with new vigor. When entrenched interests blocked them, environmentalists turned to direct democracy—the referendum, initiative, and recall—to achieve some of their most notable victories.

The decades from the 1960s through the 1980s were a creative period in resource and environmental policy. As the fate of the Peripheral Canal illustrated, state resource policies took new directions. Landmark laws and court cases established important legal principles and government functions. New agencies emerged with greater authority to regulate in the public interest. Californians pioneered methods for reducing environmental damage, while still accommodating controlled development, and taught these techniques to the rest of the nation. The ecology movement was not without contradictions and defeats. Some proposals failed to resolve conflicting needs for environmental protection and economic growth. Also, vested industries and entire sections regrouped and defeated some programs. But by the late 1980s, although their work was far from complete, environmentalists had made an indelible mark on California's future.

BUILDING A REGULATORY FRAMEWORK: CLEAN AIR

As late as the 1950s, California possessed only rudimentary environmental regulatory machinery composed of a few weak agencies relying mostly on voluntary compliance by companies, individuals, and local governments. New regulatory structures were essential to combat the postwar environmental crisis. The importance of new regulatory laws and bodies, as well as the delays and conflicts associated with environmental cleanup, are illustrated by the history of air and water pollution, two of the first problems to reach the public consciousness.

Although the outcry against smog grew intense in the late 1940s and early 1950s, authorities did little for years. The cause of

ANSEL ADAMS: CALIFORNIAN

Ansel Adams at Eighty
Photograph by William A. Bullough.

Photographer Ted Orland observed, quite accurately, that when visitors to California's best-known national park snap their camera shutters, many "hope that . . . the result will not simply look like Yosemite, . . . [but] like an *Ansel Adams photograph* of Yosemite." Adams's name became familiar to the public and synonymous with the park only in the 1960s, but the association began much earlier. In 1916, when he was a fourteen-year-old San Francisco music student, he used a box camera to make his first picture in the valley; a decade later, he ended his studies of classical piano to undertake his life's work: promoting photography as an art form distinct from painting and advancing the cause of wilderness preservation.

As a young man, Adams supported himself through commercial photography and operating Best's Studio in Yosemite. At the same time, he promoted his art by joining with Imogen Cunningham, Edward Weston, and other Californians in Group f/64 and by exhibiting his work at the De Young Museum in San Francisco (1932) and at Alfred Stieglitz's An American Place in New York City (1936). In 1940, he cofounded the Department of Photography at the New York Museum of Modern Art (MOMA), and during the remainder of the 1940s, he taught at art schools in Los Angeles and San Francisco while perfecting his own Zone System technique. He also worked for the Office of War Information during the decade and experienced his first political controversy: Adams photographed Japanese-American internees at Manzanar, but when MOMA exhibited the images, entitled "Born Free and Equal," in 1944, both his pictures and his commentaries encountered heavy censorship. During the 1950s and 1960s, however,

ANSEL ADAMS: CALIFORNIAN (continued)

Adams's photographs began to receive public attention and critical approval. In 1967, he cofounded The Friends of Photography to advance the art form, and he remained an active leader in the organization until his death in 1984.

While promoting photography, Adams advocated environmental preservation with equal energy and dedication. He joined the Sierra Club in 1919 and served the organization in capacities ranging from curator, guide and photographer to board member; in 1978, the club made him an honorary vice president. Adams also drew public attention to the conservationist cause through numerous articles, books, and portfolios of prints; he advised presidents Gerald Ford and Jimmy Carter on environmental issues; and he openly and vigorously denounced the policies of the Ronald Reagan administration and Secretary of the Interior James Watt.

For his efforts on behalf of the environment, Adams received the Sierra Club's John Muir Award (1963), the Interior Department's Conservation Service Award (1968), and the Wilderness Society's first Ansel Adams Award for Conservation (1980). In 1980, Adams also received the Presidential Medal of Freedom, his most treasured recognition. Other tributes to his work included three Guggenheim Fellowships, commendation by the state senate (1963) and assembly (1983), awards from photographic societies around the world, and honorary degrees from several universities. The most appropriate honor, however, came posthumously in 1985: a peak in Yosemite National Park was named Mount Ansel Adams. (WAB)

smog was unknown, and responsibility for solving the subtle new problem fell to fragmented local governments. Los Angeles County, the first area stung by severe smog, created an air-pollution-control district as early as 1947, but made painfully slow headway. The district did identify the basic causes of smog, but it lacked the authority and technical knowledge to clean up the air. Although the district recommended methods for reducing pollution, in the absence of compulsion, it was generally ignored. Also, like most environmental problems, smog did not respect political boundaries. The origin of much pollution lay beyond the county's jurisdiction, and other local governments refused to cooperate in adopting remedies.

Obviously, broader agencies were needed. Noted for more regional unity, the San Francisco Bay Area led the way in 1955 by founding a nine-county air-pollution-control district with authority to set air-quality standards and regulate stationary sources of pollution. Los Angeles and other areas followed suit shortly. Regional agencies banned backyard incinerators, regulated or eliminated agricultural burning, and forced reluctant industries to install emissions devices on their smokestacks. While some progress was made toward muzzling stationary polluters in the 1950s and 1960s, the automobile, responsible for ninety percent of urban smog, remained unregulated.

Public discontent over worsening smog

compelled the legislature in 1960 to pass the nation's first law to reduce automobile-exhaust pollution. The act established the country's first air-quality standards and required automobile manufacturers to equip cars sold in California with emissions devices after 1966. The state also established an Air Resources Board to sponsor research, set standards, and enforce the state's clean-air acts. In the 1970s the state tightened air-quality regulations, even to the extent of fining automakers for selling cars that violated standards.

Since auto and oil companies, as well as many other industrial polluters, were national and international concerns, difficult to regulate locally, California and other states pressed Congress to enact air-pollution legislation. Particularly important were Clean Air acts passed in 1967 and 1970, both influenced by California's two decades of experience in smog control. Under the new laws, the federal government adopted air-quality standards even tougher than California's, reduced and then banned lead in gasolines used by new cars, established timetables by which automobiles and oil companies were to produce cleaner cars and fuels, and required states to formulate plans for meeting air standards. The act of 1970 and later amendments authorized the federal government to prohibit new construction and withhold federal highway and sewer funds in states failing to meet environmental standards or to develop approved plans.

By the 1970s, state and federal laws had cleared the air somewhat. Emissions from automobiles and stationary polluters became cleaner; some types of air pollution, such as lead, declined dramatically. In seriously blighted regions, smog alerts occurred less often. Expanded bus lines, car-pooling programs, and new mass-transit systems—such as the Bay Area Rapid Transit's electric trains, which started operating in 1971, and

rail systems that opened in San Diego, Los Angeles, San José, and Sacramento in the 1980s and 1990s—began to woo commuters out of their cars in some communities.

California's war against smog, however, has had mixed results. Tough enforcement provoked the ire of motor clubs, automobile and petroleum companies, and other corporate polluters, which lobbied constantly against controls. Some regulations were weakened, particularly when the energy shortages of the 1970s provided a convenient excuse for doing so. Private citizens also sabotaged clean-air plans by illegally disconnecting smog equipment, filling the tanks of new cars with cheaper leaded fuel, or working with disreputable auto repair shops to secure fraudulent air pollution clearances for their vehicles. The number of cars and industries also soared with California's affluence and population growth. While the air freshened slightly in downtown Los Angeles and other traditional smog centers, eyes smarted in areas never troubled before, particularly southern California suburbs, the inland southern desert, and Central Valley districts. Federal-state conflicts erupted repeatedly over the most effective and economical methods to attain air-quality standards. After 1979 the federal government threatened to cut off highway funds because of California's refusal to develop a vehicle-inspection program to ensure compliance with emissions limits. The state finally adopted a watered-down inspection system in 1984.

After nearly a decade of federal and state inaction under the respective Reagan and Deukmejian administrations, the late 1980s and early 1990s were another period of air pollution reform. Again pioneering for the nation, the state greatly tightened auto tailpipe emissions standards, required much cleaner fuels, and in 1990 mandated that auto manufacturers make nonpolluting vehicles available to consumers by century's end. Also in 1990, Congress passed a new federal Clean Air Act requiring urban regions to clean up their air faster, and giving the Environmental Protection Agency greater authority to crack down on cities and states that failed to meet standards. Forced by the new, more exacting requirements, the state's air-quality districts, sometimes under EPA or court orders, began to develop comprehensive regional plans for cleaning up the air by the early twenty-first century by reducing auto use, sharply raising bridge and parking fees, enacting land-use controls, forcing employers to curtail commuting by their workers, and developing car pools and mass transit.

As before, tougher standards brought only mixed results. Though it was a pioneer in developing environmental reform regulations, California sometimes balked at implementing them, particularly when the pressure came from the federal government. Reminiscent of the conflicts of a decade before, the state in the early 1990s resisted the EPA's order to require that vehicles be inspected at state-operated stations instead of in private repair shops, which had a built-in conflict of interest. Also, since they are likely to require drastic changes in business, employment, residence, and lifestyle patterns, the new regional plans have been roundly attacked by citizens and business groups, causing delays and the enactment of plans that failed to meet EPA or court mandates. In an extreme example, Los Angeles, after much acrimony, produced a half-dozen plans, only to have the EPA reject them all. Moreover, relying as they did on what were euphemistically called "market-based incentives" (i.e., higher auto and fuel prices and vehicle-use fees) to reduce driving, many of the federal, state, and local plans raised serious equity issues. As California's air grew cleaner, it appeared, only the wealthy were to be allowed to pollute it.

As it turned out, of the state's major metropolitan areas, only the San Francisco Bay region, with naturally fresher air to begin with, easily developed a plan that met federal standards. In violation of federal orders to produce acceptable plans, Los Angeles, Ventura, and Sacramento counties were threatened by the EPA in early 1994 with severe restrictions on local economies, to take effect in early 1995. The annual cost to the state of the new federal rules for those three regions alone was estimated at between *$4 billion and $12 billion.*

In the late 1990s and early 2000s, renewed conflicts and problems erupted between the state and federal government over gasoline additives. In the mid-1990s, to satisfy new federal clean-air regulations, California ordered the oxygenate MTBE blended into reformulated gasoline required in the state. No sooner had refineries made the expensive changes, which oil companies used as an excuse for abruptly raising gasoline prices (and profits) to the highest in the nation, than MTBE was proven to be a dangerous carcinogen, particularly susceptible to leaking from underground storage tanks and destroying water supplies. When the state banned the use of the new additive, effective at the end of 2002, the administration of the newly inaugurated President George W. Bush, responding to pressures from heavily Republican midwestern states that produced ethanol, ruled in 2001 that California would have to use that corn by-product instead. At a time when largely unregulated out-of-state monopolies had also seized control of the state's electricity and natural gas, reduced production, and driven prices (and profits) up many fold, importing huge amounts of ethanol and retooling refineries yet again threatened also to raise the price of gasoline as much as fifty additional cents per gallon. Soaring prices of many forms of vital energy and the drain of capital out of the state threatened to drive out industry and jobs, dampen the economy, and sharply reduce tax revenues to state and local government. Like some other environmental programs, air-pollution control appeared to be on a treadmill in the 1990s and early 2000s, moving forward, perhaps, but only slightly faster than the problems were growing.

WATER POLLUTION CONTROL

Similar in operation to clean-air laws, state and federal water acts in the 1960s and 1970s established minimum water-quality standards, required regions to develop implementation plans, set up enforcement agencies, and allocated funds for local water purification. Heading California's water-quality program, the Water Resources Control Board sponsors research, sets water standards, regulates water quality, and inspects water projects and sewage plants. In cases such as the Sacramento-San Joaquin Delta water quality, the board has tightened purity standards and modified, delayed, or prevented developments, such as the Peripheral Canal, that would have affected water quality adversely. Nine regional boards supplement the work of the state body.

As with air pollution, California's record of cleaning its waters has been spotty. Although modern sewage treatment, highly effective against traditional organic contaminants, has recovered waterways and beaches for public use, new synthetic chemicals have been increasingly invading soils and surface and groundwater. Farmers, businesses, and homeowners casually release pesticides, herbicides, fertilizers, solvents, coolants, fuels, and industrial chemicals into the soils and waters. As only one indication of the severity of the problem, a congressional study in 1979 turned up 177 dangerous toxic dumps in California that leaked an estimated 60,000 to 70,000 different chemical compounds into water systems. The long-range effects of most new chemicals are unknown, but initial tests reveal that many cause cancer, birth defects, neurological damage, and genetic mutations. Since most toxic wastes do not decompose in nature and resist ordinary sewage processing, they lodge permanently in rivers, bays, groundwater, and the food chain.

In the 1970s and early 1980s growing public alarm prompted passage of state and federal regulations banning some chemicals, restricting their use and storage, regulating their disposal, and establishing procedures and liability for cleaning up spills. Although these restrictions were effective in a few areas—notably the banning of some particularly dangerous chemicals—most programs were small, experimental, and, at least in the case of the federal government, marred by lax enforcement, reduced budgets, and occasional collusion between public officials and corporate polluters. In California, both the powerful petrochemicals industry, which produces the substances, and agribusiness, which uses many of them, prevented tougher regulations.

The toxic-waste problem is growing much faster than solutions are being put into effect, and authorities predict that this will be a major future environmental issue. Symptomatic of this, California voters in November 1986 passed a stringent anti-toxics initiative over the strong opposition of oil, chemical, and high-tech companies that contributed $3.7 million to defeat the measure. In the tradition of the state's trend-setting environmental regulation, the new law placed the burden on would-be toxics dischargers to prove that the chemicals are safe, made it illegal to discharge chemicals causing cancer or birth defects into water supplies, held public officials criminally liable if they failed to act against illegal toxics dumping, and allowed anyone to file suit to enforce toxics laws if the government failed to take action. Full enforcement of the law, however, was hampered in the late 1980s by Governor Deukmejian's administration, which delayed in establishing lists of regulated toxic substances. Additional state laws in the 1980s and early 1990s further regulated or prohibited altogether the disposal of toxic chemicals.

ENVIRONMENTAL-IMPACT REPORTS

Also important to protecting the California environment have been comprehensive state and federal environmental-quality laws. Congress passed important environmental-policy acts in 1969 and 1970, establishing the Environmental Protection Agency (EPA), which has jurisdiction over federal environmental programs, and requiring an environmental-impact report (EIR) and public hearings for each federal action with potential environmental influences. In response to the Santa Barbara oil spill, the state legislature in 1970 passed the California Environmental Quality Act (CEQA) to supplement federal legislation. Enacted over the objections of California business and labor groups, who claimed it would stifle growth, the law required that an EIR be submitted to the appropriate state agency for each major construction project or government proposal with potential environmental impact, and it empowered agencies to reject projects on environmental grounds.

At first, government agencies and private businesses ignored or subverted these laws. In the mid-1970s, however, environmentalists began suing under their provisions, and federal and state courts applied the acts broadly. Environmental lawsuits delayed or stopped the Peripheral Canal and some other large projects that in the past would have been completed quickly without challenge. Fearing litigation, state agencies started enforcing the laws. By exposing environmental hazards, impact reports often caused projects to be altered or abandoned. Private and governmental developers began modifying proposals in advance to avoid en-

vironmental challenges. Although the EIR process in some instances proved cumbersome and obstructed innocuous projects, the EPA and state agencies have generally used their new muscle to limit harm to natural systems.

"SAVE THE BAY"

Because of dramatic postwar growth and widespread ecology sentiment, California pioneered new regulatory methods, such as the air- and water-pollution programs, on which other states and the federal government modeled their systems. The state also invented new techniques of balancing economic need and environmental protection. The most important example was the "Save the Bay" movement.

In 1846, San Francisco Bay was one of the largest and most beautiful inland estuaries, fifty miles long and 680 square miles in area. After the gold rush, settlers, eager to gain access to deep water and more level land for speculation, began diking and filling the bay's shallow edges. After World War II, population growth and more powerful earth-moving machines increased pressure on the bay. Most land under water and along the shore was in the hands of private concerns and dozens of independent, competitive local governments bent on making more room for industries, airports, warehouses, and garbage dumps. The bay shrank as never before.

By 1960 filling had cut the bay's area to four hundred square miles. The public had access to only ten miles of the bay's 276-mile shoreline. Each year tractors and paving crews gobbled up another 2,300 acres of tidal flats and marshes and fenced off more shoreline from the public. At that rate, the bay would have dwindled to a few polluted channels by the year 2000. Ocean winds would diminish in the region; air would grow stagnant; and the local weather would become hotter in summer and colder in winter. Although a few environmental groups and newspapers denounced the abuse of a valuable regional resource, the bay continued to shrink and grow more contaminated.

In 1961 several outraged Berkeley women, including Kay Kerr, the wife of the president of the University of California, started a citizen's revolution. In league with writers, naturalists, and civic leaders, they founded the Save San Francisco Bay Association. The group attracted the aid of a handful of influential legislators, particularly Nicholas Petris (Oakland), Eugene McAteer (San Francisco), and Edwin Z'berg (Sacramento). For several years, save-the-bay bills were overwhelmed in Sacramento by Bay Area pro-development industries and local governments. By 1965, however, the association had the backing of 18,000 members and eighteen of the region's nineteen legislators. Petris and McAteer finally pushed through a bill that halted filling the bay for four years and formed a temporary San Francisco Bay Conservation and Development Commission (BCDC) to develop a protection plan.

Following hearings and studies, the BCDC recommended a tough "Bay Plan" to control filling and a regional agency to enforce it. Fearing a precedent that could thwart development of their own coastlines, southern California businesses and governments joined their Bay Area counterparts in opposing the Bay Plan. Bay Area environmental and civic groups countered with a sophisticated media blitz directed against opposing legislators. When Governor Reagan appeared to oppose the bill to enact the plan, environmentalists presented him with 200,000 signatures on petitions stretching three and one half miles around the capitol.

Benefiting from overwhelming public support and the furor raised by the Santa Barbara oil spill, the bill protecting San Francisco Bay became law in 1969. The BCDC was the first regional government imposed on an urban area by legislative fiat. Composed of representatives from concerned federal, state, and local agencies, the commission acquired independent jurisdiction over the bay, tidal lands, marshes, salt ponds, and 100 feet of dry land around the shore. All projects affecting the water, bottom, shore, or shoreline structures required the BCDC's approval. Significantly, the act declared the estuary to be a regional resource, not a private or local one, and required a maximum of public access to its shore and water. The law permitted filling "only when public benefits from fill clearly exceed public detriment from the loss of water areas."

The BCDC developed the important principle of "tradeoff," or "mitigation," to combine public and private interests, preservation and exploitation. To avoid blocking all developments, the commission approved projects consistent with "public benefits" if government agencies or private builders opened up land or improved public access elsewhere on the bay. Such procedures, along with broad, representative membership, made the BCDC one of the most effective environmental agencies in the nation. Despite criticism from both extreme environmentalists and developers, the BCDC's decisions are widely supported and rarely challenged in court. Knowing requirements in advance, developers build tradeoff features into their proposals. Regional, state, and federal environmental programs have borrowed the tradeoff principle and other BCDC innovations.

Under the BCDC's guidance, the estuary recovered miraculously. After 1969 the commission not only arrested the bay's shrinkage, it opened hundreds of acres of formerly filled or diked land to the tides. Although the BCDC approved an annual average of $100 million worth of developments, the bay is larger today than in 1965. Because of the commission's actions and sewage cleanup under other state and federal laws, water purity generally improved into the early 1980s. Beaches reopened and fishing revived. The area of public access increased to ninety miles of shoreline, encompassing more than thirty parks and nature preserves. As one of its former chairmen put it, the BCDC has struck "a balance between conservation and development" that is a model for state and national environmental action.

As often happens in programs designed to manage dynamic environmental conditions, new difficulties imperiled San Francisco Bay even while cures for old problems were only beginning to take effect. Although raw sewage outflow declined in the 1970s, in the early 1980s toxic chemical discharges increased sharply, making portions of the bay among the most dangerously polluted waters in the world. At the same time, inland water projects reduced the outflows of fresh water through the estuary to forty percent of natural levels, enough to threaten the bay's ability to support animal and plant life. Planned increases in diversions from existing water facilities, as well as the possible completion of a peripheral canal and agricultural wastewater drains, would compound a serious problem. Despite decades of struggle by local citizens to save it, San Francisco Bay remains endangered.

Oil-Drilling Island
California's first offshore oil operation was hardly off shore at all. In 1957, Richfield Oil Company constructed an island connected by a quarter-mile causeway to the Ventura County shoreline. Decades later, with original palm plants grown to maturity, the island continues to function and to provide a backdrop for one of the state's favorite pastimes, surfing. Since the 1950s, however, drilling platforms have proliferated in the Santa Barbara Channel behind it. *Photograph by William A. Bullough.*

THE LIMITS OF REGIONAL PLANNING: THE COAST AND LAKE TAHOE

From the 1960s to the 1980s California attempted to solve environmental dilemmas with regional planning and regulatory agencies, many patterned after the BCDC. Duplicating the Bay Area's successes, however, proved difficult in areas where the traditions of regional consciousness and environmentalism were weaker, as suggested by the ambi-

tious and conflict-ridden Coastal and Lake Tahoe commissions.

By the 1970s, helter-skelter development, particularly in southern California, had blighted scenery and natural ecologies and lined the coast with refineries, power plants, and a jumble of commercial and residential subdivisions. Public access to the beaches, guaranteed in the state constitution, was unenforced. California's once-sublime shoreline was fast becoming "the concrete coast." Inspired by the Save-the-Bay movement, environmental activists were determined to wrest control over coastal planning from private developers and compliant local governments. Already stung by the establishment of the BCDC, worried oil and utility companies, real estate subdividers, building-trades unions, and local officials squashed several attempts to get coastal conservation bills through the legislature between 1967 and 1972.

As environmentalists did with increasing frequency, coastal conservationists appealed directly to the electorate. In 1971 they formed the nonpartisan Coastal Alliance, with the backing of seven hundred organizations across the state, representing conservationists, women, laborers, sports people, university students, senior citizens, and civic leaders. In 1972, when the legislature again rejected a coastal plan, the coalition easily collected 418,000 signatures in less than a month to place the bill on the November ballot as Proposition 20. Opponents hired a public relations firm experienced in pro-business ballot measures and mounted a lavish television ad campaign aimed at fooling voters into thinking that a "no" vote was a vote to "Save the Coast." Lacking a large fund, the alliance mustered hundreds of affiliated groups and thousands of volunteers. Supporters exploited free news space by staging events such as a "Great Coast Bike Ride" from San Francisco to San Diego and mobilized voters in precincts with the precision of a political machine. Proposition 20 passed with fifty-five percent of the vote, a showing of support for conservation that astonished experts.

The 1972 initiative instituted a temporary Coastal Commission to control development projects and draw up a permanent protection plan to submit to the legislature in 1976. When opponents regrouped to block the plan in the legislature, resourceful citizen conservationists once again demonstrated their mastery of practical politics. For several years prior to 1976, they worked to get sympathizers into the legislature and onto key committees. Holding out the threat of another initiative, they coaxed some opponents to agree to a compromise bill. When the conservationists still fell short on a crucial Senate vote, Governor Jerry Brown, a latecomer to the movement, made a valuable last-minute contribution when he arranged for a reluctant endorsement by the California AFL-CIO. The California Coastal Act of 1976 passed with virtually no votes to spare.

To reduce congestion and minimize earth slides, air and water pollution, and impairment of natural beauty, and to increase public access to the shore, the law established a state Coastal Commission and six temporary regional commissions, with development jurisdiction over the shoreline between 1,000 yards inland and three miles out to sea. The act had immediate, enormous impact. The commissions stopped or modified thousands of projects, often insisting on changes to make developments less environmentally damaging. One report on their activities concluded that the commissions were "collectively the most powerful state land-use regulatory body and the most powerful state coastal management agency in the United States."

Unlike the Bay Plan, however, coastal conservation continued to provoke controversy. The regional commissions represented local government officials and interests sympathetic toward traditional development. When local permits in favor of developments were appealed, the more preservationist state commission often overturned them, prompting localities to accuse the state body of being radical, elitist, and inexperienced in local zoning needs. Developers also resented delays and added expenses.

Groups opposed to coastal management relentlessly attacked the commission and the Coastal Act itself. Organizing a lobby called the Coastal Council, opponents introduced bills in the late 1970s and early 1980s to cut the commission's budgets, exempt areas from its jurisdiction, reduce its general authority, or repeal the coastal program entirely. Many weakening measures passed. When the regional bodies were phased out in 1981, pro-development local governments regained control of coastal management under their own conservation plans. The state commission also became less conservationist after 1981, when half its members began to be drawn from coastal-county officials. In 1982 opponents gained an important ally in the new governor, George Deukmejian, who had campaigned on the promise to cut back environmental programs, particularly coastal conservation, in the interest of jobs, energy, economy, and business growth. In 1983, as one of a number of constraints on environmental programs, Deukmejian cut the commission's budget by nineteen percent and its staff of experts by twenty-five percent. Although the governor vowed he would one day abolish the Coastal Commission, it survived into the early twenty-first century, but it remained wracked by controversy and charges that it accomplished little to avert damaging developments along the coast.

Lake Tahoe regional planning ran afoul of interstate rivalry. Straddling the California-Nevada border 6,200 feet high in the Sierra, Tahoe is one of the world's highest, deepest, and clearest large lakes. In the 1860s Mark Twain described it as "the fairest picture the whole earth affords." Recreation and population development after 1950, however, strained the environmentally sensitive lake basin. Unsightly buildings crowded the shore. Tree-cutting and land-disturbance aggravated erosion, while silt, sewage, and chemical runoff from steep surrounding mountainsides contaminated the lake, and long lines of creeping automobiles generated smog as dense as San Francisco's. Yet local developers subdivided ever more land for hotels, vacation homes, shopping centers, and, on the

Nevada side, gambling casinos.

With jurisdiction over the area divided, an interstate approach was necessary. After extended negotiations, California, Nevada, and the United States government agreed in 1969 to establish the Tahoe Regional Planning Agency (TRPA), composed of local and statewide representatives from both states, to manage growth and halt environmental decay. Since its inception, TRPA has been unable, or unwilling, to slow down development. The agency's charter made it prone to dominance by its local members, who usually represented local businesses and landowners. Moreover, although California's state-wide delegates generally favored conservation, Nevada's sought to foster development on the lake's east shore. Since a majority of each state's delegates had to approve environmental standards, Nevada could veto most protective proposals. After 1969 the sharply divided TRPA permitted building with minimal changes, and the basin's amenities continued to deteriorate, despite the state of California's independent efforts to reduce sewage discharge, erosion, and subdivision of fragile lots along its shore. In 1979, frustrated by years of friction with TRPA, California cut off its funding of the agency.

Threatened with federal intervention, Nevada agreed in 1980 to a revised contract with California requiring TRPA to devise a strict environmental plan by 1983. Local and Nevada delegates still resisted, however, and TRPA issued permits as liberally as before. After the body neared agreement on a moderately conservationist plan, Governor Deukmejian replaced California's most outspoken environmentalist representatives with pro-development people in early 1983. Finally, after years of internal wrangling and explosive meetings, TRPA adopted a twenty-year plan in April 1984. A substantial victory for developers, the document established only mild conservation standards. Most important, it returned much control over zoning and permits to local governments, which was tantamount to granting builders free rein.

Minutes after TRPA's action, California Attorney General John Van de Kamp and the League to Save Lake Tahoe sued the agency in federal court for violating the 1969 and 1980 regional contracts. In a ruling upheld by the federal Court of Appeals in July 1985, a federal judge, finding that the proposed TRPA plan "clearly violates the requirements" of the law and could lead to "the deterioration of the unique environmental and ecological qualities of the region," issued a preliminary injunction suspending the plan and halting all new construction in the region. Furious Nevada legislators threatened to withdraw their state from the TRPA compact, but some parties to the dispute continued to work for a compromise. In 1992, TRPA's long-delayed regional plan was finally announced. Although it limited building permits, traffic, and air pollution more than previously, many charged that the plan still failed to address the central problem of too-rapid development in a small, easily damaged space. TRPA repeatedly drew fire from both local development interests, who wanted the agency abolished and control over planning returned to local governments, and environmental preservationists, who denounced the agency for approving large developments along the slopes and shorelines. In early 1994, the League to Save Lake Tahoe again sued TRPA, alleging it had failed to meet its obligations. In the mid-1990s, Lake Tahoe's natural qualities continued to deteriorate rapidly.

In the summer of 1996, at a well-publicized summit meeting of Lake Tahoe regulation agencies and specialists on the lake and region, President Bill Clinton promised federal cooperation and funds for new initiatives in a massive cleanup of the lake's waters and reversal of regional forest and land development problems. Riding the crest of a wave of optimism, the University of California at Davis led an interdisciplinary and interagency project to establish a research institute at the lake to recommend solutions to the region's complex environmental problems. In the late 1990s, some progress was made in establishing programs to clear excessive forest growth and drought-killed trees in order to reduce the severe fire danger in the basin. Limited mass transit was also introduced in an attempt to reduce automobile use and air pollution.

Nevertheless, in the early 2000s the natural qualities of Lake Tahoe and its basin continued to deteriorate. The pace of new land development remained essentially unchecked. The lake's clarity, like the air quality, was still declining. MTBE increasingly concentrated in the lake, in addition to the region's groundwater, shutting down wells and producing water shortage emergencies in South Shore resort towns. Boat owners and manufacturers counterattacked, launched lawsuits, and delayed TRPA's attempts to ban the use of single-stroke boat engines, mostly on personal watercraft, which dumped up to forty percent of their gasoline directly into the lake. And President Clinton's promises of significant federal assistance for the cleanup of the region faced a problematical future after the antienvironmental administration of George W. Bush ascended to office in early 2001. The region's cleanup appeared headed for more years of conflict and litigation.

PARKS AND WILDERNESS AREAS

To preserve a vestige of California's vanishing natural lands, federal, state, and local governments expanded wilderness, recreation, and open-space preserves after 1960. Since much developed and farmed lands in the mountains, forests, and southern deserts remained under federal ownership, U.S. government actions were crucial. As they had for a century, federal land policies became battlegrounds between those who advocated reservations for wilderness or public use and those eager to lock up resources for private gain.

The Sierra Club, Friends of the Earth, and other national environmental groups worked in the 1960s for a large Redwood National Park along the northwest coast, a last-ditch effort to save a few remaining virgin redwoods, including a grove of the world's tallest trees that had recently been discovered east of Orick. The bill was vigorously opposed by the Save the Redwoods League—a traditional conservation group that protested that the state had already preserved enough representative groves—as well as by north-coast lumber companies, workers, and local governments. Governor Reagan's administration was apathetic. When asked about redwoods, the governor reportedly responded, "When you've seen one redwood tree, you've seen them all."

Nevertheless, with strong pressure from preservation-oriented President Lyndon Johnson, a compromise bill passed Congress in 1968, but the legislation created a small, discontinuous park. When logging of surrounding lands threatened to destroy the protected groves, a worldwide cry went out to "save the redwoods" by including the entire ecological zone around the groves in the national park. On the chance that the park might be expanded, lumber companies quickly clear-cut the forests right up to the old park border. By the time Congress finally enlarged the park in 1978, much of the newly protected land had been stripped of its vegetation, erosion problems had become monumental, and the unique groves were even more endangered.

Federal protection also began to be ex-

tended over remaining open space within or near cities. In 1972 the Golden Gate National Recreation Area and the San Francisco Bay Wildlife Refuge were formed to preserve hills, beaches, marshes, tidelands, and islands interspersed along the urbanizing coasts of the region. In 1994, after the federal government closed the Army base at the San Francisco Presidio, it too was converted into a national park, amidst nationwide conflict over how to establish policy and financing for an unprecedented urban national park and whether the most valuable park lands would be sold for development. To the south, the proposed Santa Monica Mountains National Recreation Area, created by Congress in 1978 to protect one of the only remaining large tracts of open land near congested Los Angeles, was stalled in the early 1980s by land developers and President Reagan's administration, which refused to spend money already appropriated to buy lands, an action the Los Angeles *Times* condemned as an "outrage against the millions of people . . . who are being robbed of a park." By the time the land began to be purchased later in the decade, shortages of national parks' operating funds prevented development of park facilities.

In the 1980s and 1990s, important decisions loomed regarding the fate of millions of acres of remote, still-unprotected federal lands in California. Environmental groups, supported by most California congressional representatives and state officials, urged that a maximum area of land be designated as wilderness and closed to economic development. Pro-development groups, championed by the Ronald Reagan and George Bush administrations, wanted most of the land to be sold or leased for grazing, mining, lumbering, and subdividing. California's U.S. senators, Alan Cranston and Pete Wilson, finally worked a compromise through Congress in 1984, designating 1.8 million acres of federal lands in California as protected wilderness or scenic areas, but opening up another 1.2 million acres to development.

The most ambitious proposal to preserve federal lands was the attempt to create new and expand existing national park and wilderness areas in the southern and eastern California deserts, which were replete with unique, stunning landscapes and endangered species, but were declining rapidly under pressure from development. Written by the Sierra Club and introduced by Senator Cranston in 1986, the California Desert Protection Act developed into one of the most controversial land-use proposals in United States history. Opponents included local development interests, mining companies, livestock grazers, hunters, and off-road vehicle users, along with Senator Pete Wilson, his successor after 1990, John Seymour, and officials of the Reagan and Bush administrations. Reintroduced each congressional session, the desert act, though widely supported by the public and in the House of Representatives, was repeatedly defeated by opponents in the Senate. The prospects for California desert protection brightened in 1992 with the simultaneous election of two

Restored San Francisco Bay Marshland
Like other new wilderness preserves, the San Francisco Bay National Wildlife Refuge was established by Congress in 1972 to protect marshes, tidal flats, and wildlife in areas such as the bay and Delta, the Farralon Islands, Humboldt Bay, and the Salinas River. Headquartered in Fremont, the refuge also operates an environmental education program for adults and elementary-school classes. At various points around San Francisco Bay, the refuge has experimented with restoring disturbed former marshland, such as the one in this photograph, to their original condition. *Courtesy of the San Francisco Bay National Wildlife Refuge.*

new Democratic senators from the state, Dianne Feinstein and Barbara Boxer, and a new president, Bill Clinton, all of whom favored the park. Nevertheless, as the 1994 congressional session drew to a close, the bill was again blocked by filibusters led by a handful of western senators opposed to wilderness preservation and Republicans hoping to embarrass the Clinton administration and Senator Feinstein, who was serving a short term and had to stand for reelection that November. Senator Feinstein, however, amended the bill to satisfy most opponents and deftly maneuvered the bill around the filibuster. In early October 1994, the desert bill, the most extensive land preservation measure in national history, cleared Congress, designating 7.5 million acres as protected wilderness, elevating Death Valley and Joshua Tree national monuments to national park status, and creating the 1.4-million-acre East Mojave National Preserve, in which hunting would be permitted.

State, local, and regional parks also expanded after the 1960s, as voters passed several large bond issues to acquire new and improve existing parks. The state park system increased by the mid-1990s to nearly three hundred units, encompassing more than one million acres.

Even while expanding as never before, wilderness areas and recreational parks continued to face problems. State budget cuts in the wake of Proposition 13 and lowered allocations for federal parks under presidents Reagan and Bush after 1981 reduced public services and jacked up user fees, inhibiting visits by low-income people. Nevertheless, recreational and economic use of public lands increased more rapidly than the population, causing congestion, erosion, and pollution, even in protected wilderness areas. Proposals to relieve pressure on these lands by controlling access to them provoked clashes among user groups and were rarely

enacted. When the severe recession in the early and mid-1990s reduced state revenues, Governor Pete Wilson and the legislature cut state parks' already slim budgets even further, causing the state to consider closing or selling some parks. The state also began to convert other parks into profit-making ventures by adding hotels, concessionaire leases, and other revenue-generating recreational facilities, thus further threatening wilderness preservation values.

FARMLAND PRESERVATION AND "SLOW GROWTH"

Among methods to slow the paving over of valuable farms and open space, none raised higher hopes than the 1965 California Agricultural Land Conservation Act, better known as the Williamson Act. This law permitted farmland in the path of expanding cities to be declared an agricultural preserve. If owners signed ten-year contracts with cities or counties agreeing to use the land for agriculture, it would be taxed at its agricultural, not subdivided, value, removing one incentive for farmers to sell out for development. From the beginning, the program fared poorly. Demand for new suburban subdivisions remained intense, land prices soared in the housing booms of the 1970s and 1980s, and many farmers sold out and reaped enormous profits. On the other hand, much of the land that was preserved was in safely rural areas, unthreatened by urban encroachment. In any case, local governments, to encourage development and new tax receipts, released landowners from contracts on any pretext. When courts began to require stricter compliance, developers pushed "reforms" of the Williamson Act through the legislature in 1981 and 1983, making escape from contracts even easier. By the early 2000s, efforts to preserve agricultural land had proven ineffective. Each year, thousands of acres of California's best farm-land yielded its final crop—of tract houses, shopping centers, industrial parks, and free-way interchanges.

Although most local governments re-mained firmly in the grasp of development interests, grassroots "no-growth" or "slow-growth" movements captured some city gov-ernments as early as 1970. First to fall were outlying San Francisco area communities such as Palo Alto, Livermore, and Petaluma. Controlling runaway expansion also became an issue in large cities. In the 1970s Janet Gray Hayes (San José) and Pete Wilson (San Diego) won mayoral elections on slow-growth platforms in two of California's most meteorically growing cities. New govern-ments tried to halt the population explosion through land-use planning and limiting building permits and new road and sewer in-stallations. In some municipalities, such as Livermore (1972), Petaluma (1973), and San José (1973), citizens passed comprehen-sive slow-growth initiatives. When developers challenged the Petaluma law, courts upheld its constitutionality, thereby firmly establish-ing an important new legal precedent: a community's right to manage its environ-ment, even by reducing or prohibiting new construction. In the 1980s and 1990s, the slow-growth movement spread to additional cities and counties across the state. In 1986, voters in Los Angeles and San Francisco passed precedent-shattering initiatives to limit construction of high-rise buildings in downtown neighborhoods. Pro-development forces remained strong in most communi-ties, however, and in the last three decades of the twentieth century, controversy over growth controls was a perennial theme of California local politics.

In sum, growth controls achieved only mixed, contradictory results. Some marginal benefits resulted, primarily the preservation of open space and quality of life in the few vigilant communities that passed and stuck with controls. But in the absence of effective regional or statewide growth regulation, run-away development all too often merely shifted to somewhat more outlying areas, re-sulting in an inexorable sprawl of California cities onto the farmlands and few remaining natural areas surrounding them. In compre-hensive studies released almost simultane-ously in early 2001, two respected research institutes reported that the Los Angeles met-ropolitan area, having expanded one hun-dred miles eastward and northward out onto the Mojave and Colorado deserts, was now out of land to accommodate further growth; the San Francisco-San Jose metropolis now reached deep into the upper San Joaquin and lower Sacramento valleys and foothills, with some commuters driving up to three hours, *each way*, to reach jobs in the Bay Area. In the Central Valley, one of the few re-maining places where space was available and reasonably economical, policy prophets predicted that a single conurbation would, within a few decades, stretch hundreds of miles from Bakersfield north to Reading.

MONO LAKE AND THE PUBLIC TRUST DOCTRINE

The crusade to save Mono Lake, a unique dead sea in the volcanic basin east of Yosemite, proved long and frustrating for en-vironmentalists. Brine shrimp thrive in the lake's salty waters, making it the breeding ground for most of the remaining popula-tion of California gulls, as well as a stopover for millions of migratory water birds. Los An-geles acquired the rights to streams feeding Mono Lake and in 1941 began diverting some of their water southward through tun-nels into the city's Owens Valley project. In 1970 the city enlarged its aqueduct and started importing the entire flow of four of Mono Lake's five tributaries, along with much of the basin's groundwater. Between 1941 and the early 1980s, the lake's level dropped fifty feet; at that rate of decline, the lake would have stabilized by the early twenty-first century at one-third of its natural area. By the late 1970s, the lake's ecosystems had changed drastically. Recreational trout fisheries in Mono Lake's tributary streams were decimated; lake water had become much saltier; the brine shrimp had begun to die off; and the receding water had exposed offshore rookery islands to predators that were devouring entire hatches of birds. The basin's fierce winds swept up billowy clouds of alkali dust from the dry, exposed lake bottom, endangering animals and humans in the region.

In the 1970s, a movement began in the locale and among scientists to preserve Mono Lake. When Los Angeles, state water agencies, and the California Farm Bureau thwarted efforts to regulate water diversions or to place the lake under federal protection, at the behest of local preservationists, the Audubon Society and Friends of the Earth sued in 1979 to challenge the city's water rights. Los Angeles and the state countered that water rights are perpetual and inviolable. The state supreme court, however, stunned water developers with a unanimous ruling against the city in 1983. Overturning more than a century of precedent, the court agreed with the environmentalists' contention that the common-law principle of "public trust" allowed water rights to be modified or abolished if water diversion causes major environmental harm. Reasoning that "the human and environmental uses of Mono Lake—protected by the public trust doctrine—deserve to be taken into account," the court ordered the case retried.

On the basis of the public trust doctrine, subsequent litigation, including some brought by fishermen and recreational interests, further undercut Los Angeles's water

rights in the basin. Particularly significant was a 1989 injunction prohibiting the city from diverting water until the lake regained the 6,377-foot elevation level deemed by some experts to be the minimum necessary to preserve basic ecosystems. Other experts, however, insisted that the lake had to be raised to its historic minimum level of 6,390 feet. Also in 1989, the state court of appeals voided the city's license to tap Mono's tributaries and directed the Water Resources Control Board to establish a new water right for the city that accounted for the public trust doctrine. Opposition mounted, increasingly isolating Los Angeles in the controversy; in 1993, even the state of California formally joined the city's opponents in the legal proceedings.

After year-long hearings, the Water Resources Control Board in the fall of 1994 suspended Los Angeles's water rights in order to allow the lake to regain the level of 6,391 feet above the sea, which may take several decades, and ordered the city to reduce its diversions thereafter to maintain the lake at that level. Although the decision still could be modified by legislation, the Mono Lake case marked the first time the board had rescinded water rights to protect environmental balances, and established a precedent for future controversies. Los Angeles stood to lose at least two-thirds of its water from the Mono Basin, or about fifteen percent of its total supply, but the city for the first time agreed not to try to overturn the ruling and, instead, to develop replacement water from conservation and reclamation projects and purchases from San Joaquin Valley farmers and the Metropolitan Water District. "It's partly facing the inevitable, partly common sense," explained Los Angeles city councilwoman and longtime Mono Lake defender Ruth Galanter, "and partly that the environmental movement is universal, even in darkest Los Angeles."

Like the defeat of the Peripheral Canal initiative in 1982, the rescue of Mono Lake illustrates the revolutionary impact of new environmental ideas on California policy. What had seemed like a looming ecological disaster in the early 1980s became by the early 1990s an example of the rehabilitation of a degraded resource through the application of science, grassroots agitation, litigation, and the interjection of public-trust considerations into water development. Born of the Mono Lake controversy, the public trust doctrine has been invoked in other lawsuits involving water and environment. If allowed to stand, it promises to transform California water law by hindering the construction of additional large water-transfer systems, such as a peripheral canal, by raising environmental safeguards on all new water projects, and even by subjecting old programs to modification when they damage natural systems.

DROUGHT AND WATER-POLICY STALEMATE

In the 1980s and 1990s, as suggested by the emergence of the public trust doctrine, legal changes and other developments heralded an ever more troubled future for California's water use. Congress in 1982, at the urging of California and other arid western states, modified the 160-acre principle of the 1902 National Reclamation Act. A compromise among agribusiness, land reformers, and environmentalists, the bill greatly increased the acreage farmers can irrigate with federally subsidized water—bringing the law more into line with California's large-scale agricultural system—while at the same time it required that farmers begin assuming the actual cost of the water. Promising some security for Delta water quality, as well as a resolution of decades of federal–state conflict, Congress in late 1986 also ratified an historic agreement between the state Department of Water Resources and the federal Bureau of Reclamation. Engineered by George Miller, the environmentalist congressman from Contra Costa County, the bill gave Delta and San Francisco Bay water quality top priority in water distribution, required the federal government to abide by California water-quality standards, merged some operations of the Central Valley Project and State Water Project, and freed an additional one million acre feet of federal water annually for flushing the Delta, conserving fish and wildlife, or shipping to southern California. Then, as the national election in the fall of 1992 approached, Congress overwhelmingly passed and a reluctant President Bush was pressured into signing the Central Valley Project Improvement Act, which held the promise of being a monumental reform of general California water policy. Spearheaded by Congressman Miller, the law diverted some CVP water from irrigation to wildlife and water-quality preservation and for the first time allowed farmers to sell project water to urban users. Bitterly opposed to the law, California agribusiness threatened to sue to block its implementation.

Ironically, during the late 1970s and early 1980s, the era of intense conflict over the Peripheral Canal bill, the rains fell abundantly. Beginning with the disappointingly dry winter of 1986–1987, however, California entered one of its longest dry periods, which lasted into the mid-1990s. In most years during this drought, state and federal deliveries of water had to be greatly curtailed. Most communities rationed water, and some farmers were forced to reduce production, causing rural unemployment and poverty to increase sharply. Some cities with particularly vulnerable supplies, such as Santa Barbara, were driven to the expensive decision of building ocean water desalinization plants. Meanwhile, slackened flow from rivers further weakened Delta water quality and threatened the very existence of several endangered fish species, particularly the winter-run salmon.

Among the many creative attempts to manage water supplies during the drought, the concept of "water marketing" stood out. Developed by the state to pool water from regions that had a surplus so it could be purchased by those short of supply, the idea quickly became a panacea for the state's complex water problems, even among some of the most powerful environmental organizations. Freeing water to be bought and sold on the open market, with price fluctuating according to its value, it was alleged, would assure that water would be used efficiently and that agricultural water (eighty-five percent of the state's developed supply) would flow toward cities and environmental uses. On the surface a quick solution to shortages, water marketing had profound and ominous implications. Critics, particularly in rural areas, charged that aggravated unemployment, poverty, and business failure were sure to follow when water was siphoned from the countryside. Others questioned the wisdom, even the sanity, of bringing yet more water, along with more development and population, to California's exhausted urban landscapes.

The great drought of the 1980s and 1990s dramatized how wide the gap between demand and water supply had grown, and how fragile the state's economy and very way of life had become. Exacerbated by serious shortages, conflict over water policy intensified and coalitions were realigned, making compromise even more difficult. Particularly unusual was the growing alliance between environmental organizations and large urban water agencies, including those in southern California and the San Francisco Bay Area. By making common cause, each of these parties hoped to achieve its water goals less painfully by seizing some of the water that agribusiness controlled.

As had been true since the 1960s, water policy conflicts revolved around the Delta and San Francisco Bay. After state courts ordered the state Water Resources Control Board to develop and enforce stricter water-quality standards for the Delta and bay by 1990, the board held several series of acrimonious hearings around the state between 1987 and 1994. When the hearings produced little besides evidence of how great the long-term water shortage was and how polarized the state was over the issue, the board issued a succession of tentative proposals to reduce slightly exports of Delta water to southern California and to divert modest amounts to maintaining fish and Delta/bay water quality. Each proposal, however, was bitterly denounced by agribusiness, which became increasingly isolated and defensive, and the board hastily withdrew each plan, leaving the state in violation of a court order and without a plan for its most vital water pool.

In the vacuum caused by state bickering and inaction, the federal government increasingly intervened in California water policy after 1990. New federal and state laws passed in the 1970s and 1980s, particularly the federal clean water acts and state and federal laws protecting endangered wildlife species, required the national government to act to preserve water purity, wildlife habitats, and endangered salmon and other species, and gave environmentalists the option of suing in federal courts to assure enforcement. As the principal environmental regulator, the federal Environmental Protection Agency assumed an increasingly aggressive role in ordering the state to comply with the new requirements. In September 1991, the EPA flatly rejected the state Water Resources Control Board's latest Delta/bay water plan and threatened to take over the setting of California water-quality standards if the state did not produce an effective plan to divert water from cities and farms to rehabilitate waterways and fisheries.

For a while, Governor Pete Wilson and his water bureaucrats tried mightily to forge a compromise among feuding urban, agricultural, environmental, and federal interest groups and to get a Delta/bay plan through the Water Resources Control Board that would satisfy the law and all groups. However, when the board in December 1992 announced its latest revised plan, which would have diverted nearly one million acre-feet to environmental conservation, all parties immediately denounced it. A month later, the EPA also rejected the plan as inadequate to protect water quality and wildlife and announced its intention to impose its own water standards. By this time, Governor Wilson's shaky water coalition had collapsed and the administration itself was deeply divided over how to proceed. In April 1993 the governor instructed the Water Resources Control Board to discontinue its work on the plan, thereby abandoning the state's effort to retain control over this important dimension of water policy.

Itself pressed by a lawsuit brought by the Sierra Club in federal court, the EPA in December 1993 announced its plan, which called for high water standards for the region and, in order to attain them, a reduction in exports from the Delta of nine percent (twenty-one percent in drought years). As part of a settlement reached in the Sierra Club lawsuit in April 1994, the EPA agreed to implement the plan by the end of the year, and the state was to be required to abide by the new standards. Making the future even murkier, in late April 1994, a federal judge in Fresno presiding over a lawsuit brought by San Joaquin Valley irrigators granted an injunction prohibiting the enforcement of the Central Valley Project Improvement Act of 1992. Then, in a last-ditch effort to avert a federal takeover of state water policy, the

EPA worked behind the scenes and in December 1994 secured a seemingly miraculous agreement of the state, environmental groups, and water agencies to a compromise Delta plan that raised water standards for the estuary, required joint federal–state enforcement, reduced water diversions by ten percent in normal years (but more than twenty percent during drought), guaranteed more predictable water supplies for farms and cities, and instituted other reforms to protect fish and other wildlife. An ecstatic Governor Wilson proclaimed that "peace has broken out amid the water wars." Despite the promising development, the agreement was only temporary, with the truly tough decisions, such as which groups would relinquish how much water, to be made over the next few years. Although immediate confrontation had been averted, little had changed fundamentally.

A new state and federal fact-gathering and water planning agency, Cal-Fed, spun off from the 1994 agreement for joint federal–state solution of complex Delta-bay water problems. After yet more meetings, hearings, and draftings of plans, Cal-Fed produced a set of compromise proposals aiming to improve water quality and increase the amount of water available for fresh water flushing, wildlife restoration, and export south, mostly by building additional water-storage facilities, essentially new reservoirs and enlarged older reservoirs up various streams and in the Delta itself, and finding ways to move the water more efficiently through the Delta. The price tag: upward of $10 billion, probably much higher. To protect themselves from losing water, San Joaquin Valley agribusiness and irrigation agencies sued to prohibit some Cal-Fed proposals from going into effect even before they were introduced into law. Conflict over the proposals continued to pit environmentalists against developers, north against south, the Sacramento Valley against the San Joaquin Valley, and especially agricultural users against the emerging environmentalist-urban coalition. Cal-Fed's proposals, the first general ones introduced into Congress in 2001, also faced an uncertain future in the environmentally unfriendly George W. Bush administration and an even more unfriendly Republican-controlled House of Representatives. The extent to which any of them would ever be enacted or, more important, funded was problematical. Meanwhile, the peripheral canal, the idea that refuses to die, continued to hold potential for unknown, but certainly revolutionary, effects on the landscape and waterscape. Many of the state's reservoirs were nearing or had exceeded their safe life spans and would have to be rebuilt or abandoned over the next few decades, at monumental cost and disruption of water supplies. And lurking in the background was the specter of global warming, predicted nearly universally by respected scientists worldwide, which for California would likely bring more rain, but less snow, resulting in increased lowland winter flooding and less capacity to store precipitation for summer dry seasons. In the early twenty-first century, with the state facing severe, permanent water shortages and rapidly deteriorating environmental systems, California water policy remained threatened by confusion, conflict, and, apparently, stalemate.

REACTION AGAINST ENVIRONMENTALISM

Resistance to the environmental movement remained strong between the 1960s and the early 2000s. Antagonists included groups with financial interests at stake—real estate development, oil, utility, and construction companies, and workers in those industries—along with people from many walks of life who clung to a traditional faith in economic and population growth, technological progress, and unregulated business. Even at the height of the ecology movement, opponents limited specific environmental protections, as in the coastal and Lake Tahoe programs. In the late 1970s, anti-environmentalism intensified. Inflation, recession, and falling government revenues caused by Proposition 13 made the public receptive to arguments that environmental regulations inhibited economic development and added to consumer prices and government costs. An energy crisis from 1978 to 1981, when Middle Eastern conflicts raised the prices of crude oil, particularly reversed many environmental gains. To increase energy supplies, the federal government weakened clean-air standards and other environmental regulations, encouraged the use of dirtier but more abundant fuels such as coal, and promoted more extraction of fuels on western public lands. Again, during the drought and recession crises from 1986 through the mid-1990s, membership and contribution to environmental organizations, particularly the Sierra Club, fell precipitously, and anti-environmentalism again experienced a resurgence.

Widely publicized events also discredited environmentalism in the eyes of some Californians. Between 1977 and 1979, projects to build a Dow Chemical factory complex in the Delta and a Standard Oil of Ohio (SOHIO) terminal for Alaskan oil at Long Beach harbor collapsed because of what critics called trivial environmental regulations. In the late 1980s and early 1990s, similar controversies erupted when the protection of particular endangered species, such as the northern spotted owl, required under federal and state laws, curtailed timber harvests; vanishing populations of salmon and other fish also threatened new water projects. Despite studies showing that environmental management did not stunt business growth, but rather channeled it in new directions, pro-development groups pointed to events such as the Dow and SOHIO defeats and to the state's dwindling lumbering industry as proof that California had become dangerously anti-business in the ecology era.

Anti-environmentalist books, speeches, newspapers, magazines, and advertisements criticized environmental regulation for being not only inefficient and anti-business, but elitist and unpatriotic. To the extent that they limited new construction, increased housing costs, and made it more difficult for newcomers and poorer people to live in sensitive areas like the coast, some environmental regulations did raise real issues of equity. The charge that environmentalists were elitists, however, was largely self-serving rhetoric, exploited by groups that had little genuine interest in the general public. One of the first provisions of the 1976 Coastal Act pro-development groups repealed, for example, was its requirement for low- and middle-income housing in coastal subdivisions.

Anti-environmentalist forces counterattacked aggressively, beginning in the 1970s. Joining the State Chamber of Commerce and California Farm Bureau were specialized pressure groups such as the California Coastal Council, the California Council for Environmental and Economic Balance, founded in 1973 by former governor Pat Brown to promote water projects, and the Pacific Legal Foundation, formed in 1973 by prominent business people and leaders of Governor Reagan's administration and supported by large contributions from individuals, corporations, foundations, and agribusiness. Borrowing environmentalist tactics, these organizations advertised against environmental values, supported pro-development political candidates, and with some success fought in the legislature, Congress, government agencies, and the courts to repeal or weaken environmental regulations.

New, more conservative political leaders coming to power in the 1970s and 1980s championed a free market, opposed restraints on business, especially environmental regulations, and advocated cheap government and lower taxes. Even Governor Jerry Brown, who took office in 1975 as a spokesman for ecology, was stung by the losses of the Dow and SOHIO facilities and bent to criticism that he was hostile to business. In 1979 Brown temporarily assumed leadership of the fight to build the Peripheral Canal and embarked on crusades to bring more business and population to the state. Anti-environmentalists took comfort in the inauguration of Ronald Reagan as president in January 1981. As governor, Reagan had rarely been more than apathetic toward environmental protection. In his bid for the presidency, Reagan vowed to harness government and free business. Anti-environmentalists worked on his campaign and went to Washington to serve in the administration. At Reagan's direction, federal agencies revoked or diluted environmental regulations adopted under presidents Johnson, Nixon, Ford, and Carter.

Reagan also discouraged vigorous enforcement by environmental agencies by cutting their staffs and budgets and entrusting them to appointees identified with anti-environmentalist causes. As his secretary of the interior, in charge of most environmental programs, Reagan appointed the president of the Rocky Mountain states' equivalent of the Pacific Legal Foundation, James Watt, who was fond of comparing environmentalists (and "liberals") to communists, Nazis, and subversives secretly trying to "bring America down." Watt halted acquisition of new parklands in California, removed some northern streams from protection as wild rivers, sidetracked plans to control environmental decline in Yosemite National Park and southern deserts, tried to remove the wilderness classification from federal lands in California, and drastically expanded the selling or leasing of hitherto protected public land to oil, lumber, and mining companies at low prices and under relaxed environmental standards. Although while campaigning for office George Bush claimed that he would be the "Environmental President," while he served between 1989 to 1993, he generally continued the Reagan administration's anti-environmentalist policies and appointments to federal office. The Bush administration particularly provoked the ire of environmentalists by its largely unsuccessful attempts to remove federal protection from wetlands and wilderness in California. Although Bush's successor, Democrat Bill Clinton, entered office in early 1993 with a plan to strengthen environmental regulation, most important efforts—most notably proposals to increase protection to federal lands and increase use fees charged miners, grazers, and lumber companies exploiting publicly owned resources—were blocked by interest groups and Congress.

Giving new momentum to anti-environmentalist forces, a new Republican Party majority took control of Congress in early 1995 committed to a program that, under the guise of promoting economic development, would sharply reduce federal enforcement of environmental laws, greatly strengthen the right of private property owners to pollute at will, and shift the enormous cost of protecting and cleaning up the environment from the polluters to the public.

Republican George W. Bush assumed the presidency in 2001, bringing with him a revival of the Reagan administration's policies and tactics, indeed returning many Reagan-era officials to office. Within the first few weeks and months of taking control, the new Bush administration delayed or reversed many Clinton administration policies, notably those tightening water pollution standards and regulations in the national parks

and forests; cut the budgets of federal agencies, including funds designated for rebuilding facilities and improving environmental conditions in Yosemite and other California national parks; attempted to stop or stall proposals to designate new wilderness areas and national monuments; pressed for environmental standards to be weakened to fuel more energy resource exploration and production; and appointed anti-environmentalists to head the Department of the Interior and various key subdepartmental agencies.

At the state level, agribusiness and pro-development groups also favored George Deukmejian's gubernatorial election in 1982. As a southern California legislator, Deukmejian had made a name for himself by opposing crime and favoring the export of northern water to the south. Convinced that environmentalism was threatening economic growth, Deukmejian committed himself to reversing the trends of the previous two decades. When he became attorney general in 1978, he broke up the unit of state attorneys that his Republican predecessor, Evelle Younger, had created to enforce environmental laws and reduced his office's legal defense of state environmental agencies. In at least one case, the attorney general sided with the Pacific Legal Foundation against the state. As governor after January 1983, Deukmejian pressed the legislature to build a peripheral canal, abolish the Coastal Commission, and weaken the California Environmental Quality Act by reducing the period of review for many types of environmental impact reports to a few days. Unlike Jerry Brown, Deukmejian also supported the efforts of President Reagan and Secretary Watt to open up most environmentally sensitive offshore waters to oil drilling. Although the Democratic-controlled legislature rejected the governor's peripheral canal project and most of his other proposed environmental cuts, Deukmejian trimmed budgets and dispensed appointments to avowed anti-environmentalists to achieve some of the same ends. The gubernatorial administrations of Pete Wilson (1991–1998) and Gray Davis (1999 and forward), lukewarm at best toward environmental protection, strongly supported the shipment of additional water to the south of the state. One of Governor Davis's principal responses to the energy crisis of his first years was to press for reduced environmental standards for refineries, power plants, and transmission lines to speed their construction.

THE LEGACY OF ENVIRONMENTAL REFORM

Although some regulations and agencies have been weakened and a few repealed altogether, environmentalism remains strong in California. Opinion polls into the early 2000s showed that most Californians favored tough environmental laws, even at the expense of higher prices and limitations on their activities. Many business leaders shared these beliefs and supported environmental regulation. Some major California firms—the Southern Pacific Railroad, Standard Oil of California, and the Bank of America, among others—developed comprehensive corporate environmental plans and complied strictly with environmental laws.

Attacks by leaders such as James Watt and George Deukmejian eroded support for environmentalism in some quarters, but strengthened it in others. Watt's policies and rhetoric, for example, swelled contributions and memberships in environmental organizations, which had dipped in the late 1970s. In the nine months after Watt's appointment, the Sierra Club raised its membership by several hundred thousand and collected one million signatures on petitions calling for his ouster. Repeatedly, Congress or the courts overturned Watt's decisions. Widely ridiculed and disowned by leaders of his own party, Watt was finally forced to resign in late

1983. Popular rejection of their environmental policies also contributed to the waning of public confidence and political support for President George Bush, who lost his reelection bid in 1992, as well as for Governor Deukmejian in the 1980s, for Pete Wilson after he took over the governor's office in 1991, and for George W. Bush after he assumed the presidency in 2001. On the other hand, in the California of the 1990s and early 2000s, divisions remained deep over almost all major environmental questions, particularly those concerning water.

Conflicts and contradictions notwithstanding, the ecology movement has left a solid legacy for California's future. Many, including government and business leaders, became more conservation-minded and willing to seek greater harmony between nature and human actions. The ecology movement also built a structure of law and regulatory machinery that survived counterattacks. Local and private control over environmental policy gave way to centralized planning by higher levels of government. Though few serious problems have been overcome entirely, a beginning has been made toward reversing generations of environmental decay. The open water and shorelines of San Francisco Bay and Mono Lake stand as shining examples.

Nevertheless, the ecology movement failed to resolve most historic resource issues, just as the defeat of the 1982 Peripheral Canal referendum failed to end conflict over water. Present and future generations still face vital questions. How can nature preservation, the public interest, and private property rights be reconciled? With soaring demand and diminishing supply, who should allocate resources, establish environmental policy, influence prices of resources, and mediate among contending parties? Should the public assert more control to assure that resources serve the best interests of the citizens? If so, what should be the limits of public power, and

Yosemite Valley in the 1980s
After World War II, Yosemite Valley, like many other popular wilderness areas, began to show the ill effects of overuse. Mobbed by millions of visitors, the tiny valley was becoming urbanized by the 1980s. Snarled traffic, overflowing parking lots, and smog that obscured the surrounding waterfalls led to the installation of a bus system. The valley also had a supermarket and numerous stores, a half-dozen crowded restaurants, and several hotels (often booked a year in advance), to say nothing of more than 1,000 developed campsites. Troubled by crime, violence, and narcotics trafficking, Yosemite now had its own police force, jail, and federal court. Plans developed by the National Park Service to reverse the valley's development were delayed or vetoed by concessionaires, some user groups, and the Reagan administration. *Photograph by Richard J. Orsi.*

should local, regional, state, or federal officers wield it? Which regions have the superior right to resources, especially water—those of origin, or those with the greatest need? What constitutes "beneficial use" of resources—economic development or preservation of natural conditions and species? And should beneficial use be measured in the short, or the long, term? Nearly everyone admits that the answers to these questions must strike a balance between conflicting extremes, but few agree on what that compromise should be. Whether Californians can resolve these critical issues remains to be seen.

CHAPTER THIRTY

CALIFORNIA CONFRONTS THE NEW MILLENNIUM

California entered the twenty-first century after a ten-year roller-coaster ride that propelled the state's economy from the depths of a severe recession to the heights of a technology-led boom to a recession after 2001. Still, in June 2001 the Los Angeles Economic Development Corporation reported that the state had surpassed France to rank as the fifth-largest economic power in the world. Silicon Valley led the recovery from recession. The development of the Internet's World Wide Web, the subsequent globalization of business, and the phenomenal growth of dot-com companies offering goods and services on the Web characterized the boom of the 90s. By late 2000, however, the dot-com, e-business bubble had burst and a period of consolidation and retrenchment ensued. In 2001 sound business plans and the ability to make a profit returned as the prerequisites for venture capital investment.

Major demographic changes also characterized the 1990s. Throughout the period, California's booming economy continued to attract thousands of immigrants, primarily from the Pacific Rim nations, such as east and southeast Asia, Mexico, and Central America. By 2000 the state had no single ethnic majority; the non-Hispanic white population had declined to just over forty-six percent; a third of the population was now Latino, while almost eleven percent was Asian and Pacific Islanders. The African-American population had stabilized at just over 6 percent. Not surprisingly, politics reflected the demographic change. Battles over services for immigrants and affirmative action were major issues of the period, contributing to the emergence of a stronger Latino and Asian political presence in the state and eventual decline in Republican electoral fortunes.

As the new millennium began, however, the state faced a major new crisis—the failure of its deeply flawed plan to deregulate the electrical utility industry. With power prices skyrocketing, rolling blackouts, its biggest electrical utility filing for bankruptcy, and the state no longer possessing progressive-era regulatory power over utilities, politicians were hard pressed to save the system.

RECESSION IN THE 1990s

When Governor Deukmejian left office in 1991 a whole new era had begun. A recession that began early in the decade had been triggered by astonishing international events. In 1989 the world watched spellbound as the Berlin Wall, the classic symbol of the Cold War, was demolished by defiant East and West Germans. Over the next two years, East and West Germany were reunited, the economy of the Soviet Union collapsed, and the Soviet Union itself disintegrated. The forty-year Cold War was suddenly over.

The event had enormous consequences for California. Dramatic cuts in defense and aerospace spending and a huge program of military base closures were quickly instituted. California's historic intimate association with the military, as well as its dominance in the defense and aerospace industries, made it especially vulnerable to the nation's new posture. Hundreds of thousands of high-paying jobs disappeared as the state's major defense companies embarked on downsizing programs that portended their permanent loss. Although the federal government promoted conversion to peacetime production, California's major defense companies, such as General Dynamics, Northrup, Rockwell International, and Lockheed, either abandoned the field, moved facilities out of the state, or simply reduced their work forces to levels necessary to continue production at lower capacities. "Conversion" became a laborious and painful process, and most replacement jobs offered much lower pay or required lengthy retraining.

Driven in part by defense cutbacks and in part by worldwide economic decline, the United States entered a severe recession in 1990, the worst economic downturn in California since the Great Depression of the 1930s. By 1994 the state had lost over 550,000 jobs, especially in the defense, aerospace, and electronics industries.

Compounding the economic troubles created by its reduction in defense expenditures, the federal government in 1989 embarked on a long-range program to close military bases around the nation, a program that was especially hard on California. In an historic decision, Congress established a Base Closure Commission to develop and submit a schedule of base closures in alternate years. In 1989, 1991, and 1993 Congress accepted the commission's proposals and the dismantling of the huge structure of military facilities in California began. By the mid-1990s some forty installations had been scheduled for closure or major reduction in force. In the south this included the famed El Toro Marine Corps Air Station, San Diego's Naval Training Station, George Air Force Base in the Mojave Desert, and San Bernardino's Norton Air Force Base. In the north the scheduled closures included Sacramento's Mather Air Force Base and Monterey's huge Fort Ord. The San Francisco Bay Area was hard hit by the scheduled closure of the San Francisco Presidio (the city's fifth-largest employer) and six naval facilities, including the Alameda Naval Air Station, Treasure Island Naval Air Station, and Vallejo's Mare Island Naval Base, the last with the loss of 30,000 direct jobs and another 30,000 indirect jobs. California lost 82,000 of the 119,000 jobs lost nationwide in the base-closing program.

It was a complicated process. A hierarchy of federal agencies had first claim on the land and buildings at each facility as it closed, followed by local reuse groups who could negotiate with the government for the property—at reduced prices. Failing such a purchase, the government could sell the property to private buyers at market prices. Environmental contamination was a problem at several bases, and Congress initially

The collapse of the double-decked Cypress freeway in Oakland during the 1989 Loma Prieta earthquake (*left*) and the widespread damage to southern California freeways in the Northridge earthquake of 1994 (*right*) finally spurred action on the state's neglected freeway "retrofit" program. *Left: Associated Press; right: Douglas C. Pizac/Associated Press.*

required complete cleanup of toxic materials before any such property could be disposed of. Eventually, California congressman Leon Panetta persuaded Congress to amend the law to allow bases to be "parcelized," permitting part of them to be put to new use while cleanup proceeded in other parts.

Results were mixed. Designation of San Diego as the Pacific Fleet's home base compensated for loss of the Training Station. Creation of California State University, Monterey Bay, and various research facilities connected as well to the University of California at Santa Cruz made good use of the facilities at Fort Ord. Treasure Island in San Francisco Bay proved useful for film production, while the San Francisco Presidio became a unique National Park. In many cases, predictions of

disaster did not materialize. At several bases local communities actually experienced growth in population, retail sales, housing markets, and employment as retired military personnel moved from PXs to local markets and new jobs were created by developers converting military property to commercial uses. Yet, ten years later, negotiations still continued at other sites as local organizations, formed to negotiate use of such facilities, found it difficult to come to agreement.

This recession also had a new twist to it. For the first time it affected upper-middle-class workers significantly, especially when high-paid Silicon Valley engineers and other staff were laid off. In the 1980s the demand for personal computers and the production of microprocessors, motherboards, disk dri-

ves, and other components, as well as software associated with this new means of mass communication, seemed nearly insatiable. Intel became the largest manufacturer of computer chips in the world. Apple Computer's MacIntosh and IBM's personal computer and its myriad clones became the leading sources of the "hardware" of the communications revolution taking place. In 1985 just over thirteen percent of U.S. households had personal computers. By 1991 that figure had doubled. The recession slowed this development drastically, with the loss of thousands of high-tech jobs.

Exacerbating the state's fiscal troubles, brought about by a sharp decline in tax revenues, the long-term impact of 1978's Proposition 13 at last took effect, especially for local governments. The public school and higher education systems were threatened with disaster, and cities and counties were so starved for funds that some were on the verge of bankruptcy. Enormous problems in education, transportation, crime, and quality of life confronted the state.

TRANSPORTATION

Governor Deukmejian's tight-fisted policies had serious consequences for the state's transportation system. Not the least was the continued disruption of the Department of Transportation's freeway "retrofit" program, which had been adopted after the 1971 San Fernando Valley earthquake but had been given little support by either Ronald Reagan or Jerry Brown. The collapse of the Cypress Freeway in Oakland during the 1989 Loma

Prieta earthquake, which killed dozens of motorists, and the enormous damage to southern California's freeway system in the 1994 Northridge quake, might well have been prevented if the Department of Transportation had not been deprived of funds earmarked to bring freeways up to new earthquake standards. By 1990 California's transportation system was in crisis: under both governors Brown and Deukmejian the state's highway system had almost ceased to expand. State per capita spending on public roads sank to dead last in the nation, while the number of automobiles doubled and, compounding the problem, an almost runaway inflation rate pushed construction costs to astronomical heights. Freeway gridlock became a daily feature of commuting in the state's large cities.

In 1990 public exasperation with the situation peaked, leading to the adoption of bond initiatives designed to restructure and rebuild the transportation system. The state gas tax was doubled to provide funds for an $18 billion highway and railroad construction program and other ambitious specific highway, mass transit, and railroad projects. The emphasis on rail transportation, ironically, was critical in securing approval of the bond issues, since public opinion had taken a decided turn in favor of rail mass transit. If there was a sense of déjà vu to these proposals, it was confirmed when the Los Angeles–Long Beach light rail transit line opened in 1990, running almost exactly along what had been the last line of the Pacific Electric (Red Car) system torn up for freeway construction.

The opening of Los Angeles's Century Freeway in 1993, at the shocking cost of over $100 million a mile, and the prominence of rail transit proposals in the 1990 bond issues led some observers to wonder if the end of the freeway era in California was at hand. However, by the mid-1990s Californians clung stubbornly to their cars. Destruction of segments of the southern California freeway system in the 1994 Northridge earthquake sent ridership on the area's rail and bus system skyrocketing, only to drop drastically when the damaged freeways were rapidly repaired by the state Department of Transportation. Still, the 1990 bond issue put the state on a long program of highway construction and repair and major extensions of rail transit systems. In the north the Bay Area Rapid Transit District (BART) made significant extensions down the peninsula to the San Francisco Airport and in the East Bay to eastern Alameda and Contra Costa counties; support was given to light rail systems in Sacramento and San José; trains were added to the Sacramento–San José CalTrain commuter line; and new fast ferries were added to the bay commuter system. In the south a downtown subway line was built in Los Angeles and light rail transit systems connected the city with Orange County in the south and Riverside and San Bernardino counties to the east. Meanwhile, planning began for high-speed rail service between the metropolitan areas of the north and south.

Disappointingly, freeway construction in the 1990s barely kept pace with the state's growth, and transportation continued to be high on the public's list of concerns in political polls. In 2000 the legislature restricted sales tax revenues on gasoline to maintenance of roads and public transit systems; and in 2001 it began considering proposals to dedicate the sales tax on motor vehicles (including trucks) to improving transportation, especially public transportation systems, in already developed cities. Public interest in the return to emphasis on public rail transit remained strong as did its support for strict anti-pollution requirements. In September 2000 the state Air Resources Board upheld its 1990 mandate requiring four percent of cars sold in 2003 to be nonpolluting and an additional six percent to be nearly nonpolluting, a standard several other states had followed in the 1990s.

RECESSION ERA POLITICS

For Republicans, the election of 1990 was crucial. They had, with good reason, blamed their failure to gain control of the state legislature in the 1980s on what they regarded as a "badly gerrymandered" apportionment of the legislature by Democrats after the census of 1980. Determined to prevent Democratic control of reapportionment after the 1990 census, party leaders sought an attractive candidate for governor when the bland George Deukmejian rejected a bid for a third term. With the support of both Ronald Reagan and President George Bush, Republicans turned to Pete Wilson, the popular, moderate, ex-mayor of San Diego who had been elected to the U.S. Senate in 1982. Wilson had handily won reelection in 1988 and seemed content to remain in the Senate; but heavily recruited by the White House and California Republicans, he finally agreed to run for governor, winning the party's nomination in the June primary. The potential of a bid for the presidency, should he become governor of California, no doubt affected his decision. Meanwhile, Democrats nominated former San Francisco mayor Dianne Feinstein, who emerged as a formidable opponent. Wilson and Feinstein proved to be remarkably close in their views on important issues, and it was only a Republican money advantage and an expensive media campaign that assured Wilson's election. As expected, Democrats retained control of the legislature and a majority of the state's congressional delegation.

The election of 1990 also brought voter approval of Proposition 140, one of the most far-reaching political reforms enacted by any state since the progressive era. The initiative established term limits of three terms (six years) for state assembly members and two terms (eight years) for state senators and key statewide officers. It also reduced the legislature's budget by forty percent and curtailed legislative pension benefits. The adoption of Proposition 140 reflected a pervasive distrust of politicians by a public convinced that special interests had too much power and influence in the governmental process. Ironically, the initiative resulted in the loss of much of the legislature's "institutional memory," as veteran members were "termed out," and increased the influence of special interest lobbyists. Legislative leaders challenged Proposition 140 in the courts, but the state supreme court upheld its constitutionality, which may account for a substantial reduction (approximately forty percent) in appropriations for the court in the next budget approved by the legislature. Nevertheless, as happened when Californians adopted Proposition 13 in 1978, term-limit proposals were soon adopted in many other states.

The issue of reapportionment came to the forefront after the election of 1990, important not only because it would affect the political power of the parties for the next decade, but also because the census of 1990 indicated California would gain several seats in the next Congress. The Democratic-controlled legislature submitted three different reapportionment plans to Governor Wilson, who vetoed all three, throwing the matter into the hands of the state supreme court, where a majority of the justices had been appointed by Republican governor George Duekmejian. The court referred the matter to three "special masters," two Republicans and one Democrat, who produced a plan that "corrected" the Democratic advantages of the 1980 reapportionment and anticipated significant Republican gains in both the legislature and Congress in the next election. Complying with the federal Voting Rights Act, the plan also established districts heavily favoring minority candidates in certain areas. Ironically, in 1992 Republicans, blamed for inept state and federal policies to cure the current economic ills, lost ground in both the legislature and the state's congressional delegation, as well as losing the state in the presidential vote to the Democrat Bill Clinton.

With the state's economy crumbling, Pete Wilson faced a projected $14.3 billion budget deficit when he took office early in 1991; only two other states had total budgets as large as California's *deficit*. To meet the crisis, Wilson proposed drastic cuts in spending, particularly welfare. Democrats rejected his proposals. After months of wrangling, the legislature passed and the governor signed a budget bill that included an increase of $7 billion in state income and sales taxes—the largest tax increase in the state's history. Taxes on business were unaffected, reflecting Wilson's determination to improve the state's business climate. The bill also included a four percent cut in payments to recipients of Aid to Families with Dependent Children and pay cuts and layoffs for state employees. Even then the budget was not completely balanced, and part of the deficit had to be carried over to the next fiscal year through a rollover accounting procedure.

The budget negotiated in 1991 by Governor Wilson and the Democratic leaders in the legislature seemed to please no one. Moreover, deficits continued to plague the governor and the legislature. In 1992 the conflict between the legislature and the governor, as well as between Democrats and conservative Republicans within the legislature itself, was so severe that a budget was not approved for weeks after the constitutional deadline had passed, and the state was reduced to paying state workers with "warrants"—essentially illegal I.O.U.s.

Natural disasters compounded the governor's problems. The 1989 Loma Prieta earthquake in the mountains east of Santa Cruz, a major temblor of 7.1 magnitude on the Richter scale, caused extensive damage in the San Francisco Bay region. Nearly a thousand homes were destroyed, and sections of the San Francisco–Oakland Bay Bridge and the double-decked Cypress Freeway in Oakland collapsed, killing sixty-three people. In 1991 five years of drought contributed to a devastating fire that raged through the hills on the eastern border of Berkeley and Oakland, destroying over 3,000 homes and killing twenty-five residents. In 1992 forest fires destroyed over 100,000 acres of northern California timberland, and the next year fire roared through the Santa Monica–Malibu area near Los Angeles, destroying more than 1,000 homes. Finally, in January 1994 another destructive earthquake, this time of 6.6 magnitude, struck Northridge, northwest of Los Angeles. Apartments, homes, and nine major freeway bridges collapsed, killing fifty-five people and creating a transportation crisis of monumental proportions. Damage estimates ran into the tens of billions of dollars. In his first three years in office, Governor Wilson issued twenty-seven declarations of emergency, covering fifty-six of the state's fifty-eight counties.

The loss of defense, aerospace, and high-technology jobs, natural disasters, and hot-button issues such as gay rights, welfare, and immigration contributed to a dramatic decline in the governor's approval ratings in state polls by early 1994. However, his handling of the Northridge disaster and his aggressive stance on crime and immigration partially revived his ratings by the summer. The kidnap-killing of Polly Klass, a Petaluma teenager, catapulted the crime issue to the top of public concerns in early 1994. Indictment of a felon with a long history of sexual crime, who had been freed on parole only shortly before the disappearance of Polly Klass, led to a rash of bills in the legislature requiring imprisonment for life of criminals convicted of a third felony. A "three strikes and you're out" initiative qualified for the 1994 ballot, and the legislature passed several "three strikes" bills, the most severe of which Governor Wilson signed. He gained politically from this action, but the state was committed to a massive increase in its prison population and the cost associated with it.

Wilson also rode the bandwagon of popular discontent over problems associated with growing ethnic diversity, adopting an aggressive approach to the issue of the cost of public services to illegal immigrants. He proposed that the state deny medical and educational services to illegal aliens and their children, that the children of illegal aliens born in the United States be denied citizenship, and that the state sue the federal government to force it to pay the full cost incurred by the state in providing such services to illegal immigrants. As the election of 1994 approached, he threw his support to an initiative, Proposition 187, designed to achieve these ends. Although he was accused of demogogic "immigrant bashing," it was an effective political move.

The timely adoption of the 1994–95 budget also aided the governor. Democrats, mindful of the negative public reaction to the 1992 delay in adopting the budget, essentially caved in to the governor's demands in order to avoid a similar situation in a crucial election year. The budget included cuts in payments for welfare and aid to the aged, blind, and disabled; a ten percent increase in fees for University of California and California State University students; no increase in per pupil spending for K–12 schools (for the third year in a row); continued suspension of the renters' income tax credit; and rollover of a $3 billion deficit. Moreover, Democrats agreed to abandon their efforts to extend an income tax surcharge on the rich, to restore funds to pay the salaries of Wilson's top polit-ical appointees, and to put $120 million in the budget to expand the prison system.

The election of 1994 brought a familiar name to the governor's race. Wilson easily won the Republican nomination for reelection, while Democrats nominated State Treasurer Kathleen Brown, daughter of former governor Edmund G. "Pat" Brown and sister of former governor Edmund G. ("Jerry") Brown, Jr. Although she attacked Wilson for the decline in California's economy, the loss of 550,000 jobs, and the nation's highest unemployment rate, Wilson was able to keep public attention on the issues of crime and illegal immigration. Brown proved especially vulnerable on the crime issue due to her stated opposition to the death penalty, even though she promised to enforce it if elected. She also adopted a more compassionate, though more risky, position on immigration, opposing denial of medical and educational services to illegal aliens and their children as shortsighted and more expensive in the long run. Moreover, Brown's attempt to present a full program of action to revive the state's economy and reform state government was drowned out by Wilson's focus on crime and immigration matters.

As the campaign progressed, the illegal alien issue, centering on Proposition 187, attracted more attention, affecting particularly the races for governor and the U.S. Senate. With Wilson's strong backing, the proposition, denying all but emergency services to illegal aliens and requiring teachers, health care providers, and other state officials to report suspected illegal aliens to federal authorities, passed by approximately a sixty to forty percent margin. Wilson defeated Brown, who opposed the initiative, by a similar margin. Opponents of the proposition immediately brought a court challenge to the constitutionality of the measure and began an organizing campaign to get a much higher percentage of the state's

Latino population to become citizens and voters. By the end of the century it was clear that the Republicans were paying dearly for Wilson's 1994 campaign, losing even more of their already small support from the state's growing ethnic population.

In a nasty and bitter campaign, one-term Santa Barbara congressman Michael Huffington, a Texas transplant with oil money, spent nearly $30 million of his own money in an attempt to unseat Senator Dianne Feinstein, one of the state's most popular politicians. Although he embraced Proposition 187 and, by a massive negative media campaign, caused Feinstein's ratings to plummet, the revelation that he had employed an undocumented alien as a nanny for his children wrecked Huffington's campaign. He eventually blamed his defeat on fraudulent voting by illegal aliens. The mood of the voters was indicated when they rejected initiatives for a single-payer health system and transportation bond issues designed to expand rail mass transit systems.

The election of 1994 was also characterized by a massive shift to the Republican Party nationally (Republican majorities in both the House of Representatives and the U.S. Senate for the first time in forty years) and at the state level. In California, Republicans picked up enough seats in Congress to attain an even split in the state's congressional delegation and won control of the state assembly by a margin of forty-one to thirty-nine. Democrats, however, retained control of the state senate by a twenty-one to seventeen margin, with two independents. A bizarre struggle for control of the assembly followed in which one Republican defected, another was expelled through parliamentary manipulation, and Willie Brown was reelected speaker. Recall campaigns restored the Republican majority, but Brown then threw his support to a maverick Republican, Doris Allen, who became the first woman to

be elected speaker of the assembly. Subsequently, Brown resigned from the assembly to run for mayor of San Francisco, Allen herself was the victim of a recall campaign, and Republicans finally gained control of the state assembly.

Despite a reviving economy and improved relations with the legislature, Governor Wilson did not escape controversy, when he embarked on a campaign for the Republican nomination for president in 1996. Since he had pledged to serve out his term if reelected in 1994, he was roundly denounced by many, even in his own party. Moreover, in the midst of his presidential campaign Wilson launched an aggressive attack on affirmative action—the practice of weighing race and gender in decisions affecting education, employment, and contracting in order to mitigate the effects of past discriminations. In 1995 the governor led the fight in the University of California Board of Regents to eliminate affirmative action in university policy affecting admissions, hiring, and contracts. In addition, he threw his support to an initiative measure on the 1996 ballot, Proposition 209, which would end affirmative action in all state and local government agencies. Wilson's campaign appealed especially to white males, many of whom felt unfairly treated by affirmative action, and the "angry white male" became an icon of the campaign. Proposition 209 was adopted in 1996 and was immediately challenged, unsuccessfully, in the courts by its opponents. Wilson's presidential bid was a bust. Campaign contributions dried up and his political status nationally sank when he tried to take his anti-immigration policies to the rest of the country. In mid-1996 he withdrew from the campaign.

THE NEW ECONOMY

Governor Wilson's reelection in 1994 coincided with California's emergence from the grip of the recession that had plagued his first administration. While the boom of the 80s was fueled largely by defense spending and the rise of Silicon Valley's computer industry, California's recovery from the recession of 1990–93 was anchored in the solid growth of foreign trade, professional services, high technology, entertainment, and tourism. Los Angeles and Orange County made the quickest recovery, benefiting from the demand for manufactured and agricultural products as the rest of the nation pulled out of the recession. In a remarkable turnaround, the region replaced lost defense and aerospace jobs with jobs in the high-tech industry, entertainment, and tourism. By 1995 Hollywood was a bigger employer than the entire defense sector, with wages at nearly the same level; by the end of the year all defense-related jobs lost in the recession had been replaced. Meanwhile, with port facilities at Long Beach and San Pedro, Los Angeles became the largest port on the Pacific Coast and by the end of 1995 had surpassed New York as the nation's largest gateway for foreign trade. Thousands of new jobs in the film industry and tourism added to the economic upturn. Moreover, the state created a friendlier business climate as state legislators slashed worker's compensation costs and streamlined permit processes, ending talk of a business exodus from the state.

After 1995, however, California's economy was driven by extraordinary changes in the high-technology industry and telecommunications. The development of the personal computer had given millions of individuals as well as business corporations all over the world access to an enormous source of information— the Internet. In the mid-1990s the Internet provided the spark for another period of explosive growth that put California in the forefront of what was called the New Economy.

The Internet evolved during the Cold War when military and scientific researchers, seeking a way to maintain communications during a nuclear war, organized networks of computers around the world. In 1983 the modern Internet was created when protocols for transmitting, routing, and receiving information in the standard Hyper Text Markup Language (HTML) were promulgated internationally. By interconnecting existing computer networks, this provided the world with an enormous source of information. In 1993 the creation of the World Wide Web made this resource available to anyone with a computer and a modem.

Access to the Web, however, required a software program called a browser. In the fall of 1993 Marc Andreesen, a young programmer working for a federal agency in Illinois, wrote one he called Mosaic, making it available on the Net. Mosaic proved to be so superior that it caused a sensation and led to an explosive growth of the World Wide Web. Moving to California, Andreesen teamed up with a Silicon Valley veteran, Jim Clark, to form a company that in 1994 produced a new, improved, web-access browser called Netscape. In a matter of weeks, Netscape took over eighty percent of the market. Still, the Internet badly needed some sort of index to its almost overwhelming resources. This was soon provided by the "search engines" that quickly appeared on the Web. Some were catalogs, the best known of which is Yahoo!, created by Stanford University students Jerry Yang and David Filo. Others were index-based engines, including Lycos, Excite!, and Infoseek. Together, browsers and search engines made the Web, as one observer noted "a resource whose breadth, depth, and value are almost beyond comprehension." And they gave individuals the ability to contact anyone, anywhere, anytime without regard to geographic boundaries.

They also made possible, as one observer claimed, the transformation of the Internet into "the biggest business and commercial

last among the states in the availability of computers to school children.

School funding continued to be an explosive political issue. The impact of Proposition 13 meant that only one quarter of the money for schools now came from local property taxes. Yet the recession of the 1990s made it difficult, indeed, for the state legislature to deal with the issue. Each year Superintendent Honig battled Governor Deukmejian and his successor Pete Wilson for additional funds, as state revenues declined and state politicians were polarized and paralyzed by the demands of conflicting interests. In 1993 Honig was removed from office when he was convicted of awarding contracts to a firm established by his wife to promote parental involvement in the schools. He was replaced by former assemblywoman Delaine Eastin, elected in 1994, but the funding issue remained unresolved.

The schools continued in the political spotlight when a school voucher initiative (Proposition 174) qualified for the ballot and was brought before the voters in 1993. The initiative proposed that the state give each California school-age child a $2,600 voucher (approximately half the state's per pupil expense for the year) that could be used to attend any school, public or private. Backed by religious and private school interests, the proposal was at first immensely attractive to those voters disenchanted with the public schools. Eventually, the state's sometimes feuding teachers, administrators, and school board associations united with public employees and other supporters of the public school system in a well-financed campaign that soundly defeated the initiative.

California's renowned system of higher education also felt the effects of the fiscal crisis of the 1990s. The system was enormous and costly. It had over one hundred community colleges enrolling over 1.5 million students; nineteen campuses of the California State University (CSU) enrolling 360,000 students and granting nearly 55,000 degrees a year—the largest system of its kind in the nation, with a budget of more than $1.6 billion a year; and nine University of California (UC) campuses enrolling 160,000 students, with state support approaching $2 billion annually. In the belief that their graduates were the wellspring of the state's prosperous economy, Californians traditionally have regarded state support of these institutions as money well spent. They took pride in the consistent ranking of the University of California as among the best in the country. Yet there were signs of trouble. Studies in the 1980s revealed the percentage of high-school graduates attending baccalaureate-degree-granting institutions had fallen below the national average. California was also below the national average in terms of the percentage of the population completing four or more years of college. College dropout rates, particularly for African Americans and Hispanics, were discouraging. The sharp decline in funding caused by Proposition 13 and other cutbacks since the 1970s, aggravated by the financial crisis of the 1990s, now threatened to end the promise of the 1960s Master Plan for Higher Education of a place for all who would profit from a college education.

From 1990 to 1994 budget cuts in all three segments of the higher education system led to the layoff of thousands of faculty, salary cuts, elimination of thousands of classes, and a dramatic increase in student fees. Students found it difficult to obtain the necessary courses to finish a bachelor's degree in four years, and thousands found the increased fees too great to contemplate or continue attending college. In a momentous 1994 decision, the Regents of the University of California raised fees in a multiyear plan that would result in 1996 fees three times those of 1990. For the first time in the university's history, the Regents also adopted a policy allowing the use of student fees for "instructional expenses," including faculty salaries—what critics called the end of free public higher education in the system. In 1995 it was estimated that fee increases, program cuts, and reduced financial aid had driven the equivalent of 58,000 students out of California colleges and universities. One administrator complained that budgets were no longer set "on the basis of what's needed to support the state's system of higher education, but on what's left that can be spent on it." In the early 1990s the percentage of the state budget going to the University of California and State University systems declined from thirteen to nine percent. After 1994 spending for prisons exceeded that for higher education. The fee increases also contributed to lower enrollments of minority students, particularly African-American and Latino students, whose numbers had steadily increased in the 1970s and 1980s. The beginning of economic recovery in California in 1994 was a long-awaited hopeful sign for higher education.

Economic recovery meant increased funding for the state's educational systems, and Governor Wilson announced his determination to be known as "the education governor." In May 1996 he proposed an appropriation in the budget as an incentive to public schools to reduce class size to twenty in the first two elementary grades, later expanding the proposal to the first three grades. Adopted in the 1996 budget, Wilson's proposal was the most important educational reform in two decades. Predicated on the simple idea that the fewer children a teacher has to deal with the better the instruction, the class size reduction program has had outstanding results. Teachers reported much faster student progress, fewer discipline problems, and greater parent involvement in school affairs. An effort to expand the program to later grades, however, has not made much progress.

Class size reduction was not accomplished without problems. It meant a corresponding increase in the number of classes, putting pressure on school districts to provide facilities. Many had to convert cafeteria, laboratory, music room, and library space to classroom use, in the absence of new construction. Increasing teaching staff by a third in many cases also put a strain on districts, with 18,000 additional teachers hired in 1996–97. Some school districts had as much as twenty percent of the staff on emergency credentials. Responding to the need, the State University system, which trains nearly sixty percent of the state's teachers, adopted programs aimed at increasing the number of teacher candidates it recommends annually by twenty-five percent and recruiting teacher training students "who represent the diversity of the public school population in California."

Despite the success of class size reduction, California's schools still languished near the bottom of the heap nationally. Nearly seventy percent of Californians indicated they would be willing to pay higher taxes if it meant better schools, but the state faced an almost overwhelming task. With over six million students, sixty-five percent of them minorities and many of them poor immigrants, the system was plagued by a high school dropout rate nearing thirty-five percent, as well as teacher shortages and strained budgets. In 1998 public concern finally led the legislature to put a $9.2 billion bond issue on the ballot (Proposition 1A) to at least rebuild the system's infrastructure, providing new schools, repairing old ones, and catching up with deferred maintenance. It passed with sixty-three percent of the vote. Then in 1999 Gray Davis, the new governor elected in 1998 promising to make education his "first, second, and third priorities," called a special session of the legislature for school reform. The result was landmark reform legislation, the Public Schools Accountability Act (PSAA) of

1999, which gave schools money to spend more time on reading, required every high school senior to pass a written examination in order to graduate, and put in place a complicated school reform plan of incentives and accountability. The law called for the establishment of an Academic Performance Index (API) that set improvement goals for each school, and established award programs for schools, certificated staff, and schoolwide staff that met or exceeded the index requirements. In Davis's first two years in office, state funding of the public schools increased by $7.1 billion (twenty percent) and per pupil spending rose by eighteen percent to $6,801. In 2000 seventy percent of all schools met their growth targets of five percent or more on standardized tests, and nearly forty percent achieved ten percent improvement.

A reform program of such a magnitude included problems, not the least of which was the whole concept of accountability, as well as the size and complexity of the program. With a school population in continual flux due to the changing demographics of the state, some critics complained that the governor and legislature expected too much, too fast. By 2001 there was talk of "reform fatigue," but the huge reform program remained popular with the public and school staff—if the resources they really needed were provided. Teachers gave it mixed reviews. Critics of the high school graduation examination requirement argued that it was "elitist," assuming that all graduates were college-bound, while ignoring the need for vocational and technical training in the new economy. Still, the Public Schools Accountability Act was a sea change (some called it a *tsunami*) in California school policy. Public confidence in the schools appeared to be returning when, in November 2000, voters approved an initiative that reduced the margin needed to pass a local school bond measure from two-thirds to fifty-five percent and

soundly defeated a voucher initiative for the second time. In 2001 the governor negotiated an agreement with teachers to lengthen the school year by fifteen days.

The state's systems of higher education also benefited from the affluence of the new economy. Operating budgets were fully funded and new programs supported. In 2000 the legislature provided for the establishment of world-class Institutes of Science and Innovation at the University of California. In December the governor announced the creation of a Nanosystems Institute at UCLA, with a partner campus at UC Santa Barbara; an Institute for Telecommunications and Information Technology at UC San Diego, with a partner campus at UC Irvine; and an Institute for Bioengineering, Biotechnology, and Quantitative Biomedical Research at UC San Francisco, with partner campuses at UC Berkeley and UC Santa Cruz. A fourth institute was planned for 2002. In addition, fees in the higher education systems were reduced, and the governor signed legislation committing the state to $1.2 billion annually for a huge financial aid program, increasing Cal Grant funding so that all qualified students would be assured of receiving the grants for tuition and supplies.

SOCIAL TRANSFORMATION

Throughout its history California's image as a western Eden, however elusive it might prove to be, has generated dramatic changes in its population. This again proved to be the case in the 1980s and 1990s; but unlike earlier changes, which were marked by massive migration from other regions of the United States, California's net population increase after 1980 came primarily from abroad. It was clear that the U.S. Immigration Acts of 1965 and 1986 had contributed to this trend by removing barriers to immigration into the United States from non-European countries.

The diversity of California's population can be seen in the faces of its schoolchildren. In 2000-2001 nearly sixty-five percent of the students enrolled in California's public schools were from ethnic minorities. Over forty-three percent were Latino and thirty-five percent non-Latino white. *Paul Chin/San Francisco*

Prior to these changes sixty percent of the nation's immigrants had come from Europe. In the 1980s and 1990s, however, more than eighty percent came from Asia and Latin America. As early as 1994 nearly forty percent of the Asian population of the United States lived in California. Los Angeles, meanwhile, had such an ethnic mix it would require more than one hundred languages to teach the city's children in their native tongues. The census of 2000 confirmed what demographers had been predicting for years: there was no longer a single ethnic majority in the state. Whites had dropped to about forty-

seven percent of the population; the Latino population had grown from less than twenty-six percent in 1990 to over thirty-two percent; Asians now accounted for almost eleven percent; and the African-American population had declined to just over six percent. For the first time the census counted persons of mixed race, which in California amounted to nearly five percent of the population. Statewide the population had grown to 33,871,648. Moreover, public school enrollment predicted an even greater shift, with forty-three percent of students Latino and only about thirty-six percent non-Latino white. As California rapidly developed into a multicultural society, the attention of the nation was focused on this transformation. Even in small ways the change was notable—by 1993, the state had a twenty percent intermarriage rate.

AFRICAN AMERICANS

Despite the successes of the civil-rights movement of the 1960s and 1970s, many persons in California's African American community continued to suffer from severe economic problems. Civil-rights and fair-employment laws, antipoverty programs, and the struggle to end school segregation brought only modest improvement in economic opportunity for blacks. While opportunity expanded greatly for educated middle-class African Americans, the lot of those less skilled and affluent worsened, in part because of a reduction in well-paying blue-collar jobs. As a result, in the mid-1980s African-American unemployment remained twice that of the general population, unemployment among black youth continued at close to forty percent, and the average annual income of black families was only sixty percent of the average white family's, a situation worsened by the recession of the 1990s. Historian John Hope Franklin saw the civil-rights movement as successful in creating the realization among most Americans that years of deprivation and disadvantage had made it difficult for blacks to compete successfully in American society, but the movement remained "unfinished," and the 1980s were characterized more by apathy than action.

The Rodney King case, however, demonstrated that racial prejudice and injustice still infused some groups. King was badly beaten in 1991 by officers of the Los Angeles Police Department after a high-speed automobile chase—an incident captured on tape by a witness with a video camera and shown re-

peatedly on network news programs. The nation was dismayed by the televised pictures of several officers beating the prostrate King with nightsticks while other officers looked on. It was then shocked when four of the officers, brought to trial in the spring of 1992, were acquitted by a San Fernando Valley jury of excessive use of force. The verdict touched off four days of multiethnic rioting, far worse than the 1965 Watts riot, resulting in $750 million in property losses and the death of over fifty persons. Outraged African Americans demanded federal action against the offending policemen, and in late 1993 two of the officers were convicted of violating King' civil rights in a federal prosecution. In 1994 a Los Angeles civil court jury also awarded King nearly $4 million in compensatory damages from the city of Los Angeles.

Still, barriers to racial justice remained subtle and, except in cases such as those revolving around the King beating and subsequent riot, seldom attracted the media attention of earlier, more blatantly discriminatory days. Unemployment, underemployment, resistance to school desegregation or improvement of inferior schools, and the complex problems of single-parent (mostly female) black families did not evoke the same sense of moral indignation that fueled much of the civil-rights movement of the 1960s and 1970s.

The riots of 1992, however, revealed significant new African American population movements. In 1965 South-Central Los Angeles (Watts) was predominantly African American; in 1992 it was predominantly Hispanic and Asian. Moreover, African Americans were resettling in greater numbers in the Central Valley and suburban areas rather than the older black communities in Oakland, San Francisco, and Los Angeles. Ironically, African Americans joined what had been termed the "white flight" from the cities, in part a reflection of a growing black middle class.

For African Americans, the changing demographics of the 1990s meant a gradual weakening of political power. For years they had exerted an influence almost incommensurate with their numbers. Organization and commitment to black issues had resulted in a powerful political presence capped by Tom Bradley's unprecedented five terms as mayor of Los Angeles and Willie L. Brown's historic fourteen years as speaker of the state assembly. Brown, often regarded as the second most powerful elected official in the state, was joined by five African-American assemblymen, two state senators in the state legislature, and three members of Congress. But as the 1990s progressed, this power seeped away. Elected mayor of San Francisco in 1995, Brown appointed many African Americans to city boards and commissions, but the black community complained they saw no real change in their condition and that African Americans had lost the cohesion and drive of earlier years. By the end of the century, African-American leaders seemed to be desperately seeking coalitions with other ethnic groups and searching for common causes. This seemed to be the case in June 2001, when African-American votes were instrumental in James Hahn's defeat of Antonio Villagairosa in the election for mayor of Los Angeles. Nevertheless, throughout the state, the momentum was shifting to Latino politicians, who were steadily replacing blacks.

Meanwhile, the state's new economy provided the economic means for thousands of blacks to move into the middle class, often fleeing the black enclaves of the big cities for the suburbs and even farther—to the high-desert towns of the south's "Inland Empire" and the Central Valley communities that were the fastest-growing sections of the state at the turn of the century. In a sense, the tide of Latino and Asian immigration was submerging California's African-American population. The decline of the state's black population was matched by the decline in the number of black legislators and county and local officials. African-American civil-rights organizations shriveled; and Latinos emerged in positions of power once held by blacks. In 2000 the African American community seemed in an identity crisis, struggling to reorganize and regain some of its earlier influence.

NATIVE AMERICANS

The census of 2000 revealed that California contained the largest Native American population in the nation, nearly 300,000. The rapid rate of growth since World War II was due largely to migration of Native Americans from other states, but much of the increase resulted from increased health care and control of Old World diseases. One remarkable feature of California Indian populations has been their survival not only demographically but tribally. In the 1980s many groups still existed as more or less viable indigenous California tribes, distinct from the non-Indian population as well as from other Native Americans who had migrated to the state. The tiny group of Tolowa of Del Norte County, for example, applied to the federal government for recognition as a tribe in 1986. Decimated by disease and nineteenth-century genocidal raids by whites, the Tolowa numbered only between 120 and 150 in 1900, but by 1986 they were estimated to number between 400 and 450, surviving in a remote section of northwestern California. Other California groups also acted to preserve their cultures. In 1974 the Cupeño established the Cupa Cultural Center at the Pala reservation near San Diego, offering classes in language, history, and culture. Near Riverside, the Cahuilla founded the Malki Museum, featuring language classes and a repository of tribal artifacts and ethnographic materials.

many and a semblance of unity. It has also made them a respected new political force in the state. But many Californians continued to oppose gambling and were quick to react with lawsuits when the tribes, now allied with out-of-state casino interests, tried to establish casinos in urban and suburban areas, instead of limiting them to reservations as voters had been assured in the 2000 constitutional amendment campaign.

ASIAN AMERICANS

Important changes in United States immigration policy fueled a dramatic increase in immigration from Asian countries. After World War II, the old anti-Asian legislation of the early twentieth century was eliminated, and in 1965 the national-origins-based policy of the 1920s was abandoned. The Immigration Act of 1965 provided for the immigration of 170,000 persons from the Eastern Hemisphere and 120,000 from the Western Hemisphere and instituted educational and occupational criteria for admission to the country. Perhaps the most important feature of the act was that it allowed United States citizens to sponsor the immigration of family members. By the 1980s earlier immigrants had become citizens and were taking advantage of this provision. By 2000 Immigration and Naturalization Service (INS) figures revealed that two-thirds of all legal immigrants were family sponsored. The Immigration Act of 1990, meanwhile, increased the 1965 ceilings even further, put greater emphasis on skilled workers, and set aside a substantial number of visas for large investors.

These changes opened California to a phenomenal growth in immigration from Asia and Latin America, only slightly diminished by the recession of the early 1990s. By that time forty percent of the Asians in the United States, primarily from China, Hong Kong, Taiwan, Korea, and the Philippines, were Cal-

Vietnamese Refugees
American withdrawal from South Vietnam in 1975 was followed by the flight of thousands of refugees fleeing the North Vietnamese take-over. Many were processed at hastily constructed camps such as this one at California's Camp Pendleton Marine Corps base near San Diego. *Roberts/Sygma.*

ifornia residents. A special category included 335,000 refugees from Southeast Asia admitted after the end of the Vietnam War, 85,000 of whom settled in Los Angeles alone.

Chinese and Filipino migrants continued to prefer San Francisco as a destination. By 2000 more than thirty-five percent of the city's population was Asian, the majority of them Chinese. Like the Japanese, Chinese Americans have established superior records for educational achievement, with a much lower school dropout rate and higher university qualification rate than whites. Chinese also became more politically active, due in part to March Fong Eu's election as California's secretary of state, and held several elective offices in San Francisco. In 1994 Secretary Eu's son Matthew K. Fong was elected

Chinese American youngsters participate in the annual Chinese New Year's parade in Los Angeles. With large Chinese American populations, both Los Angeles and San Francisco stage colorful celebrations of the Chinese New Year as one of the important cultural events of their Asian communities. *Nik Wheeler/CORBIS*

state treasurer. Since immigration law favored those with education or special skills, Chinese and, later, Indian immigrants gravitated to Silicon Valley, where they soon accounted for over a third of the scientific and engineering personnel. In the late 1990s the demand for such trained personnel led Congress to create a special visa program, H-1B, admitting 115,000 immigrants with college degrees annually. In 2000 the number of visas available under this program was increased to 195,000 annually in response to urgent pleas from the high-tech industry. One result was a huge increase in the number of migrants from India.

After 1965 the rapidly growing Filipino migration reflected in part the repressive administration of Philippine president Ferdinand Marcos, whose regime lasted until 1986. Since the 1965 Immigration Act replaced the 1920s quota limits with educational and occupational requirements, the new Filipino migrants tended to be professional people. Nevertheless, like the Filipino agricultural workers who had preceded them, as well as immigrants from all countries in general, these new arrivals, until the technology boom of the 1990s, continued to face discrimination in job placement that forced them to take positions for which they were far overqualified; but the emergence of the New Economy opened many new opportunities for Filipinos. A growing migration from South Korea was another major factor in the increase in California's Asian population. Locating primarily in Los Angeles, Koreans gave the city the largest Korean population outside of Seoul, the capital of South Korea.

For Japanese Americans, the 1980s produced important moral victories. In 1980 Congress established the Commission on Wartime Relocation and Internment of Civilians to investigate the circumstances of the mass removal of Japanese Americans from their homes in 1942. Three years later the commission reported that the evacuation resulted from "race prejudice, war hysteria, and a failure of political leadership," rather than the "military necessity" claimed at the time, and called the action "greatly unjust and deeply injurious."

The commission's investigation and passage of the federal Freedom of Information Act resulted in the release of previously suppressed documents that revealed that the government had withheld vital information relating to the alleged existence of a "military necessity" when the Supreme Court heard the Hirabayashi and Korematsu cases. This led in 1984 to the decision by U.S. District Court Judge Marilyn Hall Patel vacating Fred Korematsu's conviction for violating the evacuation order of 1942. In 1986 U.S. District Court Judge Donald Voorhees in Seattle similarly invalidated the conviction of Gordon Hirabayashi for refusal to report for evacuation. Judge Voorhees ruled the government had engaged in "misconduct of the most fundamental character" in justifying the removal and in withholding information that might have led the court to strike down the legal underpinnings of the evacuation.

The 85,000 square foot, $22 million Japanese American National Museum was built in the late 1900s in the Little Tokyo district of Los Angeles. An important cultural resource for Japanese Americans, it is effective in bringing the Japanese American experience to all visitors. *Associated Press AP, Dennis Dovarganes, Staff*

The commission's work also led President Reagan to issue a formal apology to Japanese Americans for their treatment during World War II, and Congress in 1988 appropriated $20,000 per person for reparations for all camp survivors, although such payments did not begin until 1991.

Widespread negative reaction by other groups to the report of the Commission on Wartime Relocation and Internment of Civilians, and to reparations, however, made it clear that, despite the admirable record of Japanese Americans, the general population remained colossally ignorant of the violation of their civil rights in 1942. To make matters worse, sharpened economic competition with Japan, and the tide of Asian migration in the 1990s, contributed to a revival of anti-Asian attitudes in the United States, especially in California. In January 2001 the National Asian Pacific Legal Consortium reported that incidents of violence and vandalism against Asians had increased substantially over the previous year.

Nevertheless, by 2000 Japanese Americans had become as one observer noted "the very symbol of assimilation—upwardly mobile, marrying outside their ethnic group at high rates, and dispersing throughout suburban America." Today the overwhelming number of Japanese Americans are native-born and are vastly outnumbered by recent Asian immigrants. Moreover, mixed-race births are nearly double monoracial Japanese American births. English is not a second language for Japanese Americans, and as the older generations die, there is a growing effort by their descendants to preserve the Japantowns of Los Angeles, San José, and San Francisco, and Japanese cultural values, often through social programs in their communities. The creation of the Japanese American National Museum in Los Angeles in the 1990s was an important part of this effort.

HISPANIC CALIFORNIANS

The development of California's multiethnic society is most dramatically revealed in the growth of its Hispanic population. Primarily of Mexican origin, California's eleven million Hispanics constituted more then thirty-two percent of the state's population in 2000, and state demographers predict they will equal the state's non-Latino white population by the year 2025 and become a majority by 2040.

As always, California's Latino population has been concentrated in southern California, especially East Los Angeles, which has been the focal point of Mexican American life in California since the progressive era. Its residents provided essential labor for the growth of manufacturing and industry in the city through the 1920s and again after World War II. Traditionally the distribution point for California's Mexican farm-labor force, East Los Angeles has been described as a "metropolis within a megalopolis," one of the "ethnic marvels of urban America." In 2000 ninety-seven percent of its residents were Latinos.

A number of factors spurred the growth of the state's Mexican American population and the development of East Los Angeles after World War II. The *bracero* program and postwar industrial and manufacturing development in southern California attracted a large number of migrants, both legal and illegal. By the 1980s the changing nature of the state's economy to greater emphasis on service and light-industrial-assembly occupations both attracted Mexican immigration and reflected the existence of a large pool of low-wage, unskilled labor. Declining economic conditions and a soaring birth rate in Mexico provided the push for thousands to come to the United States. East Los Angeles provided a Spanish-speaking community, inexpensive housing, restaurants, and businesses catering to Mexican tastes, and easy

Mural on the Wall of a Neighborhood Food Market, Decoto District of Union City, California
Hispanic *barrios* throughout California experienced cultural revivals after 1960, made possible by renewed immigration and ethnic pride. A flowering of traditional Mexican mural art has been one manifestation. This mural in the East Bay community of Union City celebrates Hispanic contributions to agriculture, new achievements in education, and the political activism that in the early 1970s prevented the state from replacing the Decoto *barrio* with a new freeway. *Photograph by Richard J. Orsi.*

access to Spanish-language radio, television, and theater.

As the Mexican population of East Los Angeles expanded in the 1990s, its residents expressed concern about their quality of life. Postwar freeway construction had torn through the heart of the barrio, choking the district with traffic congestion and smog; housing was scarce and of low quality; schools were overcrowded, poorly attended, and understaffed, and the dropout rate of Mexican Americans was nearly twice that of non-Latino white students. The Chicano cultural and political movement of the 1960s and 1970s and the concurrent renaissance of Mexican art

and literature contributed to the growing interest in social, economic, and political development. Meanwhile, the focus of attention on the state's Latino population shifted from farm workers to the urban residents of East Los Angeles and the San Francisco Bay region, which contained the third-largest concentration of Hispanics in the country, after Los Angeles and San Antonio, Texas.

For many years Mexican Americans lacked political representation, especially in the city and county of Los Angeles. Mexican Americans did not, like African Americans, establish effective national political organizations, and, in part because of language barriers, their political participation was minimal. In the 1970s more than half the eligible Latino voters in California were not even registered to vote. The challenge of the 1980s for California Latinos, therefore, was the translation of their numbers into political power. The emergence of successful grassroots organizations such as the United Neighborhood Organizations (UNO) in East Los Angeles and the Southwest Voter Registration Education Project, reapportionment after 1990 creating Latino districts, better educated and more experienced candidates, and the increasing Latino political consciousness by 1990 produced what some called the "dawn of Latino power." After the election of 1992 there were ten Latinos, four of them women, in the state legislature. Over 1.15 million Latinos, moreover, voted in that year's presidential election. The election of Gloria Molina to the powerful Los Angeles County Board of Supervisors was an historic breakthrough for representation of Mexican Americans in Los Angeles affairs.

The political consequences of the campaigns of the 1990s were equally important. Governor Wilson's 1994 campaign for reelection relied heavily on his support for the anti-immigrant Proposition 187, with TV spots especially galling to Latinos. His campaign for the anti-affirmative action Proposition 209 also aligned him and the Republicans against the state's minorities. Proposition 227 in 1998, which effectively ended bilingual education, was the last straw for many Latinos. While Wilson's campaigns galvanized enough white voters to ensure his reelection, they served, as some said, to "awaken the sleeping giant" of Latino political power. Latino applications for citizenship and voter registration soared; by 2000 there were half again as many Latino voters as in 1990. Whereas in 1990 there were a total of seven Latinos in the state legislature, by 1999 there were twenty-three. In 1996 Cruz Bustamante, a Central Valley

Democrat, became the first Latino speaker of the state assembly. The same year, Loretta Sanchez was the first Latina to be elected to Congress from Orange County, defeating the notorious Robert "B-1 Bob" Dornan. She repeated the feat in 1998, when Bustamante was elected lieutenant governor of California and Antonio Villaraigosa succeeded him as speaker of the assembly. *California Journal* reacted with a January 2000 issue labeled "The Latino Century."

Mexican farm labor continued to look to César Chavez for leadership in the uphill struggle against California growers. After 1975 the battleground became increasingly the makeup and bias of the state's Agricultural Labor Relations Board (ALRB). Meanwhile, the organization of farm field labor was virtually stagnant,

Dolores Huerta addresses UFW rally. Circa 1975
A cofounder, with César Chavez, of the United Farm Workers union, and one of its chief negotiators, Dolores Huerta has been called the "unheralded heroine" of the movement. She has long been an inspiration to Mexican American women. *Courtesy of Archives of Labor and Urban Affairs, Wayne State University.*

with Chavez's United Farm Workers struggling through a renewed grape boycott to maintain the small gains it had made in the 1970s, while "illegals" continued to be a major source of farm labor in the state. Chavez's death in 1993 was another contributor to the declining influence of the movement. In 1996, however, Chavez' son-in-law, Arturo Rodriguez, and Dolores Huerta revived the organization, emphasizing organizing campaigns and negotiating contracts seeking higher wages, health benefits, and paid vacations. A change in the ALRB encouraged them that they would get fair hearings, and the UFW succeeded in signing several new contracts with growers. UFW membership increased from 15,000 to 25,000.

The structure of California's Hispanic population became more complex in the 1980s, with increased legal and illegal immigration from Central America, due, in part, to the heavy involvement of the Reagan administration in the civil wars in El Salvador and Nicaragua. The Hispanic population, itself, thus became more diverse culturally and in nationality, complicating the efforts to achieve a sense of community and political power.

THE STATUS OF WOMEN

The postwar civil-rights movement profoundly changed American attitudes toward minorities. No longer just a concept of numbers, a "minority" became defined as any group subject to discrimination and denied its share of political, social, and economic power. The new concern with equality applied to women, as well as ethnic groups, and resulted in a new women's-rights movement. In the 1970s the focus of the movement became the Equal Rights Amendment (ERA), a simple amendment to the U.S. Constitution stating that "equality of rights under the law shall not be denied or abridged by the United States or by any state on account of sex." Although Congress adopted the

amendment in 1972, and California quickly ratified it, the amendment failed in 1982. Californians were heavily involved in support of the ERA and in the National Organization for Women, its chief proponent.

Failure of the ERA did not diminish the steady increase in the number of successful women politicians in California. At the local level, women continued to gain an increasing number of city council and supervisorial positions. In the early 1980s San Francisco's Board of Supervisors and San José's City Council had women majorities, and both cities, as well as San Diego and Sacramento, had women mayors.

1992 was hailed as the "Year of the Woman," in part because of the success of women candidates for office in California. When both Barbara Boxer and Dianne Feinstein were elected to the United States Senate, the state became the first ever represented in that body by two women. In addition, seven women were elected to Congress, six to the state senate, and twenty-two to the state assembly. Two women, March Fong Eu as secretary of state and Kathleen Brown as state treasurer, held statewide office that year.

California women have also played a major, though often unheralded, role in the successes of the modern environmental movement. Women were very much involved, for example, in efforts to save San Francisco Bay, to pass the initiative establishing the coastal commissions, and to establish stricter regulation of offshore oil-well operations. Contra Costa County Supervisor Sunne McPeak's critical role in the 1982 referendum campaign that defeated the bill to construct the Peripheral Canal illustrates the dedication, leadership, and political activism that women have brought to the environmental movement.

While the environmental movement contributed to increased political power and recognition for women, their economic progress was mixed. World War II provided a

Senators Dianne Feinstein and Barbara Boxer celebrate election victories in 1992. The election of two women from the same state to the United States Senate was a unique event and accentuated the growing presence of California women in politics. *Paul Sakuma/Associated Press.*

continuing stimulus for major changes affecting women in the workplace. Not only did the number of working women increase by ninety-five percent from 1960 to 1980, but the kinds of jobs they held also changed dramatically. A 1983 federal study reported that women comprised a majority in six categories of jobs that were once the province of men: insurance adjusters, examiners, and investigators; real-estate agents and brokers; photographic process workers; bill collectors; checkers, examiners, and inspectors; and production-line workers. Moreover, the percentage of women in other job categories, including lawyers, physicians, bus drivers, and bartenders, increased substantially.

A 1986 California poll reported remarkable acceptance by the state's men and women of feminist views on equality for women, government-supported child care, and equal pay for comparable work. Most also agreed, however, that working women, despite changing attitudes, still did seventy percent or more of the housework and were generally required to be better at their jobs than men in similar positions. Much of the progress of women in the job market was due to greatly increased opportunity for women to attend college, including professional and graduate schools. Women students now constitute a majority of college students and are a majority in some professional and graduate programs.

Despite modest improvement, women have failed to close the wage gap with men. In 2000 the Economic Policy Institute reported that women earned seventy-seven cents for every dollar earned by men in 1999. Accordingly, the most serious job issue for women remained the proposal to give women the same pay as men for "comparable work." Hailed as a breakthrough for women's rights, the idea received credence in a 1983 federal court decision defining the concept as "the provision of similar salaries for positions that require or impose similar responsibilities, judgments, knowledge, skills, and working conditions." It was not a new idea. During World War II the U.S. Labor Powers Board developed complex job-evaluation tables to promote equal pay for men and women in like work. The board was dismantled after the war; but following a 1981 U.S. Supreme Court decision that wage discrimination can be applied to equal as well as unequal jobs, the use of job-evaluation tables became a major weapon of the modern campaign for equal pay for comparable work. A study by the city of San José revealed major inequities, and in 1981 San José municipal workers went on strike to give women the same pay as men for comparable work. The strikers failed in their specific demands, but the city accepted the concept and began a process of funding pay raises designed to eliminate such wage discrepancies. Other cities and counties in the state have moved in a similar direction through the use of job-evaluation tables.

Sexual harrassment emerged as a key issue for women in the 1990s. The subject attracted national attention when Clarence Thomas, nominated for the U.S. Supreme Court by President Bush, was accused of sexual harassment by Anita Hill, an Oklahoma law professor and former associate of Thomas. In 1991 nationally televised hearings by the all-male United States Senate Judiciary Committee led to widespread criticism of the insensitivity of the committee members and raised public consciousness of the issue dramatically. One result was a dramatic increase in political action by women and the increased election of women officials after 1991. In 2000 both United States senators from California were women (Barbara Boxer, reelected in 1998, and Dianne Feinstein, reelected in 2000) and sixteen of California's House of Representative members were women.

GAYS AND LESBIANS

The development of sizable homosexual communities in San Francisco and Los Angeles after World War II contributed to California's cultural diversity. During the war homosexuals in the military services, as well as those dishonorably discharged because of their sexual orientation, found San Francisco a haven of tolerance. At the war's end many gay men and lesbians gravitated to the city and to Los Angeles to form the first openly homosexual communities in the state and to found important social and political organizations. By the 1970s San Francisco's gay community had developed enough political strength to elect the first openly gay politician, Harvey Milk, to the

Board of Supervisors.

Until the 1990s gay and lesbian organizations depended primarily on their "straight" supporters for political action and provided campaign workers and significant financial aid for those supporting homosexual issues. Gay political pressure and lobbying led several cities to adopt policies extending spousal benefits to partners of homosexual workers and to eliminate discrimination against homosexuals in hiring and housing. However, by the 1990s many gay and lesbian leaders had concluded that they had to seek political power themselves to obtain the full civil rights they sought. They were encouraged by the success of political figures such as Carole Migden, powerful chair of the San Francisco Board of Supervisors Budget Committee, who became a leading member of the state assembly, and Roberta Achtenberg, San Francisco Board of Supervisors member who was the first openly homosexual appointee to high federal office when President Clinton named her assistant secretary of Health and Human Services in 1993. In June 1994 the first openly gay politician to seek statewide office, Tony Miller, won the Democratic nomination for secretary of state. Openly gay and lesbian politicians also held or sought office in many local elections, although constantly under attack from what they regarded as the "rabid right" led by the Reverend Louis Sheldon's True Values Coalition of Christian fundamentalists. In San Francisco, Tom Ammiano emerged as a powerful member of the Board of Supervisors and leader of the gay community.

No issue more affected the state's homosexual community than the AIDS (Acquired Immunodeficiency Syndrome) crisis that emerged in the 1980s. AIDS was initially seen as strictly a disease related to homosexual activity; more than eighty percent of AIDS victims were homosexuals and intravenous drug users. The crisis was documented with the publication of Randy Shilts's enormously in-

fluential book *And the Band Played On* in 1987. Shocked by such statistics, the burgeoning homosexual communities in San Francisco and Los Angeles in particular adopted many changes in lifestyle. However, by the 1990s the disease was spreading increasingly among heterosexual men and women and was regarded as a national health crisis. By that time, too, medical researchers had identified the human immunodeficiency virus (HIV) that caused AIDS and had developed a drug (AZT) to fight the onset of AIDS in those infected with the virus. The virus proved unusually resistant to treatment, unfortunately, and California still had more than twenty-five percent of the nation's AIDS cases, sapping the leadership of the gay rights movement.

The AIDS crisis, along with saturation of the local job market for gays, rising housing costs, and the opening of other cities to gay populations, contributed to the decline in growth of the gay and lesbian populations in the state's major cities by the 1990s. Still, they remained a significant social and political force seeking recognition of their civil rights.

POLITICS AT THE TURN OF THE CENTURY

Governor Pete Wilson's stillborn presidential campaign of 1996 seemed a harbinger of the Republican future in California. That fall, the successes of 1994 turned sour and the Democrats regained control of the state assembly, electing Cruz Bustamente as California's first Latino speaker of the assembly, while the state voted heavily for the reelection of President Bill Clinton. Meanwhile, Loretta Sanchez's defeat of Representative Robert Dornan for Congress in Orange County was further evidence of a changing electorate that did not bode well for Republicans. The decline thus begun in 1996 accelerated so rapidly in the 1998 and 2000 elections that the *California Journal*, in 2001, was calling it the "Republican train wreck."

In the June primary of 1998 Lieutenant Governor Joseph Graham "Gray" Davis won the Democratic nomination for governor in a race against two millionaire opponents. Winning much more easily than expected, Davis's effective campaign slogan ("Experience Money Can't Buy"), his moderate, centrist political stance, as well as his overlooked money-raising ability proved decisive. Called "the best-trained governor-in-waiting California has produced," Davis certainly had a long waiting period—chief of staff to Governor Jerry Brown, 1975–81; member of the assembly, 1983–87; state controller, 1987–95; lieutenant governor, 1995–99. In fact, Davis was such a familiar, but unspectacular, public figure his nomination was viewed by many with surprise. Republicans, meanwhile nominated their own "governor-in-waiting," state attorney general Dan Lungren, who clung to the traditional Republican issues of character, crime, taxes, and immigration. Vigorously antichoice on the abortion issue, Lungren appeared, as the Washington *Post* commented, to be "searching for an electorate that had vanished." "Angry White Males," the *Post* said, "are now Content White Males" and the suburbs in California are now the "ethnoburbs." Davis defeated Lungren in the general election by almost twenty percentage points

In fact, in November 1998 Republicans suffered what one analyst called "the political equivalent of a wipeout." The wedge issues that had worked for them in recession-era 1994 failed to move voters in 1998. Gray Davis, with the support of a revived labor movement, commanded the political center on issues voters cared about—abortion rights, gun control, and health care—while putting the focus of his campaign on their number one issue, education. Davis's skillful campaign and huge political war chest produced one of the most convincing victories in California history. Moreover, the Republicans were left with only

Gray Davis celebrates his election as governor in 1998. With him is Cruz Bustamente, first Latino speaker of the state Assembly who was elected Lieutenant Governor on the Democratic ticket with Davis. Also flanking Davis is Delaine Eastin, State Superintendent of Public Instruction. The election of Davis and Democratic control of both houses of the legislature gave them control of the crucial process of reapportionment after the 2000 census. *Associated Press AP, Rich Pedroncelli, Staff*

one major statewide office, secretary of state. Democratic majorities of forty-eight to thirty-two in the state assembly and twenty-five to fifteen in the state senate made it appear impossible to prevent Democratic control of reapportionment after the census of 2000. Capping the Democratic victory, U.S. Senator Barbara Boxer, portrayed in the media as the most liberal member of the Senate and thus "vulnerable," handily defeated her opponent State Treasurer Matt Fong. The one bright spot of the election for Republicans was their pick up from the Democrats of two seats in Congress, a bright spot rubbed out in the election of 2000.

The election of 1998 revealed the frustration and rage engendered in Latinos and Asians by the wedge issues of the Wilson years. Moreover, Republican candidates were now generally on the wrong side of the issues Californians seemed to care about, such as education, abortion rights, gun control, health care reform, and the environment. Nor did national politics, the Clinton-Lewinsky scandal, and impeachment proceedings against the president drive Democrats away. Strong get-out-the-vote campaigns got them to the polls. Finally, Democrats were favored with badly managed campaigns by both Lungren and Fong.

Once in office Davis lost no time delivering on his promise to make education reform the state's number one priority, calling the legislature into special session to address the issue. Blessed with a budget surplus of major proportions, the legislature responded with the Public School Accountability Act of 1999, establishing a huge, expensive, controversial, and complex program of reform and accountability for the state's public schools. Over $7 billion was appropriated for California schools in 1999.

Davis also moved to cement Latino ties to the Democrats and his administration, entertaining Mexican president Ernesto Zedillo early in 1999, the first Mexican president to visit the state. In March 2001 the new president of Mexico, the charismatic Vicente Fox, visited California at Davis's invitation, addressed the state legislature, and was greeted across the state, as one reporter wrote, "like a rock star." Fox and Davis vowed to promote continued good relations between Mexico and California and to deal with the stubborn problems between them of illegal immigration and drug trafficking. The visit reflected California's growing Mexican American population as well as California's expanding economic ties with Mexico.

By the fall of 2000 the roaring prosperity of the late 1990s had produced a satisfied electorate that shoved California Republicans farther toward political oblivion. Although they failed to win the presidency, Democrats took comfort in the twelve-point margin Vice President Gore scored over Texas governor George W. Bush, while Senator Dianne Feinstein buried her opponent, former congressman Tom Campbell, by twenty points in her reelection bid. Democratic majorities in the state assembly and state senate were also increased. In a year in which, nationally, Democrats needed to take seven seats from Republicans to regain control of the House of Representatives in Congress, California Democrats did their part, picking up five—raising their majority in the state's congressional delegation to thirty to twenty-two.

Two hard-fought initiatives were also on the ballot in November 2000. Proposition 38, which would have the state provide parents with a $4,000 voucher to help pay for private school tuition, was promoted as an alternative for students in low-performing schools. Opponents termed it a risky experiment that would erode school accountability and drain resources from the state's already fiscally troubled public schools. Like the voucher intitiative of 1993, Proposition 38 was defeated by a seventy-one percent to twenty-nine percent vote.

Proposition 39 was significant in that it was the first important change in the 1978 landmark Proposition 13. Approved by a fifty-three percent to forty-seven percent vote, Proposition 39 amended the state constitution to allow voters to approve local school bonds with a fifty-five percent vote instead of the two-thirds vote required under Proposition 13. Proponents argued that the demonstrated difficulty school districts had in reaching the two-thirds vote and the need to repair the state's schools and house the booming

student population made the change absolutely necessary. Strong backing for the
amendment came from Silicon Valley businesspeople concerned that the state's schools
were not producing the trained workers the
new economy demanded. Opponents, led by
the Howard Jarvis Taxpayer's Association,
warned the change would drive up property
taxes and complained that it lacked adequate
spending oversight. With passage of the measure, the association began consideration of a
challenge to the initiative in 2002.

Republicans may have been in a political
train wreck after 2000, but there was a train
coming down another track. By the end of
winter in 2001, the state's economy was being
buffeted by bad news with the collapse of the
Internet commerce craze of the 90s, followed by massive layoffs, and huge costs associated with an energy crisis of almost overwhelming proportions. Governor Davis who,
a few months previously, was considered a
logical contender for the Democratic presidential nomination in 2004, was now fighting
for his political life, with even his reelection
in 2002 threatened, political analysts said, if
he didn't "fix the energy problem." Even
with their majorities in the legislature, Democrats seemed puzzled and ineffective in
the crisis, while Republicans, with enough remaining members to block the two-thirds
vote needed for most fiscal actions, could
still demand to be dealt with. Some Democrats feared their own political train wreck.

ANOTHER ENERGY CRISIS

The year 2001 began as though it would be
remembered as the year of California's worst
energy crisis ever, although there was a pre-
view of the crisis in the summer of 2000,
when San Diego residents were surprised
with a tripling of their electric bills. San
Diego's experience was the first sign that the
state's utility deregulation plan was a disaster.

The genesis of California's pioneering
1996 effort to deregulate the power industry
lay in the Reagan era's free-market philosophy. Based on the belief that freeing markets
from government regulation would increase
competition and reduce prices, the federal
government had deregulated airlines, communications, and other industries. In California, with utility rates as much as forty percent higher than in the rest of the country,
the California Manufacturer's and Technology Association and other business groups
pressed Governor Wilson and his Public Utilities Commission (PUC) to move toward
deregulating the state's electric utilities. The
state's three major private utilities, San Diego
Gas and Electric, Southern California Edison, and Pacific Gas and Electric (PG&E),
also lobbied for such action, claiming it
would bring utility rates down dramatically.
During 1994–95, the PUC worked up various
deregulation plans, and in 1996, at Wilson's
urging, the state legislature took up the PUC
recommendations.

The legislaure's consideration of deregulation exposed the consequences of the term-
limits initiative (Proposition 140) adopted in
1990. Pushed by a lame-duck governor and in
the hands of inexperienced legislators, the
measure was so complicated and complex
that it was ignored for weeks and shuttled between committees whose members admit-
tedly did not understand it. The bill, AB1890,
was finally adopted unanimously in 1996 and
went into effect, some say appropriately, on
April 1, 1998. It became a classic illustration
of how term limits had removed knowledge,
experience, and accountability from the
state's lawmaking bodies and given industry
lobbyists unusual opportunities to influence
legislation. An initiative put on the ballot by
consumer groups in the fall of 1998 would
have reversed major portions of AB1890; but
the initiative was so complicated that confused voters rejected it.

ONE-ARMED BANDIT, NEVADA

JACKPOT

ONE-ARMED BANDIT, CALIFORNIA

POWER CO

Most Californians were convinced during the energy crisis of 2001 that energy suppliers were taking advantage of the state's flawed deregulation legislation to manipulate supply in order to drive up the price. This cartoon seemed to sum up public opinion. By the end of the summer a number of agencies were investigating the energy "shortages." © 2001 Tom Meyer, San Francisco Chronicle. Reprinted by permission.

Deregulation was designed to end the power monopoly of California's big private utilities. They were forced to sell off their fossil-fuel generating plants, which were bought by big, largely unregulated, out-of-state energy conglomerates such as Duke Power, Enron, Reliant Energy Services, and others, located mainly in Texas and the southeast. California's utilities, which retained the system's transmission and distribution lines, were then required to purchase power on the wholesale market, anticipating that the competition for the California market would drive prices down. Discouraged from making long-term contracts for power, the utilities were forced to buy on the short-term "spot" market. Initially, the Federal Energy Regulatory Commission (FERC) set a cap of $150 per megawatt hour on what generators could charge the California utilities, well above the

1998 going rate of $40. However, the FERC removed this cap in the fall of 2000, when it appeared the generators would not sell power at that rate. Meanwhile, the rates utilities could charge their customers were frozen. The legislation also established the Independent System Operator (ISO) to manage the state's immense power grid, matching supply to demand, and the California Power Exchange to conduct auctions through which independent generators bid to sell power to the California utilities. A curious provision of the law was that the price offered by the highest bidder became the price all received.

What happened? Many observers argue that the fundamental problem was California's failure to build generating plants during the 1990s, during which demand rose fifteen percent. However, there is little agreement on the causes of this failure. The utilities and business groups maintain that the state's strict environmental laws and permit requirements discouraged construction of new plants. Others point out that in the 1990s the utilities themselves were discouraging new construction on the grounds that the state already had an adequate supply. The fact is that no new plants were built in California in a decade, and that, by the year 2000, the state was importing twenty-five percent of its energy.

Contributing to the failure of deregulation was the flawed legislation itself. Forcing the utilities to sell their generating plants, discouraging long-term power contracts, fully freeing wholesale prices, thus forcing the utilities to buy power on the spot market, and freezing retail rates all gave the independent generators and power brokers enormous power over the California energy market, which they were willing to use for profit.

Unfortunately, the situation was worsened by other circumstances. Two years of drought in the Northwest reduced hydroelectric power available to California from the region. In addition, natural gas supply was diminished, and natural gas prices skyrocketed because of eastern weather conditions, a break in the main pipeline supplying the state, and near-monopoly control by El Paso Natural Gas on the only pipeline into southern California. Since most of California's generating plants are gas-fired, energy costs rose precipitously. Finally, there was the suspicion that power brokers and the independent electrical generators were manipulating or "gaming" the system, withholding supply to force higher prices, and "gouging" California buyers. An inordinate number of plant shutdowns "for maintenance" in critical supply situations, for example, led the state PUC to begin an investigation, while the state attorney general also launched an investigation into charges of manipulated rates.

Cold weather in the winter of 2000–2001 brought the crisis to a head. The demand for electricity rose moderately, but supply was suddenly inadequate, and the state's utilities had to cut power temporarily to large sections of the state, what came to be called "rolling blackouts." The cost of energy skyrocketed, and the utilities finally announced that, $12 billion in debt, their credit was exhausted and the independent generators would no longer sell them power. The state was forced to act.

For six months Governor Davis and state legislators attempted to deal with the crisis. The governor's cautious plan, after the San Diego crisis, was to try to save the utilities; expedite construction of small "peaker" plants that could come online quickly during peak summer loads; speed up the permit process for new generating plants; and promote conservation by the public. He also sought help from the federal government, pleading with the FERC to reinstate a temporary cap on the price that generators and power brokers could charge the state for electric power. He had only modest success. Early in 2001 the legislature authorized a $10 billion bond fund for the state to puchase power on behalf of the utilities; from then on the state itself purchased power, and the California Power Exchange was eliminated. Davis tried to negotiate state takeover of the utilities' transmission lines in return for bailing them out, but PG&E filed for bankruptcy instead. The governor, meanwhile, began negotiating long-term power contracts with the independent producers at prices that, while almost double the 1999 rates, were much less than the spot market and eventually contributed to stabilizing power cost on the open market. In January 2001 the state PUC approved an electricity rate increase of ten percent, and another one, in May, that was tiered and calculated on baselines. Customers using over one hundred and thirty percent of their baseline were hit with a rate increase that could go as high as forty percent.

The state's relations with the federal government did not improve with the inauguration of Texas oilman and governor George W. Bush as president. An avowed fossil-fuel advocate, Bush appointed Curt Hebert, a free-market ideologue, as chairman of the FERC. Hebert adamantely rejected the pleas of Governor Davis, the state's two senators, and most of its congressional delegation to place a temporary cap on the prices independent generators could charge the state for power. Nor was the administration sympathetic to the state's charges of manipulation and collusion by the generators; Vice President Cheney dismissed California's problem as "self-inflicted," and scoffed at Davis' call for conservation by the state's people as unrealistic. When the Texas firm, Reliant Energy charged the state $1,900 per megawatt hour for electricity during a May 2001 heat spell, Davis denounced the FERC and the Bush administration for contributing to an economic disaster that could overtake the state and affect the whole country.

Responding to public outrage, and with the possibility of rolling blackouts looming as the heat of the summer approached, an exasperated legislature also acted. In May it adopted in a bill, that the governor quickly signed, authorizing the state to sell $5 billion in revenue bonds to buy, build, and operate its own generating plants. The way was thus opened to public power that had been urged for months by State Treasurer Phil Angelides, Democratic legislators, and consumer action groups. In addition the legislature and the state attorney general intensified their investigations of alleged price manipulation by power brokers and generators.

By mid-summer, however, the crisis had surprisingly eased. When Vermont Senator James Jeffords resigned from the Republican party in May, the Democrats regained control of the United States Senate and immediately began hearings into the FERC's refusal to bring power prices under control in California. Suddenly, the FERC placed a cap on energy prices in the western states and began its own investigation into charges of price gouging by the generators. Chairman Hebert soon resigned and his replacment was far less ideological in outlook. In June gas prices declined dramatically and energy costs plummeted. Meanwhile, three new power plants came online in California just as Californians, responding to the governor's call for conservation, were cutting demand by 10 to 12 percent in May, June, and July, a huge saving of energy. By August the blackouts and energy crisis feared in the spring had failed to materialize, and California reported periodic power surpluses.

California, however, still faced a long-term energy crisis and continued strain on its economic resources. With the state spending millions of dollars a day for power, the budget surpluses contemplated in 2000 were rapidly shrinking under the pressure of a weakening economy and the intractable energy crisis.

THE NEW MILLENNIUM

Just when California entered the new millennium was a matter for some conjecture. Most assumed, as did the worldwide majority, that it began on January 1, 2000, and there were spectacular celebrations all over the world on New Year's Eve, December 31, 1999. But purists maintained that the millennium began on January 1, 2001, and held their own celebrations a year later. Oddly, the two celebrations took place in considerably different circumstances. On January 1, 2000, Californians were celebrating good times—a roaring economy, a dazzling new information age, and widespread prosperity. On January 1, 2001, the euphoria was gone. The great Internet business bubble was collapsing, hundreds of high-flying dot-com companies had failed, and there were daily announcements of layoffs by major companies throughout the nation. And the state was in the midst of an energy crisis that was soaking up billions of dollars and exporting them out of state just "to keep the lights on." It did not appear to be an auspicious beginning to the new millennium.

Looked at in perspective, however, the state still had great potential. The state's new economy was one of the most powerful in the world; it led the nation in high technology and its entertainment industry was unmatched; it remained the leading agricultural state in the union; and tourism continued to pour billions into the economy. There was even a kind of consensus that the state would muddle through the energy crisis. After all, in 2001 there were six new generating plants under construction in the state and nine more approved by the State Energy Commission ready for construction. It was anticipated that within eighteen months to two years, the crisis would be a thing of the past. By that time, too, it was thought, the national and state economies would have recovered from the uncertainty and dislocations caused by the destruction of the New York World Trade Center on September 11, 2001.

California entered the new millennium as a state with a minority/majority, and its people expressed general satisfaction with what they had become. Double the national rate described themselves for the 2000 census as of "mixed race," and the rate of mixed-race marriages remained high. At the start of the millennium, California continued to be regarded as a western Eden, however elusive, leading the nation in developing a multicultural society. For a century and a half the state had absorbed an astonishing number and diversity of new migrants. It continued to give them the conviction that the California Dream was real and that California remained a land of promise.

SUGGESTIONS FOR ADDITIONAL READING

Water, the Delta, and the Peripheral Canal

Norris Hundley, Jr., *The Great Thirst: Californians and Water, 1770s–1990s* (2001); W. Turrentine Jackson and Alan M. Paterson, *The Sacramento–San Joaquin Delta and the Evolution and Implementation of Water Policy: An Historical Perspective* (1977); California Department of Water Resources, *Delta Water Facilities: Program for Delta Protection and Water Transfer, Water Conservation, Water Recycling, Surface and Ground Water Storage* (1978); Roger Minick, *Delta West: The Land and People of the Sacramento-San Joaquin Delta* (1969); Janet Lokke, "'Like a Bright Tree of Life': Farmland Settlement of the Sacramento River Delta," *California History* (1980); John Thompson and Edward A. Dutra, *The Tule Breakers: The Story of the California Dredge* (1983); Harry Dennis, *Water and Power: The Peripheral Canal and Its Alternatives* (1981); John Hart, "The Delta: The Living (or Dying?) Heart of California," *Cry California* (1977); Frank Stead and Walt Anderson, "The California Water Plan: Onward and Upward," *Cry California* (1976);

Elizabeth Johnson, "Get Ready for the Water War of the 80's," *California Journal* (1980); Dan Walters, "The Evaporation of Consensus on Brown's $7 Billion Water Plan," *California Journal* (1979); Daniel J. Blackburn, "The Farm Bureau's Big Switch on the Big Ditch," *California Journal* (1981); Antonio Rossman, "Water: Where Do We Go From Here?" *California Journal* (1982); Dan Meyers, "Searching for a Solution to the Delta's Costly Problems," *California Journal* (1983); William Karhl, ed., *The California Water Atlas* (1979); Ronald B. Robie, "Water Issues Facing California," in Institute of Governmental Studies, University of California, Berkeley, *Four Persistent Issues* (1978); Paul S. Taylor, "California Water Project: Law and Politics," *Ecology Law Quarterly* (1975); Michael Storper and Richard A. Walker, *The Price of Water: Surplus and Subsidy in the California State Water Project* (1984); Cheryl Clark, "Breaking the Faith; Southern California Dissidents: We Don't Need Northern Water Now," *California Journal* (1985); Tom Harris, *Death in the Marsh* [Kesterson Wildlife Refuge] (1991); Ted Williams, "Death in a Black Desert [Kesterson Wildlife Refuge],"*Audubon* (January–February 1994); Robert Kelley, *Battling the Inland Sea: American Political Culture, Public Policy, and the Sacramento Valley, 1950–1986* (1989); Marc Reisner, *Cadillac Desert: The American West and Its Disappearing Water* (1986); John Walton, *Western Times and Water Wars: State, Culture, and Rebellion in California* (1992); Robert Gottlieb and Margaret FitzSimmons, *Thirst for Growth: Water Agencies as Hidden Government in California* (1991).

Environmental History, General

Carolyn Merchant, ed., *Green Versus Gold: Sources in California's Environmental History* (1998); Raymond F. Dasmann, *The Destruction of California* (1965), and *California's Changing Environment* (1981); Ed Salzman, ed., *California Environment and Energy: Text and Readings on Contemporary Issues* (1980); Michael Barbour, et al., *California's Changing Landscapes: Diversity and Conservation of California Vegetation* (1993); Tim Palmer, ed., *California's Threatened Environment: Restoring the Dream* (1993); Burton L. Gordon, *The Monterey Bay Area: Natural History and Cultural Imprints* (1996); Lois J. Roberts, *San Miguel Island: Santa Barbara's Fourth Island West* (1991); Joseph M. Petulla, *American Environmental History: The Exploitation and Conservation of Natural Resources* (1977); Roderick Nash, *Wilderness and the American Mind* (1973); Richard White, "American Environmental History: The Development of a New Historical Field," *Pacific Historical Review* (1985); John Hart, ed., *The New Book of California Tomorrow: Reflections and Projections from the Golden State* (1984); Carolie Sly, coord., *The California State Environmental Education Guide: A Curriculum Guide for Kindergarten Through Sixth Grade* (1988); Joseph B. Knox and Ann Foley Scheuring, eds., *Global Climate Change and California: Potential Impacts and Responses* (1991); Peter Steinhart, *California's Wild Heritage: Threatened and Endangered Animals in the Golden State* (1990); Biosystems Books, *Life on the Edge: A Guide to California's Endangered Natural Resources: Wildlife* (1994); James C. Williams, *Energy and the Making of Modern California* (1997).

The Rise of Environmental Ideas and Groups

Samuel E. Wood and Alfred E. Heller, *California, Going, Going. . .* (1962); Richard G. Lillard, *Eden in Jeopardy; Man's Prodigal Meddling with His Environment: The Southern California Experience* (1966); William Bronson, *How to Kill a Golden State* (1968); Barry Commoner, *The Closing Circle* (1971); Ansel Adams, *Ansel Adams: An Autobiography* (1985); A. E. Keir Nash, Dean E. Mann, and Phil G. Olson, *Oil Pollution and the Public Interest: A Study of the Santa Barbara Oil Spill* (1972); Robert Easton, *Black Tide: The Santa Barbara Oil Spill and Its Consequences* (1972); Holway R. Jones, "John Muir, The Sierra Club, and the Formulation of the Wilderness Concept," *The Pacific Historian* (1981); David R. Brower, *For Earth's Sake: The Life and Times of David Brower* (1990); "A Century of Environmental Action: The Sierra Club, 1892–1992," special issue of *California History* (Summer 1992); Michael P. Cohen, *The History of the Sierra Club, 1892–1970* (1988); Douglas H. Strong, *Dreamers and Defenders: American Conservationists* (1988); Samuel P. Hays, *Beauty, Health, and Permanence: Environmental Politics in the United States, 1955–1985* (1987).

Clean Air and Water

James E. Krier and Edmund Ursin, *Pollution and Policy: A Case Essay on California and Federal Experience with Motor Vehicles Air Pollution, 1940–1975* (1977); Douglas

Foster, "The Growing Battle over Pesticides in Drinking Water," *California Journal* (1983); Jennifer F. Sugar, "Hazardous Waste Disposal in Southern California," *California Journal* (1984); Stephen Green, "Glitches, Gremlins, and Swoap: Staggering along the Road to Toxic Waste Reform in California," *California Journal* (1985); Mary Ellen Leary, "The Water Resources Control Board: Overwhelmed with Work, It Struggles to Correct Past Failures," *California Journal* (1985).

Saving San Francisco Bay

Mel Scott, *The Future of San Francisco Bay* (1963); Harold Gilliam, *Between the Devil and the Deep Blue Bay: The Struggle to Save San Francisco Bay* (1969), and *For Better or for Worse* (1972); T. J. Conomos, ed., *San Francisco Bay—The Urbanized Estuary* (1979); Janine M. Dolezel and Bruce N. Warren, "Saving San Francisco Bay: A Case Study in Environmental Legislation," *Stanford Law Review* (1971); Charles A. Gulick, *The Fight for San Francisco Bay: The First Ten Years* (1971); Rice Odell, *The Saving of San Francisco Bay* (1972); Robert Fernbaum, "The Growing Use of Tradeoffs to Solve Development Problems," *California Journal* (1978).

The Coast

Jared Orsi, "Restoring the Common to the Goose: Citizen Activism and the Protection of the California Coastline, 1969–1982," *Southern California Quarterly* (1996); Stanley Scott, *Governing California's Coast* (1975); Robert G. Healy, ed., *Protecting the Golden Shore: Lessons from the California Coastal Commission* (1978); Drew Liebert, "Another Crisis Ahead for Coastal Commission," *California Journal* (1980); California Coastal Commission, *California Coastal Access Guide* (1981); Stanley Scott, ed., *Coastal Conservation: Essays on Experiments in Governance* (1981); Stephen Green, "'Death of a Thousand Cuts': The Governor's Campaign against the California Coastal Commission," *California Journal* (1985); Joseph E. Petrillo and Peter Grenell, eds., *The Urban Edge: Where City Meets the Sea* (1985).

Lake Tahoe

Douglas H. Strong, *Tahoe: An Environmental History* (1984); "Lake Tahoe: The Future of a National Asset—Land Use, Water, and Pollution," *California Law Review* (1964); Ron Roach, "Jerry's Suit for Divorce from Pat's Tahoe Marriage," *California Journal* (1978); Hal Rubin, "Lake Tahoe: A Tale of Two States," *Sierra* (1981); Urban Land Institute, *Lake Tahoe: An Evaluation of Governmental, Planning, Environmental, and Infrastructure Financial Issues in the Tahoe Basin* (1985); Peter Goin, et al., *Stopping Time: A Photographic Survey of Lake Tahoe* (1992).

Mono Lake

John Hart, *Storm over Mono Lake: The Mono Lake Battle and the California Water Future* (1996); Ron Bass, "The Troubled Waters of Mono Lake: Unique Ecological Resource or Wasteful Brine Sink?" *California Journal* (1979); D. J. Chasan, "Mono Lake vs. L. A.: A Tug of War for Precious Water," *Smithsonian Magazine* (1981); H. Dunning, "The Meaning of the Mono Lake Decision," *California Journal* (1983); G. Young, "Troubled Waters of Mono Lake," *National Geographic* (1981); Mono Lake Committee, *Mono Lake: Endangered Oasis* (1993); David Gaines, *Mono Lake Guidebook* (Revised by Lauren Davis, 1989); Scott Stine, "Geomorphic, Geographic, and Hydrographic Basis for Resolving the Mono Lake Controversy," *Environmental Geology and Water Science*, Vol. 17 (1991).

Controlling Growth and Preserving Land

Yvonne Olson Jacobson, *Passing Farms, Enduring Values: California's Santa Clara Valley* (1985); California Land-Use Task Force, *The California Land: Planning for People* (1975); Valerie C. Kircher, "The Legislative Battle over Preserving Agricultural Land," *California Journal* (1976); John H. Dresslar, "Agricultural Land Preservation in California: Time for a New View," *Ecology Law Quarterly* (1979); People for Open Space, *Endangered Harvest: The Future of Bay Area Farmland* (1980); Dan Walters, "Punching Holes in the Williamson Act," *California Journal* (1983); Jim Churchill, "Mapping the Present and Future of California's Farmland Resources," *California Journal* (1983); Malca Chall and Willa Baum, eds., *Statewide and Regional Land-Use Planning in California, 1950–1980 Project* (3 vols., 1983); John Hart, "Petaluma: The Little City that Could," *Cry California* (1976); Rob Kling, Spencer Olin, and Mark Foster, eds., *Postsuburban California: The Transformation of Orange County Since World War II* (1991); David E.

Dowall, *The Suburban Squeeze: Land Conversion and Regulation in the San Francisco Bay Area* (1984).

Forestry

Alfred Runte, *Public Lands, Public Heritage: The National Forest Idea* (1991); Reed F. Noss, ed., *The Redwood Forest: History, Ecology, and Conservation of the Coast Redwoods* (2000); Timothy P. Duane, *Shaping the Sierra: Nature, Culture, and Conflict in the Changing West* (1999); C. Raymond Clar, *California Government and Forestry* (1959); Lee T. Burcham, *California Range Land* (1957); Gerald D. Nash, "The California State Board of Forestry, 1883–1960," *Southern California Quarterly* (1965); William G. Robbins, *American Forestry: A History of National, State, and Private Cooperation* (1985).

Parks and Wilderness

Joseph H. Engbeck, *State Parks of California from 1864 to the Present* (1980); Jennifer Jennings, "Why the State Parks Face a Troubled Future," *California Journal* (1981); Susan R. Schrepfer, *The Fight to Save the Redwoods: A History of Environmental Reform, 1917–1978* (1983); John Muir, *Our National Parks* (1901); Mimi Stein, A *Vision Achieved: Fifty Years of East Bay Regional Park District* (1984); John L. Harper, *Mineral King: Public Concern with Government Policy* (1982); "Yosemite and Sequoia," special issue of *California History* (Summer 1990); Richard J. Orsi, Alfred Runte, and Marlene Smith-Baranzini, eds., *Yosemite and Sequoia: A Century of California National Parks* (1993), especially the last chapter, "Planning Yosemite's Future: A Historical Perspective," by Alfred Runte; Alfred Runte, *National Parks: The American Experience* (Second Edition, Revised, 1987), and *Yosemite: The Embattled Wilderness* (1990); Lary M. Dilsaver and William C. Tweed, *Challenge of the Big Trees: A Resource History of Sequoia and Kings Canyon National Parks* (1990); Richard West Sellars, *Preserving Nature in the National Parks: A History* (1997); Frank Wheat, *California Desert Miracle: The Fight for Desert Parks and Wilderness* (1999).

Reaction Against Environmentalism

Charles Zurhorst, *The Conservation Fraud* (1970); Bernard J. Frieden, *The Environmental Protection Hustle* (1979); Joseph Gughemetti and Eugene D. Wheeler, *The Taking* (1981); C. Brant Short, *Ronald Reagan and the Public Lands: America's Conservation Debate, 1979–1984* (1989); David Brodsly, *L. A. Freeway: An Appreciative Essay* (1983); Wesley Marx, "Offshore Oil: A California Battleground," *California Journal* (1983); Rush Shay, "The Sagebrush Rebellion," *Sierra* (1980); Tony Quinn, "Pacific Legal Foundation: Nemesis of the Environmentalists," *California Journal* (1979), and "Deukmejian and the Environmentalists," *California Journal* (1980); Donald H. Harrison, "The Deukmejian Dilemma: Promises Meet Reality," *California Journal* (1982); "Our Faltering Conservation Crusade," special issue of *Cry California* (1979); Katherine A. Kohm, *Balancing on the Brink of Extinction: The Endangered Species Act and Lessons for the Future* (1991).

Recession in the 90s

"California: The Endangered Dream," Special Issue, *Time* (November 18, 1991); Bénédicte Raybaud and Danielle Starkey, "California's Film Industry Beats the Recession," *California Journal* (1993); Richard Zeiger, "A Bittersweet Farewell: George Deukmejian Kept His Word, but Was It Enough?" *California Journal* (1991); Danielle Starkey and Vic Pollard, "The Prision Dilemma," *California Journal* (1994); Mary Beth Barber, "Transportation in California," *California Journal* (1993), and "Base Closures," *California Journal* (1994); Lisa M. Benton, *The Presidio: From Army Base to National Park* (1998); James W. Sweeney, "The Joads Go Home: Has the Golden State Lost Its Luster?" *California Journal* (1992); Dan Walters, *"The New California: Facing the 21st Century* (Second Ed., 1992); Jackson K. Putnam, "The Pattern of Modern California Politics," *Pacific Historical Review* (1992); Mark Nollinger, "The New Crusaders: The Christian Right Storms California's Political Bastions," *California Journal* (1993); Danielle Starkey, "Immigrant Bashing: Good Policy or Good Politics?" *California Journal* (1993), and "Pete to Immigrants: 'Don't Huddle Here': Governor Says Breathing Here Ain't Free," *California Journal* (1992); "Los Angeles—A Special Report," *California Journal* (1997); Steve Scott, "The No-Party System," *California Journal* (1999).

The New Economy

Wade Rowland, *Spirit of the Web: The Age of Information from Telegraph to Internet* (1999); Ward Winslow, ed., *The Making of Silicon Valley: One Hundred Year Renaissance* (1995); Rebecca S. Lowen, *Creating the Cold War University: The Transformation of Stanford* (1997); "Silicon Valley: A Special Issue," *California Journal* (2000); Emelyn Rodriguez, "The New Economy Comes of Age in the Capitol," *California Journal* (2001); Hal K. Rothman, "Stumbling toward the Millennium: Tourism, the Postindustrial World, and the Transformation of the American West," *California History* (1998); Peter Schrag, *Paradise Lost: California's Experience, America's Future* (1998); Gray Brechin and Robert Dawson, *Farewell Promised Land: Waking from the California Dream* (1999); Gray Brechin, *Imperial San Francisco: Urban Power, Earthly Ruin* (1999); Allen J. Scott and Edward W. Soja, eds., *The City: Los Angeles and Urban Theory at the End of the Twentieth Century* (1997).

Education

"Education in California: Facing the Future," *California Journal* (1986); Lynne G. Zucker, *California's Proposition 13: Early Impact on Education and Health Services* (1982); Laura A. Locke and Steve Scott, "Education in California: The Age of Turmoil and Hope," *California Journal* (1993); Laura A. Locke, "Crime Issue Knocks Education out of Spotlight," *California Journal* (1994), and "The Voucher Initiative: Breakthrough or Break-up for California Schools?" *California Journal* (1993); Steve Scott, "Pay as You Go: Privatizing California's 'Public' Higher Education System," *California Journal* (1994); Charles Wollenberg, *Golden Gate Metropolis: Perspectives on Bay Area History* (1985); Steve Scott, "Doing More with Less," *California Journal* (1997); Emelyn Rodriguez, "The State's Schools Gamble," *California Journal* (2001).

Social Transformation

Ron Chepesiuk, "Spokesman for Civil Rights: John Hope Franklin Offers Historical Perspective," *Modern Maturity* (1986); Joan Walsh," You Can See the World in Their Faces, *"Image"* (February 9, 1992); David Rieff, *Los Angeles: Capital of the Third World* (1991); Hans P. Johnson, "How Many Californians? A Review of Population Projections for the State," *California Counts* (1999); Sonya M. Tafoya, "Check One or More: Mixed Race and Ethnicity in California," *California Counts* (2000); Mark Baldassare, *California in the New Millennium: The Changing Social and Political Landscape (2000);* "An Interview with Mr. Speaker," *California Journal* (1986); Lydia Chávez, *Color Bind: California's Struggle to End Affirmative Action* (1998); Russell Thornton, "History, Structure, and Survival: A Comparison of the Yuki (Ukomno'm) and Tolowa (Hush) Indians of Northern California," *Ethnology* (1986); Steve Wiegand, "The Canvas Casino: California Indian Tribes Battle over Gaming," *California Journal* (1993); Bill Ainsworth, "Betting on Politics," *California Journal* (1997); Ioana Partringenaru, "Tribes Come of Age," *California Journal* (1999); Claudia Buck, "A Gamble That Paid Off," *California Journal* (1998); Steve Scott, "Proposition 5's Legacy," *California Journal* (1999); Rodolfo Acuña, *Occupied America: A History of Chicanos* (1981); Albert S. Herrera, "The Mexican American in Two Cultures," in Ed Ludwig and James Santibañez, eds., *The Chicanos: Mexican American Voices* (1971); Matt S. Meier and Feliciano Rivera, *The Chicanos: A History of Mexican Americans* (1972); Mario T. García, *Mexican Americans* (1991); David G. Guttiérrez, *Wall and Mirrors: Mexican Americans, Mexican Immigrants and the Politics of Ethnicity* (1995); Ricardo Romo, *East Los Angeles: History of a Barrio* (1983); R. Michael Alvarez and Tara L. Butterfield, "Latino Citizenship and Participation in California Politics: A Los Angeles County Case Study," *Pacific Historical Review* (1999); "The Latino Century," *California Journal* (2000); Richard A. García, "César Chávez: A Personal and Historical Testimony," *Pacific Historical Review* (May 1994); Ellen Carol DuBois and Vicki Ruiz, *Unequal Sisters* (1990); "The Asians," *California Journal* (1986); Sucheng Chan, *Asian Californians* (1991); Roger Daniels, Sandra C. Taylor, and Harry H. L. Kitano, eds., *Japanese Americans: From Relocation to Redress* (1986); Leland Saito, *Race and Politics: Asian Americans, Latinos and Whites in a Los Angeles Suburb* (1999); California Commission on the Status of Women, "Comparability: An Issue for the 80s" (1981), and *California Women* (monthly bulletin); Mildred Hamilton, "Pay Equity—Most Explosive Job Issue of the 80s," San Francisco *Examiner* (April 22, 1984); Melvin I. Urofsky, *Affirmative Action on Trial: Sex Discrimination in Johnson v. Santa Clara* (1997); John D'Emilio, *Sexual Politics, Sexual Communities: The Making of a Homosexual Minority in the United States* (1983); Brian J. Godfrey, *Neighbor-*

hoods in Transition: The Making of San Francisco's Ethnic and Nonconformist Communities (1988); Randy Shilts, *And the Band Played On: Politics, People and the AIDS Epidemic* (1987); J. S. Taub, "Gay Politics," *California Journal* (1993).

Politics at the Turn of the Century

A.G.Block, "The Republican Bust of 1998," *California Journal* (1998); William Booth, "California Recasts Itself to Play the Lead," *Washington Post Weekly* (July 5, 1999); Lou Cannon and A.G. Block, "Surviving the Republican Train Wreck," *California Journal* (2001); Carl M. Cannon, "D.C. Eyes Gray Davis," *California Journal* (2001); "Rating Gray Davis," *California Journal* (2000).

Energy

Richard Nemec, "Electricity in California: A Political and Economic Crossroads," *California Journal* (2001); Peter Asmus, "California's New Energy Legacy," *California Journal* (2001).

INDEX

Note: Page numbers in *italics* refer to illustrations; those followed by *(m)* refer to maps.